S0-BAH-656

ATLA BIBLIOGRAPHY SERIES

edited by Dr. Kenneth E. Rowe

1. *A Guide to the Study of the Holiness Movement,* by Charles Edwin Jones. 1974.
2. *Thomas Merton: A Bibliography,* by Marquita E. Breit. 1974.
3. *The Sermon on the Mount: A History of Interpretation and Bibliography,* by Warren S. Kissinger. 1975.
4. *The Parables of Jesus: A History of Interpretation and Bibliography,* by Warren S. Kissinger. 1979.
5. *Homosexuality and the Judeo-Christian Tradition: An Annotated Bibliography,* by Thom Horner. 1981.
6. *A Guide to the Study of the Pentecostal Movement,* by Charles Edwin Jones. 1983.
7. *The Genesis of Modern Process Thought: A Historical Outline with Bibliography,* by George R. Lucas, Jr. 1983.
8. *A Presbyterian Bibliography,* by Harold B. Prince. 1983.
9. *Paul Tillich: A Comprehensive Bibliography . . .,* by Richard C. Crossman. 1983.
10. *A Bibliography of the Samaritans,* by Alan David Crown. 1984.
11. *An Annotated and Classified Bibliography of English Literature Pertaining to the Ethiopian Orthodox Church,* by Jon Bonk. 1984.
12. *International Meditation Bibliography, 1950 to 1982,* by Howard R. Jarrell. 1984.
13. *Rabindranath Tagore: A Bibliography,* by Katherine Henn. 1985.
14. *Research in Ritual Studies: A Programmatic Essay and Bibliography,* by Ronald L. Grimes, 1985.
15. *Protestant Theological Education in America,* by Heather F. Day. 1985.
16. *Unconscious: A Guide to Sources,* by Natalino Caputi. 1985.
17. *The New Testament Apocrypha and Pseudepigrapha,* by James H. Charlesworth. 1987.
18. *Black Holiness,* by Charles Edwin Jones. 1987.
19. *A Bibliography on Ancient Ephesus,* by Richard Oster. 1987.
20. *Jerusalem, the Holy City: A Bibliography,* by James D. Purvis. 1987.
21. *An Index to English Periodical Literature on the Old Testament and Ancient Near Eastern Studies,* Volume I, by William G. Hupper. 1987.

An Index to English Periodical Literature on the Old Testament and Ancient Near Eastern Studies

Volume I

Compiled and Edited by

William G. Hupper

ATLA Bibliography Series, No. 21

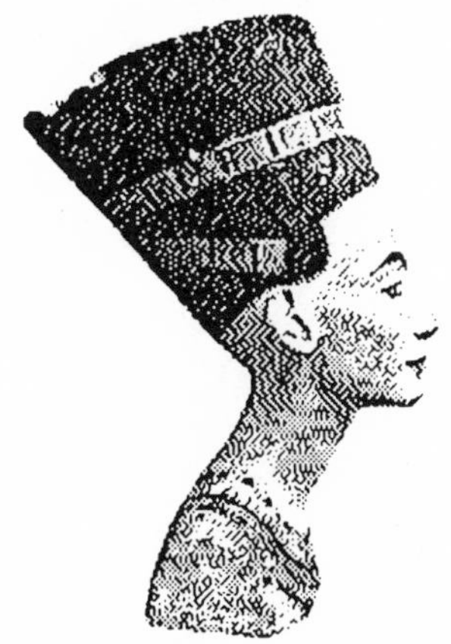

It is better to be last among lions than first among foxes.
. . . Aboth, 4.15

The American Theological Library Association, and
The Scarecrow Press, Inc.
Metuchen, NJ, & London 1987

Library of Congress Cataloging-in-Publication Data

Hupper, William G.
An index to English periodical literature on the Old Testament and ancient Near Eastern studies.

(ATLA bibliography series; no. 21)
Includes bibliographies.
1. Bible. O.T.--Periodicals--Indexes.
2. Near East--Periodicals--Indexes.
I. American Theological Library Association.
II. Title III. Series.
Z7772.A1H86 1987 [BS1171.2] 016.221 86-31448
ISBN 0-8108-1984-8 (v. 1)

Manufactured in the United States of America

To my wife Louise,
my daughter Susan,
and my son Adam,
whose sacrifice of
husband and father
was greater than
my sacrifice
of time.

Editor's Foreword

The American Theological Library Association Bibliography Series is designed to stimulate and encourage the preparation of reliable bibliographies and guides to the literature of religious studies in all its scope and variety. Compilers are free to define their field, make their own selections, and work out internal organization as the unique demands of the subject require. We are pleased to publish William G. Hupper's *An Index to English Periodical Literature on the Old Testament and Ancient Near Eastern Studies* as number 21 in the series.

William G. Hupper studied at Florida Beacon College and Gordon College. He continued scholarly pursuits in biblical languages and their interpretation as an avocation while serving as a transportation administrator for a large multi-national corporation. He has authored articles in *Journal for the Study of the Old Testament* and the *Journal of the Evangelical Theological Society* and has developed software for Macintosh™ computers to produce Egyptian hieroglyphics. A lay member of the Assemblies of God, Mr. Hupper is also a member of the Society of Biblical Literature.

Kenneth E. Rowe
Series Editor

Drew University Library
Madison, NJ 07940

Table of Contents *

*Section numbers shown in parentheses indicate that no entries will be found in the index proper. Sections have been kept to maintain continuity to the outline.

Table of Contents

Table of Contents

Table of Contents

Table of Contents

Table of Contents

Table of Contents

Table of Contents

Preface

This is the work of an independent scholar, "a layman" is probably a more acceptable term to the academic community. This preliminary statement is not meant to be an apology, but it should be explained at the outset that Ancient Near Eastern Studies is not the editor's métier. It is the undertaking of one who has not been in a constant academic environment, though in some ways, despite certain handicaps, this may well have been an advantage. It has been completed without the aid of a staff, or a computer,[1] until the final draft was typed. Rather, it has been accomplished by spending innumerable hours in cloistered carrels physically leafing through thousands of pages of dusty volumes, and searching hundreds of reels of microfilm.[2] Oftentimes the transcription of entries had to be handwritten. Looking back, perhaps this should not have been attempted as a solo enterprise, not from lack of expertise, though certainly there are others more qualified, but rather from the disproportionate consumption of time. This first volume is just now presented after over 16 years of labor. What was originally conceived as a project taking a few years, has become an oeuvre, and is a labor of love, being totally self-funded, except for a small, one-time grant from the American Theological Library Association which was used to purchase a typewriter.

The idea for this index was first conceived while researching articles for an exegetical paper in partial fulfillment of a seminary course in New Testament Greek. Numerous articles on the Old Testament which were discovered while attempting to locate other material became at once both fascinating and troubling, as further

1. When this project was initiated, the idea of wordprocessing was still on the drawing boards, or at best, in its infancy. It has been only in the past few years that a computer with the capability to do a project of this nature including all the various languages and diacritics has been available. This entire manuscript is a reproduction of the computer printout from a Macintosh™ ImageWriter II™. This includes the Greek, Hebrew, Cuneiform, and Egyptian Hieroglyphic fonts which were developed by the editor.

2. The editor was fortunate to be able to obtain much of this material while it was still in bound form. (But there is something very painful about handling periodicals which literally crumble at the slightest touch because of the acid in the paper.) Much of it now has been reduced to microform. Needless to say, it is difficult to deal with microfilm, microfiche, and especially microcards. While it is a method of preserving deteriorating material, it is not itself a final solution as it is said that the shelf life of microfilm is estimated at 50 years. Often microform material is available only within certain hours and reproduction to hard copy is difficult to secure. While libraries deal with the problem of storage space *vs.* access, thought should be given to reprints of these series. Indeed, some of them have been reprinted, but limited markets make it expensive. Perhaps in a few years duplication on laser disk will be possible, with hard copies of specific articles obtainable on request.

investigation revealed that there was only limited access to the wide scope of journals dealing with the Ancient Near East.[3] The need for access to these publications became even more apparent as the project progressed. Various discussions, rejoinders, surrejoinders, and rebuttals on a particular subject were not confined to a single series, but often crossed into other journals, while occasionally contemporary articles dealing with the same subject went totally unnoticed and were never cited.[4]

Scholars and students actively involved in research cannot individually keep pace with the literal deluge of information which is constantly inundating Ancient Near Eastern Studies. As early as 1934, Wilbur M. Smith stated that "the bibliography of Biblical and theological literature is probably the most neglected field in bibliographic science".[5] Fortunately, great strides have been made by the abstracting and indexing services since then, but even as recently as 1973, Moberg pointed out very dramatically:

> We must live with the tower of Babel; one illustration of this is the fact that in 1907 there were 400 periodicals with literature about chemistry in three languages of German, English, and French, but today there are 12,000 periodicals in 54 languages.[6]

The same is true in Ancient Near Eastern Studies and the Old Testament in particular. Since beginning the compilation of this index (acronym *IEPLOT*) in May, 1969, more than two dozen new journals have begun publication bearing directly or indirectly on Ancient Near Eastern Studies. It was not until *IEPLOT* was

3. For a list of indexes in series which have been published see: Michael J. Walsh, *Religious bibliographies in serial literature: a guide* (1981); Ronald E. Diener, "Handbook and Guide for the BTI Libraries, I. Serialized Bibliographic Tools," *Religious and Theological Resources* 1 (1970) p. 227ff.; also, William G. Hupper, "An Index to English Periodical Literature on the Old Testament (A Prospectus)," *Journal for the Study of the Old Testament* #8 (1978) p. 54f., notes 1 & 3. Diener estimates that only 45.5% of the U.S. and Canadian titles on religion are presently indexed, and this with nearly one-third duplication. (Diener, "The Present Status of the Indexing of Theological and Religious Periodical Literature," *R&TR* 1 (1970) p. 317.)

4. This, and "academic politics" (see p. xvii, n. 16), was poignantly illustrated in an article concerning Joel Block, a High School science teacher in Norwalk, Connecticut, whose paper regarding the Exodus written in 1974, was overlooked because he could not get it published in any scholarly journal of note. Fred M. Hechinger of the *New York Times* picked up the story (*New York Times*, June 2, 1981) after an article appeared on May 4, 1981 regarding Professor Hans Goedicke's new thesis entitled "Theory Ties Exodus Flood to Tidal Wave"; a proposal which Block had made seven years earlier! The story has been retold in *Independent Scholar's Handbook* by Ronald Gross, Addison-Wesley: Reading, MA, (1982) p. 100f.

5. "Some Much Needed Books in Biblical and Theological Literature," *BS* 91 (1934) p. 49.

6. David O. Moberg, "Documentation and Publishing," *ADRIS Newsletter* 2 (1973) #4, p. 37. Statistics indicate it takes just eight years for the information stored in libraries and computers to double! (*Reader's Digest*, July, 1985, p.40)

underway that the quantum dimensions of the material published on the Ancient Near East was realized. Perhaps this preliminary lack of knowledge worked to its own advantage, since if the extent had been fully understood, this work might not have been attempted.

Prior to compiling any articles, a schema had to be developed for classifying entries. Since Ancient Near Eastern Studies encompass such a wide range of subjects, a schema similar to that used by Metzger[7] was chosen. An outline was prepared with more than 900 divisions and subdivisions. This in itself required over 200 hours of initial preparation. It has since undergone more than six revisions and is the basis for the present Table of Contents.

Since no computer was available for random input and storage, a card catalog system matching the outline was implemented and entries were interfiled under appropriate headings on 3 x 5 cards.[8] Two additional card files were kept; one for each journal and its history; and a second set to list abbreviations in order that no duplication should occur.[9]

This index includes all English Language articles from over 600 journals which have reference to the Ancient Near East generally, the Old Testament, Intertestamental Literature, Rabbinic Studies, the Dead Sea Scrolls, and ancient contemporary languages and literature. All publications listed have been indexed completely from the first year of issue (unless otherwise indicated) through 1969/70 or until publication ceased prior to 1969/70.[10] In some cases this is a span of nearly two centuries! The central focus of this index is Old Testament Studies and the classification of articles tends to converge around this theme. The Old Testament, however, was

7. Bruce M. Metzger, *Index to Periodical Literature on Christ and the Gospels*, Leiden: E. J. Brill, 1966.

8. Special thanks go to Alan Stiffler of the Episcopal Divinity School, Cambridge, MA, for the loan of 45 card catalog drawers to facilitate indexing.

9. *International glossary of abbreviations for theology and related subjects* by Siegfried Schwertner; *Periodical Title Abbreviations* by E. Edward Wall; and "Instructions for Contributors. 34. Abbreviations of Commonly Used Periodicals, Reference Works, and Serials," *JBL* 95 (1976) p. 339ff. have all been consulted for abbreviations. Standard abbreviations have been used whenever possible, but a large number are by necessity original, since the journals cited have not otherwise been indexed. This is particularly true of retroactive material which has long ceased publication.

10. Journals which are published within a calendar year are covered only through 1969. Those which overlap years are covered through 1970, hence the reference 1969/70. Some exceptions do occur and are noted in the Periodicals Abbreviations list.

not produced in a vacuum, and peripheral topics which may bear only indirectly on the Old Testament have been included.[11] Classical Studies, on the other hand, have been avoided, except where they are found within the journals indexed, though interaction between the Aegean area and the Fertile Crescent is recognized.

While some have criticized that only English Language articles have been indexed, it is hoped that the enormity of the entries listed will, to some extent, compensate for the lack of foreign language citations.[12] As stated in the list of Periodical Abbreviations, foreign language journals have been searched for their English Language contents.

Several major problems arise in constructing an index of this nature, particularly in setting parameters. A three dimensional approach to this problem was taken. The first major problem was chronological. One of the main objectives of this index was to concentrate particularly on 19th Century Literature which for the most part has been neglected.[13] A number of series began in the late 1700's however, and inclusion of these journals has allowed for some reflection from the close of the age of enlightenment. The current termination has been discussed above.[14] Secondly, the problems of the limits of the primary discipline (Ancient Near Eastern Studies) had to be addressed. Dealing with the history and cultures of civilizations which in some cases span several millenia, it was easy to stray outside the intended parameters into the fields of art, law, mathematics, medicine, science, indeed into all facets of life. While each of these subjects is listed in the index, they have

11. Eg., [Henry Tattam], "A Catalogue of the rev. H. Tattam's Coptic and Sahidic Manuscripts purchased or copied in Egypt," *ZDMG* 7 (1853) 94-97; Raphael Patai, "Note to the Gnostic Background of the Rabbinic Adam Legends," *JQR, N.S.*, 36 (1945-46) 416-417; and Samuel Daiches, "Notes on the Gezer Calendar and Some Babylonian Parallels," *PEFQS* 41 (1909) 113-118. These are randomly chosen entries.

12. This was a major consideration, but much beyond the editor's capability, since the inclusion of foreign language articles would no doubt more than double the size of the present work. Perhaps W. F. Albright's remark in *From Stone Age to Christianity*[2] p. 53 is appropriate: ". . . an imperfect classification is better than no classification at all." This is in no way intended to minimize the many fine articles in foreign languages, but the foothold English has gained only increases the necessity for indexing these articles. It should be noted that even *Revue Biblique*, the bastion of French Biblical Studies, has yielded to accepting English Language articles as of 1970.

13. Hupper, *op. cit.*, p. 51.

14. *Supra.*, note 7.

been entered, qualified by the confines of the primary discipline.[15] The third limitation was the extent of coverage with regard to the nature of periodicals to be included. The identification of periodical literature appears to vary from library to library. Some have elected not to include certain annuals and proceedings as part of their periodicals card catalog, while others do so. For the purposes of *IEPLOT*, a "Byzantine" position (borrowing a term from New Testament Textual Criticism) toward periodical literature was taken in order to include articles from a wide spectrum of divergent sources. Therefore, while including the standard periodicals, e.g., *JAOS*, *JBL*, *JNES*, and *JTS*, an attempt has been made to cover annuals, proceedings, transactions; and particularly journals which have been neglected by the mainstream abstracting and indexing services.[16] In addition, third world publications, and journals from smaller colleges and seminaries, which are by no means less important, but frequently overlooked, have been of particular concern. This decision has often assumed the aspects of a good detective adventure. In one case the search for a single fascicle to an otherwise complete series took over 5 years of correspondence to locate.[17]

15. Several noteworthy articles tramontane to Ancient Near Eastern Studies include: R. P. Dow, "The Vengeful Brood of Lilith and Samaël," *Bulletin of the Brooklyn Entomological Society* 12 (1917) 1-9; A. S. Freidus, "Bibliography of Lilith," *BBES* 12 (1917) 9-12, cited in *Encyclopedia Judaica* "Lilith," Vol. XI, p. 249; D. I. Macht, "An Experimental Pharmacological Appreciation of Leviticus 11 and Deuteronomy 4," *Bulletin of the History of Medicine* 27 (1953) 444-450, noted by P. C. Craigie in *The Book of Deuteronomy*, p. 230, n. 9; J. Boss, "The Character of Childbirth According to the Bible," *Journal of Obstetrics and Gynaecology of the British Commonwealth* 69 (1962) 508-513, referred to in *Theological Dictionary of the Old Testament* IV, p. 188. n.; and Jacob J. Finkelstein, "The Goring Ox: Some Historical Perspectives on Deodands, Forfeitures, Wrongful Death and the Western Notion of Sovereignty," *Temple Law Quarterly* 46 (1973) #2, 169-290, mentioned in "The Atrahasis Epic and Its Significance for Our Understanding of Genesis 1-9," *BA* 40 (1977) p. 148, by Tikva Frymer-kensky. In fact, Biblical Studies seem to appear in the most unlikely places, cf.: "Putting the Biblical Pieces Together," by Richard F. Dempewolff, *Popular Mechanics* (May, 1978) pp. 103-107, 278, 280-283!

16. Diener, "Indexing," p. 318ff. indicates three problems concerning the present status of periodical indexing: 1) Duplication (*supra*., note 1); 2) Religious bias or prejudice; and 3) Academic "politics". With particular reference to the last point, Deiner lists 25 journals not currently indexed by abstracting and indexing services. Nearly all of these have been included in *IEPLOT* when they fell within the discipline of Ancient Near Eastern Studies.

17. Volume 1, number 2, of *Indian Ecclesiastical Studies* was finally located through contact with the Christian Institute for the Study of Religion & Society. Dr. M. M. Thomas directed the editor to The United Theological College in Bangalore, India. With the aid of the librarian, Mrs. E. Adiappa, a copy was obtained and duly indexed. It has since been deposited at St. John's Seminary, Brighton, MA. As far as is known, St. John's has the only complete set of this journal in the United States.

Occasionally some journals have devoted an entire volume to a single article written by one individual,[18] taking on the nature of a monograph. Other series which began as multi-authored volumes end up as monographs.[19] Monographs, as a rule, however, have not been included.

It has been the editor's good fortune to be based in the Greater Boston Area. Because of such a location, it has been possible to obtain the majority of journals with minimal difficulty, particularly very early volumes which might not have been available elsewhere. Most of the compiling was completed through access to the resources of the Boston Theological Institute consortium which consists of the following libraries: The Franklin Trask Library of Andover-Newton Theological School; The Bapst Library at Boston College; Boston University School of Theology Library; the combined libraries of the Episcopal Divinity School and Weston School of Theology; Goddard Library at Gordon-Conwell Theological Seminary; St. John's Seminary Library; and Andover-Harvard Library at Harvard Divinity School.[20]

These were supplemented by additional local libraries: Boston Athenaeum; Boston Public Library; The Congregational Library;[21] Goldfarb Library at Brandeis University; Harvard Law School Library; Harvard-Yenching Library; Tozzer Library at the Peabody Museum of Archaeology and Ethnology; Pusey and Widener Libraries at Harvard University.

Additionally, trips to Moulton Library, Bangor Theological Seminary; Rose Memorial Library, Drew University; the Jewish Theological Seminary of America; New York Public Library; Speer Library, Princeton Theological Seminary; Union Theological Seminary; and Yale Divinity School were made over several years, during vacations and holidays. Further, letters were written worldwide to over 40 libraries, the publishers of

18. Eg., B. D. Eerdmans, "The Hebrew Book of Psalms," *OTS* 4 (1947) 1-610.

19. Eg., *University of California. Publications in Semitic Philology*.

20. Also included in BTI is Holy Cross Greek Orthodox School of Theology, but it was unnecessary to utilize their facilities.

21. Particular gratitude is extended to Evelyn E. Vradenburg, former head of the Congregational Library, and her assistant, Velma Clifford, who were kind enough to allow the editor to withdraw entire series, sometimes amounting to over 100 volumes at a time. This facilitated indexing outside the confines of the library.

several journals.[22] The British (Museum) Library, and numerous individuals. The gracious response of librarians in the United States and overseas has been extraordinary, and it would be amiss not to acknowledge the assistance of these unsung guardians of literature. It is their cooperation that has contributed to the completion of many series which might not otherwise be included.[23]

The editor wishes to express his sincerest thanks for the exceptional assistance rendered by a number of individuals who cannot go unnamed: Mrs. Florence Hall, former reference librarian at Melrose Public Library, whose overwhelming enthusiasm in indefatigably proofreading the whole computer printout and checking it against every entry in the card catalog was indispensable, and to Norman E. Anderson, Associate Librarian at Gordon-Conwell for his technical assitance, re-reading the entire manuscript, pointing out a number of misprints and omissions. Thanks also to Ms. Marialice Wade, Melrose Public Library, for obtaining several interlibrary loans; to Andrew Schrimgeour, former head of BTI for his suggestions and encouragement early in the project; and to Ms. Bernadette Perrault, Periodicals Librarian at Andover-Harvard, for her continual help over the past sixteen years. The services of Rabbi Frederick E. Greenspahn to develop the classification of Rabbinic Literature is profoundly appreciated; and to Dr. James Moyer, Southwest Missouri State University, for offering his expertise on cuneiform documents and languages. Additional thanks go to James S. Irvine, and Barbara MacHaffie, Speer Library, Princeton Theological Seminary; and to Curtis Bochanyin, The Joseph Regestine Library, University of Chicago, who many times extended themselves beyond the call of duty for faithfully answering the many letters sent to them. Tribute is also offered to Robert Petersen of the Far Eastern Library, also at the University of Chicago.[24] It is especially gratifying for the cordial relationship with Dr. Kenneth E. Rowe of the American Theological Library Association, who expressed the first professional interest in

22. *Christian News from Israel*; *Ghana Bulletin of Theology*; *Journal of Theology*; and *Yavneh Review* provided information not otherwise available, especially confirming if specific issues were published.

23. The editor is indebted to Eric C. Watchman, the University of Durham, for supplying articles from *Durham University Journal (Original Series)* which is not available in the United States, and Ms. Harriet V. Leonard, Duke University, for forwarding a listing of articles from *Ministry* which was originally thought to be unavailable locally, as well as many others who have filled in the gaps to a number of series that were incomplete in the libraries visited.

24. Mr. Petersen, with the financial support provided by the Japan-United States Friendship Commission, supplied copies of *Nihon Orient Gakkai Getto* to the editor at no cost. These were subsequently given to the Harvard-Yenching Library.

the project. Another individual, who could not possibly be repaid, is Mr. Peter F. Jensen. As a senior at Gordon-Conwell, he spent several hours each week for over a year, patiently teaching the editor Classical Hebrew. Above all, my deepest gratitude is given to Dr. William L. Lane, presently at Western Kentucky State University, for first introducing the editor to the world of Biblical scholarship, and who has been a constant encouragement and mentor.

While every effort has been taken to eliminate omissions[25] and errors, the editor takes full responsibility for any which exist, and would be grateful for any correspondence from the readers of this work in helping to detect any which remain.

Finally, it is perhaps appropriate to heed the words of Qohelet:

. . . עשות ספרים הרבה אין קץ ולהג הרבה יגעת בשר׃

(Ecclesiastes 12:12b)

All Saints' Day, November, 1986

25. In a project such as this, it is nearly impossible to be absolutely sure all entries have been included. Even as the final copy was run off, additional entries were located and inserted.

Introduction

This work is divided into seven basic sections. While it is unnecessary to duplicate the table of contents here, the following quick overview will perhaps allow the user to be more comfortable with the format.

- 1.1 Bibliographical Articles - General Studies[26]
- 2.1 Biographical, Geographical, Historical, and Scientific Studies
- 3.1 Critical Studies of the Old Testament
  - 1.2 Textual Criticism - General Studies
  - 2.2 Literary Criticism
  - 3.2 Exegetical Studies
- 4.1 Contemporary Ancient Near Eastern Literature (including the Apocrypha and Pseudepigrapha)
- 5.1 Theological Studies related to the Old Testament
- 6.1 The Influence and Interpretation of the Old Testament in Worship, the Fine Arts, and Culture in General
- 7.1 Studies on the Dead Sea Scrolls and the Qumran Community

Two numbering systems have been employed in developing the Table of Contents which correspond to the division in the main body of the index. The first is a "numeric outline" which incorporates the use of decimal points for subdivisions rather than the traditional Roman Numerals, capital letters, etc. This allows for subdivisions *ad infinitum*. A cursory glance at the table of contents should be adequate for the user who is unfamiliar with this schema to understand the structural concept. Additionally, each division heading is marked with a section number. This also appears on the upper inside header of each page in the index proper. This will allow the user to locate divisions either by the outline or by specific section numbers.

Articles are listed chronologically by date under each heading (exceptions noted in the Table of Contents and below). Entries included are listed without regard to their scholarly integrity. Occasionally an editorial remark has been made indicating an outstanding bibliography or to show that an article was not continued. These remarks will be found at the end of a particular entry in brackets and italics. Review articles are included only when they are *not* part of a specific review section.

26. Sections 1.1 & 2.1 make up the first two volumes.

Observation of several points regarding the classification in general are important. 1) The section entitled "Literary Criticism" is to be understood more as containing articles dealing with specific subjects within a given Old Testament book which do not lend themselves to entry by chapter and verse. 2) "Exegetical Articles" are arranged according to the Hebrew Bible (i.e., The Pentateuch; The Prophets; and The Hagiographa). Entries are then subdivided by chapter and verse under each book of the Old Testament in an inverted pyramid fashion: articles dealing with larger blocks of passages being first and narrowing ultimately to a single verse or portion of a verse, e.g.:

Multiple Mixed Texts
Chapters 1-10
Chapters 1-3
Chapters 1:1-3:5
Chapter 1
vss. 1-15 of Chapter 1
v. 3 of Chapter 1
Chapters 2:1-3:8
etc.

The scope of articles covered under this section may actually cross over into "Literary Criticism" but are placed here for convenience since they make reference to a specific Old Testament passage. 4) Lexicographical Studies are arranged alphabetically where possible. The section on hieroglyphics has been classified according to Gardiner's sign lists from his *Egyptian Grammar*[3]. Articles dealing with "phrases" are listed separately by key words. 5) Two sections of biographical articles are listed. The first deals with persons specifically mentioned in the Old Testament, while the second deals with individuals who were contemporary historical figures. 6) There are also two sections of geographical entries. The first covers "Palestine" proper as defined by the area shown in Plate XVIII of *The Westminster Historical Atlas of the Bible*[2] (in Biblical terms: "from Dan to Beer-sheba") but in actuality as far south as Petra. While at first this may seem slightly cumbersome, it has allowed entries to be considerably more manageable. Very few cross-references within the geographical section have been included because of the elusiveness of assured identification of particular sites, especially in earlier journals.[27] 7) In the section dealing with contemporary literature, articles dealing with cuneiform documents refer to the registration numbers whenever possible. While the understanding of cuneiform documents is far superior today, some of the early references in the lexicographical section may be valuable from an historical standpoint.

27. Concerning identification problems of historical geography see: David A. Dorsey, "The Location of Biblical Mekkedah," *Tel Aviv* 7 (1980) #3/4, pp. 185-193.

Those familiar with other analytical indexes should realize the necessity for looking in several locations within this index for articles dealing with specific scriptural references, i.e., specific subjects, specific passages, as well as word studies and peripheral topics. An attempt has been made to minimize the necessity for checking many different listings. Articles often fall into more than one classification and a large number of multiple entries has been included. These articles are indicated by an asterisk * before the entry, but do not reference the location of any additional citations. Aricles may not necessarily follow all the present library conventions, as more attention has been given to listing entries as near as possible to the exact title shown in the periodical from which they were derived. This includes variant spellings, italics, and underscores as they actually appear. Titles of some articles have been given in an abbreviated form or are taken from the table of contents of a journal, or some other source. These are noted by the use of a dagger † before the entry. This is particularly true of very early periodicals where an article is referred to only at the top of a page, or is untitled altogether. Bibliographical articles on specific subjects are located within a given subject and are prefixed with a double dagger ‡ for quick location. These may include references to foreign language articles. Subdivisions of articles are listed in brackets at the end of a particular title, sometimes with page numbers, especially for lengthy articles. Since the publication of periodical literature is somewhat inconsistent in its approach to volumes numbers, jounals published by issue are noted by the number sign # before an issue number (eg. *BASOR*). Issue numbers are only given elsewhere when distinction of pagination demands it. Section headings followed by → or ← indicates cross-reference within this *Index*, though references may not be within a specific volume. The Periodical Abbreviations List incorporates all journals covered, even though no reference to them may appear in the first few volumes. A subject and author index is planned since the entry headings can only begin to approximate the scope of specific topics covered.

Periodical Abbreviations*

A

A&A	*Art and Archaeology; the arts throughout the ages* (Washington, DC, Baltimore, MD, 1914-1934)
A/R	*Action/Reaction* (San Anselmo, CA, 1967ff.)
A&S	*Antiquity and Survival* (The Hague, 1955-1962)
AA	*Acta Archaeologica* (Copenhagen, 1930ff.)
AAA	*Annals of Archaeology and Anthropology* (Liverpool, 1908-1948; Suspended, 1916-1920)
AAAS	*Annales archéologiques arabes de Syriennes* (Damascus, 1951ff.) [Volumes 1-15 as: *Les Annales archéologiques de Syrie*)
AAASH	*Acta Antiqua Academiae Scientiarum Hungaricae* (Budapest, 1951ff.)
AAB	*Acta Archaeologica* (Budapest, 1951ff.)
AAI	*Anadolu Araştirmalari Istanbul Üniversitesi Edebiyat Fakültesi eski Önasya Dilleri ve Kültürleri Kürsüsü Tarafindan Čikarilir* (Istanbul, 1955ff.) [Supersedes: *Jahrbuch für Kleinasiatische Forschungen*]
AAOJ	*American Antiquarian and Oriental Journal* (Cleveland, Chicago 1878-1914)
AASCS	*Antichthon. The Australian Society for Classical Studies* (Sydney, 1967ff.)
ABBTS	*The Alumni Bulletin [of] Bangor Theological Seminary* (Bangor, ME; 1926ff.)
ABenR	*The American Benedictine Review* (St. Paul, 1950ff.)
ABR	*Australian Biblical Review* (Melbourne, 1951ff.)
Abr-N	*Abr-Nahrain, An Annual Published by the Department of Middle Eastern Studies, University of Melbourne* (Melbourne, 1959ff.)

*All the journals indexed are listed in the Periodical Abbreviations even though no specific citation may appear in the first volume. Although the titles of many foreign language journals have been listed, only English Language articles are included in this index (except as noted). Articles from Modern Hebrew Language Journals are referred to by their English summary page.

Periodical Abbreviations

ACM — *The American Church Monthly* (New York, 1917-1939) [Volumes 43-45 as: *The New American Church Monthly*]

ACQ — *American Church Quarterly* (New York, 1961ff.) [Volume 7 on as: *Church Theological Review*]

ACQR — *The American Catholic Quarterly Review* (Philadelphia, 1876-1929)

ACR — *The Australasian Catholic Record* (Sydney, 1924ff.)

ACSR — *American Catholic Sociological Review* (Chicago, 1940ff.) [From Volume 25 on as: *Sociologial Analysis*]

ADAJ — *Annual of the Department of Antiquities of Jordan* (Amman, 1957ff.) [Volume 14 not published - destroyed by fire at the publishers]

AE — *Annales d'Ethiopie* (Paris, 1955ff.)

AEE — *Ancient Egypt and the East* (New York, London, Chicago, 1914-1935; Suspended, 1918-1919)

Aeg — *Aegyptus: Revista Italiana di Egittologia e di Papirologi* (Milan,1920ff.)

AER — *American Ecclesiastical Review* (Philadelphia, New York, Cincinnati, Baltimore, 1889ff.) [Volumes 11-19 as: *Ecclesiastical Review*]

AfER — *African Ecclesiastical Review: A Quartlerly for Priests in Africa* (Masaka, Uganda, 1959ff.)

Aff — *Affirmation* (Richmond, VA, 1966ff.) [Volume 1 runs from 1966 to 1980 inclusive]

AfO — *Archiv für Orientforschung; Internationale Zeitschrift für Wissenschaft vom Vorderen Orient* (Berlin, 1923ff.)

AfRW — *Archiv für Religionswissenschaft* (Leipzig, 1898-1941)

AHDO — *Archives d'histoire du droit oriental et Revue internationale des droits de l'antiquité* (Brussels, 1937-38, 1947-1951, *N.S.*, 1952-53)

AIPHOS — *Annuaire de l'institut de philologie et d'histoire orientales et slaves* (Brussels, 1932ff.)

AJ — *The Antiquaries Journal. Being the Journal of the Society of Antiquaries of London* (London, 1921ff.)

AJA — *The American Journal of Archaeology* (Baltimore, 1885ff.) [Original Series, 1885-1896 shown with *O. S.*; Second Series shown without notation]

AJBA — *The Australian Journal of Biblical Archaeology* (Sydney, 1968ff.) [Volume 1 runs from 1968 to 1971 inclusive]

Periodical Abbreviations

AJP	*The American Journal of Philology* (Baltimore, 1880ff.)
AJRPE	*The American Journal of Religious Psychology and Education* (Worcester, MA, 1904-1911)
AJSL	*The American Journal of Semitic Languages and Literatures* (Chicago, 1884-1941) [Volumes 1-11 as: *Hebraica*]
AJT	*American Journal of Theology* (Chicago, 1897-1920)
AL	*Archivum Linguisticum: A Review of Comparative Philology and General Linguistics* (Glasgow, 1949-1962)
ALUOS	*The Annual of the Leeds University Oriental Society* (Leiden,1958ff.)
Amb	*The Ambassador* (Wartburg Theological Seminary, Dubuque, IA, 1952ff.)
AmHR	*American Historical Review* (New York, Lancaster, PA, 1895ff.)
AmSR	*American Sociological Review* (Washington, DC, 1936ff.)
Anat	*Anatolica: Annuaire International pour les Civilisations de l'Asie Anterieure* (Leiden, 1967ff.)
ANQ	*Newton Theological Institute Bulletin* (Newton, MA, 1906ff.) [Title varies as: *Andover-Newton Theological Bulletin; Andover-Newton Quarterly, New Series,* beginning 1960ff.]
Anthro	*Anthropos; ephemeris internationalis ethnologica et linguistica* (Salzburg, Vienna, 1906ff.)
Antiq	*Antiquity: A Quarterly Review of Archaeology* (Gloucester, England, 1927ff.)
Anton	*Antonianum. Periodicum Philosophico-Theologicum Trimestre* (Rome, 1926ff.)
AO	*Acta Orientalia ediderunt Societates Orientales Bœtava Donica, Norvegica* (Lugundi Batavorum, Havniæ, 1922ff.)
AOASH	*Acta Orientalia Academiae Scientiarum Hungaricae* (Budapest, 1950ff.)
AOL	*Annals of Oriental Literature* (London, 1820-21)
APST	*Aberdeen Philosophical Society, Transactions* (Aberdeen, Scotland, 1840-1931)
AQ	*Augustana Quarterly* (Rock Island, IL, 1922-1948)
AQW	*Anthropological Quarterly* (Washington, DC, 1928ff.) [Volumes1-25 as: *Primitive Man*]
AR	*The Andover Review* (Boston, 1884-1893)
Arch	*Archaeology* (Cambrige, MA, 1948ff.)

Periodical Abbreviations

Archm	*Archaeometry. Bulletin of the Research Laboratory for Archaeology and the History of Art, Oxford University* (Oxford,1958ff.)
ARL	*The Archæological Review* (London, 1888-1890)
ArOr	*Archiv Orientální. Journal of the Czechoslovak Oriental Institute, Prague* (Vlašska, Czechoslovakia,1929ff.)
AS	*Anatolian Studies: Journal of the British Institute of Archaeology at Ankara* (London, 1951ff.)
ASAE	*Annales du service des antiquités de l'Égypte* (Cairo, 1899ff.)
ASBFE	*Austin Seminary Bulletin. Faculty Edition* (Austin, TX; begins with volume 71 */sic/*, 1955ff.)
ASR	*Augustana Seminary Review* (Rock Island, IL, 1949-1967) [From volume 12 on as: *The Seminary Review*]
ASRB	*Advent Shield and Review* (Boston, 1844-45)
ASRec	*Auburn Seminary Record* (Auburn, NY, 1905-1932)
ASSF	*Acta Societatis Scientiarum Fennicae* (Helsinki, 1842-1926) [Suomen tideseura]
ASTI	*Annual of the Swedish Theological Institute (in Jerusalem)* (Jerusalem, 1962ff.)
ASW	*The Asbury Seminarian* (Wilmore, KY, 1946ff.)
AT	*Ancient Times: A Quarterly Review of Biblical Archaeology* (Melbourne, 1956-1961)
ATB	*Ashland Theological Bulletin* (Ashland, OH, 1968ff.)
ATG	*Advocate for the Testimony of God* (Richmond, VA, 1834-1839)
AThR	*The American Theological Review* (New York, 1859-1868) [*New Series* as: *American Presbyterian and Theological Review*, 1863-1868]
'Atiqot	*'Atiqot: Journal of the Israel Department of Antiquities* (Jerusalem, 1955ff.)
ATJ	*Africa Theological Journal* (Usa River, Tanzania, 1968ff.)
ATR	*Anglican Theological Review* (New York, Lancaster, Pa; 1918ff.)
AubSRev	*Auburn Seminary Review* (Auburn, NY, 1897-1904)
Aug	*Augustinianum* (Rome, 1961ff.)
AULLUÅ	*Acta Universitatis Lundensis. Lunds Universitets Årsskrift. Första Avdelningen. Teologi, Juridik och Humanistika Åmnen* (Lund, 1864-1904; *N. S.*, 1905-1964)

Periodical Abbreviations

AUSS *Andrews University Seminary Studies* (Berrien Springs, MI, 1963ff.)

AusTR *The Australasian Theological Review* (Highgate, South Australia, 1930-1966)

B

B *Biblica* (Rome, 1920ff.)

BA *The Biblical Archaeologist* (New Haven; Cambridge, MA; 1938ff.)

Baby *Babyloniaca Etudes de Philologie Assyro-Babylonienne* (Paris, 1906-1937)

BASOR *Bulletin of the American Schools of Oriental Research* (So. Hadley, MA; Baltimore, New Haven, Philadelphia, Cambridge, MA;1919ff.)

BASP *Bulletin of the American Society of Papyrologists* (New Haven, 1963ff.)

BAVSS *Beiträge zur Assyriologie und vergleichenden semitischen Sprachwissenschaft* (Leipzig, 1889-1927)

BBC *Bulletin of the Bezan Club* (Oxford, 1925-1936)

BC *Bellamire Commentary* (Oxon., England; 1956-1968)

BCQTR *British Critic, Quarterly Theological Review and Ecclesiastical Record* (London, 1793-1843) [Superseded by: *English Review*]

BCTS *Bulletin of the Crozer Theological Seminary* (Upland, PA, 1908-1934)

Bery *Berytus. Archaeological Studies* (Copenhagen, 1934ff.)

BETS *Bulletin of the Evangelical Theological Society* (Wheaton, IL, 1958ff.)

BFER *British and Foreign Evangelical Review, and Quarterly Record of Christian Literature* (Edinburgh, London, 1852-1888)

BH *Buried History. Quarterly Journal of the Australian Insitute of Archaeology* (Melbourne, 1964-65; 1967ff.)

BibR *Biblical Repertory* (Princeton, NJ; New York, 1825-1828)

BibT *The Bible Today* (Collegeville, MN, 1962ff.)

Periodical Abbreviations

BIES — *Bulletin of the Israel Exploration Society* (Jerusalem, 1937-1967) [*Yediot* - ידיעות ארץ־ישראל החברה ועאיקותיה לחקירת - Begun as: *Bulletin of the Jewish Palestine Exploration Society* through volume 15. English summaries discontinued from volume 27 on as translations published in: *Israel Exploration Journal*]

BIFAO — *Bulletin de l'institut français d'archéologie orientale au Caire* (Cairo, 1901ff.)

BJ — *Biblical Journal* (Boston, 1842-1843)

BJRL — *Bulletin of the John Rylands Library* (Manchester, 1903ff.)

BM — *Bible Magazine* (New York, 1913-1915)

BMB — *Bulletin du Musée de Byrouth* (Paris, 1937ff.)

BN — *Bible Numerics: a Periodical Devoted to the Numerical Study of the Scriptures* (Grafton, MA; 1904)

BO — *Bibliotheca Orientalis* (Leiden, 1944ff.)

BofT — *Banner of Truth* (London, 1955ff.)

BOR — *The Babylonian and Oriental Record: A Monthly Magazine of the Antiquities of the East* (London, 1886-1901)

BQ — *Baptist Quarterly* (Philadelphia, 1867-1877)

BQL — *Baptist Quarterly* (London, 1922ff.)

BQR — *Baptist Quarterly Review* (Cincinnati, New York, Philadelphia,1879-1892)

BQRL — *The British Quarterly Review* (London, 1845-1886)

BR — *Biblical Review* (New York, 1916-1932)

BRCM — *The Biblical Review and Congregational Magazine* (London, 1846-1850)

BRCR — *The Biblical Repository and Classical Review* (Andover, MA,1831-1850) [Title varies as: *Biblical Repository; The Biblical Repository and Quarterly Observer; The American Biblical Repository*]

BRec — *Bible Record* (New York, 1903-1912) [Volume 1, #1-4 as: *Bible Teachers Training School, New York City, Bulletin*]

BRes — *Biblical Research: Papers of the Chicago Society of Biblical Research* (Amsterdam, Chicago, 1956ff.)

BS — *Bibliotheca Sacra* (New York, Andover, Oberlin, OH; St. Louis, Dallas, 1843, 1844ff.)

BSAJB — *British School of Archaeology in Jerusalem, Bulletin* (Jerusalem, 1922-1925)
BSOAS — *Bulletin of the School of Oriental and African Studies. University of London* (London, 1917ff.)
BSQ — *Bethel Seminary Quarterly* (St. Paul, MN; 1952ff.) [From Volume 13 on as: *Bethel Seminary Journal*]
BT — *Biblical Theology* (Belfast, 1950ff.)
BTF — *Bangalore Theological Forum* (Bangalore, India, 1967ff.)
BTPT — *Bijdragen Tijdschrift voor philosophie en theologie* (Maastricht,1938ff.) [Title varies as: *Bijdragen. Tijdschrift voor filosofie entheologie*]
BTr — *Bible Translator* (London, 1950ff.)
BUS — *Bucknell University Studies* (Lewisburg, PA; 1941ff.) [From Volume 5 on as: *Bucknell Review*]
BW — *Biblical World* (Chicago, 1893-1920)
BWR — *Bible Witness and Review* (London, 1877-1881)
BWTS — *The Bulletin of the Western Theological Seminary* (Pittsburgh, 1908-1931)
BZ — *Biblische Zeitschrift* (Paderborn, 1903-1939; *New Series*, 1957ff.) [*N.S.* shown without notation]

C

C&C — *Cross and Crown. A Thomistic Quarterly of Spiritual Theology* (St. Louis, 1949ff.)
CAAMA — *Cahiers archéologiques fin de l'antiquité et moyen age* (Paris, 1961ff.)
CAAST — *Connecticut Academy of Arts and Sciences, Transactions* (New Haven, 1866ff.)
Carm — *Carmelus. Commentarii ab instituto carmelitano editi* (Rome, 1954ff.)
CBQ — *Catholic Biblical Quarterly* (Washington, DC; 1939ff.)
CC — *Cross Currents* (West Nyack, NY; 1950ff.)
CCARJ — *Central Conference of American Rabbis Journal* (New York,1953ff.)
CCBQ — *Central Conservative Baptist Quarterly* (Minneapolis, 1958ff.) [From volume 9, #2 on as: *Central Bible Quarterly*]

Periodical Abbreviations

CCQ — *Crisis Christology Quarterly* (Dubuque, IA, 1943-1949) [Volume 6 as: *Trinitarian Theology*]

CD — *Christian Disciple* (Boston, 1813-1823) [Superseded by: *Christian Examiner*]

CdÉ — *Chronique d'Égypte* (Brussels, 1925ff.)

CE — *Christian Examiner* (Boston, New York, 1824-1869)

Cent — *Centaurus. International Magazine of the History of Science and Medicine* (Copenhagen, 1950ff.)

Center — *The Center* (Atlanta, 1960-1965)

CFL — *Christian Faith and Life* (Columbia, SC, 1897-1939) [Title varies: Original Series as: *The Bible Student and Relgious Outlook*, volume 1 & 2 as: *The Religious Outlook;* New Series as: *The Bible Student;* Third Series as: *The Bible Student and Teacher;* Volumes as: *Bible Champion*]

ChgoS — *Chicago Studies* (Mundelein, IL; 1962ff.)

CJ — *Conservative Judaism* (New York, 1945ff.)

CJL — *Canadian Journal of Linguistics* (Montreal, 1954ff.)

CJRT — *The Canadian Journal of Religious Thought* (Toronto, 1924-1932)

CJT — *Canadian Journal of Theology* (Toronto, 1955ff.)

ClR — *Clergy Review* (London, 1931ff.)

CM — *The Clergyman's Magazine* (London, 1875-1897)

CMR — *Canadian Methodist Review* (Toronto, 1889-1895) [Volumes 1-5 as: *Canadian Methodist Quarterly*]

CNI — *Christian News from Israel* (Jerusalem, 1949ff.)

CO — *Christian Opinion* (New York, 1943-1948)

Coll — *Colloquium. The Australian and New Zealand Theological Review* (Auckland, 1964ff.) [Volume 1 through Volume 2, #1 as: *The New Zealand Theological Review*]

CollBQ — *The College of the Bible Quarterly* (Lexington, KY, 1909-1965) [Break in sequence between 1927 and 1937, resumes in 1938 with volume 15 duplicated in number]

ColTM — *Columbus Theological Magazine* (Columbus, OH; 1881-1910)

CongL — *The Congregationalist* (London, 1872-1886)

CongML — *The Congregational Magazine* (London, 1818-1845)

CongQB — *The Congregational Quarterly* (Boston, 1859-1878)

CongQL — *The Congregational Quarterly* (London, 1923-1958)

CongR — *The Congregational Review* (Boston, Chicago, 1861-1871) [Volumes 1-6 as: *The Boston Review*]

Periodical Abbreviations

CongRL — *The Congregational Review* (London, 1887-1891)
ConstrQ — *The Constructive Quarterly. A Journal of the Faith, Work, and Thought of Christendom* (New York, London, 1913-1922)
Cont — *Continuum* (St. Paul, 1963-1970)
ContextC — *Context (Journal of the Lutheran School of Theology at Chicago)* (Chicago, 1967-1968)
ContR — *Contemporary Review* (London, New York, 1866ff.)
CovQ — *The Covenant Quarterly* (Chicago, 1941ff.) [Volume 1, #1 as: *Covenant Minister's Quarterly*]
CQ — *Crozer Quarterly* (Chester, PA; 1924-1952)
CQR — *Church Quarterly Review* (London, 1875-1968)
CR — *The Church Review* (New Haven, 1848-1891) [Title varies; Volume 62 not published]
CraneR — *The Crane Review* (Medford, MA; 1958-1968)
CRB — *The Christian Review* (Boston, Rochester; 1836-1863)
CRDSB — *Colgate-Rochester Divinity School Bulletin* (Rochester, NY;1928-1967)
Crit — *Criterion* (Chicago, 1962ff.)
CRP — *The Christian Review: A Quarterly Magazine* (Philadelphia, 1932-1941)
CS — *The Cumberland Seminarian* (McKenzie, TN; Memphis; 1953-1970)
CSQ — *Chicago Seminary Quarterly* (Chicago, 1901-1907)
CSQC — *The Culver-Stockton Quarterly* (Canton, MO; 1925-1931)
CSSH — *Comparative Studies in Society and History: An International Quarterly* (The Hague, 1958ff.)
CT — *Christian Thought* (New York, 1883-1894)
CTJ — *Calvin Theological Journal* (Grand Rapids, 1966ff.)
CTM — *Concordia Theological Monthly* (St. Louis, 1930ff.)
CTPR — *The Christian Teacher [and Chronicle]* (London, 1835-1838; *N.S.*, 1838-1844 as: *A Theological and Literary Journal*) [Continues as: *The Prospective Review; A Quarterly Journal of Theology and Literature*)
CTSB — *Columbia Theological Seminary Bulletin* (Columbia, SC; Decatur, GA; 1907ff.) [Title varies]
CTSP — *Catholic Theological Society, Proceedings* (Washingon, DC; Yonkers, NY; 1948ff.)
CTSQ — *Central Theological Seminary Quarterly* (Dayton, OH; 1923-1931)
CUB — *Catholic University Bulletin* (Washington, DC;1895-1914) [Volumes 1-20 only]

Periodical Abbreviations

D

DDSR — *Duke Divinity School Review* (Durham, NC; 1936ff.) [Volumes 1-20 as: *The Duke School of Religion Bulletin;* Volumes 21-29 as: *Duke Divinity School Bulletin*]

DG — *The Drew Gateway* (Madison, NJ; 1930ff.)

DI — *Diné Israel. An Annual of Jewish Law and Israeli Family Law* דיני ישואל שנתון למשט עברי ולדיני משחה ביראל (Jerusalem, 1969ff.)

DJT — *Dialogue: A Journal of Theology* (Minneapolis, 1962ff.)

DQR — *Danville Quarterly Review* (Danville, KY; Cincinnati; 1861-1864)

DownsR — *Downside Review* (Bath, 1880ff.)

DR — *Dublin Review* (London, 1836-1968) [Between 1961 and 1964 as: *Wiseman Review*]

DS — *Dominican Studies. A Quarterly Review of Theology and Philosophy* (Oxford, 1948-1954)

DSJ — *The Dubuque Seminary Journal* (Dubuque, IA; 1966-1967)

DSQ — *Dubuque Seminary Quarterly* (Dubuque, IA; 1947-1949) [Volume 3, #3 not published]

DTCW — *Dimension: Theology in Church and World* (Princeton, NJ; 1964-1969) [Volumes 1 & 2 as: *Dimension*; New format beginning in 1966 with full title, beginning again with Volume 1]

DTQ — *Dickinson's Theological Quarterly* (London, 1875-1883) [Superseded by *John Lobb's Theological Quarterly*]

DUJ — *The Durham University Journal* (Durham, 1876ff.; *N.S.*, 1940ff.) [Volume 32 of *O.S.* = Volume 1 of *N.S.*]

DUM — *Dublin University Magazine* (Dublin, London, 1833-1880)

DunR — *The Dunwoodie Review* (Yonkers, NY; 1961ff.)

Periodical Abbreviations

E

EgR *Egyptian Religion* (New York, 1933-1936)

EI *Eretz-Israel. Archaeological, Historical and Geographical Studies* (Jerusalem, 1951ff.) מחקרים
ארץ־ישראל בידיעת הארץ ועתיקותיה
[English Summaries from Volume 3 on]

EJS *Archives européennes de Sociologie / European Journal of Sociology / Europäisches Archiv für Soziologie* (Paris, 1960ff.)

EN *The Everlasting Nation* (London, 1889-1892)

EQ *Evangelical Quarterly* (London, 1929ff.)

ER *Evangelical Review* (Gettysburg, PA; 1849-1870) [From Volume 14 on as: *Evangelical Quarterly Review*]

ERCJ *Edinburgh Review, or Critical Journal* (Edinburgh, London, 1802-1929)

ERG *The Evangelical Repository: A Quarterly Magazine of Theological Literature* (Glasgow, 1854-1888)

ERL *The English Review, or Quarterly Journal of Eccesiastical and General Literature* (London, 1844-1853) [Continues *British Critic*]

ESS *Ecumenical Study Series* (Indianapolis, 1955-1960)

ET *The Expository Times* (Aberdeen, Edinburgh, 1889ff.)

ETL *Ephemerides Theologicae Lovanienses* (Notre Dame, 1924ff.)

Eud *Eudemus. An International Journal Devoted to the History of Mathematics and Astronomy* (Copenhagen, 1941)

Exp *The Expositor* (London, 1875-1925)

Exped *Expedition* (Philadelphia, 1958ff.) [Continues: *The University Museum Bulletin*]

Periodical Abbreviations

F

F&T	*Faith and Thought* (London, 1958ff.) [Supersedes: *Journal of the Transactions of the Victoria Institute, or Philosophical Society of Great Britain*]
FBQ	*The Freewill Baptist Quarterly* (Providence, London, Dover, 1853-1869)
FDWL	*Friends of Dr. Williams's Library (Lectures)* (Cambridge, Oxford, 1948ff.)
FLB	*Fuller Library Bulletin* (Pasadena, CA; 1949ff.)
FO	*Folia Orientalia* (Kraków, 1960ff.)
Focus	*Focus. A Theological Journal* (Willowdale, Ontario, 1964-1968)
Folk	*Folk-Lore: A Quarterly Review of Myth, Tradition, Institution & Custom being the Transactions of the Folk-Lore Society And Incorporating the Archæological Review and the Folk-Lore Journal* (London, 1890ff.)
Found	*Foundations (A Baptist Journal of History and Theology)* (Rochester, NY; 1958ff.)
FUQ	*Free University Quarterly* (Amsterdam-Centrum, 1950-1965)

G

GBT	*Ghana Bulletin of Theology* (Legon, Ghana; 1957ff.)
GJ	*Grace Journal* (Winona Lake, IN; 1960ff.)
GOTR	*Greek Orthodox Theological Review* (Brookline, MA; 1954ff.)
GR	*Gordon Review* (Boston; Beverly Farms, MA; Wenham, MA; 1955ff.)
GRBS	*Greek, Roman and Byzantine Studies* (San Antonio; Cambridge, MA; University, MS; Durham, NC; 1958ff.) [Volume1 as: *Greek and Byzantine Studies*]

Greg — *Gregorianum; Commentarii de re theologica et philosophica* (Rome, 1920ff.) [Volume 1 as: *Gregorianum; rivista trimestrate di studi teologici e filosofici*]

GUOST — *Glasgow University Oriental Society, Transactions* (Glasgow, 1901ff.)

H

H&T — *History and Theory: Studies in the Philosophy of History* (The Hague, 1960ff.)

HA — *Hebrew Abstracts* (New York, 1954ff.)

HDSB — *Harvard Divinity School Bulletin* (Cambridge, MA; 1935-1969)

Herm — *Hermathena; a Series of Papers on Literature, Science and Philosophy by Members of Trinity College, Dublin* (Dublin, 1873ff.) [Volumes 1-20; changes to issue number from #46 on]

HeyJ — *The Heythrop Journal* (New York, 1960ff.)

HJ — *Hibbert Journal* (London, Boston, 1902-1968)

HJAH — *Historia. Zeitschrift für alte Geschichte / Revue d'Histoire Ancienne / Journal of Ancient History / Di Storia Antica* (Baden, 1950ff.)

HJud — *Historia Judaica. A Journal of Studies in Jewish History Especially in the Legal and Economic History of the Jews* (New York, 1938-1961)

HQ — *The Hartford Quarterly* (Hartford, CT; 1960-1968)

HR — *Homiletic Review* (New York, 1876-1934)

HRel — *History of Religions* (Chicago, 1961ff.)

HS — *Ha Sifrut. Quarterly for the Study of Literature* הסרות רבצון למדצ הסרות (Tel-Aviv, 1968ff.)

HSR — *Hartford Seminary Record* (Hartford, CT; 1890-1913)

HT — *History Today* (London, 1951ff.)

HTR — *Harvard Theological Review* (Cambridge, MA; 1908ff.)

HTS — *Hervormde Teologiese Studien* (Pretoria, 1943ff.)

HUCA — *Hebrew Union College Annual* (Cincinnati, 1904, 1924ff.)

Periodical Abbreviations

I

IA	*Iranica Antiqua* (Leiden, 1961ff.)
IALR	*International Anthropological and Linguistic Review* (Miami, 1953-1957)
ICHR	*Indian Church History Review* (Serampore, West Bengal, 1967ff.)
ICMM	*The Interpreter. A Church Monthly Magazine* (London, 1905-1924)
IEJ	*Israel Exploration Journal* (Jerusalem, 1950ff.)
IER	*Irish Ecclesiastical Record (A Monthly Journal under Episcopal Sanction)* (Dublin, 1864-1968)
IES	*Indian Ecclesiastical Studies* (Bangalore, India, 1962ff.)
IJA	*International Journal of Apocrypha* (London, 1905-1917) [Issues #1-7 as: *Deutero-Canonica,* pages unnumbered]
IJT	*Indian Journal of Theology* (Serampore, West Bengal, 1952ff.)
ILR	*Israel Law Review* (Jerusalem, 1966ff.)
Inter	*Interchange: Papers on Biblical and Current Questions* (Sydney, 1967ff.)
Interp	*Interpretation; a Journal of Bible and Theology* (Richmond,1947ff.)
IPQ	*International Philosophical Quarterly* (New York, 1961ff.)
IR	*The Iliff Review* (Denver, 1944ff.)
Iran	*Iran: Journal of the British Institute of Persian Studies* (London, 1963ff.)
Iraq	*Iraq. British School of Archaeology in Iraq* (London, 1934ff.)
IRB	*International Reformed Bulletin* (London, 1958ff.)
IRM	*International Review of Missions* (Edinburgh, London, Geneva, 1912ff.)
Isis	*Isis. An International review devoted to the history of Science and civilization* (Brussels; Cambridge, MA; 1913ff.)
ITQ	*Irish Theological Quarterly* (Dublin, Maynooth, 1906ff.)

Periodical Abbreviations

J

JAAR — *Journal of the American Academy of Religion* (Wolcott, NY; Somerville, NJ; Baltimore; Brattleboro, VT) [Volumes1-4 as: *Journal of the National Association of Biblical Instructors;* Volumes 5-34 as: *Journal of Bible and Religion*]

JANES — *Journal of the Ancient Near Eastern Society of Columbia University* (New York, 1968ff.)

Janus — *Janus; Archives internationales pour l'Histoire de la Médecine et pour la Géographie Médicale* (Amsterdam; Haarlem; Leiden; 1896ff.)

JAOS — *Journal of the American Oriental Society* (Baltimore, New Haven, 1843ff.)

JAOSS — *Journal of the American Oriental Society, Supplements* (Baltimore, New Haven, 1935-1954)

JARCE — *Journal of the American Research Center in Egypt* (Gluckstadt, Germany; Cambridge, MA; 1962ff.)

JASA — *Journal of the American Scientific Affiliation* (Wheaton, IL, 1949ff.)

JBL — *Journal of Biblical Literature* (Middletown, CT; New Haven; Boston; Philadelphia; Missoula, MT; 1881ff.)

JC&S — *The Journal of Church and State* (Fresno, CA; 1965ff.)

JCP — *Christian Philosophy Quarterly* (New York, 1881-1884) [From Volume 2 on as: *The Journal of Christian Philosophy*]

JCS — *Journal of Cuneiform Studies* (New Haven; Cambridge, MA;1947ff.)

JCSP — *Journal of Classical and Sacred Philology* (Cambridge, England, 1854-1857)

JEA — *Journal of Egyptian Archaeology* (London, 1914ff.)

JEBH — *Journal of Economic and Business History* (Cambridge, MA;1928-1932)

JES — *Journal of Ethiopian Studies* (Addis Ababa, 1963ff.)

JESHO — *Journal of the Economic and Social History of the Orient* (Leiden, 1958ff.)

JHI — *Journal of the History of Ideas. A Quarterly Devoted to Intellectual History* (Lancaster, PA; New York; 1940ff.)

JHS — *The Journal of Hebraic Studies* (New York; 1969ff.)

Periodical Abbreviations

JIQ — *Jewish Institute Quarterly* (New York, 1924-1930)

JJLP — *Journal of Jewish Lore and Philosophy* (Cincinnati, 1919)

JJP — *Rocznik Papirologii Prawniczej - Journal of Juristic Papyrology* (New York, Warsaw, 1946ff.) [Suspended 1947 & 1959-60]

JJS — *Journal of Jewish Studies* (London, 1948ff.)

JKF — *Jahrbuch für Kleinasiatische Forschungen* (Heidelberg, 1950-1953) [Superseded by *Anadolu Araştirmalari Istanbul Üniversitesi Edebiyat Fakültesi eski Önasya Dilleri ve Kültürleri Kürsüsü Tarafindan Čikarilir*]

JLTQ — *John Lobb's Theological Quarterly* (London, 1884)

JMUEOS — *Journal of the Manchester Egyptian and Oriental Society* (Manchester, 1911-1953) [Issue #1 as: *Journal of the Manchester Oriental Society*]

JMTSO — *Journal of the Methodist Theological School in Ohio* (Delaware, OH; 1962ff.)

JNES — *Journal of Near Eastern Studies* (Chicago, 1942ff.)

JOEL — *Jaarbericht van het Vooraziatisch-Egyptisch Gezelschap Ex Oriente Lux* (Leiden, 1933ff.)

JP — *The Journal of Philology* (Cambridge, England; 1868-1920)

JPOS — *Journal of the Palestine Oriental Society* (Jerusalem, 1920-1948) [Volume 20 consists of only one fascicle]

JQR — *Jewish Quarterly Review* (London, 1888-1908; *N.S.*, Philadelphia, 1908ff.) [Includes 75th Anniversary Volume as: *JQR, 75th*]

JR — *Journal of Religion* (Chicago, 1921ff.)

JRAS — *Journal of the Royal Asiatic Society of Great Britain and Ireland* (London, 1827ff.) [*Transactions*, 1827-1835 as *TRAS; Journal* from 1834 on: (Shown without volume numbers)]

JRelH — *Journal of Religious History* (Sydney, 1960ff.)

JRH — *Journal of Religion and Health* (Richmond, 1961ff.)

JRT — *Journal of Religious Thought* (Washington, DC; 1943ff.)

JSL — *Journal of Sacred Literature and Biblical Record* (London,1848-1868)

JSOR — *Journal of the Society of Oriental Research* (Chicago, 1917-1932)

JSP — *The Journal of Speculative Philosophy* (St. Louis, 1868-1893)

JSS	*Journal of Semitic Studies* (Manchester, 1956ff.)
JTALC	*Journal of Theology of the American Lutheran Conference* (Minneapolis, 1936-1943) [Volumes 1-5 as: *American Lutheran Conference Journal;* continued from volume 8, #3 as: *Lutheran Outlook* (not included)]
JTC	*Journal for Theology and the Church* (New York, 1965ff.)
JTLC	*Journal of Theology: Church of the Lutheran Confession* (Eau Claire, WI; 1961ff.)
JTS	*Journal of Theological Studies* (Oxford, 1899-1949; *N.S.,* 1950ff.)
JTVI	*Journal of the Transactions of the Victoria Institute, or Philosophical Society of Great Britain* (London, 1866-1957) [Superseded by *Faith & Thought*]
Jud	*Judaism. A Quarterly Journal of Jewish Life and Thought* (New York, 1952ff.)
JWCI	*Journal of the Warburg and Courtauld Institutes* (London,1937ff.)
JWH	*Journal of World History - Cahiers d'Histoire Mondiale - Cuadernos de Historia Mundial* (Paris, 1953ff.)

K

Kêmi	*Kêmi. Revue de philologie et d'archéologie égyptiennes et coptes* (Paris, 1928ff.)
Klio	*Klio. Beiträge zur alten Geschichte* (Leipzig, 1901ff.)
Kobez	*Kobez (Qobeṣ);* קובץ החברה העברית לחקירת ארץ־ישראל ועתיקותיה (Jerusalem, 1921-1945)
KSJA	*Kedem; Studies in Jewish Archaeology* (Jerusalem, 1942, 1945)
Kuml	*Kuml. Årbog for Jysk Arkæologisk Selskab* (Århus, 1951ff.)
Kush	*Kush. Journal of the Sudan Antiquities Service* (Khartoum, Sudan, 1953-1968)
KZ	*Kirchliche Zeitschrift* (St. Louis; Waverly, IA; Chicago; Columbus; 1876-1943)
KZFE	*Kadmos. Zeitschrift für vor-und frühgriechische Epigraphik* (Berlin, 1962ff.)

L

L	*Levant (Journal of the British School of Archaeology in Jerusalem)* (London, 1969ff.)
Lang	*Language. Journal of the Linguistic Society of America* (Baltimore, 1925ff.)
LCQ	*Lutheran Church Quarterly* (Gettysburg, PA; 1928-1949)
LCR	*Lutheran Church Review* (Philadelphia, 1882-1927)
Lěš	*Lěšonénu. Quarterly for the Study of the Hebrew Language and Cognate Subjects* לשוננו (Jerusalem, 1925ff.) [English Summaries from volume 30 onward]
Listen	*Listening* (Dubuque, IA; 1965ff.) [Volume numbers start with "zero"]
LofS	*Life of the Spirit* (London, 1946-1964)
LQ	*The Quarterly Review of the Evangelical Lutheran Church* (Gettysburg, PA; 1871-1927; revived in1949ff.) [From 1878 on as: *The Lutheran Quarterly*]
LQHR	*London Quarterly and Holborn Review* (London, 1853-1968)
LS	*Louvain Studies* (Louvain, 1966ff.)
LSQ	*Lutheran Synod Quarterly* (Mankato, MN, 1960ff.) [Formerly *Clergy Bulletin* (Volume 1 of *LSQ* as *Clergy Bulletin*, Volume 20, #1 & #2)
LTJ	*Lutheran Theological Journal* (North Adelaide, South Australia, 1967ff.)
LTP	*Laval Theologique et Philosophique* (Quebec, 1945ff.)
LTQ	*Lexington Theological Quarterly* (Lexington, KY; 1966ff.)
LTR	*Literary and Theological Review* (New York; Boston, 1834-1839)
LTSB	*Lutheran Theological Seminary Bulletin* (Gettysburg, PA; 1921ff.)
LTSR	*Luther Theological Seminary Review* (St. Paul, MN; 1962ff.)
LWR	*The Lutheran World Review* (Philadelphia, 1948-1950)

M

Man	*Man. A Monthly Record of Anthropological Science* (London,1901-1965; *N. S.*, 1966ff.) [Articles in original series referred to by *article* number not by *page* number - New Series subtitled: *the journal of the Royal Anthropological Institute*]
ManSL	*Manuscripta* (St. Louis, 1957ff.)
MB	*Medelhavsmuseet Bulletin* (Stockholm, 1961ff.)
MC	*The Modern Churchman* (Ludlow, England; 1911ff.)
McQ	*McCormick Quarterly* (Chicago, 1947ff.) [Volumes 1-13 as: *McCormick Speaking*]
MCS	*Manchester Cuneiform Studies* (Manchester, 1951-1964)
MDIÄA	*Mitteilungen des deutsches Instituts für ägyptische Altertumskunde in Kairo* (Cairo, 1930ff.)
Mesop	*Mesopotamia* (Torino, Italy, 1966ff.)
MH	*The Modern Humanist* (Weston, MA; 1944-1962)
MHSB	*The Mission House Seminary Bulletin* (Plymouth, WI; 1954-1962)
MI	*Monthly Interpreter* (Edinburgh, 1884-1886)
MidS	*Midstream (Council on Christian Unity)* (Indianapolis, 1961ff.)
Min	*Ministry. A Quarterly Theological Review for South Africa* (Morija, Basutolan, 1960ff.)
Minos	*Minos. Investigaciones y Materiales Para el Estudio de los Textos Paleocretenses Publicados Bajo la Direccion de Antonio Tovar y Emilio Peruzzi* (Salamanca, 1951ff.) [From Volume 4 on as: *Minos Revista de Filologia Egea*]
MIO	*Mitteilungen des Instituts für Orientforschung [Deutsche Akademie der Wissenschaften zu Berlin Institut für Orientforschung]* (Berlin, 1953ff.)
Miz	*Mizraim. Journal of Papyrology, Egyptology, History of Ancient Laws, and their Relations to the Civilizations of Bible Lands* (New York, 1933-1938)
MJ	*The Museum Journal. Pennsylvania University* (Philadelphia,1910-1935)

MMBR — *The Monthly Magazine and British Register* (London, 1796-1843) [*1st Ser.*, 1796-1826, Volumes 1-60; *N.S.*, 1826-1838, Volumes 1-26; *3rd Ser.*, 1839-1843, Volumes 1-9, however, Volumes 7-9 are marked 95-97 *[sic]*]

ModR — *The Modern Review* (London, 1880-1884)

Monist — *The Monist. An International Quarterly Journal of General Philosophical Inquiry* (Chicago; La Salle, IL; 1891ff.)

Mosaic — *Mosaic* (Cambridge, MA; 1960ff.)

MQ — *The Minister's Quarterly* (New York, 1945-1966)

MQR — *Methodist Quarterly Review (South)* (Louisville, Nashville,1847-1861; 1879-1886; 1886-1930) [*3rd Ser.* as: *Southern Methodist Review*; Volume 52 (1926) misnumbered as 53; Volume 53 (1927) misnumbered as 54; and the volume for 1928 is also marked as 54]

MR — *Methodist Review* (New York, 1818-1931) [Volume 100 not published]

MTSB — *Moravian Theological Seminary Bulletin* (Bethlehem, PA; 1959-1970) [Volume for 1969 apparently not published]

MTSQB — *Meadville Theological School Quarterly Bulletin* (Meadville, PA;1906-1933) [From Volume 25 on as: *Meadville Journal*]

Muséon — *Le Muséon. Revue d'Études Orientales* (Louvain, 1882-1915;1930/32ff.)

MUSJ — *Melánges de l'Université Saint-Joseph. Faculté orientale* (Beirut, 1906ff.)

Mwa-M — *Milla wa-Milla. The Australian Bulletin of Comparative Religion* (Parkville, Victoria, 1961ff.)

N

NB — *Blackfriars. A Monthly Magazine* (Oxford, 1920ff.) [From Volume 46 on as: *New Blackfriars*]

NBR — *North British Review* (Edinburgh, 1844-1871)

NCB — *New College Bulletin* (Edinburgh, 1964ff.)

NEAJT — *Northeast Asia Journal of Theology* (Kyoto, Japan, 1968ff.)

NEST — *The Near East School of Theology Quarterly* (Beirut, 1952ff.)
Nexus — *Nexus* (Boston, 1957ff.)
NGTT — *Nederduitse gereformeerde teologiese tydskrif* (Kaapstad, N.G., Kerk-Uitgewers, 1959ff.)
NOGG — *Nihon Orient Gakkai geppo* (Tokyo, 1955-1959) [Being the *Bulletin of the Society for Near Eastern Studies in Japan* - Continued as: *Oriento*]
NPR — *The New Princeton Review* (New York, 1886-1888)
NOP — *New Orient* (Prague, 1960-1968)
NQR — *Nashotah Quarterly Review* (Nashotah, WI; 1960ff.)
NT — *Novum Testamentum* (Leiden, 1955ff.)
NTS — *New Testament Studies* (Cambridge, England; 1954ff.)
NTT — *Nederlandsch Theologisch Tijdschrift* (Wageningen, 1946ff.)
NTTO — *Norsk Teologisk Tidsskrift* (Oslo, 1900ff.)
Numen — *Numen; International Review for the History of Religions* (Leiden, 1954ff.)
NW — *The New World. A Quarterly Review of Religion, Ethics and Theology* (Boston, 1892-1900)
NYR — *The New York Review. A Journal of The Ancient Faith and Modern Thought (St. John's Seminary)* (New York, 1905-1908)
NZJT — *New Zealand Journal of Theology* (Christchurch, 1931-1935)

O

OA — *Oriens Antiquus* (Rome, 1962ff.)
OBJ — *The Oriental and Biblical Journal* (Chicago, 1880-1881)
OC — *Open Court* (Chicago, 1887-1936)
ONTS — *The Hebrew Student* (Morgan Park, IL; New Haven; Hartford;1881-1892) [Volumes 3-8 as: *The Old Testament Student;* Volume 9 onwards as: *The Old and New Testament Student*]
OOR — *Oriens: The Oriental Review* (Paris, 1926)
OQR — *The Oberlin Quarterly Review* (Oberlin, OH; 1845-1849)
Or — *Orientalia commentarii de rebus Assyri-Babylonicis, Arabicis, and Aegyptiacis, etc.* (Rome 1920-1930)

Or, N.S.	*Orientalia: commentarii, periodici de rebus orientis antiqui* (Rome, 1932ff.)
Oriens	*Oriens. Journal of the International Society of Oriental Research* (Leiden, 1948ff.)
Orient	*Oriento. The Reports of the Society for Near Eastern Studies in Japan* (Tokyo, 1960ff.)
Orita	*Orita. Ibadan Journal of Religious Studies* (Ibadan, Nigeria, 1967ff.)
OrS	*Orientalia Suecana* (Uppsala, 1952ff.)
OSHTP	*Oxford Society of Historical Theology, Abstract of Proceedings* (Oxford, 1891-1968 [Through 1919 as: *Society of Historical Theology, Proceedings*]
Osiris	*Osiris* (Bruges, Belgium; 1936-1968) *[Subtitle varies]*
OTS	*Oudtestamentische Studiën* (Leiden, 1942ff.)
OTW	*Ou-Testamentiese Werkgemeenskap in Suid-Afrika, Proceedings of die* (Pretoria, 1958ff.) [Volume 1 in Volume 14 of: *Hervormde Teologiese Studies*]

P

P	*Preaching: A Journal of Homiletics* (Dubuque, IA; 1965ff.)
P&P	*Past and Present* (London, 1952ff.) *[Subtitle varies]*
PA	*Practical Anthropology* (Wheaton, IL; Eugene, OR; Tarrytown, NY; 1954ff.)
PAAJR	*Proceedings of the American Academy for Jewish Research* (Philadelphia, 1928ff.)
PAOS	*Proceedings of the American Oriental Society* (Baltimore, New Haven; 1842, 1846-50, 1852-1860) [After 1860 all proceedings are bound with *Journal*]
PAPA	*American Philological Association, Proceedings* (Hartford, Boston, 1896ff.) [*Transactions* as: *TAPA. Transactions* and *Proceedings* combine page numbers from volume 77 on]
PAPS	*Proceedings of the American Philosophical Society* (Philadelphia, 1838ff.)
PBA	*Proceedings of the British Academy* (London, 1903ff.)

Periodical Abbreviations

PEFQS — *Palestine Exploration Fund Quarterly Statement* (London, 1869ff.) [From Volume 69 (1937) on as: *Palestine Exploration Quarterly*]

PEQ — *Palestine Exploration Quarterly* [See: *PEFQS*]

PER — *The Protestant Episcopal Review* (Fairfax, Co., VA; 1886-1900) [Volumes 1-5 as: *The Virginian Seminary Magazine*]

Person — *Personalist. An International Review of Philosophy, Religion and Literature* (Los Angeles, 1920ff.)

PF — *Philosophical Forum* (Boston, 1943-1957; *N.S.*, 1968ff.)

PHDS — *Perspectives. Harvard Divinity School* (Cambridge, MA; 1965-1967)

PIASH — *Proceedings of the Israel Academy of Sciences and Humanities* (Jerusalem, 1967ff.)

PIJSL — *Papers of the Institute of Jewish Studies, London* (Jerusalem,1964)

PJT — *Pacific Journal of Theology* (Western Samoa, 1961ff.)

PJTSA — *Jewish Theological Seminary Association, Proceedings* (New York, 1888-1902)

PP — *Perspective* (Pittsburgh, 1960ff.) [Volumes 1-8 as: *Pittsburgh Perspective*]

PQ — *The Presbyterian Quarterly* (New York, 1887-1904)

PQL — *The Preacher's Quarterly* (London, 1954-1969)

PQPR — *The Presbyterian Quarterly and Princeton Review* (New York, 1872-1877)

PQR — *Presbyterian Quarterly Review* (Philadlephia, 1852-1862)

PR — *Presbyterian Review* (New York, 1880-1889)

PRev — *The Biblical Repertory and Princeton Review* (Princeton, Philadelphia, New York, 1829-1884) [Volume 1 as: *The Biblical Repertory, New Series;* Volumes 2-8 as: *The Biblical Repertory and Theological Review*]

PRR — *Presbyterian and Reformed Review* (New York, Philadelphia, (1890-1902)

PSB — *The Princeton Seminary Bulletin* (Princeton, 1907ff.)

PSTJ — *Perkins School of Theology Journal* (Dallas, 1947ff.)

PTR — *Princeton Theological Review* (Princeton, 1903-1929)

PUNTPS — *Proceedings of the University of Newcastle upon the Tyne Philosophical Society* (Newcastle-upon-Tyne, 1967ff.)

Periodical Abbreviations

Q

QCS	*Quarterly Christian Spectator* (New Haven, 1819-1838) *[1st Series* and *New Series* as: *Christian Spectator]*
QDAP	*The Quarterly of the Department of Antiquities in Palestine* (Jerusalem, 1931-1950)
QRL	*Quarterly Review* (London, 1809-1967)
QTMRP	*The Quarterly Theological Magazine, and Religious Repository* (Philadelphia, 1813-1814)

R

R&E	*[Baptist] Review and Expositor* (Louisville, 1904ff.)
R&S	*Religion and Society* (Bangalore, India, 1953ff.)
RAAO	*Revue d'Assyriologie et d'Archéologie Orientale* (Paris, 1886ff.)
RdQ	*Revue de Qumran* (Paris, 1958ff.)
RHA	*Revue Hittite et Asianique* (Paris, 1930ff.)
RIDA	*Revue internationale des droits de l'antiquité* (Brussels, 1948ff.)
RJ	*Res Judicatae. The Journal of the Law Students' Society of Victoria* (Melbourne, 1935-1957)
RL	*Religion in Life* (New York, 1932ff.)
RChR	*The Reformed Church Review* (Mercersburg, PA; Chambersburg, PA; Philadelphia; 1849-1926) [Volumes 1-25 as: *Mercersburg Review;* Volumes 26-40 as: *Reformed Quarterly Review; 4th Series* on as: *Reformed Church Review*]
RCM	*Reformed Church Magazine* (Reading, PA; 1893-1896) [Volume 3 as: *Reformed Church Historical Magazine*]
RDSO	*Rivista degli Studi Orientali* (Rome, 1907ff.)
RÉ	*Revue Égyptologique* (Paris, 1880-1896; *N.S.*, 1919-1924)
RÉg	*Revue d'Égyptologie* (Paris, 1933ff.)
RefmR	*The Reformation Review* (Amsterdam, 1953ff.)

RefR — *The Reformed Review. A Quarterly Journal of the Seminaries of the Reformed Church in America* (Holland, MI; New Brunswick, NJ; 1947ff.) [Volumes 1-9 as: *Western Seminary Bulletin*]

RelM — *Religion in the Making* (Lakeland, FL; 1940-1943)

Resp — *Response—in worship—Music—The arts* (St. Paul, 1959ff.)

RestQ — *Restoration Quarterly* (Austin, TX; Abeline, TX; 1957ff.)

RFEASB — *The Hebrew University/Jerusalem: Department of Archaeology. Louis M. Rabinowitz Fund for the Exploration of Ancient Synagogues, Bulletin* (Jerusalem, 1949-1960)

RO — *Rocznik Orjentalistyczny. (Wydaje Polskie towarzystwo orjentalisyczne)* (Kraków, Warsaw, 1914ff.)

RP — *Records of the Past* (Washington, DC; 1902-1914)

RR — *Review of Religion* (New York, 1936-1958)

RS — *Religious Studies* (London, 1965ff.)

RTP — *Review of Theology and Philosophy* (Edinburgh, 1905-1915)

RTR — *Recueil de travaux relatifs à la philologie et à l'archéologie egyptiennes et assyriennes* (Paris, 1870-1923)

RTRM — *The Reformed Theological Review* (Melbourne, 1941ff.)

S

SAENJ — *Seminar. An Annual Extraordinary Number of the Jurist* (Washington, DC; 1943-1956)

SBAP — *Society of Biblical Archæology, Proceedings* (London, 1878-1918)

SBAT — *Society of Biblical Archæology, Transactions* (London, 1872-1893)

SBE — *Studia Biblica et Ecclesiastica* (Oxford, 1885-1903) Volume 1 as: *Studia Biblica*]

SBFLA — *Studii (Studium) Biblici Franciscani. Liber Annuus* (Jerusalem, 1950ff.)

SBLP — *Society of Biblical Literature & Exegesis, Proceedings* (Baltimore, 1880)

Periodical Abbreviations

SBO	*Studia Biblica et Orientalia* (Rome 1959) [Being Volumes 10-12 respectively of *Analecta Biblica. Investigationes Scientificae in Res Biblicas*]
SBSB	*Society for Biblical Studies Bulletin* (Madras, India, 1964ff.)
SCO	*Studi Classici e Orientali* (Pisa, 1951ff.)
Scotist	*The Scotist* (Teutopolis, IL; 1939-1967)
SCR	*Studies in Comparative Religion* (Bedfont, Middlesex, England, 1967ff.)
Scrip	*Scripture. The Quarterly of the Catholic Biblical Association* (London, 1944-1968)
SE	*Study Encounter* (Geneva, 1965ff.)
SEÅ	*Svensk Exegetisk Årsbok* (Uppsala-Lund, 1936ff.)
SEAJT	*South East Journal of Theology* (Singapore, 1959ff.)
Sefunim	*Sefunim (Bulletin)* [היפה] סינים (Haifa, 1966-1968)
SGEI	*Studies in the Geography of Eretz-Israel* (Jerusalem, מחקרים בגיאוגרפיה של ארץ-ישראל 1959ff.) [English summaries in Volumes 1-3 only; continuing the *Bulletin of the Israel Exploration Society (Yediot)*]
SH	*Scripta Hierosolymitana* (Jerusalem, 1954ff.)
Shekel	*The Shekel* (New York, 1968ff.)
SIR	*Smithsonian Institute Annual Report of the Board of Regents* (Washington, DC; 1846-1964; becomes: *Smithsonian Year* from 1965 on]
SJH	*Seminary Journal* (Hamilton, NY; 1892)
SJT	*Scottish Journal of Theology* (Edinburgh, 1947ff.)
SL	*Studia Liturgica. An International Ecumenical Quarterly for Liturgical Research and Renewal* (Rotterdam, 1962ff.)
SLBR	*Sierra Leone Bulletin of Religion* (Freetown, Sierra Leone;1959-1966)
SMR	*Studia Montes Regii* (Montreal, 1958-1967)
SMSDR	*Studi e Materiali di Storia Delle Religioni* (Rome, Bologna, 1925ff.
SO	*Studia Orientalia* (Helsinki, 1925ff.)
SOOG	*Studi Orientalistici in Onore di Giorgio Levi Della Vida* (Rome, 1956)
Sophia	*Sophia. A Journal for Discussion in Philosophical Theology* (Parkville, N.S.W., Australia, 1962ff.)
SP	*Spirit of the Pilgrims* (Boston, 1828-1833)

SPR	*Southern Presbyterian Review* (Columbia, SC; 1847-1885)
SQ/E	*The Shane Quarterly* (Indianapolis, 1940ff.) [From Volume 17 on as: *Encounter*]
SR	*The Seminary Review* (Cincinnati, 1954ff.)
SRL	*The Scottish Review* (London, Edinburgh, 1882-1900; 1914-1920)
SS	*Seminary Studies of the Athenaeum of Ohio* (Cincinnati, 1926-1968) [Volumes 1-15 as: *Seminary Studies*]
SSO	*Studia Semitica et Orientalia* (Glasgow, 1920, 1945)
SSR	*Studi Semitici* (Rome, 1958ff.)
ST	*Studia Theologica* (Lund, 1947ff.)
StEv	*Studia Evangelica* (Berlin, 1959ff.) [Being miscellaneous volumes of: *Text und Untersuchungen zur Geschichte der altchristlichen Literatur,* beginning with Volume 73]
StLJ	*The Saint Luke's Journal* (Sewanee, TN; 1957ff.) [Volume 1, #1 as: *St. Luke's Journal of Theology*]
StMR	*St. Marks Review: An Anglican Quarterly* (Canberra, N.S.W., Australia, 1955ff.)
StP	*Studia Patristica* (Berlin, 1957ff.) [Being miscellaneous volumes of: *Text und Untersuchungen zur Geschichte der altchristlichen Literatur,* beginning with Volume 63]
StVTQ	*St. Vladimir's Theological Quarterly* (Crestwood, NY; 1952ff. [Volumes 1-4 as: *St. Vladimir's Seminary Quarterly*]
Sumer	*Sumer. A Journal of Archaeology in Iraq* (Bagdad, 1945ff.)
SWJT	*Southwestern Journal of Theology* (Fort Worth, 1917-1924; *N.S.,* 1950ff.)
Syria	*Syria, revue d'art oriental et d'archéologie* (Paris, 1920ff.)

T

T&C	*Theology and the Church / SÎN-HÁK kap kàu-Hōe (Tainan Theological College)* (Tainan, Formosa, 1957ff.)
T&L	*Theology and Life* (Lancester, PA; 1958-1966)

Periodical Abbreviations

TAD — *Türk tarih, arkeologya ve etnoğrafya dergisi* (Istanbul, 1933-1949; continued as: *Türk arkeoloji Dergisi*, (Ankara, 1956ff.)

TAPA — *American Philological Society, Transactions* (See: *PAPA*)

TAPS — *Transactions of the American Philosophical Society* (Philadelphia, 1789-1804; *N.S.*, 1818ff.)

Tarbiz — *Tarbiz. A quarterly review of the humanities;* תרביץ רעזן למדעי היהדות. שנת (Jerusalem , 1929ff.) [English Summaries from Volume 24 on only]

TB — *Tyndale Bulletin* (London, 1956ff.) [Numbers 1-16 as: *Tyndale House Bulletin*]

TBMDC — *Theological Bulletin: McMaster Divinity College* (Hamilton, Ontario, 1967ff.)

TE — *Theological Education* (Dayton, 1964ff.)

Tem — *Temenos. Studies in Comparative Religion* (Helsinki, 1965ff.)

TEP — *Theologica Evangelica. Journal of the Faculty of Theology, University of South Africa* (Pretoria, 1968ff.)

Text — *Textus. Annual of the Hebrew University Bible Project* (Jerusalem, 1960ff.)

TF — *Theological Forum* (Minneapolis, 1929-1935)

TFUQ — *Thought . A Quarterly of the Sciences and Letters* (New York, 1926ff.) [From Volume 15 on as: *Thought. Fordham University Quarterly*]

ThE — *Theological Eclectic* (Cincinnati; New York, 1864-1871)

Them — *Themelios, International Fellowship of Evangelical Students* (Fresno, CA; 1962ff.)

Theo — *Theology; A Journal of Historic Christianity* (London, 1920ff.)

ThSt — *Theological Studies* (New York; Woodstock, MD; 1940ff.)

TLJ — *Theological and Literary Journal* (New York, 1848-1861)

TM — *Theological Monthly* (St. Louis, 1921-1929)

TML — *The Theological Monthly* (London, 1889-1891)

TPS — *Transactions of the Philological Society* (London, 1842ff.) [Volumes 1-6 as: *Proceedings*]

TQ — *Theological Quarterly* (St. Louis, 1897-1920)

Tr — *Traditio. Studies in Ancient and Medieval History, Thought and Religion* (New York, 1943ff.)

Trad — *Tradition. A Journal of Orthodox Jewish Thought* (New York, 1958ff.)

TRep — *Theological Repository* (London, 1769-1788)

TRFCCQ	*Theological Review and Free Church College Quarterly* (Edinburgh, 1886-1890)
TRGR	*The Theological Review and General Repository of Religious and Moral Information, Published Quarterly* (Baltimore, 1822)
TRL	*Theological Review: A Quarterly Journal of Religious Thought and Life* (London, 1864-1879)
TT	*Theology Today* (Lansdown, PA; 1944ff.)
TTCA	*Trinity Theological College Annual* (Singapore, 1964-1969) [Volume 5 apparently never published]
TTD	*Teologisk Tidsskrift* (Decorah, IA; 1899-1907)
TTKB	*Türk Tarih Kurumu Belleten* (Ankara, 1937ff.)
TTKF	*Tidskrift för teologi och kyrkiga frågor (The Augustana Theological Quarterly)* (Rock Island, IL; 1899-1917)
TTL	*Theologisch Tijdschrift* (Leiden, 1867-1919) [English articles from Volume 45 on only]
TTM	*Teologisk Tidsskrift* (Minneapolis, 1917-1928)
TUSR	*Trinity University Studies in Religion* (San Antonio, 1950ff.)
TZ	*Theologische Zeitschrift* (Basel, 1945ff.)
TZDES	*Theologische Zeitschrift (Deutsche Evangelische Synode des Westens, North America)* (St. Louis, 1873-1934) [Continued from Volumes 22 through 26 as: *Magazin für Evangel. Theologie und Kirche;* and from Volume 27 on as: *Theological Magazine*]
TZTM	*Theologische Zeitblätter, Theological Magazine* (Columbus,1911-1919)

U

UC	*The Unitarian Christian* (Boston, 1947ff.) [Volumes 1-4 as: *Our Faith*]
UCPSP	*University of California Publications in Semitic Philology* (Berkeley, 1907ff.)
UF	*Ugarit-Forschungen. Internationales Jahrbuch für die Altertumskunde Syrien-Palästinas* (Neukirchen, West Germany; 1969ff.)

ULBIA — *Univeristy of London. Bulletin of the Institute of Archaeology* (London, 1958ff.)
UMB — *The University Museum Bulletin (University of Pennsylvania* (Philadelphia, 1930-1958)
UMMAAP — *University of Michigan. Museum of Anthropology. Anthropological Papers* (Ann Arbor, 1949ff.)
UPQR — *The United Presbyterian Quarterly Review* (Pittsburgh, 1860-1861)
UQGR — *Universalist Quarterly and General Review* (Boston, 1844-1891)
UnionR — *The Union Review* (New York, 1939-1945)
URRM — *The Unitarian Review and Religious Magazine* (Boston, 1873-1891)
USQR — *Union Seminary Quarterly Review* (New York, 1945ff.)
USR — *Union Seminary Review* (Hampton-Sidney, VA; Richmond; 1890-1946) [Volumes 1-23 as: *Union Seminary Magazine*]
UTSB — *United Theological Seminary Bulletin* (Dayton, 1905ff.) [Including: *The Bulletin of the Evangelical School of Theology; Bulletin of the Union Biblical Seminary,* later, *Bonebrake Theological Bulletin*]
UUÅ — *Uppsala Universitets Årsskrift* (Uppsala, 1861-1960)

V

VC — *Virgiliae Christianae: A Review of Early Christian Life and Language* (Amsterdam, 1947ff.)
VDETF — *Deutsche Vierteljahrsschrift für englisch-theologische Forschung und Kritik / herausgegeben von M. Heidenheim* (Leipzig, Zurich, 1861-1865) [Continued as: *Vierteljahrsschrift für deutsch-englisch- theologische Forschung und Kritik. . .* 1866-1873]
VDI — *Vestnik Drevnei Istoriĭ. Journal of Ancient History* (Moscow, 1946ff.) [English summaries from 1967 on only]
VDR — *Koinonia* (Nashville, 1957-1968) [Continued as: *Vanderbilt Divinity Review,* 1969-1971]

VE — *Vox Evangelica. Biblical and Historical Essays by the Members of the Faculty of the London Bible College* (London, 1962ff.)
Voice — *The Voice* (St. Paul, 1958-1960) [Subtitle varies]
VR — *Vox Reformata* (Geelong, Victoria, Australia, 1962ff.)
VT — *Vetus Testamentum* (Leiden, 1951ff.)
VTS — *Vetus Testamentum, Supplements* (Leiden, 1953ff.)

W

Way — *The Way. A Quarterly Review of Christian Spirituality* (London, 1961ff.)
WBHDN — *The Wittenberg Bulletin (Hamma Digest Number)* (Springfield, OH; 1903ff.) [Volumes 40-60 (1943-1963) only contain *Hamma Digest Numbers*]
WesTJ — *Wesleyan Theological Journal. Bulletin of the Wesleyan Theological Society* (Lakeville, IN; 1966ff.)
WLQ — *Wisconsin Lutheran Quarterly* (Wauwatosa, WI; Milwaukee;1904ff.) [Also entitled: *Theologische Quartalschrift*]
WO — *Die Welt des Orients. Wissenschaftliche Beiträge zur Kunde des Morgenlandes* (Göttingen, 1947ff.)
Word — *Word: Journal of the Linguistic Circle of New York* (New York, 1945ff.)
WR — *The Westminster Review* (London, New York, 1824-1914)
WSQ — *Wartburg Seminary Quarterly* (Dubuque, IA; 1937-1960) [Volumes 1-9, #1 as: *Quarterly of the Wartburg Seminary Association*]
WSR — *Wesleyan Studies in Religion* (Buckhannon,WV; 1960-1970) [Volumes 53-62 only *[sic]*]
WTJ — *Westminster Theological Journal* (Philadelphia, 1938ff.)
WW — *Western Watch* (Pittsburgh, 1950-1959) [Superseded by: *Pittsburgh Perspective*]
WZKM — *Wiener Zeitschrift für die Kunde des Morgenlandes* (Vienna, 1886ff.)

Periodical Abbreviations

Y

YCCAR	*Yearbook of the Central Conference of American Rabbis* (Cincinnati, 1890ff.)
YCS	*Yale Classical Studies* (New Haven, 1928ff.)
YDQ	*Yale Divinity Quarterly* (New Haven, 1904ff.) [Volumes 30-62 as: *Yale Divinity News,* continued as: *Reflections*]
YR	*The Yavneh Review. A Religious Jewish Collegiate Magazine* (New York, 1961ff.) [Volume 2 never published]

Z

Z	*Zygon. Journal of Religion and Science* (Chicago, 1966ff.)
ZA	*Zeitschrift für Assyriologie und verwandte Gebiete* (Leipzig, Strassburg, Berlin, 1886ff.)
ZÄS	*Zeitschrift für ägyptische Sprache und Altertumskunde* (Leipzig, Berlin, 1863ff.)
ZAW	*Zeitschrift für die alttestamentliche Wissenschaft* (Giessen, Berlin, 1881ff.)
ZDMG	*Zeitschrift der Deutschen Morgenländischen Gesellschaft* (Leipzig, Wiesbaden, 1847ff.)
ZDPV	*Zeitschrift des Deutschen Palästina-Vereins* (Leipzig, Wiesbaden, 1878ff.) [English articles from Volume 82 on only]
Zion	*Zion. A Quarterly for Research in Jewish History, New Series* ציון סדרה חדשה רבעון לחקר תולדות ישראל (Jerusalem, 1935ff.) [English summaries from Volume 3 on only]
ZK	*Zeitschrift für Keilschriftforschung* (Leipzig, 1884-1885)
ZNW	*Zeitschrift für die neutestamentliche Wissenschaft und die Kunde des Urchristentums (. . . Kunde der älteren Kirche,* 1921— *)* (Giessen, Berlin, 1900ff.)
ZS	*Zeitschrift für Semitistik und verwandte Gebiete* (Leipzig, 1922-1935)

Anonymous, "Literary and Scientific Intelligence," *AOL* 1 (1820-21) 562-565. [2. Catalogue of Printed Books from Pera and Scutari, Turkey Since 1782, pp. 562-564]

†Anonymous, "Manuals of Ancient History," *ERCJ* 132 (1870) 154-176. *(Review)*

Chas. H. S. Davis, "Index of Articles on Archaeology, Anthropology and Ethnology, Which have appeared in American and English Periodicals during 1879," *OBJ* 1 (1880) 100-103.

Anonymous, "Semitic and Old Testament Bibliography," *ONTS* 2 (1882-83) 254-256, 286-287, 331-332; 3 (1883-84) 32, 62-64, 95-96, 127-128, 175-176, 221-224, 271-272, 319-320, 367-368, 414-416; 4 (1884-85) 46-48, 94-96, 142-144, 191-192, 240, 287-288, 335-336, 383-384, 431-432, 475-476; 5 (1885-86) 48, 95-96, 143-144, 189-192, 239-240, 286-288.

Anonymous, "Semitic Bibliography," *AJSL* 1 (1884-85) 23-24, 48, 72, 135-136, 199-200, 263-264; 2 (1885-86) 63-64, 127-128, 191-192, 255-256; 3 (1886-87) 62-64, 127-128, 191-192, 273-274; 4 (1887-88) 63-64, 126-128, 192, 253-254; 5 (1888-89) 94-96, 207-208, 297-298; 6 (1889-90) 77-80, 158-160, 237-239, 317-320; 7 (1890-91) 80, 159-160, 239-240, 306; 8 (1891-92) 109-112; 9 (1892-93) 232-243; 10 (1893-94) 218-224.

Anonymous, "What to Write Upon and Where to Read on It," *ET* 1 (1889-90) 211-214.

A. Neubauer, "Bibliography 1890-91," *JQR* 4 (1891-92) 307-318.

A. Neubauer, "Bibliography 1891-2," *JQR* 5 (1892-93) 281-294.

Ira M. Price, "Semitic Bibliography," *AJSL* 11 (1894-95) 111-117, 245-253; 12 (1895-96) 126-132.

Anonymous, "Semitic Bibliography," *AJSL* 12 (1895-96) 274-283; 13 (1896-97) 81-88, 154-162, 240-248, 318-328; 14 (1897-98) 51-56.

W. Muss-Arnolt, "Bibliography," *AJT* 1 (1897) 271-288, 555-576, 858-882, 1130-1150.

W. Muss-Arnolt, "Theological and Semitic Literature: A Bibliographical Supplement," *AJSL* 14 (1897-98) i-xxxii (*following pp. 136, 216, 296 respectively*); 15 (1898-99) i-xxxvi (*following p. 64*), i-xvi (*following p. 128*), i-xxxii (*following p.192*); i-xxxii (*following p. 260*); 16 (1899-1900) i-xvi (*following p. 64*), i-xvi (*following p. 128*), i-xxxii (*following p.192*)

W. Muss-Arnolt, "Theological and Semitic Literature," *AJT* 2 (1898) [(*in four parts, each section numbered with Roman numerals*) sections follow pp. 240, 480, 736, 976 respectively. (*sometimes bound together at end of volume*)]

W. Muss-Arnolt, "Theological and Semitic Literature," *BW* 12 (1898) i-xxxvi. (*following p. 288*)

W. Muss-Arnolt, "Theological and Semitic Literature,1899," *AJT* 3 (1899) [(*in four parts, each section numbered with Roman numerals*) sections follow pp.224, 432, 640, 884 respectively. (*sometimes bound together at end of volume*)]

W. Muss-Arnolt, "Theological and Semitic Literature, 1900," *AJT* 4 (1900) [(*in four parts, each section numbered with Roman numerals*) sections follow pp. 256, 464 respectively. (*sometimes bound together at end of volume*)]

Benjamin B. Warfield, "The Century's Progress in Biblical Knowledge," *HR* 39 (1900) 195-202.

W. Muss-Arnolt, "Theological and Semitic Literature for the Year 1900," *AJSL* 17 (1900-01) #3, 1-108. (*following p. 196 - paged separately*)

W. Muss-Arnolt, "Theological and Semitic Literature for the Year 1900," *AJT* 5 (1901) 1-108. (*following p. 432 - paged separately*)

W. Muss-Arnolt, "Theological and Semitic Literature for the Year 1901," *AJSL* 18 (1901-02) 1-112. (*following p. 192 - paged separately*)

W. Muss-Arnolt, "Theological and Semitic Literature for the Year 1901," *AJT* 6 (1902) 1-112. *(following p. 416 - paged separately)*

Anonymous, "The Young Pastor's Library," *PQ* 16 (1902-03) 407-409.

I. Abrahams, "Bibliography of Hebraica and Judaica," *JQR* 17 (1904-05), 598-608, 810-822; 18 (1905-06) 191-207, 391-398, 571-586, 772-782; 19 (1906-07) 198-208, 429-440.

George F. Moore, "Christian Writers of Judaism," *HTR* 14 (1921) 197-254. [I. To the End of the Eighteenth Century; II. The Nineteenth Century to the Present]

Herbert H. Gowen, "Spiritual Movements in the Oriental Religions: A Reading Course," *ATR* 11 (1928-29) 159-164.

Anonymous, "Dropsie College Theses," *JQR, N.S.* 24 (1933-34) 101-102.

Wilbur M. Smith, "Some Much Needed Books in Biblical and Theological Literature," *BS* 91 (1934) 47-64, 191-201.

John McConnachie, "Notes on books," *CCQ* 4 (1946-47) #1, 49-51.

Joseph L. Mihelic, "Books for the Pastors' Library," *DSQ* 1 (1947) #2, 18-20.

Richard N. Frye, "Orientalia in Germany and Scandinavia," *JAOS* 67 (1947) 139-141.

A. Theissen, "Catholic English Bibliography of General Questions Bearing on Sacred Scriptures," *Scrip* 2 (1947) 116-118; 3 (1948) 27-29, 59-61. [Ecclesiastical Documents; Catholic English Bible Texts; The Canon of Sacred Scripture; Inspiration; Hermeneutics; Introduction to Sacred Scripture, O.T. and N.T.; Bible History; Biblical Geography; Biblical Archaeology; Texts and Versions of the Bible; History of Exegesis; Dictionaries; Concordances; Periodicals]

Richard N. Frye, "Further note on Orientalia in Germany," *JAOS* 68 (1948) 68.

G. Graystone, "Catholic English Bibliography of General Questions on the Scriptures," *Scrip* 6 (1953-54) 84-94. [1. General; 2. The Church and the Bible; 3. Catholic English Bible Texts; 4. The Canon of Sacred Scripture; 5. Inspiration; 6. Hermeneutics; 7. General Introduction to Sacred Scripture; 8. Bible History; 9. Biblical Geography; 9. */sic/* Biblical Archaeology, (a) General, (b) The Dead Sea Scrolls; 10. Texts and Versions, (a) General, (b) Greek and Latin, (c) English Versions; 11. History of Exegesis; 12. Biblical Theology (General); 13. Preaching, reading and the Liturgy; 4. */sic/* Miscellaneous Questions.]

Ignatius J. Hunt, "Trends in Biblical Study," *ABenR* 11 (1960) 280-301.

Ignatius J. Hunt, "Recent Biblical Study, 1960-61," *ABenR* 12 (1961) 328-360.

*W. C. Heiser, "Theology Digest magazine list," *TD* 10 (1962) 152-170. [VI. a. Biblical Archaeology, pp. 159-160; The Bible, pp. 160-161]

A. F. Walls, "Some Biblical Studies of 1961," *Them* 1 (1962-63) #2, 16-23.

Ignatius J. Hunt, "Recent Biblical Study, 1961-63," *ABenR* 14 (1963) 590-621.

S. O. Hills and J. A. Walther, "Biblical Studies. General," *PP* 7 (1965) #3, 4-5.

Ignatius [J.] Hunt, "Recent Biblical Study, 1963-1965," *ABenR* 16 (1965)120-170.

Ignatius [J.] Hunt, "Recent Biblical Study," *ABenR* 17 (1966) 533-580.

Ignatius [J.] Hunt, "Recent Biblical Study: Part I," *ABenR* 20 (1969) 28-64.

Ignatius [J.] Hunt, "Recent Biblical Study: Part II," *ABenR* 20 (1969) 171-197.

§2 *1.1 Bibliographical Articles on the Old Testament [For Articles on the Dead Sea Scrolls see: Studies in the Dead Sea Scrolls, Bibliographical Material →]*

Anonymous, "Commentaries on the Scriptures, I. Old Testament," *BS* 7 (1850) 379-387.

†Anonymous, "Recent Introductions to the Old Testament," *BFER* 10 (1861) 725-762. *(Review)*

W. R[obertson] Smith, "The Study of the Old Testament in 1876," *BFER* 26 (1877) 779-805.

A. B. Davidson, "Review of Works on Old Testament Exegesis in 1878," *BFER* 28 (1879) 337-367.

†Anonymous, "Clark's Foreign Theological Library," *LQHR* 52 (1879) 265-285. *(Review) [Some Reference to O.T. Commentaries]*

Revere F. Weidner, "Letter II.—To a Pastor Who Wishes to Invest $200 in Books Pertaining to Old Testament Study," *ONTS* 7 (1887-88)116-119.

John P. Peters, "Professor Weidner's Lists," *ONTS* 7 (1887-88) 146-149.

W. R. Harper, "An Old Testament Library," *ONTS* 7 (1887-88) 223-225.

S. R. Driver, "Recent Old Testament Literature," *ContR* 55 (1889) 393-402. *(Review)*

A. J. Maas, "The Library of A Priest. Second Article. Department of Sacred Scripture, comprising Introduction, Auxiliary Sciences and Exegesis," *AER* 12 (1895) 138-150.

Henry Bond, "The Best Bible Commentaries," *ET* 14 (1902-03) 151-155.

Anonymous, "Notes on 'The Best Bible Commentaries, Old Testament'," *ET* 14 (1902-03) 270-271.

*John M[erlin] P[owis] Smith, "Annotated List of Books on Early Old Testament History," *BW* 28 (1906) 421-423.

John Merlin Powis Smith, "Books for Old Testament Study," *BW* 30 (1907) 135-162.

Crawford H. Toy, "Survey of Recent Literature: The Old Testament," *HTR* 1 (1908) 377-381.

Wm. J. Hinke, "A Selected Bibliography for Old Testament Study," *ASRec* 8 (1912-13) 32-46.

*J[ohn] M[erlin] Powis Smith, "A Professional Reading Course on the Religion of the Hebrews and Modern Scholarship," *BW* 42 (1913) 234-239, 305-308, 373-377.

Stanley A. Cook, "Survey of Some Recent Literature on the Old Testament," *RTP* 9 (1913-14) 1-21, 61-81.

*J[ohn] M[erlin] Powis Smith, "A Professional Reading Course on the Religion of the Hebrews and Modern Scholarship IV," *BW* 43 (1914) 44-48.

G. H. Box, "Some Recent Contributions to Old Testament Studies," *CQR* 80 (1915) 50-113. *(Review)*

F. C. Porter and George Dahl, "A Bibliography. Books for a Minister's Study. II. Old Testament," *YDQ* 13 (1916-17) 216-220.

James A. Kelso, "Bibliography. Old Testament," *BWTS* 10 (1917-18) 11-30.

William J. Hinke, "A Bibliography for Old Testament Study," *ASRec* 15 (1919) 147-192.

H[oward] C. Ackerman, "An Old Testament Bibliography for 1914 to 1917 Inclusive," *ATR* 1 (1918-19) 214-239, 314-332.

Howard C. Ackerman, "An Old Testament Bibliography for 1914 to 1917 Inclusive," *ATR* 2 (1919-20) 43-70.

George William Brown, "Some Helpful Books on the Old Testament," *CollBQ* 10 (1919-20) #4, 31-32.

W. B. Stevenson, "The Ten Best Books on the Value and Use of the Old Testament," *Exp, 9th Ser.*, 1 (1924) 404-415.

John A. Maynard, "A Current Bibliography of Old Testament Studies for the Years 1918 to 1923," *JSOR* 8 (1924) 182-195.

Anonymous, "The Value of the Old Testament for To-day," *HR* 89 (1925) 29.

Samuel A. B. Mercer, "General Introduction to the Old Testament. A Reading Course," *ATR* 12 (1929-30) 51-52.

Carl A. Anderson, "Recent Developments in the Field of Old Testament Literature," *AugQ* 13 (1934) 256-290.

*Robert H. Pfeiffer, "The History, Religion, and Literature of Israel. Research in the Old Testament, 1914-1925," *HTR* 27 (1934) 241-325.

John Paterson, "The Student and the Old Testament," *DG* 6 (1934-35) #4, 1-3, 9.

H. Wheeler Robinson, "The Best Books on the Old Testament," *ET* 48 (1936-37) 151-154.

Robert H. Pfeiffer, "Articles on the Old Testament Published in English During 1937," *JAAR* 6 (1938) 39-41.

*Beatrice L. Goff, "Books Suitable for Use in Undergraduate Courses in the Old Testament," *JAAR* 6 (1938) 140-143, 171.

W. A. Irwin, "Fifty Years of Old Testament Scholarship," *JAAR* 10 (1942)131-135, 183.

S[amuel] L. Terrien, "A Survey of Recent Theological Literature. The Old Testament," *USQR* 1 (1945-46) #1, 27-29.

James Percival Berkley, Paul Sevier Minear, Russell Chase Tuck, and John Humphrey Scammon, "Theological Bibliographies. I. The Bible and Biblical Interpretation," *ANQ* 38 (1946) #2, 3-8; 43 (1951) #4, 5-9.

Robert H. Pfeiffer, "Research in the Old Testament (1946)," *JAAR* 15 (1947) 171-173.

James Muilenburg, "A Survey of Recent Theological Literature, The Old Testament," *USQR* 2 (1946-47) #1, 23-25.

Anonymous, "A Theological Bibliography," *AugQ* 26 (1947) 160-177. [Old Testament References, pp. 162-164]

Samuel L. Terrien, "A Survey of Recent Theological Literature. Current Old Testament Books," *USQR* 3 (1947-48) #4, 21-23.

Samuel L. Terrien, "A Survey of Recent Theological Literature, Old Testament," *USQR* 5 (1949-50) #2, 29-34.

Claude V. Roebuck, "A Bibliography for Ministers—II. Old Testament," *USQR* 5 (1949-50) #3, 21-26.

*Wilbur M. Smith, "Some Recently Published (1950-1952) Bibliographies in Books of Biblical Interpretation, Theology, and Church History," *FLB* #17-18 (1953) 3-13. [O.T. - General, p. 5; Old Testament Books, p. 6; The Jews - Israel, p. 13]

Anonymous, "A Book List. The Old Testament," *SR* 2 (1955-56) #4, 12-17.

Anonymous, "Theological Bibliographies. The Old Testament," *ANQ* 48 (1956) #4, 6-15.

Donald H. Gard, "Old Testament Periodical Literature 1954," *Interp* 10 (1956) 72-84.

Anonymous, "A List of Recent Master's Theses in Bible and Bible Related Studies at Abilene Christian College," *RestQ* 1 (1957) 130-132; 2 (1958) 11-12.

Alex Humphrey Jr., "A List of Some Doctors of Philosophy and Doctors of Theology Dissertations by Members of Churches of Christ," *RestQ* 2 (1958) 71-72. *[Some O.T. Subjects]*

James Muilenberg and George Landes, "Bibliography for Ministers, Old Testament," *USQR* 14 (1958-59) #2, 41-51.

G. R. Driver, A. R. Johnson, John Mauchline, H. H. Rowley, N. H. Snaith, and D. Winton Thomas, "Old Testament Commentaries," *ET* 71 (1959-60) 4-7.

Anonymous, "Old Testament Bibliography," *R&E* 59 (1962) 71-75.

Theordore N. Swanson, "The New Relevance of Old Testament Study," *ASR* 15 (1963) #4, 9-15.

Anonymous, "Bibliographies: Biblical Literature," *ASW* 17 (1963) #1, 5-31. [The Bible, pp. 6-11; Old Testament, pp. 12-21]

Calvin Katter, "Some Biblical Commentaries for the Pastor's Study," *CovQ* 21 (1963) #2, 3-10. [O.T. References, pp. 4-5.]

Anonymous, "Theological Bibliographies. The Old Testament," *ANQ, N.S.* 4 (1963-64) #1, 10-20.

James R. Brown, "An Old Testament Bookshelf," *NQR* 4 (1963-64) #4, 10-25.

George W. Anderson, "Old Testament Survey 1939-1964," *ET* 76 (1964-65) 9-14.

Carrol Stuhlmuller*[sic]*, "The Bible and the World of Books," *CC* 15 (1965) 305-323.

Frederick Holgren, "Some Recent Literature on the Old Testament," *CovQ* 23 (1965) #3, 9-18.

S. O. Hills (and staff), "Biblical Studies. Old Testament," *PP* 7 (1965) #3, 6-11.

Frederick L. Moriarty, "Boston College Select Bibliography of the Bible," *BibT* #23 (1966) 1548-1557. [Section II - The Old Testament, pp.1550-1552]

R. E. Clements, "I Recommend You Read. I. Some Recent Books on the Old Testament," *ET* 78 (1966-67) 4-8.

§3 *1.1.1 The Pentateuch*

*C. H. H. Wright, "Advice About Commentaries: I. The Pentateuch and Joshua," *Exp, 3rd Ser.*, 7 (1888) 228-239; 8 (1888) 462-472.

*Lewis B. Paton, "Aids to the Study of the Pentateuch and Joshua," *HSR* 8 (1897-98) 138-145.

*James Gale Inglis, "The Pentateuch and the Book of Genesis as Treated in the 'Biblical World'," *BW* 13 (1899) 263-265.

A. S. Peake, "The Movement of Old Testament Scholarship in the Nineteenth Century. Some Leading Dates in Pentateuch Criticism," *BJRL* 1 (1903-08) 65-66.

John A. Maynard, "A Bibliography of Pentateuch Studies for 1918 to 1923," *JSOR* 9 (1925) 41-72.

[J. Giblet], "Pentateuch and recent research," *TD* 4 (1956) 184.

§4 *1.1.1.1 Genesis*

*James Gale Inglis, "The Pentateuch and the Book of Genesis as Treated in the 'Biblical World'," *BW* 13 (1899) 263-265.

Elmer Harding, "Genesis. Hints for Study," *ET* 11 (1899-1900) 28-29.

§5 *1.1.1.2 Exodus*

Francis Brown, "Commentaries on Exodus," *ONTS* 6 (1886-87) 84-91.

J. A. Emerton, "Commentaries on Exodus," *Theo* 66 (1963) 453-456.

(§6) *1.1.1.3 Leviticus*

(§7) *1.1.1.4 Numbers*

§8 *1.1.1.5 Deuteronomy*

L. B. Cross, "Commentaries on Deuteronomy," *Theo* 64 (1961) 184-189.

§9 *1.1.2 The Prophets - General Studies*

G. H. Box, "The Ten Best Books on the Prophetic Literature," *Exp, 9th Ser.*, 2 (1924) 167-182.

[G. H. Box(?)], "The Ten Best Books on the Prophetic Literature," *HR* 89 (1925) 28-29.

John A. Maynard, "A Critical Bibliography of the Prophetical Books of the Old Testament since 1918," *JSOR* 9 (1925) 131-167.

§10 *1.1.2.1 The Former Prophets - General Studies*

*Barnabas Lindars, "Commentaries on Samuel and Kings," *Theo* 67 (1964) 11-15.

§11 *1.1.2.1.1 Joshua*

*C. H. H.Wright, "Advice About Commentaries: I. The Pentateuch and Joshua," *Exp, 3rd Ser.*, 7 (1888) 228-239; 8 (1888) 462-472.

*Lewis B. Paton, "Aids to the Study of the Pentateuch and Joshua," *HSR* 8 (1897-98) 138-145.

(§12) *1.1.2.1.2 Judges*

§13 *1.1.2.1.3 The Books of Samuel*

Elmer Harding, "First Book of Samuel, Hints for Study," *ET* 2 (1890-91) 235.

§14 *1.1.2.1.4 The Books of Kings*

*Barnabas Lindars, "Commentaries on Samuel and Kings," *Theo* 67 (1964) 11-15.

§15 *1.1.2.2 The Latter Prophets - General Studies*

W. Muss-Arnolt, "Helps to the Study of the Earlier Prophets," *BW* 9 (1897) 443-456. [Amos, Hosea, Micah, Isaiah (1-39), Nahum]

T. Witton Davies, "Recent Literature on the Prophecy and the Prophetical Writings of the Old Testament," *RTP* 8 (1911-12) 577-596, 641-657.

John Drese, "Friends of the Prophets," *BibT* #28 (1967) 1947-1951.

§16 *1.1.2.2.1 The Major Prophets*

George Adam Smith, "A Survey of Recent Criticism of the Books of Isaiah and Jeremiah," *RTP* 3 (1907-08) 1-12, 65-77.

§17 *1.1.2.2.1.1 Isaiah*

J. H. Eaton, "Commentaries on the Book of Isaiah," *Theo* 60 (1957) 451-455.

§18 *1.1.2.2.1.2 Jeremiah*

J. A. Emerton, "Commentaries on the Book of the Prophet Jeremiah," *Theo* 63 (1960) 319-323.

Anonymous, "Bibliography for a Study of Jeremiah," *SWJT, N.S.* 4 (1961-62) #1, 81-82.

§19 *1.1.2.2.1.3 Ezekiel*

W. O. E. Oesterley, "The Book of Ezekiel: A Survey of Recent Literature," *CQR* 116 (1933) 187-200.

Peter R. Ackroyd, "Commentaries on Ezekiel," *Theo* 62 (1959) 97-100.

§ 20 *1.1.2.2.2 The Minor Prophets - General Studies*

T. Witton Davies, "Survey: Recent Literature on the Minor Prophets," *RTP* 6 (1910-11) 129-142, 197-213.

J. H. Eaton, "Commentaries on the Minor Prophets," *Theo* 64 (1961) 405-409.

§21 *1.1.3 The Hagiographa - General Studies*

John A. Maynard, "A Critical Bibliography of the Hagiographa (Ketubim) from 1918 to 1924," *JSOR* 9 (1925) 249-274.

(§22) *1.1.3.1 The Poetical Books*

§23 *1.1.3.1.1 Job*

T. H. Robinson, "The Ten Best Books on the Book of Job," *Exp, 9th Ser.*, 3 (1925) 357-377.

Robert W. Rogers, "Recent Commentaries on Job," *MR* 104 (1921) 966-971.*(Review)*

John Baker, "Commentaries on Job," *Theo* 66 (1963) 179-185.

§24 *1.1.3.1.2 The Psalms*

T. H. Robinson, "The Ten Best Books on the Psalms," *Exp, 9th Ser.*, 1 (1924) 6-23.

Edmund F. Sutcliffe, "The Psalms. Aids by Catholic Writers in English,"*Scrip* 1 (1946) 91-93.

G. Graystone, "Catholic English Bibliography on the Psalms," *Scrip* 6 (1953-54) 116-117.

§25 *1.1.3.1.3 Proverbs*

John P. Naish, "The Ten Best Books on Proverbs," *Exp, 9th Ser.*, 4 (1925) 111-119.

(§26) *1.1.3.2 The Megilloth - General Studies*

§27 *1.1.3.2.1 The Song of Solomon (Canticles)*

†Anonymous, "Recent Commentaries on the Song of Solomon," *BFER* 3 (1854) 221-247. *(Review)*

Roland E. Murphy, "Recent Literature on the Canticle of Canticles," *CBQ* 16 (1954) 1-11.

(§28) *1.1.3.2.2 Ruth*

(§29) *1.1.3.2.3 Lamentations*

(§30) *1.1.3.2.4 Ecclesiastes*

(§31) *1.1.3.2.5 Esther*

(§32) *1.1.3.3 The Historical Books*

§33 *1.1.3.3.1 Daniel*

Douglas R. Jones, "Commentaries on Daniel," *Theo* 66 (1963) 276-280.

(§34) *1.1.3.3.2 Ezra*

(§35) *1.1.3.3.3 Nehemiah*

(§36) *1.1.3.3.4 1 & 2 Chronicles*

§37 *1.1.4 The Non-Canonical Writings - General Studies*

*John A. Maynard, "A Critical Bibliography of Literature on the Apocrypha and Pseudepigrapha from 1918 to 1924," *JSOR* 11 (1927) 225-233.

§38 *1.1.4.1 The Apocrypha*

*John A. Maynard, "A Critical Bibliography of Literature on the Apocrypha and Pseudepigrapha from 1918 to 1924," *JSOR* 11 (1927) 225-233.

G. H. Box, "Survey of Recent Literature on the Apocrypha," *RTP* 2 (1906-07) 543-555.

Anonymous, "Theological Bibliographies. The Intertestamental Period," *ANQ* 48 (1956) #4, 15.

Donald E. Gowan (and staff), "Biblical Studies. Intertestamental Period," *PP* 7 (1965) #3, 11-12.

§39 *1.1.4.2 The Pseudepigrapha*

*John A. Maynard, "A Critical Bibliography of Literature on the Apocrypha and Pseudepigrapha from 1918 to 1924," *JSOR* 11 (1927) 225-233.

§40 *1.1.4.3 The Rabbinical Writings*

A. Neubauer, "Post-Biblical Bibliography," *JQR* 2 (1888-89) 191-204.

*G. H. Box, "Survey of Recent Contributions to the Study of Judaism and the Rabbinical Literature," *RTP* 10 (1914-15) 437-456, 497-513.

§41 *1.1.4.4 Theological Articles*

Anonymous, "An Index to Current Literature in Theology," *ET* 13 (1901-02) 280-282.

Anonymous, "A Subject-Index to Current Theological Literature," *ET* 13 (1901-02) 377-378.

Anonymous, "Subject-Index to Recent Theological Literature. Periodicals," *ET* 13 (1901-02) 475-476.

Anonymous, "Index of Subjects in Recent Theology," *ET* 14 (1902-03) 43-47; 378-382; 522-526; 15 (1903-04) 216-220; 16 (1904-05) 90-94.

Anonymous, "Theology in Recent Serial Literature, June to December1902," *ET* 14 (1902-03) 236-240.

Anonymous, "Index of Subjects in Recent Theology," *ET* 14 (1902-03) 378-382.

Anonymous, "Index of Subjects in Recent Theological Literature," *ET* 14 (1902-03) 522-526.

Anonymous, "Religious, Ethical, and Theological Articles in the Periodicals of 1903," *ET* 15 (1903-04) 324-329.

Anonymous, "Index of Subjects in Recent Theological Literature," *ET* 15 (1903-04) 216-220.

Anonymous, "Recent Theological Literature," *ET* 15 (1903-04) 465-469.

Anonymous, "Index of Subjects in Recent Theological Literature," *ET* 16 (1904-05) 90-94.

Anonymous, "Index to the Theology in Recent Books," *ET* 16 (1904-05) 280-284.

Anonymous, "Religious, Ethical, and Theological Articles in the Periodicals of 1904,"*ET* 16 (1904-05) 372-376, 415-418.

Anonymous, "Recent Theological Literature. Index of Subjects," *ET* 16 (1904-05) 508-512; 17 (1905-06) 78-82, 367-372; 18 (1906-07) 83-87.

Anonymous, "Religious, Ethical, and Theological Articles in the Periodicals of1905," *ET* 17 (1905-06) 463-469.

W. H. Bennett, "Survey of Recent Literature on Old Testament Theology," *RTP* 2 (1906-07) 345-351; 4 (1908-09) 349-356.

George W. Knox, "Some Recent Works on Systematic Theology," *HTR* 1 (1908) 189-206.

William W. Fenn, "Some Recent Books on Theology," *HTR* 1 (1908) 513-517.

W. H. Bennett, "Survey of Recent Theological Literature—Old Testament Theology," *RTP* 5 (1909-10) 665-681.

W. H. Bennett, "Survey of Some Recent Literature on Old Testament Theology," *RTP* 7 (1911-12) 65-79.

James P. Berkeley and Philip A. Nordell, "Theological Bibliographies. III. Old Testament," *ANQ* 6 (1913-14) #2, 5-10.

Theodore B. Foster, "A Bibliography of Dogmatics," *ATR* 2 (1919-20) 298-317.

Francis J. Hall, "The Study of Dogmatic Theology. A Reading Course for Clergy," *ATR* 10 (1927-28) 358-363.

Frank H. Hallock, "The Study of Moral Theology. A Reading Course," *ATR* 11 (1928-29) 356-361.

David E. Roberts, "A Survey of Recent Theological Literature, Theology and Philosophy of Religion," *USQR* 2 (1946-47) #4, 19-21.

Murray L. Newman, "Survey of Recent Theological Literature. Old Testament," *USQR* 9 (1953-54) #1, 18-20.

Robert McAfee Brown, and Albert R. Vogeler, "Philosophy of Religion and Systematic Theology, Part I: Survey of Recent Theological Literature," *USQR* 10 (1954-55) #3, 35-39.

Albert R. Vogeler, "Theological Literature Today," *USQR* 10 (1954-55) #4, 27-38.

Robert McAfee Brown, "Bibliography for Ministers, Systematic Theology," *USQR* 14 (1958-59) #4, 35-43.

§42 *1.1.4.5 Bibliography of Ancient Near Eastern Scholars - Alphabetical Listing*

William F. Hill, "Father Arbez: Bibliography" *CBQ* 23 (1961) 123-124. [**Edward P. Arbez**]

Joseph Reider, "Selected Bibliograpy of **Cyrus Adler**," *JAOS* 61 (1941) 193-194.

David Noel Freedman, "Bibliography of **W[illiam] F[oxwell] Albright**," *EI* 9 (1969) 1-5. [Non-Hebrew Section]

Anonymous, "Bibliography of **M. Avi-Yonah**," *BIES* 18 (1953-54) 113-120.

Anonymous, "Bibliography of Sir **Harold Idris Bell**," *JEA* 40 (1954) 3-6.

J. David Thomas, "Bibliography of Sir **Harold Idris Bell**: Additions and corrections to the list published in *JEA* 40 (1954) 3-6," *JEA* 53 (1967) 139-140.

[F. Willesen], "Bibliography of **Aage Bentzen**," *VTS* 1 (1953) IX-XV.

M. B., "Bibliography of **Yitzhak Ben-Zvi**," *EI* 4 (1956) 1-8.

T[errien] de L[acouperie], "Bibliography of the late **George Bertin**, Assyriologist," *BOR* 5 (1891) 71-72.

E. A. Wallis Budge, "Memoir of **Samuel Birch**, LL.D., D.C.L., F.S.A, &c., President," *SBAT* 9 (1886-93) 1-41. [Bibliography, pp. 23-41]

U. Bahadır Alkın, "Bibliographie von **Helmuth Theodor Bossert**," *AAI* 2 (1965) XVII-XXVIII.

J. Philip Hyatt and Raymond P. Morris, "A Bibliography of **Millar Burrows**' Works," *VT* 9 (1959) 423-432.

Joseph A. Grispino and Richard T. Cochran, "Father **Butin**: Bibliography," *CBQ* 24 (1962) 391-393. [**Romain François Butin**]

Milka Cassuto Salzmann, "Bibliografia scelta delle pubblicazioni scientifiche di **Umberto Cassuto**," *RDSO* 28 (1953) 229-238.

M[ilka] Cassuto-Salzmann, "Bibliography of the Writings of **M.D.U. Cassuto**," *EI* 3 (1954) 3-12.

C. H. S. Spaull, "Bibliography of **Jaroslav Černý**," *JEA* 54 (1968) 3-8.

Ettalene M. Grice, "Select Bibliography of **Albert T. Clay**, Ph.D., LL.D., Litt.D.," *JAOS* 45 (1925) 295-300.

Anonymous, "A Bibliography of **Walter Ewing Crum**," *JEA* 25 (1939) 134-138. [Additions, *JEA* 30 (1944) p. 66]

James Strachan, "The Writings of the Late Professor **A. B. Davidson**," *ET* 15 (1903-04) 450-455.

Guy Brunton, "**Reginald Engelbach**," *ASAE* 48 (1948) 1-7. [Bibliography, pp. 5-7]

Harald Riesenfeld, "**Ivan Engnell** 1906-1964," *SEÅ* 28&29 (1964) 5-8.

Johanne Vindenas, "Bibliography of **Henri Frankfort**," *JNES* 14 (1955) 4-13.

I. Sugi, "The Late Prof. **Henri Frankfort**," *NOGG* 1 (1955-58) #4, 14-17. *[Bibliography (Japanese Text)]*

A. R. M., "A Bibliography of **C. J. Gadd**," *Iraq* 31 (1969) 184-188.

R. O. Faulkner, "Bibliography of Sir **Alan Henderson Gardiner**," *JEA* 35 (1949) 1-12.

K. Enoki, "Dr. **Roman Ghirshman**: A Sketch of His Academic Career and Achievements," *NOGG* 2 (1959) #9, 1-10. [(Bibliography, pp. 5-10) *(Text in Japanese)*]

Ida A. Pratt, "Selected Bibliography of **R. J. H. Gottheil**," *JAOS* 56 (1936) 480-489.

I. Abrahams, "The Writings of Prof. **Graetz**," *JQR* 4 (1891-92) 194-203. [**Hirsch (Heinrich) Graetz**]

S. Halberstam, "The Works of Professor **Graetz**," *JQR* 4 (1891-92) 502. [**Hirsch (Heinrich) Graetz**]

Joseph H. Dulles, "**William Henry Green** Bibliography," *PRR* 7 (1896) 509-521.

Abou-Ghazi Dia', "**Selim Hassan**: His Writings and Excavations," *ASAE* 58 (1964) 61-84.

Cyrus Adler, "Announcement of a proposed complete edition of the works of **Edward Hincks**, with a biographical introduction and portrait of the author," *JAOS* 13 (1889) ccxcvi-ccci. [Bibliography, pp. ccxcvii-ccci.]

Cyrus Adler, "Note on the proposed edition of the Life and Writings of **Edward Hincks**," *JAOS* 14 (1890) ci-civ. [Additional List of Dr. Hincks's Papers, pp. cii-ciii; Further Additions to List of Dr. Hincks's Papers, pp. ciii-civ.]

Theodor Dombart, "**Fritz Hommel**," *EgR* 2 (1934) 161-168. [(Bibliography, pp. 164-165) *(German Text)*]

George C. O. Haas, "Bibliography of **A. V. Williams Jackson**," *JAOS* 58 (1938) 241-257. [addenda, p. 473]

Albert T. Clay and James A. Montgomery, "Bibliography of **Morris Jastrow Jr**.," *JAOS* 41 (1921) 337-344.

Erich Winter, "**Hermann Junker** Verzeichnis Seiner Schriften," *WZKM* 54 (1957) VII-XV.

W. C. Van Manen, "The Writings of Prof. **Kuenen**," *JQR* 4 (1891-92) 471-489. [**A. Kuenen**]

Zbyněk Žába, "Bibliographie des œuvres de **František Lexa**," *ArOr* 20 (1952) 7-14.

John A. Maynard, "A Bibliography of **D. D. Luckenbill**," *AJSL* 45 (1928-29) 90-93.

U. Ben-Horin, "Bibliography of Prof. **L. A. Mayer**," *BIES* 12 (1946) 1-9.

H. Z. (J. W.) Hirschberg, "The Works of Professor **L. A. Mayer**," *EI* 7 (1964) XIX-XXVII.

H. Beinart, "Bibliography of **Benjamin Mazar**," *EI* 5 (1958) 1-8.

E. A. Speiser, "Bibliography of **James Alan Montgomery**," *BASOR* #117 (1950) 8-13.

L. C. Casartelli, "**James Hope Moulton** as an Irānian Scholar," *JMUEOS* #6 (1916-17) 25-28. [Bibliography, pp. 27-28]

Wilfrid Bonser, "A Bibliography of the Writings of Dr **Murray**," *Folk* 72 (1961) 560-566. [**Margaret Alice Murray**]

H. S. K. Bakry, "A Tribute to a Centenarian Archaeologist and Folklorist," *ASAE* 59 (1966) 1-13. [**Margaret Alice Murray** - Bibliography, pp. 6-8]

David H. Bobo, "Bibliography of **Toyozo W. Nakarai**," *SQ/E* 26 (1965) 293-297.

Bezalel Narkiss, "Bibliography of **Mordecai Narkiss**," *EI* 6 (1960) 5-19.

W. Muss-Arnolt, "The Works of **Jules Oppert**," *BAVSS* 2 (1894) 523-556.

H. W. Fairman, "Bibliography of Professor **T. E. Peet**," *EgR* 2 (1934) 158-160.

J. P. Peters Jr., "Selected Bibliography of **John Punnett Peters**," *JBL* 41 (1922) 246-248.

Milka Cassuto-Salzmann, "Bibliography of **A. Reifenberg**," *IEJ* 4 (1954) 143-149.

W. H. Rylands, "Chronological List of Publications of the late Sir **P. Le Page Renouf**," *SBAP* 19 (1897) 317-341.

Emery Percell, "Bibliography of Works by **Martin Rist**," *IR* 18 (1961) #2, 49-50.

Anonymous, "Bibliography of the Published Writings of the Rev. Professor **James Robertson**, D.D., LL.D," *SSO* 1 (1920) 126-127.

C. Bradford Welles, "Bibliography—**M. Rostovtzeff**," *HJAH* 5 (1956) 358-381.

G. Henton Davies, "Select Bibliography of the Writings of **Harold Henry Rowley**," *VTS* 3 (1955) XI-XIX.

Walter G. Williams, "A List of the Publications of **J[ohn] M[erlin] Powis Smith**," *AJSL* 49 (1932-33) 169-171, 272.

James Henry Breasted Jr., "The Writings of **George Steindorff**," *JAOS* 66 (1946) 76-87.

James Henry Breasted Jr., "**Steindorff** Bibliography: Additions," *JAOS* 67 (1947) 141-142. [**George Steindorff**]

Anonymous, "Bibliography of the Published Writings of **William Barron Stevenson**, D.Litt., D.D. (Edinburgh and Wales), LL.D.," *SSO* 2 (1945) 138-140.

U. Ben-Horin, "Bibliography of the Writings of **E. L. Sukenik**," *EI* 8 (1967) כא־כז.

Anonymous, "A Bibliography of the Published Works of the late **Henry Barclay Swete**," *JTS* 19 (1917-18) 1-19.

Dorothy Burr Thompson, "**Mary Hamilton Swindler**, Bibliography," *AJA* 54 (1950) 293.

Richard Cull, "A Bibliographical Notice of the Late **William Henry Fox Talbot**, F.R.S.," *SBAT* 6 (1878-79) 543-559. [Bibliography, pp. 556-559]

Caspar Rene Gregory, "**Tischendorf**. The Writings of Professor Tischendorf," *BS* 33 (1876) 183-193. [**Constantin Tischendorf**]

Anonymous, "Necrology," *AJA* 67 (1963) 83-84. [*Bibliography of:* **Elizabeth Douglas Van Buren**]

Harry A. Butler, "Bibliography of the Writings of **Walter G. Williams**," *IR* 24 (1967) #3, 51-52.

J. A., "Bibliography of **S. Yeivin**," *BIES* 13 (1947) 67-74.

§43 *1.1.4.6 Studies on Ancient Near Eastern & Old Testament Scholars - Their Lives and Contributions [Selected Listing]*

W[illiam] F[oxwell] Albright, "†**Albrecht Alt**," *JBL* 75 (1956) 169-173.

*H[oward] Osgood, "**Jean Astruc**," *PRR* 3 (1892) 83-102.

A. R. S. Kennedy, "**Jean Astruc**," *ET* 8 (1896-97) 24-27, 61-65.

Howard Osgood, "Was **Astruc** a Bad Man?" *ET* 8 (1896-97) 141.

Anonymous, "Whitewashing **Jean Astruc**," *HR* 39 (1900) 157.

E. G. Turner and T. C. Skeat, "Sir **Harold Idris Bell**," *JEA* 53 (1967) 131-139.

B[enjamin] Mazar, "The Debt of Biblical Research to **Izhak Ben-Zvi**," *Text* 3 (1963) VII-VIII.

George Sarton, "**James Henry Breasted** (1865-1935): The Father of American Egyptology," *Isis* 34 (1942-43) 289-291.

Martin Sprengling, "**Edward Chiera** August 5, 1885—June 20, 1933," *AJSL* 49 (1933-34) 273-274.

G. H. Box, "**Samuel Davidson's** Work in Old Testament Scholarship," *CQR* 115 (1932-33) 49-66.

Hermann V. Hilprecht, "**Franz Delitzsch** in His Relation to Israel," *LCR* 6(1887) 115-127.

William Copely Winslow, "The Queen of Egyptology," *AAOJ* 14 (1892) 305-315. [Miss **Amelia B. Edwards**]

John M[erlin] P[owis] Smith, "**Heinrich Ewald** and the Old Testament," *BW* 22 (1903) 407-415.

George Adam Smith, "Memorials of **William Rainey Harper**: As an Old Testament Interpreter," *BW* 27 (1906) 200-203.

Julian Morgenstern, "**Morris Jastrow Jr**. as a Biblical Critic," *JAOS* 41 (1921) 322-327.

George A. Barton, "The Contributions of **Morris Jastrow Jr**. to the History of Religion," *JAOS* 41 (1921) 327-333.

Albert T. Clay, "Professor **Jastrow** as an Assyriologist," *JAOS* 41 (1921) 333-336. [**Morris Jastrow Jr**.]

*B. Pick, "**Jerome** as an Old Testament Student," *LCR* 6 (1887) 230-243, 287-295; 7 (1888) 137-149, 272-293. [**Jerome (Hieronymus) Sophronius Eusebius**]

Moshe Greenberg, "**Kaufmann** on the Bible: An Appreciation," *Jud* 13 (1964) 77-89. [**Yehezkel Kaufmann**]

G. W. Anderson, "**Johannes Lindblom's** Contribution to Biblical Studies," *ASTI* 6 (1967-68) 4-19.

Israel Abrahams, "**Samuel David Luzzato** as Exegete," *JQR, N.S.* 57 (1966-67) 83-100, 179-199.

Henry Englander, "**Mendelssohn** as Translator and Exegete," *HUCA* 6 (1929) 327-348. [**Moses Mendelssohn**]

*D. R. Ap-Thomas, "An Appreciation of **Sigmund Mowinckel's** Contribution to Biblical Studies," *JBL* 85 (1966) 315-325.

J. T. E. Renner, "Old Testament Notes and Comments," *LTJ* 3 (1969) 26-27. [**Martin Noth**]

Max Schloessinger, "**Rashi**, His Life and Work," *YCCAR* 15 (1905) 223-245. [**Shelomoh Yishaqi (Solomon ben Isaac) Rashi**]

S. D. F. Salmond, "Professor **Ryle's** Contributions to Old Testament Scholarship," *ET* 4 (1892-93) 341-345. [**Herbert Edward Ryle**]

Theodore E. Schmauk, "Prof. **A. B. Sayce** and the Tendencies of His Works," *LCR* 25 (1906) 75-87.

W. Irving Carroll, "Professor **Robert Dick Wilson** and the Bible," *CFL, 3rd Ser.*, 29 (1923) 233-234.

A. A. Berle, "Tributes to the Memory of **George Frederick Wright**," *CFL, 3rd Ser.*, 27 (1921) 227-234.

§44 *1.2 Bibliographical Studies of Old Testament Figures*

†Anonymous, "Robinson's Scripture Characters," *BCQTR* 4 (1794) 260-263. *(Review)*

†Anonymous, "Geography and Biography of the Old Testament," *QRL* 106 (1859) 368-419. *(Review)*

Anonymous, "The Heroes of Hebrew History," *WR* 98 (1872) 285-310.

*Claude R. Conder, "The Moslem Mukams," *PEFQS* 9 (1877) 89-103. [II. *Bible Characters*, pp. 92-97]

*Geo. F. Herrick, "A Study in Biblical Biography," *BS* 37 (1880) 209-220.

Albert A. Isaacs, "The Exemplars of the Old Testament," *EN* 3 (1891) 289-292.

J. Hogan, "The Old Testament Saints," *AER* 8 (1893) 100-105, 161-171, 290-294.

S. Schechter, "Algazi's Chronicle and the Names of the Patriarchs' Wives," *JQR* 2 (1889-90) 190.

George Matheson, "The Characteristics of Bible Portraiture," *LQHR* 94 (1900) 1-12.

George S. Goodspeed, "The Men Who Made Israel," *BW* 29 (1907) 34-40. [I. Introductory]

*George S. Goodspeed, "The Men Who Made Israel," *BW* 30 (1907) 266-274. [The Judges and the Preparation for the Kingdom]

J. Fry, "The Preachers of the Old Testament and Their Preaching," *LCR* 34 (1915) 112-120.

*W[illiam] F[oxwell] Albright, "Contributions of Biblical Archaeology and Philology," *JBL* 43 (1924) 363-393. [4. The Role of Post-Deluvian Patriarchs in Hebrew History, pp. 385-393]

Frieda Clark Hyman, "Women of the Bible," *Jud* 5 (1956) 338-347.

*B[enjamin] Mazar, "The Military Élite of King David," *VT* 13 (1963) 310-320.

H. McKeating, "Some Saints and Sinners in the Old Testament," *PQL* 13 (1967) 5-11.

§45 *1.2.1 Alphabetical Listing of Old Testament Persons*

A

Aaron

M. Forbes, "'Areos,' 'Arisu,' or 'Aarsu' of the 'Harris Papyrus,' 'Aaron' of Exodus," *PEFQS* 29 (1897) 226-230.

*Lewis Bayles Paton, "Outline Studies of Obscurer Prophets—II. Aaron and Miriam," *HR* 49 (1904) 197-198.

*H. G. Judge, "Aaron, Zadok, and Abiathar," *JTS, N.S.,* 7 (1956) 70-74.

Abel

*Rachel J. Fox, "Cain-Abel-Seth," *ET* 18 (1906-07) 522-524.

*Joseph Offord, "Archaeological Notes on Jewish Antiquities. XII. *Abel and Cuneiform* Ibila," *PEFQS* 48 (1916) 138-139.

*Fredeick [L.] Moriarty, "Abel, Melchizedek, Abraham," *Way* 5 (1965) 95-104.

Abiathar

*H. G. Judge, "Aaron, Zadok, and Abiathar," *JTS, N.S.,* 7 (1956) 70-74.

Abijam

*S. Yeivin, "Abijam, Asa and Maachah the Daughter of Abishalom," *BIES* 10 (1942-44) #4, III.

Abimelech

Anonymous, "Abimelech," *ET* 29 (1917-18) 511-515.

Abishalom

*S. Yeivin, "Abijam, Asa and Maachah the Daughter of Abishalom," *BIES* 10 (1942-44) #4, III.

Abraham (Abram)

Anonymous, "A Biographical Sketch of the Life of the Patriarch Abraham, Illustrated with Observations Drawn from Natural History, and Ancient Manners," *QTMRP* 3 (1814) 63-92.

Kurtz (of Dorphat), "Abraham," *RChR* 8 (1856) 131-141.

*Anonymous, "Abraham's Position in Sacred History," *DQR* 4 (1864) 611-631.

*S. S. Hebberd, "The Religion of Abraham," *UQGR, N.S.*, 16 (1879) 341-359.

[W.] Hanna, "A Table of Abraham's Life," *ONTS* 1 (1882) #1, 15.

[Richard] Allen, "The Time of Abraham's Birth," *ONTS* 4 (1884-85) 174-175.

*G[eorge] Rawlinson, "Biblical Topography. VI.—Sites connected with the History of Abraham—Harran, Damascus, Hebron," *MI* 4 (1886) 241-252. *[Part IV not published]*

W. St. Chad Boscawen, "Historical Evidence of the Migration of Abram," *JTVI* 20 (1886-87) 92-133.[(Letter by H. G. Thomkins, p. 137; by D. Howard, p. 138)(Discussion by Robinson Thornton, pp. 138-139; E. A. W. Budge, pp. 139-141; W. Wright, pp. 141-142; M. Bertin, pp. 142-143; W. St. Chad Boscawen, pp. 142-144]

A. H. Sayce, "Notes on Mr. Boscawen's Paper: Historical Evidences of the Migration of Abram," *JTVI* 20 (1886-87) 134-137.

Abraham cont.

P. D. Cowan, "How was Abraham Saved?" *BS* 44 (1887) 494-503.

*W. O. Sproull, "The Native Language of Abraham," *AJSL* 4 (1887-88) 186.

John Henry Hopkins, "Abraham and his Seed," *CR* 60 (1891) 30-34.

R. W. Dale, "Abraham," *Exp, 5th Ser.,* 3 (1896) 434-444.

*R. W. Dale, "The Place of Abraham in Religious History," *Exp, 5th Ser.,* 4 (1896) 338-350.

*D. S. Margouliouth, "The Name 'Abraham'," *ET* 9 (1897-98) 45.

*Hormuzd Rassam, "Abraham and the Land of his Nativity," *SBAP* 20 (1898) 70-92.

*Fritz Hommel, "The True Date of Abraham and Moses," *ET* 10 (1898-99) 210-212.

*Fritz Hommel, "Additional Note to: 'The True Date of Abraham and Moses'," *ET* 10 (1898-99) 278.

Benjamin W. Bacon, "Abraham the Heir of Yahweh," *NW* 8 (1899) 674-690.

G. A. Kohut, "Abraham's Lesson in Tolerance," *JQR* 15 (1902-03) 104-111.

*Constantine Grethenbach, "Hammurabi and Abraham," *OC* 17 (1903) 760.

Eb. Nestle, "Abraham, the Friend of God," *ET* 15 (1903-04) 46-47.

Wilson D. Sexton, "Abraham, the Man of Vision," *CFL, 3rd Ser.,* 1 (1904) 756-759.

*James Henry Breasted, "The Earliest Occurrence of the Name Abram," *AJSL* 21(1904-05) 22-36.

Robert Dick Wilson, "'Was Abraham a Myth?'," *CFL, 3rd Ser.,* 3 (1905) 90-103.

Abraham cont.

*Andrew Craig Robinson, "The Bearing of Recent Oriental Discoveries on Old Testament History," *JTVI* 38 (1906) 154-176. {(Discussion, pp. 176-181.) [The Connection of Israel with Babylonia in the Early Times. *Abraham*, pp. 156-158]}

Francis E. Gigot, "Abraham: A Historical Study," *NYR* 2 (1906-07) 37-48.

George S. Goodspeed, "The Men Who Made Israel," *BW* 29 (1907) 133-137. [II. Abraham and the Forefathers of Israel]

Albert T. Clay, "Abraham in the Light of the Monuments," *CFL, 3rd Ser.*, 6 (1907) 95-97.

Willis J. Beecher, "Abraham: A Man or a Myth?" *CFL, 3rd Ser.*, 6 (1907) 435-438.

Eduard König, "The Historicity of the First Patriarch. A Critical Essay," *BW* 32 (1908) 103-112, 174-182. *[Abraham]*

*R. A. S[tewart] Macalister (trans.), "Tales of the Prophets," *PEFQS* 40 (1908) 310-317. [Of Abraham, pp. 310-312]

Anonymous, "Was There Ever an Abraham?" *CFL, 3rd Ser.*, 10 (1909) 294. *(Editorial)*

G. A. Barton, "Abraham and Archaeology," *JBL* 28 (1909) 152-168.

*Stephen Langdon, "The Name Abraham in Babylonian," *ET* 21 (1909-10) 88-90.

Anonymous, "Abraham," *MR* 92 (1910) 479-481.

*M. G. Kyle, "Hammurabi, Abraham, and the Reviewers," *BS* 70 (1913) 528-531.

*James A. Montgomery, "Abraham as the Inventor of an Improved Plow," *MJ* 4 (1913) 55-56.

*[James A. Montgomery(?)], "Abraham as the Inventor of the Improved Plow," *RP* 13 (1914) 57.

Abraham cont.

*W. T. Pilter, "The Personal Names Abram and Abraham," *SBAP* 37 (1915) 175-191.

W. M. Patton, "The View of Abraham in the Late Second Century B.C.," *IJA* #46 (1916) 43-45.

William Manson, "Abraham not an Astrologer, but a Prophet," *CJRT* 2 (1925) 164-165.

*Wilfred Lawrence Knox, "Abraham and the Quest for God," *HTR* 28 (1935) 55-60.

*W[illiam] F[oxwell] Albright, "The Names *Shaddai* and *Abram*," *JBL* 54 (1935) 173-204.

D. M. McIntyre, "The Faith of Abraham," *EQ* 8 (1936) 65-74.

Joshua Finkel, "An Arabic Story of Abraham," *HUCA* 12&13 (1937-38) 387-409.

Robert Henry Miller, "An Appreciation of Abraham," *CFL, 3rd Ser.*, 44 (1938) 72-73.

*Clive A. Thomson, "Certain Bible Difficulties," *BS* 96 (1939) 459-478. [II. The age of Abraham, pp. 463, 470-472]

Michael J. Gruenthaner, "Archaeological Corner. The Date of Abraham," *CBQ* 4 (1942) 360-363.

Michael J. Gruenthaner, "Archaeological Corner. The Date of Abraham, II," *CBQ* 5 (1943) 85-87.

*Samuel Sandmel, "Abraham's Knowledge of the Existence of God," *HTR* 44 (1951) 137-139.

*Samuel Sandmel, "Philo's Place in Judaism: A Study of Conceptions of Abraham in Jewish Literature," *HUCA* 25 (1954) 209-237.

Edward D. O'Connor, "The Faith of Abraham and the Faith of the Virgin Mary," *AER* 132 (1955) 232-238.

Abraham cont.

Walter J. Harrelson, "Kierkegaard and Abraham," *ANQ* 47 (1955), #3, 12-16.

*Samuel Sandmel, "Philo's Place in Judaism: A Study of Conceptions of Abraham in Jewish Literature, II," *HUCA* 26 (1955) 151-332.

Martin Buber, "Abraham the Seer," *Jud* 5 (1956) 291-305.

*Edwin M. Good, "Two Notes on Aqhat," *JBL* 77 (1958) 72-74. [I. Abraham and the Aqhat Legend, pp. 72-73]

*Cyrus H. Gordon, "Abraham and the Merchants of Ura," *JNES* 17 (1958) 28-31.

S[tanley] B. Frost, "Bible Characters. I: Abraham," *PQL* 4 (1958) 297-303.

H. H. Rowley, 'The Migration of Abram," *ET* 70 (1958-59) 54.

J. W. Wenham, "The Migration of Abram," *ET* 70 (1958-59) 54.

M. D. W. Jeffreys, "Braima alias Abraham: A Study in Diffusion," *Folk* 70 (1959) 323-333.

*W[illiam] F[oxwell] Albright, "Abram the Hebrew: A New Archaeological Interpretation," *BASOR* #163 (1961) 36-54.

*Isabel Speyart Van Woerden, "The Iconography of the Sacrifice of Abraham," *VC* 15 (1961) 214-255.

*David S. Shapiro, "The Book of Job and the Trial of Abraham," *Trad* 4 (1961-62) 210-220.

Frederick L. Moriarty, "'My Father was a Wandering Aramean'," *BiBT* #2 (1962) 97-99, 102-106. *[Abraham]*

*Ben Zion Wacholder, "How Long Did Abram Stay in Egypt?" *HUCA* 35 (1964) 43-56.

Abraham concluded

*J. Massingberd Ford, "'You are "Abraham" and upon this rock' (A study of stone symbolism)," *HeyJ* 6 (1965) 289-301.

*James Muilenburg," Abraham and the Nations. *Blessing and World History,*" *Interp* 19 (1965) 387-398.

*Allan A. MacRae, "Abraham and the Stars," *JASA* 17 (1965) 65-67.

*Frederick [L.] Moriarty, "Abel, Melchizedek, Abraham," *Way* 5 (1965) 95-104.

Henry Wansbrough, "Event and Interpretation. I. Abraham our Father," *ClR* 52 (1967) 658-664.

*Samuel Belkin, "Some Obscure Tradition Mutually Clarified in Philo and Rabbinic Literature," *JQR 75th* (1967) 80-103. [2. Abraham's Name, pp. 83-86]

*J. Massingberd Ford, "'You are "Abraham" and upon this rock'," *TD* 15 (1967) 134-137.

*Louis H. Feldman, "Abraham the Greek Philosopher in Josephus," *TAPA* 99 (1968) 143-156.

Adam

W. Hoffman, "Adam," *RChR* 8 (1856) 141-151.

Anonymous, "The First and Second Man," *DR, N.S.,* 9 (1867) 441-472. *(Review) [Original Numbering as volume 61]*

[Carl von] Buchrucker, "Adam," *LQ* 8 (1878) 244-248. *(Trans. by G. F. Behringer)*

*William Adamson, "Did Adam Excuse or Confess His Sin?" *ERG, 7th Ser.,* 3 (1880-81) 233-244.

Philip S. Moxom, "The Natural Headship of Adam," *BQR* 3 (1881) 273-287.

A. N. Scott, "Adam," *ERG, 9th Ser.,* 1 (1886-87) 275-286.

Adam concluded

Chas. S. Robinson, "How was Adam the Son of God?" *HR* 15 (1888) 126-129.

*Alexander Kohut, "Parsic and Jewish Literature of the First Man," *JQR* 3 (1890-91) 231-250.

*Morris Jastrow Jr., "Adam and Eve in Babylonian Literature," *AJSL* 15 (1898-99) 193-214.

*A. H. Sayce, "The Name of Adam," *ET* 17 (1905-06) 416-417.

*R. A. S[tewart] Macalister (trans.), "Tales of the Prophets," *PEFQS* 41 (1909) 35-41. [Of Adam, pp. 40-41]

Eb. Nestle, "'Adam'," *ET* 21 (1909-10) 139.

*Arthur E. Whatham, "Are Adam and Eve Historical Characters?" *AAOJ* 32 (1910) 85-93.

William H. Bates, "Life of Adam," *CFL, 3rd Ser.,* 23 (1917) 115-117.

*S[tephen] Langdon, "The Sumero-Babylonian Origin of the Legend of Adam," *ET* 43 (1931-32) 45.

*A. C. Graham, "Adam and Enosh," *ET* 51 (1939-40) 205.

*P. Middlekoop, "A Question," *BTr* 6 (1955) 30-31. [Translation of the name "Adam"]

*A. J. Campbell, "Adam," *Theo* 69 (1966) 215-222. [O.T. refs., pp. 216-218]

Martha Shaw, "The Unknown Adam," *C&C* 21 (1969) 40-50.

Ahasuerus

*G. B., "Ahasuerus and Artaxerxes," *JSL, 3rd Ser.,* 6 (1857-58) 171.

*I. */sic/* W. Bosanquet, "Who was Ahasuerus of the Seed of the Medes, whose Son Darius was set over the realm of the Chaldeans, when about sixty-two years old? *Dan.* v. 31; ix. 1," *JSL, 3rd Ser.,* 4 (1856-57) 452-462.

Ahasuerus concluded

*(   ) G., "Kai-Khosiu and Ahasuerus," *JSL, 3rd Ser.,* 11 (1860) 385-416.

*[Joseph Fullonton], "Esther," *FBQ* 16 (1868) 205-216. [Who was Ahasuerus? pp. 206-207]

*Anonymous, "The Possible Identification of the Ahasuerus of Esther with Astyages," *RP* 8 (1909) 170.

Amos

*W. G. Jordan, "Amos the Man and the Book in the Light of Recent Criticism," *BW* 17 (1901) 265-271.

*S. Lawrence Brown, "Amos: The Man and His Message," *ICMM* 3 (1906-07) 296-304.

*J. W. Jack, "Recent Biblical Archaeology," *ET* 53 (1941-42) 367-370. [Archæology and the Biblical Text: II. The 'Herdsman' Amos, p. 370]

Simon Cohen, "Amos *Was* a Navi," *HUCA* 32 (1961) 175-178.

Nolan P. Howington, "Toward an Ethical Understanding of Amos," *R&E* 63 (1966) 405-412.

A. Murtonen, "The Prophet Amos—A Hepatoscoper?" *VT* 2 (1952) 170-171.

W. R. Parker, "Amos, the herdsman prophet of Tekoah," *CMR* 4 (1892) 289-331.

L. P. Smith, Amos a North Israelite," *JBL* 55 (1936) vii.

Carroll Stuhlmueller, "Amos, Desert-Trained Prophet," *BibT* #4 (1963) 224-230.

John D. W. Watts, "Amos, the Man," *R&E* 63 (1966) 387-392.

Rolland Emerson Wolfe, "The Call of the Prophet Amos," *CQ* 18 (1941) 323-328.

Araunah

William Glynne, "Araunah the Jebusite," *ET* 28 (1916-17) 425.

Arpachshad (Arpakaxad)

*Fritz Hommel, "Arpakshad," *ET* 8 (1896-97) 283-284.

T. K. Cheyne, "Prof. Hommel on Arpharad," *ET* 8 (1896-97) 474.

T. K. Cheyne, "Prof. Hommel on Arphaxad," *Exp, 5th Ser.,* 5 (1897) 145-148.

*T. K. Cheyne, "Arpachshad," *ZAW* 17 (1897) 190.

Fritz Hommel, "The True Meaning of Arpakshad," *ET* 13 (1901-02) 285.

Asenath

*V. Aptowitzer, "Asenath, the Wife of Joseph—A Haggadic, Literary-Historical Study," *HUCA* 1 (1924) 221-238.

*Bernhard Pick, "Joseph and Asenath," *OC* 27 (1913) 467-496. *[Legend concerning Joseph's marriage to Asenath]*

B

Balaam

Anonymous, "Reflections on the Life and Character of Balaam," *PRev* 6 (1834) 200-213.

J. T. Smith, "Balaam, The Prophet of Syria," *BQ* 3 (1869) 464-485.

[Selah(?)] Merrill, "Balaam's Birthplace," *ONTS* 1 (1882) 75.

*J. A. Seiss, "Balaam and His Prophecy," *LCR* 14 (1895) 213-225.

A. H. Sayce, "Who was Balaam?" *ET* 15 (1903-04) 405-406.

Balaam concluded

Lewis Bayles Paton, "Outline Studies of Obscurer Prophets—Balaam," *HR* 49 (1905) 357-358. *[Part IV]*

Henry M. Whitney, "Balaam," *BS* 63 (1906) 150-163.

Randolph H. McKim, "The Study of the Character of Balaam," *HR* 51 (1906) 125-128.

*G. A. Smith, "The Experience of Balaam as Symbolic of the Origins of Prophecy," *Exp, 8th Ser.,* 5 (1913) 1-11.

W[illiam] F[oxwell] Albright, "The Home of Balaam," *JAOS* 35 (1915) 386-390.

James Atkins, "Balaam: The Man in the Prophet," *MQR, 3rd Ser.,* 44 (1918) 447-456.

*Cuthbert Lattey, "Balaam: Prophet or Soothsayer? (Numbers XXII.-XXIV.)," *IER, 5th Ser.,* 22 (1923) 166-76.

*Alexander Krappe, "The Story of Eriphyle in Arabic Legend," *AJSL* 41 (1924-25) 194-197. *[Balaam]*

Gilmore H. Guyot, "Balaam," *CBQ* 3 (1941) 235-242.

J. Liver, "The Figure of Balaam in Biblical Tradition," *EI* 3 (1954) IV.

Laurentia Digges, "Balaam: A Man in a Corner," *BibT* #13 (1964) 869-874.

Barzillai

Anonymous, "Barzillai," *ET* 29 (1917-18) 411-415.

Benjamin

*Stanley A Cook, "Notes on Old Testament History, IV, Saul and Benjamin," *JQR* 18 (1905-06) 528-543.

James Muilenberg, "The Birth of Benjamin," *JBL* 75 (1956) 194-201.

Bildad

*W[illiam] F[oxwell] Albright, "The Name of Bildad the Shuhite," *AJSL* 44 (1927-28) 31-36.

*E. A. Speiser, "The Name Bildad," *AfO* 6 (1930-31) 23.

C

Cain

*Rachel J. Fox, "Cain-Abel-Seth," *ET* 18 (1906-07) 522-524.

Cain's Wife

J. W. M. Dawson, "Requests and Replies," *ET* 8 (1896-97) 154. *[Cain's Wife]*

Arthur E. Whatham, "Cain's Wife," *ET* 8 (1896-97) 476.

Caleb

J. T. L. Preston, "Caleb, a Bible Study," *SPR* 35 (1884) 251-264.

D

Daniel

Franke Parker, "The Three First Years of Daniel's Captivity," *JSL, 4th Ser.,* 1 (1862) 165-168.

Hezekiah Butterworth, "The Education of the Young Prophet Daniel," *BW* 10 (1897) 444-453.

*Charles Melancthon Jones, "Daniel the Man of Prayer," *HR* 66 (1913) 395-396.

Deborah

A. B. Davidson, "The Prophetess Deborah," *Exp, 3rd Ser.,* 5 (1887) 38-55.

Lewis Bayles Paton, "Outline Studies of Obscurer Prophets—IV. The Prophetess Deborah," *HR* 49 (1905) 281-282. *[Misnumbered as IV, but should be III]*

*Ed. König, "Deborah and Hannah," *HR* 51 (1906) 130.

*John Hendrick de Vries, "Higher Criticism and the Sunday School," *CFL, 3rd Ser.,* 8 (1908) 209-212. *[Deborah & Jael]*

E

Elhanan

*Norvelle Wallace Sharpe, "David, Elhanan, and the Literary Digest," *BS* 86 (1929) 319-326.

Eli

Anonymous, "Eli," *ET* 31 (1919-20) 457-462.

L. O. Lineberger, "Eli: The Parent's Eye-Opener," *BS* 85 (1928) 145-154.

Eliakim

*S. Klein, "Eliakim, Steward of Joiachin," *BIES* 5 (1937-38) IV.

*H. J. Katzenstein, "The House of Eliakim, a Family of Royal Stewards," *EI* 5 (1958) 89*-90*.

Eliezer

Eb. Nestle, "318 = Eliezer," *ET* 17 (1905-06) 44-45.

Elihu

H. D. Beeby, "Elihu—Job's Mediator?" *SEAJT* 7 (1965-66) #2, 33-54.

Elijah

*Idiota, "On the Elijah foretold by Malachi," *TRep* 6 (1788) 135-175.

*†Anonymous, "Discourses on Elijah and John the Baptist," *BCQTR, 4th Ser.*, 17 (1835) 295-309. *(Review)*

*W. G. Keady, "The Typical Significance of Elijah and Elisha.—2 Kings ii," *PQPR* 6 (1877) 745-754.

G. F. Genung, "A Study of Elijah," *BQR* 2 (1880) 163-181.

[Cunningham] Geikie, "Elijah, the Great Prophet Reformer," *ONTS* 2 (1882-83) 243-245.

Joseph Longking, "'Elijah the Tishbite' a Gentile," *MR* 70 (1888) 900-908. (Rejoinder by J. W. Mendenhall, pp. 908-911)

Norman L. Walker, "The Ministry of Elijah: A Theory," *ET* 4 (1892-93) 252-254.

Arthur T. Pierson, "Elijah the Tishbite," *HR* 26 (1893) 541-542.

C. H. Cornill, "Elijah," *OC* 9 (1895) 4463-4465.

Ed. König, "Elijah the Tishbite," *ET* 12 (1900-01) 383.

*Archibald Fairly Carr, "Elijah as an Illustration of Prayer," *CFL, N.S.*, 4 (1901) 111-117.

Sylvester Burnham, "The Mission and Work of Elijah," *BW* 24 (1904) 180-187.

Daniel S. Gregory, "The International Lessons in Their Literary and Historical Setting. Elijah's Environment and Mission," *CFL, 3rd Ser.*, 1 (1904) 477-485.

Elijah concluded

Willis J. Beecher, "The Biography of Elijah," *CFL, 3rd Ser.,* 1 (1904) 485-491.

*R. A. S[tewart] Macalister (trans.), "Tales of the Prophets," *PEFQS* 41 (1909) 35-41. [Of El-Khidr, son of 'Abbas, brother of Elijah, pp. 39-40]

*W. H. Marquess, "Elijah as a Man of Prayer," *BRec* 8 (1911) 223-228.

J. E. Hanauer, "Folk-lore and other Notes from Damascus, etc.," *PEFQS* 57 (1925) 31-36. [Elijah *(folklore about),* pp. 32-33]

*R. B. Y. Scott, "The Expectation of Elijah," *CJRT* 3 (1926) 490-502.

George Ferguson Finnie, "Elijah—Jehovah's Champion," *CQ* 14 (1937) 5-10.

F. Brenner, "Spirit and Power of Elijah," *WLQ* 34 (1937) 16-26; 35 (1938) 183-193.

*J. S. McArthur, "Elijah or Elisha?" *ET* 50 (1938-39) 363-367.

*Paschal P. Parente, "Ascetical and Mystical Traits of Moses and Elias," *CBQ* 5 (1943) 183-190.

Julian Obermann, "Two Elijah Stories in Judeao-Arabic Transmission," *HUCA* 23 (1950-51) Part 1, 387-404.

Donald M. Englert, "Elijah—An Old Testament Layman," *T&L* 3 (1960) 95-102.

Stanley B. Frost, "Old Testament Characters: X. Elijah," *PQL* 7 (1961) 7-15.

Van Wanroy Macarius, "The Prophet Elijah example of solitary and contemplative Life?" *Carm* 16 (1969) 251-263.

*R. P. Carroll, "The Elijah-Elisha Sagas: Some Remarks on Prophetic Succession in Ancient Israel," *VT* 29 (1969) 400-415.

Elisha

*W. G. Keady, "The Typical Significance of Elijah and Elisha.—2 Kings ii," *PQPR* 6 (1877) 745-754.

A. A. Pfanstiehl, "Elisha and His Times," *RChR* 38 (1891) 362-369.

Willis J. Beecher, "The Biography of Elisha," *CFL, 3rd Ser.*, 1 (1904) 546-553.

Daniel S. Gregory, "International Lessons in Their Literary and Historical Setting. The Career of Elisha as Leader for Jehovah," *CFL, 3rd Ser.*, 1 (1904) 607-617.

*Daniel S. Gregory, "The International Lessons in Their Historical and Literary Setting," *CFL, 3rd Ser.*, 14 (1911-12) 179-193. [The Career of Elisha, pp. 179-187]

James Donald, "The Call of Elisha," *ET* 24 (1912-13) 70-72.

*J. S. McArthur, "Elijah or Elisha?" *ET* 50 (1938-39) 363-367.

*R. P. Carroll, "The Elijah-Elisha Sagas: Some Remarks on Prophetic Succession in Ancient Israel," *VT* 29 (1969) 400-415.

Enoch

Moshe Gil, "Enoch in the Land of Eternal Life," *Tarbiz* 38 (1968-69) #4, I-III.

*J. P. Lesley, "Notes on Hebrew Etymologies from Egyptian ANX. Enoch; Anoki; Enos," *PAPS* 29 (1891) 17-20.

*C. Taylor, "Two Notes on Enoch in Sir. xliv 16," *JTS* 4 (1902-03) 589-590.

*J. H. A. Hart, 'Two Notes on Enoch in Sir. xliv 16," *JTS* 4 (1902-03) 590-591.

Enos

*J. P. Lesley, "Notes on Hebrew Etymologies from Egyptian ANX. Enoch; Anoki; Enos," *PAPS* 29 (1891) 17-20.

*A. C. Graham, "Adam and Enosh," *ET* 51 (1939-40) 205.

Esau

Thomas Whitelaw, "The House of Esau," *BFER* 37 (1888) 293-308.

C[laude] R. Conder, "Esau's Head," *PEFQS* 22 (1890) 123-124.

*T. K. Cheyne, "The Connection of Esau and Usöos," *ZAW* 17 (1897) 189.

R. M'Cheyne Edgar, "Esau, an Old Testament 'Rob Roy'," *CFL, N.S.,* 6 (1902) 222-226.

Ernest Elliot, "Esau," *ET* 29 (1917-18) 44-45.

L. O. Lineberger, "Esau: A Man of the World," *R&E* 25 (1928) 39-47.

Esther

*[Joseph Fullonton], "Esther," *FBQ* 16 (1868) 205-216.

Marcus Dods, "Esther," *Exp, 3rd Ser.,* 5 (1887) 401-410.

*C. H. Toy, "Esther as a Babylonian Goddess," *NW* 7 (1898) 130-144.

*W. B. Stevenson, "Esther in the Apocrphya," *IJA* #5 (1906) 1-2.

*A. S. Yahuda, "The Meaning of the name Esther," *JRAS* (1946) 174-178.

Eve

*A. H. Sayce, "Miscellaneous Notes," *ZA* 4 (1889) 382-393. [33. The name of Eve in Assyrian, p. 393]

*Morris Jastrow Jr., "Adam and Eve in Babylonian Literature," *AJSL* 15 (1898-99) 193-214.

*Arthur E. Whatham, "Are Adam and Eve Historical Characters?" *AAOJ* 32 (1910) 85-93.

Thomas J. Motherway, "The Creation of Eve in Catholic Tradition," *ThSt* 1 (1940) 97-116.

Ezekiel

*R. P. Stebbins, "Did the Prophet Ezekiel Write or Edit or Remodel Any Portion of the Pentateuch?" *ONTS* 3 (1883-84) 289-295.

E. H. Plumptre, "Ezekiel: An Ideal Biography," *Exp, 2nd Ser.*, 7 (1884) 1-18, 161-174, 267-281, 401-416; 8 (1884) 1-17, 161-176, 281-293, 419-430.

Walter R. Betteridge, "Ezekiel, the Prophet of the Exile," *BW* 5 (1895) 248-257.

*John Rothwell Slater, "Individualism and Solidarity as Developed by Jeremiah and Ezekiel," *BW* 14 (1899) 172-183.

*A. W. Ackerman, "Ezekiel's Contribution to Sociology," *BW* 17 (1901) 112-117.

J. H. Light, "The Son of Buzi: The Up-standing Man Face to Face with the Issues of the Day," *MQR, 3rd Ser.*, 39 (1913) 721-732.

John F. Humphrey, "The Personality of Ezekiel," *LQHR* 166 (1941) 208-214.

Edwin C. Broome Jr., "Ezekiel's Abnomal Personality," *JBL* 65 (1946) 277-292.

Dora Askowith, "Ezekiel and St. Augustine. A Comparative Study," *JAAR* 15 (1947) 224-227.

Harold Knight, "The Personality of Ezekiel—Priest or Prophet?" *ET* 59 (1947-48) 115-120.

M. G. Stalker, "Ezekiel and Jesus," *GUOST* 13 (1947-49) 16-18.

Ezekiel concluded

G. B. F. Cook, "A Prophet to Displaced Persons," *MC* 39 (1949) 43-49.

J. C. Whitney, "The Ministry According to Ezekiel," *BQL* 14 (1951-52) 34-38, 84-87.

*Dane R. Gordon, "Two Problems in the Book of Ezekiel," *EQ* 28 (1956)148-151. *[Ezekiel's Knowledge of Jerusalem; Was Ezekiel a prophet?]*

Walter R. Roehrs, "The Dumb Prophet," *CTM* 29 (1958) 176-186.

Moshe Greenberg, "On Ezekiel's Dumbness," *JBL* 77 (1958) 101-105.

Cameron Mackay, "Ezekiel in the New Testament," *CQR* 162 (1961) 4-16.

Ezra

Thomas E. Thomas, "Ezra, the Model of the Biblical Divine," *PQPR* 1 (1872) 160-180.

C[rawford] H[owell] Toy, "Ezra the Scribe," *BQ* 9 (1875) 339-349.

[Crawford Howell] Toy, "Ezra the Scribe," *DTQ* 2 (1876) 191-199.

Marcus Dods, "Ezra," *Exp, 3rd Ser.,* 7 (1887) 53-64.

*R. P. Stebbins, "Did Ezra Write or Amend any Portion of the Pentateuch?" *URRM* 20 (1883) 221-229.

*R. P. Stebbins, "Did Ezra Write or Amend any Portion of the Pentateuch?" *ONTS* 3 (1883-84) 234-240.

A. B. Hyde, "Ezra the Scribe," *MR* 72 (1890) 809-817.

*C. H. Cornill, "Ezra and Nehemiah," *OC* 9 (1895) 4599-4601.

*A. [E.] Cowley, "Ezra's Recension of the Law," *JTS* 11 (1909-10) 542-545.

Henry Englander, "Ezra the Scribe," *JJLP* 1 (1919) 319-328.

Ezra concluded

Norman H. Snaith, "The Date of Ezra's Arrival in Jerusalem," *ZAW* 63 (1950-51) 53-66.

*Donald Fay Robinson, "Was Ezra Nehemiah?" *ATR* 37 (1955) 177-189.

J. A. Emerton, "Did Ezra go to Jerusalem in 428 B. C.?" *JTS, N.S.,* 17 (1966) 1-19.

David W. Searle, "Ezra the Historian," *BH* 5 (1969) 56-59.

G

Gad

Lewis Bayles Paton, "Outline Studies of Obscurer Prophets—VII. The Prophet Gad," *HR* 50 (1905) 121-122.

Gesham

William Creighton Graham, "Gashmu, the Arabian," *AJSL* 42 (1925-26) 276-278.

Frank Moore Cross Jr., "Gesham the Arabian," *BA* 18 (1955) 46-47.

*Anonymous, "Gesham the Arab," *AT* 1 (1956-57) #3, 13.

Gideon

W. G. Elmslie, "Gideon," *Exp, 4th Ser.,* 5 (1892) 50-65.

*Barnabas Lindars, "Gideon and Kingship," *JTS, N.S.,* 16 (1965) 315-326.

Goliath

( ) B., "Was there Only One Giant 'Goliath'?" *CFL, 3rd Ser.,* 9 (1908) 357-359.

H

Habakkuk

*E. A. Chown, "Habakkuk—the prophet and prophecy," *CMR* 6 (1894) 34-48.

Hadad

*T. K. Cheyne, "The N. Arabian Land of Muṣri in Early Hebrew Tradition," *JQR* 11 (1898-99) 551-560. [I. The History of Hadad the Edomite, pp. 551-556]

Hagar

Anonymous, "Hagar. A Study in Providence," *ET* 28 (1916-17) 554-559.

*S. M. Zwemer, "Hagar and Ishmael," *EQ* 22 (1950) 32-39.

Hananiah

C. G. Tuland, Hanani—Hananiah," *JBL* 77 (1958) 157-161.

Hannah

*Ed. König, "Deborah and Hannah," *HR* 51 (1906) 130.

Hazael

H. B. 2nd, "Hazael," *UQGR* 10 (1853) 158-166.

*J. F. McCurdy, "Light on Scriptural Texts from Recent Discoveries. Bible Personages. II. Benhadad and Hazael," *HR* 36 (1898) 23-26.

Heber

*J. Blunt Chesire Jr., "Jael, the Wife of Heber the Kenite," *PER* 2 (1888-89) 277-284.

Hosea

*Emery Barnes, "The Prophet of the Love of God," *Exp, 8th Ser.,* 9 (1915) 97-108.

Paul Haupt, "Hosea's Birthplace," *JBL* 34 (1915) 182-183.

*I. H. Eybers, "The matrimonial life of Hosea," *OTW* 7&8 (1964-65) 11-34.

I

Ira

*Moshe Aberbach, "The Relations between Ira the Jairite and King David according to Talmudic Legend," *Tarbiz* 33 (1963-64) #4, III.

Isaac

W. Hanna, "The Table of Isaac's Life," *ONTS* 1 (1882) #2, 14.

Thomas Whitelaw, "The Life of Isaac," *BFER* 36 (1887) 114-128.

John Watson, "Isaac, the Type of Quietness," *Exp, 6th Ser.,* 11 (1905) 123-132.

*R. A. S[tewart] Macalister (trans.), "Tales of the Prophets," *PEFQS* 40 (1908) 310-317. [Of Isaac, pp. 312-313]

Anonymous, "A Study in the Life of Isaac," *ET* 21 (1909-10) 171.

Harold M. Wiener, "The Age of Isaac," *BS* 68 (1911) 705-707.

*Walter R. Alexander, "His Sons, Isaac and Ishmael," *CQ* 16 (1939) 210-214.

Isaac concluded

*A. van Selms, "Isaac in Amos," *OTW* 7&8 (1964-65) 157-165.

Isaiah

A. G. L., "Isaiah," *UQGR* 14 (1857) 261-285.

E. H. Plumptre, "Isaiah: An Ideal Biography," *Exp, 2nd Ser.,* 5 (1883) 23-40, 81-86, 87-101, 210-229, 296-317, 449-468. [I. The Youth and Training of the Prophet; II. Under Jotham, B.C. 758-741; III. Under Ahaz, B.C. 741-726; IV. Under Hezekiah, B.C. 726-698; V. Under Hezekiah-The Egyptian Alliance; VI. The Last Labours of the Prophet]

( ) Dunning, "Character of Isaiah," *ONTS* 4 (1884-85) 82.

William R. Harper, "The Work of Isaiah," *BW* 10 (1897) 48-57.

*A. H. Sayce, "The Politics of Isaiah and Jeremiah," *ET* 1 (1889-90) 65.

James S. Wallace, "Isaiah as a Statesman," *BRec* 4 (1907) 21-24.

Charles Edward Smith, "The Greatness of Isaiah," *CFL, 3rd Ser.,* 7 (1907) 274-279.

Alexander R. Gordon, "The Prophets as Internationalists. Isaiah," *BW* 51 (1918) 212-215, 269-271.

Robert George Raymer, "Isaiah the Statesman," *MQR, 3rd Ser.,* 45 (1919) 708-726; 46 (1920) 147-159.

Archibald Duff, "The Actual Story of Isaiah," *ICMM* 20 (1923-24) 142-149.

C. B. Reynolds, "Isaiah's Wife," *JTS* 36 (1935) 182-185.

John Paterson, "Isaiah: Prophet of Faith," *RL* 14 (1944-45) 422-428.

*Ivan Engnell, "The Call of Isaiah. An exegetical and comparative study," *UUÅ* (1949) Band 1, #4, 1-68.

Isaiah concluded

W. Norman Pittenger, "The Prophet Isaiah," *ATR* 32 (1950) 199-203.

*John Gray, "The Period and Office of the Prophet Isaiah in the Light of a New Assyrian Tablet," *ET* 63 (1951-52) 263-265.

Silvester Humphries, "The Mystical Life of Isaias, I," *LofS* 9 (1954-55) 158-165.

Silvester Humphries, "The Mystical Life of Isaias, II," *LofS* 9 (1954-55) 212-216.

C. F. Whitley, "The Call and Mission of Isaiah," *JNES* 18 (1959) 38-48.

Robert T. Anderson, "Was Isaiah a Scribe?" *JBL* 79 (1960) 57-58.

Stanley B. Frost, "Old Testament Characters: XI. Isaiah," *PQL* 7 (1961) 128-135.

*Frederick L. Moriarty, "Hezekiah, Isaiah and Imperial Politics," *BiBT* #19 (1965) 1270-1276.

*Alfred E. McBride, "The Preaching Technique of Isaiah," *P* 1 (1966) #3, 1-4.

*Peter R. Ackroyd, "Historians and Prophets," *SEÅ* 33 (1968) 18-54. [Isaiah and Ahaz, pp. 23-37]

R. Knierm, "The Vocation of Isaiah," *VT* 18 (1968) 47-68.

Ishmael

*Walter R. Alexander, "His Sons, Isaac and Ishmael," *CQ* 16 (1939) 210-214.

*S. M. Zwemer, "Hagar and Ishmael," *EQ* 22 (1950) 32-39.

Israel (see: Jacob)

J

Jabez

*John Campbell, "Jabez," *BFER* 29 (1880) 291-313.

Jacob (Israel)

Thomas Whitelaw, "The History of Jacob," *BFER* 36 (1887) 285-298, 480-496, 708-722.

*Lysander Dickerman, "The Names of Jacob and Joseph in Egypt," *ONTS* 7 (1887-88) 181-185.

P. Carnegie Simpson, "Jacob's Wrestle: A Man and His Fate," *Exp, 5th Ser.,* 8 (1898) 391-400.

*S. R. Driver, "Jacob's Route from Haran to Shechem," *ET* 13 (1901-02) 457-460.

R. McCheyne Edgar, "Jacob, the Prince Among the Patriarchs," *CFL, N.S.,* 6 (1902) 342-349.

A. B. Davidson, "Jacob at Peniel," *Exp, 6th Ser.,* 5 (1902) 176-188.

*Arthur Babbitt Fairchild, "Jacob or Israel," *BS* 62 (1905) 698-712.

John E. McFadyen, "The Original Conception of the Character of Jacob," *HR* 53 (1907) 209-210.

*H. M. Du Bose, "Shechem and the Historicity of Jacob," *BR* 13 (1928) 528-548.

Leroy Waterman, "Jacob the Forgotten Supplanter," *AJSL* 55 (1938) 25-43.

*J. W. Jack, "Recent Biblical Archaeology," *ET* 51 (1939-40) 544-548. [The Name Jacob, p. 547]

S[tanley] B. Frost, "Old Testament Characters. II: Jacob," *PQL* 5 (1959) 18-23.

Arthur Gold, "The Personality of Jacob," *Mosaic* 2 (1961) #2, 3-9.

Jacob (Israel) concluded

*D. N. Freedman, "The Original Name of Jacob," *IEJ* 13 (1963) 124-125.

*John Van Seters, "Jacob's Marriages and Ancient Near East Customs: A Re-examination," *HTR* 62 (1969) 377-395.

Jael

*J. Blunt Chesire Jr., "Jael, the Wife of Heber the Kenite," *PER* 2 (1888-89) 277-284.

*John Hendrick de Vries, "Higher Criticism and the Sunday School," *CFL, 3rd Ser.,* 8 (1908) 209-212. *[Deborah & Jael]*

*Anonymous, "Jael. A Study in Early Ethics," *ET* 28 (1916-17) 349-354.

*Edgar J. Bruns, "Judith or Jael?" *CBQ* 16 (1954) 12-14.

Japhet

*A. H. Sayce, "On the names Shem and Japhet," *SBAP* 5 (1882-83) 154-155.

*A. H. Sayce, "The Explanation of the Biblical Names Shem and Japhet," *ONTS* 3 (1883-84) 120-121.

Javan

E. Robertson, "Notes on Javan," *JQR* 20 (1907-08) 466-508.

E. Robertson, "Notes on Javan. II.," *JQR* 20 (1907-08) 812-824.

A. H. Sayce, "Javan," *JRAS* (1921) 53-54.

Jehoezer

*Sergio J. Grintz, "Jehoezer—Unknown High Priest?" *JQR, N.S.,* 50 (1959-60) 338-347.

Jephthah (See also: Judges, Literary Criticism →)

J[ohn] D. D[avis], "Editorial Notes," *CFL, N.S.,* 3 (1901) 306-309. *[Jephthah] (Editorial)*

Jeremiah

R. Payne Smith, "Short Papers Upon the Prophet Jeremiah. No. 1.—Jeremiah's Call," *Exp, 1st Ser.,* 7 (1878) 241-248.

*J. Edwin Odgers, "Jeremiah and the Fall of Judah," *ModR* 5 (1884) 211-237.

A. W. Stearne, "Traditions Relating to Jeremiah," *ONTS* 5 (1884-85) 279-280.

*Archibald Duff, "Jeremiah, the Prophet of Personal Godliness: A Study in Hebrew Religion," *BS* 43 (1886) 652-662.

Wm. G. Ballantine, "Jeremiah's Temperament," *ONTS* 8 (1888-89) 181-183.

*A. H. Sayce, "The Politics of Isaiah and Jeremiah," *ET* 1 (1889-90) 65.

A[rchibald] Duff, "The Prophet Jeremiah. A Study of his Development in Thought and Utterance," *Exp, 4th Ser.,* 4 (1891) 241-255.

James Stalker, "Jeremiah: The Man and His Message," *Exp, 5th Ser.,* 1 (1895) 66-73, 108-118, 309-316. [I. His Call; II. His Times; III. Ideal]

James Stalker, "Jeremiah: The Man and His Message," *Exp, 5th Ser.,* 2 (1895) 118-128, 199-209, 278-286, 356-365. [IV. Degeneration; V. Retribution; VI. God; VII. The Future]

*John Rothwell Slater, "Individualism and Solidarity as Developed by Jeremiah and Ezekiel," *BW* 14 (1899) 172-183.

George G. Findlay, "The Inner Life of Jeremiah," *ET* 18 (1906-07) 296-299, 351-355, 412-414.

Jeremiah cont.

L. W. Grensted, "The Significance of Jeremiah," *ICMM* 9 (1912-13) 271-281.

Lindsay B. Longacre, "Jeremiah as His Neighbors Knew Him," *BW* 48 (1916) 283-287.

B. R. Downer, "The Pathos of the Life and Ministry of Jeremiah," *R&E* 15 (1918) 45-56.

S. Arthur Peake, "Jeremiah," *MR* 105 (1922) 800-806.

James Gilroy, "Jeremiah as Patriot and Statesman," *GUOST* 5 (1923-38) 35-36.

H. A. Williamson, "Jeremiah and Jesus—In Comparison and Contrast," *ET* 34 (1922-23) 535-538.

H. A. Williamson, "Jeremiah and Jesus—In Comparison and Contrast. II.," *ET* 35 (1923-24) 39-42.

Theophile J. Meek, "Was Jeremiah a Priest?" *Exp, 8th Ser.,* 25 (1923) 215-222.

Johann Hempel, "God and the World in the Religious Faith of Jeremiah," *JR* 4 (1924) 32-45.

W. T. Davison, "The Prophet as Hero," *LQHR* 141 (1924) 253-256.

Alexander Steward, "Jeremiah—The Man and His Message," *PTR* 26 (1928) 1-40.

Edmund F. Sutcliffe, "Was Jeremias Sanctified in the Womb?" *IER, 5th Ser.,* 34 (1929) 130-138.

Herbert C. Alleman, "Jeremiah, the Preacher's Prophet," *LCQ* 5 (1932) 73-83.

*Shalom Spiegel, "Josiah and Jeremiah," *JBL* 61 (1942) iv.

*Harry F. Baughman, "Jeremiah and the Word of the Lord," *LCQ* 18 (1945) 223-240. [I. The Man Who Was Inspired. II. How Did the Word of the Lord Come to Jeremiah?]

Jeremiah cont.

W. F. Lofthouse, "Prophet and Apostle: Jeremiah and Paul," *OSHTP* (1945-46) 5-26.

*W[illiam] F[oxwell] Albright, "A Brief History of Judah from the Days of Josiah to Alexander the Great," *BA* 9 (1946) 1-16. [Jeremiah and the Fall of Judah, pp. 4-5]

*Walter G. Williams, "Prayer in the Life of Jeremiah," *RL* 15 (1946) 436-445.

Harris E. Kirk, "The Hammer and the Anvil. *A Subjective Approach to a Pivotal Moment in the Life of a Prophet*," *Interp* 1 (1947) 33-40.

James T. Veneklasen, "The Religion of Jeremiah," *JAAR* 15 (1947) 90-99.

Margaret Smith, "Jeremy," *LofS* 2 (1947-48) 503-509.

G. B. F. Cook, "Jeremiah: The Prophet of Universal, Spiritual and Personal Religion," *MC* 37 (1947-48) 146-154.

E. C. Broome Jr., "The Personality of Jeremiah," *JBL* 70 (1951) v.

*M. B. Rowton, "Jeremiah and the Death of Josiah," *JNES* 10 (1951) 128-130.

M. D. Goldman, "Was Jeremiah Married?" *ABR* 2 (1952) 42-47.

Leslie J. Dunstan, "Kierkegaard and Jeremiah," *ANQ* 47 (1955) #3, 17-24.

*P. E. Broughton, "The Call of Jeremiah: The Relation of Deut. 18:9-22 to the Call and Life of Jeremiah," *ABR* 6 (1958) 39-46.

Robert Dobbie, "Jeremiah and the Preacher," *CJT* 4 (1958) 37-45.

Carroll Stuhlmueller, "Jeremias—The Successful Failure," *C&C* 12 (1960) 146-163.

Ulrich Simon, "The Mysticism of Jeremiah," *CQR* 161 (1960) 270-279.

Jeremiah concluded

George Orvick, "The Personality and Work of Jeremiah," *LSQ* 1 (1960-61) #3, 10-16; #4, 6-14.

Stanley B. Frost, "Old Testament Characters: XII. Jeremiah," *PQL* 7 (1961) 205-214.

*David Smith, "Jeremiah in Political Context," *R&E* 58 (1961) 417-427.

John D. W. Watts, "Jeremiah—A Character Study," *R&E* 58 (1961) 428-437.

T. T. Crabtree, "The Prophet's Call—A Dialogue with God," *SWJT, N.S.*, 4 (1961-62) 33-56.

John H. Marks, "The Image of Jeremiah's Call," *McQ* 16 (1962-63) #4, 29-38.

*Julien Harvey, "The Prayer of Jeremias," *Way* 3 (1963) 165-173. *(Trans. by Peter Hebblethwaite)*

M. Catherine Cenkner, "A Model for Teachers," *C&C* 16 (1964) 338-343.

Ronald F. Youngblood, "The Prophet of Loneliness," *BSQ* 13 (1964-65) #3, 3-19.

Donald J. Patrick, "Jeremiah and Human Affection," *C&C* 18 (1966) 297-310.

*M. Philotea, "Jeremiah, Prophet of Affliction," *BibT* #36 (1968) 2513-2516.

*Peter R. Ackroyd, "Jeremiah and the fall of Jerusalem," *SEÅ* 33 (1968) 37-54.

*Gerard Reedy, "Jeremiah and the Absurdity of the Prophet," *BibT* #40 (1969) 2781-2787.

M. Margaret O'Connor, "Jeremiah the Man: A Word Spoken by God," *BibT* #40 (1969) 2788-2798.

Job

†Cantabrigensis, "The Patience of Job Questioned," *TRep* 2 (1770) 301-303.

G. P., "Sketch of the Life and Character of Job," *CongML* 4 (1821) 234-240, 343-350, 689-695.

J. S., "Kant's View on the Moral Lesson Conveyed in the Vindication of Job," *BRCM* 6 (1849-50) 566-569.

Josiah Royce, "The Problem of Job," *NW* 6 (1897) 261-281.

M. Kaufmann, "Was Job an Agnostic?" *Exp, 5th Ser.,* 7 (1898) 377-389.

*Edward M. Merrins, "The Patience of Job," *BS* 64 (1907) 224-249.

*R. A. S[tewart] Macalister (trans.), "Tales of the Prophets," *PEFQS* 40 (1908) 310-317. [Of Job, pp. 315-317]

Rufus J. Wyckoff, "Job and the Man of the Sermon on the Mount," *MR* 93 (1911) 257-263.

Edwin H. Gomes, "The Impatience of Job," *HR* 66 (1913) 487.

[Frank M. Thomas], "Hamlet and Job," *MQR, 3rd Ser.,* 45 (1919) 3-16.

*J. Hugh Michael, "Paul and Job: A Neglected Analogy," *ET* 36 (1924-25) 67-70.

Alice Belmer Nickles, "The Greatest of all the Men of the East," *CFL, 3rd Ser.,* 42 (1936) 286-288.

*Herbert Gordon May, "Prometheus and Job: The Problem of the God of Power and the Man of Worth," *ATR* 34 (1952) 240-246.

D. H. Gard, "The Concept of Job's Character According to the Greek Translator of the Hebrew Text," *JBL* 71 (1952) xii.

Morris Stockhammer, "Job's Problem," *Jud* 2 (1953) 247-253.

*Robert Gordis, "The Temptation of Job—Tradition Versus Experience in Religion," *Jud* 4 (1955) 195-208.

Job concluded

Morris Stockhammer, "The Righteousness of Job," *Jud* 7 (1958) 64-71.

André Néher, "Job: The Biblical Man," *Jud* 13 (1964) 37-47.

Elmer F. Suderman, "The Character of Job," *CraneR* 8 (1965) 74-82.

Lionel Swain, "The Bible and the People. The Suffering of Job," *ClR* 51 (1966) 624-631.

H. L. Ginsberg, "Job the Patient and Job the Impatient," *CJ* 21 (1966-67) #3, 12-28.

Peter R. Ackroyd, "Job the Agnostic," *ContextC* 1 (1967-68) #2, 15-26.

Job's Wife

Anonymous, "Job's Wife," *ET* 29 (1917-18) 363-366.

Harris E. Kirk, "Job's Wife," *BR* 5 (1920) 439-448.

Jonah

John Foster, "Observations on the History of Jonah," *CongML* 27 (1844) 253-260.

W. Quance, "Jonah the fugitive prophet," *CMR* 4 (1892) 456-479.

Earl A. Weis, "Jonah: Prophet and Type," *MH* 11 (1954-55) #2, 38-42.

D. M. Deed, "Jonah," *SCR* 2 (1968) 26-31.

Meir Havazelet, "Jonah and the Prophet Experience," *Trad* 10 (1968-69) #4, 29-32.

Jonathan

D. J. Woods, "The Career and Character of Jonathan," *CFL, N.S.,* 8 (1903) 267-273.

*George Henslow, "Did Jonathan taste Hachish?" *ET* 15 (1903-04) 336.

*Julian Morgenstern, "David and Jonathan," *JBL* 78 (1959) 322-325.

Joseph

†Anonymous, "On the History of Joseph," *MMBR* 32 (1811-12) 27-28.

H. G. Tomkins, "The Life of Joseph, Illustrated from Sources External to Holy Scripture," *JTVI* 15 (1881-82) 83-113. [Discussion, pp.113-119]

*L. Lund, "The Epoch of Joseph: Amenhotep IV as the Pharaoh of the Famine," *SBAP* 4 (1881-82) 96-102. (Remarks by H. Villiers Stuart, pp. 95-96; by St. Vincent Beechey, p. 102; by Samuel Birch, p. 102)

Robert Rainy, "Joseph's Forgetting," *Exp, 3rd Ser.,* 4 (1886) 401-411.

*J. G. Lansing, "Egyptian Notes," *AJSL* 4 (1887-88) 43-45. [II. The Egyptian Name of Joseph, pp. 44-45]

*Lysander Dickerman, "The Names of Jacob and Joseph in Egypt," *ONTS* 7 (1887-88) 181-185.

Thomas Whitelaw, "The History of Joseph: The Story of his Fortunes," *BFER* 37 (1888) 491-507, 706-725.

*A. H. Sayce, "Miscellaneous Notes," *ZA* 4 (1889) 382-393. [27. *Asipu* and Joseph, pp. 387-388]

James Monroe, "Joseph as a Statesman," *BS* 54 (1897) 484-500.

Charles Foster Kent, "The Boyhood of Joseph," *BW* 10 (1897) 414-421.

Joseph cont.

Armstrong Black, "Joseph: an Ethical and Biblical Study," *Exp, 6th Ser.*, 1 (1900) 63-78, 111-121, 217-230, 289-308, 444-459; 2 (1900) *[1.The Youth and His Dreams; 2. Joseph and His Brethren; 3. The Blank in the Tent; 4. The Choice of a Side; 5. The Life Within Bars; 6. The Prisoner in the Palace; 7. The Second to Pharaoh, the Saviour of Egypt]*

S[amuel] M. S[mith], "Editorial Notes," *CLF, N.S.*, 4 (1901) 181-185. *[Joseph] (Editorial)*

*Jas. A. Quarles, "The Sociology of Joseph's Day. Ethical," *CFL, N.S.*, 6 (1902) 110-116.

William J. Frazer, "Where Was Joseph Buried?" *HR* 50 (1905) 440.

Ed., König, "Is Joseph Forever Lost to us as a Real Person?" *MR* 87 (1905) 345-350.

Melvin Grove Kyle, "Joseph in His Times—A Portrait," *CFL, 3rd Ser.*, 6 (1907) 417-419.

*P. Scott-Moncrieff, "Note on the name Zaphnath Paaneaḥ," *SBAP* 29 (1907) 87-88. *[The Egyptian Name of Joseph]*

*E[douard] Naville, "The Egyptian Name of Joseph," *SBAP* 32 (1910) 203-210.

*Harold M. Wiener, "The Egyptian Name of Joseph," *BS* 68 (1911) 156-159.

M. Gaster, "The Age of Joseph," *ET* 23 (1911-12) 237.

*Bernhard Pick, "Joseph and Asenath," *OC* 27 (1913) 467-496. *[Legend concerning Joseph's marriage to Asenath]*

*Oswald [T.] Allis, "The Name Joseph," *PTR* 18 (1920) 646-659.

M. Ryerson Turnbull, "Joseph—A Character Study," *USR* 32 (1920-21) 133-144.

*Maurice Bloomfield, "Joseph and Potiphar in Hindu Fiction," *PAPA* 54 (1923) 141-167.

Joseph cont.

*J. P. Wilson, "The Story of Joseph in the Septuagint," *GUOST* 5 (1923-28)16-17.

*R. Engelbach, "The Egyptian Name of Joseph," *JEA* 10 (1924) 204-206.

Eduard Koenig, "Is the Biblical Joseph a Product of Poetizing Folk-Phantasy?" *CFL, 3rd Ser.,* 31 (1925) 496-499. *(Trans. by E. W. Hammer)*

*Howard Tillman Kuist, "Shechem and the Bones of Joseph," *BR* 11 (1926) 412-420.

*Edouard Naville, "The Egyptian Name of Joseph," *JEA* 12 (1926) 16-18.

A. S. Yahuda, "Joseph in Egypt in the Light of the Monuments," *JTVI* 65 (1933) 39-54. [Discussion, pp. 54-56]

P. E. Kretzmann, "The Story of Joseph in the Light of Recent Research," *CTM* 5 (1934) 611-614.

E. W. Heaton, "The Joseph Saga," *ET* 59 (1947-48) 134-136.

*A. W. Argyle, "Joseph the Patriarch in Patristic Teaching," *ET* 67 (1955-56) 199-201.

C. A. Wilson, "The Local Colour of the Bible Records: Part 2. The Israelites in Egypt: Joseph as Vizier in Egypt," *AT* 1 (1956-57) #2, 11-13.

S[tanley] B. Frost, "Old Testament Characters. III: Joseph," *PQL* 5 (1959) 107-113.

W. A. Ward, "The Egyptian Office of Joseph," *JSS* 5 (1960) 144-150.

Robert S. Kinsey, "An Archaeologist Looks at Joseph," *WBHDN* 60 (1963) #4 16-22.

Joseph concluded

Anonymous, "Joseph, Ruler of Egypt. A Study of the court officials of ancient Egypt and the ceremonies associated with their installation or their being honoured by the king shows that the Joseph narrative fits perfectly into a genuine Egyptian background," *BH* 2 (1965) #2, 22-28.

W. Gunther Plaut, "Understanding Joseph," *CCARJ* 16 (1969) #2, 20-23.

Joshua

*Anonymous, "Who was Sesostris?" *MMBR* 23 (1807) 560-562.

*W. Bacher, "The Supposed Inscription upon 'Joshua the Robber'," *JQR* 3 (1890-91) 354-357.

George S. Goodspeed, "The Men Who Made Israel," *BW* 30 (1907) 202-207. [Joshua and the Promised Land]

*Eb. Nestle, "The Genealogy and the Name Joshua," *ET* 20 (1908-09) 45.

William H. Bates, "Joshua, the Man: A Study in Character," *CFL, 3rd Ser.,* 27 (1921) 57-60.

Stanley B. Frost, "Old Testament Characters. V: Joshua," *PQL* 5 (1959) 321-327.

Judah

*Anonymous, "Notes on Bishop Colenso's New Book," *JSL, 4th Ser.,* 2 (1862-63) 385-401. *(Review)* [III. The Family of Judah: marginal Chronology of the Bible]

*B. J. van der Merwe, "Judah in the Pentateuch," *TEP* 1 (1968) 37-52.

K

Korah

*Greta Hort, "The Death of Qorah," *ABR* 7 (1959) 2-26.

W. Gunther Plaut, "Some Unanswered Questions About Korah," *CCARJ* 16 (1969) #4, 74-78.

L

Lot

Joseph Offord, "The Worship of the Patriach Lot in Palestine," *PEFQS* 47 (1915) 91-92.

Lot's Wife

*Anonymous, "Lot's Wife. A Study in Detatchment," *ET* 28 (1916-17) 445-449.

*Parray Marshall, "Life from the Dead Sea," *ContR* 169 (1946) 296-299. *[Lot's Wife]*

M

Maachah

*S. Yeivin, "Abijam, Asa and Maachah the Daughter of Abishalom," *BIES* 10 (1942-44) #4, III.

*B[enjamin] Mazar, "Geshur and Maacah," *JBL* 80 (1961) 16-28.

Melchizedek *(Note: Some articles refer to N.T. book of Hebrews)*

†Paulinus, "Observations on St. Paul's Reasoning concerning Melchizedec," *TRep* 2 (1770) 283-290.

W. W., "Observations on Christ's Answer to the Sadducees, and St. Paul's Reasoning concerning Melchizedec, in Answer to Paulinus," *TRep* 2 (1770) 458-461.

B. E. T., "On the character of Melchisedec," *QCS* 3 (1821) 516-525.

Isaac Headley, "Who was Melchisedec?" *BRCR, 3rd Ser.,* 4 (1848) 495-502.

Anonymous, "Melchizedek," *BRCM* 5 (1848-49) 217-229.

Henry A. Sawtelle, "The Eternal Life and Priesthood of Melchisedek," *BS* 16 (1859) 528-557. [Condensed from the German of Carl August Auberlen]

J. B. Gross, "Melchisedec," *ER* 20 (1869) 50-58.

Anonymous, "The Melchizedekan Priesthood," *SPR* 25 (1874) 431-459.

*C. V. Anthony, "The Order of Melchisedec," *ONTS* 3 (1883-84) 209-210.

Jos. H. Alexander, "Who was Melchizedek?" *PQ* 1 (1887-88) 454-476.

John Henry Hopkins, "Who Was Melchizedek?" *CR* 60 (1891) 24-30.

George C. Currie, Melchisedec," *PER* 5 (1891-92) 443-447.

Anonymous, "Melchizadek," *ONTS* 14 (1892) 121.

J. N. Fradenburgh, "The Order of Melchizedek," *MR* 75 (1893) 426-437.

A. H. Sayce, "Melchizedek," *ET* 7 (1895-96) 478.

S. R. Driver, "Melchizedek II.," *ET* 7 (1895-96) 478-480.

Melchizedek cont.

A. H. Sayce, "Melchizedek," *ET* 7 (1895-96) 565-566.

S. R. Driver, "Melchizedek," *ET* 8 (1896-97) 43-44.

A. H. Sayce, "Melchizedek. I," *ET* 8 (1896-97) 94.

F[ritz] Hommel, "Melchizedek. II," *ET* 8 (1896-97) 94-96.

S. R. Driver, "Melchizedek," *ET* 8 (1896-97) 142-144.

*R. Balgarnie, "'Could Jesus Err?'," *ET* 8 (1896-97) 475. *[Melchizedek]*

Anonymous, "Melchizedek, the Priest-King," *MR* 87 (1905) 301-303.

Anonymous, "The Melchizedek Priesthood (Continued)," *MR* 87 (1905) 478-479, 642-645.

Anonymous, "New Light on 'Melchizedek' from the Cuneiform Inscriptions," *CFL, 3rd Ser.,* 6 (1907) 169-171. *(Editorial Note)*

F. P. Mayser, "Melchizedek the Most Perfect Type of Christ," *LCR* 30 (1911) 692-697.

F. P. Mayser, "Melchizedek the Most Perfect Type of Christ. II," *LCR* 31 (1912) 88-97.

*Paul Haupt, "Zerubbabel and Melchizedek," *JSOR* 2 (1918) 76-82.

H. K. Doerman, "Melchisedec," *TZTM* 9 (1919) 188-214.

J. P. Arendzen, "Melchisedek," *IER, 5th Ser.,* 27 (1926) 113-126.

W. J. McGarry, "'Priest According to the Order of Melchisedech'," *TFUQ* 8 (1933-34) 257-271.

H. M. DuB[ose], "Melchizedek's Title," *CFL, 3rd Ser.,* 40 (1934) 182-184.

Guy Brinkworth, "Melchisedech, King of Salem," *CIR* 10 (1935) 342-357.

Melchizedek concluded

Patrick F. Cremin, "According to the Order of Melchisedech," *IER, 5th Ser.,* 51 (1938) 469-487.

Patrick F. Cremin, "According to the Order of Melchisadech: II An Objection," *IER, 5th Ser.,* 52 (1938) 37-45.

Patrick F. Cremin, "According to the Order of Melchisedech: III Melchisedech, a Type of the Eucharist," *IER, 5th Ser.,* 53 (1939) 487-500.

*Patrick F. Cremin, "According to the Order of Melchisedech: IV The Patristic Interpretation and Its Value," *IER, 5th Ser.,* 54 (1939) 385-391.

Cameron Mackay, "The Order of Melchizedek," *CQR* 138 (1944) 175-191.

*Paul Leo, "Melchizedek and Christ," *WSQ* 1 (1948-49) #1, 3-9.

Jakob J. Petuchowski, "The Controversial Figure of Melchizedek," *HUCA* 28 (1957) 127-136.

*Y. Yadin, "A Note on Malchizedek and Qumran," *IEJ* 15 (1965) 152-154.

*Frederick [L.] Moriarty, "Abel, Melchizedek, Abraham," *Way* 5 (1965) 95-104.

*Anonymous, "The Mysterious Figure of Melchisedec. A Comment From the Dead Sea Scrolls," *BH* 3 (1967) #2, 5-8.

*Joseph A. Fitzmyer, "Further Light on Melchizedek from Qumran Cave 11," *JBL* 86 (1967) 10-24.

*H. H. Rowley, "Melchizedek and David," *VT* 17 (1967) 485.

Micah

I. H. Eybers, "Micah, the Morasthite: the man and his message," *OTW* 11 (1968) 9-24.

Michal

Anonymous, "Michal," *ET* 29 (1917-18) 221-224.

*Paul H. Levenson, "David and Michal: A Tragic Marriage," *CCARJ* 16 (1969) #4, 79-82.

Milcah

*John Moncure, "Sarah and Milkah," *R&E* 27 (1930) 62-64.

Miriam

*Lewis Bayles Paton, "Outline Studies of Obscurer Prophets—II. Aaron and Miriam," *HR* 49 (1904) 197-198.

Mordecai

Siegfried H. Horn, "Mordecai, a Historical Problem," *BRes* 9 (1964) 14-25.

Moses

Anonymous, "Observations on the Divine Mission of Moses," *TRep* 5 (1786) 366-384.

Mosaicus, "Observations on the Divine Mission of Moses [continued from Vol. V. p. 384]," *TRep* 6 (1788) 39-49.

S. C. L., "The Authority of Moses," *UQGR* 4 (1847) 196-209.

W. T. Hamilton, "The Character of Moses," *SPR* 5 (1851-52) 504-535.

Moses cont.

*(   ) G., "The Burial of Moses: With Remarks on Mal. IV. 5, 6, and the Reappearance of Enoch and Elijah as the Apocalyptic Witnesses," *JSL, 2nd Ser.,* 6 (1854) 135-165.

E. G. B., "Moses: or the Providential Method of Human Elevation," *UQGR* 13 (1856) 221-243.

J. W. N., "Death and Burial of Moses," *DQR* 1 (1861) 450-460.

[D. Waterman], "Life of Moses," *FBQ* 15 (1867) 1-25.

[D. Waterman], "Life of Moses. Part II," *FBQ* 15 (1867) 170-183.

*[S. N. Tufts], "The Hebrew Lawgiver," *FBQ* 15 (1867) 430-445; 16 (1868) 143-161. *[Moses]*

J. H. Martin, "Moses," *SPR* 18 (1867-68) 235-245.

Jacob Fry, "The Meekness of Moses," *ER* 21 (1870) 283-290.

J. P. Thompson, "Moses," *DTQ* 1 (1875) 88-107.

Anonymous, "Jewish Legendary Account of the Death of Moses," *DTQ* 1 (1875) 146-148.

A. Lowy, "Old Jewish Legends on Biblical Topics. No. 1. A Legend on the Death of Moses," *SBAP* 9 (1886-87) 40-47.

Anson D., Morse, "The Task and Education of Moses," *ONTS* 7 (1887-88)16-20.

*A. Wiedemann, "On the Legends concerning the Youth of Moses," *SBAP* 11 (1888-89) 29-43, 267-282.

Thomas Whitelaw, "The Choice of Moses; or, the Turning-Point in a Great Career," *TML* 2 (1889) 274-283.

Isaac H. Hall, "The Story of Arsâniš," *AJSL* 6 (1889-90) 81-88. [Nestorian legend of Moses]

Moses cont.

*E. de Bunsen, "The Pharaohs of Moses according to Hebrew and Egyptian Chronology," *SBAP* 12 (1889-90) 157-166.

Isaac H. Hall, "The Colloquy of Moses on Mount Sinai," *AJSL* 7 (1890-91) 161-177.

*Thomas Nixon Carver, "Moses as a Political Economist," *MR* 74 (1892) 598-605.

William Henry Green, "The Moses of the Critics," *PRR* 5 (1894) 369-397.

*C[arl] H[einrich] Cornill, "The Religion of Moses," *OC* 9 (1895) 4455-4458.

*G. G. Cameron, "Dr. Driver's 'Deuteronomy', The Use of the Name Moses," *ET* 7 (1895-96) 62-67.

Nathaniel Schmidt, "Moses: His Age and His Work (Illustrated)," *BW* 7 (1896) 30-38, 105-119.

A. R. S. Kennedy, "Requests and Replies," *ET* 8 (1896-97) 154. *[The Fasting of Moses]*

Charles P. Fagnani, "The Boyhood of Moses," *BW* 10 (1897) 422-432.

H. H. Hall, "Moses as a Scholar," *LQ* 27 (1897) 531-544.

Anonymous, "The Education of Moses," *MR* 79 (1897) 809-812.

*S. Krauss, "Names of Moses," *JQR* 10 (1897-98) 726.

*Fritz Hommel, "The True Date of Abraham and Moses," *ET* 10 (1898-99) 210-212.

*Fritz Hommel, "Additional Note to 'The True Date of Abraham and Moses'," *ET* 10 (1898-99) 278.

J. T. Marshall, "The Contest for the Body of Moses," *ET* 11 (1899-1900) 390-391.

Moses cont.

H. L. Reed, "Moses: His Personal Character," *CFL, N.S.*, 6 (1902) 227-231.

James M. Ludlow, "Moses—An Up-To-Date Statesman," *HR* 44 (1902) 3-9, 201-206.

*J. A. Selbie, "Moses and Hammurabi," *ET* 14 (1902-03) 363-364.

*Anonymous, "Hammurabi and Moses," *MR* 86 (1904) 132-136.

*C. M. Cobern, "Moses and Hammurabi and Their Laws," *MR* 86 (1904) 697-703.

A. H. Sayce, "Moses in Archaeology and Criticism," *R&E* 3 (1906) 356-367.

George S. Goodspeed, "The Men Who Made Israel," *BW* 29 (1907) 361-369. [Moses and the Beginnings of Israel]

John E. McFadyen, "What Did Moses Do?" *HR* 53 (1907) 368-370.

J. H. Sammis, "'What Did Moses Do?'," *CFL, 3rd Ser.*, 7 (1907) 20-22.

*R. A. S[tewart] Macalister (trans.), "Tales of the Prophets," *PEFQS* 41 (1909) 35-41. [Of Moses, pp. 37-38]

C[arl] H[einrich] Cornill, "Moses," *Monist* 20 (1910) 161-184.

Frank Crane, "Moses, An Interpretation," *MR* 92 (1910) 774-783.

Samuel Krauss, "A Moses Legend," *JQR, N. S.*, 2 (1911-12) 339-364.

Israel Friedlaender, "Note on 'A Moses Legend' by Professor Krauss," *JQR, N.S.*, 3 (1912-13) 179-180.

J. Francis Lamb, "Prof. Kent's 'Bible' and 'Science'," *CFL, 3rd Ser.*, 21 (1916) 55-58. [The Call of Moses]

Ernest Ward Burch, "The Character of Moses," *CFL, 3rd Ser.*, 23 (1917) 165-167.

Moses cont.

George H. Schodde, "Editorial Notes and Comments. The Moses of the Critics," *TZTM* 7 (1917) 383-384. *(Editorial)*

*J[ohn] M[erlin] Powis Smith, "The Name Moses," *AJSL* 35 (1918-19) 110-112.

*Harold M. Wiener, "The Religion of Moses," *BS* 76 (1919) 323-358.

*Harold M. Wiener, "Professor Barton on 'The Religion of Moses'," *BS* 77 (1920) 334-344.

Thomas Whitehead Murrell, "An Estimate of Moses," *MQR, 3rd Ser.,* 47 (1921) 650-673.

*D. S. Cairns, "The Divine Providence Illustrated from the Life of Moses," *BR* 7 (1922) 31-47.

Anonymous, "The Historicity of Moses," *TZDES* 50 (1922) 355-369.

*R. B. Henderson, "Akhnaton and Moses," *CQR* 97 (1923-24) 109-131.

J. Rendel Harris, "The Traditional Burial of Moses on Mount Sinai," *BJRL* 8 (1924) 404-405.

Martin Kegel, "What Do We Know Concerning Moses?" *MQR, 3rd Ser.,* 50 (1924) 3-10.

D[avid] S. K[ennedy], "Christ and Moses," *CFL, 3rd Ser.,* 31 (1925) 291-292.

*J. W. Jack, "Moses and the New Sinai Inscriptions," *ET* 37 (1925-26) 327-330.

W. J. Gruffyee, "Moses in the Light of Comparative Folklore," *ZAW* 46 (1928) 260-270.

David Russell, "Moses' Last Birthday—An Interview," *HR* 98 (1929) 238-241.

*Albert Abbott, "Was Moses the Meekest of Men?" *ET* 45 (1933-34) 524-525.

Moses cont.

*J. R. Towers, "The Name Moses," *JTS* 36 (1935) 407-409.

*Theophile James Meek, "Moses and the Levites," *AJSL* 56 (1939) 113-120.

*J. Philip Hyatt, "Freud on Moses and the Genesis of Monotheism," *JAAR* 8 (1940) 85-88. *(Review)*

L[eroy] Waterman, "Moses, the Pseudo-Levite," *JBL* 59 (1940) vii.

Leroy Waterman, "Moses, the Pseudo Levite," *JBL* 59 (1940) 397-404.

*Paschal P. Parente, "Ascetical and Mystical Traits of Moses and Elias," *CBQ* 5 (1943) 183-190.

*Michael J. Gruenthaner, "The Name of Moses," *AER* 111 (1944) 72-73.

*Herbert G. May, "Moses and the Sinai Inscriptions," *BA* 8 (1945) 93-99.

*Richard Hanson, "Moses in the Typology of St Paul," *Theo* 48 (1945) 174-177.

*T. C. Skeat, "Two Notes on the Passover 'Haggadah'," *JTS* 50 (1949) 53-57. *[The "virgin-birth" of Moses(?)]*

E. F. Sutcliffe, "Moses. A Sketch of his Life and Achievements," *Scrip* 4 (1949-51) 169-174.

*J. Gwyn Griffiths, "The Egyptian Derivation of the Name Moses," *JNES* 12 (1953) 225-231.

N. Wieder, "The Idea of a Second Coming of Moses," *JQR, N.S.,* 46 (1955-56) 356-364. [Reply by Solomon Zeitlin, pp. 364-366]

Eugene Arden, "How Moses Failed God," *JBL* 76 (1957) 50-52.

Arvid S. Kapelrud, "How Tradition Failed Moses," *JBL* 76 (1957) 242.

Moses cont.

Samuel E. Loewenstamm, "The Death of Moses," *Tarbiz* 27 (1957-58) #2-3, II-V.

Carl Armerding, "Moses, the Man of God," *BS* 116 (1959) 350-356.

C. Umhau Wolf, "Moses in Christian and Islamic Tradition," *JAAR* 27 (1959) 102-108.

Stanley B. Frost, "Old Testament Characters: IV: Moses," *PQL* 5 (1959) 207-213.

John Macdonald, "The Samaritan Doctrine of Moses," *SJT* 13 (1960) 149-162.

*Edward Ullendorff, "The 'Death of Moses' in the Literature of the Falashas," *BSOAS* 24 (1961) 419-443.

Alan M. Stibbs, "Exposition: The Call of Moses," *Them* 1 (1962-63) #2, 1-4.

Ivar Lissner, "The Tomb of Moses is Still Undiscovered," *BA* 26 (1963)106-108.

E[lmer] G. Suhr, "The Horned Moses," *Folk* 74 (1963) 387-395.

*Neal Kozodoy (trans.), "The Death of Moses. A Midrash," *Mosaic* 4 (1963) #2, 20-28.

R. C. Foster, "The Choice of Moses," *SR* 10 (1963-64) 1-10.

*Claude Chavasse, "The Suffering Servant and Moses," *CQR* 165 (1964) 152-163.

*William L. Holladay, "The Background of Jeremiah's Self-Understanding: Moses, Samuel, and Psalm 22," *JBL* 83 (1964) 153-164.

E. L. Allen, "Jesus and Moses in the New Testament," *ET* 67 (1966-67) 104-106.

Edward J. Young, "The Call of Moses—I," *WTJ* 29 (1966-67) 117-135.

Moses concluded

Edward J. Young, "The Call of Moses—II," *WTJ* 30 (1967-68) 1-23.

John G. Garger Jr., "Moses and Alpha," *JTS, N.S.,* 20 (1969) 245-248.

N

Naamah

*C. J. Ball, "Israel and Babylon," *SBAP* 16 (1893-94) 188-200. [2. Tubalcain and Naamah, pp. 191-193]

Nahor

*B. Maisler, "The Genealogy of the Sons of Nahor and the Historical Background of the Book of Job," *Zion* 11 (1945-46) #1, I.

Nahum

G. Nestle, "Where is the Birthplace of the Prophet Nahum to be Sought?" *PEFQS* 11 (1879) 136-138.

Nedabiah

*J. W. Jack, "Nedabiah in the Lachish Letters," *ET* 47 (1935-36) 430-431.

Nehemiah

Anonymous, "Nehemiah the Tirshatha," *JSL, 3rd Ser.,* 14 (1861-62) 444-449.

I. W. Bosanquet, "Nehemiah the Tirshatha," *JSL, 4th Ser.,* 1 (1862) 169-173.

Marcus Dods, "Nehemiah," *Exp, 3rd Ser.,* 6 (1887) 414-435.

Nehemiah concluded

Amasa B. McMackin, "Nehemiah," *LQ* 17 (1887) 40-60.

*C[arl] H[einrich] Cornill, "Ezra and Nehemiah," *OC* 9 (1895) 4599-4601.

Nathaniel Schmidt, "Nehemiah and His Work," *BW* 14 (1899) 329-343.

James Oscar Boyd, "Nehemiah Twelve Years at Jerusalem," *CFL, N.S.,* 2 (1900)176.

W. Emery Barnes, "Nehemiah," *ICMM* 2 (1905-06) 32-42.

*W[illiam] F[oxwell] Albright, "A Brief History of Judah from the Days of Josiah to Alexander the Great," *BA* 9 (1946) 1-16. [The Work of Nehemiah, pp. 10-13]

*Donald Fay Robinson, "Was Ezra Nehemiah?" *ATR* 37 (1955) 177-189.

Nimrod

W. T., "Nimrod and His Dynasty," *JSL, 3rd Ser.,* 11 (1860) 61-76.

Henry Crossley, "Dean Alford on Slavery.—Nimrod and His Dynasty," *JSL, 3rd Ser.,* 11 (1860) 442-449 [Nimrod, pp. 446-448]

W. T., "Nimrod," *JSL, 3rd Ser.,* 12 (1860-61) 173-174.

*[G. H. Ball], "Nimrod and Babel," *FBQ* 15 (1867) 412-429.

*A. H. Sayce, "Nimrod and the Assyrian Inscriptions," *SBAT* 2 (1873) 243-249.

*†Fritz Hommel, "The Babylonian Gish-du-barra to be identified with Biblical Nimrod," *SBAP* 8 (1885-86) 119-120.

*Fritz Hommel, "Gish-dubarra, Gibil-gamish, Nimrod," *SBAP* 15 (1892-93) 291-300.

Nimrod concluded

*Fritz Hommel, "A Supplementary Note to Gibil-Gamish," *SBAP* 16 (1893-94) 13-15. *[Nimrod]*

A. H. Sayce, "Nimrod," *ET* 24 (1912-13) 38-40.

C. Van Gelderen, "Who was Nimrod?" *Exp, 8th Ser.*, 8 (1914) 274-282.

Parke P. Flournoy, "Nimrod and the Beginning of His Kingdom," *USR* 27 (1915-16) 27-38.

*J. Dyneley Prince, "A possible Sumerian original of the Name Nimrod," *JAOS* 40 (1920) 201-202.

*E. G. H. Kraeling, "The Origin and Real Name of Nimrod," *AJSL* 38 (1921-22) 214-220.

*Joseph Poplicha, "The Biblical Nimrod and the Kingdom of Eanna," *JAOS* 49 (1929) 303-317.

E[phraim] A. Speiser, "In Search of Nimrod," *EI* 5 (1958) 32*-36*.

Noah

A. H. Sayce, "Noah," *ET* 15 (1903-04) 514.

*R. A. S[tewart] Macalister (trans.), "Tales of the Prophets," *PEFQS* 41 (1909) 35-41. [Of Noah, pp. 35-37]

*M. Milman, "Noah and His Family," *Monist* 29 (1919) 259-292. [Index shows author as: *Max Müller!*]

O

Oded

*Frank H. Wilkinson, "Oded: Proto-type of the Good Samaritan," *ET* 69 (1957-58) 94.

Og

C. Rabin, "Og," *EI* 8 (1967) 75*-76*.

Orpah

*Anonymous, "Orpah. A Study in Internationalism," *ET* 28 (1916-17) 508-512.

P

Pekah

*B. Oded, "The Historical Background of the War between Rezin and Pekah against Ahaz," *Tarbiẓ* 38 (1968-69) #3, I-II.

Phinehas

Abram Spiro, "The Ascension of Phinehas," *PAAJR* 22 (1953) 91-114.

Potiphar

*Maurice Bloomfield, "Joseph and Potiphar in Hindu Fiction," *PAPA* 54 (1923) 141-167.

Y. M. Grintz, "Potifar—The Chief Cook," *Lĕš* 30 (1965-66) #1, n. p. n.

G. M. Mackie, "Who was Potiphar?" *ET* 8 (1896-97) 430.

J. A. Selbie, "Who was Potiphar?" *ET* 8 (1896-97) 474-475.

R

Rachel

*E. G. H. Kraeling, "Geographical Notes," *AJSL* 41 (1924-25) 193-194. [II. The Names "Rachel" and "Reu"]

Rahab

H. H. Moore, "Rahab and Another," *ET* 4 (1892-93) 555-556.

George A. Barton, "Rahab," *ET* 22 (1910-11) 331-332.

Cavendish Moxon, "Rahab," *ET* 22 (1910-11) 423-424.

Anonymous, "Rahab," *ET* 29 (1917-18) 267-271.

D. J. Wiseman, "Rahab of Jericho," *THB* #14 (1964) 8-11.

Rezin

*B. Oded, "The Historical Background of the War between Rezin and Pekah against Ahaz," *Tarbiẕ* 38 (1968-69) #3, I-II.

Rizpah

*Ed., König, "Ruth and Rizpah," *HR* 50 (1905) 440.

*Anonymous, "Rizpah. A Study in Motherhood," *ET* 28 (1916-17) 413-418.

Ruth

*Ed., König, "Ruth and Rizpah," *HR* 50 (1905) 440.

H. H. Rowley, "The Marriage of Ruth," *HTR* 40 (1947) 77-99.

S

Samson

*Geo. F. Herrick, "A Study in Biblical Biography," *BS* 37 (1880) 209-220. *[Samson]*

*Anonymous, "The Samson-Saga and the Myth of Herakles," *WR* 121 (1884) 305-328. *(Review)*

Samson concluded

Wm. Ormiston, "The Character of Samson," *HR* 13 (1887) 470-476.

George Dana Boardman, "The Story of Samson," *ONTS* 8 (1888-89) 88-96.

W. G. Elmslie, "Samson," *Exp, 4th Ser.,* 4 (1891) 360-373.

Anonymous, "Is Samson a Sun Myth?" *ONTS* 14 (1892) 374.

W. Garden Blaikie, "Samson: Was He Man or Myth?" *ET* 4 (1892-93) 543-546.

[Paul Carus], "Mythical Elements in the Samson Story," *Monist* 17 (1907) 33-83.

*Geo[rge] W. Shaw, "Samson and Shemesh Once More," *Monist* 17 (1907) 620-626.

Otto Pfleiderer, "Dr. Pfleiderer on the Samson Story," *Monist* 17 (1907) 626-627.

Martin L. Rouse, "Hercules and Samson," *AJA* 14 (1910) 75.

J. A. MacCulloch, "Was Samson a Solar Hero?" *IJA* #36 (1914) 5-6. *(Review)*

*(Mrs.) J. W. Kilgo, "The Hebrew Samson and Milton's Samson," *MQR, 3rd Ser.,* 50 (1924) 312-316.

Walter W. Moore, "The Story of a Wasted Life," *USR* 50 (1938-39) 193-199.

J. Blenkinsopp, "Some Notes on the Saga of Samson and the Heroic Milieu," *Scrip* 11 (1959) 81-89.

Samuel

*R. Payne Smith, "Samuel and the Schools of the Prophets," *Exp, 1st Ser.,* 3 (1876) 241-251, 342-355, 401-414.

*C[onrad] Schick, "Ramathaim-Zophim—The Home of Samuel the Prophet," *PEFQS* 30 (1898) 7-20.

Samuel concluded

*Lucien Gautier, "The Home of Samuel," *PEFQS* 30 (1898) 135-137.

R. B. Girdlestone, "To What Tribe Did Samuel Belong?" *Exp, 5th Ser.*, 10 (1899) 385-388.

Henry E. Dosker, "The Place of Samuel in the History of Israel," *CFL, N.S.*, 6 (1902) 326-333.

*James Oscar Boyd, "Samuel and the Rise of the Prophetic Order," *CFL, N.S.*, 8 (1903) 25-30.

*James Oscar Boyd, "Samuel and the Law of Sacrifice," *CFL, N.S.*, 8 (1903) 69-74.

F. L. H. Millard, "Samuel's Revenge," *ICMM* 6 (1909-10) 309-315.

*Martin Buber, "Samuel and the Evolution of Authority in Israel," *Zion* 4 (1938-39) #1, I-II.

*Edward Robertson, "Samuel and Saul," *BJRL* 28 (1944) 175-206.

Rolland Emerson Wolfe, "Samuel, the Enigma," *JAAR* 14 (1946) 203-208.

Stanley B. Frost, "Old Testament Characters: VI: Samuel," *PQL* 6 (1960) 45-52.

*Clive A. Thomson, "Samuel, the Ark, and the Priesthood," *BS* 118 (1961) 259-263.

*A. H. van Zyl, "The meaning of the name Samuel," *OTW* 12 (1969) 122-129.

Sanballat

*Claude R. Conder, "Notes on New Discoveries," *PEFQS* 41 (1909) 266-275. [Sanballat, p. 275]

Joseph Offord, "Archaeological Notes on Jewish Antiquities. LVI. *Sanballat in Josephus and in the Elephantine Papyri*," *PEFQS* 51 (1919) 86-87.

Sanballat concluded

Charles C. Torrey, "Sanballat 'The Horonite'," *JBL* 47 (1928) 380-389.

I. Press, "Where did Sanballat the Horonite live?" *BIES* 9 (1941-42) #4, II.

*H. H. Rowley, "Sanballat and the Samaritan Temple," *BJRL* 38 (1955-56)166-198.

Sarah

*John Moncure, "Sarah and Milkah," *R&E* 27 (1930) 62-64.

Serah

*Fritz Hommel, "Serah the Cushite," *ET* 8 (1896-97) 378-379.

Seth

*Rachel J. Fox, "Cain-Abel-Seth," *ET* 18 (1906-07) 522-524.

*J. Gwyn Griffiths, "Seth or Anubis?" *JWCI* 22 (1959) 367. [Rejoinder by A. A. Barb, pp. 367-371]

Shamgar

E. Nestle, "The Judge Shamgar," *JTS* 13 (1911-12) 424-425.

B. Maisler, "Shamgar ben 'Anat," *PEFQS* 66 (1934) 192-194.

F. Charles Fensham, "Shamgar ben 'Anath," *JNES* 20 (1961) 197-198.

Eva Danelius, "Shamgar ben 'Anath," *JNES* 22 (1963) 191-193.

A. van Selms, "Judge Shamgar," *VT* 14 (1964) 294-309.

Shem

*A. H. Sayce, "On the names Shem and Japhet," *SBAP* 5 (1882-83) 154-155.

*A. H. Sayce, "The Explanation of the Biblical Names Shem and Japhet," *ONTS* 3 (1883-84) 120-121.

Sheshbazzar

*J. A. Selbie, "Sheshbazzar—Zerubbabel," *ET* 12 (1900-01) 255-256.

T

Tamar

Eb. Nestle, "Tamar," *ET* 15 (1903-04) 141.

Terah

*W[illiam] F[oxwell] Albright, "Was the Patriarch Terah a Canaanite Moon-God?" *BASOR* #71 (1938) 35-40.

Tubalcain

*C. J. Ball, "Israel and Babylon," *SBAP* 16 (1893-94) 188-200. [2. Tubalcain and Naamah, pp. 191-193]

V

Vashti

J. Dyneley Prince, "Note on Vashti," *JBL* 33 (1914) 87-90.

Z

Zakok

*H. H. Rowley, "Zadok and Nehushtan," *JBL* 58 (1939) 113-142.

*H. G. Judge, "Aaron, Zadok, and Abiathar," *JTS, N.S.,* 7 (1956) 70-74.

Christian E. Hauer Jr., "Who was Zadok? *JBL* 82 (1963) 89-94.

*J. R. Bartlett, "Zadok and His Successors at Jerusalem," *JTS, N.S.,* 19 (1968) 1-18.

Zechariah

*Sheldon H. Blank, "The Death of Zechariah in Rabbinic Literature," *HUCA* 12&13 (1937-38) 327-346.

Zephaniah

J. E. Ford, "Zephaniah, a leader of an ancient forward movement," *CMR* 6 (1894) 403-410, 515-527.

G. Buchanan Gray, "The Royal Ancestry of Zephaniah," *Exp, 6th Ser.,* 2 (1900) 76-80.

Zerah

Fritz Hommel, "Zerah the Cushite," *ET* 8 (1896-97) 378-379.

Zerubbabel

P[aul] Haupt, "The coronation of Zerubbabel," *JBL* 37 (1918) 209-218.

*Paul Haupt, "Zerubbabel and Melchizedek," *JSOR* 2 (1918) 76-82.

*J. A. Selbie, "Sheshbazzar—Zerubbabel," *ET* 12 (1900-01) 255-256.

Zipporah

*Hugh Rose Rae, "Had Moses a Scolding Wife?" *HR* 42 (1901) 257-260.

§46 *1.2.2 The Kings of Israel and Judah - General Studies (See also: Institution of Kingship §133→)*

*N. Rouse, "Chronology of the Kings of Judah and Israel," *JSL, 2nd Ser.*, 1 (1851-52) 217-220.

*Anonymous, "The Prophets and Kings of the Old Testament," *CTPR, 3rd Ser.*, 9 (1853) 1-17. *(Review)*

*W. J. Beecher, "The Chronology of the Kings of Israel and Judah," *PR* 1 (1880) 211-246.

*J. P. Lesley, "Notes on an Egyptian element in the Names of the Hebrew kings, and its bearing on the History of the Exodus," *PAPS* 19 (1880-81) 409-435.

*H. G. Mitchell, "Chronological," *ONTS* 3 (1883-84) 110-115. [Chronology of the Kings]

*Anonymous, "The Chronology of the Kings of Israel and Judah Compared with the Monuments," *CQR* 21 (1885-86) 257-271.

J. A. Howlett, "Rénan and the Kings of Israel," *IER, 3rd Ser.*, 12 (1891) 193-212. *(Review)*

*E. Elmer Harding, "Kings and their Counsellors," *ET* 4 (1892-93) 460-461.

*Frederick Gard Fleay, "On the Synchronous Chronology of the Kings of Israel and Judah," *JTVI* 36 (1904) 253-274, 282-285. (Discussion, pp. 274-281)

*Stanley A. Cook, "Notes on the Dynasties of Omri and Jehu," *JQR*, 20 (1907-08) 597-630. [I. Introduction; II. The Aramaean Wars; III. Judah and Israel; IV. The History of the Period; V. Conclusion]

*E. Day, "The Deuteronomic Judgments of the Kings of Judah," *JTS* 11 (1909-10) 74-83.

*Eduard König, "Alleged Mythological Character of the Patriarchs and Kings," *HR* 62 (1911) 30-32.

*Oscar J. Boyd, "The House of David," *PSB* 15 (1921) #4, 9-12.

L. W. Batten, "A Crisis in the History of Israel," *JBL* 49 (1930) 55-60. [Royal Lineage; Succession to the Throne by Birthright]

*A. G. Shortt, "The Chronology of the Kings of Israel and Judah," *JTVI* 64 (1932) 11-20, 28. [(Discussion, pp. 20-23.) (Communications by Norman S. Denham, pp. 23-25; G. B. Michell, pp. 25-27)]

*Grace Harriet Macurdy, "Jewish Queens under the Roman Empire," *PAPA* 64 (1933) lvi.

Edward Robertson, "The Disruption of Israel's Monarchy—Before and After," *BJRL* 20 (1936) 134-156.

*Julian Morgenstern, "Chronological Data of the Dynasty of Omri," *JBL* 59 (1940) 385-396.

*Edwin R. Thiele, "The Chronology of the Kings of Judah and Israel," *JNES* 3 (1944) 137-186.

*J. A. Thompson, "Extra-Biblical Data and the Omri Dynasty," *ABR* 3 (1953) 24-40.

*E[dwin] R. Thiele, "Certain Peculiarities in the Chronological Data of the Hebrew Kings," *JBL* 72 (1953) viii.

J. Edgar Bruns, "The Davidic Dynasty in Post-Exilic Palestine," *Scrip* 7 (1955) 2-5.

*Edwin R. Thiele, "New Evidence on the Chronology of the Last Kings of Judah," *BASOR* #143 (1956) 22-27.

*Hayim Tadmor, "Chronology of the Last Kings of Judah," *JNES* 15 (1956) 226-230.

Edwin R. Thiele, "The Synchronisms of the Hebrew Kings—A Re-Evaluation: I," *AUSS* 1 (1963) 121-138.

Edwin R. Thiele, "The Synchronisms of the Hebrew Kings—A Re-Evaluation: II," *AUSS* 2 (1964) 120-136.

*G. Coleman Luck, "Israel's Demand for a King," *BS* 120 (1963) 56-64.

*A[braham] Malamat, "Aspects of the Foreign Policies of David and Solomon," *JNES* 22 (1963) 1-17. [A. David and the Kingdom of Hadadezer; B. Israel and Hamath; C. David's and Solomon's Foreign Marriages; D. The Historical Implications of Solomon's Marriage with the Daughter of Pharaoh]

*Barnabas Lindars, "Gideon and Kingship," *JTS, N.S.* 16 (1965) 315-326.

E[dwin] R. Thiele, "Pekah to Hezekiah," *VT* 16 (1966) 83-102.

*E[dwin] R. Thiele, "The Azariah and Hezekiah Synchronisms, with Table," *VT* 16 (1966) 103-107.

*Matitiahu Tsevat, "The Biblical Narrative of the Foundation of Kingship in Israel," *Tarbiz* 36 (1966-67) #2, I.

*Larry R. Thornton, "God's Standards for the Kings of Judah," *CCBQ* 11 (1968) #3, 16-30.

*A[braham] Malamat, "The Last Kings of Judah and the Fall of Jerusalem," *IEJ* 18 (1968) 137-156.

§47 *1.2.2.1 Alphabetical Listing of Specific Kings & Queens*

Ahab

*J. Boehmer, "The Name 'Ahab'," *ET* 17 (1905-06) 564-566.

*A. H. Sayce, "Ahab's Palace at Samaria," *ET* 22 (1910-11) 527-528.

W. S. Auchincloss, "New Light Breaking on King Ahab," *CFL, 3rd Ser.,* 14 (1911-12) 69-70.

*B. C. Napier, "The Omrides of Jezreel," *VT* 9 (1959) 366-378. *[Ahab]*

Joan Gorell, "*Kings of Israel and Judah:* The Successful King Who Failed," *AT* 4 (1959-60) #3, 8-11. *[Ahab]*

Ahab concluded

D. W. Gooding, "Ahab according to the Septuagint," *ZAW* 76 (1964) 269-280.

J. M. Miller, "The Fall of the House of Ahab," *VT* 17 (1967) 307-324.

Ahaz

*J. W. Bosanquet, "Synchronous History of the Reigns of Tiglath-Pileser. . and . . Azariah. Shalmanezer . . and . . Jotham. Sargon . . and . . Ahaz. Sennacherib . . and . . Hezekiah," *SBAT* 3 (1874) 1-8

*Peter R. Ackroyd, "Historians and Prophets," *SEÅ* 33 (1968) 18-54. [Isaiah and Ahaz, pp. 23-37]

*B. Oded, "The Historical Background of the War between Rezin and Pekah against Ahaz," *Tarbiẕ* 38 (1968-69) #3, I-II.

*J. Barton Payne, "The Relationship of the Reign of Ahaz to the Accession of Hezekiah," *BS* 125&126 (1969) 40-52.

Amon

A[braham] Malamat, "The Historical Background of the Assasination of Amon, King of Judah," *IEJ* 3 (1953) 26-29.

A[braham] Malamat, "The Historical Background of the Assasination of Amon, King of Judah," *JBL* 72 (1953) vi.

Asa

*S. Yeivin, "Abijam, Asa and Maachah the Daughter of Abishalom," *BIES* 10 (1942-44) #4, III.

*Larry R. Thornton, "Asa and Jehoshaphat," *CCBQ* 12 (1969) #1, 31-41.

Athaliah

H. J. Katzenstein, "Who Were the Parents of Athaliah?" *IEJ* 5 (1955) 194-197.

Azariah

*J. W. Bosanquet, "Synchronous History of the Reigns of Tiglath-Pileser. . and . . Azariah. Shalmanezer . . and . . Jotham. Sargon . . and . . Ahaz. Sennacherib . . and . . Hezekiah," *SBAT* 3 (1874) 1-8

*C[laude] R. Conder, "Notes on Biblical Antiquities. 2. *Uzziah and Azariah*," *PEFQS* 37 (1905) 156.

*Howell M. Haydn, "Azariah of Judah and Tiglath-pileser III," *JBL* 28 (1909) 182-199.

D. D. Luckenbill, "Azariah of Judah," *AJSL* 41 (1924-25) 217-232.

*E[dwin] R. Thiele, "The Azariah and Hezekiah Synchronisms, with Table," *VT* 16 (1966) 103-107.

*Hayyim Tadmor, "Azioyau of Yaudi," *SH* 8 (1961) 232-271. *[Azariah-Uzziah]*

David

Crito, "The Reign of David—No. IV," *QCS* 6 (1824) 23-34.

John Kitto, "The Youth of David, Illustrated from the Psalms," *JSL, 1st Ser.,* 2 (1848) 59-79.

*G. M. Bell, "Thoughts on the Literary Character of David," *JSL, 1st Ser.,* 4 (1849) 335-342.

*E. P. Barrows, "The Relation of David's Family to the Messiah," *BS* 11 (1854) 306-328.

J. R., "David, from his Annointing to his Accession," *JSL, 3rd Ser.,* 1 (1855) 33-55.

David cont.

H. B., "Age of David," *JSL, 3rd Ser.,* 2 (1855-56) 443.

*(   ) Q., "The Typical Character of David: with a Digression concerning certain Words," *JSL, 4th Ser.,* 5 (1864) 14-27.

*Claude R. Conder, "The Scenery of David's Outlaw Life," *PEFQS* 7 (1875) 41-48.

C[unningham] Geikie, "The Character of David," *ONTS* 1 (1882) 73.

*A. H. Sayce, "The Names of the First Three Kings of Israel," *ModR* 5 (1884)158-169. *[David]*

G. C. M. Douglas, "David's Religion and David's Morality," *ET* 3 (1891-92) 173.

Benjamin W. Bacon, "The Historical David," *NW* 4 (1895) 540-559.

*R. Balgarnie, "'Could Jesus Err?'," *ET* 8 (1896-97) 475. *[David]*

O. P. Gifford, "The Boyhood of David. (Illustrated.)," *BW* 10 (1897) 433-442.

*T. K. Cheyne, "The Witness of Amos to David as a Psalmist (Amos VI. 5)," *ET* 9 (1897-98) 334.

*J[ohn] D. D[avis], "Editorial Notes," *CFL, N.S.,* 2 (1900) 181-184. ["The Historical David", pp. 182-183]

Willis J. Beecher, "The International Lessons in Their Literary Setting. II.," *CFL, N. S.,* 8 (1903) 78-84. [Spiritual Aim of the Biblical Narratives; These Points Illustrated; Narrative of the Beginnings of David's Career; An Alleged Contradiction; Narrative of David's Becoming an Outlaw; Narrative Concerning David the Blameless Outlaw; Psalm Titles Referring to these Events; Narrative Concerning David's Deterioration After Samuel's Death]

J. D. Irons, "The David of History and the David of the Psalms," *CFL, N.S.,* 8 (1903) 260-267.

David cont.

Ross F. Murison, "The Character of David," *ET* 15 (1903-04) 416-418.

J. E. Roberts, "The Anointing of David," *ET* 15 (1903-04) 474-475.

*Stanley A. Cook, "Notes on Old Testament History, I, The Life of David," *JQR* 17 (1904-05) 782-799.

J. F. Stenning, "The Critical Study of the Life of David," *ICMM* 1 (1905) 394-405, 491-501.

J. F. Stenning, "The Critical Study of the Life of David (*continued*)," *ICMM* 2 (1905-06) 61-71.

*Stanley A. Cook, "Notes on Old Testament History, VIII, Saul and David," *JQR* 19 (1906-07) 363-382.

*William H. Bates, "Saul, David, and the Critics," *CFL, 3rd Ser.,* 9 (1908) 266-269. [I. Saul's Alleged Ignorance of David; II. Alleged Contradictions Regarding David's Age]

John Urquhart, "The Empire of David," *CFL, 3rd Ser.,* 9 (1908) 269-272.

Anonymous, "David's Radical Failure as a Father," *CFL, 3rd Ser.,* 9 (1908) 272-274.

Andrew C. Zenos, "David the Ideal King of Israel," *HR* 56 (1908) 302-304.

Andrew C. Zenos, "David's Clouded Days," *HR* 56 (1908) 386-388.

*P[atrick] V. Higgins, "David's Life a Key to the Psalms and Vice Versa," *IER, 4th Ser.,* 24 (1908) 283-289.

W. Emery Barnes, "The David of the Book of Samuel and the David of the Book of Chronicles," *Exp, 7th Ser.,* 7 (1909) 49-59.

*C. F. Burney, "David as a Poet," *ICMM* 6 (1909-10) 49-65.

*Eb. Nestle, "David in the Book of Job," *ET* 22 (1910-11) 91.

David concluded

*H. F. B. Compston, "The Name 'David' in the O.T.," *ET* 22 (1910-11) 140-141.

Paul Haupt, "Was David an Aryan?" *OC* 33 (1919) 27-38, 85-97.

*Norvelle Wallace Sharpe, "David, Elhanan, and the Literary Digest," *BS* 86 (1929) 319-326.

(Miss) M. D. R. Willink, "David and Baber," *Theo* 19 (1929) 146-156.

J. M. P. Smith, "The Character of King David," *JBL* 52 (1933) 1-11.

*S. Yeivin, "The Beginnings of the Davidids," *Zion* 9 (1943-44) #3. I.

*W. D. McHardy, "Religious Education. David and Jerusalem," *ET* 65 (1953-54) 123-125.

*Julian Morgenstern, "David and Jonathan," *JBL* 78 (1959) 322-325.

Stanley B. Frost, "Old Testament Characters: VIII. David," *PQL* 6 (1960) 267-274.

*Moshe Aberbach, "The Relations between Ira the Jairite and King David according to Talmudic Legend," *Tarbiz* 33 (1963-64) #4, III.

*H. H. Rowley, "Melchizedek and David," *VT* 17 (1967) 485.

*Paul H. Levenson, "David and Michal: A Tragic Marriage," *CCARJ* 16 (1969) #4, 79-82.

Hezekiah

*J. W. Bosanquet, "Synchronous History of the Reigns of Tiglath-Pileser. . and . . Azariah. Shalmanezer . . and . . Jotham. Sargon . . and . . Ahaz. Sennacherib . . and . . Hezekiah," *SBAT* 3 (1874) 1-82.

*John D. Davis, "The Fourteenth Year of Hezekiah," *PRR* 1 (1880) 100-105.

Hezekiah concluded

*Joseph Horner, "Hezekiah, Sargon, and Sennacherib—A Chronological Study," *MR* 75 (1893) 74-89.

*Harry M. Orlinsky, "The Kings-Isaiah Recensions of the Hezekiah Story," *JQR, N.S.,* 30 (1939-40) 33-49.

T. Nicklin, "When Did Hezekiah Reign?" *ET* 53 (1941-42) 243.

H. H. Rowley, "Hezekiah's Reform and Rebellion," *BJRL* 44 (1961-62) 395-431.

*Siegfried H. Horn, "The Chronology of King Hezekiah's Reign," *AUSS* 2 (1964) 40-52.

*John McHugh, "The Date of Hezekiah's Birth," *VT* 14 (1964) 446-453.

*Frederick L. Moriarty, "Hezekiah, Isaiah and Imperial Politics," *BibT* #19 (1965) 1270-1276.

*Siegfried H. Horn, "Did Sennacherib Campaign Once or Twice Against Hezekiah?" *AUSS* 4 (1966) 1-28.

*J. Barton Payne, "The Relationship of the Reign of Ahaz to the Accession of Hezekiah," *BS* 125&126 (1969) 40-52.

*Larry R. Thornton, "Hezekiah and Josiah," *CCBQ* 12 (1969) #2, 30-48.

Hoshea

*H. L. Ginsberg, "An Unrecognized Allusion to Kings Pekah and Hoshea of Israel (Isa. 8:23)," *EI* 5 (1958) 61*-65*.

Jehoiakim

G. G. Garner, "*Writing and the Bible:* A King in Exile," *AT* 2 (1957-58) #1, 12-14. *[Jehoiakim]*

Jehoiachin

*Herbert Gordon May, "Three Hebrew Seals and the Status of Exiled Jehoiakin," *AJSL* 56 (1939) 146-148.

*J. W. Jack, "Recent Biblical Archaeology," *ET* 52 (1940-41) 229-233. [Jehoiachin, King of Judah, p. 233]

*W[illiam] F[oxwell] Albright, "King Joiachin in Exile," *BA* 5 (1942) 49-55.

G. R. Driver, "Jehoiakin in Captivity," *ET* 56 (1944-45) 317-318.

Jehoram

*Paul Haupt, "Biblical Studies," *AJP* 43 (1922) 238-249. [2. Jehoram's Fatal Illness, p. 239]

Jehoshaphat

*K. T. Frost, "The Navy of Tharshish and the Failure of Jehoshaphat," *ET* 16 (1904-05) 177-180.

S. Yeivin, "King Yehoshaphat," *EI* 7 (1964) 165*-166*.

*Larry R. Thornton, "Asa and Jehoshaphat," *CCBQ* 12 (1969) #1, 31-41.

Jehu

*Stanley A. Cook, "Notes on the Dynasties of Omri and Jehu," *JQR*, 20 (1907-08) 597-630. [I. Introduction; II. The Aramaean Wars; III. Judah and Israel; IV. The History of the Period; V. Conclusion]

*Anonymous, "Jehu. A Study of Divine Instrumentality," *ET* 29 (1917-18) 75-79.

Joan Gorell, "*Kings of Israel and Judah:* Jehu, the Bible Speedster," *AT* 4 (1959-60) #4, 12-15.

Jeroboam

Charles Foster Kent, "Jeroboam and the Disruption," *BW* 4 (1894) 38-48.

*M. Gaster, "The Feast of Jeroboam and the Samaritan Calendar," *ET* 14 (1912-13) 198-201.

M[enahem] Haran, "The Rise and Fall of the Empire of Jeroboam II," *Zion* 31 (1966) #1/2, II-IV.

Menahem Haran, "The Rise and Decline of the Empire of Jeroboam ben Joash," *VT* 17 (1967) 266-297.

Eva Danelius, "The Sins of Jeroboam ben-Nabat," *JQR, N.S.,* 58 (1967-68) 95-114, 204-223.

*Moses Aberbach and Leivy Smolar, "Jeroboam and Solomon: Rabbinic Interpretations," *JQR, N.S.,* 59 (1968-69) 118-132.

Moses Aberbach and Leivy Smolar, "Jeroboam's Rise to Power," *JBL* 88 (1969) 69-72.

Jezebel

Stanley B. Frost, "Judgment on Jezebel, or a Woman Wronged," *TT* 20 (1963-64) 503-517.

Joash

F. W. Farrar, "Notes on the Reign of Joash," *Exp, 4th Ser.,* 10 (1894) 81-98.

E. L. Curtis, "The Coronation of Joash," *BW* 17 (1901) 272-275.

*Daniel S. Gregory, "The International Lessons in Their Historical and Literary Setting," *CFL, 3rd Ser.,* 14 (1911-12) 179-193. [Joash, the Boy King; Josash Repairs the Temple; pp. 187-190]

Anonymous, "'Joash the Samaritan'," *BH* 5 (1969) 10-11.

Joash concluded

*Stephanie Page, "Joash and Samaria in a New Stela Excavated at Tell al Rim," *VT* 19 (1969) 483-484.

Josiah

*( ) G., "The Scythians Dominion in Asia (as recorded by Herodotus) in its Connexion with Josiah's Exercise of Sovereign Power in the Territory of the Ten Tribes," *JSL, 2nd Ser.*, 4 (1853) 1-34.

*Fritz Hommel, "The Hebrew Name Josiah," *ET* 8 (1896-97) 562-563.

*Fritz Hommel, "Supplementary Note on the Hebrew Name Josiah," *ET* 9 (1897-98) 144.

*A. T. Olmstead, "Notes and Suggestions. The Reform of Josiah and its Secular Aspects," *AmHR* 20 (1914-15) 566-570.

*Walter T. McCree, "Josiah and Gadd's Babylonian Tablet," *CJRT* 1 (1924) 307-312.

Adam C. Welch, "The death of Josiah," *ZAW* 43 (1925) 255-260.

W. W. Cannon, "A note on Dr. Welch's article 'The death of Josiah'," *ZAW* 44 (1926) 63-64.

*P. E. Kretzmann, "Josiah and the Battle of Meggido," *CTM* 2 (1931) 38-45.

*M. B. Rowton, "Jeremiah and the Death of Josiah," *JNES* 10 (1951) 128-130.

*Frank M. Cross Jr. and David Noel Freedman, "Josiah's Revolt Against Assyria," *JNES* 12 (1953) 56-58.

Stanley Brice Frost, "The Death of Josiah: A Conspiracy of Silence," *JBL* 87 (1968) 369-382.

*Larry R. Thornton, "Hezekiah and Josiah," *CCBQ* 12 (1969) #2, 30-48.

Jotham

*J. W. Bosanquet, "Synchronous History of the Reigns of Tiglath-Pileser. . and . . Azariah. Shalmanezer . . and . . Jotham. Sargon . . and . . Ahaz. Sennacherib . . and . . Hezekiah," *SBAT* 3 (1874) 1-8

Omri

*Stanley A. Cook, "Notes on the Dynasties of Omri and Jehu," *JQR*, 20 (1907-08) 597-630. [I. Introduction; II. The Aramaean Wars; III. Judah and Israel; IV. The History of the Period; V. Conclusion]

Daniel S. Gregeroy, "The International Lessons in Their Historical and Literary Setting. Lessons from the Conflict with Idolatry and Baalism," *CFL, 3rd Ser.*, 14 (1911-12) 51-65. [Dr. Beecher's View of the Conditions Under the Dynasty of Omri, pp. 58-60]

*Herbert Parzen, "The Prophets and the Omri Dynasty," *HTR* 33 (1940) 69-96.

*Julian Morgenstern, "Chronological Data of the Dynasty of Omri," *JBL* 59 (1940) 385-396.

J. A. Thompson, "Extra-Biblical Data and the Omri Dynasty," *ABR* 3 (1953) 24-40.

*B. C. Napier, "The Omrides of Jezreel," *VT* 9 (1959) 366-378.

Joan Gorell, "Omri, King of Israel," *AT* 4 (1959-60) #2, 18-20.

Pekah

*H. L. Ginsberg, "The Unrecognized Allusion to Kings Pekah and Hoshea of Israel (Isa. 8:23)," *EI* 5 (1958) 61*-65*. *[Heb. vs.]*

H. J. Cook, "Pekah," *VT* 14 (1964) 121-135.

Rehoboam

Anonymous, "Rehoboam," *ET* 29 (1917-18) 314-318.

*Geoffrey D. Evans, "Rehoboam's Advisers at Shechem, and Political Institutions in Israel and Sumer," *JNES* 25 (1966) 273-279. [I. The Elders of Israel and Judah under King David; II. The Crisis of Succession; III. The Councils at Shechem; IV. The Assemblies at Uruk]

Saul

*A. H. Sayce, "The Names of the First Three Kings of Israel," *ModR* 5 (1884) 158-169. *[Saul]*

Robert Kerr Eccles, "Saul ben-Kish," *BW* 4 (1894) 432-443.

Claude R. Shaver, "Saul, King of Israel.—A Character Study," *CFL, N.S.,* 6 (1902) 271-285.

*J. A. Stokes Little, "Was Saul a Hachish-Eater?" *ET* 15 (1903-04) 239.

*Benj[amin] W. Bacon, "Was Saul a Hachish-Eater?" *ET* 15 (1903-04) 380.

Edward M. Merrins, "The Malady of Saul, King of Israel," *BS* 61 (1904) 752-773.

Ed. König, "A Modern Attempt to Reduce King Saul to a Mythological Figure," *ET* 16 (1904-05) 422-425.

*Stanley A. Cook, "Notes on Old Testament History, II, Saul," *JQR* 18 (1905-06) 121-134.

John E. McFadyen, "The Character of Saul," *BW* 25 (1905) 103-116.

*Stanley A. Cook, "Notes on Old Testament History, IV, Saul and Benjamin," *JQR* 18 (1905-06) 528-543.

*Stanley A. Cook, "Notes on Old Testament History, VIII, Saul and David," *JQR* 19 (1906-07) 363-382.

Saul concluded

J. C. Gregory, "The Life and Character of Saul," *ET* 19 (1907-08) 510-513.

*William H. Bates, "Saul, David, and the Critics," *CFL, 3rd Ser.*, 9 (1908) 266-269. [I. Saul's Alleged Ignorance of David; II. Alleged Contradictions Regarding David's Age]

T. H. Weir, "The Election of Saul," *ET* 21 (1909-10) 376.

H. C. Ackerman, "Saul: A Psychotherapeutic Analysis," *ATR* 3 (1920-21) 114-124.

Chas. W. Budden, "Was Saul an Epileptic?" *ET* 35 (1923-24) 477.

W. W. Cannon, "The Reign of Saul," *Theo* 25 (1932) 326-335.

*Clive A. Thomson, "Certain Bible Difficulties," *BS* 96 (1939) 459-478. [The age of King Saul, pp. 461-463, 467-470]

*Edward Robertson, "Samuel and Saul," *BJRL* 28 (1944) 175-206.

*Alcuin Kirberg, "Saul and the Grace of God," *Scotist* 6 (1947) 84-93.

A. Spiro, "The Vilification of King Saul in Biblical Literature," *JBL* 71 (1952) ix.

Clovis Savard, "Saul: The Elect of God and The Man," *MH* 11 (1954-55) #2, 7-11.

Stanley B. Frost, "Old Testament Characters. VII: Saul," *PQL* 6 (1960) 105-111.

G. Coleman Luck, "The First Glimpse of the First King of Israel," *BS* 123 (1966) 60-66.

Robert North, "The Trauma of King Saul," *BibT* #29 (1967) 2048-2059.

Stephen S. Yonick, "The Rejection of Saul: A Study of Sources," *AJBA* 1 (1968-71) #4, 29-50.

Solomon

*Anonymous, "Chronological Remark on the Time of Solomon, &c.," *MMBR* 3 (1797) 9-10.

( ) F., "The Reign of Solomon," *QCS* 4 (1822) 131-142.

E. Nestle, "How Old was Solomon When He Began to Reign?" *ONTS* 2 (1882-83) 23-24.

*A. H. Sayce, "The Names of the First Three Kings of Israel," *ModR* 5 (1884) 158-169. *[Solomon]*

*J. Cheston Morris, "The Ethics of Solomon," *PAPS* 33 (1894) 310-332.

Benjamin W. Bacon, "Solomon in Tradition and in Fact," *NW* 7 (1898) 212-228.

Moncure D. Conway, "Solmonic Literature," *OC* 12 (1898) 1-9.

*Moncure D. Conway, "The Judgment of Solomon," *OC* 12 (1898) 72-79.

Moncure D. Conway, "The Wives of Solomon," *OC* 12 (1898) 200-206.

Andrew C. Zenos, "The Strength and Weakness of Solomon," *HR* 56 (1908) 478-480.

*R. A. S[tewart] Macalister (trans.), "Tales of the Prophets," *PEFQS* 41 (1909) 35-41. [Of Solomon, pp. 38-39]

C. C. McCown, "The Christian Tradition as to the Magical Wisdom of Solomon," *JPOS* 2 (1922) 1-24.

*Alexander Haggerty Krappe, "Solomon and Ashmodai," *AJP* 54 (1933) 260-268.

D. M. Vaughan, "The Modern Estimate of Solomon," *CQR* 121 (1935-36) 23-33.

*J. W. Jack, "Recent Biblical Archaeology. Mummy of Solomon's Father-in-Law," *ET* 51 (1939-40) 423. *[Psusennes II]*

Solomon concluded

Philip J. Hyatt, "'Solomon and All His Glory'," *JAAR* 8 (1940) 27-30.

*R. B. Y. Scott, "Solomon and the beginnings of wisdom in Israel," *VTS* 3 (1955) 262-279.

Stanley B. Frost, "Old Testament Characters: IX. Solomon," *PQL* 6 (1960) 327-333.

*Stanley M. Horton, "Critical Notes: A Suggestion Concering the Chronology of Solomon's Reign," *BETS* 4 (1961) 3-4.

*H. J. Katzenstein, "Is There any Synchronism Between the Reigns of Hiram and Solomon?" *JNES* 24 (1965) 116-117.

*D. W. Gooding, "The Septuagint's Version of Solomon's Misconduct," *VT* 15 (1965) 325-335.

Allan A. MacRae, "The voice of the stones," *RefmR* 13 (1965-66) 213-224. *[Solomon]*

Edmund Leach, "The Legitimacy of Solomon. Some structural aspects of Old Testament History," *EJS* 7 (1966) 58-101.

*Siegfried H. Horn, "Who was Solomon's Father-in-Law?" *BRes* 12 (1967) 3-17.

Abraham Malamat, "Comments on E. Leach: 'The Legitimacy of Solomon—Some Structural Aspects of Old Testament History'," *EJS* 8 (1967) 165-167.

*Harold M. Parker Jr., "Solomon and the Queen of Sheba," *IR* 24 (1967) #3, 17-24.

*G. W. Ahlström, "Solomon, the Chosen One," *HRel* 8 (1968-69) 93-110.

*Moses Aberbach and Leivy Smolar, "Jeroboam and Solomon: Rabbinic Interpretations," *JQR, N.S.,* 59 (1968-69) 118-132.

Uzziah (see also: Azariah)

*J. F. McCurdy, "Uzziah and the Philistines," *Exp, 4th Ser.*, 4 (1891) 388-396.

*C[laude] R. Conder, "Notes on Biblical Antiquites. 2. *Uzziah and Azariah*," *PEFQS* 37 (1905) 156.

*W[illiam] F[oxwell] Albright, "The Discovery of an Aramaic Inscription Relating to King Uzziah," *BASOR* #44 (1931) 8-10.

*Anonymous, "A Gravestone of Uzziah, King of Judah," *BA* 1 (1938) 8-9.

*Hayyim Tadmor, "Aziyau of Yaudi," *SH* 8 (1961) 232-271. *[Azariah-Uzziah]*

§48 *1.2.3 Priests (including High Priests) - General Studies [For Duties of a High Priest see: The High Priest →]*

*S. Baring-Gould, "Priest and Prophet," *ContR* 76 (1899) 832-841.

*A. S. Laidlaw, "The Priest and the Prophet," *ET* 11 (1899-1900) 168-170.

*Ed. König, "The Priests and the Levites in Ezekiel XLIV. 7-15," *ET* 12 (1900-01) 300-303.

*A. van Hoonacker, "Ezekiel's Priests and Levites—A Disclaimer," *ET* 12(1900-01) 383.

*A. van Hoonacker, "Ezekiel's Priests and Levites," *ET* 12 (1900-01) 494-498.

*William R. Harper, "Prophet and Priest," *BW* 20 (1902) 83-88. *(Editorial)*

*Charles Callaway, "The Prophet and the Priest in Hebrew Ethics," *WR* 161 (1904) 533-539.

*E. F. Morison, "The Relation of Priest and Prophet in the History of Israel Before the Exile," *JTS* 11 (1909-10) 211-245.

*Charles Lynn Pyatt, "The Prophet and the Priest in Judaism," *CollBQ* 14 (1923-24) #2, 15-29.

Theophile James Meek, "Aaronites and Zadokites," *AJSL* 45 (1928-29)149-166.

*Adam C. Welch, "Prophet and Priest in Old Israel," *ET* 48 (1936-37) 187.

*Ismar J. Perita, "The New Biblical Approach to Social Problems," *JAAR* 5 (1937) 107-116. [III. The Principle of Differentiation in Biblical Opinion, *II. The Social Ideals of the Priests*, pp. 112-114]

Julian Morgenstern, "A Chapter in the History of the High-Priesthood," *AJSL* 55 (1938) 1-24, 183-197, 360-377.

*N. W. Porteous, "Living Issues in Biblical Scholarship. Prophet and Priest in Israel," *ET* 62 (1950-51) 4-9.

*Walter G. Williams, "Studies in Prophecy. Part II. Priest and Prophet," *IR* 10 (1953) 110-115.

*Sergio J. Grintz, "Jehoezer—Unknown High Priest?" *JQR, N.S.*, 50 (1959-60) 338-347.

*Nicol Milne, "Prophet, Priest and King and their Effect on Religion in Israel," *Abr-N* 2 (1960-61) 55-67.

*E. Mary Smallwood, "High Priests and Politics in Roman Palestine," *JTS, N.S.*, 13 (1962) 14-34.

*Saul Christensen, "Priest and Prophets—Old Testament Controversy," *Scotist* 20 (1964) 19-31.

*Martin A. Cohen, "The Role of the Shilonite Priesthood in the United Monarchy of Ancient Israel," *HUCA* 36 (1965) 59-98.

*Marten H. Woudstra, "The Religious Problem—Complex of Prophet and Priest in Contemporary Thought," *CTJ* 1 (1966) 39-66. [O. T. refs., pp. 42-47]

*C. H. R. Martin, "Alexander and the High Priest," *GUOST* 23 (1969-70) 102-115.

§49 *1.2.4 Prophets - General Studies* *[See §44 ← for specific Prophets]*

(   ) Volens, "Remarks on the Jewish Prophets," *CongML* 4 (1821) 621-626.

C. W., "Ancient Prophets and Modern Ministers," *CTPR, N.S.,* 1 (1838-39) 55-72.

E[noch] Pratt, "Sublimity of the Prophetic Visions," *BJ* 2 (1843) 262-268.

N. L. F., "The Jewish Prophet," *CE* 42 (1847) 402-408.

*Anonymous, "The Prophets and Kings of the Old Testament," *CTPR, 3rd Ser.,* 9 (1853) 1-17. *(Review)*

J. H. A[llen], "The Hebrew Prophets," *CE* 56 (1854) 374-397. *(Review)*

Anonymous, "The Old Testament Idea of a Prophet," *PRev* 31 (1859) 698-717.

[Friedrich Wilhelm Carl] Umbriet, "The Prophets of the Old Testament: The Oldest and Worthiest Popular Orators," *RChR* 13 (1861) 513-525. *(Trans. by Samuel T. Lowrie)*

J. F. Hirst, "The Prophets and Their Prophecies," *MR* 44 (1862) 270-289. *(Review)*

*Hermann Hupfeld, "The Political Principles of the Old Testament Prophets," *AThR, N.S.,* 2 (1864) 223-233.

*Anonymous, "Prophets and Prophecy," *SPR* 26 (1875) 138-159. [Signification of the Name; The Prophetic Order; The Prophetic Gift; Their Manner of Life; The Prophetic Inspiration; Dreams; The Vision; The Prophetic Ecstasy; As to the Mode of Prophetic Communication; The Criteria of Prophecy]

*William Henry Green, "The Prophets and Prophecy in Israel," *DTQ* 4 (1878) 544-572.

*William Henry Green, "The Prophets and Prophecy in Israel," *PRev* 54 (1878) Part 2, 281-328.

*John W. Chadwick, "Prophets and Prophecy in Israel," *URRM* 9 (1878) 361-382. *(Review)*

O. Cone, "Studies in Hebrew Prophecy—The Inspiration of the Prophets," *UQGR, N.S.,* 16 (1879) 115-126.

I. C. Knowlton, "A Prophet," *UQGR, N.S.,* 19 (1882) 92-100.

R[ufus] P[hineas] Stebbins, "Office, Mission, and Influence of the Hebrew Prophets," *URRM* 17 (1882) 318-332.

R[ufus] P[hineas] Stebbins, "The Hebrew Prophets. No. II. *The Preparation of the Prophets for their Work, and the Formulas of Authority with which they Speak,*" *URRM* 18 (1882) 409-421.

Charles A. Briggs, "Robertson Smith's 'Prophets of Israel'," *ONTS* 2 (1882-83) 8-14. *(Review)*

William Henry Green, "Dr. W. Robertson Smith on the Prophets of Israel," *BFER* 32 (1883) 201-260. *(Review)*

Anonymous, "Prophetism," *DTQ, N.S.,* 2 (1883) 125-127.

J. Frederick Smith, "The Prophets of the Old Testament," *ModR* 4 (1883) 649-674.

R[ufus] P[hineas] Stebbins, "The Hebrew Prophets. The Style of Delivery of the Prophets, and Their Rhetorical Ornaments. No. III," *URRM* 19 (1883) 289-300.

R[ufus] P[hineas] Stebbins, "The Hebrew Prophets. The Fundamental Principles of the Prophetic Teaching. IV.," *URRM* 20 (1883) 524-536.

Israel E. Dwinell, "Professor Robertson Smith's Lectures on the Prophets of Israel," *BFER* 33 (1884) 552-572. *(Review)*

Israel E. Dwinell, "The Prophets of Israel and Their Place in History to the Close of the Eighth Century B.C.: Eight Lectures by W. Robertson Smith, LL.D.," *BS* 41 (1884) 327-349.

*R[ufus] P[hineas] Stebbins, "The Hebrew Prophets. No. V. Rules to be Observed in Interpreting the Prophets," *URRM* 22 (1884) 240-251.

F. B. Denio, "The Work of the Prophets," *ONTS* 4 (1884-85) 49-59.

*C. J. Bredenkamp, "The Covenant and the Early Prophets," *ONTS* 4 (1884-85) 123-127. *(Trans. by George H. Schodde)*

John Stuart Mill, "The Prophetic Order," *ONTS* 4 (1884-85) 375-376.

R[ufus] P[hineas] Stebbins, "The Hebrew Prophets. No. VI. The Grounds of Prophetic Authority and Assurance," *URRM* 22 (1885) 493-504.

Anonymous, "Model Preachers," *ONTS* 5 (1885-86) 87-88.

*S. R. Calthrop, "The Prophets," *URRM* 26 (1886) 67-77, 128-140.

*S. R. Calthrop, "The Prophets and the Exile," *URRM* 26 (1886) 206-219.

Edward L. Curtis, "The Old Testament Prophet," *ONTS* 6 (1886-87) 25-26.

*R. V. Foster, "Hebrew Prophets and Prophecy," *ONTS* 6 (1886-87) 110-113, 150-153, 166-170.

W. H. Bennett, "Ancient and Modern Prophets," *Exp, 3rd Ser.*, 8 (1888) 69-80.

Loring W. Batten, "The Preachers of the Old Testament," *HR* 17 (1889) 410-415.

*A. H. Sayce, "Miscellaneous Notes," *ZA* 4 (1889) 382-393. [27. *Asipu* and Joseph, pp. 387-388 *(Assyrian word for Prophet*]

George B. Spaulding, "The Hebrew Prophet and the Christian Preacher," *AR* 14 (1890) 280-291.

*Anonymous, "Prophecy and History," *ONTS* 10 (1890) 243.

Anonymous, "Prophets and Seers," *ONTS* 10 (1890) 314.

Stilon Henning, "A Prophet—what is he?" *TML* 4 (1890) 48-64.

*Anonymous, Who Were the Seers (Chozim)?" *HR* 22 (1891) 266-269.

*E. Elmer Harding, "Kings and Their Counsellors," *ET* 4 (1892-93) 460-461. *[The Prophets]*

*Karl Budde, "The Folk-Song of Israel in the Mouth of the Prophets," *NW* 2 (1893) 28-51.

W. St. Chad Boscawen, "Hebrew Prophetism," *BOR* 7 (1893-94) 185-190.

*Andrew Harper, "The Prophets and Sacrifice," *Exp, 4th Ser.,* 9 (1894) 241-253.

Anonymous, "Prophets in Israel and Judah," *HR* 28 (1894) 252. *[Chart]*

Talbot W. Chambers, "The Function of the Prophet," *PRR* 5 (1894) 49-68.

*C[arl] H[einrich] Cornill, "The Reaction Against the Prophets," *OC* 9 (1895) 4503-4505.

Anonymous, "'Prof. C. H. Cornill on the Prophets of Israel'," *OC* 9 (1895) #44, 4693-4694. *(Review)*

Arthur S. Hoyt, "The Prophet's Spirit," *AubSRev* 1 (1897) 240-250.

John Taylor, "The Qualifications of an Old Testament Prophet," *ET* 9 (1897-98) 359-361.

*George Stibitz, "The Old Testament Prophets as Social Reformers," *BW* 12 (1898) 20-28.

Edward B. Pollard, "The Prophet as a Poet," *BW* 12 (1898) 327-332.

W. M. McPheeters, "Current Criticism and Interpretation of the Old Testament. 'The Prophet As a Poet'," *CFL, O.S.,* 3 (1899) 232-233.

*S. Baring-Gould, "Priest and Prophet," *ContR* 76 (1899) 832-841.

E. R. Hendrix, "The Prophet as a Spokesman of God," *MQR, 3rd Ser.*, 25 (1899) 323-336.

*A. S. Laidlaw, "The Priest and the Prophet," *ET* 11 (1899-1900) 168-170.

Walter R. Betteridge, "The Historical and Religious Significance of the Old Testament Prophets," *AJT* 4 (1900) 757-769.

William R. Harper, "The Methods of the Prophets in Teaching," *BW* 15 (1900) 245-249. *(Editorial)*

T. S. Wynkoop, "The Prophetic Office of the Christian Ministry," *HR* 40 (1900) 315-320. [O. T. Word Studies, pp. 315-317]

K. D. Macmillan, "Prophets and Seers," *CFL, N.S.*, 3 (1901) 239.

R. Bruce Taylor, "Prophetic Ecstasy," *ET* 13 (1901-02) 150-156, 223-228.

*William R. Harper, "Prophet and Priest," *BW* 20 (1902) 83-88. *(Editorial)*

F. A. Gast, "The Making of a Prophet," *RChR, 4th Ser.*, 6 (1902) 289-309.

*James Oscar Boyd, "Samuel and the Rise of the Prophetic Order," *CFL, N.S.*, 8 (1903) 25-30.

*Wilbert Webster White, "Some distinguishing features of Old Testament prophets and prophecy," *BRec* 1 (1903-04) 221-228.

*Charles Callaway, "The Prophet and the Priest in Hebrew Ethics," *WR* 161 (1904) 533-539.

Francis B. Denio, "The Authority of the Hebrew Prophets," *BS* 62 (1905) 105-125, 287-303.

Lewis Bayles Paton, "Outline Studies of Obscurer Prophets—The Seventy Elders," *HR* 49 (1905) 121-122. *[Part I]*

Ed. König, "On the Origin of Jewish Prophetism," *HR* 49 (1905) 356-357.

Lewis Bayles Paton, "Outline Studies of Obscurer Prophets—VI. The Prophet at Shiloh," *HR* 50 (1905) 41-42.

Arthur S. Hoyt, "The Prophet's Spirit," *HR* 50 (1905) 168-171.

Lewis Bayles Paton, "Outline Studies of Obscurer Prophets—VIII. The Ecstatic Prophets," *HR* 50 (1905) 197-198.

C. H. W. Johns, "The Prophets in Babylonia," *ICMM* 2 (1905-06) 297-304.

*Jacob H. Kaplan, "Psychology of Prophecy," *AJRPE* 2 (1906-07) 168-203.

Wm. Deans, "'The Prophet's Badge'," *ET* 18 (1906-07) 144.

Honoré Coppieters, "Hebrew Prophetism Before the Eighth Century," *NYR* 3 (1907-08) 617-634.

Ambrose White Vernon, "The Prophet of Israel and the Minister of Christ," *YDQ* 4 (1907-08) 51-68.

Henry W. A. Hanson, "The Prophets of Israel," *LQ* 38 (1908) 335-349.

*Henry Preserved Smith, "Reforms and Reformers in Israel," *MTSQB* 3 (1908-09) #1, 3-18.

*E. F. Morison, "The Relation of Priest and Prophet in the History of Israel Before the Exile," *JTS* 11 (1909-10) 211-245.

J. Ross Stevenson, "The Perils of a Prophet," *USR* 21 (1909-10) 263-269.

*James B. Smiley, "Prophecy and Inspiration," *OC* 24 (1910) 405-423.

Irving King, "The Psychology of the Prophet," *BW* 37 (1911) 402-410; 38 (1911) 8-17.

John Gamble, "Prophets: Ancient and Modern," *MC* 1 (1911-12) 550-559; 640-650.

*Alex. R. Gordon, "The Prophets as Models for the Preacher," *BW* 40 (1912) 338-351.

Floyd W. Tomkins, "The Marks of the Prophet," *RChR, 4th Ser.,* 16 (1912) 316-329. *(Sermon)*

*G. A. Smith, "The Experience of Balaam as Symbolic of the Origins of Prophecy," *Exp, 8th Ser.,* 5 (1913) 1-11.

F. C. Eiselen, "A Prophetic Ministry," *MR* 95 (1913) 230-242.

A. Boissier, "The Soothsayers of the Old Testament," *SBAP* 35 (1913) 189-190.

*D. E. Thomas, "The Psychological Approach to Prophecy," *AJT* 18 (1914) 241-256. [I. The Prophet's Antecedents and Inheritances; II. The Prophet's Environment; III. The Prophet's Temperament; IV. The Prophet's Experience]

F. B. Stockdale, "The Prophet," *MR* 96 (1914) 732-737.

J. Willcock, "Prophetic Trances," *ET* 26 (1914-15) 92-93.

H. H. B. Ayles, "The Office and Work of a Hebrew Prophet," *ICMM* 13 (1916-17) Part 2, 31-37.

Edward G. King, "The Lord's Rememberancers," *ICMM* 15 (1918-19) 149-151.

*Adam C. Welch, "The Prophets and the World-Order," *Exp, 8th Ser.,* 18 (1919) 81-99.

*Alfred E. Garvie, "The Hebrew Prophet and the Christian Preacher," *ET* 32 (1920-21) 421-425.

*G. A. Cooke, "Some Principles of Reconstruction from the Old Testament Prophets," *ICMM* 17 (1920-21) 17-26.

T. H. Robinson, "The Ecstatic Element in Old Testament Prophecy," *Exp, 8th Ser.,* 21 (1921) 217-238.

B. A. Copass, "The Hebrew Prophets as Preachers," *SWJT* 5 (1921) #1, 31-42.

W. J. Cleal, "Ecstasy and Prophecy," *BQL* 1 (1922-23) 391-392. *(Review)*

*J. M. T. Winther, "Prophet and Prophecy," *BR* 8 (1923) 213-228, 400-416.

William H. Bates, "The Prophet," *CFL, 3rd Ser.,* 29 (1923) 139-140, 339-343. [I. What and Who the Prophet Is; II. The Origin, Rise, and Development of the Prophetic Order; III. Some Characteristics of the Prophet]

Herbert W. Hines, "The Prophet as Mystic," *AJSL* 40 (1923-24) 37-71.

W. F. Lofthouse, "'Thus Hath Jahveh Said'," *AJSL* 40 (1923-24) 231-251.

Charles Lynn Pyatt, "The Prophets of Israel and a Prophetic Ministry," *CollBQ* 13 (1923-24) #4, 19-31.

*Charles Lynn Pyatt, "The Prophet and the Priest in Judaism," *CollBQ* 14 (1923-24) #2, 15-29.

Hermann Gunkel, "The Secret Experiences of the Prophets," *Exp, 9th Ser.,* 1 (1924) 356-366, 427-435; 2 (1924) 23-32.

*Fleming James, "The Attitude of the Hebrew Prophets Toward War," *ACM* 17 (1925) 43-57.

*Samuel Teitelbaum, "The Political and Social Ideas of the Prophets," *JIQ* 2 (1925-26) #2, 15-17.

*G. M. Bruce, "The Prophets as a Moral Code," *TTM* 9 (1925-26) 285-297.

Harlan Creelman, "The Liberty of Prophesying in Ancient Israel," *ASRec* 22 (1926-27) 129-142.

*Moses Buttenwieser, "The Prophets and Nationalism," *YCCAR* 37 (1927) 271-291.

Edward R. Hamme, "The Present-Day Value of the Hebrew Prophet and His Message," *CTSQ* 5 (1927-28) #2, 5-13.

R. C. Gillie, "Prophetic Vocation: A Comparison," *ET* 39 (1927-28) 311-315.

George Ricker Berry, "Some Anonymous Prophets of the Old Testament," *CRDSB* 2 (1929-30) 318-332.

*Robert C. Horn, "Symbolic Acts of Greek Philosophers and Hebrew Prophets," *LCQ* 5 (1932) 190-201.

H. H. Rowley, "Prophetic Ministry," *BQL* 6 (1932-33) 1-13.

Fleming James, "Were the Writing Prophets *Nebi'im* ?" *JBL* 54 (1935) ii.

*A. R. Johnson, "Some Outstanding Old Testament Problems, VI. The Prophet in Israelite Worship," *ET* 47 (1935-36) 312-319.

*Adam C. Welch, "Prophet and Priest in Old Israel," *ET* 48 (1936-37) 187.

*Alexander Moffatt, "The Prophet as Orator, with Illustrations from Micah and Isaiah of Jerusalem," *GUOST* 8 (1936-37) 32-33.

Carl A. Anderson, "The Message of the Prophets of Israel," *AugQ* 16 (1937) 347-357.

*Ismar J. Perita, "The New Biblical Approach to Social Problems," *JAAR* 5 (1937) 107-116. [III. The Principle of Differentiation in Biblical Opinion, *II. The Social Ideas of the Prophets;* p. 112]

Harold L. Creager, "How God Inspired the Prophets," *LCQ* 10 (1937) 284-294. [I. Divine Influence; II. Inner Convictions; III. Subjective Qualities; IV. External Conditions; V. Mental Activity]

*H. Th. Obbink, "The Forms of Prophetism," *HUCA* 14 (1939) 23-28.

*J. Hempel, "Prophet and Poet," *JTS* 40 (1939) 113-132.

*H. C. Leupold, "Old Testament Prophets and Social Life," *KZ* 63 (1939) 201-214, 276-290, 338-352. [I. The Modern Approach; II. The Social Teachings of Moses and the Non-Literary Prophets; III. The Social Teachings of the Literary Prophets]

*Th. Laetsch, "The Prophets and Political and Social Problems," *CTM* 11 (1940) 241-258, 337-351.

*Herbert Parzen, "The Prophets and the Omri Dynasty," *HTR* 33 (1940) 69-96.

H[enry] S. Gehman, "The 'Burden' of the Prophets," *JBL* 59 (1940) vii.

*Henry S. Gehman, "The 'Burden' of the Prophets," *JQR, N.S.*, 31 (1940-41) 107-121.

I. G. Matthews, "The Old Testament Prophet in His Background," *CQ* 18 (1941) 3-13.

*C. Lattey, "The Prophets and Sacrifice: A Study in Biblical Relativity," *JTS* 42 (1941) 155-165.

*Robert Henry Pfeiffer, "The Patriotism of Israel's Prophets," *HDSB* 7 (1941-42) 45-54.

*H. Wheeler Robinson, "Hebrew Sacrifice and Prophetic Symbolism," *JTS* 43 (1942) 129-139.

*Paul S. Minear, "The Conception of History in the Prophets and Jesus," *JAAR* 11 (1943) 156-161.

*H. Wheeler Robinson, "The Council of Yahweh," *JTS* 45 (1944) 151-157.

*James E. Coleran, "The Prophets and Sacrifice," *ThSt* 5 (1944) 411-438.

*Norman H. Snaith, "The Prophets and Sacrifice and Salvation," *ET* 58 (1946-47) 152-153.

*Harold Garner, "Exodus, Prophet and West Africa," *ET* 58 (1946-47) 278-279.

*H. H. Rowley, "The Prophets and Sacrifice," *ET* 58 (1946-47) 305-307.

H. A. Fischel, "Martyr and Prophet," *JQR, N.S.,* 37 (1946-47) 265-280, 363-386.

John Bright, "The Prophets Were Protestants," *Interp* 1 (1947) 153-182.

†J. P. Arendzen, "The Marks of the True Prophet," *Scrip* 2 (1947) 21-22.

George W. Richards, "The Drama of Redemption. *God Seeks in History,*" *Interp* 2 (1948) 17-23.

*L H. Brockington, "Audition in the Old Testament," *JTS* 49 (1948) 1-8.

*A. H. Edelkoot, "Prophet and Prophet," *OTS* 5 (1948) 179-189.

*Geo Widengern, "Literary and Psychological Aspects of the Hebrew Prophets," *UUÅ* (1948) #10, 1-138.

*Sidney Jellicoe, "The Prophets and the Cultus," *ET* 60 (1948-49 256-258.

A. S. Herbert, "The Prophet as Intercessor," *BQL* 13 (1949-50) 76-80.

*John Bowman, "Prophets and Prophecy in Talmud and Midrash," *EQ* 22 (1950) 107-114, 205-220, 255-275. [I. Israelite and Gentile Prophets; II. Israel and the Prophets; III. The Prophets and the Law]

*A. S. Kapelrud, "Cult and Prophetic Words," *ST* 4 (1950) 5-12.

*N. W. Porteous, "Living Issues in Biblical Scholarship. Prophet and Priest in Israel," *ET* 62 (1950-51) 4-9.

Roland Potter, "God Spoke Through the Prophets," *LofS* 6 (1951-52) 343-347.

Walter G. Williams, "Studies in Prophecy. Part I. Prophecy as a Profession," *IR* 10 (1953) 102-109.

*Walter G. Williams, "Studies in Prophecy. Part II. Priest and Prophet," *IR* 10 (1953) 110-115.

*Kelvin Van Nuys, "Evaluating the Pathological in Prophetic Experience (Particularly in Ezekiel)," *JAAR* 21 (1953) 244-251.

*A. Marmostein, "Greek Poet and Hebrew Prophet," *LQHR* 178 (1953) 42-44.

*George H. Mennenga, "The Prophets and Domestic Relations," *RefR* 7 (1953-54) #3, 1-4.

J. Y. Muckle, "The Call to the Ministry in the Bible," *LQHR* 179 (1954) 181-184.

*Julian N. Hartt, "The Philosopher, the Prophet, and the Church: Some Reflections on Their Roles as Critics of Culture," *JR* 35 (1955) 147-159.

*Sheldon H. Blank, "The Relevance of Prophetic Thought for the American Rabbi," *YCCAR* 65 (1955) 163-177.

*H. H. Rowley, "Ritual and the Hebrew Prophets," *JSS* 1 (1956) 338-360.

Jacob B. Agus, "The Prophet in Modern Hebrew Literature," *HUCA* 28 (1957) 289-324.

E. H. Burgmann, "The Hebrew Prophets," *StMR* #9 (1957) 5-12.

R. L. P. Milburn, "Prophets and sibyls," *OSHTP* (1958-59) 3-17.

Ernest Best, "Prophets and Preachers," *SJT* 12 (1959) 129-150. [1. The Old Testament; 2. The Prophet of the Old Testament and the Preacher; 3. The Prophet in the New Testament; 4. Conclusion]

Edward Robertson, "The Role of the Early Hebrew Prophet," *BJRL* 42 (1959-60) 412-431.

S. Herbert Bess, "The Office of the Prophet in Old Testament Times," *GJ* 1 (1960) #1, 7-12.

*Nicol Milne, "Prophet, Priest and King and Their Effect on Religion in Israel," *Abr-N* 2 (1960-61) 55-67.

*Samuel C. Kincheloe, "Social Unrest and Prophet Expression," *Center* 2 (1961) #2, 1-13.

*Norman Walker, "What is a Nābhî?" *ZAW* 73 (1961) 99-100.

Bruce Vawter, "The Prophets: Men for Our Times," *BibT* #1 (1962) 23-29.

Victor Paul Furnish, "Prophets, Apostles, and Preachers. *A Study in the Biblical Concept of Preaching*," *Interp* 17 (1963) 48-60. [O.T. ref. to *prophets*, I., pp. 48-52]

Abraham J. Heschel, "Prophetic Inspiration: An Analysis of Prophetic Consciousness," *Jud* 11 (1962) 3-13.

*L. Johnston, "The Prophets and Politics," *Scrip* 14 (1962) 43-47.

*Edwin C. Kingsbury, "The Prophets and the Council of Yahweh," *JBL* 83 (1964) 279-286.

*Saul Christensen, "Priests and Prophets—Old Testament Controversy," *Scotist* 20 (1964) 19-31.

George MacRae, "Prepare the way of the Lord," *Way* 4 (1964) 247-257.

*Frederick L. Moriarty, "Prophet and Covenant," *Greg* 46 (1965) 817-833.

Edmond Jacob, "Interpretation in Contemporary Theology. V. The Biblical Prophets: Revolutionaries or Conservatives," *Interp* 19 (1965) 47-58. *(Trans. by James H. Farley)*

H[arry] M. Orlinsky, "The Seer in Ancient Israel," *OA* 4 (1965) 153-174.

*N. Habel, "The Form and Significance of the Call Narratives," *ZAW* 77 (1965) 297-323. [I. The Calls of Gideon and Moses; II. The Call of Jeremiah; III. The Calls of Isaiah and Ezekiel; IV. The Call of II Isaiah; V. Form, Significance and Origin]

Leon J. Wood, "Ecstasy and Israel's Early Prophets," *BETS* 9 (1966) 125-138.

Robert L. Alden, "Ecstasy and the Prophets," *BETS* 9 (1966) 149-156.

*Marten H. Woudstra, "The Religious Problem-Complex of Prophet and Priest in Contemporary Thought," *CTJ* 1 (1966) 39-66. [O. T. refs., pp. 42-47]

*Page H. Kelley, "Contemporary Study of Amos and Prophetism," *R&E* 63 (1966) 375-386.

C. F. Myer, 'The Prophet—A Heavenly Messenger," *RestQ* 9 (1966) 290-294.

Elizabeth Achtemeier, "On Being a Prophet. *A Reflection About the Ministry,*" *T&L* 9 (1966) 199-205.

*A. van Selms, "Church and state according to the Old Testament prophets," *Min* 7 (1966-67) 155-159.

James Smith, "The Life and Thought of the Pre-Literary Prophets," *SR* 13 (1966-67) 91-112.

*John A. Lucal, "God of Justice—The Prophets as Social Reformers," *BibT* #32 (1967) 2221-2228.

Clyde M. Woods, "The Nature, Activities and Teachings of the Non-Literary Prophets," *RestQ* 10 (1967) 12-24.

Reuven Kimelman, "Prophets and Others: Comparisons and Contrasts," *YR* 6 (1967) 51-60.

Klaus Baltzer, "Considerations Regarding the Office and Calling of the Prophet," *HTR* 61 (1968) 567-581.

*Peter R. Ackroyd, "Historians and Prophets," *SEÅ* 33 (1968) 18-54.

W. Pierce Matheney Jr., "Interpretation of Hebrew Prophetic Symbolic Act," *SQ/E* 29 (1968) 256-267.

*Gerard Reedy, "Jeremiah and the Absurdity of the Prophets," *BibT* #40 (1969) 2781-2787.

Werner E. Lemke, "The Prophets in the Time of Crisis," *CovQ* 27 (1969) #3, 3-25.

Donald L. Jones, "Ecstaticism in the Hebrew Prophets," *JMTSO* 7 (1969) 33-45.

David Monkton, "Media and Prophetic Symbolism," *PQL* 15 (1969) #4, 16-18.

James M. Ward, "The Jackson Lectures, 1969: The Prophets and the Church: Who Speaks for God?" *PSTJ* 22 (1969) #2/3, 14-21.

§50 *1.2.4.1 "Schools of the Prophets"*

*R. Payne Smith, "Samuel and the Schools of the Prophets," *Exp, 1st Ser.,* 3 (1876) 241-251, 342-355, 401-414.

R. Payne Smith, "The Schools of the Prophets After the Time of Samuel," *Exp, 1st Ser.,* 4 (1876) 35-46.

[Robert Ainslie] Redford, "Samuel's Schools of the Prophets," *ONTS* 4 (1884-85) 177-178.

Ira M. Price, "The Schools of the Sons of the Prophets," *ONTS* 8 (1888-89) 244-249.

*Hugh Duncan, "The Sons of the Prophets," *GUOST* 2 (1901-07) 24-27.

*James Oscar Boyd, "Samuel and the Rise of the Prophetic Order," *CFL, N.S.,* 8 (1903) 25-30.

Anonymous, "'Company of the Prophets', 'Sons of the Prophets', 'Schools of the Prophets'," *CFL, 3rd Ser.,* 9 (1908) 53-54.

H. O. Hendrickson, "The Prophet Schools of Israel," *TTM* 12 (1928) 69-80.

A. W. Meyer, "Schools of the Prophets in Old Testament Times," *CTM* 1 (1930) 754-759.

J. W. Parker, "An Old Testament Group Movement," *Theo* 30 (1935) 162-166. *[The Sons of the Prophets]*

Howard Jacobson, "The 'Sons of the Prophets'," *YR* 1 (1961) 10-16.

Jack P. Lewis, "The Schools of the Prophets," *RestQ* 9 (1966) 1-10.

§51 *1.2.4.2 False Prophets*

J. C. Matthes, "The False Prophets of Israel," *ModR* 5 (1884) 417-445.

A. B. Davidson, "The False Prophets," *Exp, 5th Ser.,* 2 (1895) 1-17.

Ed. Koenig, "The Origin of the False Prophetic Office in Israel," *TZTM* 4 (1914) 549-552. *(Trans. by T[heophilus] M[ees])*

Willis Thompson, "The Counter-Prophets," *BR* 15 (1930) 347-365.

*H. Wheeler Robinson, "The Council of Yahweh," *JTS* 45 (1944) 151-157. *[False Prophets]*

Lloyd Mooney, "False Prophets," *CCBQ* 2 (1959) #1, 39-42.

L. Yaure, "Elymas-Nehelamite-Pethor," *JBL* 79 (1960) 297-314. *[False Prophets]*

*R. Davidson, "Orthodoxy and the Prophetic Word. A Study in the Relationship between Jeremiah and Deuteronomy," *VT* 14 (1964) 407-416. *[False Prophets]*

§52 *1.2.5 Studies concerning Genealogies*

Arthur Hervey, "Lord Arthur Hervey on the Genealogies," *JSL, 3rd Ser.,* 3 (1856) 172-175.

H. M. G., "Lord Hervey on the Genealogies of Our Lord," *JSL, 3rd Ser.,* 4 (1856-57) 439-448.

*Anonymous, "Notes on Bishop Colenso's New Book," *JSL, 4th Ser.,* 2 (1862-63) 385-401. *(Review)* [I. The Genealogy of Genesis xlvi, pp. 385-394]

Daniel Hy. Haigh, "Egyptian genealogies," *ZÄS* 7 (1869) 43-47.

George Mooar, "The Favorable References to the Foreign Element in Hebrew History," *BS* 27 (1870) 614-624.

*Frederic Gardiner, "The Chronological Value of the Genealogy in Genesis V," *BFER* 22 (1873) 566-575.

*Frederic Gardiner, "The Chronological Value of the Genealogy in Genesis V," *BS* 30 (1873) 323-333.

*Françios Lenormant, "The Genealogies between Adam and the Deluge. A Biblical Study," *ContR* 37 (1880) 565-589.

*Anonymous, "Genealogy of the Edomites," *SBAP* 8 (1885-86) 41.

*Anonymous, "Genealogy of the Horites," *SBAP* 8 (1885-86) 41.

Vinc. Goehlert, "Statistical Observations upon Biblical Data," *ONTS* 7 (1887-88) 76-83. *(Trans. by Charles E. Dennis) [Genealogies]*

H. B. Carrington, "On Hebrew Genealogy," *JAOS* 13 (1889) cxlvi.

*Fritz Hommel, "The Ten Patriarchs of Berosus," *SBAP* 15 (1892-93) 243-246.

*H. W. Hogg, "The Genealogy of Benjamin: A Criticism of 1 Chronicles VIII," *JQR* 11 (1898-99) 102-114.

*M. Berlin, "Notes on Genealogies of the Tribe of Levi in 1 Chron. XXIII-XXVI," *JQR* 12 (1899-1900) 291-298.

*H. W. Hogg, "The Ephraim Genealogy," *JQR* 13 (1900-01) 147-154.

*J. Marquart, "The Genealogy of Benjamin," *JQR* 14 (1901-02) 343-351.

Parke P. Flournoy, "The Ancestry of David," *CFL, N.S.,* 6 (1902) 338-342.

*William F. McCauley, "Bible Chronology and the Archæologists," *CFL, 3rd Ser.,* 1 (1904) 733-743. [The Genealogies, pp. 734-735]

*A. H. Sayce, "The Archaeological Analysis of the Book of Genesis. The Genealogy of Abraham," *ET* 18 (1906-07) 232-233.

*Eb. Nestle, "Job the Fifth, and Moses the Seventh, from Abraham," *ET* 19 (1907-08) 474-475.

*Eb. Nestle, "The Genealogy and the Name of Joshua," *ET* 20 (1908-09) 45.

Thomas à Kempis O'Reilly, "Literary Truth and Historicity in Their Bearing on the Biblical Genealogies," *CUB* 19 (1913) 30-51.

*Herbert H. Gowen, "The Cainite and Sethite Genealogies of Gen. 4 and 5," *ATR* 2 (1919-20) 326-327.

M. A. Murray, "Notes on Some Genealogies of the Middle Kingdom," *AEE* 12 (1927) 45-51.

G. W. Dunham, "Are the Genealogies Trustworthy and Chronological?" *CFL, 3rd Ser.,* 38 (1932) 400-403.

*B[enjamin] Maisler, "A Genealogical List from Ras Shamra," *JPOS* 16 (1936) 150-157.

*Theodor H. Gaster, "A Genealogical List from Ras Shamra," *JPOS* 17 (1937) 105-107.

S. Klein, "A Genealogical Record Found in Jerusalem," *Zion* 4 (1938-39) #1, II-III.

*Leroy Waterman, "Some Repercussions from Late Levitical Genealogical Accretions in P and the Chronicler," *AJSL* 58 (1941) 49-56.

*B[enjamin] Maisler, "The Genealogy of the Sons of Nahor and the Historical Background of the Book of Job," *Zion* 11 (1945-46) #1, I.

*A. Guillaume, "The Habiru, The Hebrews, and the Arabs," *PEQ* 78 (1946) 64-85. [I. The Hebrew Genealogical Tradition, pp. 64-68]

*Philip Whitwell Wilson, "Names in the Bible," *BS* 108 (1951) 315-322.

*S. Schuller, "Some Problems Connected with the Supposed Common Ancestry of Jews and Spartans and Their Relations During the Last Three Centuries B.C.," *JSS* 1 (1956) 257-268.

Jacob Liver, "The Problem of the Genealogy of the Davidic Family after the Biblical Period," *Tarbiz* 26 (1956-57) #3, I-III.

*Andres Ibanez Arana, "The age of man and biblical genealogies," *TD* 8 (1960) 149-153.

*Eric Young, "Some Notes on the Chronology and Genealogy of the Twenty-first Dynasty," *JARCE* 2 (1963) 99-111.

*J. J. Finkelstein, "The Genealogy of the Hammurapi Dynasty," *JCS* 20 (1966) 95-118. [B.M. 80328]

*Abraham Malamat, "King Lists of the Old Babylonian Period and Biblical Genealogies," *JAOS* 88 (1968) 163-173.

§53 *2. Ancient Near Eastern Civilization - General Studies*

Anonymous, "On an Argument for the Antiquity of Human Civilization," *MMBR* 1 (1796) 377-379.

Anonymous, "Greece and Rome, A Brief Comparison of the Influence of Greece and Rome on Civilization," *MMBR, N.S.*, 18 (1834) 327-330.

†Anonymous, "An Essay on Primæval History," *CTPR, 3rd Ser.,* 2 (1846) 243-254. *(Review)*

M. P. Case, "Vestiges of Culture in Early Ages," *BS* 9 (1852) 686-700.

D. S., "The Origin of Civilization," *UQGR* 14 (1857) 27-41. *(Review)*

*Anonymous, "The Greek Schools of Alexandria," *CE* 80 (1866) 14-25. *(Review)*

†Anonymous, "History of the World," *BQRL* 46 (1867) 289-323. *(Review)*

J. H. Titcomb, "On the Antiquity of Civilisation," *JTVI* 3 (1868-69) 1-14. (Discussion, pp. 14-25)

†Anonymous, "Tylor *on Primitive Culture,*" *ERCJ* 135 (1872) 88-121. *(Review)*

*A. H. Sayce, "The Origin of Semitic Civilisation, chiefly upon Philological Evidence," *SBAT* 1 (1872) 294-309.

John Elliot Howard, "On the Early Dawn of Civilization, considered in the Light of Scripture," *JTVI* 9 (1874) 239-268. [(Appendices, pp. 269-275.) (Discussion, pp. 275-280)]

Anonymous, "Early Phases of Civilization," *WR* 106 (1876) 43-80.

J. F. Garrison, "The Schools of Alexandria and the Alexandrian School," *DTQ* 4 (1878) 361-379.

Anonymous, "The Antiquity of Civilization," *LQHR* 61 (1883-84) 250-267. *(Review)*

[Theodor] Benfrey, "Semitic and Indo-European Culture," *ONTS* 4 (1884-85) 170-171. *(Trans. by G. H. Schodde)*

W. S. Ralph, "The Dawn of Civilization," *UQGR, N.S.,* 22 (1885) 276-292.

*J. A. Smith, "Religion as a Element in Civilization," *ONTS* 6 (1886-87) 106-109.

William Hayes Ward, "Light on Scriptural Texts from Recent Discoveries. III. The Beginnings of Civilization," *HR* 25 (1893) 320-321.

*H. M. Mackenzie, "Abstract of British Museum Lectures (W. St. Chad Boscawen) on Assyrian History and Civilization," *BOR* 7 (1893-94) 211-216.

F. Legge, "The Origin of Our Civilisation," *SRL* 24 (1894) 366-386. *(Review)*

*Hormuzd Rassam, "Biblical Lands, Their Topography, Races, Religions, Languages and Customs, Ancient and Modern," *JTVI* 30 (1896-97) 29-82. [Discussion, pp. 83-85]

*A[rthur] J. Evans, "The Neolithic Settlement at Knossos and its Place in the History of Early Ægean Culture," *Man* 1 (1901) #146.

[Stephen D. Peet], "The Earliest Home of the Human Race," *AAOJ* 25 (1903) 191-206. *(Editorial)*

*Carl Josef Grimm, "Babylonia, Glimpses of its Civilization and Culture," *LQ* 37 (1907) 377-384.

*Phillips Endecott Osgood, "The Temple of Solomon. A Deductive Study of Semitic Culture," *OC* 23 (1909) 449-468, 526-549, 588-609.

N. Kolpin, "Can We Obtain any Definite Knowledge of the Beginning of Civilized Life?" *AAOJ* 32 (1910) 195-202.

*A. S. Zerbe, "Hebrew Civilization in the Mosaic Age," *CFL, 3rd Ser.*, 15 (1912) 17-20.

*G. Elliot Smith, "Ships as Evidence of the Migrations of Early Culture," *JMUEOS* #5 (1915-16) 63-102.

George Hempl, "New Light on the Earliest History of Mediterranean Civlization," *AJA* 20 (1916) 91-92.

*A. Kampmeier, "Roman Tolerance Toward the Greek Language," *OC* 35 (1921) 243-248.

O. G. S. Crawford, "The Origins of Civilisation," *ERCJ* 239 (1924) 101-116.

*I. O. Nothstein, "The Civilization of Ur Older than that of Egypt," *AugQ* 7 (1928) 169.

*George A Barton, "The Origins of Civilization in Africa and Mesopotamia, their Relative Antiquity and Interplay," *PAPS* 68 (1929) 303-312.

Isaac Herzog, "The Outlook of Greek Culture upon Judaism," *HJ* 29 (1930-31) 49-60.

M. B. Crook, "Some Cultural Practices in Hebrew Civilisation," *JBL* 50 (1931) 156-175.

*Harold L. Creager, "Cultural and Religious Influence of Babylonia and Assyria on Western Asia," *LCQ* 4 (1931) 345-367.

A. H. Sayce, "The antiquity of civilized man," *SIR* (1931) 515-529.

E. A. Speiser, "The Ethnic Background of the Early Civilizations of the Near East," *AJA* 37 (1933) 459-466.

*William Creighton Graham, "Recent Light on the Cultural Origins of the Hebrews," *JR* 14 (1934) 306-329.

W[illaim] F[oxwell] Albright, "How well can we know the Ancient Near East?" *JAOS* 56 (1936) 121-144.

J. Penrose Harland, "1400 B.C. the Fourteenth Century in the Ancient World," *AJA* 41 (1937) 114-115.

*Warren R. Dawson, "The First Egyptian Society," *JEA* 23 (1937) 259-260.

V. Gordon Childe, "The Orient and Europe," *AJA* 43 (1939) 10-26.

*Hermann Ranke, E[phraim] A. Speiser, W. Norman Brown, and Carl W. Bishop, "The Beginnings of Cilivlization in the Orient. A Symposium at the Meetings of the American Oriental Society, Baltimore,April 13, 1939," *JAOSS* #4 (1939) 3-61. [The Beginnings of Civilization in Egypt, pp. 3-16(R); The Beginnings of Civilization in Mesopotamia, pp. 17-31(S)]

*[C.] Leonard Woolley, "North Syria as a Cultural Link in the Ancient World," *Man* 43 (1943) #19.

M. E. Kirk, "An Outline of the Cultural History of Palestine Down to Roman Times," *PEQ* 75 (1943) 9-49.

*T. Fish, "The Place of the Small State in the Political and Cultural History of Ancient Mesopotamia," *BJRL* 18 (1944) 83-98.

M. E. Kirk, "An Outline of the Ancient Cultural History of Transjordan," *PEQ* 76 (1944) 180-198.

*Dorothy Mackay, "Ancient River Beds and Dead Cities," *Antiq* 19 (1945) 135-144.

*B[enjamin] Maisler, "The History of Settlement in Ancient Times," *Kobez* 4 (1945) XVII-XVIII.

John R. Swanton, "The Primary Centers of Civilization," *SIR* (1947) 367-378.

Theodore Burton Brown, "1600-1400 B.C. in the Eastern Mediterranean," *AAA* 28 (1948) 8-26.

G. Ernest Wright, "The Old Testament Attitude toward Civilization," *TT* 5 (1948-49) 327-339.

*John L. Myres, "The Geographical Background of the Aegean Civilization," *ArOr* 17 (1949) Part 2, 196-204.

*M. E. L. Mallowan, "Mesopotamia and Syria. Unity and Diversity of the Earliest Civilizations," *Sumer* 5 (1949) 1-7.

Arnaldo Momigliano, "Ancient History and the Antiquarian," *JWCI* 13 (1950) 285-315.

George M. A. Hanfmann, "The Bronze Age in the Near East: A Review Article," *AJA* 55 (1951) 355-365; 56 (1952) 27-38. *(Review)*

V. G[ordon] Childe, "The Birth of Civilization," *P&P* #2 (1952) 1-10.

Anonymous, "The Neolithic Cultures of Palestine," *BIES* 17 (1952-53) #1/2, I.

Julian Huxley, "The Birth of Civilization," *HT* 3 (1953) 390-400.

John Waechter, "The Beginnings of Civilization in the Middle East," *PEQ* 85 (1953) 124-131.

*V. Gordon Childe, "Science in Preliterate Societies and the Ancient Oriental Civilization," *Cent* 3 (1953-54) 12-23.

*Winifred Lamb, "The Culture of North-East Anatolia and its Neighbours," *AS* 4 (1954) 21-32.

A[braham] Malamat, "Cushan Rishathaim and the Decline of the Near East Around 1200 B.C.," *JNES* 13 (1954) 231-242.

*Hans Julius Wolff, "Roman Law as Part of Ancient Civilization: Reflections on Leopold Wenger's Last Work," *Tr* 11 (1956) 381-394. *(Review)*

*S. Yeivin, "The Land of Israel and the Birth of Civilization in the Near East," *A&S* 2 (1957) #2/3, 111-120.

V. Gordon Childe, "The Bronze Age," *P&P* #12 (1957) 2-15.

*Samuel Noah Kramer, "Love, Hate, and Fear. Psychological Aspects of Sumerian Culture," *EI* 5 (1958) 66*-74*.

*Robert M. Adams, "Survey of Ancient Water Courses and Settlements in Central Iraq," *Sumer* 14 (1958) 101-103.

*Vladimír Souček, "Tracing Ancient Cultures in Armenia," *NOP* 1 (1960) #6, 12-14.

W. J. Beasley, "*Abraham and His Ancestors:* New Light on the Precision of Early Semitic Peoples," *AT* 5 (1960-61) #2, 17-20.

*John Alexander, "Greeks, Italians and the Earliest Balkan Iron Age," *Antiq* 36 (1962) 123-130.

*Roderick A. F. MacKenzie, "The City and Israelite Religion," *CBQ* 25 (1963) 60-70.

*E. A. Speiser, "Cuneiform Law and the History of Civilization," *PAPS* 107 (1963) 536-541.

*C. J. Bleeker, "The pattern of the Ancient Egyptian Culture," *Num* 11 (1964) 75-82.

*Stanley D. Walters, "The Development of Civilization in Ancient Mesopotamia," *JASA* 17 (1965) 68-73.

*(Mrs.) E. C. L. During Caspers, "Further Evidence for Cultural Relations Between India, Baluchistan, and Iran and Mesopotamia in Early Dynastic Times," *JNES* 24 (1965) 53-56.

*Josef Klíma, "The Periphery of Mesopotamian Culture," *NOP* 4 (1965) 17-19.

*Robert Erwin, "Civilization as a Phase of World History," *AmHR* 71 (1965-66) 1181-1198.

*John E. Rexine, "Hebrew and Greek Thought and Culture Compared," *StVSQ N.S.,* 9 (1965) 138-144.

*James Mellaart, "Anatolian Trade with Europe and Anatolian Geography and Culture Provinces in the Late Bronze Age," *AS* 18 (1968) 187-202.

*David Daube, "The Culture of Deuteronomy," *Orita* 3 (1969) 27-52.

Mario Liverani, "Problems and Trends of Studies in the History of the Ancient Near East," *VDI* (1969) #4, 67.

§54 *2.1 Historiography & Ancient Near Eastern History - General Studies*

Anonymous, "Reflections on the Origin of History," *MMBR* 34 (1812-13) 402-405.

*Anonymous, "Outlines of History," *QRL* 45 (1831) 450-471. *[Subtitled:* "Subversion of Ancient Governments"*]*

†Anonymous, "Beke's *Origines Biblicæ*," *QRL* 52 (1834) 496-519. *(Review)*

E. D. Sanborn, "Ancient and Modern Historians," *BRCR, 3rd Ser.*, 2 (1846) 338-360.

*I. Trautmann, "The Hellenes, Romans, and Israelites. Their Position, Secular and Religious, in the History of the World," *CRB* 16 (1851) 96-105.

*G. B., "Xenophon as an Historian, and as a Writer of the Anabasis," *JSL, 3rd Ser.*, 5 (1857) 438-439.

[M. Philips], "Philosophy of the Rise and Fall of Empires," *FBQ* 10 (1862) 22-38.

*Anonymous, "Abraham's Position in Sacred History," *DQR* 4 (1864) 611-631.

R. O., "On the Correct Treatment of Ancient History," *IER, N.S.*, 10 (1873-74) 389-406.

*Henry Coppée, "Art as an Interpreter of History," *PRev* 54 (1878) Part 2, 352-383.

*Philip H. Wicksteed, "The Place of the Israelites in History," *ModR* 2 (1881) 548-564. *(Review)*

*E. Hull, "The Physical Features of Egypt and Syria in Relation to Bible History," *PEFQS* 18 (1886) 53-54. *(Review)*

J. H. Young, "The Science of History," *MQR, 3rd Ser.*, 3 (1887-88) 199-204.

J. D. Tadlock, "Materials of History," *PQ* 3 (1889) 1-16.

*Norman Macleod, "Israel's Place in the World's History," *EN* 2 (1890) 409-413, 454-458.

Theo. G. Soares, "Hebrew Historiography," *BW* 2 (1893) 178-188.

W. W. Moore, "Echoes of Bible History," *USR* 4 (1892-93) 97-111.

*George H. Schodde, "Israel's Place in Universal History," *BW* 10 (1897) 272-276.

*William C. Conant, "The Prophetic Scope of Sacred History," *HR* 34 (1897) 353-355.

*D. S. Gregory, "Philosophy of History and the Old Testament," *HR* 35 (1898) 167-173.

*A. C. Zenos, "The Philosophy of History in the Philosophy of Religion," *CFL, N.S.,* 7 (1903) 67-74.

John A. W. Haas, "A New Old Testament History," *LCR* 23 (1904) 45-57. *(Review)*

Stephen D. Peet, "The Beginnings of History," *AAOJ* 29 (1907) 65-80.

John E. McFadyen, "Sacred Versus Secular History," *HR* 54 (1907) 451-453.

William Hazen, "Discussions of Old Testament History in India. 'Difficulties in Bible History'," *CFL, 3rd Ser.,* 9 (1908) 396-397.

Edgar M. Wilson,"Discussions of Old Testament History in India. 'Difficulties in Bible History': A Reply," *CFL, 3rd Ser.,* 9 (1908) 397-400. (Editorial note, by William Hazen, pp. 400-401)

*G. B. Grundy, "Herodotus the Historian," *QRL* 210 (1909) 115-140. *(Review)*

*E. G. Richardson, "Israel's Thread in History," *MR* 92 (1910) 605-609.

Henry Preserved Smith, "Light on Some Ancient History," *MTSQB* 6 (1911-12) #2, 11-23.

*Ellsworth Huntington, "Changes in Climate and History," *AmHR* 18 (1912-13) 213-232.

J. T. Shotwell, "The Interpretation of History," *AmHR* 18 (1912-13) 692-709.

C. L. Bedale, "The Ancient History of the Near East. A Review," *JMUEOS* #2 (1912-13) 69-72. *(Review)*

G. H. Stevenson, "Ancient historians and their sources," *JP* 35 (1919-20) 204-224.

George W. Gilmore, "A Background of Biblical History," *HR* 80 (1920) 299-300.

*Leon Legrain, "Reconstructing Ancient History," *MJ* 11 (1920) 169-180.

W. M. Flinders Petrie, "The Transmission of History," *AEE* 6 (1921) 44-45.

*Anonymous, "God in History," *MR* 105 (1922) 132-133.

[W. M.] Flinders Petrie, "Current Fallacies About History," *AEE* 8 (1923) 78-84.

John E. McFadyen, "Telescoped History," *ET* 36 (1924-25) 103-109.

*Darwin A. Leavitt, "Some Aspects of History-Writing in the Old Testament," *MTSQB* 20 (1925-26) #3, 16-28.

Tenney Frank, "Roman Historiography before Caesar," *AmHR* 32 (1926-27) 232-240.

[W. M.] Flinders Petrie, "The Materialization of Old Testament History," *JTVI* 61 (1929) 260-270, 277. [(Discussion, pp. 270-275) (Communications by W. R. Rowlatt-Jones, p. 275; J. W. Thirtle, pp. 275-277)]

*Henry Thatcher Fowler, "Herodotus and the Early Hebrew Historians," *JBL* 49 (1930) 207-217.

*Frank Richards, "The Foundations of Bible History," *LQHR* 156 (1932) 307-317.

H. Wheeler Robinson, "Israel's Contribution to the Philosophy of History," *OSHTP* (1932) 5-23.

S[tanley] A. Cook, "'The Foundations of Bible History'," *PEFQS* 64 (1932) 88-96. *(Review)*

G. B. Grundy, "The Cambridge Ancient History," *QRL* 258 (1932) 341-362. *(Review)*

*Kurt von Fritz, "Herodotus and the Growth of the Greek Historiography," *TAPA* 67 (1936) 315-340.

*Stanley A. Cook, "Biblical Criticism and the Interpretation of History," *MC* 26 (1936-37) 121-129, 183-194.

Carl Becker, "What is Historiography?" *AmHR* 44 (1938-39) 20-28.

Edgar M. Carlson, "The Prophetic Interpretation of History," *AugQ* 18 (1939) 322-332.

*John Derby, "God and History," *Theo* 44 (1942) 24-31.

*John Derby, "History and Eschatology," *Theo* 44 (1942) 90-99.

James A. Montgomery, "The Contribution of the Near Orient to the Concept of Universal History," *CQ* 20 (1943) 98-104.

*Paul S. Minear, "The Conception of History in the Prophets and Jesus," *JAAR* 11 (1943) 156-161.

*A. T. Olmstead, "History, Ancient World, and the Bible. Problems of Attitude and of Method," *JNES* 2 (1943) 1-34.

Merle William Boyer, "Philosophy of History for Bible Classes," *LCQ* 16 (1943) 410-413.

W. J. Phythian-Adams, "Shadow and Substance. *The Meaning of Sacred History*," *Interp* 1 (1947) 419-435.

E. L. Allen, "Biblical and Secular History," *CongQL* 26 (1948) 120-127.

Anonymous, "Biblical History," *Interp* 2 (1948) 63-65.

*Burr C. Brundage, "The Ancient Near East as History," *AmHR* 54 (1948-49) 530-547.

Hajo Holborn, "Greek and Modern Concepts of History," *JHI* 10 (1949) 3-13.

*D. S. Russell, "The Apocalyptic Conception of the Unity of History," *BQL* 13 (1949-50) 68-75.

C[yrus] H. Gordon, "The Origin of Hebrew Historiography," *JBL* 69 (1950) viii-ix.

H. D. Schmidt, "Palestine Trends of Power: A Survey of Three Thousand Years of Palestine History," *JNES* 10 (1951) 1-12.

Ephraim A. Speiser, "The Ancient Near East and Modern Philosophies of History," *PAPS* 95 (1951) 583-588.

Gunnar Östborn, "Yahweh's Words and Deeds. A Preliminary Study into the Old Testament Presentation of History," *UUÅ* (1951) #7, 1-80.

B[enjamin] Maisler, "Ancient Israelite Historiography," *IEJ* 2 (1952) 82-88.

*M. A. C. Warren, "Eschatology and History," *IRM* 41 (1952) 337-350.

*John A. Wilson, "Oriental History: Past and Present," *JAOS* 72 (1952) 49-55.

*Francis Rue Steele, "God in History," *JTVI* 84 (1952) 1-16, 25. [(Discussion, pp. 16-18) (Communications by, J. Stafford Wright, pp. 18-20; R. E. D. Clark, pp. 20-21; B. B. Knopp, pp. 21-22; L. Merson Davies, pp. 22-23; H. W. F. Saggs, pp. 23-25)]

*S[amuel] N[oah] Kramer, "Sumerian Historiography," *IEJ* 3 (1953) 217-232.

David N[oel] Freedman and David M. Thompson, "The Key to Old Testament History," *WW* 4 (1953) #4, 15-19.

*Truesdell S. Brown, "Herodotus and His Profession," *AmHR* 59 (1953-54) 829-843. *[Historiography]*

*Lionel Pearson, "Real and Conventional Personalities in Greek History," *JHI* 15 (1954) 136-145.

Virgil H. Todd, "The Old Testament View of History," *CS* 2 (1954-55) #1, 1-4.

*Paul E. Brown, "The Basis for Hope. *The Principle of the Covenant as a Biblical Basis of a Philosophy of History*," *Interp* 9 (1955) 35-40.

*A[braham] Malamat, "Doctrines of Causality in Hittite and Biblical Historiography: A Parallel," *VT* 5 (1955) 1-12.

*Frank M. Cross Jr., "A Footnote to Biblical History," *McQ* 9 (1955-56) #2, 7-10. *[Unsolved problems of Biblical History and Archaeology]*

*Constant de Wit, "Egyptian Methods of Writing History," *EQ* 28 (1956) 158-169.

T. Foster Lindley Jr., "The History of Historiography," *Person* 37 (1956) 379-387.

*William Connolly, "God and History in the Old Testament," *MH* 12 (1956-57) #1, 11-18.

C. A. Simpson, "Old Testament Historiography," *OSHTP* (1956-57) 22-23.

E. A. Speiser, "The Biblical Idea of History in its Common Near Eastern Setting," *IEJ* 7 (1957) 201-216.

*Maurice Blanchard, "Uniqueness of the Hebrew Concept of History as Seen in the Books of Kings," *IJT* 6 (1957) 122-130.

*George E. Ladd, "Revelation, History, and the Bible," *JASA* 9 (1957) #3, 15-18.

*J. D. Thomas, "Time and History," *RestQ* 1 (1957) 17-20.

Arnold Toynbee, "Uniqueness and Recurrence in History," *Sumer* 13 (1957) 23-29.

*C. A. Simpson, "Old Testament Historiography and Revelation," *HJ* 56 (1957-58) 319-332.

*N. H. Tur-Sinai, "On Some Historical References in the Bible," *EI* 5 (1958) 87*-88*.

*Maurice Blanchard, "Uniqueness of Hebrew History," *IJT* 7 (1958) 24-32.

*L. Johnston, "Prophecy and History," *ClR* 44 (1959) 602-615.

*G. Ernest Wright, "Modern Issues on Biblical Studies: History and the Patriarchs," *ET* 71 (1959-60) 292-296.

*F. W. Walbank, "History and Tradgedy," *HJAH* 9 (1960) 216-234.

*A. E. Wardman, "Myth in Greek Historiography," *HJAH* 9 (1960) 403-413.

*David N[oel] Freedman, "History and Eschatology. *The Nature of Biblical Religion and Prophetic Faith,*" *Interp* 14 (1960) 143-154.

*G[erhard] von Rad, "History and the Patriarchs," *ET* 72 (1960-61) 213-216.

*William O. Walker Jr., "Critical Study and 'Historical' Traditions in the Old Testament," *TUSR* 7 (1960-63) 100-117.

S. G. F. Brandon, "The Jewish Philosophy of History," *HT* 11 (1961) 155-164.

Jack Riemer, "The Jewish View of History," *Jud* 10 (1961) 34-39.

Daniel J. Elazar, "A Constitutional View of Jewish History," *Jud* 10 (1961) 256-264.

J. L. Seeligman, "Aetiological Elements in Biblical Historiography," *Zion* 26 (1961) #3/4, I-II.

*R. H. Altus, "God's Revelation and History," *AusTR* 33 (1962) 3-7.

Leonard S. Kravitz, "Some Reflections on the Teaching of Jewish History," *CCARJ* 18 (1962-63) #3, 30-32.

*Truesdell S. Brown, "The Greek Sense of Time in History as suggested by their Accounts of Egypt," *HJAH* 11 (1962) 257-270.

Wilfrid Harrington, "A Biblical View of History," *ITQ* 29 (1962) 207-222.

Morton Smith, "Judaism and the Academy. III. *Hebrew Studies Within the Study of History,*" *Jud* 11 (1962) 333-344.

*Arthur L. Merrill, "The Old Testament and the Future," *MHSB* 7 (1962) #1, 3-14. [History, pp. 6-10]

S[igmund] Mowinckel, "Israelite Historiography," *ASTI* 2 (1963) 4-26.

Eugene H. Maly, "The Nature of Biblical History," *BibT* #5 (1963) 276-285.

William R. Foster, "The Meaning of Biblical History," *GJ* 4 (1963) #2, 3-8.

John Briggs Curtis, "A Suggested Interpretation of the Biblical Philosophy of History," *HUCA* 34 (1963) 115-123.

J. J. Finkelstein, "Mesopotamian Historiography," *PAPS* 107 (1963) 461-472.

*James Barr, "Revelation Through History in the Old Testament and in Modern Theology," *PSB* 56 (1963) #3, 4-14.

*Miriam Lichtheim, "Ancient Egypt: A Survey of Current Historiography," *AmHR* 69 (1963-64) 30-46.

E. D. Phillips, "The Greek Vision of Prehistory," *Antiq* 38 (1964) 171-178.

*Josef Meysha, "Jewish Coins in Ancient Historiography," *PEQ* 96 (1964) 46-52.

*James Muilenburg, "Abraham and the Nations. *Blessing and World History,*" *Interp* 19 (1965) 387-398.

Hartmut Gese, "The Idea of History in the Ancient Near East and the Old Testament," *JTC* 1 (1965) 49-64.

Bernhard W. Anderson, "The Problem of Old Testament History," *LQHR* 190 (1965) 5-11.

*Robert Erwin, "Civilization as a Phase of World History," *AmHR* 71 (1965-66) 1181-1198.

A. W. Mosley, "Historical reporting in the Ancient World," *NTS* 12 (1965-66) 10-26.

Wayne E. Barr, "Novelty and Tradition in the Old Testament," *UTSB* 65 (1965-66) #3, 20-26.

*Elaine Marie Prevallet, "The Use of the Exodus in Interpreting History," *CTM* 37 (1966) 131-145.

*Jacob Neusner, "The Religious Uses of History: Judaism in First-Century A.D. Palestine and Third Century Babylonia," *H&T* 5 (1966) 153-171.

*David B. Richardson, "Linear History and the Unity of Mankind," *Person* 47 (1966) 5-15.

*Mircea Eliade, "Cosmic Myth and 'Sacred History'," *RS* 2 (1966-67) 171-184.

*Bruce Vawter, "History and the Word," *CBQ* 29 (1967) 512-523.

David Noel Freedman, "The Biblical Idea of History," *Interp* 21 (1967) 32-49.

*William R. Murdock, "History and Revelation in Jewish Apocalypticism," *Interp* 21 (1967) 167-187.

*John Van Seters, "History and Myth in Biblical Interpretation," *ANQ, N.S.,* 8 (1967-68) 154-162.

*W. Den Boer, "Graeco-Roman Historiography in its Relation to Biblical and Modern Thinking," *H&T* 7 (1968) 60-75.

*R. F. Hathaway, "Cicero, *De Re Publica* II, and his Socratic View of History," *JHI* 29 (1968) 3-12.

*Gordon D. Kaufman, "God's Purposes and World History," *PP* 9 (1968) 9-28.

*Peter R. Ackroyd, "Historians and Prophets," *SEÅ* 33 (1968) 18-54.

Menahem Haran, "Problems in Biblical History," *Tarbiẕ* 38 (1968-69) #1, I-II.

*Solomon Zeitlin, "A Survey of Jewish Historiography: From the Biblical Books to the *Sefer Ha-Kabbalah* with Special Emphasis on Josephus," *JQR, N.S.*, 59 (1968-69) 171-214.

*Solomon Zeitlin, "A Survey of Jewish Historiography: From the Biblical Books to the *Sefer Ha-Kabbalah*," *JQR, N.S.*, 60 (1969-70) 37-68.

§55 *2.2 General History of the Nation of Israel*

†Anonymous, "A Connection of Sacred and Profane History, from the death of Joshua to the Decline of the Kingdoms of Israel and Judah," *BCQTR, 4th Ser.,* 3 (1828) 395-420. *(Review)*

†Anonymous, "History of the Jews," *BCQTR, 4th Ser.,* 7 (1830) 374-408. *(Review)*

Anonymous, "The History of the Jews, from the Earliest Period. By Rev. H. H. Milman," *CE* 9 (1830) 290-304. *(Review)*

Φιλαλήθης, "Illustrations of Jewish History, from Tacitus," *CongML* 16 (1833) 657-662; 17 (1834) 8-16.

†Anonymous, "Connection of Sacred and Profane History, from the Death of Joshua to the Decline of the Kingdoms of Israel and Judah," *BCQTR, 4th Ser.,* 23 (1838) 396-438. *(Review)*

†E. W., "History of the Jews," *CE* 45 (1848) 48-60. *(Review)*

*I. Trautmann, "The Hellenes, Romans, and Israelites. Their Position, Secular and Religious, in the History of the World," *CRB* 16 (1851) 96-105.

Anonymous, "Jews in China," *JAOS* 2 (1851) 341-342.

J. A. Seiss, "History of the Jews," *ER* 3 (1851-52) 255-274.

J. H. A., "Ewald's Hebrew History," *CE* 55 (1853) 161-187. *(Review)*

†Anonymous, "Kurtz's History of the Old Testament," *BFER* 5 (1856) 809-838. *(Review)*

†Anonymous, "Edersheim's History of the Jewish Nation," *BFER* 5 (1856) 910-927. *(Review)*

H. I. Schmidt, "Israel and the Gentiles," *ER* 8 (1856-57) 485-500.

Anonymous, "Canon Stanley's Lectures on the Jewish Church," *JSL, 4th Ser.,* 3 (1863) 257-272. *(Review)*

†Anonymous, "Dean Milman *and* Dean Stanley *on Jewish History,*" *ERCJ* 119 (1864) 137-167. *(Review)*

*R. Payne Smith, "The Samaritan Chronicle of Abu'l Fatah, the Arabic text from the manuscript in the Bodleian Library with a literal English translation," *VDETF* 2 (1865) 303-335, 431-459.

*J. S. Howson, "Dean Stanley on the Hebrew Kings and Prophets," *ContR* 1 (1866) 615-641. *(Review)*

J. A. H., "Milman's Historical Works," *BFER* 16 (1867) 570-598. *(Review)* [The History of the Jews, pp. 571-580]

*J. S. Howson, "Dean Stanley on the Hebrew Kings and Prophets," *ThE* 4 (1867) 105-136. *(Review)*

G. Collins, "Notes on Ancient Hebrew Civilization," *UQGR, N.S.,* 10 (1873) 133-146.

William Salmond, "Ewald's History of Israel," *MR* 56 (1874) 396-422. *(Review) [Abridged]*

A. J. Canfield, "Ewald's History of Israel," *UQGR, N.S.,* 11 (1874) 54-69. *(Review)*

[John Peter(?)] Lange, "Side-Lights. The Israelitish People," *DTQ* 1 (1875)144-145.

†Anonymous, "Ewald's *History of Israel,*" *ERCJ* 142 (1875) 432-471. *(Review)*

Josiah Miller, "On the Numbers of the Jews in all Ages," *SBAT* 4 (1875) 315-331.

C. H. Brigham, "Characteristics of the Jewish Race," *URRM* 5 (1876) 156-178.

*Alfred Cave, "The Critical Estimate of Mosaism," *DTQ* 5 (1879) 449-470.

*Alfred Cave, "The Critical Estimate of Mosaism," *PRev* 55 (1879) Part 1, 579-614. *(Review)*

*Philip H. Wicksteed, "The Place of the Israelites in History," *ModR* 2 (1881) 548-564. *(Review)*

Robert R. Doherty, "The Wandering Jew and His Congeners," *MR* 56 (1882) 489-506.

Anonymous, "Renan's 'History of Israel'," *WR* 128 (1887) 1126-1135. *(Review)*

†Anonymous, "M. Renan's History of the People Israel," *ERCJ* 167 (1888) 482-519. *(Review)*

Anonymous, "Renan's History of Israel," *CQR* 27 (1888-89) 391-408. *(Review)*

T. Cartwright, "The History of Israel," *CR* 53 (1889) 217-221. *(Review)*

S. H. Kellogg, "The Antiquity of the Jewish Race," *EN* 1 (1889) 11-13.

Cyrus Adler, "Jewish History in Arabian Historians," *JQR* 2 (1889-90) 106-107.

A. Bernstein, "The Book and the People," *EN* 2 (1890) 228-231, 272-277, 316-318, 360-364, 405-408, 462-464, 505-510, 545-551; 3 (1891) 24-31, 76-81, 120-124, 169-172, 214-218, 265-269, 312-316, 356-360.

*Norman Macleod, "Israel's Place in the World's History," *EN* 2 (1890) 409-413, 454-458.

J. A. Howlett, "Rénan's 'Israel' Down to the Time of the Kings," *IER, 3rd Ser.*, 11 (1890) 158-175. *(Review)*

R. T. Polk, "Wellhausen's History of Israel," *UQGR, N.S.*, 27 (1890) 413-426. *(Review)*

C[laude] R. Conder, "The Oriental Jews," *SRL* 18 (1891) 1-23.

Anonymous, "Graetz's History of the Jews," *CQR* 35 (1892-93) 68-97. *(Review)*

John Taylor, "Renan's 'History of the People of Israel'," *ET* 4 (1892-93) 546-548. *(Review)*

*S. Krauss, "The Jews in the Works of the Church Fathers," *JQR* 5 (1892-93) 122-157.

†Anonymous, "Israel," *QRL* 176 (1893) 106-139. *(Review)*

*S. Krauss, "The Jews in the Works of the Church Fathers II," *JQR* 6 (1893-94) 82-99.

*S. Krauss, "The Jews in the Works of the Church Fathers III," *JQR* 6 (1893-94) 225-261.

*F. Meinhold, "The Origins of the Religion and History of Israel," *NW* 4 (1895) 98-121.

*George H. Schodde, "Israel's Place in Universal History," *BW* 10 (1897) 272-276.

*A. H. Sayce, "The Limitations of Archaeology as a Substitue for Old-Testament History," *HR* 34 (1897) 195-199.

*[George H. Schodde], "Biblical Research Notes," *ColTM* 17 (1897) 117-121. [Egyptian References to the Israelites, pp. 117-119]

C[arl] H[einrich] Cornill, "History of the People of Israel. From the Beginning to the Destruction of Jerusalem," *OC* 11 (1897) 385-400. [Introductory Observations.—Land and People. —Race Migrations of the Orient in Ancient Times] *(Trans. by W. H. Carruth)*

Joseph Bruneau, "Biblical Research. V. History of Israel," *AER* 18 (1898) 57-58.

G. Buchanan Gray, "Professor Sayce's 'Early History of the Hebrews'," *Exp, 5th Ser.*, 7 (1898) 337-355. *(Review)*

*H. W. Hogg, "'Dan to Beersheba': The Literary History of the Phrase and the Historical Problems it Raises," *Exp, 5th Ser.*, 8 (1898) 411-421.

*I[srael] Abrahams, "Professor Schürer on Life Under the Jewish Law," *JQR* 11 (1898-99) 626-642.

*I[srael] Abrahams, "Professor Schürer on Life Under the Jewish Law," *OSHTP* (1898-99) 33-37.

*W. H. Bennett, "Two Important Works on the Old Testament," *Exp, 6th Ser.*, 2 (1900) 312-320. *(Review)*

E. N. Heimann, "Israel in the History of the World," *TTKF* 3 (1901) 40-52.

*William R. Harper, "Was Israel Really a Separate Nation?" *BW* 19 (1902) 163-167. *(Editorial)*

Walter M. Patton, "The Composite Character of Israel," *BW* 20 (1902) 432-440.

T. R. English, "The Diasporae Before the Diaspora," *CFL, N.S.*, 6 (1902) 349-353.

W. M. Ramsay, "The Jews in the Graeco-Asiatic Cities," *Exp, 6th Ser.*, 5 (1902) 19-33, 92-109.

Willis J. Beecher, "Smith's 'Old Testament History'," *CFL, 3rd Ser.*, 1 (1904) 183-189. *(Review)*

B. D. Hahn, "'Israel of the Schools'," *CFL, 3rd Ser.*, 2 (1905) 28-38.

Henry Wace, "Diverse Critical Views of Jewish History," *CFL, 3rd Ser.*, 5 (1906) 346-355.

Stanley A. Cook, "The Jews of Syene in the Fifth Century B.C.," *PEFQS* 39 (1907) 68-73.

B. D. Eerdmans, "Have the Hebrews been Nomads?" *Exp, 7th Ser.*, 6 (1908) 118-131.

G. A. Smith, "'Have the Hebrews been Nomads?' A Reply to Professor Eerdmans," *Exp, 7th Ser.*, 6 (1908) 254-272.

B. D. Eerdmans, "The Nomads Again: a Reply to Professor G. A. Smith," *Exp, 7th Ser.*, 6 (1908) 345-358.

F. Hugh Pope, "Israel in Egypt after the Exodus," *ITQ* 3 (1908) 342-356.

*[F.] Hugh Pope, "The Temple of Onias at Leontopolis," *ITQ* 3 (1908) 415-424.

*Henry Preserved Smith, "Reforms and Reformers in Israel," *MTSQB* 3 (1908-09) #1, 3-18.

*Stanley A. Cook, "Palestine Excavations and the History of Israel," *Exp, 7th Ser.,* 8 (1909) 97-114.

W. F. Lofthouse, "The Reconstruction of the World of the Hebrews," *LQHR* 112 (1909) 258-267. *(Review)*

A. H. Sayce, "The Influence of the Sudan upon Jewish History," *R&E* 6 (1909) 539-549.

Herbert C. Alleman, "A New Theory of Hebrew Origins," *LQ* 40 (1910) 275-288. *(Review)*

*E. G. Richardson, "Israel's Thread in History," *MR* 92 (1910) 605-609.

T. K. Cheyne, "Survey of Recent Literature Relative to the External or Internal History of Israel," *RTP* 6 (1910-11) 385-392.

*Stephen Langdon, "Franz Böhl, *Kanaanäer und Hebäer,*" *Baby* 6 (1912) 54-55. *(Review)*

*A. S. Zerbe, "Hebrew Civilization in the Mosaic Age," *CFL, 3rd Ser.,* 15 (1912) 17-20.

J. Willcock, "Tacitus on the Jews," *ET* 24 (1912-13) 234.

A. Nairne, "The People of God," *CQR* 76 (1913) 176-181. *(Review)*

F. J. Foakes-Jackson, "A Literary Appreciation of the History of Israel," *ICMM* 10 (1913-14) 53-61.

Charles W. Super, "The Jews in History," *LQ* 44 (1914) 519-538.

Pietro Romanelli, "The Jewish Quarters in Ancient Rome," *PEFQS* 46 (1914) 134-140.

Herbert Strong, "The Jews as Viewed Through Roman Spectacles," *HJ* 13 (1914-15) 300-313.

*Joseph Offord, "Archaeological Notes. IV. *The Jewish Community at Delos,*" *PEFQS* 47 (1915) 201-203.

*Julian Morgenstern, "The Foundations of Israel's History," *YCCAR* 25 (1915) 221-287. {(I. The Conception of Revelation in Ancient Israel, pp. 221-238; II. Biblical Science and Judaism, pp. 239-256; III. The Sources of Israel's Early History, pp. 256-259; IV. Israel in the Desert, pp. 259-275; V. Israel in Canaan, pp. 275-284; Conclusion, pp. 284-287.) (Comments by [Max] Heller, pp. 287-288; [William] Rosenau, p. 288; [Samuel] Schulman, pp. 288-289; L[ouis] Grossmann, 289-290; [Isaac] Landman, p. 290; [David] Philipson, pp. 290-291; [Moses] Buttenwieser, pp. 291-292; F[elix] Levy, pp. 292-293; [Joseph] Stolz, p. 293; D[avid] Lefkowitz, pp. 293-294; [Joel] Blau, p. 294; Reply byJ. Morgenstern, pp. 294-299)}

*Jacob Mann, "The Responsa of the Babylonian Geonim as a Source of Jewish History," *JQR, N.S.*, 7 (1916-17) 457-490; 8 (1917-18) 339-366.

*Jacob Mann, "The Responsa of the Babylonian Geonim as a Source of Jewish History," *JQR, N.S.*, 9 (1918-19) 139-179. [I. Appendix to Chapter I (concluded)]

*Jacob Mann, "The Responsa of the Babylonian Geonim as a Source of Jewish History," *JQR, N.S.*, 10 (1919-20) 121-152, 309-366. [II. The Political Status of the Jews; III. The Economic Conditions of the Jews; IV. The Power of the Bêt-Din and the Organization of Communities]

*Joseph Offord, "Archaeological Notes on Jewish Antiquities. XVIII. *Jewish Communities in Egypt*," *PEFQS* 49 (1917) 96-98.

*Joseph Offord, "Archaeological Notes on Jewish Antiquities. XXIX *Jewish Colony in the Fayoum*," *PEFQS* 49 (1917) 98-99.

*Joseph Offord, "Archaeological Notes on Jewish Antiquities. XXXIX *Jewish Colonists in the Nile Delta*," *PEFQS* 49 (1917) 184.

D. D. Luckenbill, "On Israel's Origins," *AJT* 22 (1918) 24-53.

*Paul Haupt, "Semites, Hebrews, Israelites, Jews," *OC* 32 (1918) 753-760.

Theophile J. Meek, "A Proposed Reconstruction of Early Hebrew History," *MTSQB* 14 (1919-20) #3, 3-12.

Theophile J. Meek, "A Proposed Reconstruction of Early Hebrew History," *AJT* 24 (1920) 209-216.

*Jacob, Mann, "Addenda to 'The Responsa of the Babylonian Geonim as a Source of Jewish History'," *JQR, N.S.,* 11 (1920-21) 433-471.

Harold M. Wiener, "Some Factors in Early Hebrew History," *BS* 78 (1921) 201-231, 376-399.

*Paul F. Bloomhardt, "Zionism in the Sixth Century B.C.," *LQ* 55 (1925) 13-28.

S. Baron, "The Study of Jewish History," *JIQ* 4 (1927-28) #2, 7-14.

S. Baron, "Research in Jewish History," *JIQ* 4 (1927-28) #4, 1-8.

*C. Moss, "Jews and Judaism in Palmyra," *PEFQS* 60 (1928) 100-107.

William Fairweather, "Concerning the Jewish Dispersion," *JR* 9 (1929) 224-236.

W. J. Phythian-Adams, "Early Israelite History: A New Light from Archaeology," *CQR* 114 (1932) 43-59.

Norman Bentwich, "Of Jews and Hebraism in the Greek Anthology," *JQR, N.S.,* 23 (1932-33) 181-186.

E. Silberschlag, "The Earliest Record of Jews in Asia Minor," *JBL* 52 (1933) 66-77.

T. H. Robinson, "Some Economic and Social Factors in the History of Israel. I. In External Relations," *ET* 45 (1933-34) 264-269.

T. H. Robinson, "Some Economic and Social Factors in the History of Israel. II. In Domestic Relations," *ET* 45 (1933-34) 294-300.

‡*Robert H. Pfeiffer, "The History, Religion, and Literature of Israel. Research in the Old Testament, 1914-1925," *HTR* 27 (1934) 241-325.

*Solomon Zeitlin, "The Jews: Race, Nation or Religion—Which?" *JQR, N.S.,* 26 (1935-36) 313-347.

*Erwin R. Goodenough, "Archaeology and Jewish History," *JBL* 55 (1936) 211-220.

C. D. Matthews, "Significance of Nomadism for Hebrew Origins," *JBL* 57 (1938) vi.

*Michael J. Gruenthaner, "The Jews as a Race," *TFUQ* 14 (1939) 36-51.

*G. Ernest Wright, "Hebrew Origins in the Background of Near Eastern History," *BA* 3 (1940) 27-40. [1. The Palestine Hill Country; 2. People of the Desert and People of the Town; The Fall of Jericho; The Fall of other Cities; Some Historical Conclusions]

*Solomon Zeitlin, "Rashi and the Rabbinate, The Struggle Between the Secular and Religious Forces for Leadership," *JQR, N.S.,* 31 (1940-41) 1-58.

*Nelson Glueck, "How Archaeology Has Contributed to Our Knowledge of the Bible and the Jew," *YCCAR* 51 (1941) 299-327. {Discussion by [Samuel B.] Freehof, p. 327; Nelson Glueck, pp. 327-330; [Joshua] Trachtenburg, p. 327; [Israel] Harburg, p. 328; [Ephriam] Frisch, p. 328; [David] Philipson, p. 328; Max Raisin, p. 329; Leo Shubow, p. 329; Clifton Herby Levy, p. 330; [Ahron] Opher, p. 330; W. Gunter Plaut, p. 330}

*Isaiah Sonne, "The Use of Rabbinic Literature as Historical Sources," *JQR, N.S.,* 36 (1945-46) 147-169.

*Alexander Marx, "The Importance of the Geniza for Jewish History," *PAAJR* 16 (1946-47) 183-204.

*A. Guillaume, "The Habiru, the Hebrews, and the Arabs, *PEQ* 78 (1946) 64-85.

*A. Guillaume, "The Ḫābiru, the Hebrews, and the Arabs," *Man* 47 (1947) #77.

Isaac Heinemann, "The Relationship Between the Jewish People and their Land in Hellenistic-Jewish Literature," *Zion* 13&14 (1948-49) I.

*Aage Bentzen, "Biblical Criticism, History of Israel, and Old Testament Theology," *EQ* 23 (1951) 85-88.

*B. Dinaburg, "Zion and Jerusaelm: Their Role in the Historic Consciousness of Israel," *Zion* 16 (1951) #1/2, I-II.

‡*Wilbur M. Smith, "Some Recently Published (1950-1952) Bibliographies in Books of Biblical Interpretation, Theology, and Church History," *FLB* #17-18 (1953) 3-13. [The Jews - Israel, p. 13]

*Solomon Zeitlin, "The Names Hebrew, Jew and Israel: A Historical Study," *JQR, N.S.,* 43 (1952-53) 365-379.

W. H. Gispen, "The Old Testament on Israel," *FUQ* 3 (1954-55) 248-264.

B. Z. Lurie, "On the History of the Jewish Community of Damascus from the Babylonian Exile to the Conclusion of the Talmud," *EI* 4 (1956) VII-VIII.

*Arie Kindler, "Coins as Documents for Israel's Ancient History," *A&S* 2 (1957) #2/3, 225-236.

David Diringer, "The origins of the Hebrew people," *RDSO* 32 (1957) 301-313.

Ellis Rivkin, "The Utilization of Non-Jewish Sources for the Reconstruction of Jewish History," *JQR, N.S.,* 48 (1957-58) 183-203.

*G. Ernest Wright, "Israelites, Samaria and Iron Age Chronology," *BASOR* #155 (1959) 13-29.

*John Gray, "Archaeology and the History of Israel," *LQHR* 184 (1959) 13-21.

*G. Ernest Wright, "Modern Issues in Biblical Studies. History and the Patriarchs," *ET* 71 (1959-60) 292-296.

Y. Gutman, "Jewish History in the Light of Papyrology," *JQR, N.S.,* 50 (1959-60) 279-287.

I. Ben-zvi, "The Origins of the Settlement of Jewish Tribes in Arabia," *EI* 6 (1960) 35*-37*.

*Jakob J. Petuchowski, "Diaspora Judaism—An Abnormality? The Testimony of History," *Jud* 9 (1960) 17-28.

*Gerhard Von Rad, "History and the Patriarchs," *ET* 72 (1960-61) 213-216.

*John C. L. Gibson, "Observations on Some Important Ethnic Terms in the Pentateuch," *JNES* 20 (1961) 217-238. [Hebrews, pp. 234-237]

Jacob Neusner, "The Jews in Pagan Armenia," *JAOS* 84 (1964) 230-240.

*Sami S. Ahmed, "The Jewish Colony at Elephantine," *IR* 22 (1965) #2, 11-20.

*R. Alan Cole, "Wandering Arameans. How far were the Patriarchs truly nomadic, when in Mesopotamia?" *TTCA* 2 (1965) 10-15. *[A Contribution towards a Social History of Israel]*

*B[enjamin] Mazar, "The Philistines and the Rise of Israel and Tyre," *PIASH* 1 (1967) #7, 1-22.

Solomon Zeitlin, "The Need for a Systematic Jewish History," *JQR, N.S.* 58 (1967-68) 261-273.

E. C. B. MacLaurin, "The Beginnings of the Israelite Diaspora," *AJBA* 1 (1968-71) #4, 82-95.

Ben-Zion Dinur, "Jewish History—Its Uniqueness and Continuity," *JWH* 11 (1968-69) 15-29.

*Aaron Hendin, "Jewish History as Portrayed in Coins," *Shekel* 2 (1969) #1, 25; #2, 24-25; #3, 15, 22; #4, 8-9, 25.

*R. Laird Harris, "Problem Periods in Old Testament History," *SR* 16 (1969-70) 3-26. [I. The Patriarchal Age; II. The Conquest; III. The Postexilic Period]

§56 *2.2.1 Israel in Egypt*

*†Anonymous, "Allwood's Literary Antiquities of Greece," *BCQTR* 15 (1800) 539-549, 608-618; 16 (1800) 65-77. [*Israel in Egypt*, pp. 612-613, 66-73]

Anonymous, "Increase of the Israelites in Egypt," *JSL, 1st Ser.*, 3 (1849) 170-171.

O. Seeleys, "Israel in Egypt," *JSL, 2nd Ser.*, 7 (1854-55) 398-402.

Anonymous, "Studies on the Bible, No. II. *Israel in Egypt*," *DQR* 2 (1862) 445-472.

B. W. Savile, "Israel in Egypt," *JSL, 4th Ser.*, 6 (1864-65) 1-26.

*H. Moule, "Israel in Egypt: The Period of their Sojourn and their numbers at the Exodus and in the Wilderness," *JTVI* 5 (1870-71) 378-393. [Discussion, pp. 394-441]

B. W. Savile, "On the Evidence of the Egyptian Monuments to the Sojourn of Israel in Egypt," *JTVI* 6 (1872-73) 93-107, 119-125. [Discussion, pp. 107-119]

Ernest de Bensen, "The Times of Israel's Servitude and Sojourning in Egypt," *SBAP* 3 (1880-81) 79-80. (Remarks by Charles James Ball, pp. 80-81; by Villiers Stuart, pp. 81-82]

*John Campbell, "The Pharaoh of Joseph," *SBAP* 3 (1880-81) 87. [Ra-*aa-peh-ti*]

William C. Wilson, "What Says Egypt of Israel?" *CR* 42 (1883) 137-157.

Alexander W. Thayer, "The Bene Israel in Egypt," *CR* 48 (1886) 143-163.

Albert A. Isaacs, "Israel in Egypt," *EN* 2 (1890) 193-197.

H. B. Pratt, "On the Length of the Sojourn in Egypt," *PQ* 4 (1890) 433-442.

*A[lexander] W. Thayer, "Critical Theology. The Hebrews in Egypt and the Exodus," *URRM* 33 (1890) 253-268. *(Review)*

Arthur C. Hervey, "The Sojourn of the Israelites in Egypt," *Exp, 4th Ser.,* 8 (1893) 446-455.

C. H. Toy, "Israel in Egypt," *NW* 2 (1893) 121-141.

*A. A. Berle, "Semitic and Oriental Note. Israel in Egypt," *BS* 53 (1896) 745-747.

*W. W. Moore, "The Hyksos and the Hebrews," *USR* 8 (1896-97) 263-266.

*James Orr, "Israel in Egypt and the Exodus. With Reference to Prof. Flinders Petrie's Recent Discovery," *Exp, 5th Ser.,* 5 (1897) 161-177.

*W. W. Moore, "Israel's Attitude Towards Canaan During the Egyptian Sojourn," *USR* 9 (1897) 188-193.

W. W. Moore, "The Period of the Israelitist Sojourn in Egypt, in the Light of Archaeological Research," *PQ* 13 (1899) 24-43.

John D. Davis, "Israel in Egypt," *CFL, N.S.,* 4 (1901) 251-253.

William G. Moorehead, "Duration of Israel's Sojourn in Egypt," *CFL, N.S.,* 4 (1901) 278-283.

*J. V. Prasek, "The Sojourn in Goshen and the Exodus," *ET* 16 (1904-05) 223-225.

B. D. Eerdmans, "The Hebrews in Egypt," *Exp, 7th Ser.,* 6 (1908) 193-207.

Colin Campbell, "The Oppression of the Children of Israel from an Egyptian Standpoint," *GUOST* 4 (1913-22) 56-58.

*Joseph Offord, "A New Inscription Concerning the Jews in Egypt," *PEFQS* 46 (1914) 45-46.

*I. G. Matthews, "The Hebrew Bondage and Its Influence on Hebrew Morals," *CJRT* 1 (1924) 300-306.

A. Cowper Field, "The Evidence in the Pentateuch of the Sojourn in Egypt," *JTVI* 68 (1936) 92-113, 118-123. [(Discussion, pp. 113-114.) (Communications by E. Cecil Curwen, p. 114; A. S. Yahuda, pp. 114-118)]

C. A. Wilson, "The Local Colour of the Bible Record: Israel in Egypt," *AT* 1 (1956-57) #1, 4-6.

*C. A. Wilson, "The Local Colour of the Bible Records: Part 3. The Israelites in Egypt: The Egyptian Titles Used," *AT* 1 (1956-57) #3, 6-8.

*John Rea, "The Time of the Oppression and the Exodus," *BETS* 3 (1960) 58-66.

*John Rea, "The Time of the Oppression and the Exodus," *GJ* 2 (1961) #1, 5-14.

Philip J. King, "'When Israel was a Child. ,'" *BibT* #5 (1963) 286-293.

§57 *2.2.2 Israel's Conquest of Palestine*

*( ) D., "The Canaanitish Wars. How are the Canaanitish Wars to be Reconciled with the Principles of Christianity?" *CRB* 13 (1848) 345-365.

*Claude R. Conder, "The First Traveller in Palestine," *PEFQS* 8 (1876) 74-88.

*Claude R. Conder, "Palestine Before Joshua from the Records of Egyptian Conquest," *PEFQS* 8 (1876) 87-97, 140-148.

*Claude R. Conder, "Samaritan Topography," *PEFQS* 8 (1876) 182-197.

*E. P. Evans, "Biblical Exegesis and Historical Criticism," *URRM* 24 (1885) 237-254. *[The Conquest of Palestine]*

*Carl Heinrich Cornill, "The Conquest of Palestine and the Founding of the Kingdom of Israel," *OC* 3 (1889-90) 1643-1647. *(Trans. by γνλν)*

*C[laude] R. Conder, "Shishak's List," *PEFQS* 25 (1893) 245-246.

*W. Garden Blaikie, "The Part of Judah in the Conquest of Caanan," *ET* 5 (1893-94) 521-523.

*Martin L. Rouse, "Procopius's African Monument of Joshua's Conquest of Canaan: *Narrative of a visit to the Site*," *JTVI* 34 (1902) 234-250. (Discussion, pp. 251-252)

(Mrs.) Louise Seymour Houghton, "When Did Israel Enter Canaan?" *BS* 61 (1904) 496-510.

*L. W. Batten, "The Conquest of Northern Canaan: Joshua xi. 1-9; Judges iv-v," *JBL* 24 (1905) 31-40.

*K. T. Frost, "The Siege of Jericho and the Strategy of the Exodus," *ET* 18 (1906-07) 464-467.

Lewis Bayles Paton, "Israel's Conquest of Canaan," *JBL* 32 (1913) 1-53.

*Harold M. Wiener, "The Exodus and the Conquest of the Negeb," *BS* 76 (1919) 468-474.

*George A. Barton, "The Habiri of the El-Amarna Tablets and the Hebrew Conquest of Palestine," *JBL* 48 (1929) 144-148.

*Harold M. Wiener, "The Conquest Narrative," *JPOS* 9 (1929) 1-26.

S. Yeivin, "Archaeology and the Israelite Invasion," *PEFQS* 62 (1930) 226-227.

*Frank Richards, "The Foundations of Bible History," *LQHR* 156 (1932) 307-317. [II. The Israelite Invasion, pp. 312-317]

*T. H. Robinson, "The Exodus and the Conquest of Palestine," *Theo* 25 (1932) 267-275.

Abraham Bergman, "The Israelite Occupaton of Eastern Palestine," *JAOS* 54 (1934) 169-177.

*B[eatrice] L. Goff, "The Lost Jahwistic Account of the Conquest of Canaan," *JBL* 53 (1934) x.

*Beatrice L. Goff, "The Lost Jahwistic Account of the Conquest of Canaan," *JBL* 53 (1934) 241-249.

W[illiam] F[oxwell] Albright, "Archaeology and the Date of the Hebrew Conquest of Palestine," *BASOR* #58 (1935) 1-18.

*W. J. Phythian-Adams, "Mirage in the Wilderness," *PEFQS* 67 (1935) 69-78; 114-127. [I. The Settlement in Canaan; II. Horeb and Kadesh-barnea]

Theophile J. Meek, "The Israelite Conquest of Ephraim," *BASOR* #61 (1936)17-19.

Merton French, "The Israelite Tribal Invasions during the Late Bronze Age," *JBL* 55 (1936) vi.

W[illiam] F[oxwell] Albright, "The Israelite Conquest of Canaan in the Light of Archaeology," *BASOR* #74 (1939) 11-23.

G. Ernest Wright, "Epic of Conquest," *BA* 3 (1940) 25-27.

*W[illiam] F[oxwell] Albright, "A Case of Lèse-Majesté in Pre-Israelite Lachish, with some Remarks on the Israelite Conquest," *BASOR* #87 (1942) 32-38.

O. R. Sellers, "From Joshua to Ehud," *JBL* 66 (1947) vi.

*J. Simons, "Two Connected Problems Relating to the Israelite Settlement in Transjordan," *PEQ* 79 (1947) 27-39, 87-101. [I. The meaning of מִן + a Proper name in Dt. III, 16 and some other Geographical Texts; II. 'From Arnon unto Yabboq']

G. Ernest Wright, "Holy War in Israel," *McQ* 6 (1952-53) #4, 3-6. *[Conquest of Palestine]*

*G. Ernest Wright, "Hazor and the Conquest of Canaan," *BA* 18 (1955) 106-108.

Y[ohanan] Aharoni, "Problems of the Israelite Conquest in the light of Archaeological Discoveries," *A&S* 2 (1957) #2/3, 131-150.

Mary Neely, "*The Exodus:* Through the Transjordan," *AT* 3 (1958-59) #2, 7-9.

*Edward F. Campbell Jr., "The Amarna Letters and the Amarna Period," *BA* 23 (1960) 2-22. [The Amarna Letters and the Israelite Conquest, pp. 10-12]

*Walter R. Roehrs, "The Conquest of Canaan According to Joshua and Judges," *CTM* 31 (1960) 746-760.

John Rea, "New Light on the Wilderness Journey and the Conquest," *GJ* 2 (1961) #2, 5-13.

George E. Mendenhall, "The Hebrew Conquest of Palestine," *BA* 25 (1962) 66-87.

A. J. Mattill Jr., "Representative Universalism and the Conquest of Canaan," *CTM* 35 (1964) 8-17.

Paul W. Lapp, "The Conquest of Palestine in the Light of Archaeology," *CTM* 37 (1967) 283-300.

*M. Weinfeld, "The Period of the Conquest and of the Judges as seen by the earlier and later sources," *VT* 17 (1967) 93-113.

*P. C. Craigie, "The Conquest and Early Hebrew Poetry," *TB* #20 (1969) 76-94.

*R. Laird Harris, "Problem Periods in Old Testament History," *SR* 16 (1969-70) 3-26. [II. The Conquest, pp. 9-18]

§58 *2.2.3 Pre-Exilic Israel - General Studies (includes Period of the Judges)*

*Anonymous, "A Bird's Eye View of the Church Under the Patriarchs and Moses," *SPR* 28 (1877) 415-436.

J. B. Walker, "Ancient Judea and Its Institutions," *MQR, 3rd Ser.,* 4 (1888) 63-75.

*Carl Heinrich Cornill, "Rise of the People of Israel," *OC* 3 (1889-90) 1619-1620. *(Trans by γνλν)*

C[laude] R. Conder, "The Earliest Ages of Hebrew History," *SRL* 22 (1893) 274-292.

Ira M. Price, "Important Movements in Israel Prior to 1000 B.C.," *BW* 7 (1896) 472-482.

Edward T. Harper, "Important Movements in Israel Prior to the Establishment of the Kingdom," *BW* 7 (1896) 483-496.

[W. M.] Flinders Petrie, "The Period of the Judges," *SBAP* 18 (1896) 243-249.

C[arl] H[einrich] Cornill, "History of the People of Israel. From the Beginning to the Destruction of Jerusalem," *OC* 11 (1897) 483-497. [II. Israel Prior to the Origin of the National Kingdom] *(Trans. by W. H. Carruth)*

Charles Foster Kent, "The History of Israel to the Founding of the Kingdom," *BW* 28 1906) 374-387.

A. H. McNeile, "Israel in the Time of the Judges," *ICMM* 3 (1906-07) 141-161.

*George S. Goodspeed, "The Men Who Made Israel," *BW* 30 (1907) 266-274. [The Judges and the Preparation for the Kingdom]

Daniel S. Gregory, "The International Lessons in Their Historical and Literary Setting. Lessons on the Educative Struggle of Elijah and Elisha to Save Israel," *CFL, 3rd Ser.*, 14 (1911-12) 109-120.

Yehezkel Kaufmann, "Traditions Concerning Early Israelite History in Canaan," *SH* 8 (1961) 303-334.

§59 *2.2.4 Studies concerning the 12 Tribes of Israel*

*(   ) Newbold, "On the Mountainous Country, the portion of Asher, between the Coasts of Tyre and Sidon, and the Jordan," *JRAS* (1850) 348-371.

*W. Robertson Smith, "Animal worship and animal tribes among the Arabs and the Old Testament," *JP* 19 (1880) 75-100.

*Joseph Jacobs, "Are there Totem-Clans in the Old Testament?" *SBAP* 8 (1885-86) 39-41.

Edmund Davys, "The Rivalry between Ephraim and Judah and its Consequences," *EN* 1 (1889) 289-294.

Carl Heinrich Cornill, "The Migrations of the Tribes of Israel," *OC* 3 (1889-90) 1633-1637. *(Trans by γνλν)*

*W. Garden Blaikie, "The Part of Judah in the Conquest of Caanan," *ET* 5 (1893-94) 521-523.

*C[laude] R. Conder, "Notes on the Antiquities of the Book of Judges," *PEFQS* 31 (1899) 162. *[The Levites]*

*M. Berlin, "Notes on Genealogies of the Tribe of Levi in 1 Chron. XXIII-XXVI," *JQR* 12 (1899-1900) 291-298.

James Oscar Boyd, "The Simeonites in Arabian Tradition," *CFL, N.S.,* 2 (1900) 175-176.

*J[ohn] D. D[avis], "Editorial Notes," *CFL, N.S.,* 5 (1902) 191-192. [Tribes Individualized in the O.T.; The Principle not Ignorable in Gen. v. and xi.] *(Editorial)*

G. Buchanan Gray, "The Lists of the Twelve Tribes, *Exp, 6th Ser.,* 5 (1902) 225-240.

*Ed. König, "'A Fateful Dogma'," *ET* 16 (1904-05) 332-334. *[The 12 Tribes]*

*Caleb Hauser, "Cities in the Negeb, and Tribal Boundaries," *PEFQS* 38 (1906) 213-221.

*Geo. St. Clair, "Israel in Camp: A Study," *JTS* 8 (1906-07) 185-217. *[The Origin of the 12 Tribes]*

Stanley A. Cook, "Simeon and Levi: The Problem of the Old Testament," *AJT* 13 (1909) 370-388.

*M. H. Segal, "The Settlement of Manasseh East of the Jordan," *PEFQS* 50 (1918) 124-131.

*W[illiam] F[oxwell] Albright, "The Topography of the Tribe of Issachar," *ZAW* 44 (1926) 225-236.

J. A. Maynard, "The rights and revenues of the tribe of Levi," *JSOR* 14 (1930) 11-17.

Abraham Bergman, "The Israelite Tribe of Half-Manasseh," *JPOS* 16 (1936) 224-254.

*Dwight F. Putman, "War and Religion: An Unholy Alliance," *LCQ* 9 (1936) 197-205. [1. War and Religion in the Tribe of Dan, pp. 197-200]

*P[atrick] P. McKenna, "The Hill Country of Gad," *IER, 5th Ser.,* 50 (1937) 164-173.

Leroy Waterman, "Some Determining Factors in the Northward Progress of Levi," *JAOS* 57 (1937) 375-380.

*H. H. Rowley, "The Danite Migration to Laish," *ET* 51 (1939-40) 466-471.

*H. H. Rowley, "Early Levite History and the Question of Exodus," *JNES* 3 (1944) 73-78.

C. Umhau Wolf, "Tribes or Individuals? *A Study in the Problem of the Development of the Twelve Tribes,*" *AugQ* 24 (1945) 320-326.

C. Umhau Wolf, "Some Remarks on the Tribes and Clans of Israel," *JQR, N.S.,* 36 (1945-46) 287-295.

C. Umhau Wolf, "Terminology of Israel's Tribal Organization," *JBL* 65 (1946) 45-49.

H. L. Ginsberg, "The Eleven Tribes," *JBL* 67 (1948) xii.

*Robert North, "Israel's Tribes and Today's Frontier," *CBQ* 16 (1954) 146-153.

*Z. Kallai-Kleinmann, "Notes on the Topography of Benjamin," *IEJ* 6 (1956) 180-187.

W[illiam] F[oxwell] Albright, "The Biblical Tribe of Massa' and some congeners," *SOOG* 1 (1956) 1-14.

L. M. Muntingh, "The Period of the Judges," *OTW* 2 (1959) 29-34.

*A. H. van Zyl, "The Relationship of the Israelite Tribes to the Indigenous Population of Canaan according to the Book of Judges," *OTW* 2 (1959) 51-60.

*A[braham] Malamat, "Mari and the Bible: Some Patterns of Tribal Organization and Institutions," *JAOS* 82 (1962) 143-150.

H[arry] M. Orlinsky, "The Tribal System of Israel and Related Groups in the Period of the Judges," *OA* 1 (1962) 11-20.

*Isaiah Rackovsky, "Tribe and Family," *Trad* 7 (1964-66) #3, 15-20.

*Martin A. Cohen, "The Role of the Shilonite Priesthood in the United Monarchy of Ancient Israel," *HUCA* 36 (1965) 59-98. [Excursus on the Origin of the Tribe of Judah, pp. 94-98.]

*B. D. Rahtjen, "Philistine and Hebrew Amphictyonies," *JNES* 24 (1965) 100-104.

*J. J. Groen, "Historical and Genetic Studies on the Twelve Tribes of Israel and Their Relation to the Present Ethnic Composition of the Jewish People," *JQR, NS.,* 58 (1967-68) 1-13.

*B. J. van der Merwe, "Judah in the Pentateuch," *TEP* 1 (1968) 37-52.

*Yigael Yadin, "'And Dan, why did he remain in ships?' (Judges, V, 17)," *AJBA* 1 (1968-71) #1, 9-23.

§60 *2.2.4.1 The Jerahmeel Theory*

*T. K. Cheyne, "From Isaiah to Ezra. A Study of Ethanites and Jerahmeelites," *AJT* 5 (1901) 433-444.

*Hugo Winckler, "North Arabia and the Bible: A Defense," *HJ* 2 (1903-04) 571-590. *[Jerahmeel]*

Henry Preserved Smith, "Israel or Jerahmeel?" *AJT* 11 (1907) 553-568.

W. W. Everts, "The 'Jerahmeel' of Professor Cheyne," *CFL, 3rd Ser.,* 7 (1907) 350.

*Nathaniel Schmidt, "The 'Jerahmeel' Theory and the Historic Importance of the Negeb," *HJ* 6 (1907-08) 322-342.

*†T. Witton Davies, "Traditions and Beliefs of Ancient Israel," *RTP* 3 (1907-08) 689-708. [(Subtitle: †"The Early Traditions of Genesis," pp. 697-706) *(Jerahmeel)*]

T. K. Cheyne, "The 'Jerahmeel Theory': A Mistaken Name for a Genuine Thing," *HJ* 7 (1908-09) 132-151.

H. J. Dukinfield Astley, "The 'Jerahmeel Theory'," *HJ* 7 (1908-09) 441-443.

T. K. Cheyne, "Criticisms of the North Arabian Theory," *HJ* 7 (1908-09) 673-675.

H. J. Dukinfield Astley, "Some Strictures on the 'Jerahmeel Theory'," *CFL, 3rd Ser.,* 12 (1910) 168-170.

§61 *2.2.4.2 The Habiru / Hebrew Question*

C[laude] R. Conder, "Notes by Major Conder. VI. The Khabiri or Abiri," *PEFQS* 23 (1891) 72.

*William Hayes Ward, "The Latest Palestinian Discoveries," *HR* 24 (1892) 403-407. *[Habiru]*

W. W. Moore, "Who were the Habiri?" *USR* 6 (1894-95) 273-278.

George A. Reisner, "Ḫabiri in the El-Amarna Tablets," *JBL* 16 (1897) 143-145.

*W. M. McPheeters, "Light on Early Egyptian History," *CFL, O.S.,* 3 (1899)151-153. *[Habiru]*

Ed. König, "On the Ḫabiri Question," *ET* 11 (1899-1900) 238-240.

A. H. Sayce, "On the Khabiri Question," *ET* 11 (1899-1900) 377.

*T. G. P[inches], "Talmudische und midrashische Parallelen zum Babylonischen Weltschöpfungsepos," *JRAS* (1904) 369-370. [Habiri, p. 370]

Joseph Offord, "Archaeological Notes on Jewish Antiquities. XIV. *The Habiri of the Tell-el-Amarna Tablets and the Hebrews,*" *PEFQS* 48 (1916) 140-141.

S[tephen] H. Langdon, "The Habiru and the Hebrews. New Material in the Problem," *ET* 31 (1919-20) 324-329.

W. H. Whitlock, "Who were the Habiri? *MR* 103 (1920) 971-973.

A. H. Sayce, "The Khabiri," *ET* 33 (1921-22) 43-44.

*George A. Barton, "The Habiri of the El-Amarna Tablets and the Hebrew Conquest of Palestine," *JBL* 48 (1929) 144-148.

Edward Chiera, "Habiru and Hebrews," *AJSL* 49 (1932-33) 115-124.

Julius Lewy, "Ḫābirū and Hebrews," *HUCA* 14 (1939) 587-623.

Julius Lewy, "A New Parallel between Ḫābirū and Hebrews," *HUCA* 15 (1940) 47-58.

*H. H. Rowley, "Ras Shamra and the Habiru Question," *PEQ* 72 (1940) 90-94.

J. W. Jack, "New Light on the Habiru-Hebrew Question," *PEQ* 72 (1940) 95-115.

Eugen Täubler, "The First Mention of Israel," *PAAJR* 12 (1942) 115-120.

H. H. Rowley, "Habiru and Hebrews," *PEQ* 74 (1942) 41-53.

*A. Guillaume, "The Habiru, The Hebrews, and the Arabs," *PEQ* 78 (1946) 64-85.

*A. Guillaume, "The Ḫābiru, the Hebrews, and the Arabs," *Man* 47 (1947) #77.

*T. Säve-Söderbergh, "The *ʿprw* as Vintagers in Egypt," *OrS* 1 (1952) 5-14.

Moshe Greenberg, "On the Habiru Problem," *Tarbiẓ* 24 (1954-55) #4, I-II.

Meredith G. Kline, "The Ḫa-BI-ru—Kin or Foe of Israel?" *WTJ* 19 (1956-57) 1-24.

Meredith G. Kline, "The Ḫa-BI-ru—Kin or Foe of Israel?—II.," *WTJ* 19 (1956-57) 129-140.

Meredith G. Kline, "The Ḫa-BI-ru—Kin or Foe of Israel?—III.," *WTJ* 20 (1957-58) 46-70.

‡Mary P. Gray, "The Ḫâbirū-Hebrew Problem in the Light of the Source Material Available at Present," *HUCA* 29 (1958) 135-202. *[Good Bibliography]*

*J. P. Oberholzer, "The 'ibirim in I Samuel," *OTW* 3 (1960) 54. *[Habiru]*

*Shemuel Yeiven, "The Age of the Patriarchs," *RDSO* 38 (1963) 227-302. [I. - *The Patriarchs and the Ḫab|piru,* pp. 277-285]

§62 *2.2.5 The United Kingdom*

D. G. Lyon, "Sketch of Babylonian and Assyrian History with Special Reference to Palestine Down to the Division of the Kingdom," *BW* 7 (1896) 425-437.

Lewis B[ayles] Paton, "The Social, Industrial, and Poltical Life of Israel Between 950 B.C. and 621 B.C.," *BW* 10 (1897) 24-32.

*Carl Heinrich Cornill, "The Conquest of Palestine and the Founding of the Kingdom of Israel," *OC* 3 (1889-90) 1643-1647. *(Trans. by γνλν)*

C[arl] H[einrich] Cornill, "History of the People of Israel. From the Beginning to the Destruction of Jerusalem," *OC* 11 (1897) 542-548. [III. The National Kingdom.—Saul and David] *(Trans. by W. H. Carruth)*

*Walter R. Roehrs, "Recent Studies in the Chronology of the Period of the Kings," *CTM* 18 (1947) 738-746.

John Bright, "The Age of King David: A Study in the Institutional History of Israel," *USR* 53 (1941-42) 87-109.

Howard F. Vos, "The Glories of the Reign of Solomon," *BS* 110 (1953) 321-332.

*Roland E. Murphy, "Israel and Moab in the Ninth Century B.C.," *CBQ* 15 (1953) 409-417.

*S. Yeivin, "Religious and Cultural Trends in Jerusalem under the Davidic Dynasty," *VT* 3 (1953) 149-166.

Merrill F. Unger, "Archaeology and the Reign of David," *BS* 111 (1954) 11-26.

Merrill F. Unger, "Archaeology and Solomon's Empire," *BS* 111 (1954) 112-124.

Melvin A. Stuckey, "The Solomonic Era and Archaeology," *TUSR* 4 (1954-56) 68-77.

*Stanley M. Horton, "Critical Note: A Suggestion Concerning the Chronology of Solomon's Reign," *BETS* 4 (1961) 3-4.

*William R. Griffiths, "Covenant and Charisma as Related to the Establishment and Dissolution of the United Monarchy of Israel," *IR* 24 (1967) #3, 43-50.

Walter Brueggemann, "Israel's Moment of Freedom," *BibT* #42 (1969) 2917-2925.

Gordon H. Lovik, "Events during the Reign of Saul," *CCBQ* 12 (1969) #3, 11-15.

§63 *2.2.6 The Divided Kingdom - General Studies*

*Daniel Kerr, "Chronology of the Kingdoms of Israel and Judah," *JSL, 1st Ser.,* 4 (1849) 241-257.

*N. Rouse, "Chronology of the Kings of Judah and Israel," *JSL, 2nd Ser.,* 1 (1851-52) 217-220.

*John D. Davis, "The Chronology of the Divided Kingdom," *PRR* 2 (1891) 98-114.

George S. Goodspeed, "A Sketch of Assyrian History, with Special Reference to Palestine, from the Division of the Kingdom (Illustrated)," *BW* 9 (1897) 401-412.

Ira M. Price, "Important Events in Israel, 950-621 B.C.," *BW* 9 (1897) 429-442.

C[arl] H[einrich] Cornill, "History of the People of Israel. From the Beginning to the Destruction of Jerusalem," *OC* 11 (1897) 585-601. [IV. Solomon.-The Division of the Kingdom. —The Early Years of the Divided Kingdom] *(Trans. by W. H. Carruth)*

Edward T. Harper, "Historical Movements in Israel from the Reform of Josiah to the Completion of the Second Temple," *BW* 11 (1898) 382-396.

Oscar L. Joseph, "An Indian Summer in the History of Israel," *MR* 92 (1910) 769-773. [*cir.* 782-741 B.C.]

*E. Power, "Another view on the line of demarcation between the kingdoms of Juda and Israel," *B* 7 (1926) 87-95.

Herbert Parzen, "A Chapter of Israelitish History. The Division of the Kingdom," *BS* 85 (1928) 188-223.

*Edwin R. Thiele, "The Chronology of the Kings of Judah and Israel," *JNES* 3 (1944) 137-186.

*W[illiam] F[oxwell] Albright, "The Chronology of the Divided Monarchy of Israel," *BASOR* #100 (1945) 16-22.

*W[illiam] F[oxwell] Albright, "New Light from Egypt on the Chronology and History of Israel and Judah," *BASOR* #130 (1953) 4-11.

*Erwin R. Thiele, "A comparison of the chronological data of Israel and Judah," *VT* 4 (1954) 185-195.

*Walter R. Wifall Jr., "The Chronology of the Divided Monarchy of Israel," *ZAW* 80 (1968) 319-337.

§64 *2.2.6.1 The Northern Kingdom & Assyrian Captivity (includes articles on the so-called Ten "Lost" Tribes of Israel)*

*T. M. Dickinson, "An Inquiry into the Fate of the Ten Tribes of Israel after the Fall of Samaria; with a View of the History of the Assyrian Empire at that period, as derived from a comparison of what is recorded on the Subject in the Histories of the Jews, the Greeks, and the Persians," *JRAS* (1837) 217-253.

*( ) G., "The Sythian Dominion in Asia (as Reported by Herodotus) in its Connexion with Josiah's Exercise of Sovereign Power in the Territory of the Ten Tribes," *JSL, 2nd Ser.,* 4 (1853) 1-34.

A. M. Osborn, "Were the Ten Tribes of Israel Ever Lost?" *MR* 37 (1855) 419-440.

G. B., "The Lost Tribes of Israel," *JSL, 3rd Ser.,* 2 (1855-56) 179-187.

Anonymous, "The Lost Ten Tribes," *PQR* 10 (1861-62) 652-669.

( ) G., "The Ten Tribes," *JSL, 4th Ser.,* 1 (1862) 195-204.

John H. Shedd, "The Remnants of the Ten Tribes," *PQPR* 2 (1873) 308-319.

Anonymous, "Anglo-Israelite Theory," *BFER* 35 (1886) 65-79.

C[laude] R. C[onder], "The Ten Tribes," *PEFQS* 20 (1888) 144-150.

A. Neubauer, "Where are the Ten Tribes?" *JQR* 1 (1888-89) 14-28, 95-114, 185-201, 408-423.

L. N. Dembitz, "The Lost Tribes," *AR* 12 (1889) 169-185.

J. M. Boland, "The Lost Tribes of Israel," *MQR, 3rd Ser.,* 11 (1891-92) 104-110.

Albert A. Isaacs, "The Anglo-Israelite Theory," *EN* 4 (1892) 97-102, 145-151.

*W. Francis Ainsworth, "The Two Captivities. Habor and Chebar," *SBAP* 15 (1892-93) 70-76.

Marcus N. Adler, "Jewish Pilgrims to Palestine," *PEFQS* 26 (1894) 288-300. (Note by C. R. Conder, *PEFQS* 27 (1895) p. 87) *[The Ten Tribes]*

J. F. McCurdy, "Light on Scriptural Texts from Recent Discoveries. The Kingdom of the 'Ten Tribes'," *HR* 32 (1896) 218-220.

J. F. McCurdy, "Light on Scriptural Texts from Recent Discoveries. The Fate of the People of Northern Israel," *HR* 32 (1896) 311-314.

*Daniel S. Gregory, "The International Lessons in Their Literary and Historical Setting," *CFL, 3rd Ser.,* 1 (1904) 725-733. [Captivity of the Ten Tribes, pp. 729-730]

Max Kellner, "The Fall of the Kingdom of Israel," *BW* 25 (1905) 8-19.

William Cowper Conant, "'The Lost Tribes'—A Hypothesis," *CFL, 3rd Ser.,* 2 (1905) 154-156.

*C. H. W. Johns, "The Lost Ten Tribes of Israel," *SBAP* 30 (1908) 107-115, 137-141.

R. M. Lithgow, "An Important Discovery," *ET* 22 (1910-11) 520-521. *[Exile of the Northern Tribes]*

Henry Proctor, "The Migration of Dan," *AAOJ* 33 (1911) #2, 22-23. *[The Lost Tribes]*

F. J. Foakes-Jackson, "A Consideration of the History of Northern Israel," *Exp, 8th Ser.,* 4 (1912) 451-459.

F. J. Foakes-Jackson, "Our Debt to Northern Israel," *ICMM* 9 (1912-13) 292-299.

Harold M. Wiener, "The Reunions of Israel and Judah," *LQHR* 138 (1922) 102-104.

*William Rosenau, "Ezekiel 37:15-28. What Happened to the Ten Tribes," *HUCA, Jubilee Volume* (1925) 79-88.

*W. W. Everts, "The Dispersion and the Restoration of the Twelve Hebrew Tribes," *BS* 84 (1927) 465-470.

John Mocure, "The Lost Ten Tribes of Israel," *R&E* 24 (1927) 321-323.

V. Burch, "The Myth of the Lost Tribes of Israel," *CQR* 111 (1930-31) 293-305.

Harry Rimmer, "The Anglo-Saxon People and the Ten Lost Tribes of Israel," *CFL, 3rd Ser.,* 44 (1938) 10-15.

S. Spiegel, "Unrecorded Deportations," *JBL* 58 (1939) xvi.

H. G. May, "The Ten Lost Tribes," *BA* 6 (1943) 55-60. *[Anglo-Israelism; The Deportation of Israel]*

*B[enjamin] Maisler, "The Israelite Exiles in Gozan," *BIES* 15 (1949-50) #3/4, III.

†J. M. T. Barton, "The Northern Tribes after 722 B.C.," *Scrip* 4 (1949-51) 182.

*Yigael Yadin, "Some Aspects of the Material Culture of Northern Israel during the Canaanite and Israelite Periods, in the light of Excavations at Hazor," *A&S* 2 (1957) #2/3, 165-186.

§65 *2.2.6.2 The Southern Kingdom - General Studies*

*( ) G., "The Sythian Dominion of Asia (as Reported by Herodotus) in its Connexion with Josiah's Exercise of Sovereign Power in the Territory of the Ten Tribes," *JSL, 2nd Ser.,* 4 (1853) 1-34.

*J. Edwin Odgers, "Jeremiah and the Fall of Judah," *ModR* 5 (1884) 211-237.

C[arl] H[einrich] Cornill, "History of the People of Israel. From the Beginning to the Destruction of Jerusalem," *OC* 11 (1897) 654-670. [V. To the Destruction of Jerusalem by the Chaldeans] *(Trans. by W. H. Carruth)*

Robert Gordis, "Sectional Rivalry in the Kingdom of Judah," *JQR, N.S.,* 25 (1934-35) 237-259.

*W[illiam] F[oxwell] Albright, "A Brief History of Judah from the Days of Josiah to Alexander the Great," *BA* 9 (1946) 1-16. [The Great Reform of Josiah; The Prophet Jeremiah and the Fall of Judah; The Exile; The Restoration; The Work of Nehemiah; From Ezra to the Fall of the Perisan Empire]

*D. Winton Thomas, "The Age of Jeremiah in the Light of Recent Archaeological Discovery," *PEQ* 82 (1950)1-15.

*Edwin R. Thiele, "New Evidence on the Chronology of the Last Kings of Judah," *BASOR* #143 (1956) 22-27.

*Hayim Tadmor, "Chronology of the Last Kings of Judah," *JNES* 15 (1956) 226-230.

*William W. Hallo, "From Qarqar to Carchemish: Assyria and Israel in the Light of New Discoveries," *BA* 23 (1960) 34-61. (Correction, p. 132) [I. The Assyrian Resurgence (859-829); II. Revolt and Restoration (828-783); III. Assyria in Retreat (783-745); IV. Divide et Impera (745-705) V. Pax Assyriaca (705-648); VI. Decline and Fall (648-609)]

*A. van Selms, "The Southern Kingdom in Hosea," *OTW* 7&8 (1964-65) 100-111.

§66 *2.2.6.2.1 The Babylonian Period - the captivity [c. 587-559 B.C.]*

*F. W. Farrar, "The Results of the Exile and the Origin of Pharisaism," *Exp, 1st Ser.,* 5 (1877) 87-98.

*W. St. Chad Boscawen, "The Cuneiform Inscriptions and the Era of the Jewish Captivity," *JTVI* 18 (1884-85) 99-134. (Discussion, pp. 135-139)

*S. R. Calthrop, "The Prophets and the Exile," *URRM* 26 (1886) 206-219.

Frederic Gardiner, "On the Number of the Babylonian Captives," *ONTS* 9 (1889) 118-119.

*W. Francis Ainsworth, "The Two Captivities. The Habor and Chebar," *SBAP* 15 (1892-93) 70-76.

Julius Wellhausen, "The Babylonian Exile," *NW* 2 (1893) 601-611.

C[arl] H[einrich] Cornill, "The Babylonian Exile," *OC* 9 (1895) 4537-4538.

William Rainey Harper, "The Jews in Babylon," *BW* 14 (1899) 104-111.

Joseph D. Wilson, "The Seventy Years Captivity," *CFL, 3rd Ser.,* 9 (1908)161-164.

R. W. Moss, "The Babylonian Jews During the Exile," *LQHR* 115 (1911) 125-127.

*J. M. Powis Smith, "The Effect of the Disruption on the Hebrew Thought of God," *AJSL* 32 (1915-16) 261-269.

John Franklin Genung, "The Inner History of the Chaldean Exile," *BS* 73 (1916) 13-43.

E. G. Sihler, "The Older Diaspora," *BR* 10 (1925) 544-568.

*W.W. Everts, "The Dispersion and the Restoration of the Twelve Hebrew Tribes," *BS* 84 (1927) 465-470.

*S. F. Hunter, "Babylonia during the Latter Half of the Jewish Exile," *NZJT* 2 (1932-33) 205-213.

Charles C. Torrey, "The Exile and the Return: A Correction," *ET* 47 (1935-36) 380-381.

*J. W. Jack, "Recent Biblical Archaeology," *ET* 53 (1941-42) 113-117. [The Jewish Diaspora, pp. 116-117]

*W[illiam] F[oxwell] Albright, "King Joiachin in Exile," *BA* 5 (1942) 49-55.

*J. W. Jack, "Recent Biblical Archaeology," *ET* 54 (1942-43) 78-82. [The Israelite Deportations, pp. 81-82]

*J. M. Wilkie, "Nabonidus and the Later Jewish Exiles," *JTS, N.S.,* 2 (1951) 36-44.

D. Winton Thomas, "The Sixth Century B.C.: A Creative Epoch in the History of Israel," *JSS* 6 (1961) 33-46.

B. Oded, "When Did the Kingdom of Judah Become Subjected to Babylonian Exile?" *Tarbiẓ* 35 (1965-66) #2, II.

C[lifford] A. W[ilson], "Your Questions Answered. Seventy or Fifty Years' Captivity?" *BH* 3 (1967) #4, 23-24.

Gerhard Larsson, "When Did the Babylonian Captivity Begin?" *JTS, N.S.,* 18 (1967) 417-423.

Peter R. Ackroyd, "The Interpretation of the Exile and Restoration," *CJT* 14 (1968) 3-12.

Henry Wansbrough, "Event and Interpretation: IV. At the Waters of Babylon," *ClR* 53 (1968) 961-967.

‡Jacob Neusner, "Jews and Judaism under Iranian Rule: Bibliographical Reflections," *HRel* 8 (1968-69) 159-177.

§67 *2.2.6.2.1 The Persian Period - [c. 559-331 B.C.]*

Anonymous, "Import of Hebrew History," *SPR* 9 (1855-56) 582-610. *(Review)*

R. Hill, "Israel under the Second Great Monarchy," *ER* 11 (1859-60) 369-388; 12 (1860-61) 135-149. *[536 B.C. - 335 B.C.]*

*†Anonymous, "Prophecies concerning Israel after the Captivity," *LQHR* 53 (1879-80) 1-23.

Willis J. Beecher, "The Postexilic History of Israel," *ONTS* 9 (1889) 29-37, 90-99, 170-177, 224-232, 291-297, 344-352; 10 (1890) 26-34, 100-108, 160-168, 220-227, 294-300, 348-357.

Andrew Gray, "The Post-Exilian Period," *ET* 6 (1894-95) 382-383.

William Hayes Ward, "Light on Scriptural Texts from Recent Discoveries. Cyrus and the Return of the Jews," *HR* 29 (1895) 121-123.

C[arl] H[einrich] Cornill, "The Return from the Captivity," *OC* 9 (1895) 4587-4589.

G. W. Thatcher, "Kosters' Reconstruction of Jewish History in the Persian Period," *OSHTP* (1895-96) 49-51.

A. R. S. Kennedy, "Recent Foreign Theology. Did the Jews return under Cyrus?" *ET* 8 (1896-97) 268-271.

J. A. Selbie, "Israel's Return from Exile," *ET* 8 (1896-97) 320-322.

A. van Hoonaker, "The Return of the Jews under Cyrus," *ET* 8 (1896-97) 351-354.

C[arl] H[einrich] Cornill, "History of the People of Israel. From the Beginning to the Destruction of Jerusalem," *OC* 11 (1897) 733-749. [VI. From the Return of the Babylonian Captivity to the Outbreak of the Rebellion of the Maccabees] *(Trans. by W. H. Carruth)*

J. A. Selbie, "Kosters on Israel's Return from Exile," *ET* 9 (1897-98) 66-68.

J. A. Selbie, "Israel's Return from Exile," *ET* 9 (1897-98) 275, 305-306.

*Elkan N. Adler, "The Persian Jews: Their Books and Their Ritual," *JQR* 10 (1897-98) 584-625.

‡George S. Goodspeed, "A Selected Bibliography. From Ezra to the Maccabees," *BW* 13 (1899) 399-400.

E. C. Gordon, "The Restoration of Israel from the Babylonian Exile. A Historical Outline with Notes," *CFL, 3rd Ser.*, 3 (1899) 178-183.

William Rainey Harper, "The Return of the Jews from Exile," *BW* 14 (1899) 157-163.

*J. F. McCurdy, "Light on Scriptural Texts from Recent Discoveries. *My city he'll build, and my exiles he'll free, Not for a price, and not for a fee.* – Isa. xlv. 13," *HR* 37 (1899) 124-127. [Cyrus and the return of the exiles]

J. Dick Fleming, "Israel's Restoration in the Persian Period," *ET* 11 (1899-1900) 296-300. *(Review)*

L. W. Batten, "The Israel of the Post-Exilic Period," *HR* 65 (1913) 272-277.

Amos I. Dushaw, "The Post-Exilic Period," *OC* 32 (1918) 626-637.

*Henry Englander, "Problems of Chronology in the Persian Period of Jewish History," *JJLP* 1 (1919) 83-103.

W[illiam] F[oxwell] Albright, "Light on the Jewish State in Persian Times," *BASOR* #53 (1934) 20-22.

W. O. E. Oesterley, "Some Outstanding Old Testament Problems. VII. The Early Post-Exilic Community," *ET* 47 (1935-36) 341-345, 394-398.

*U[mberto] Cassuto, "The Gods of the Jews of Elephantine," *KSJA* 2 (1945) VI.

*J. L. Myres, "Persia, Greece and Israel," *PEQ* 85 (1953) 8-22.

J. Liver, "The Return from Babylon, Its Time and Scope," *EI* 5 (1958) 90*.

*Peter R. Ackroyd, "Two Old Testament Historical Problems of the Early Persian Period," *JNES* 17 (1958) 13-27. [A. The First Years of Darius I and the Chronology of Haggai, Zechariah 1-8, pp. 13-22; B. The "Seventy Year" Period, pp. 22-27]

R. Borger, "An Additional Remark on P. R. Ackroyd," *JNES* 17 (1958) 23-27.

*E. E. Ubrach, "The Laws Regarding Slavery as a Source for Social History of the Period of the Second Temple, the Mishnah and Talmud," *PIJSL* 1 (1964) 1-94.

Frank Moore Cross Jr., "Aspects of Samaritan and Jewish History in Late Persian and Hellenistic Times," *HTR* 59 (1966) 201-211.

*I. H. Eybers, "Relations between Jews and Samaritans in the Persian Period," *OTW* 9 (1966) 72-89.

Henry Wansbrough, "Event and Interpretation: V. The Presence of God in the Poverty of Man," *ClR* 54 (1969) 285-291.

A. F. Rainey, "The Satrapy 'Beyond the River'," *AJBA* 1 (1968-71) #2, 51-78.

§68 *2.2.6.2.3 The Greek Period - General Studies [c. 331-63 B.C.]*

R. M. Patterson, "The Biblical Blank," *PR* 2 (1881) 738-756.

*Shailer Mathews, "Antiochus Ephiphanes and the Jewish State," *BW* 14 (1899) 13-26.

*A. H. Sayce, "Jewish Tax-gatherers in Thebes," *JQR* 2 (1889-90) 400-405.

George Holley Gilbert, "The Hellenization of the Jews Between 334 B.C. and 70 A.D.," *AJT* 13 (1909) 520-540.

Carolus P. Harry, "Apocryphal History," *LCR* 28 (1909) 36-51.

Leonard S. Alban Wells, "The Successors of the Prophets," *ICMM* 7 (1910-11) 158-175.

*A. H. Godbey, "The Influence of Alexander's Conquest upon Jewish Life," *BW* 38 (1911) 171-184.

H. Offermann, "Between the Testaments," *LCR* 38 (1919) 213-217.

*Solomon Zeitlin, "Megillat Taanit as a Source for Jewish Chronology and History in the Hellenistic and Roman Periods, Chapters I to III," *JQR, N.S.,* 9 (1918-19) 71-102.

*Solomon Zeitlin, "Megillat Taanit as a Source for Jewish Chronology and History in the Hellenistic and Roman Periods, Chapters IV to XII," *JQR, N.S.,* 10 (1919-20) 49-80, 237-290.

J. Simon, "Hellenism and the Jews in the Three Centuries Preceding Christianity," *ACQR* 45 (1920) 243-254.

Robert George Raymer, "Tendencies and Developments in Judaism of the Intertestamental Period," *MQR, 3rd Ser.,* 47 (1921) 727-739.

W. G. Jordon, "Hebraism and Hellenism in the Second Century B.C.," *CJRT* 2 (1925) 337-347.

Charles W. Harris, "The Hellenistic Conflict with Judaism," *JBL* 55 (1936) v.

*V. Tscherikower, "Palestine under the Ptolemies (A Contribution to the Study of the Zenon Papyri)," *Miz* 4&5 (1937) 9-90.

(Mrs.) K. M. Atkinson, "The Jews in the Hellenistic World," *JMUEOS* #23 (1942) 7-8. *(Summary)*

‡Ralph Marcus, "A Selected Bibliography (1920-1945) of the Jews in the Hellenistic-Roman Period," *PAAJR* 16 (1946-47) 97-181.

‡*Ramond F. Surburg, "Intertestmental Studies 1946-1955," *CTM* 27 (1956) 95-114. [IV. Hellenistic Judaism, pp. 106-107]

*Abraham Schalit, "The Letter of Antiochus III to Zeuxis Regarding the Establishment of Jewish Military Colonies in Phrygia and Lydia," *JQR, N.S.,* 50 (1959-60) 289-318.

D. Barag, "The Effects of the Tennes Rebellion on Palestine," *BASOR* #183 (1966) 6-12.

D. S. Russell, "The Intertestamental Period," *BQL* 22 (1967-68) 215-224.

§69 *2.2.6.2.3.1 The Maccabean Period [168 - 63 B.C.]*

Franz Delitzsch, "A June Date in Jerusalem," *BS* 31 (1874) 528-544. *(Trans. by Selah Merrill) [History of the Jews just prior to the Birth of Christ]*

A. G. Laurie, "The Jew—From the Maccabees to Christ. Part I," *UQGR, N.S.,* 20 (1883) 389-411.

A. G. Laurie, "The Jew—From the Maccabees to Christ. Part II," *UQGR, N.S.,* 21 (1884) 133-146.

A. G. Laurie, "The Jew—From the Maccabees to Christ. Part III," *UQGR, N.S.,* 21 (1884) 389-405.

A. G. Laurie, "The Jew—From the Maccabees to Christ. Part IV," *UQGR, N.S.,* 23 (1886) 22-39.

Anonymous, "The Maccabean Period," *ONTS* 10 (1890) 380.

C[arl] H[einrich] Cornill, "History of the People of Israel. From the Beginning to the Destruction of Jerusalem," *OC* 12 (1898) 10-27. [VII. The Maccabeean *[sic]* Rebellion to the Establishment of the Hereditary High-Priesthood and Principality Under Simon] *(Trans. by W. H. Carruth)*

C[arl] H[einrich] Cornill, "History of the People of Israel. From the Beginning to the Destruction of Jerusalem," *OC* 12 (1898) 80-96. [VIII.—From Simon the Maccabean to Herod the Great] *(Trans. by W. H. Carruth)*

W. G. Jordan, "The Significance of the Maccabean Period," *BW* 38 (1911) 294-305.

*Julian Obermann, "The Sepulchre of Maccabean Martyrs," *JBL* 50 (1931) 250-265.

F. D. Coggan, "Intercanonical Period," *EQ* 5 (1933) 138-143.

W. Harvey-Jellie, "Bridging the Gulf Between the Testaments. I. In History," *HR* 107 (1934) 19-22.

*Lawrence H. Davis, "Attitudes and Policies toward Gentiles during the Maccabean Period," *YR* 4 (1965) 5-20.

Menahem Stern, "The Hasmonean Revolt and Its Place in the History of Jewish Society and Religion," *JWH* 11 (1968-69) 92-106.

*Wolf Wirgin, "Judah Maccabee's Embassy to Rome and the Jewish-Roman Treaty," *PEQ* 101 (1969) 15-20.

§70 *2.2.6.2.4 The Roman Period [c. 63 B.C. - A.D. 135] (Generally speaking to A.D. 70 only)*

*[Isak Marus] Jost, "The Condition and Belief of the Jews at the time of the coming of Christ," *BRCR, N.S.,* 2 (1839) 174-183. *(Trans. by James Murdock)*

(   ) B., "The Jewish War under Hadrian and Trajan," *JSL, 1st Ser.,* 7 (1851) 439-446.

J. H. W. Stuckenberg, "Condition of the Jews in the days of Christ," *ER* 16 (1865) 61-85.

Franz Delitzsch, "A June Day in Jerusalem, B.C.," *DTQ* 1 (1875) 67-75. *(Trans. by Selah Merrill)*

Franz Delitzsch, "A June Day in Jerusalem During the Last Decade Before Christ," *DTQ, N.S.,* 2 (1883) 77-87. *(Trans. by P. C. Croll)*

Anonymous, "Jewish Life in the Time of Christ," *LQHR* 67 (1886-87) 205-223. *(Review)*

Terrien de Lacouperie, "On the entrance of the Jews into China during the first century of our Era," *BOR* 5 (1891) 131-134.

M. Alder, "The Emperor Julian and the Jews," *JQR* 5 (1892-93) 591-651.

Claude R. Conder, "The Jews under Rome," *PEFQS* 26 (1894) 47-79.

*J. A. Howlett, "Josephus and the Language of Palestine in the Days of Christ," *IER, 3rd Ser.,* 16 (1895) 735-750.

C[arl] H[einrich] Cornill, "History of the People of Israel. From the Beginning to the Destruction of Jerusalem," *OC* 12 (1898) 168-184. [IX.—The House of Herod—Judea as a Roman Province] *(Trans. by W. H. Carruth)*

C[arl] H[einrich] Cornill, "History of the People of Israel. From the Beginning to the Destruction of Jerusalem," *OC* 12 (1898) 257-273. [X.—The War in Judea and the Destruction of Jerusalem] *(Trans. by W. H. Carruth)*

J. C. Nevin, "The Siege of Jerusalem. Diary of the Principal Events Connected with the Memorial Siege of Jerusalem by Titus, Drawn from Josephus: with some Accompanying Notes and Observations," *PEFQS* 39 (1907) 34-42.

*Joseph Offord, "Jewish Notes," *PEFQS* 46 (1914) 46-47. [The Jews in Rome]

William M. Ramsay, "The Old Testament in the Roman Phrygia," *ET* 26 (1914-15) 168-174.

[William M. Ramsay(?)], "The Old Testament in the Roman Phrygia," *HR* 69 (1915) 200-201.

*Joseph Offord, "Archaeological Notes on Jewish Antiquities. LV. *Fresh Light on Hadrian's Jewish War,*" *PEFQS* 51 (1919) 37-38.

W. A. Heidel, "Why Were the Jews Banished from Italy in 19 A.D.?" *AJP* 41 (1920) 38-47.

*William D. Gray, "The Founding of Aelia Capitolina and the Chronology of the Jewish War under Hadrian," *AJSL* 39 (1922-23) 248-256.

W. M. Christie, "The Jamnia Period in Jewish History," *JTS* 26 (1924-25) 347-364. *[A.D. 70 - A.D. 135]*

Frederic G. Kenyon, "The Jews in Roman Egypt," *ERCJ* 242 (1925) 32-47.

J. P. Arendzen, "The Jews Outside Palestine in the Days of Christ," *IER, 5th Ser.,* 27 (1926) 468-480.

George La Piana, "Foreign Groups in Rome During the First Centuries of the Empire," *HTR* 20 (1927) 183-403.

Frederick J. Foakes-Jackson, "Professor Moore's *Judaism,*" *ATR* 10 (1927-28) 23-36. *(Review)*

George Brockwell King, "'The Root of the Fatness of the Olive Tree'. A Review of Professor Moore's *Judaism,*" *CJRT* 5 (1928) 28-37. *(Review)*

*S. Tolkowsky, "The Destruction of the Jewish Navy at Jaffa in the Year 68 A.D.," *PEFQS* 60 (1928) 153-163.

Harry J. Leon, "New Material About the Jews of Ancient Rome," *JQR, N.S.,* 20 (1929-30) 301-312.

Michael S. Ginsburg, "Fiscus Judaicus," *JQR, N.S.,* 21 (1930-31) 281-291.

*Grace Harriet Macurdy, "Jewish Queens under the Roman Empire," *PAPA* 64 (1933) lvi.

M. Avi-Yonah, "Problems of the Roman Period in Palestine," *Kobez* 4 (1945)XXIII-XXIV.

*Sh. Applebaum, "Notes on the Jewish Revolt under Trajan," *JJS* 2 (1950-51) 26-30. [1. The Date of the Revolt; 2. Cyprus, Pappus, and Lulianus; 3. The Sibylline Oracles as Military Evidence]

*Sh. Applebaum, "The Jewish Revolt in Cyrene in 115-117, and the Subsequent Recolonisation," *JJS* 2 (1950-51) 177-186. [I. Cyrene, Additional Evidence of Damage during the Revolt; II. The Other Towns of the Pentapolis and the Countryside]

*M. B. Dagut, "The Habbakuk Scrolls and Pompey's Capture of Jerusalem," *B* 32 (1951) 542-548.

Harry J. Leon, "The Jews of Venusia," *AJA* 57 (1953) 109.

H. M. Matter, "Israel and the New Testament," *FUQ* 3 (1954-55) 265-269.

Alexander Scheiber, "Jews at Intercisa in Pannonia," *JQR, N.S.,* 45 (1954-55) 189-197.

‡*Raymond F. Surburg, "Intertestamental Studies 1946—1955," *CTM* 27 (1956) 95-114. [VI. Palestinian Judaism and Christianity, pp. 108-111]

G. M. FitzGerald, "Palestine in the Roman Period. 63 B.C.—A.D. 324," *PEQ* 88 (1956) 38-48.

S. G. F. Brandon, "Rome and Jewry," *HT* 8 (1958) 485. *(Review)*

*Cecil Roth, "The Jewish Revolt Against the Romans (66-73) in the Light of the Dead Sea Scrolls," *PEQ* 90 (1958) 104-121.

L. W. Barnard, "Judaism in Egypt—A.D. 70-135," *CQR* 160 (1959) 320-334.

*Cecil Roth, "The Zealots in the War of 66-73," *JSS* 4 (1959) 332-355.

*Cecil Roth, "Did Vespasian Capture Qumran?" *PEQ* 91 (1959) 122-129.

Raphael Loewe, "A Jewish Counterpart of the Acts of the Alexandrians," *JJS* 12 (1961) 105-122.

E. Bammel, "The Organization of Palestine by Gabinius," *JJS* 12 (1961) 159-162.

M. Stern, "The Relations between Judea and Rome during the Rule of John Hyrcanus," *Zion* 26 (1961) #1, I.

*Cecil Roth, "The Pharisees in the Jewish Revolution of 66-73," *JSS* 7 (1962) 63-80.

*S. Safrai, "The Status of Provincia Judaea after the Destruction of the Second Temple," *Zion* 27 (1962) #3/4, VII.

V. A. Tcherikover, "The Decline of the Jewish Diaspora in Egypt in the Roman Period," *JJS* 14 (1963) 1-32.

P. J. Sijpesteijn, "The Legationes ad Gaium," *JJS* 15 (1964) 87-96.

Solomon Zeitlin, "The Edict of Augustus Caesar in Relation to the Judaeans of Asia," *JQR, N.S.,* 55 (1964-65) 160-163.

E. Mary Smallwood, "Jews and Romans in the Early Empire: Part I," *HT* 15 (1965) 232-239.

E. Mary Smallwood, "Jews and Romans in the early Empire: Part II," *HT* 15 (1965) 313-319.

*S. G. F. Brandon, "The Zealots: the Jewish resistance against Rome A.D. 6-73," *HT* 15 (1965) 632-641.

*Menaḥem Stern, "The Politics of Herod and the Jewish Society towards the End of the Second Commonwealth," *Tarbiẕ* 35 (1965-66) #3, III.

*L. W. Barnard, "Hadrian and Judaism," *JRelH* 5 (1968-69) 285-298. [Appendix: The Second Jewish Revolt and the Discoveries by the Dead Sea, pp. 295-298]

§71 *2.3* *Sociological Studies; Cultural Studies & Customs - General Studies*

†Anonymous, "Confirmation of Scripture History," *QTMRP* 1 (1813) 369-371. *[Custom of Tattooing]*

†Anonymous, "Manners of the Athenians," *QRL* 23 (1820) 245-279. *(Review)*

Anonymous, "Manners and Customs of the Ancient Egyptians," *QRL* 63 (1839) 120-151. *(Review)*

E. G. Wait, "On Customs illustrative of the Bible," *JSL, 1st Ser.*, 3 (1849) 309-319.

*Anonymous, "The Reproduction of Biblical Life in its Bearing on Biblical Exposition," *JSL, 3rd Ser.*, 4 (1856-57) 1-16.

*W. S. Tyler, "Athens, or Aesthetic Culture and the Art of Expression," *BS* 20 (1863) 152-180.

A. D. Savage, "'Ῥαδαμάνθυος ὅρκος, or Did the notion of irreverence in swearing exist among the Greeks?" *PAPA* 10 (1877-78) 27-28. [Bound with *Transactions*, but paged separately]

Selah Merrill, "History and Life Illustrated by the Inscriptions from Eastern Palestine," *JAOS* 10 (1880) clxiv-clxv.

J. E. Hananer, "The Place of Stoning," *PEFQS* 13 (1881) 318-319.

C[laude] R. Conder, "Jewish Superstitions," *PEFQS* 14 (1882) 145-146.

Jas. Neil, "The Study of Palestinian Life," *ONTS* 3 (1883-84) 20.

A. S. Carrier, "Tiele on Babylonian-Assyrian Culture," *ONTS* 8 (1888-89) 170-176, 214-219, 266-270, 290-296, 335-341. *(Review)*

William Hayes Ward, "Light on Scriptural Texts from Recent Discoveries. VIII. Manners and Customs of the Ancient East," *HR* 26 (1893) 221-223.

Frants Buhl, "Some Observations on the Social Institutions of the Israelites," *AJT* 1 (1897) 728-740.

*G. M. Mackie, "Giving: A Study in Oriental Manners," *ET* 9 (1897-98) 367-370.

E. W. G. Mastermann, "Social Customs in Palestine," *BW* 15 (1900) 262-272.

*A. W. Ackerman, "Ezekiel's Contribution to Sociology," *BW* 17 (1901) 112-117.

(Miss) Lucia C. C. Grieve, "The Dead who are not Dead," *AJA* 6 (1902) 37-38.

*James A. Quarles, "Sociology of Joseph's Day," *CFL, N.S.,* 5 (1902) 97-108. [Slavery, Food & Drink, Dress, Death]

*James A. Quarles, "Sociology of Joseph's Day," *CFL, N.S.,* 5 (1902) 340-352. [Political, Military, Educational & Esthetic]

*James A. Quarles, "Sociology of Joseph's Day," *CFL, N.S.,* 6 (1902) 164-175. [Religious]

*(Mrs.) Harriet Boyd Hawes, "Minoans and Mycenaeans: A Working Hypothesis for the Solution of Certain Problems of Early Mediterranean Race and Culture," *AJA* 11 (1907) 57-58.

Arthur Stanley Pease, "Notes on Stoning among the Greeks and Romans," *TAPA* 38 (1907) 5-18.

*Campbell Bonner, "Notes on a Certain Use of the Reed, with Special Reference to Some Doubtful Passages," *TAPA* 39 (1908) 35-48.

*David Heumark, "Crescas and Spinoza. A Memorial Paper in Honor of the Five Hundredth Anniversary of the 'Or Adonoi'," *YCCAR* 18 (1908) 277-318. [Introduction; I. Chisdai Crescas; II. Spinoza; III. Excursus on Urim ve-Thummim, Choshen, and Goral; Introduction, I. The Choshen (Breastplate), II. Urim ve-Thummim, III. The Goral in the Priestly Code, Annotation (Lev. 16), IV. The Goral in the Book of Joshua, V. The Goral in the Book of Chronicles, VI. Urim ve-Thummim—Conclusion]

M. N. Dhalla, "The Use of Ordeals Among the Ancient Iranians," *Muséon* 29 (1910) 121-133.

Joseph Offord, "Life in Ancient Babylonia Four Thousand Years Ago; as Depicted by the Dilbat Tablets," *AAOJ* 33 (1911) #2, 15-21.

A. L. Frothingham, "Ancient Orientation from Babylon to Rome," *AJA* 19 (1915) 73.

*Herbert L. Willett, "The Religious and Social Ideals of Israel," *BW* 46 (1915) 193-200, 258-263, 326-333, 398-404. (Suggestions to Leaders by Georgia L. Chamberlin, pp. 263-266, 333-336, 404-406); 47 (1916) 63-72, 133-144, 207-216, 279-288, 351-360, 421-430. (Suggestions to Leaders by Georgia L. Chamberlin, pp. 142-144, 215-216, 286-288, 358-360, 428-430)

*(Lady) Ramsey, "'Her that kept the Door'," *ET* 27 (1915-16) 314-316.

Jacob Mann, "'Her that kept the Door'," *ET* 27 (1915-16) 424-425.

*S[tephen] Langdon, "The early Chronology of Sumer and Egypt and the Similarities in their Culture," *JEA* 7 (1921) 133-153.

John A. Maynard, "A Spurious Jewish Custom," *ATR* 3 (1920-21) 330. *[Cutting a boy's hair for the first time]*

*Harold Bennett, "On the Meaning of 'gollere' and 'suscipere' as Applied to Infants," *PAPA* 53 (1922) xvii-xviii.

*Julian Morgenstern, "Trial by Ordeal Among the Semites and in Ancient Israel," *HUCA, Jubilee Volume* (1925) 113-144.

Louis Finkelstein, "The Persistence of Rejected Customs in Palestine," *JQR, N.S.,* 29 (1938-39) 179-186.

*Cyrus H. Gordon, "Biblical Customs and the Nuzu Tablets," *BA* 3 (1940) 1-12. [The Patriarchal Age; Parallels to Other Biblical Laws and Customs; Hebrews and Horites]

W. B. Stevenson, "Property Marks in the Ancient World," *GUOST* 12 (1944-46) 34-42. *[Branding]*

*Rafael Taubenschlag, "Customary Law and Custom in the Papyri," *JJP* 1 (1946) 41-54.

H. H. Rowley, "Recent Foreign Theology. Nomadic Culture and the Old Testament," *ET* 58 (1946-47) 249.

J. S. van der Poleg, "The Social Study of the Old Testament," *CBQ* 10 (1948) 72-80.

Eva Matthews Sanford, "Roman Avarice in Asia," *JNES* 9 (1950) 28-36.

*Franz Rosenthal, "Sedâḳâ, Charity," *HUCA* 23 (1950-51) 411-430.

*G. Ernest Wright, "The Israelite Law for the Common Life," *McQ* 4 (1950-51) #4, 7-10.

*Helen North, "The Use of Poetry in the Training of the Ancient Orator," *Tr* 8 (1952) 1-33.

*Charles Lee Feinberg, "The Old Testament in Jewish Thought and Life," *BS* 111 (1954) 27-38, 125-136.

*G. Ernest Wright, "Israelite Daily Life," *BA* 18 (1955) 50-79. [Farming; The Town; Dress; Arts & Crafts]

*Ernest Wiesenberg, "Related Prohibitions: Swine Breeding and the Study of Greek," *HUCA* 27 (1956) 213-233.

G. F. Mobbs, "The Eastern Way," *ET* 68 (1956-57) 210-212.

G. J. Polkinghorne, "The Eastern Way," *ET* 68 (1956-57) 382.

*Yigael Yadin, "Some Aspects of the Material Culture of Northern Israel during the Canaanite and Israelite Periods, in the light of the Excavations at Hazor," *A&S* 2 (1957) #2/3, 165-186.

*K. V. Mathew, "Ancient Religions of the Fertile Crescent—and the Sanathana Dhrama," *IJT* 8 (1959) 83-90. [The Social Customs and Legal Usages of Hurrians, p. 89]

D. Cracknell, "*Abraham and Ur:* Early Mesopotamian Culture," *AT* 4 (1959-60) #4, 3-5.

A. Brelich, "The Historical Development of the Institution of Initiation in the Classical Ages," *AAASH* 9 (1961) 267-283.

Ernest Lussier, "Daily Life in Ancient Israel," *AER* 144 (1961) 327-331.

*Alan Rowe, "Studies in the Archaeology of the Near East: I. The Derivations of the Nomenclatures of the Cultures of the Egyptian Palaeolithic and Predynastic Periods," *BJRL* 43 (1960-61) 480-491.

Joh. Lindblom, "Lot-Casting in the Old Testament," *VT* 12 (1962) 164-178.

*John E. Rexine, "Hebrew and Greek Thought and Culture Compared," *StVSQ, N.S.,* 9 (1965) 138-144.

Abraham Malamat, "The ban in Mari and in the Bible," *OTW* 9 (1966) 40-49.

Abraham Goldberg, "Rabbi Ze'ira and Babylonian Custom in Palestine," *Tarbiẓ* 36 (1966-67) #4, I-III.

*Karl Oberhuber, "Polytheism and High Culture," *NOP* 6 (1967) 11-15.

*Yitzhak F. Baer, "Social Ideas of the Second Jewish Commonwealth: *The Mishnah as a historical record of the social and religious life during the Second Commonwealth,*" *JWH* 11 (1968-69) 69-91.

Alin M. Dincol and Sönmez Kantman, "Arkeolojide Yeni Kavramlar ve Metodolojik Araştirma Plânlamasi," *AAI* 3 (1969) 15-36. [English Summary, p. 34]

*Melford E. Spiro, "Religious Symbolism and Social Behavior," *PAPS* 113 (1969) 341-349. [Some Similarities Between Judaism and Buddhism, pp. 344-349]

§72 *2.3.16 Social Structures*

*Anonymous, "Essays on the Institutions, Government, and Manners of the States of Ancient Greece," *QRL* 22 (1819-20) 163-203. *(Review)*

*J. J. Ampere, "The Castes of Ancient Egypt," *BS* 9 (1852) 529-540. *(Trans. by John W. May)*

Josiah K. Bennet, "Aliens in Israel," *BS* 13 (1856) 564-574.

*Perceval M. Laurence, "On the Character of the agnatic guardianship of minors and women—Note on Gaius I. 168," *JP* 19 (1880) 24-28.

*W. Robertson Smith, "Animal worship and animal tribes among the Arabs and the Old Testament," *JP* 9 (1880) 75-100.

*†Theo. G. Pinches, "Assyriological Notes," *SBAP* 8 (1885-86) 240-245. [Âgarrūtu, "workmen", p 241]

*Alfred W. Benn, "The Alleged Socialism of the Prophets," *NW* 2 (1893) 60-88.

*C[arl] H[einrich] Cornill, "The Reaction Against the Prophets," *OC* 9 (1895) 4503-4505.

*Harris R. Schenck, "The Old Testament Eldership—Its Origins and Functions," *PQ* 11 (1897) 433-466.

L. W. Batten, "The Social Life of the Hebrews from Josiah to Ezra," *BW* 11 (1898) 397-409.

Charles Foster Kent, "The Social Life of the Jews Between 444 and 160 B.C.," *BW* 13 (1899) 369-379.

L. W. Batten, "The Social Life of the Hebrews from Josiah to Ezra. II," *BW* 13 (1899) 150-161.

*David Werner Amram, "Zekenim or council of elders," *JBL* 19 (1900) 34-52.

*Maurice Thorner, "The Biblical Conception of Poverty and Riches," *HR* 49 (1905) 360-362.

*Alan H. Gardiner, "*Kjj-bm* 'foreigners'," *ZÄS* 43 (1906) 160.

Lewis B[ayles] Paton, "The Social Problem in Israel in the Time of the Prophets," *HSR* 18 (1908) 247-283.

Ralph Van Deman Magoffin, "The Quinquennales," *AJA* 13 (1909) 61.

*Earle Bennett Cross, "Traces of the Matronymic Family in the Hebrew Social Organization," *BW* 36 (1910) 407-414.

*S[tephen] Langdon, "The Babylonian *Zuḫaru*," *SBAP* 33 (1911) 121-127.

F. J. Foakes-Jackson, "Social Organization of Israel," *ICMM* 9 (1912-13) 165-174.

*A. R. S. Kennedy, "The Mishnah Treatise Shabbath as a Reflection of Jewish Social Life," *GUOST* 4 (1913-22) 34-35.

*Israel Lebendiger, "The Minor in Jewish Law. I-III," *JQR, N.S.*, 6 (1915-16) 459-493.

*Eduard König, "Israel's Attitude Respecting Alien-Right and Usages War in Antiquity," *HR* 72 (1916) 184-189.

*Paul Haupt, "Askari, *'soldier,'* and Lascar, *'sailor,'*" *JAOS* 36 (1916) 417-418.

*Otto H. Boström, "The Babylonian Temple and its Place in the Ancient Community," *TTKF* 19 (1917) 28-36.

H. Oscherowitz, "The Social Bases of Judaism," *OC* 32 (1918) 141-154.

*M. Rostovtzeff, "The Foundations of Social and Economic Life in Egypt in Hellenistic Times," *JEA* 6 (1920) 161-178.

*Joseph Offord, "Archaeological Notes on Jewish Antiquities. LXI. *The Sukkiim*," *PEFQS* 52 (1920) 42.

H[arold] Idris Bell, "Hellenic Culture in Egypt," *JEA* 8 (1922) 139-155.

*John Gavin Tait, "The Strategi and Royal Scribes in the Roman Period," *JEA* 8 (1922) 166-173.

*Mayer Sulzberger, "The Status of Labor in Ancient Israel," *JQR, N.S.,* 13 (1922-23) 245-302, 397-459.

*J. W. Flight, "The Nomadic Idea and Ideal in the Old Testament," *JBL* 42 (1923) 158-226.

[W. M.] Flinders Petrie, "Assyrian and Hittite Society," *AEE* 9 (1924) 18-28.

*[W. M.] Flinders Petrie, "The Palace Titles," *AEE* 9 (1924) 109-122.

*[W. M.] Flinders Petrie, "The Royal Magician," *AEE* 10 (1925) 65-70.

*[W. M.] Flinders Petrie, "The Cultivators and Their Land," *AEE* 10 (1925) 105-110.

*J. Penrose Harland, "The Calaurian Amphictyony," *AJA* 29 (1925) 160-171.

*John E. McFadyen, "Poverty in the Old Testament," *ET* 37 (1925-26) 184-189.

*Samuel Teitelbaum, "The Political and Social Ideas of the Prophets," *JIQ* 2 (1925-26) #2, 15-17.

[W. M.] Flinders Petrie, "Supplies and Defence[sic],*" *AEE* 11 (1926) 15-23.

W. K. Prentice, "The Fall of Aristocracies and the Emancipation of Men's Minds," *AJA* 30 (1926) 81.

A. Buchler, "The Levitical Impurity of the Gentile in Palestine Before the Year 70," *JQR, N.S.,* 17 (1926-27) 1-81.

Harold Mattingly, "Doles in Ancient Egypt," *ERCJ* 246 (1927) 47-60.

Samuel Loomis Mohler, "Notes on Public Meals," *PAPA* 59 (1928) xxv.

Zevi Diesendruck, "The Ideal Social Order in Judaism," *YCCAR* 42 (1932) 283-315.

*Anonymous, "The Beisan Expedition and the Beth-shan Society," *UMB* 4 (1932-33) 144-145.

*G[eorge] M[cLean] Harper Jr., "The Relation of Ἀρχώνης, Μέτοχοι, and Ἔγγυοι to each other, to the Government and to the Tax Contract in Ptolemaic Egypt," *Aeg* 14 (1934) 269-285.

*W. H. McClellan, "Rich Men in Ancient Israel. I. The Patriarchal Period," *TFUQ* 10 (1935-36) 437-452.

*W. H. McClellan, "Rich Men in Ancient Israel. II. The Period of Gradual Conquest and the Age of the Kings," *TFUQ* 10 (1935-36) 602-620.

*T. C. Skeat, "A Forthcoming Catalogue of Nome Strategi," *Miz* 2 (1936) 30-35.

*Ismar J. Perita, "The New Biblical Approach to Social Problems," *JAAR* 5 (1937) 107-116. [I. The Method of Imparting Knowledge of Social Ideas; II. The Development of Biblical Social Ideas, *The Epochs of Biblical History;* III. The Principle of Differentiation in Biblical Opinion, *I. The Social Ideals of the Prophets; II. The Social Ideals of the Priests; III. The Social Ideals of the Sages; IV. The Social Ideals of the Apocalyptist;* IV. The Bible and Social Progress, *I. The Authority of the Bible; II. The Authority of Christ*]

*William Linn Westermann, "Enslaved Persons Who Are Free. Rainer Papyrus (PER) Inv. 24,552," *AJP* 59 (1938) 1-30.

*G. R. Driver and John C. Miles, "The *Sal-Zikrum* 'Woman-Man' in Old Babylonian Texts," *Iraq* 6 (1939) 66-70.

*N. W. Goldstein, "Cultivated Pagans and Ancient Anti-Semitism," *JR* 19 (1939) 346-364.

*H. C. Leupold, "Old Testament Prophets and Social Life," *KZ* 63 (1939) 201-214, 276-290, 338-352.

*W. S. Ferguson, "*Polis* and *Idia* in Periclean Athens. The Relation between Public Service and Private Activities," *AmHR* 45 (1939-40) 269-278.

*Th. Laetsch, "The Prophets and Political and Social Problems," *CTM* 11 (1940) 241-258, 337-351.

*J. W. Jack, "Recent Biblical Archaeology," *ET* 52 (1940-41) 353-357. [Guilds of Workman, pp. 356-357]

*Franklin P. Johnson, "Stamnoi," *AJA* 45 (1941) 89-90.

*I. Mendelsohn, "The Canaanite term for 'Free Proletarian'," *BASOR* #83 (1941) 36-39.

Henry L. F. Lutz, "The Racial Relationship of the Ancient Hebrews," *KZ* 65 (1941) 413-419, 466-471.

*Alan Rowe, "The '𓌀-sceptre' sub-gang of workmen at Meydum," *ASAE* 41 (1942) 339-341.

*Mary S. Shaw, "Individuality according to the thought and practice of Ancient Egypt," *JMUEOS* #23 (1942) 11-12.

*I. Mendelsohn, "Free Artisans and Slaves in Mesopotamia," *BASOR* #89 (1943) 25-29.

*Hans Julius Wolff, "Marriage Law and Family Organization in Ancient Athens: A Study in the Interrrelation of Public and Private Law in the Greek City," *Tr* 2 (1944) 43-96.

Eva J. Ross, "Judaic Social Thought," *ACSR* 7 (1946) 33-42.

Paul Claudel, "Paul Claudel: Old Age According to Sacred Scripture," *IER, 5th Ser.*, 68 (1946) 227-231. *(Trans. by P. J. Doyle)*

Frank M. Snowden Jr., "The Negro in Ancient Greece," *TAPA* 77 (1946) 322-323.

T. Fish, "Some Ancient Mesopotamian Traditions Concerning Men and Society," *BJRL* 30 (1946-47) 41-56.

*O. W. Reinmuth, "The Ephebate and Citizenship in Attica and Egypt," *TAPA* 78 (1947) 433-434.

*J. L[awrence] Angel, "Health and Society in Greece," *AJA* 52 (1948) 373.

*Robert North, "The Biblical Jubilee and Social Reform," *Scrip* 4 (1949-51) 323-335.

R[afael] Taubenschlag, "The herald in the law of the papyri," *AHDO* 5 (1950-51) 189-194.

Stanislaw Plodzień, "The Origin and Competence of the πράκτωρ ξενικῶν," *JJP* 5 (1951) 217-227.

Kathleen Chrimes Atkinson, "Some observations on Ptolemaic Ranks and Titles," *Aeg* 32 (1952) 204-214.

*John Gray, "Feudalism in Ugarit and Early Israel," *ZAW* 64 (1952-53) 49-55.

Richard H. Randall Jr., "The Erechtheum Workmen," *AJA* 57 (1953) 199-210.

*William J. Ahern, "Social Justice in the Prophets of the Old Testament," *MH* 9 (Spring, 1953) 19-25.

*John W. Wilson, "Egyptian Technology, Science, and Lore," *JWH* 2 (1954-55) 209-213. [Government and Society, pp. 210-212]

*Joseph H. Heinemann, "The Status of the Labourer in Jewish Law and Society in the Tannaitic Period," *HUCA* 25 (1954) 263-325.

*Rodolfo Mondolfo, "The Greek Attitude to Manual Labor," *P&P* #6 (1954) 1-5, *(Trans. by D. S. Duncan)*

*I. Mendelsohn, "New Light on the Ḫupšu," *BASOR* #139 (1955) 9-11.

*P. A. H. de Boer, "The counsellor," *VTS* 3 (1955) 42-71.

*B. Gemser, "The *rîb*- or controversy-pattern in Hebrew mentality," *VTS* 3 (1955) 120-137. [1. The Frequency of Disputes in Israelite Life, pp. 120-122]

*James G. Leovy and Greer M. Taylor, "Law and Social Development in Israel," *ATR* 39 (1957) 9-24.

*Kentarô Murakawa, "Demiurges," *HJAH* 6 (1957) 385-415.

*William McKane, "The *Gibbôr Ḥayil* in the Israelite Community," *GUOST* 17 (1957-58) 28-37.

*Jacob J. Rabinowitz, "Miscellanea Papyrologica," *JJP* 11&12 (1957-58) 167-183. [III. A Note on the ΠΡΑΚΤΩΡ ΞΕΝΙΚΩΝ, pp. 180-181]

*Howard Becker, "Culture Case Study and Greek History: Comparison Viewed Sociologically," *AmSR* 23 (1958) 489-504.

*H. J. Katzenstein, "The House of Eliakim, a Family of Royal Stewards," *EI* 5 (1958) 89*-90*.

Peter Green, "Roman Satire and Roman Society I: The Republican Tradition," *HT* 7 (1957) 106-114.

Peter Green, "Roman Satire and Roman Society II: The Imperial Knife-Walkers," *HT* 7 (1957) 243-250.

*E[phraim] A. Speiser, "The *muškênum*," *Or, N.S.*, 27 (1958) 19-28.

*Folker Willesen, "The Yālīd in Hebrew Society," *ST* 12 (1958) 192-210.

*J. L. McKenzie, "The Elders in the Old Testament," *B* 40 (1959) 522-540.

Mabel Lang, "Allotment by Tokens," *HJAH* 8 (1959) 80-89.

*J. L. McKenzie, "The elders in the Old Testament," *SBO* 1 (1959) 388-406.

*Henry W. F. Saggs, "Two Administrative Officals at Erech in the 6th Century B.C.," *Sumer* 15 (1959) 29-38. [shatammu and resh sharri bel piqitti]

*C. L. Gibson, "Life and Society at Mari and in Old Israel," *GUOST* 18 (1959-60) 15-29.

Walter C. Klein, "The Model of a Hebrew Man: The Standards of Manhood in Hebrew Culture," *BRes* 4 (1960) 1-7.

*Naphtali Lewis, "*Leitourgia* and Related Terms," *GRBS* 3 (1960) 175-184.

*Edward Neufeld, The Emergence of a Royal-Urban Society in Ancient Israel," *HUCA* 31 (1960) 31-53.

*H. J. Katzenstein, "The Royal Steward (*Asher al ha-Bayith*)," *IEJ* 10 (1960) 149-154.

*Geoffrey Evans, "An Old Babylonian Soldier: Notes on the Archive of Ubarrum," *JCS* 14 (1960) 34-42.

*William W. Hallo, "A Sumerian Amphictyony," *JCS* 14 (1960) 88-114.

Ronald Syme, "Bastards in the Roman Aristocracy," *PAPS* 104 (1960) 323-327.

*Frank M. Snowden Jr., "Some Greek and Roman Observations on the Ethiopian," *Tr* 16 (1960) 19-38.

Rivkah Harris, "On the Process of Secularization under Hammurapi," *JCS* 15 (1961) 117-120.

*M. Haran, "The Gibeonites, the Nethinim, and the sons of Solomon's Servants," *VT* 11 (1961) 159-169.

*H. C. Thomson, "*Shophet* and *Mishpat* in the Book of Judges," *GUOST* 19 (1961-62) 74-85.

K. J. Narr, "Approaches to the Social Life of Earliest Man," *Anthro* 57 (1962) 604-620.

*I. Mendelsohn, "The Corvee Labor in Ancient Canaan and Israel," *BASOR* #167 (1962) 31-35.

*Maria Jaczynowaska, "The Economic Differentiation of the Roman Nobility at the End of the Republic," *HJAH* 11 (1962) 486-499.

*F. Charles Fensham, "Widow, Orphan and the Poor in Ancient Near Eastern Legal and Wisdom Literature," *JNES* 21 (1962) 129-139.

Z[byněk] Žába, "The Development of Primitive and Class Societies in Ancient Egypt," *NOP* 3 (1962) 35-40, 60.

*Ephraim A. Speiser, "Background and Function of the Biblical *nāśī*," *CBQ* 25 (1963) 111-117.

*A[nson] F. Rainey, "A Canaanite at Ugarit," *IEJ* 13 (1963) 43-45.

*D. G[eoffrey] Evans, "The Incidence of Labour-service in the Old Babylonian Period," *JAOS* 83 (1963) 20-26.

*[D.] Geoffrey Evans, "The Incidence of Labour-Service at Mari," *RAAO* 57 (1963) 65-78. [I. Work upon the canals and irrigation system; II. Agricultural corvées; III. Conclusions; IV. Periods of Labour-service]

*Rivkah Harris, "The organization and administration of the cloister in Ancient Babylonia," *JESHO* 6 (1963) 121-157.

*L. M. Muntingh, "A Few Social Concepts In The Psalms And Their Relation To The Canannite Residental Area," *OTW* 6 (1963) 48-57.

*John F. Oates, "The Status Designation: ΠΕΡΣΗΣ, ΤΗΣ ΕΠΙΓΟΝΗΣ," *YCS* 18 (1963) 1-129.

*Moshe Beer, "Were the Babylonian Amoraim Exempt from Taxes and Customs?" *Tarbiẕ* 33 (1963-64) #3, III-IV.

*Angelo P. O'Hagan, "Poverty in the Bible," *ABR* 12 (1964) 1-9.

*Pierre Biard, "Biblical Teaching on Poverty," *CC* 14 (1964) 433-440. *(Trans. by M. de Montfort)*

M. A. H. el-Abbadi, "The *Gerousia* in Roman Egypt," *JEA* 50 (1964) 164-169.

*T. Donald, "The Semantic Field of Rich and Poor in the Wisdom Literature of Hebrew and Accadian," *OA* 3 (1964) 27-41.

*Derek Kidner, "Wealth," *TB* #15 (1964) 2-9.

*Paul E. Davies, "'The Poor You Have With You Always'. *(The Biblical View of Poverty)*," *McQ* 18 (1964-65) #2, 37-48.

R. J. Rowland Jr., "The Number of Grain Recipients in the Late Republic," *AAASH* 13 (1965) 81-83.

D. Hegyi, "Notes on the Origin of Greek Tyrannis," *AAASH* 13 (1965) 303-318.

*Naphtali Lewis, "*Leitourgia* and Related Terms (II)," *GRBS* 6 (1965) 227-230.

*Hanna E. Kassis, "Gath and the Structure of the 'Philistine' Society," *JBL* 84 (1965) 259-271.

*Simon Pembroke, "Last of the Matriarchs: A Study in the Inscriptions of Lycia," *JESHO* 8 (1965) 217-247.

*Menaḥem Stern, "The Politics of Herod and Jewish Society towards the End of the Second Commonweatlh," *Tarbiẓ* 35 (1965-66) #3, III.

E. E. Urbach, "Class-Status and Leadership in the World of the Palestinian Sages," *PIASH* 2 (1965-67) #4, 1-37.

*Robert Bierstedt, Gregory Vlastos, and Lewis A. Coser, "Review Symposium: Alvin W. Gouldner. *Enter Plato: Classical Greece and the Origins of Social Theory*," *AmSR* 31 (1966) 548-550.

*A[nson] F. Rainey, "^{LÚ}maskim at Ugarit," *Or, N.S.,* 35 (1966) 426-428.

*P. A. Brunt, "The Roman Mob," *P&P* #35 (1966) 3-27.

*Pierre Biard, "Biblical Teaching on Poverty," *TD* 14 (1966) 153-154. *(Synopsis)*

Michael Michels, "Community and Biblical Patterns," *BibT* #28 (1967) 1961-1967.

*James Kelly, "The Biblical Meaning of Poverty and Riches," *BibT* #33 (1967) 2282-2290.

*Michael Grant, "The Gladiators," *HT* 17 (1967) 610-617.

Ignace J. Gelb, "Approaches to the Study of Ancient Society," *JAOS* 87 (1967) 1-8.

A. Leo Oppenheim, "A new look at the structure of Mesopotamian society," *JESHO* 10 (1967) 1-16.

John Briscoe, "Rome and the Class Struggle in the Greek States 200-146 B.C.," *P&P* #36 (1967) 3-20.

*P. R. C. Weaver, "Social Mobility in the Early Roman Empire: The Evidence of the Imperial Freedman and Slaves," *P&P* #37 (1967) 3-20.

K. K. Zelyin, "Principles of Morphological Classification of Forms of Dependence," *VDI* (1967) #2, 30-31.

*M. Heltzer, "Royal Dependents (bnš mlk) and Units (gt) of the Royal Estate in Ugarit," *VDI* (1967) #2, 47.

*Joseph Vogt, "Free Arts and Unfree People in Ancient Rome," *VDI* (1967) #2, 103.

Ye. S. Golubtsova, "Forms of Dependence in Rural Areas of Hellenistic Asia Minor," *VDI* (1967) #3, 44.

*I. M. Diakonoff, "Problems of Property. The Structure of Near Eastern Society to the Middle of the Second Millenium B.C.," *VDI* (1967) #4, 35. *[Numbers 1 & 2]*

*Horst Klengel, "On the Economic Basis of Nomadism in Ancient Mesopotamia," *VDI* (1967) #4, 69-70.

*H. S. Smith, "A Note on Amnesty," *JEA* 54 (1968) 209-214.

V. A. Belyavsky, "The Descendents of Ēa-ilūta-bāni (from the history of the middle strata of New Babylonian society)," *VDI* (1968) #1, 119.

*I. M. Diakonoff, "Problems of Economics. The Structure of the Near Eastern Society to the Middle of the Second Millenium B.C. 3. The Structure of the Communal Sector of the Economy in Western Asia," *VDI* (1968) #3, 26-27.

A. G. Perikhanian, "Agnatic Groups in Ancient Iran," *VDI* (1968) #3, 52-53.

*I. M. Diakonoff, "Problems of Economics. The Structure of Near Eastern Society to the Middle of the Second Millenium B.C.," *VDI* (1968) #4, 38-40. [4. The Structure of the State Sector of the Economy in Western Asia; 5. General Conclusions. The Strucutre of Society and the Mode of Production]

*Howard Wohl, "Towards a Definition of *muškênum*," *JANES* 1 (1968-69) #1, 5-10.

*A[nson] F. Rainey, "'The King's Son' at Ugarit and among the Hittites," *Lěš* 33 (1968-69) #4, 3.

Anonymous, "Amnesty for Prisoners," *BH* 5 (1969) 78-81.

*Francis I. Andersen, "Israelite Kinship Terminology and Social Structure," *BTr* 20 (1969) 29-39.

*Naphtali Lewis, "The Limited Role of the Epistrategos in Liturgical Appointments," *CdÉ* 44 (1969) 339-344.

*F. G. Gordon, "The Egyptian Harpedonaptai," *JEA* 55 (1969) 217-218. [Ἀρπεδονάπται]

*C. D. Darlington, "The Genetics of Society," *P&P* #43 (1969) 3-33.

*I. V. Kuklina, "Ἄβιοι in the Ancient Literary Tradition," *VDI* (1969) #3, 130.

Yu. V. Andreyev, "The Spartan 'Knights'," *VDI* (1969) #4, 36.

Ye. M. Shtaerman, "On the Class Structure of Roman Society," *VDI* (1969) #4, 59.

§73 *2.3.16.1 Women in Society*

*Anonymous, "Essays on the Institutions, Government, and Manners of the States of Ancient Greece," *QRL* 22 (1819-20) 163-203. *(Review) [Women in Society]*

Anonymous, "The Position of Woman in Barbarism and among the Ancients," *WR* 64 (1855) 378-436. *(Review)*

D. R. Cady, "The Biblical Position of Woman," *CongQB* 12 (1870) 370-377.

Edward Thomas, "On the Position of Women in the East in Olden Time," *JRAS* (1879) 1-60.

*Perceval M. Laurence, "On the Character of the agnatic guardianship of minors and women—Note on Gaius I. 168," *JP* 9 (1880) 24-28.

Jeremiah Chaplin, "The Position of Women among the Ancient Romans," *BQR* 3 (1881) 466-491.

Geo. Bertin, "Rules of Life among the Ancient Akkadians," *SBAP* 4 (1881-82) 87-88. (Remarks by Samuel Birch, p. 88)

J. Chotzner, "On the Life and Social Position of Hebrew Women in Biblical Times," *SBAP* 6 (1883-84) 137.

†J. Marshall, "Remarks on Dr. Chotzner's Paper, 'On the Life and Social Position of Hebrew Women in Biblical Times,'" *SBAP* 6 (1883-84) 222-224.

Otis T. Mason, "Woman's Share in Primitive Culture," *AAOJ* 11 (1889) 3-13.

James Donaldson, "The Position of Women in Ancient Rome," *ContR* 54 (1889) 558-574.

*Elsie Davis, "Woman in the Midrash," *JQR* 8 (1895-96) 529-533.

Anonymous, "Woman in Antiquity," *MR* 78 (1896) 314-317.

*W. M. McPheeters, "Woman in the Ancient Hebrew Cult," *CFL, O.S.,* 3 (1899) 72-74.

*Phililp J. Baldensperger, "Woman in the East," *PEFQS* 31 (1899) 132-160. *[Modern Status]*

*Phililp J. Baldensperger, "Woman in the East. Part II," *PEFQS* 32 (1900) 171-190. *[Modern Status]*

*Phililp J. Baldensperger, "Woman in the East," *PEFQS* 33 (1901) 66-90, 167-184, 252-273. *[Modern Status]*

*Lewis R. Farnell, "Sociological hypothesis concerning the position of women in ancient religion," *AfRW* 7 (1904) 70-94.

Anonymous, "Place of Women Among the Hittites," *RP* 7 (1908) 258.

*Caroline M. Breyfogle, "The Religious Status of Woman in the Old Testament," *BW* 35 (1910) 405-419.

*Earle Bennett Cross, "Traces of the Matronymic Family in the Hebrew Social Organization," *BW* 36 (1910) 407-414.

Joseph Strauss, "Woman's Position in Ancient and Modern Jewry," *WR* 174 (1910) 620-628.

H. J. Rose, "On the Alleged Evidence for Mother-Right in Early Greece," *Folk* 22 (1911) 276-291, 493.

A. Lang, "Mother-Right in Early Greece," *Folk* 22 (1911) 494.

Elizabeth Bruin, "Judaism and Womanhood," *WR* 180 (1913) 125-132.

*Theophilus G. Pinches, "Sumerian Women for Field-Work," *JRAS* (1915) 457-463.

John H., Strenge, "The Ancient Position of Women," *LCR* 34 (1915) 410-417.

*C. C. Edgar, "A Women's Club in Ancient Alexandria," *JEA* 4 (1916) 253-254.

(Miss) Helen McClees, "Notes on Women in Attic Inscriptions," *AJA* 23 (1919) 73.

Franz M. Th. Böhl, "The Position of Women in Ancient Babylon and Israel," *BS* 77 (1920) 4-13, 186-197.

H. J. Rose, "Mother-Right in Ancient Italy," *Folk* 31 (1920) 93-108.

Belinda May Briggs, "The Bible Estimate of Woman," *MR* 103 (1920) 879-896.

Aylward M. Blackman, "On the Position of Women in the Ancient Egyptian Hierarchy," *JEA* 7 (1921) 8-30.

Beatrice Allard Brooks, "Some Observations Concerning Ancient Mesopotamian Women," *AJSL* 39 (1922-23) 187-194.

Edith M. Guest, "Women's Titles in the Middle Kingdom," *AEE* 11 (1926) 46-50.

H. J. Rose, "Prehistoric Greece and Mother-Right," *Folk* 37 (1926) 213-244.

*Grace H. Macurdy, "Queen Eurydice and the Evidence for Woman-Power in Early Macedonia," *AJP* 48 (1927) 201-214.

L. A. Post, "Feminism in Greek Literature," *QRL* 248 (1927) 354-373. *(Review)*

Wilhelm Spiegelberg, "Note on the Feminine Character of the New Empire," *JEA* 15 (1929) 199.

*Samuel I Feigin, "The Captives in Cuneiform Inscriptions," *AJSL* 50 (1933-34) 217-245. [1. *asirtu*, "Captive Women," in the Omen Text K.3, pp. 217-220; 7. *i-sar-ti-* and *napṭarti-* Women in Hittite Texts, pp. 232-234; 8. *esrêti-* Women in Nuzi Documents, p. 234-237; 9. The ŠU.GE$_4$-Women in the Code of Hammurabi and the Contracts of that Period, pp. 237-243]

Cyrus H. Gordon, "The Status of Woman Reflected in the Nuzi Tablets," *ZA* 43 (1936) 147-169.

*G. R. Driver and John C. Miles, "The *Sal-Zikrum* 'Woman-Man' in Old Babylonian Texts," *Iraq* 6 (1939) 66-70.

L. A. Post, "Woman's Place in Meander's Athens," *TAPA* 71 (1940) 420-459.

J. P. V. D. Balsdon, "Women in Republican Rome," *HT* 9 (1959) 455-461.

J. P. V. D. Balsdon, "Women in Imperial Rome," *HT* 10 (1960) 24-31.

*Rivkah Harris, "Biographical Notes on the *nadītu* women of Sippar," *JCS* 16 (1962) 1-12.

*F. Charles Fensham, "Widow, Orphan and the Poor in Ancient Near Eastern Legal and Wisdom Literature," *JNES* 21 (1962) 129-139.

*L. M. Muntingh, "The Social and Legal Status of a Free Ugaritic Female," *JNES* 26 (1967) 102-112.

Simon Pembroke, "Women in Charge: The Function of Alternatives in Early Greek Tradition and the Ancient Idea of Matriarchy," *JWCI* 30 (1967) 1-35.

*M. Philotea, "Jeremiah, Prophet of Affliction," *BibT* #36 (1968) 2513-2516. [Woman's Progress in the Bible, pp. 2520-2521]

Gail Morlan, "Toward a Biblical understanding of womanhood," *Min* 8 (1968) 3-9. [I. Woman in the Old Testament, pp. 3-7]

*Emmanuel Levinas, "Judaism and the Feminine Element," *Jud* 18 (1969) 30-38. *(Trans. by Edith Wyschogrod)*

*R[ivkah] Harris, "Notes on the Babylonian Cloister and Hearth: A Review Article," *Or, N.S.,* 38 (1969) 133-145. *(Review)*

*David [Noel] Freedman, "A New Approach to the Nuzi Sistership Contract," *JANES* 2 (1969-70) 77-85.

§74 *2.3.16.2 Slavery & Manumission*

[B. B. Edwards], "Slavery in Ancient Greece," *BRCR* 5 (1835) 138-163.

William C. Wisner, "The Biblical Argument on Slavery," *BRCR, N.S.,* 11 (1844) 302-339.

J. O. Lincoln, "Roman Slavery," *BS* 2 (1845) 565-584.

O. P., "Slavery in the Old Testament," *JSL, 2nd Ser.,* 4 (1853) 125-145. *(Review)*

George B. Cheever, "The Historical and Legal Judgment of the Old Testament Scriptures Against Slavery," *BS* 12 (1855) 739-770; 13 (1856) 1-48, 359-387, 575-609.

J. W. Lindsay, "Roman Slavery," *MR* 37 (1855) 441-456.

Anonymous, "Slavery," *SPR* 9 (1855-56) 345-364.

[Joseph Fullonton], "Slavery," *FBQ* 7 (1858) 259-272. [Egyptian Servitude, pp. 260-261, Hebrew Servitute, pp. 261-264]

*H. C., "The Origin and History of the Sacred Slaves of Israel in Hivitia, Mount Se'yr, and the Hivite Tetrapolis," *JSL, 3rd Ser.,* 10 (1859-60) 266-283.

M. Mielziner, "Slavery among the Ancient Hebrews," *AThR* 3 (1861) 423-438.

Anonymous, "Slavery and Ancient Rome," *FBQ* 9 (1861) 394-400.

Philip Schaff, "Slavery and the Bible," *RChR* 13 (1861) 288-317. [The Origin of Slavery; The Curse of Noah; Patriarchal Slavery; Jewish Slavery; Greek and Roman Slavery; The New Testament and Slavery]

Thomas Beveridge, "The Hebrew Servant," *UPQR* 1 (1860) 481-505; 2 (1861) 356-369.

H. I. Schmidt, "Slavery among the Ancient Hebrews," *ER* 13 (1861-62) 311-355.

E. P. Barrows, "Saalschutz on Hebrew Servitude," *BS* 19 (1862) 32-75.

E. P. Barrows, "The Bible and Slavery," *BS* 19 (1862) 574-606.

M. E. F., "Does the Bible Sustain Slavery?" *CRB* 27 (1862) 584-594.

( ) H., "Slavery and the Bible," *BFER* 12 (1863) 801-823. *(Review)*

Anonymous, "The Bible and Slavery," *CE* 77 (1864) 191-200. *(Review)*

Orientalist, "Slavery Not Sanctioned in the Bible," *JSL, 4th Ser.*, 8 (1865-66) 315-320.

*Theo. G. Pinches, "Documents relating to Slave-dealing in Babylonia in Ancient Times," *SBAP* 7 (1884-85) 32-36.

*Theo. G. Pinches, "Tablets Referring to the Apprenticeship of *Slaves at Babylon*," *BOR* 1 (1886-87) 81-85.

*J. P. Mahaffy, "The Slave Wars against Rome," *Herm* 7 (1889-90) 167-182.

Anonymous, "Jews and Slavery," *EN* 3 (1891) 41-42.

Thomas D. Seymour, "Slavery and Servitude in Homer," *AJA* 5 (1901) 23-24.

*James A. Quarles, "Sociology of Joseph's Day," *CFL, N.S.*, 5 (1902) 97-108. [Slavery, pp. 97-100]

S. Zabarowski, "Ancient Greece and its slave population," *SIR* (1912) 597-608.

Beatrice Allard Brooks, "The Babylonian Practice of Marking Slaves," *JAOS* 42 (1922) 80-90.

*Eli Ginzberg, "Studies in the Economics of the Bible," *JQR, N.S.*, 22 (1931-32) 343-408. [I. Laws Pertaining to Slavery, pp. 345-351]

Tenney Frank, "The Sacred Treasure and the Rate of Manumission," *AJP* 53 (1932) 360-363.

*Samuel I Feigin, "The Captives in Cuneiform Inscriptions," *AJSL* 50 (1933-34) 217-245. *[Slavery]*

*Samuel I Feigin, "The Captives in Cuneiform Inscriptions—*continued*," *AJSL* 51 (1934-35) 22-29.

*A. Saarisalo, "New Kirkuk documents relating to slaves," *SO* 5 (1934) #3, i-viii, 1-101.

*I. Mendelsohn, "The Conditional Sale into Slavery of Free-born Daughters in Nuzi and the Law of Exodus 21:7-11," *JAOS* 55 (1935) 190-195.

*S. L. Mohler, "Slave Education in the Roman Empire," *TAPA* 71 (1940) 262-280.

I. Mendelsohn, "State Slavery in Ancient Palestine," *BASOR* #85 (1942) 14-17.

*I. Mendelsohn, "Free Artisans and Slaves in Mesopotamia," *BASOR* #89 (1943) 25-29.

Rafael Taubenschlag, "Some notes on W. L. Westermann's article, Slave Maintenance and Slave Revolts. Classical Philology XL (1945) 1ff.," *JJP* 1 (1946) 151.

*I. Mendelsohn, "Slavery in the Ancient Near East," *BA* 9 (1946) 74-88. [I. Sources of Slavery, 1. Prisoners of War, 2. Sale of Minors, 3. Self-Sale, Defaulting Debtors; II. Legal Status, 1. Branding, 2. Treatment, 3. Manumission; III. The Economic Role of Slavery, 1. State Slaves, 2. Temple Slavery, 3. Slaves in Agriculture, 4. Slaves in Industry; Attitude of Religion Toward Slavery]

A. M. Bakir, "Slavery in Pharaonic Egypt," *ASAE* 45 (1947) 135-144.

William Linn Westermann, "The Paramone as General Service Contract," *JJP* 2 (1948) 9-50. *[Manumission]*

M. David, "The Manumission of Slaves Under Zedekiah," *OTS* 5 (1948) 63-79.

*C. Bradford Wells, "Manumission and Adoption," *RIDA, 1st Ser.,* 3 (1949) 507-520.

*B[enjamin] Maisler, "The Israelite Exiles at Gozan," *BIES* 15 (1949-50) #3/4, III. *[Manumission]*

William Linn Westermann, "Extinction of Claims in Slave Sales at Delphi," *JJP* 4 (1950) 49-61.

*F. Pringsheim, "A suggestion on P. Columbia Inv. No 480 (198—197 B.C.)," *JJP* 5 (1951) 115-120. *[Slavery in Egypt]*

*F. Sokolowski, "The Real Meaning of Sacral Manumission," *HTR* 47 (1954) 173-181.

*Zeev W. Falk, "The Deeds of Manumission of Elephantine," *JJS* 5 (1954) 114-117.

*Franz Steiner, "Enslavement and the Early Hebrew Lineage System: An Explanation of Genesis 47:29-31, 48:1-16," *Man* 54 (1954) #102.

*(Miss) S. Strizower, "Enslavement and the Early Hebrew Lineage System," *Man* 54 (1954) #264.

*I. Mendelsohn, "On Slavery in Alalakh," *IEJ* 5 (1955) 65-72.

Reuven Yaron, "Alienation and Manumission," *RIDA, 3rd Ser.,* 2 (1955) 381-387.

*Clarence A. Forbes, "The Education and Training of Slaves in Antiquity," *TAPA* 86 (1955) 321-360.

*Jaan Puhvel, "'Servant' in Hieroglyphic Hittite," *JAOS* 77 (1958) 137-139.

*Julius Lewy, "The Biblical Institution of *D^e^rôr* in the Light of Akkadian Documents," *EI* 5 (1958) 21*-31*.

Z[eev] W. Falk, "Manumission by Sale," *JSS* 3 (1958) 127-128.

*M. I. Finley, "Was Greek Civilisation based on Slave Labor?" *HJAH* 8 (1959) 145-164.

Reuven Yaron, "Redemption of Persons in the Ancient Near East," *RIDA, 3rd Ser.*, 6 (1959) 155-176.

*Jacob J. Rabinowitz, "Manumission of Slaves in Roman Law and Oriental Law," *JNES* 19 (1960) 42-44.

M. I. Finley, "The Significance of Ancient Slavery (a Brief Reply)," *AAASH* 9 (1961) 285-286.

*Edward Neufeld, "*Ius redemptionis* in Ancient Hebrew Law," *RIDA, 3rd Ser.*, 8 (1961) 29-40.

*M. Haran, "The Gibeonites, the Nethinim, and the sons of Solomon's Servants," *VT* 11 (1961) 159-169.

P. Oliva, "The Significance of Ancient Slavery (Some Remarks to 'Brief Reply')," *AAASH* 10 (1962) 417.

M. I. Finley, "The Black Sea and Danubian Regions and the Slave Trade in Antiquity," *Klio* 40 (1962) 51-59.

Solomon Zeitlin, "Slavery During the Second Commonwealth and the Tannaitic Period," *JQR, N.S.*, 53 (1962-63) 185-218.

Anonymous, "Selling the Poor," *BH* 1 (1964) #2, 3-6, 13.

*E. E. Ubrach, "The Laws Regarding Slavery as a Source for Social History of the Period of the Second Temple, the Mishnah and the Talmud," *PIJSL* 1 (1964) 1-94.

Alan E. Samuel, "The Role of *Paramone* Clauses in Ancient Documents," *JJP* 15 (1965) 221-311.

*Edwin Yamauchi, "Slaves of God," *BETS* 9 (1966) 31-50. [Slavery in Antiquity, pp. 36-43]

Victoria Cuffel, "The Classical Greek Concept of Slavery," *JHI* 27 (1966) 323-342.

*Lionel Casson, "Galley Slaves," *TAPA* 97 (1966) 35-44.

*P. R. C. Weaver, "Social Mobility in the Early Roman Empire: The Evidence of the Imperial Freedman and Slaves," *P&P* #37 (1967) 3-20.

V. I. Velkov, "Thracian Slaves in the Ancient Greek Cities (6th-2nd Centuries B.C.)," *VDI* (1967) #4, 79-80.

*M. A. Dandamayev, "The Testimony of Slaves in Babylonian Courts," *VDI* (1968) #1, 12.

*R. Ye. Lyast, "Manumissions of Slave Craftsmen in the First Century B.C.," *VDI* (1968) #2, 120.

*M. L. Heltzer, "Slaves, Slaveowning and the Role of Slavery in Ugarit [in the Fourteenth and Thirteenth Centuries B.C.]," *VDI* (1968) #3, 96.

*V. P. Popov, "The Status of Slaves in the Hittite Kingdom (based on §§93-99 of the Hittite laws)," *VDI* (1969) #3, 81.

M. A. Dandamayev, "The Condition of Slaves in Late Babylonia (Dayān-bel-uṣur, a slave in the house of Egibi)," *VDI* (1969) #4, 16-17.

§75 *2.3.16.3 Urban Studies*

[G. H. Ball], "Lessons from Ancient Cities," *FBQ* 10 (1862) 463-476. [The Rise and Influence of Cities; Cities of Opposite Character and Mission; Opposite Example; How They Multiplied; Commerce a Civilizer]

Thomas Laurie, "Ancient and Modern Cities," *HSR* 1 (1890-91) 146-148.

*Anonymous, "The Size of Babylon," *RP* 7 (1908) 261-262.

H. R. Fairclough, "Some Aspects of City Planning in Ancient Rome," *AJA* 18 (1914) 83-84.

*F. W. Read, "Boats or fortified villages?" *BIFAO* 13 (1917) 145-151.

Guido Calza, "The Aesthetics of the Antique City," *A&A* 12 (1921) 211-217.

*W. M. Ramsay, "Specimens of Anatolian Words," *OOR* 1 (1926) #2, 1-7. [VII. Kume and Rume, Village and Steet: */sic/* Ros, Head, p. 5]

*Jotham Johnson, "City Planning at Minturnae," *AJA* 37 (1933) 110.

J. Walter Graham, "The City Plan at Olynthus," *AJA* 38 (1934) 185-186.

*J. W. Jack, "Recent Biblical Archaeology," *ET* 51 (1939-40) 420-423. [Houses, Streets, Gates, pp. 420-421]

*J. W. Jack, "Recent Biblical Archaeology," *ET* 51 (1939-40) 544-548. [Cities and Villages, p. 544]

*Dorothy Mackay, "Ancient River Beds and Dead Cities," *Antiq* 19 (1945) 135-144.

*B[enjamin] Maisler, "The History of Settlement in Ancient Times," *Kobez* 4 (1945) XVII-XVIII.

*Alex Boëthius, "Ancient Town Architecture and the New Material from Olynthus," *AJP* 69 (1948) 396-407.

*M. Avnimelech, "Notes on the Geological History of the Yakron Valley and its Influence on Ancient Settlements," *IEJ* 1 (1950-51) 77-83.

G. Downey, "The City Plan of Antioch," *AJA* 55 (1951) 154-155.

Marcus Wheeler, "Self-Sufficiency and the Greek City," *JHI* 16 (1955) 416-420.

Paul MacKendrick, "Roman Town Planning," *Arch* 9 (1955) 126-133.

Mortimer Wheeler, "The First Towns?" *Antiq* 30 (1956) 132-136.

Leonard Woolley, "The First Towns?" *Antiq* 30 (1956) 224-225. [Reply by Mortimer Wheeler, p. 225]

*Robert M. Adams, "Survey of Ancient Water Courses and Settlements in Central Iraq," *Sumer* 14 (1958) 101-103.

*Y[ehuda] Karmon, "Geographical Conditions in the Sharon Plain and Their Impact on Its Settlement," *BIES* 23 (1959) #3/4, I-III.

Alexander Badawy, "Orthogonal and Axial Town Planning in Egypt," *ZÄS* 85 (1960) 1-12.

*Edward Neufeld, The Emergence of a Royal-Urban Society in Ancient Israel," *HUCA* 31 (1960) 31-53.

*Mortimer Wheeler, "Size and Baalbek," *Antiq* 36 (1962) 6-9.

Alexander M. Badawi*[sic]*, "The Modular System of Egyptian Town Plans," *BO* 19 (1962) 206-213.

*Peder Mortensen, "On the Chronology of Early Village farming Communities in Northern Iraq," *Sumer* 18 (1962) 73-80.

[D.(?)] Geoffrey Evans, "'Gates' and 'Streets': Urban Institutions in Old Testament Times," *JRelH* 2 (1962-63) 1-14.

*Roderick A. F. MacKenzie, "The City and Israelite Religion," *CBQ* 25 (1963) 60-70.

*V. A. Tcherikover, "Was Jerusalem a 'Polis'?" *IEJ* 14 (1964) 61-78.

*Peder Mortensen, "Additional Remarks on the Chronology of Early Village-Farming Communities," *Sumer* 20 (1964) 28-36.

*John H. Kroll, "Bronze Allotment Plates from Aeolis," *AJA* 73 (1969) 239.

Robert McC. Adams, "The Study of Ancient Mesopotamian Settlement Patterns and the Problem of Urban Origins," *Sumer* 25 (1969) 111-124.

§76 *2.3.9 Homes and Domestic Life*

( ) G., "Observations on the Hebrew mode of living in tents, or moveable habitations; with a view to illustrate the scriptures," *QCS* 1 (1819) 125-128.

†R. P. S., "Manners and Customs of the Ancient Egyptians, including their Private Life, Goverment, Laws, Arts, Manufactures, Religion, and Early History. By J. G. Wilkinson," *CE* 31 (1841-42) 38-60. *(Review)*

J. L. Lincoln, "Roman Private Life," *BS* 3 (1846) 217-241.

†Anonymous, "Private Life of the Greeks and Romans," *QRL* 79 (1846-47) 336-372. *(Review)*

*†Theo. G. Pinches, "Babylonian Tablets relating to Householding," *SBAP* 5 (1882-83) 67-71.

A[ndrew] Lang, "The Early History of the Family," *ContR* 44 (1883) 406-422.

[M. E.] Harkness, "Assyrian Domestic Affairs," *ONTS* 4 (1884-85) 323-325.

*G. Bertin, "The Babylonians at Home," *ContR* 49 (1886) 212-218.

F. B. Jevons, "Kin and Custom," *JP* 16 (1887-88) 87-110.

†Anonymous, "Provincial Life under the Roman Republic," *QRL* 167 (1888) 427-447. *(Review)*

Joseph Strauss, "Table Fellowship (Tischgemeinschaft) of Jew and Gentile," *ET* 4 (1892-93) 307-309.

*Theo. G. Pinches, "Notes upon some of the Recent Discoveries in the Realm of Assyriology, with Special Reference to the Private Life of the Babylonians," *JTVI* 26 (1892-93) 123-171, 184. [(Discussion, pp. 171-177) (Remarks by C. R. Conder, pp. 177-181; H. G. Tomkins, 182-183)]

*W. St. Chad Boscawen, "The Laws of the Family," *ET* 6 (1894-95) 371-372.

Edmund Belfour, "A Few Facts About the Domestic and Social Life of the Jews [Prior to] the Christic Period," *LCR* 14 (1895) 117-125.

F. E. Peiser, "A Sketch of Babylonian Society," *SIR* (1898) 579-599.

James Wells, "Bible Hospitality," *ET* 10 (1898-99) 62-64.

Gustaf Dalman, "Grinding in Ancient and Modern Palestine," *BW* 19 (1902) 9-18.

F. P. Ramsay, "The Next of Kin; His Rights and Duties," *CFL, N.S.*, 6 (1902) 333-338.

*E. W. G. Masterman, "Jewish Customs of Birth, Marriage, and Death," *BW* 22 (1903) 248-257.

*Caroline L. Ransom, "Chronological Survey of the Forms of Egyptian Stools, Chairs, and Couches," *AJA* 10 (1906) 81-82.

*Earle Bennett Cross, "Traces of the Matronymic Family in the Hebrew Social Organization," *BW* 36 (1910) 407-414.

Anonymous, "Daily Life of the Babylonians," *RP* 9 (1910) 284.

*W. T Pilter, "A Legal Episode in Ancient Babylonian Family Life," *SBAP* 32 (1910) 81-92, 129-142.

*Charles Newton Smiley, "Athenian Thought and Life as Reflected in the Parthenon Sculptures," *A&A* 4 (1916) 27-46.

*Archibald Robert Stirling Kennedy, "Jewish Everyday Life *as reflected in the Mishnah treatise shabbath,*" *SSO* 1 (1920) 35-48.

La Rue Van Hook, "The Exposure of Infants at Athens," *TAPA* 51 (1920) 134-145.

*Cornelia G. Harcum, "Roman Cooking Utensils in the Royal Ontario Museum of Archaeology," *AJA* 25 (1921) 37-54.

*Max Radin, "Teknonymy in the Old Testament," *HTR* 15 (1922) 293-297. *[Naming of a son after a father]*

Geo. P. G. Sobhy, "Customs and Supersitions of the Egyptians Connected with Pregnancy and Child-Birth," *AEE* 8 (1923) 9-16.

Brenda Z. Seligman, "Studies in Semitic Kinship," *BSOAS* 3 (1923-25) 51-68. (Errata, p. 279)

Brenda Z. Seligman, "Studies in Semitic Kinship, Part II," *BSOAS* 3 (1923-25) 263-279.

Ludwig Keimer, "Egyptian Formal Bouquets (Bouquets Montés)," *AJSL* 41 (1924-25) 145-161.

*Paul Haupt, "Ass. *talîmu,* full brother," *BAVSS* 10 (1927) Heft 2, 114-120.

John M. Cooper, "The Early History of the Family," *AQW* 3 (1930) 56-68.

Mary S. Shaw, "Family Life in Ancient Egypt," *JMUEOS* #18 (1932) 37-48.

*S[tephen] Langdon, "Notes on Sumerian Etymology and Syntax," *JRAS* (1933) 857-866. [V. Arûtu "relatives, relations," pp. 860-861]

James L. Kelso, "Living Again in Bible Houses," *BS* 92 (1935) 427-432.

Hjalmar Larsen, "On Baking in Egypt during the Middle Kingdom. An Archaeological Contribution," *AA* 7 (1936) 51-57.

*W. S. Ferguson, "*Polis* and *Idia* in Periclean Athens. The Relation between Public Service and Private Activities," *AmHR* 45 (1939-40) 269-278.

*Lucy Talcott, "From a Fifth Century Kitchen," *AJA* 45 (1941) 94.

*Steven T. Byington, "Hebrew Marginalia I," *JBL* 60 (1941) 279-288. [Terms of Hebrew Daily Life Surviving Only in Metaphor and Similie, pp. 279-281]

*J. W. Jack, "Recent Biblical Archaeology," *ET* 53 (1941-42) 113-117. [Israelite Baking Methods, pp. 113-115]

*W. E. Crum, "Bricks as Birth-Stool," *JEA* 28 (1942) 69.

*W. E. Crum, "Corrections to Brief Communication, vol. XXVIII, p. 69," *JEA* 29 (1943) 79. *[Bricks as Birth-Stool]*

*Hans Julius Wolff, "Marriage Law and Family Organization in Ancient Athens: A Study in the Interrelation of Public and Private Law in the Greek City," *Tr* 2 (1944) 43-96.

*J. L. Angel, "Health and Society in Greece," *AJA* 52 (1948) 373.

*I. Mendelsohn, "The Family in the Ancient Near East," *BA* 11 (1948) 24-40. [I. Monogamy and Polygamy; II. Marriage and Divorce; III. Women and Children]

*Josef Klíma, "The *patria potestas* in the Light of the Newly Discovered pre-Hammurabian Sources of Law," *JJP* 4 (1950) 275-288.

*George H. Mennenga, "The Prophets and Domestic Relations," *RefR* 7 (1953-54) #3, 1-4.

*(Miss) S. Strizower, "Enslavement and the Early Hebrew Lineage System," *Man* 54 (1954) #264.

*Robert Shafer, "System of Relationship in Lukian," *WO* 2 (1954-59) 484-501.

M. Theophane, "Family Customs in the Old Testament," *ACSR* 16 (1955) 198-210.

P. Buringh, "Living Conditions in the Lower Mesopotamian Plain in Ancient Times," *Sumer* 13 (1957) 30-46.

*Jacob J. Rabinowitz, "Miscellanea Papyrologica," *JJP* 11&12 (1957-58) 167-183. [I P. LOND. 1711 AND JEWISH TALMUDIC SOURCES, 2. The Husband's Undertaking to Maintain and Clothe the Wife; 3. The Husband's Undertaking not to Divorce the Wife Except for Certain Causes; 4. Proof by Three or More Villagers or City-dwellers, pp. 170-174]

*Dorothy Kent Hill, "Chairs and Tables of the Ancient Egyptians," *Arch* 11 (1958) 276-280.

*I. Mendelsohn, "On the Preferential Status of the Eldest Son," *BASOR* #156 (1959) 38-40.

*James Muilenburg, "Father and Son," *T&L* 3 (1960) 177-187.

Solomon Zeitlin, "The Offspring of Intermarriage," *JQR, N.S.,* 51 (1960-61) 135-140.

L. A. Lipin, "The Assyrian Family in the Second Half of the Second Millennium B.C.," *JWH* 6 (1960-61) 628-643.

*Nicholas M. Verdelis, "A Private House Discovered at Mycenae," *Arch* 14 (1961) 12-17.

*Lawrence E. Toombs, "Daily Life in Ancient Shechem," *DG* 32 (1961-62) 166-172.

*C. J. Gadd, "Two Sketches from the Life at Ur," *Iraq* 25 (1963) 177-188.

*John H. Chamberlayne, "Kinship Relationships among the early Hebrews," *Numen* 10 (1963) 153-166.

*Andrew F. Key, "The Giving of Proper Names in the Old Testament," *JBL* 83 (1964) 55-59.

*Isaiah Rackovsky, "Tribe and Family," *Trad* 7 (1964-66) #3, 15-20.

A[nson] F. Rainey, "Family Relationships at Ugarit," *Or, N.S.,* 34 (1965) 10-22.

R. E. Clements, "The Relation of Children to the People of God in the Old Testament," *BQL* 21 (1965-66) 195-205.

*B. Spooner, "Iranian Kinship and Marriage," *Iran* 4 (1966) 51-59. [O.T. refs., p. 54]

*Josef Klíma, "Marriage and Family in Ancient Mesopotamia," *NOP* 5 (1966) 99-103.

Cyril S. Rodd, "The Family in the Old Testament," *BTr* 18 (1967) 19-26.

*N. Postowskaja, "The *Familia* in Egypt of the Old Kingdom," *VDI* (1967) #1, 37.

*John Van Seters, "The Problem of Childlessness in Near Eastern Law and the Patriarchs of Israel," *JBL* 87 (1968) 401-408.

*Harry A. Hoffner Jr., "Birth and Name-Giving in Hittite Texts," *JNES* 27 (1968) 198-203.

E. Grace (Kazakevich), "Concubines in Classical Athens," *VDI* (1968) #1, 52.

*Bernard M. Boyle, "The Ancient Italian Town-house Reconsidered," *AJA* 73 (1969) 231-232.

*Anonymous, " The Problem of Childlessness in Near Eastern Law," *BH* 5 (1969) 106-114.

*F. C. Fensham, "Aspects of Family Law in the Covenant Code in Light of Ancient Near Eastern Parallels," *DI* 1 (1969) v-xix.

Aaron Skaist, "The Authority of the Brother at Arrapha and Nuzi," *JAOS* 89 (1969) 10-17.

§77 *2.3.9.1 Marriage & Divorce, and Sexual Morés*

*J. M. Sturtevant, "The Levitical Law of Incest," *BRCR, N.S.* 8 (1842) 423-444.

Edward Robinson, "Marriage of a Wife's Sister. The Biblical Argument," *BS* (1843) 283-301.

[Hermann] Zeller, "Marriage.—Translated from Zeller's Biblisches Wörterbuch," *ER* 16 (1865) 526-549.

*[Moses] Mielziner, "Rabbinical Sayings Concerning Marriage," *ONTS* 4 (1884-85) 180-181.

(Miss) ( ) Simcox, "Egyptian and Basque Marriage Contracts," *SBAP* 10 (1887-88) 479-487.

*B. Pick, "The Rites, Ceremonies and Customs of the Jews," *HR* 17 (1889) 119-206. [VI. Marriage, p. 202]

( ) Salomon, "Ancient and Modern Marriage Customs," *EN* 3 (1891) 225-229.

Noah Lathrop, "The Holy Scriptures and Divorce," *BS* 56 (1899) 266-277.,

Lysander Dickerman, "On Marriage and Divorce in Ancient Egypt," *JAOS* 13 (1889) lxvi.

James A. Quarles, "The Sociology of Joseph's Day: The Relations of the Sexes," *CFL, N.S.,* 4 (1901) 207-216.

*E. W. G. Masterman, "Jewish Customs of Birth, Marriage, and Death," *BW* 22 (1903) 248-257.

*S. L. Bowman, "Does the Bible Sanction Polygamy? 2 Sam. xii., 1-10," *CFL, 3rd Ser.,* 1 (1904) 221-223.

Ernest D[e Witt] Burton, "The Biblical Teaching concerning Divorce: I. Old Testament Teaching and Jewish Usage," *BW* 29 (1907) 121-127.

*C. H. W. Johns, "A Marriage Contract from the Chabour," *SBAP* 29 (1907) 177-184.

*W. J. Oldfield, "Marriage in the Apocrypha," *IJA* #16 (1908) 14-17.

Kerr D. Macmillan, "Marriage Among the Early Babylonians and Hebrews," *PTR* 6 (1908) 211-245.

*Claude R. Conder, "Notes on New Discoveries," *PEFQS* 41 (1909) 266-275. [Divorce (Deut. 24:1), pp. 271-272]

*F. Ll. Griffith, "A Demotic Marriage Contract of the Early Ptolemaïc Type," *SBAP* 31 (1909) 47-56.

*F. Ll. Griffith, "The Earliest Egyptian Marriage Contracts," *SBAP* 31 (1909) 212-220.

Ephraim Feldman, "Intermarriage Historically Considered," *YCCAR* 19 (1909) 271-301.

*Edward Carpenter, "On the Connection Between Homo-sexuality and Divination and the Importance of the Intermediate Sexes Generally in Early Civilizations," *AJRPE* 4 (1910-11) 219-243.

C. W. Emmet, "The Biblical Teaching on Divorce," *CQR* 70 (1910) 154-179.

*J. H. Bernard, "The Levitical Code and the Table of Kindred and Affinity," *Exp, 8th Ser.*, 4 (1912) 20-31.

William Frederic Badè, "Notes on the Stepmother Marriage among the Hebrews and Arabs," *PAPA* 45 (1913) lxxvi-lxxvii.

G. Margoliouth, "The Calendar, the Sabbath, and the Marriage Law in the Geniza-Zadokite Documents," *ET* 25 (1913-14) 560-564. [III. The Marriage Law]

W. A. Jarrell, "The Redemption of Sex," *SWJT* 3 (1919) #4, 57-65. [O.T. refs., pp. 57-59]

*George A. Barton, "An Important Social Law of the Ancient Babylonians—A Text Hitherto Misunderstood," *AJSL* 37 (1920-21) 62-71. *[Prostitution, and the rights of Prostitutes]*

*Morris Jastrow Jr., "*Ḫuruppati*, 'betrothal gifts'," *JAOS* 41 (1921) 314-316.

Eugene S. McCartney, "Sex Determination and Control in Antiquity," *AJP* 43 (1922) 62-70.

Allen Howard Godbey, "Blood; Marriage Contracts," *MQR, 3rd Ser.*, 49 (1923) 481-491.

*Nathaniel Reich, "Marriage and Divorce in Ancient Egypt: Papyrus Documents discovered at Thebes by the Eckley B. Coxe Jr. Expedition to Egypt," *MJ* 15 (1924) 50-57.

R. Campbell Thompson, "Note," *JRAS* (1925) 81. *[Semitic Kinship - Cousin Marriages]*

*Paul Haupt, "Ass. *napšu*, lust," *BAVSS* 10 (1927) 148-149.

Jacob Z. Lauterbach, "Talmudic-Rabbinic View on Birth Control," *YCCAR* 37 (1927) 369-384.

Anonymous, "Notes and Comments. Babylonian Wife-Insurance," *A&A* 26 (1928) 148.

Frederick C. Grant, "Divorce: Another View," *ATR* 11 (1928-29) 1-22. [O.T. refs., pp. 2-3]

W. O. E. Oesterley, "Jewish Marriage in Ancient and Modern Times," *CQR* 106 (1928) 89-104.

J[ulian] Morgenstern, "*Benna* Marriage (Matriarchat) in Ancient Israel and Its Historical Implications," *ZAW* 47 (1929) 91-110.

Julian Morgenstern, "Additional Notes on '*Benna* marriage (Matriarchat) in Ancient Israel'," *ZAW* 49 (1931) 46-58.

A. Mackenzie, "Marriage with a Deceased Wife's Sister Prohibited," *AusTR* 3 (1932) 127-166.

J. Paterson, "Divorce and Desertion in the Old Testament," *JBL* 51 (1932) 161-170.

*Clive H. Carruthers, "More Hittite Words," *Lang* 9 (1933) 151-161. [4. *pupus* 'paramour, lover, adulterer', pp. 155-156]

Solomon Zeitlin, "The Origin of the Ketubah, A Study in the Institution of Marriage," *JQR, N.S.*, 24 (1933-34) 1-7.

F. J. Smith, "Marriage Customs in the Bible," *CIR* 7 (1934) 395-402.

Louis M. Epstein, "The Institution of Concubinage among the Jews," *PAAJR* 6 (1934-35) 153-187.

Norman E. Himes, "Forerunners of the Modern Condom," *Janus* 42 (1938) 1-6.

*Charles F. Nims, "Notes on Univeristy of Michigan Demotic Papyri from Philadelphia," *JEA* 24 (1938) 73-82. [2. The *sš n s'nḫ* of Marriage Settlements, pp. 74-77]

*G. R. Driver and John C. Miles, "The *Sal-Zikrum* 'Woman-Man' in Old Babylonian Texts," *Iraq* 6 (1939) 66-70.

*J. W. Jack, "Recent Biblical Archaeology," *ET* 51 (1939-40) 420-423. [The Nuzi Tablets. Marriage Customs, p. 422]

Bayard H. Jones, "Marriage and Divorce," *ATR* 24 (1942) 38-62. [I. Pre-Christian Development of Matrimony, pp. 38-41]

Fritz Mezger, "Promised but not engaged," *JAOS* 64 (1944) 28-31.

E. Douglas Van Buren, "The Sacred Marriage in Early Times in Mesopotamia," *Or, N.S.,* 13 (1944) 1-72.

*Hans Julius Wolff, "Marriage Law and Family Organization in Ancient Athens: A Study in the Interrelation of Public and Private Law in the Greek City," *Tr* 2 (1944) 43-96.

Michael J. Gruenthaner, "Hebrew Tribal Intermarriage," *AER* 113 (1945) 149.

A. S. Herbert, "Marriage in the Bible and the Early Christian Church. I. The Old Testament Foundation," *ET* 59 (1947-48) 12-13.

*I. Mendelsohn, "The Family in the Ancient Near East," *BA* 11 (1948) 24-40. [I. Monogamy and Polygamy, pp. 24-25; II. Marriage and Divorce, pp. 25-36]

Fritz Mezger, "The Origin of a Specific Rule on Adultery in the Germanic Laws," *JAOS* 68 (1948) 145-148. *[Near Eastern Background Material]*

Boaz Cohen, "On the Theme of Betrothal in Jewish and Roman Law," *PAAJR* 18 (1948-49) 67-135.

H[arold] I. Bell, "Brother and sister marriage in Graeco-Roman Egypt," *RIDA, 1st Ser.,* 2 (1949) 83-92.

*A. Van Selms, "The Best Man and Bride—From Sumer to St. John, with a New Interpretation of Judges, Chapters 14 and 15," *JNES* 9 (1950) 65-75.

*Elise Baumgartel, "Tomb and fertility," *JKF* 1 (1950-51) 56-65.

Boaz Cohen, "Concerning Divorce in Jewish and Roman Law," *PAAJR* 21 (1952) 3-34.

Boaz Cohen, "Dowry in Jewish and Roman Law," *AIPHOS* 13 (1953) 57-85.

Jacob J. Rabinowitz, "Marriage Contracts in Ancient Egypt in the Light of Jewish Sources," *HTR* 46 (1953) 91-97.

Robert Gordis, "The Jewish Concept of Marriage," *Jud* 2 (1953) 225-238.

Jaroslav Černeý, "Consanguineous Marriages in Pharaonic Egypt," *JEA* 40 (1954) 23-29.

Emanuel Rackman, "Ethical Norms in the Jewish Law of Marriage," *Jud* 3 (1954) 221-228.

M. I. Finley, "Marriage, Sale, and Gift in the Homeric World," *SAENJ* 12 (1954) 7-33.

M. I. Finley, "Marriage, Sale, and Gift in the Homeric World," *RIDA, 3rd Ser.,* 2 (1955) 166-194.

S. B. Gurewicz, "Divorce in Jewish Law," *RJ* 7 (1955-57) 357-362.

Zeev W. Falk, "Mutual Obligations in the Ketubah," *JJS* 8 (1957) 215-217.

Reuven Yaron, "On Divorce in Old Testament Times," *RIDA, 3rd Ser.,* 4 (1957) 117-128.

*D. Daube, "Origin and the Punishment of Adultery in Jewish Law," *StP* 2 (1957) 109-113.

*Jacob J. Rabinowitz, "Miscellanea Papyrologica," *JJP* 11 & 12 (1957-58) 167-183. [I P. LOND. 1711 AND JEWISH TALMUDIC SOURCES, 1. The General Hypothec Formula, 2. The Husband's Undertaking to Maintain and Clothe the Wife; 3. The Husband's Undertaking not to Divorce the Wife Except for Certain Causes; 4. Proof by Three or More Villagers or City-dwellers; 5. ἔργῳ καὶ δυνάμει; 6. Ἀξιόπιστος and ἐλεύθερος; II ARAMAIC PAPYRUS BROOKLY */sic/* 7 AND P. FREIB. III 29; III A NOTE ON THE ΠΡΑΚΤΩΡ ΞΕΝΙΚΩΝ; IV THE MEANING OF ΑΛΛΑΣΣΩ IN SOME PAPYRI FROM KARANIS]

David Hallivni (Weiss), "Notes on the Mishna and Baraita," *Tarbiẓ* 27 (1957-58) #1, III-IV.

S. Lowy, "The Extent of Jewish Polygamy in Talmudic Times," *JJS* 9 (1958) 115-138.

*Reuven Yaron, "Aramaic Marriage Contracts from Elephantine," *JSS* 3 (1958) 1-39.

*Matitiahu Tsevat, "Marriage and Monarchial Legitimacy in Ugarit and Israel," *JSS* 3 (1958) 237-243.

Jean-Paul Audet, "Love and Marriage in the Old Testament," *Scrip* 10 (1958) 65-83. *(Trans. by F. Burke)*

*J[acob] J. Rabinowitz, "The puzzle of the 'Tirhatum bound in the bride's girdle'," *BO* 16 (1959) 188-190.

*Jacob J. Rabinowitz, "The 'Great Sin' in Ancient Egyptian Marriage Contracts," *JNES* 18 (1959) 73. [חטאה גדולה]

*W. L. Moran, "The Scandal of the 'Great Sin' at Ugarit," *JNES* 18 (1959) 280-281. [חטאה גדולה]

Solomon Zeitlin, "Family Life in Israel," *JQR, N.S.,* 51 (1960-61) 335-339.

*Reuven Yaron, "Aramaic Marriage Contracts: Corrigenda and Addenda," *JSS* 5 (1960) 66-70.

*Paul Ramsey, "The Marriage of Adam and Eve," *MTSB, Fall,* (1960) 35-56.

*William McKane, "Ruth and Boaz," *GUOST* 19 (1961-62) 29-40. *[Marriage]*

Herbert McCabe, "Sex and Sacred," *LofS* 16 (1961-62) 70-80.

Russell Middleton, "Brother-Sister and Father-Daughter Marriage in Ancient Egypt," *AmSR* 27 (1962) 603-611.

*J. Hoftijzer, and P. W. Pestman, "Hereditary Rights as laid down in the Marriage Contract Krael. 2," *BO* 19 (1962) 216-219.

Z. W. Falk, Endogamy in Israel," *Tarbiz* 32 (1962-63) #1, II-III.

*W. G. Lambert, "Celibacy in the World's Oldest Proverbs," *BASOR* #169 (1963) 63-64.

*E. K. Borthwick, "The Oxyrhynchus Musical Monody and Some Ancient Fertility Superstitions," *AJP* 84 (1963) 225-243.

*Hugh Ross Williamson, "Sodom and Homosexuality," *ClR* 48 (1963) 507-514.

E. Holloway, "'The Sin of Sodom'," *ClR* 48 (1963) 650-651.

*Nathaniel S. Lehrman, "Moses, Monotheism, and Marital Fidelity," *JRH* 3 (1963-64) 70-89.

*Reuven Yaron, "Matrimonial Mishaps at Eshnunna," *JSS* 8 (1963) 1-16.

Robert C. Campbell, "Teachings of the Old Testament Concerning Divorce," *Found* 6 (1963) 174-178.

R[euven] Yaron, "A Royal Divorce at Ugarit," *Or, N.S.,* 32 (1963) 21-31.

*John H. Chamberlayne, "Kinship Relationships among the early Hebrews," *Numen* 10 (1963) 153-166.

*Samuel Noah Kramer, "Cuneiform Studies and the History of Literature: The Sumerian Marriage Texts," *PAPS* 107 (1963) 485-527.

Mustafa El-Amir, "Monogamy, Polygamy, Endogamy and Consanguinity in ancient egyptian marriage," *BIFAO* 62 (1964) 103-107.

Jacob J. Rabinowitz, "On the Definition of Marriage as a 'Consortium Omnis Vitae'," *HTR* 57 (1964) 55-56.

*David Halivni Weiss, "The Use of קנה in Connection with Marriage," *HTR* 57 (1964) 244-248.

F. E. Frenkel, "Sex-Crime and Its Socio-Historical Background," *JHI* 25 (1964) 333-352. [III. Origins in Antiquity, pp. 335-337; X. An Example of Persistence of Ancient Thought in Modern Law, pp. 348-349; XI. Latent Influences of Ancient Thought on Present-day Attitude, pp. 349-350]

*L. M. Muntingh, "Married life in Israel according to the book of Hosea," *OTW* 7&8 (1964-65) 77-84.

Keith Hopkins, "Contraception in the Roman Empire," *CSSH* 8 (1965-66) 124-151.

Eric Young, "A Possible Consanguinous Marriage in the Time of Philip Arrhidaeus," *JARCE* 4 (1965) 69-71.

*B. Spooner, "Iranian Kinship and Marriage," *Iran* 4 (1966) 51-59. [O.T. refs., p. 54]

*J. J. Finkelstein, "Sex Offenses in Sumerian Laws," *JAOS* 86 (1966) 355-372.

S. Greengus, "Old Babylonian Marriage Ceremonies and Rites," *JCS* 20 (1966) 55-72.

R[euven] Yaron, "The Restoration of Marriage," *JJS* 17 (1966) 1-11.

*Josef Klíma, "Marriage and Family in Ancient Mesopotamia," *NOP* 5 (1966) 99-103.

*Anonymous, "Archaeology Sheds Light on A Marriage Contract," *BH* 3 (1967) #1, 18-21.

Bruce Vawter, "The Biblical Theology of Divorce," *CTSP* 22 (1967) 223-243. [I. Marriage in the Old Testament, pp. 223-227; II. Divorce in the Old Testament, pp. 227-230; III. Marriage and Divorce in the New Testament; IV. The New Testament Theology of Divorce]

Philip J. Murnion, "The Biblical Teaching on Sexuality," *DunR* 7 (1967) 162-176.

Robert Holst, "Polygamy and the Bible," *IRM* 56 (1967) 205-213.

Hans Goedicke, "Unrecognized Sportings," *JARCE* 6 (1967) 97-109. *[Egyptian Sexual Practices and Taboos]*

*Samuel Belkin, "Some Obscure Tradtion Mutually Clarified in Philo and Rabbinic Literature," *JQR, 75th* (1967) 80-103. [8. Marital Abstinence, pp. 98-100 (Gen. 8:18)]

Alan F. Guttmacher, "Traditional Judaism and Birth Control," *Jud* 16 (1967) 159-165.

Thomas D. McGonigle, "Sex in the Scriptures," *Listen* 2 (1967) #2 113-120.

Isaac Klein, "Abortion-A Jewish View," *DR* 241 (1967-68) 382-390.

Peter Staples, "Occasions for Sexual Abstinence in the Bible," *MC, N.S.,* 11 (1967-68) 26-29.

Panos D. Bardis, "Contraception in Ancient Egypt," *Cent* 12 (1968) 305-307.

*Kalonomos Kalman Epstein, "Sexual Purity and Redemption," *Jud* 17 (1968) 65-67.

Gerhard Jasper, "Polygyny*[sic]* in the Old Testament," *ATJ* #2 (1969) 27-57.

*William R. Eichhorst, "Ezra's Ethics on Intermarriage and Divorce," *GJ* 10 (1969) #3, 16-29.

*John Van Seters, "Jacob's Marriages and Ancient Near East Customs: A Re-examination," *HTR* 62 (1969) 377-395.

*Samuel Greengus, "The Old Babylonian Marriage Contract," *JAOS* 89 (1969) 505-532.

*Samuel Noah Kramer, "Sumerian Sacred Marriage Songs and the Biblical 'Song of Songs'," *MIO* 15 (1969) 262-274.

David Cohen, "Birth Control in Jewish Law," *NB* 50 (1969) 760-765.

*Samuel Greengus, "A Textbook Case of Adultery in Ancient Mesopotamia," *HUCA* 40&41 (1969-70) 33-44.

§78 *2.9.3.2 Levirate Marriage*

Samuel S. Cohon, "Marrying a Deceased Brother's Wife," *YCCAR* 35 (1925) 364-371. {Discussion by: Jacob Z. Lauterbach, pp. 372-376; [David] Philipson, p. 376; [Samuel] Schulman, pp. 376-379}

S[amuel] Belkin, "Levirate Marriage, Biblical and Post-Biblical," *JBL* 57 (1938) ix.

Millar Burrows, "The Ancient Oriental Background of Hebrew Levirate Marriage," *BASOR* #77 (1940) 2-15.

Millar Burrows, "Levirate Marriage in Israel," *JBL* 59 (1940) 23-33.

*Lambert Nolle, "Old Testament Laws of Inheritance and St. Luke's Genealogy of Christ," *Scrip* 2 (1947) 38-42. [II. The Levirate Marriage, pp. 39-40]

Dwight Acomb, "Levirate Marriage," *JC&S* 4 (1968) #2, 41-48.

*Samuel Belkin, "Levirate and Agnate Marriage in Rabbinic and Cognate Literature," *JQR, N.S.,* 60 (1969-70) 275-329.

§79 *2.3.9.3 Adoption*

*August C. Merriam, "Law Code of the Kretan Gortyna," *AJA, O.S.,* 1 (1885) 324-350; 2 (1886) 24-45. *[Greek Law Codes on Adoption & Property Rights]*

Theo. G. Pinches, "'Sonhood,' or Adoption Among the Early Babylonians," *AJSL* 7 (1890-91) 186-189.

*S. Feigin, "Some Cases of Adoption in Israel," *JBL* 50 (1931) 186-200. [I. The Adoption of Jephthah (Judges 11:1-3; II. Adoption of Foreign Step Children in the Time of Ezra]

Cyrus H. Gordon, "Fratriarcy in the Old Testament," *JBL* 54 (1935) 223-231. *[adoption // "brothership"]*

*Alan H. Gardiner, "Adoption Extraordinary," *JEA* 26 (1940) 23-29.

*Lambert Nolle, "Old Testament Laws of Inheritance and St. Luke's Genealogy of Christ," *Scrip* 2 (1947) 38-42. [I. Adoption, pp. 38-39]

*C. Bradford Wells, "Manumission and Adoption," *RIDA, 1st Ser.*, 3 (1949) 507-520.

W. H. Rossell, "New Testament Adoption, Graeco-Roman or Semitic?" *JBL* 70 (1951) xi.

W. H. Rossell, "New Testament Adoption, Graeco-Roman or Semitic?" *JBL* 71 (1952) 233-234.

*Samson Kardimon, "Adoption as a Remedy for Infertility in the Period of the Patriarchs," *JSS* 3 (1958) 123-126.

*I Mendelsohn, "A Ugaritic Parallel to the Adoption of Ephraim and Manasseh," *IEJ* 9 (1959) 180-183.

*Martin W. Schoenberg, "Huiothesia: The Word and the Institution," *Scrip* 15 (1963) 115-123. [Adoption in the Old Testament, pp. 119-120]

Anonymous, "Children by Proxy. Archaeology Reveals a Custom of Patriarchal Times," *BH* 2 (1965) #4, 11-16.

R. Yaron, "Varia on Adoption," *JJP* 15 (1965) 171-183.

§80 *2.3.9.4 Inheritance and Property Rights [See also: Land Tenure §89 ←]*

*August C. Merriam, "Law Code of the Kretan Gortyna," *AJA, O.S.*, 1 (1885) 324-350; 2 (1886) 24-45. *[Greek Law Codes on Adoption & Property Rights]*

*Theo. G. Pinches, "Babylonian Legal Documents referring to House Property, and the Law of Inheritance," *SBAT* 8 (1883-84) 271-298.

Theo. G. Pinches, "The Law of Inheritance in Ancient Babylonia," *AJSL* 3 (1886-87) 13-21.

*Joseph Jacobs, "The Junior-Right in Genesis," *ARL* 1 (1888) 331-342.

Gordon Calthrop, "The Mosaic Idea of Property," *TML* 2 (1889) 307-315.

*(Miss) M. A. Murray, "The Descent of Property in the Early Periods of Egyptian History," *SBAP* 17 (1895) 240-245.

Franklin Dudley Stone, "The Scriptural Doctrine of Property. *First Article,*" *CFL, N.S.*, 4 (1901) 155-160.

Franklin Dudley Stone, "The Scriptural Doctrine of Property. *Second Article,*" *CFL, N.S.*, 4 (1901) 222-226.

J. E. Hartman, "The Idea of Heredity in Israel," *HR* 47 (1904) 218-221.

*Milton G. Evans, "Biblical Teaching on the Righteous Acquisition of Property," *BW* 27 (1906) 275-285.

*Willard Brow Thorp and J. W. A. Stewart, "Biblical Teaching on the Righteous Acquisition of Property: Comment and Criticism," *BW* 27 (1906) 359-361.

Anonymous, "Crown Lands Given by the Ptolemies," *RP* 6 (1907) 342. *[Inheritance]*

Albert T. Clay, "The Son's Portion in the Oldest Laws Known," *ET* 27 (1915-16) 40-42.

E. Herman, "Ultimo-geniture in the Old Testament," *HR* 77 (1919) 196-197.

M. A. Murray, "Royal Inheritance in the XIXth Dynasty," *AEE* 10 (1925) 100-104.

Boaz Cohen, "An Essay on Possession in Jewish Law," *PAAJR* 6 (1934-35) 123-137.

*Samuel Atlas, "Rights of Private Property and Private Profit," *YCCAR* 54 (1944) 212-241. {Discussion by: [Jacob] Singer, pp. 241-242; [Herman I.] Pollack, p. 242; [Ferdinand M.] Isserman, pp. 242-243; Isaiah Sonne, pp. 243-246; Julius Gordon, pp. 246-247; [Moses] Landau, p. 247; [Abraham] Shinedling, pp. 247-248; Eric Werner, pp. 248-249; Solomon B. Freehof, p. 249; [Bernard J.] Bamberger, pp. 249-251; Reply by Samuel Atlas, pp. 251-256]}

Pierre M. Purves, "Commentary on Nuzi Real Property in the Light of Recent Studies," *JNES* 4 (1945) 68-86.

John Lurye, "The Evolution and Philosophy of Property," *RJ* 3 (1946-47) 181-186. [The Occupation Theories of Property *(Roman Law)*, p. 183]

Hildegard Lewy, "A Propos of Nuzi Real Property," *JNES* 6 (1947) 180-181.

Perrie M. Purves, "Additional Remarks on Nuzi Real Property," *JNES* 6 (1947) 181-185.

*Lambert Nolle, "Old Testament Laws of Inheritance and St. Luke's Genealogy of Christ," *Scrip* 2 (1947) 38-42. [III. Heiresses, pp. 40-41]

Robert Samuel Rogers, "The Roman Emperors as Heirs and Legatees," *TAPA* 78 (1947) 140-158.

*Rafael Taubenschlag, "The Inviolability of Domicle in Graeco-Roman Egypt," *ArOr* 18 (1950) Part 4, 293-297.

*E. Neufeld, "The status of the male minor in Talmud," *RIDA, 1st Ser.,* 6 (1951) 121-140.

*O. R. Sellers, "Progeniture in Israel," *JBL* 71 (1952) vi.

*Franz Steiner, "Enslavement and the Early Hebrew Lineage System: An Explanation of Genesis 47:29-31, 48:1-16," *Man* 54 (1954) #102.

*(Miss) S. Strizower, "Enslavement and the Early Hebrew Lineage System," *Man* 54 (1954) #264.

*J[acob] J. Rabinowitz, "A Legal Formula in the Susa Tablets in an Egyptian Document of the Twelfth Dynasty, in the Aramaic Papyri, and in the Book of Daniel [4, 14]," *B* 36 (1955) 223-226. *[Property Rights]*

*I Mendelsohn, "On the Preferential Status of the Eldest Son," *BASOR* #156 (1959) 38-40.

*Zeev W. Falk, "Testate Succession in Jewish Law," *JJS* 12 (1961) 67-77.

*J. Hoftijzer, and P. W. Pestman, "Hereditary Rights as laid down in the Marriage Contract Krael. 2," *BO* 19 (1962) 216-219.

A. Ehrman, 'Gentile Interest in Jewish Law: A Chapter from Selden's 'De Successionibus'," *CNI* 13 (1962) #3/4, 31-37.

*Alan [H.] Gardiner, "The Gods of Thebes as Guarantors of Personal Property," *JEA* 48 (1962) 57-69.

*David Asheri, "Laws of Inheritance, Distribution of Land and Political Constitutions in Ancient Greece," *HJAH* 12 (1963) 1-21.

*N. H. Snaith, "The Daughters of Zelophehad," *VT* 16 (1966) 124-127.

*J. Weingreen, "The Case of the Daughters of Zelophchad," *VT* 16 (1966) 518-522.

Solomon Zeitlin, "Testamentary Succession: A Study in Tannaitic Jurisprudence," *JQR, 75th,* (1967) 574-581.

*N. Postowskaja, "The *Familia* in Egypt of the Old Kingdom," *VDI* (1967) #1, 37 *[Heirs]*

*I. M. Diaknoff, "Problems of Property. The Structure of Near Eastern Society to the Middle of the Second Millenium B.C.," *VDI* (1967) #4, 35. [Numbers 1 & 2]

*Jac. J. Janssen and P. W. Pestman, "Burial and inheritance in the community of the necropolis workmen at Thebes," *JESHO* 11 (1968) 137-170.

*R[ivkah] Harris, "Notes on the Babylonian Cloister and Hearth: A Review Article," *Or, N.S.*, 38 (1969) 133-145. *(Review) [Inheritance]*

§81 *2.3.10 Education*

Albert Smith, "Greek and Roman Education," *BRCR, N.S.,* 8 (1842) 21-50.

Anonymous, "Hebrew Education," *BRCM* 5 (1848-49) 70-92.

Dom. Augustin Calmet, "The Schools of the Hebrews," *JSL, 1st Ser.,* 3 (1849) 87-103. [Note by editor, pp. 103-107] *(Trans. by Alexander J. D. D'Orsey)*

N. C. Schaeffer, "School Life in Ancient Athens," *RChR* 26 (1879) 217-230.

O. H. P. Corprew, "Ancient Greek Education," *MQR, 2nd Ser.,* 5 (1883) 265-281.

Charles G. Herbermann, "Education in Ancient Babylonia, Phoenicia and Judea," *ACQR* 18 (1893) 449-480, 562-587, 719-733.

A. A. Berle, "Education Among the Semites," *BS* 53 (1896) 370-372.

Carl Heinrich Cornill, "The Education of Children in Ancient Israel," *Monist* 13 (1902-03) 1-23. *(Trans. by W. H. Carruth)*

*James A. Quarles, "Sociology of Joseph's Day," *CFL, N.S.,* 5 (1902) 340-352. [Educational & Esthetic, pp. 348-352]

*Anonymous, "Asia:—Babylonia," *RP* 2 (1903) 347. *[Excavations of a school house]*

Anonymous, "A Babylonian School," *MQR, 3rd Ser.,* 30 (1904) 394-395.

*Ernest G. Loosey, "Jewish Home Teaching and Old Testament Criticism," *LQHR* 106 (1906) 288-298.

C. Robinson, "Schoolmasters in Ancient Greece," *ContR* 102 (1912) 257-260.

A. Buchler, "Learning and Teaching in the Open Air in Palestine," *JQR, N.S.,* 4 (1913-14) 485-491.

*F. H. Colson, "Philo on Education," *JTS* 18 (1916-17) 151-162.

Fletcher H. Swift, "Hebrew Education During the Pre-Exilic Period," *OC* 31 (1917) 725-740.

Fletcher H. Swift, "Hebrew Education in the Family After the Exile," *OC* 32 (1918) 9-29.

*Fletcher H. Swift, "Hebrew Education in School and Society. During the Period of Reaction to Foreign Influence," *OC* 32 (1918) 228-253.

*Fletcher H. Swift, "Hebrew Education in School and Society," *OC* 32 (1918) 312-316. [II. Woman and the Education of Girls]

*John A. Maynard, "The Problem of the Formation of Character in the Light of the History of Hebrew Education," *ATR* 3 (1920-21) 228-235.

Jacob Z. Lauterbach, "The Names of the Rabbinical Schools and Assemblies in Babylonia," *HUCA, Jubilee Volume,* (1925) 211-222.

*Emil Johnson, "The Ancient Hebrew Education. *A Study in Proverbs, Ecclesiastes, and Talmud,*" *AugQ* 4 (1925) 215-227, 338-349; 5 (1926) 8-24.

Meyer Waxman, "The Conception of Education in the Old Testament," *OC* 41 (1927) 220-231.

John B. Stentz, "The Instruction and Education of Children in Pre-Christian Israel," *SS* 3 (1929) #1, 4-17.

*S. L. Mohler, "Slave Education in the Roman Empire," *TAPA* 71 (1940) 262-280.

S. Krauss, "Outdoor Teaching in Talmudic Times," *JJS* 1 (1948-49) 82-84.

*Samuel Noah Kramer, "Schooldays: a Sumerian Composition Relating to the Education of a Scribe," *JAOS* 69 (1949) 199-215.

*Clarence A. Forbes, "The Education and Training of Slaves in Antiquity," *TAPA* 86 (1955) 321-360.

Moshe Aberbach, "Educational Institutions and Problems during the Talmudic Age," *HUCA* 37 (1966) 107-120.

Alan Cameron, "The End of Ancient Universities," *JWH* 10 (1966-67) 653-673.

J. Katz, "Jewish Civilization as Reflected in the Yeshivot—Jewish Centers of Higher Learning," *JWH* 10 (1966-67) 674-704.

Kenan T. Erim, "The School of Aphrodisias," *Arch* 20 (1967) 18-25.

*Z. E. Kurzweil, "Fundamental Principles of Jewish Education in the Light of the Halachah," *Jud* 16 (1967) 176-185.

*Bernard M. W. Knox, "Silent Reading in Antiquity," *GRBS* 9 (1968) 421-435.

Shmuel Safrai, "Elementary Education, Its Religious and Social Significance in the Talmudic Period," *JWH* 11 (1968-69) 147-169.

§82 *2.3.10.1 The Development of Writing & Book Production [See also: The Alphabet→]*

Anonymous, "Writing Instruments," *CongML* 14 (1831) 341-342.

*[Joseph Fullonton], "Invention of Writing;—The Alphabet;—and Printing," *FBQ* 10 (1862) 431-441. [Writing, pp. 432-436]

A. H. Sayce, "The Use of Papyrus as Writing Material among the Accadians," *SBAT* 1 (1872) 343-345.

Hermann L. Strack, "Writing Among the Hebrews," *AJSL* 2 (1885-86) 209-217.

*†Theo. G. Pinches, "Assyriological Notes," *SBAP* 8 (1885-86) 240-245. [[cuneiform] = *šaṭāru*, "a written document", p. 241]

Henry Preserved Smith, "Ancient Book-Making," *BS* 43 (1886) 690-710.

*T[errien] de Lacouperie, "Did Cyrus Introduce Writing into India?" *BOR* 1 (1886-87) 58-64.

John P. Peters, "Did the Hebrews Use Clay Writing Tablets," *JBL* 8 (1888) 125-128.

Anonymous, "The Antiquity of Writing," *MR* 76 (1894) 478-481.

Morris Jastrow Jr., "An Arabic tradition of writing on clay," *ZA* 10 (1895-96) 99.

Ira M. Price, "Recent Thought on the Origin of the Cuneiform Writing," *AJSL* 15 (1898-99) 145-156.

Anonymous, "Antiquity of Writing," *MR* 84 (1902) 304-307.

*Stephen D. Peet, "Ancient Alphabets and Sacred Books," *AAOJ* 27 (1905) 265-280.

*C[laude] R. Conder, "Notes on Biblical Antiquities. 3. *Writing with Lead*," *PEFQS* 37 (1905) 156.

*Andrew Craig Robinson, "The Bearing of Recent Oriental Discoveries on Old Testament History," *JTVI* 38 (1906) 154-176. (Discussion, pp. 176-181) [The Literary Conditions of the Mosaic Age, pp. 171-173]

Henry Proctor, "The Origin of the Art of Writing," *AAOJ* 31 (1909) 168-169.

*Anonymous, "Remains of Roman Ink," *RP* 8 (1909) 318.

*James H. Breasted, "The Physical Processes of Writing in the Early Orient and Their Relation to the Origin of the Alphabet," *AJSL* 32 (1915-16) 230-249.

*A. H. Godbey, "'Men of a Name'," *AJSL* 43 (1926-27) 42-44. *[Use of Seals]*

*C. Ainsworth Mitchell, "Marking-Ink in Ancient Egypt," *AEE* 12 (1927) 18.

Raymond P. Dougherty, "Writing upon Parchment and Papyrus among the Babylonians and Assyrians," *JAOS* 48 (1928) 109-135.

S. H. Hooke, "The Early History of Writing," *Antiq* 11 (1937) 261-277.

*Doreen Canaday Spitzer, "Ancient Ink-wells," *AJA* 46 (1942) 125.

*J. Philip Hyatt, "The Writing of an Old Testament Book," *BA* 6 (1943) 71-80. [The First Edition of Jeremiah's Book; Writing was a Learned Profession; Materials on Which Scribes Wrote; Ancient Pens and Ink; The Scribe's Kit]

*H. L. Ginsberg, "Ugaritic Studies and the Bible," *BA* 8 (1945) 41-58. [II. Writing in Western Asia in General and at Ugarit in Particular, pp. 45-48]

*H. L. Lorimer, "Homer and the Art of Writing: A Sketch of Opinion between 1713 and 1939," *AJA* 52 (1948) 11-23. [Corrections, *AJA* 54 (1950) p. 203]

*David Diringer, "Early Hebrew Writing," *BA* 13 (1950) 74-95. [Literary Sources; Paucity of Hebrew Inscriptions; Early Hebrew Inscriptions—Script and Language; The Origin of the Early Hebrew Script; Early Hebrew Epigraphy—Development of Early Hebrew Writing; End of Early Hebrew Writing; Styles of Early Hebrew Writing; Early Hebrew Monumental or Lapidary Style of Writing; Early Hebrew Current Hand; Early Hebrew Book-Hand]

C. H. Roberts, "The Codex," *PBA* 40 (1954) 169-204.

*D. J. Wiseman, "Assyrian Writing Boards," *Iraq* 17 (1955) 3-13.

Margaret Howard, "Technical Descripton of the Ivory Writing Boards from Nimrud," *Iraq* 17 (1955) 14-20 *[misnumbered as pp. 1-7]*

*T. C. Skeat, "The Use of Dictation in Ancient Book-Production," *PBA* 42 (1956) 179-208.

*G. G. Garner, "Writing in the Ancient World: Writing and the Books of Moses," *AT* 1 (1956-57) #1, 14-16.

Jerome Quinn, "Take a Scroll and Write—Jer. 36:2," *BibT* #2 (1962) 87-95.

Kenneth Willis Clark, "The Posture of the Ancient Scribe," *BA* 26 (1963) 63-72.

Maurice Pope, "The Origins of Writing in the Near East," *Antiq* 40 (1966) 17-23.

*F. N. Hepper and T. Reynolds, "Papyrus and the adhesive properties of its cell sap in relation to paper-making," *JEA* 53 (1967) 156-157.

§83 *2.3.10.2 Libraries*

Convers, Francis, "On the Historical Credibility of the Reported Burning of the Alexandrian Library by order of the Caliph Omar," *JAOS* 7 (1862) liv.

Anonymous, "Assyrian Libraries," *DTQ* 2 (1876) 155-156.

Morris Jastrow Jr., "The text-books of the Babylonians and Assyrians," *JAOS* 14 (1890) clxx-clxxi.

A. H. Sayce, "The Libraries of Assyria and Babylonia," *Janus* 2 (1897-98) 547-549.

*Percy E. Newberry, "Extracts from my Notebooks (IV.)," *SBAP* 23 (1901) 218-224. [22. The Site of the Library of Akhenaten, p. 219]

*John P. Peters, "The Nippur Library," *JAOS* 26 (1905) 145-164.

Morris Jastrow Jr., "Did the Babylonian Temples have Libraries?" *JAOS* 27 (1906) 147-182.

Fayette L. Thompson, "The Temple Library at Nippur," *CFL, 3rd Ser.*, 7 (1907) 122-125.

Alan S. Hawkesworth, "The Temple Library of Nippur," *OC* 24 (1910) 770.

Frederic Kenyon, "The Library of a Greek of Oxyrhynchus," *JEA* 8 (1922) 129-138.

*H. R. Hall, "An Egyptian Royal Bookplate: The *Ex Libris* of Amenophis III and Teie," *JEA* 12 (1926) 30-33.

George H. Bushnell, "The Alexandrian Library," *Antiq* 2 (1928) 196-204.

A. H. Sayce, "The Libraries of David and Solomon," *JRAS* (1931) 783-790.

*T. C. Skeat, "The Use of Dictation in Ancient Book-Production," *PBA* 42 (1956) 179-208.

*James T. Hooker, "Sets and Files within the Knossos Tablets," *KZFE* 4 (1965) 86-95.

*Bernard M. W. Knox, "Silent Reading in Antiquity," *GRBS* 9 (1968) 421-435.

§84 *2.3.11 Amusements, Athletics, Entertainment, Games, Recreation (including Hunting), & Sectarian Festivals and Holidays*

†Anonymous, "Field Sports of the Ancient Greeks and Romans," *QRL* 118 (1865) 468-498. *(Review)*

*Franz Delitzsch, "Dancing and Pentateuch Criticism in Correlation," *Exp, 3rd Ser.,* 4 (1886) 81-95.

W. Knighton, "The Sportsman in Ancient Greece and Italy," *DUM* 89 (1877) 231-240.

*Karl Blind, "Ale-Drinking in Old Egypt and the Thrako-Germanic Race," *SRL* 25 (1895) 23-41.

Daniel Quinn, "The Games of Olympia," *CUB* 2 (1896) 172-179.

John Patterson, "Pulvis Olympicus," *SRL* 27 (1896) 276-292.

William KcKendree Bryant, "The Greek Games," *NW* 9 (1900) 301-323.

E. Towry Whyte, "Types of Egyptian Draughts-men," *SBAP* 24 (1902) 261-263.

W. L. Nash, "Ancient Egyptian Draughts-boards and Draughts-men," *SBAP* 24 (1902) 341-348.

Walton Brooks McDaniel, "Some Passages concerning Ball-games," *TAPA* 37 (1906) 121-134.

Anonymous, "Liquor Saloons Four Thousand Years Ago," *MQR, 3rd Ser.,* 33 (1907) 611.

*Alfred Emerson, "The Case of Kyniska," *AJA* 15 (1911) 60.

F. B. Jevons, "Masks and the Origin of the Greek Drama," *Folk* 27 (1916) 171-192.

*Julian Morganstern, "The Etymological History of the Three Hebrew Synonyms for 'to Dance.' ḤGG, ḤLL, and KRR, and their Cultural Significance," *JAOS* 36 (1916) 321-332.

Ella Bourne, "Ancient Bull Fights," *A&A* 5 (1917) 142-153.

*Charles Newton Smiley, "Olympia and Greek Athletics," *A&A* 10 (1920) 177-189.

Joseph William Hewitt, "The Comic Aspect of the Greek Athletic Meet," *AJA* 30 (1926) 82.

James E. Dunlap, "The Swimming-Stroke of the Ancients," *A&A* 26 (1928) 26-35.

[W. M.] Flinders Petrie, "A Ptolemaic Holiday," *AEE* 12 (1927) 75-76.

Lillian B. Lawler, "The Ancient Greek Dance: The Maenads," *AJA* 31 (1927) 91-92.

*Paul Haupt, "The Cuneiform Terms for Sport," *BAVSS* 10 (1927) Heft 2, 127-132.

Paul Haupt, "Throw-stick and Clap-net," *BAVSS* 10 (1927) Heft 2, 185-192.

Casper J. Kraemer, "A Greek Element in Egyptian Dancing," *AJA* 35 (1931) 125-138.

*John A. Wilson, "Ceremonial Games of the New Kingdom," *JEA* 17 (1931) 211-220.

Anita E. Klein, "Some Greek Playthings," *PAPA* 62 (1931) xxvii-xxviii.

W. L. Westermann, "Entertainment in the villages of Graeco-Roman Egypt," *JEA* 18 (1932) 16-27.

W[illiam] F[oxwell] Albright, "A Set of Egyptian Playing Pieces and Dice from Palestine," *Miz* 1 (1933) 130-134.

C. J. Gadd, "An Egyptian Game in Assyria," *Iraq* 1 (1934) 45-50.

Irene Ringwood Arnold, "The Festivals of Rhodes," *AJA* 39 (1935) 113.

Irene Ringwood Arnold, "The Shield of Argos," *AJA* 40 (1936) 128. *[Festival]*

Irene Ringwood Arnold, "Festivals of Rhodes," *AJA* 40 (1936) 432-436.

Zaki Saad, "Khazza Lawizza," *ASAE* 37 (1937) 212-218. *[Games]*

E. Douglas Van Buren, "A Gaming Board from Tall Ḫalaf," *Iraq* 4 (1937) 11-15.

*Zaki Y. Saad, "Handles for copper piercers or gaming pieces?" *ASAE* 38 (1938) 333-344. (Reply by Walter B. Emery, pp. 345-346)

R. G. Austin, "Greek Board Games," *Antiq* 14 (1940) 257-271.

Walter F. Snyder, "Public Anniversaries in the Roman Empire: The Epigraphical Evidence for their Observance during the First Three Centuries," *YCS* 7 (1940) 223-317.

A. M. G. Little, "The Social Archaeology of the Attic Theater," *AJA* 45 (1941) 96.

*Marcus N. Tod, "Big Game Hunters in Ptolemaic and Roman Libya," *JEA* 27 (1941) 159-160.

*J. W. Jack, "Recent Biblical Archaeology," *ET* 53 (1941-42) 367-370. [Children's Games, p. 370]

C. J. Gadd, "Babylonian Chess?" *Iraq* 8 (1946) 66-72.

Harry J. Leon, "Ball Playing at Rome," *TAPA* 77 (1946) 320.

E[dward] Robertson, "The Sport of the Assyrian Kings," *JMUEOS* #24 1947) 33-38. *[Lion Hunting]*

Robert Scranton, "A Hot Bath of the Greek Period at Corinth," *AJA* 54 (1950) 259.

William Bell Dinsmor, "The Athenian Theater in the Fifth Century," *AJA* 54 (1950) 260.

Dorothy Barr Thompson, "Parks and Gardens of the Ancient Empires," *Arch* 3 (1950) 101-106.

Cyrus H. Gordon, "Belt-Wrestling in the Bible World," *HUCA* 23 (1950-51) Part 1, 131-136.

Dorothy Barr Thompson, "Ancient Gardens in Greece and Italy," *Arch* 4 (1951) 41-47.

Cyrus H. Gordon, "Marginal Notes on the Ancient Middle East," *JKF* 2 (1952-53) 50-61. [V. Hebraica: d. The Wrestling Belt, pp. 55-56]

Winifred Needler, "A Thirty-Square Draught-Board in the Royal Ontario Museum," *JEA* 39 (1953) 60-75.

B. H. Stricker, "The Origin of the Greek Theatre," *JEA* 41 (1955) 34-47.

*George E. Bean, "Victory in the Pentathlon," *AJA* 60 (1956) 361-368.

George Highmore, "The Victor of the Greek Pentathlon," *Folk* 67 (1956) 129-141.

*Alexander Badawy, "Maru-Aten: Pleasure Resort or Temple?" *JEA* 42 (1956) 58-64.

*Anonymous, "When Kings, Hunted Lions, and Men. No. 1. Palace Pictures of nearly 3000 years ago Support the Scriptures," *AT* 3 (1958-59) #2, 11-14.

Brian A. Sparkes, "Kottabos: An Athenian After-Dinner Game," *Arch* 13 (1960) 202-207.

Frantisek Lexa, "Physical Culture in Ancient Egypt," *NOP* 1 (1960) #2, 19.

Harold E. Winter, "Recreation in the Old Testament," *LQHR* 186 (1961) 55-57.

Bernard Ashmole, "Torch-Racing at Rhamnus," *AJA* 66 (1962) 233-234.

*Osamu Sudzuki, "Royal Lion-hunting Scene on the Silver Cup of Solokha," *Orient* 2 (1962) 37-43.

Robert L. Alexander, "The Royal Hunt," *Arch* 16 (1963) 243-250.

A. Leo Oppenheim, "On Royal Gardens in Mesopotamia," *JNES* 24 (1965) 328-333.

Richard S. Ellis and Briggs Buchanan, "An Old Babylonian Gameboard with Scuptured Decoration," *JNES* 25 (1966) 192-201.

*Henry R. Immerwahr, "An Inscribed Terracotta Ball in Boston," *GRBS* 8 (1967) 255-266.

*Michael Grant, "The Gladiators," *HT* 17 (1967) 610-617.

Anne Ward, "The Cretan Bull Sports," *Antiq* 42 (1968) 117-122.

Foad Yacoub, "A Private Bath Discovered at Kîmân-Fâris, Fayûm," *ASAE* 60 (1968) 55-56.

Kamal Sedky, "Ptolemaic Baths of Kôm Ganâdy," *ASAE* 60 (1968) 221-225.

*George F. Dales, "Of Dice and Men," *JAOS* 88 (1968) 14-23.

Kassem Hassan Al Mindlawi, "Physical Culture in Ancient Iraq," *NOP* 7 (1968) 77-79.

§85 *2.3.12 Music and Musical Instruments [See also: Studies concerning Accents, Rhyme and Metre and Musical Notations →]*

C. I. Smyth, "Observations on certain Musical Terms, used by the Ancient Greeks; in a Letter to a Friend," *MMBR* 29 (1810) 121-122.

Musicus, "On the Music of Ancient Greece and Rome," *MMBR* 58 (1824-25) 407-408.

[Friedrich] Pfeiffer, "Pfeiffer on the Music of the Ancient Hebrews," *BRCR* 6 (1835) 136-172, 357-411. *(Trans. by O. A. Taylor)*

Oliver A. Taylor, "What kind of Instruments of Music were in use among the Egyptians?" *BRCR* 9 (1837) 273-300.

A. H. W., "On the Ancient Music of the Hebrews in General, and their Temple Music in Particular. Part I," *DUM* 41 (1853) 675-683.

A. H. W., "On the Ancient Music of the Hebrews in General, and their Temple Music in Particular. Part II.—Conclusion," *DUM* 42 (1853) 21-31.

Anonymous, "Biblical and Classical Hymnology," *CRB* 21 (1856) 283-291.

Anonymous, "Music in its Religious Uses," *DR, N.S.,* 2 (1864) 128-158. *(Review) [Original numbering as volume 54]*

*Dunbar I. Heath, "The Orders for Musical Services at Hamath," *PEFQS* 13 (1881) 118-124.

†Anonymous, "Sacred Music," *LQHR* 56 (1881) 51-64. *(Review) [Brief reference to Music in the Bible]*

Anonymous, "The Organ," *MQR, 2nd Ser.,* 4 (1882) 358-367. [O.T. refs, pp. 358-360]

[John Stainer], "The Music of the Bible," *ONTS* 3 (1883-84) 55-57.

*Erastus Wentworth, "Musical Instruments in the Revision," *MR* 68 (1886) 546-564.

Cyrus Adler, "The Shofar, its use and origin," *JAOS* 14 (1890) clxxi-clxxv. *[cornet]*

*Anonymous, "Music in the Old Testament," *ONTS* 11 (1890) 114.

S. A. Binion, "Critical Remarks," *JAOS* 15 (1893) cix-cx. *[The Shofar]*

*Alexander Renshaw De Witt, "Early Hebrew Song Life," *PER* 9 (1895-96) 435-452. [Patriot Songs and the Messiah; Psalmody; Prophecy; Secular Song]

E. Towry Whyte, "Egyptian Musical Instrument," *SBAP* 21 (1899) 143-144.

Eneas B. Goodwin, "Early Maccabean War Songs," *AER* 23 (1900) 120-128.

*Walter L. Nash, "A Wooden Handle for Small Cymbals, from Egypt," *SBAP* 22 (1900) 117-118.

H. G. Simpson, "The Music of the Bible," *MR* 83 (1901) 359-373.

William Ridgeway, "The Origin of the Guitar and Fiddle," *Man* 8 (1908) #7.

Waldo S. Pratt, "Music and Musical Instruments in the Bible," *HR* 57 (1909) 53-55.

Carl Heinrich Cornill, "Music in the Old Testament. Lecture Given for the Benefit of the Home for Aged Music Teachers at Breslau, February 9, 1906," *Monist* 19 (1909) 240-264.

Phillips Barry, "The Bagpipe not a Hebrew Instrument," *Monist* 19 (1909) 459-461.

Jacob Singer, "Jewish Music Historically Considered," *YCCAR* 23 (1913) 232-248. [Biblical Times, pp. 233-235; Temple Origins; Traditional Variants; Musical Forms; Synagogal Music; Paytanim; Period of Decadence; Reform; Modern Status; Our Problem and Its Solution]

Anonymous, "Old Testament Music," *HR* 67 (1914) 197.

W. H. Grattan Flood, "The Music of the Bible," *AER* 53 (1915) 298-305. *(Review)*

*N. de Garis Davies, "An Alabaster Sistrum dedicated by King Teta," *JEA* 6 (1920) 69-72.

*A[braham] Z[ebi] Idelson *[sic]*, "Hebrew Music with special reference to the Musical Intonations in the Recital of the Pentateuch," *JPOS* 1 (1920-21) 80-94.

*S[tephen] Langdon, "Babylonian and Hebrew Musical Terms," *JRAS* (1921) 169-191.

*F. W. Read, "A New Interpretation of the Phaestos Disk: The Oldest Music in the World?" *PEFQS* 53 (1921) 29-54.

A[braham] Z[ebi] Idelsohn, "Synagog Music—Past and Present," *YCCAR* 33 (1923) 344-355.

Henry George Farmer, "The Evolution of the Ṭanbūr or Pandore," *GUOST* 5 (1923-28) 26-28.

O. R. Sellers, "Intervals in Egyptian Music," *AJSL* 41 (1924-25) 11-16.

Sol Baruch Finesinger, "Musical Instruments in the O.T.," *HUCA* 3 (1926) 21-76.

*L. B. Ellis, "The Sistrum of Isis," *AEE* 12 (1927) 19-25.

H[enry] G[eorge] Farmer, "Ancient Egyptian Instruments of Music," *GUOST* 6 (1929-33) 30-34.

H[enry] G[eorge] Farmer, "The Study of Musical Instruments in Primitive Culture," *GUOST* 8 (1936-37) 29-31.

Ovid R. Sellers, "Musical Instruments of Israel," *BA* 4 (1941) 33-47. [The Hand Drum; The Lyre; The Harp(?); The Zither(?); The Oboe; The Trumpet; Cymbals; The Sistrum; Other Instruments; Tunes Still Unknown]

Henry George Farmer, "The Importance of Ethnological Studies," *GUOST* 11 (1942-44) 27-30. *[Musical Instruments]*

*Miriam Lichteim, "The Songs of the Harpers," *JNES* 4 (1945) 178-212.

Nicholas B. Bodley, "The Auloi of Meroë," *AJA* 50 (1946) 217-240.

Howard F. Vos, "The Music of Israel," *BS* 106 (1949) 446-457.

P. R. Kirby, "The Trumpets of Tut-ankh-amen and their Successors," *Man* 49 (1949) #13.

Howard F. Vos, "The Music of Israel (Concluded)," *BS* 107 (1950) 64-70.

*(Sister) St. Catherine Nestor, "Music in the Psalms," *ABenR* 2 (1951) 190-193.

James H. Wente, "Music of Old Testament Times," *Amb* 3 (1954-55) #6, 14.

‡Ruth Needham, "Music in Bible History; A Bibliography," *FLB* #30 (1956) 3-6.

*William M. Calder III, "An Unrecognized Metrical Text from Temple G at Selinus," *AJA* 61 (1957) 182. [Greek Marching Song (Embaterion)]

*William Green, "Ancient Comment on Instrumental Music in the Psalms," *RestQ* 1 (1957) 3-8.

*J. Leibovitch, "The Statuette of an Early Harper and String-Instruments in Egyptian History," *JEA* 46 (1960) 53-59.

Isadore Freed, "Organs—Biblical and Modern," *CCARJ* 8 (1960-61) #2, 43-45.

*Edward F. Wente, "Egyptian 'Make Merry' Songs Reconsidered," *JNES* 21 (1962) 118-128.

*Samuel Noah Kramer, "The Biblical 'Song of Songs' and the Sumerian Love Songs," *Exped* 5 (1962-63) #1, 25-31.

*Robert North, "The Cain Music," *JBL* 83 (1964) 373-389.

*Eric Werner, "The Role of Tradition in the Music of the Synagogue," *Jud* 13 (1964) 156-163.

*D. M. Dixon and K. P. Wachsman, "A Sandstone Statue of an Auletes from Meroe," *Kush* 12 (1964) 119-125.

James Mountford, "Music and the Romans," *BJRL* 47 (1964-65) 198-211.

*R. Ross Holloway, "Music at the Panathenaic Festival," *Arch* 19 (1966) 112-119.

*Ulrich S. Leupold, "Worship Music in Ancient Israel: Its Meaning and Purpose," *Resp* 9 (1967-68) 116-124.

Walter E. Buszin, "Religious Music Among the Jews," *CTM* 39 (1968) 422-431.

David Wulstan, "The Tuning of the Babylonian Harp," *Iraq* 30 (1968) 215-228.

*O. R. Gurney, "An Old Babylonian Treatise on the Tuning of the Harp," *Iraq* 30 (1968) 229-233.

*Ulrich S. Leupold, "Worship Music in Ancient Israel: Its Meaning and Purpose," *CJT* 15 (1969) 176-186.

*Eugene W. Bushala, "ῥόπτρον as a Musical Instrument," *GRBS* 10 (1969) 169-172.

R. D. Barnett, "New Facts About Musical Instruments from Ur," *Iraq* 31 (1969) 96-103. [Appendix: A Short Note on African Lyres in Use Today, by Jean Jenkins, p. 103]

*Samuel Noah Kramer, "Sumerian Sacred Marriage Songs and the Biblical 'Song of Songs'," *MIO* 15 (1969) 262-274.

§86 *2.3.13 Nutrition (Includes Methods of Dining)*

*†Anonymous, "Lemons," *MMBR* 29 (1810) 250. *(Misnumbered as p. 242)*

†Philo-Antiquarias, "Opinions of the ancients respecting Salt," *MMBR* 41 (1816) 319-321.

Leonard Withington, "Man and His Food," *BS* 11 (1854) 139-155.

J. H. Swainson, "On the position of the guests at a Roman dinner-table," *JP* 6 (1875-76) 219-221.

*E. Bonavia, "Bananas and Melons as Dessert Fruits of Assyrian Monarchs and Courtiers," *BOR* 4 (1889-90) 169-175.

*Karl Blind, "Ale-Drinking in Old Egypt and the Thrako-Germanic Race," *SRL* 25 (1895) 23-41.

*E. W. G. Masterman, "Food and Its Preparation in Modern Palestine," *BW* 17 (1901) 407-419.

*James A. Quarles, "Sociology of Joseph's Day," *CFL, N.S.,* 5 (1902) 97-108. [Food & Drink, pp. 100-103]

*Joseph Offord, "Notes and Queries. (1) *Garlic,*" *PEFQS* 40 (1908) 338-339.

Anonymous, "Pork in Ancient Babylonia," *RP* 9 (1910) 120.

*St[ephen] Langdon, "Babylonian Wisdom," *Baby* 7 (1913-23) 129-229. [The supposed Rules of Monthly Diet, pp. 221-229]

*S[tephen] Langdon, "Lexicographical and epigraphical notes," *RAAO* 13 (1916) 1-4. [(1) *Li-ga, ga-li = duḫdu,* "Cream", p. 1]

George Farmer, "Leaven," *ET* 30 (1918-19) 142.

*A. Lucas, "Egyptian Use of Beer and Wine," *AEE* 13 (1928) 1-5.

*Julius Grant, "Brewing in Ancient Times," *Antiq* 4 (1930) 232-233.

*J. W. Jack, "Recent Biblical Archaeology," *ET* 51 (1939-40) 544-548. [Barley Food, p. 547]

Ahmed Zaky */sic/* and Iskander Zaky, "Ancient Egyptian Cheese," *ASAE* 41 (1942) 295-313.

*Louis F. Hartman and A. L. Oppenheim, "On Beer and Brewing Techniques in Ancient Mesopotamia According to the XXIIIrd Tablet of the Series ḪAR.ra=*ḫubullu*," *JAOSS* #10 (1950) 1-55.

Naum Jasny, "The daily bread of the ancient Greeks and Romans," *Osiris* 9 (1950) 227-253.

*A[braham] Malamat, "Scales of Rationing in Pap. Anastasi I and the Bible," *BIES* 19 (1955) #3/4 ii.

*Hildegard Lewy, "On Some Old Assyrian Cereal Names," *JAOS* 76 (1956) 201-204.

*Alfred C. Andrews, "The Mints of the Greeks and Romans and Their Condimentary Uses," *Osiris* 13 (1958) 127-149.

*Alfred C. Andrews, "Thyme as a Condiment in the Graeco-Roman Era," *Osiris* 13 (1958) 150-156.

*Thalia Phillies Howe, "Linear B and Hesiod's Breadwinners," *TAPA* 89 (1958) 44-65.

*Thalia Phillies Howe, "Linear B and Hesiod's Breadwinners," *AJA* 63 (1959) 189.

*Martin Levey, "Food and its Technology in Ancient Mesopotamia: the Earliest Chemical Processes and Chemicals," *Cent* 6 (1959) 36-51.

Hans Helbaek, "Studying the Diet of Ancient Man," *Arch* 14 (1961) 95-101.

Hans Helbaek, "Isin Larsa and Horian Food Remains at Tell Barmosian in the Dokan Valley," *Sumer* 19 (1963) 27-35.

Hans Helbaek, "Early Hussunan Vegetable Food at Tell as-Sawwan near Samarra," *Sumer* 20 (1964) 45-48.

*Jack R. Harlan, "A Wild Wheat Harvest in Turkey," *Arch* 19 (1966) 197-201.

*Vít Bubeník, "The World's First Beer Brewers," *NOP* 5 (1966) 163-165.

§87 *2.3.14 Dietary Laws*

[John Gorham] Palfrey, "The Law of Meats," *JSL, 1st Ser.,* 7 (1851) 456.

Anonymous, "The Bible and Strong Drink," *WR* 103 (1875) 50-64. [O.T. refs., pp. 55-59]

*Henry Hayman, "The Teaching of Holy Scripture regarding fermented Liquors," *CM* 9 (1879) 65-81.

*Anonymous, "The Scriptural View of Wine and Strong Drink," *CQR* 8 (1879) 413-436.

*A. B. Rich, "Do the Scriptures Prohibit the Use of Alcoholic Beverages?" *BS* 37 (1880) 99-133, 305-327, 401-418. *[Word Studies of Old Testament Terms]*

G. Lansing, "A Kid in its Mother's Milk," *ONTS* 3 (1883-84) 19-20.

*B. Felsenthal, "'Gamaliel ben Pedahzur'—Fermented or Unfermented Wine?" *ONTS* 4 (1884-85) 131-132.

*B. Felsenthal, "Use of Wine by the Jews," *ONTS* 4 (1884-85) 184-185. (Correction, p. 230)

C. G. Montefiore, "Dr. Weiner on the Dietary Laws," *JQR* 8 (1895-96) 392-413.

(Mrs.) M. Joseph, "The Dietary Laws from a Woman's Point of View," *JQR* 8 (1895-96) 643-651.

M. Hyamson, "Another Word on the Dietary Laws," *JQR* 9 (1896-97) 294-310.

J. G. Frazer, "Not to seethe a Kid in its Mother's Milk," *Man* 7 (1907) #96.

*Andrew Lang, "Seething the Kid," *Man* 7 (1907) #103.

Irwin Hoch De Long, "Prohibitory Food Laws in Israel," *RChR, 4th Ser.*, 11 (1907) 222-228.

Henry Preserved Smith, "Animal Sources of Pollution," *JBL* 30 (1911) 55-60.

*T. B. McCorkindale, "An Ancient Ritual Prohibition," *HR* 67 (1914) 227. *[On not seething a kid in its mother's milk]*

*Paul Haupt, "Alcohol in the Bible," *JBL* 36 (1917) 75-83.

*Royden Keith Yerkes, "The Unclean Animals of Leviticus 11 and Deuteronomy 14," *JQR, N.S.*, 14 (1923-24) 1-29.

*Ira M. Price, "Swine in Old Testament Taboo," *JBL* 44 (1925) 154-157.

*Max Radin, "The Kid and Its Mother's Milk," *AJSL* 40 (1923-24) 209-218.

Jacob Singer, "Taboos of Food and Drink," *OC* 41 (1927) 368-380.

*G. B. Gray, "Passover and Unleavened Bread: The Laws of J, E, and D," *JTS* 37 (1936) 241-253.

*D. Daube, "A Note on a Jewish Dietary Law," *JTS* 37 (1936) 289-291. *[On not seething a kid in its mother's milk]*

*Norman Golb, "The Dietary Laws of the Damascus Covenant in Relation to Those of the Ḳaraites," *JJS* 8 (1957) 51-69.

*Herold S. Stern, "The Ethics of the Clean and the Unclean," *Jud* 6 (1957) 319-327.

*S. Stein, "The Dietary Laws in Rabbinic and Patristic Literature," *StP* 2 (1957) 141-154.

Samuel H. Dresner, "The Mitzvah of Kashrut. The Meaning of the Dietary Laws for Our Time," *CJ* 12 (1957-58) #1, 1-15.

*Jacob Milgorm, "The Biblical Diet Laws as an Ethical System. *Food and Faith*," *Interp* 17 (1963) 288-301.

*J. M. Grintz, "'Ye Shall not Eat *on* the Blood'," *Zion* 31 (1966) #1/2, I-II.

§88 *2.3.1 Agriculture and Husbandry - General Studies [For Irrigation see §107→]*

*Henricus Ehrenfried Warnekros, "On the Fertility of Palestine, and its Principal Advantages, Compared with those of Egypt," *BibR* 1 (1825) 155-197, 437-446.

†[Thomas Gisborne], "Ancient Agricultural Literature," *QRL* 87 (1850) 141-189. *(Review)*

†Anonymous, "The Roman at his Farm," *QRL* 104 (1858) 451-474. *(Review)*

*Claude R. Conder, "The Fertility of Ancient Palestine," *PEFQS* 8 (1876) 120-132.

A. H. Sayce, "Horticulture in the Time of Merodach-Baladan," *OBJ* 1 (1880) 202-203.

A. H. Sayce, "Horticulture in the Time of Merodach-Baladan," *AAOJ* 3 (1880-81) 128-129.

*A. H. Sayce, "Miscellaneous Notes," *ZA* 2 (1887) 331-340. [17. Agricultural Calendar, pp. 333-335]

Anonymous, "Solomon's Stables," *EN* 4 (1892) 523.

G. M. Mackie, "Requests and Replies," *ET* 8 (1896-97) 109-110. *[Rods and Staffs]*

E. W. G. Masterman, "Agricultural Life in Palestine," *BW* 15 (1900) 185-192.

J. T. Gracey, "The Bible and Shepherd Life in the Orient," *HR* 43 (1902) 341-344.

*Alan H. Gardiner, "The Egyptian Word for 'herdsman' &c.," *ZÄS* 42 (1905) 116-123. [hieroglyph]

*Jas. P. Conry, "Some Old Biblical Customs in Modern Palestine," *AER* 39 (1908) 169-175.

*L. W. King, "An Early mention of Cotton: the Cultivation of *Gossypium Arboreum,* or Tree-Cotton, in Assyria in the Seventh Century, B.C.," *SBAP* 31 (1909) 339-343.

*A. T. Clay, "Babylonian Section. An Ancient Plow," *MJ* 1 (1910) 4-6.

Mahmoud effendi Roushdy, "The treading of sown seed by swine," *ASAE* 11 (1911) 162-163.

*(Miss) Marie N. Buckman, "The Mystery of the Predynastic Egyptian Furnace Solved," *HR* 66 (1913) 114-115. *[Ovens for Grain Preparation]*

*James A. Montgomery, "Abraham as the Inventor of an Improved Plow," *MJ* 4 (1913) 55-56.

*[James A. Montgomery(?)], "Abraham as the Inventor of the Improved Plow," *RP* 13 (1914) 57.

*Theophilus G. Pinches, "Sumerian Women for Field-Work," *JRAS* (1915) 457-463.

*W. Sherwood Fox, "A Problem of Cultus and Agriculture," *PAPA* 47 (1915) xvi-xvii.

*(Miss) Deette Rolfe, "Enviromental Influences in the Agriculture of Ancient Egypt," *AJSL* 33 (1916-17) 157-168.

Eugene Tavenner, "The Roman Farmer and the Moon," *TAPA* 49 (1918) 67-82.

*A. H. Pruessner, "Date Culture in Ancient Babylonia," *AJSL* 36 (1919-20) 213-232.

*Aylward M. Blackman, "A Painted Pottery Model of a Granary in the collection of the late Jeremiah James Colman, Esq., of Carrow House, Norwich," *JEA* 6 (1920) 206-208.

*Albert Hiorth, "Concerning Irrigation in Ancient and Modern Times, the Cultivation and Electrification of Palestine with the Mediterranean as the Source of Power," *JTVI* 55 (1923) 133-144, 154-157. (Discussion, pp. 145-154)

*W. L. Westermann, "Orchard and Vineyard Taxes in the Zenon Papyri," *JEA* 12 (1926) 38-51.

*E. A. Marples, "Ancient Reaping Hooks," *Man* 29 (1929) #37.

James H. Hoban, "The Shepherd of Palestine. A Figure of the Eternal Shepherd," *SS* 3 (1929) #1, 18-23.

Anonymous, "Notes and Comments. Hittite Horse Training," *A&A* 32 (1931) 186.

*David M. Robinson, "Bouzyges and the First Plough on a Krater by the Painter of the Naples Hephaistos," *AJA* 35 (1931) 152-160.

*A. E. Watkins, "The Origin of Cultivated Plants," *Antiq* 7 (1933) 73-80.

*S[tephen] Langdon, "Notes on Sumerian Etymology and Syntax," *JRAS* (1933) 857-866. [I. Šandanaku "Gardener", p. 857]

Arthur Stanley Pease, "Notes on Ancient Grafting," *TAPA* 64 (1933) 66-76.

*Shlomo Marenof, "Digging in Talmud Archaeology," *AJSL* 50 (1933-34) 93-95. *[Agriculture]*

G. W. B. Huntingford, "Prehistoric Ox-Yoking," *Antiq* 8 (1934) 456-459.

F. Ll. Griffith and Mrs. G. M. Crowfoot, "On the Early Use of Cotton in the Nile Valley," *JEA* 20 (1934) 5-12.

*George Sarton, "The artificial fertilization of date-palms in the time of Ashur-nasir-pal B.C. 885-860," *Isis* 21 (1934) 8-13.

*Cecil E. Curwen, "Agriculture and the Flint Sickle in Palestine," *Antiq* 9 (1935) 62-66.

*Max Hilzheimer, "The Evolution of the Domestic Horse," *Antiq* 9 (1935) 133-139.

*Solomon Gandz, "Artifical fertilization of date-palms in Palestine and Arabia," *Isis* 23 (1935) 245-250.

*George Sarton, "Additional note on date culture in ancient Babylonia," *Isis* 23 (1935) 251-252.

*George Sarton, "Third note on date culture in ancient Babylonia," *Isis* 26 (1936) 95-98.

G. Ernest Wright, "The Good Shepherd," *BA* 2 (1939) 44-48.

*N. M. Davies and N. de G. Davies, "Harvest Rites in a Theban Tomb," *JEA* 25 (1939) 154-156.

*Richard A. Parker, "A Late Demotic Gardening Agreement. Medinet Habu Ostracon 4038," *JEA* 26 (1940) 84-113.

*J. W. Jack, "Recent Biblical Archaeology," *ET* 52 (1940-41) 353-357. [Agriculture, pp. 353-355]

*J. W. Jack, "Recent Biblical Archaeology," *ET* 52 (1940-41) 454-458. [After the Harvest, pp. 454-456]

*J. W. Jack, "Recent Biblical Archaeology," *ET* 53 (1941-42) 208-212. [Israelite Horticulture, pp. 211-212]

J. G. Winter and H. C. Youtie, "Cotton in Graeco-Roman Egypt," *AJP* 65 (1944) 249-258.

*Hildegard Lewy, "Assyro-Babylonian and Israelite Measures of Capacity and Rates of Seeding," *JAOS* 64 (1944) 65-73.

A. Leo Oppenheim and Louis F. Hartman, "The Domestic Animals of Ancient Mesopotamia," *JNES* 4 (1945) 152-177.

*N. Shalem, "The Desert and the Sown in Judea," *Kobez* 4 (1945) X.

*I. Mendelsohn, "Slavery in the Ancient Near East," *BA* 9 (1946) 74-88. [III. The Economic Role of Slavery, 3. Slaves in Agriculture, p. 87]

*N. Wilbush, "Olive-Oil Industry in Ancient Times," *BIES* 13 (1946-47) #1/2, III.

*T. Burton Brown, "Early Bread Wheat," *Antiq* 24 (1950) 40.

*Robert J. Braidwood, "Jarmo: A Village of Early Farmers in Iraq," *Antiq* 24 (1950) 189-195.

*Philip Keep Reynolds, "Earliest Evidence of Banana Culture," *JAOSS* #12 (1951) 1-28. [Graeco-Roman References, pp. 9-11]

T. Reekmans, "Ἐὰν μηθεὶς ἔαθῆι στρατεύσασθαι in *UPZ 110* (164 B.C.) 1. 162," *Aeg* 32 (1952) 286-292. *[Agriculture]*

D. Zohary, "Notes on Ancient Agriculture in the Central Negev," *IEJ* 4 (1954) 17-25.

*Elinor M. Husselman, "The Granaries of Karanis," *TAPA* 83 (1952) 56-73.

G. Goossens, "Sennacherib's Experiment: Cotton Reaches the West," *HT* 3 (1953) 122-127.

*T. Fish, "Seasonal Labour according to GURUŠ Texts from Umma," *MCS* 4 (1954) 1-8.

*A. L[eo] Oppenheim, "A Note on *ṣôn barzel*," *IEJ* 5 (1955) 89-92. *[Legal Idiom concerning Husbandry]*

*G. Ernest Wright, "Israelite Daily Life," *BA* 18 (1955) 50-79. [Farming, pp. 50-56]

*Ernest Wiesenberg, "Related Prohibitions: Swine Breeding and the Study of Greek," *HUCA* 27 (1956) 213-233.

*J. *[sic]* Kedar, "The Problem of the Mounds or 'Tuleilat el 'Anab' and Their Relation to Ancient Agriculture in the Central Negev," *BIES* 20 (1955-56) #1/2, III.

*William L. Reed, "A Recent Analysis of Grain from Ancient Dibon in Moab," *BASOR* #146 (1957) 6-10.

Y. Kedar, "Ancient Agriculture at Shivtah in the Negev," *IEJ* 7 (1957) 178-189.

Martín S. Ruipérez, "Notes on Mycenaean Land-Division and Livestock-Grazing," *Minos* 5 (1957) 174-206.

*D. G. Reder, "Ancient Egypt, a Center of Agriculture," *JWH* 4 (1957-58) 801-817.

*J. A. Thompson, "The Economic Significance of Transjordan in Old Testament Times," *ABR* 6 (1958) 143-168. [Agriculture and Pastoral Pursuits in Transjordan in the Iron Age, pp. 152-156]

*Carl O. Sauer, "Jericho and Composite Sickles," *Antiq* 32 (1958) 187-189.

Y. Kedar, "Ancient Agriculture in the Niṣṣanah-Beerothaim Region," *BIES* 22 (1958) #3/4, n.p.n.

*M. Evenari, Y. Ahaoroni, L. Shanan, and N. H. Tadmor, "The Ancient Desert Agriculture of the Negev. III. Early Beginnings," *IEJ* 8 (1958) 231-268. {Part I published in *Ktavim* 8 (1958); Parts II & IV in *Ktavim* 9 (1959) *[Hebrew Text]*}

Hans Helbaek, "How Farming Began in the Old World," *Arch* 12 (1959) 183-189.

*Philip Mayerson, "Ancient Agricultural Remains in the Central Negeb: The Teleilât el-'Anab," *BASOR* #153 (1959) 19-31.

Y. Kedar, "The Ancient Agriculture in the 'Avdat Area," *BIES* 23 (1959) #3/4, V-VI.

M. W. Prausnitz, "The First Agricultural Settlements in Galilee," *IEJ* 9 (1959) 166-174.

Y. Kedar, "The Ancient Agriculture in the 'Avdat Area, *SGEI* #1 (1959) V-VI.

Y. Karmon, "Soil Utilisation in the Safed Area," *BIES* 24 (1959-60) #4, I-II. *[Modern Usage]*

*Philip Mayerson, "The Ancient Agricultural Remains of the Central Negeb: Methodology and Dating Criteria," *BASOR* #160 (1960) 27-37.

*Y[ohanan] Aharoni, M. Evenari, L. Shanan, N. H. Tadmor,"The Ancient Desert Agriculture of the Negev. V: An Israelite Agricultural Settlement at Ramat Maṭred," *IEJ* 10 (1960) 23-36, 97-111.

Y. Karmon, "Soil Utilisation in the Safed Area," *SGEI* #2 (1960) I-II. *[Modern Usage]*

Hans Helbaek, "Ancient Crops in the Shahrzoor Valley in Iraqi Kurdistan," *Sumer* 16 (1960) 79-81.

I. Chiva, "Cypro-Mycenæan and Early Agriculture," *Man* 60 (1960) #182.

Hans Helbaek, "Late Bronze Age and Byzantine Crops at Beycesultan in Anatolia," *AS* 11 (1961) 77-97.

*Peder Mortensen, "On the Chronology of Early Village farming Communities in Northern Iraq," *Sumer* 18 (1962) 73-80.

*Miguel Civil, "Sumerian Harvest Time," *Exped* 5 (1962-63) #4, 37-39.

K. D. White, "Wheat-Farming in Roman Times," *Antiq* 37 (1963) 207-212.

*Geoffrey Evans, "The Incidence of Labour-Service at Mari," *RAAO* 57 (1963) 65-78. [II. Agricultural corvées, pp. 70-72]

Hans Helbaek, "First Impressions of Çatal Hüyük Plant Husbandry," *AS* 14 (1964) 121-123.

*Yehuda Kedar, "More about the Teleilât el-'Anab in the Negeb," *BASOR* #176 (1964) 47-49.

*Anonymous, "Villas and Victuals," *BH* 1 (1964) #1, 3-7. *[Agriculture]*

Paul Huard, "A propos des Buchânes a corne déformée de Faras," *Kush* 12 (1964) 63-79. [English Summary, pp. 80-81]

*Peder Mortensen, "Additional Remarks on the Chronology of Early Village-Farming Communities," *Sumer* 20 (1964) 28-36.

*J. G. D. Clark, "Radiocarbon Dating and the Spread of Farming Economy," *Antiq* 39 (1965) 45-48.

K. D. White, "The Productivity of Labour in Roman Agriculture," *Antiq* 39 (1965) 102-107.

*Philip Mayerson, "The Issue of the Teleilât el-'Anab," *BASOR* #178 (1965) 69.

Douglas Young, "Some Puzzles about Minoan woolgathering," *KZFE* 4 (1965) 111-122.

*George Devereux, "The abduction of Hippodameia as 'aition' of a Greek animal husbandry rite. A structural analysis," *SMSDR* 36 (1965) 3-25.

K. D. White, "The Gallo-Roman Harvesting Machine," *Antiq* 40 (1966) 49-50.

*Jack R. Harlan, "A Wild Wheat Harvest in Turkey," *Arch* 19 (1966) 197-201.

Z. Ron, "Agricultural Terraces in the Judean Mountains," *IEJ* 16 (1966) 33-49, 111-122.

*F. Charles Fensham, "An Ancient Tradition of the Fertility of Palestine," *PEQ* 98 (1966) 166-167.

*Philip Mayerson, "A Note on Demography and Land Use in the Ancient Negeb," *BASOR* #185 (1967) 39-43.

*I. J. Gelb, "Growth of a Herd of Cattle in Ten Years," *JCS* 21 (1967) 64-69.

*M. Heltzer, "Royal Dependants (bnš mlk) and Units (gt) of the Royal Estate in Ugarit," *VDI* (1967) #2, 47.

(Mrs.) Mary Aiken Littauer, "The Function of the Yoke Saddle in Ancient Harnessing," *Antiq* 42 (1968) 27-31.

Jane M. Renfrew, "A Note on the Neolithic Grain from Can Hasan," *AS* 18 (1968) 55-56.

*J. J. Finkelstein, "An Old Babylonian Herding Contract and Genesis 31:38f.," *JAOS* 88 (1968) 30-36.

John T. Killen, "Minoan woolgathering: a reply," *KZFE* 7 (1968) 105-123; 8 (1969) 23-38.

E. S. Higgs and M. R. Jarman, "The Origins of Agriculture: a Reconsideration," *Antiq* 43 (1969) 31-41.

*(Mrs.) Mary Aiken Littauer, "Bits and Pieces," *Antiq* 43 (1969) 289-300. *[Horse Bits]*

*Edith Porada, "Iranian Art and Archaeology: A Report of the Fifth International Congress, 1968," *Arch* 22 (1969) 54-65. [The Emergence of Early Farming Communities p. 54; Early Farming Communities and Their External Relations, pp. 54 & 56; Early Farming Communities of Western Iran, pp. 56-58]

Douglas Young, "Minoan woolgathering: a rejoinder," *KZFE* 8 (1969) 39-42.

Linda Braidwood and Robert Braidwood, "Current thoughts on the beginnings of food-production in southwestern Asia," *MUSJ* 45 (1969) 147-155.

*Henry T. Wright, "The Administration of Rural Production in an Early Mesopotamian Town," *UMMAAP* #38 (1969) i-xiii, 1-162.

§89 *2.3.1.1 Land Tenure & Land Laws*

*T[homas] B. Thayer, "The Land-Laws of Moses," *UQGR, N.S.*, 9 (1872) 220-228.

John Fenton, "The Primitive Hebrew Land Tenure," *TR* 14 (1877) 489-503.

Anonymous, "The System of Land Tenure in Ancient Palestine," *CQR* 10 (1880) 404-435.

James Neil, "Land Tenure in Ancient Times, as Preserved by the Present Village-Communities in Palestine," *JTVI* 24 (1890-91) 155-183, 196-203. [(Discussion, pp. 183-192) (Remarks by E. A. Finn, pp. 192-196)]

*P. T. Forsyth, "Land Laws of the Bible," *ContR* 104 (1913) 496-504.

H. Stuart Jones, "Land Problems in Ancient Rome," *ERCJ* 224 (1916) 60-79.

*Joseph Offord, "Archaeological Notes on Jewish Antiquities. XLI. *Land Ownership in Ancient Palestine and Egypt and the Jubliee Year,*" *PEFQS* 50 (1918) 37-39.

*M. Cary, "The land legislation of Caesar's first consulship," *JP* 35 (1919-20) 174-190.

*Robert H. Pfeiffer, "On Babylonian-Assyrian Feudalism (*ilku*)," *AJSL* 39 (1922-23) 66-68.

Albert T. Olmstead, "Land Tenure in the Ancient Orient," *AmHR* 32 (1926-27) 1-9.

*Knud Fabricius, "The Hittite System of Land Tenure in the Second Millennium B.C. (Saḫḫan and luzzi)," *AO* 7 (1928-29) 275-292.

Thomas Robert Shannon Broughton, "Roman Landholding in Asia Minor," *TAPA* 65 (1934) 207-239.

*Russel M. Geer, "Notes on the Land Law of Tiberius Gracchus," *TAPA* 70 (1939) 30-36.

H. Lewy, "The Nuzian Feudal System," *Or, N.S.,* 11 (1942) 1-40, 209-250, 297-349.

John Bradford, "A Technique for the Study of Centuriation," *Antiq* 21 (1947) 197-204.

*Allan Chester Johnson, "The ἐπιβολή of land in Roman Egypt," *Aeg* 32 (1952) 61-72.

*John Gray, "Feudalism in Ugarit and Early Israel," *ZAW* 64 (1952-53) 49-55.

Emile Marmorstein, "The Origins of Agricultural Feudalism in the Holy Land," *PEQ* 85 (1953) 111-117.

K. H. Henry, "Land Tenure in the Old Testament," *PEQ* 86 (1954) 5-15.

*Emmett L. Bennett Jr., "The Landholders of Pylos," *AJA* 59 (1955) 176; 60 (1956) 103-133.

W. Edward Brown, "Land Tenure in Mycenaean Pylos," *HJAH* 5 (1956) 385-400.

M. I. Finley, "Homer and Mycenae: Property and Tenure," *HJAH* 6 (1957) 133-159.

*David Asheri, "Laws of Inheritance, Distribution of Land and Political Constitutions in Ancient Greece," *HJAH* 12 (1963) 1-21.

A. French, "Land Tenure and the Solon Problem," *HJAH* 12 (1963) 242-247.

*Geoffrey Evans, "The Incidence of Labour-Service at Mari," *RAAO* 57 (1963) 65-78. [V. Royal Policies upon labor service and land use, pp. 76-78]

J. D. Thomas, "Some recently published Leases of Land," *JJP* 15 (1965) 129-134.

V. N. Andreyev, "Attic Public Landownership from the Fifth to the Third Centuries B.C.," *VDI* (1967) #2, 76.

G. F. Polyaskova, "Teojo Doero/Ra in the Pylos System of Land Tenure," *VDI* (1968) #1, 27.

L. M. Gluskina, "The Renting of Land in Fourth Century Attica," *VDI* (1968) #2, 58.

R. T. Pritchard, "Land Tenure in Sicily in the First Century B.C.," *HJAJ* 18 (1969) 545-556.

I. V. Vinogradov, "The So-Called 'Landholders' in the Wilbur Papyrus," *VDI* (1969) #1, 44.

I. S. Sventsitskaya, "The Destruction of the Citizen Collective and Polis Property in the Province of Asia," *VDI* (1969) #3, 141-142.

I. V. Vinogradov, "The Qualitative Definition of Land: Evidence of the Wilbur Papyrus," *VDI* (1969) #4, 23.

§90 *2.3.1.2 Viticulture [Vineyard Keeping] (includes Brewing)*

*[H. Rood], "The Grapes of Eshcol," *BJ* 1 (1842) 94-99.

Eli Smith, "The Wines of Mount Lebanon," *BS* 3 (1846) 385-389.

Henry Homes, "The Produce of the Vineyard in the East," *BS* 5 (1848) 283-295.

Anonymous, "The Wine of the Bible, of Bible Lands, and of the Lord's Supper," *PRev* 43 (1871) 564-595.

Peter Mearns, "The Fruit of the Vine in Palestine," *BFER* 26 (1877) 56-70.

F. D. Hemenway, "Bible Wines," *MR* 60 (1878) 480-490.

Dunlop Moore, "Bible Wines," *PR* 2 (1881) 80-113.

Leon C. Field, "The Wines of the Bible," *MR* 56 (1882) 284-320.

Dunlop Moore, "Sacramental Wine," *PR* 3 (1882) 78-107.

Norman Kerr, "Passover Wine," *CM* 16 (1883) 184-192.

(   ) St., "Wine in the Bible," *ColTM* 3 (1883) 148-163.

*B. Felsenthal, "'Gamaliel ben Pedahzur'—Fermented or Unfermented Wine?" *ONTS* 4 (1884-85) 131-132.

*B. Felsenthal, "Use of Wine by the Jews," *ONTS* 4 (1884-85) 184-185. (Correction, p. 230)

Franz Delitzsch, "The Bible and Wine," *Exp, 3rd Ser.,* 3 (1886) 58-69.

*Alvah Hovey, "Bible Wine: The Meanings of Yayin and Oinos in Scripture," *BQR* 9 (1887) 151-180.

Conrad Schick, "Reports by Dr. Conrad Schick. VI. *Ancient Rock-cut Jewish Wine-presses at Ain Karim,*" *PEFQS* 31 (1899) 41-42.

R. A. Stewart Macalister, "Reports by R. A. Stewart Macalister, M.A., F.S.A. X. A. Rock-cut Press near Jerusalem," *PEFQS* 34 (1902) 248-249.

*Morris Jastrow Jr., "Wine in the Pentateuchal Codes," *JAOS* 33 (1913) 180-192.

Paul Haupt, "Alcohol in the Bible," *JBL* 36 (1917) 75-83.

*Walton Brooks McDaniel, "The So-Called Athlete's Ring," *AJA* 22 (1918) 295-303.

*A. Lucas, "Egyptian Use of Beer and Wine," *AEE* 13 (1928) 1-5.

*Julius Grant, "Brewing in Ancient Times," *Antiq* 4 (1930) 232-233.

*Louis F. Hartman and A. L. Oppenheim, "On Beer and Brewing Techniques in Ancient Mesopotamia According to the XXIIIrd Tablet of the Series ḪAR.ra=*ḫubullu*," *JAOSS* #10 (1950) 1-55.

*T. Säve-Söderbergh, "The *ʿprw* as Vintagers in Egypt," *OrS* 1 (1952) 5-14.

*Charles Seltman, "The Wine Trade in Ancient Greece," *HT* 5 (1955) 860-866.

James B. Pritchard, "The Wine Industry at Gibeon: 1959 Discoveries," *Exped* 2 (1959-60) #1, 17-25.

*Alan Millard, "Ezekiel XXVII. 19: The Wine Trade of Damascus," *JSS* 7 (1962) 201-203.

William Y. Adams, "The Vintage of Nubia," *Kush* 14 (1966) 262-283.

*Vít Bubeník, "The World's First Beer Brewers," *NOP* 5 (1966) 163-165.

*John Chadwick, "Mycenaean Wine and the Etymology of γλυκύς," *Minos* 9 (1968) 192-197.

*L. A. Yelnitsky, "The Ancient Greek Wine Trade and Ceramics Production,". *VDI* (1969) #3, 105.

J. P. Brown, "The Mediterranean Vocabulary of the Vine," *VT* 19 (1969) 146-170.

§91 *2.3.3 Arts and Crafts, Industry & "Technology"*

*F. M. Hubbard, "Commerce and Manufacturing of Ancient Babylon, intended to illustrate some parts of the Prophetic Scripture," *BRCR* 7 (1836) 364-390.

†E. C., "The Ancient Egyptians: Their Arts and Manufactures," *WR* 36 (1841) 1-19. *(Review)*

*S. Louis, "On the Handicrafts and Artizans mentioned in Talmudical Writings," *SBAP* 6 (1883-84) 117-119.

*A. Lowy, "On Technological Terms in Ancient Semitic Culture and Foke-lore," *SBAP* 6 (1883-84) 138-144.

*S. Louis, "On the Handicrafts and Artizans mentioned in Talmudical Writings," *SBAT* 8 (1883-84) 398-411.

T[errien] de L[acouperie], "Note on Fire-Making in Ancient Egypt," *BOR* 6 (1892-93) 42-43.

*E. W. G. Masterman, "Occcupations and Industries in Bible Lands," *BW* 16 (1900) 199-209, 272-282; 17 (1901) 276-291.

*F. M. Barber, "An Ancient Egyptian Mechanical Problem. Papyrus Anastasi I. About 1300 B.C.," *OC* 26 (1912) 705-716.

W. M. F[linders] P[etrie], "For Reconsideration. Glass Blowing," *AEE* 1 (1914) 33.

*Ernest Mackay, "On the Use of Beeswax and Resin as Varnishes in Theban Tombs," *AEE* 5 (1920) 35-38. (Note by [W. M.] Fl[inders] P[etrie], p. 38)

Gustavus Eisen, "The Origin of Glass Blowing," *AJA* 20 (1916) 134-143.

M. A. Murray, "Knots," *AEE* 7 (1922) 14-19.

*George A. Barton, "On Binding-Reeds, Bitumen, and other Commodities in Ancient Babylonia," *JAOS* 46 (1926) 297-302.

*George Morey, "The Mystery of Ancient Glassware," *A&A* 28 (1929) 199-205.

Anonymous, "Notes and Comments. Steam Heat 2400 Years Ago," *A&A* 30 (1930) 144.

H. C. Beck, "Glass Before 1500 B.C.," *AEE* 19 (1934) 7-21.

*S. Yeivin, "Miscellanea Archæologica," *ASAE* 34 (1934) 114-124. [I. Ovens and Baking in Roman Egypt, pp. 114-121]

Shirley H. Weber and Earle R. Caley, "Theophrastus: The Treatise on Stones in the Light of Archaeological Discoveries," *AJA* 42 (1938) 128.

*J. d'A. Waechter, V. M. Seton-Williams, Dorothea M. A. Bate, and L. Pichard, "The Excavations at Wadi Dhobai, 1937-1938 and the Dhobaian Industry," *JPOS* 18 (1938) 172-186.

*J. W. Jack, "Recent Biblical Archaeology. Beth-Shemesh (1 S^{6})," *ET* 52 (1940-41) 113-114. [Industries, p. 113]

Eric Manx, "Ancient Egyptian Woodworking," *Antiq* 20 (1946) 127-133.

*I. Mendelsohn, "Slavery in the Ancient Near East," *BA* 9 (1946) 74-88. [III. The Economic Role of Slavery, pp. 86-87; 4. Slaves in Industry, pp. 87-99]

*N. Wilbush, "Olive-Oil Industry in Ancient Times," *BIES* 13 (1946-47) #1/2, III.

*Girgis Mattha, "The ἀρτοκοπεῖον in demotic texts," *BIFAO* 45 (1947) 59-60 *[Bakehouse]*

M. Stekelis, "A New Neolithic Industry: The Yarmukian of Palestine," *IEJ* 1 (1950-51) 1-19.

*John W. Wilson, "Egyptian Technology, Science, and Lore," *JWH* 2 (1954-55) 209-213.

*Tahsin, Özguç, "Report on a work shop belonging to the late phase of the Colony Period (Ib)," *TTKB* 19 (1955) 77-80. *[Kaniş]*

Martin Levey, "Technology of Oils, Fats and Waxes in Ancient Mesopotamia," *Cent* 5 (1956-57) 151-163.

*Ruth Amiran, "The Millstone and the Potter's Wheel," *EI* 4 (1956) V.

*Viggo Nielsen, "Famed for Its Many Pearls," *Kuml* (1958) 157-160.

*Aage Roussell, "A Hellenistic Terra-Cotta Workshop in the Persian Gulf," *Kuml* (1958) 198-200.

*Philip C. Hammond, "The Nabataean Bitumen Industry at the Dead Sea," *AJA* 63 (1959) 188.

Frederic Schuler, "Ancient Glassmaking Techniques: The Molding Process," *Arch* 12 (1959) 47-52.

Frederic Schuler, "Ancient Glassmaking Techniques: The Blowing Process," *Arch* 12 (1959) 116-122.

*Philip C. Hammond, "The Nabataean Bitumen Industry at the Dead Sea," *BA* 22 (1959) 40-48.

Ida Bobula, "Sumerian Technology: A Survey of Early Material Advancements in Mesopotamia," *SIR* (1959) 637-675.

Muzaffer [Süleyman] Şenyürek, "A Note on the Palaeolithic Indusry of the Plugged Cave," *TTKB* 23 (1959) 27-58.

W. F. Leemans, "Some marginal remarks on ancient technology," *JESHO* 3 (1960) 217-237.

Muzaffer [Süleyman] Şenyürek, "The Upper Acheulean Industry of Altindere," *TTKB* 25 (1961) 163-168.

Gladys Davidson Weinberg, "Evidence for Glass Manufacture in Ancient Thessaly," *AJA* 66 (1962) 129-133.

Frederic Schuler, "Ancient Glassmaking Techniques: *The Egyptian Core Vessel Process*," *Arch* 15 (1962) 32-37.

*H. S. K. Bakry, "On the Technique of restoration and mending in the first Dynasty," *ASAE* 57 (1962) 15-17.

*W. Winton, "Bagdad Batteries B.C.," *Sumer* 18 (1962) 87-88.

Anita Engle, "Does Western Galilee Contain the Secrets of Glass-Blowing?" *CNI* 15 (1964) #4, 13-18.

Eugene D. Stockton, "Stone Age Factory Site at Arafa near Bethlehem," *SBFLA* 15 (1964-65) 124-130.

*Albert Al-Haik, "The Rabbou'a Galvanic Cell," *Sumer* 20 (1964) 103-104.

Frank J. Frost, "Scyllias: Diving in Antiquity," *AJA* 70 (1966) 189.

Rudolf M. Reifstahl, "Ancient Glass: A Reconstruction of Sand Core Technology," *AJA* 71 (1967) 193.

*Clare L. Goff, L. Vanden Berghe, Frank Hole, Murray B. Nicol, Henry T. Wright, Ezat O. Negahban, C. A. Burney, Robert H. Dyson Jr., Oscar White Muscarella and Mary M. Voigt, Maurizio Tosi, David Whitehouse, M.-J. Steve, C. C. Lamburg-Karlovsky, R. B. R. Kearton, Wolfram Kleiss, Ralph S. Solecki, Theodore A. Wertime, Paul Gotch, Dietrich Huff, "Survey of Excavations in Iran, 1967-8," *Iran* 7 (1969) 169-193 [Survey of Man's fire-using industries in Afghanistan, Iran and Turkey, p 190]

§92 *2.3.3.1 Occupations, Professions, and Trades - not including Religious Professions [For Scribes as a religious group see: The Scribes →]*

*S. Louis, "On the Handicrafts and Artizans mentioned in Talmudical Writings," *SBAP* 6 (1883-84) 117-119.

*S. Louis, "On the Handicrafts and Artizans mentioned in Talmudical Writings," *SBAT* 8 (1883-84) 398-411.

*†Theo. G. Pinches, "Assyriological Notes," *SBAP* 8 (1885-86) 240-245. [Âgarrūtu, "workmen", p 241]

Terrien de Lacouperie, "The Fabulous Fisherman of Babylonia in Ancient Chinese Legends," *BOR* 2 (1887-88) 221-226.

*W. St. Chad Boscawen, "The Merchants of Ur," *ET* 6 (1894-95) 120-122.

*E. W. G. Masterman, "Occupations and Industries in Bible Lands," *BW* 16 (1900) 199-209, 272-282; 17 (1901) 276-291.

E. W. G. Masterman, "Occupations of the Jews in Palestine," *BW* 22 (1903) 88-97.

R. A. Stewart Macalister, "The Craftsmen's Guild of the Tribe of Judah," *PEFQS* 37 (1905) 243-253, 328-342.

A. H. Godbey, "The Ḳêpu," *AJSL* 22 (1905-06) 81-88.

R. A. Stewart Macalister, "Some Further Observations on the 'Craftsmen's Guild' of Judah," *PEFQS* 40 (1908) 71-75.

E. W. G. Masterman, "The Fisheries of Galilee," *PEFQS* 40 (1908) 40-51.

*James Henry Breasted, "Studio of an Egyptian Portrait Sculptor in the Fourteenth Century B.C.," *A&A* 4 (1916) 233-242.

*Archibald C. Dickie, "The Jews as Builders," *PEFQS* 48 (1916) 26-33.

*Alan H. Gardiner, "Professional Magicians in Ancient Egypt," *SBAP* 39 (1917) 31-44.

*Alan H. Gardiner, "Postscripta," *SBAP* 39 (1917) 133-140. [4. Professional Magicians in Ancient Egypt, 139-140]

Joseph Offord, "The Princes of the Bakers and the Cup-Bearers," *PEFQS* 50 (1918) 139-142.

[W. M.] Flinders Petrie, "Professions and Trades," *AEE* 11 (1926) 73-84.

*S. Yeivin, "Miscellanea Archæologica," *ASAE* 34 (1934) 114-124. [I. Ovens and Baking in Roman Egypt, pp. 114-121]

R. D. Middleton, "Shebna 'The Scribe'," *Theo* 28 (1934) 342.

Colin Roberts, Theodore C. Skeat, and Arthur Darby Nock, "The Gild of Zeus Hypsistos," *HTR* 29 (1936) 39-88.

A. E. R. Boak, "The Organization of Gilds in Greco-Roman Egypt," *TAPA* 68 (1937) 212-220.

Pierre M. Purves, "The Early Scribes of Nuzi," *AJSL* 57 (1940) 162-187.

I. Mendelsohn, "Guilds in Ancient Palestine," *BASOR* #80 (1940) 17-21.

I. Mendelsohn, "Gilds in Babylonia and Asyria," *JAOS* 60 (1940) 68-72.

*J. W. Jack, "Recent Biblical Archaeology," *ET* 52 (1940-41) 353-357. [Guilds of Workman, pp. 356-357]

*Alan Rowe, "The '[illegible]-sceptre' sub-gang of workmen at Meydum," *ASAE* 41 (1942) 339-341.

*J. Philip Hyatt, "The Writing of an Old Testament Book," *BA* 6 (1943) 71-80. [Writing was a Learned Profession, p. 72]

*Charles C. Torrey, "The Evolution of a Financier in the Ancient Near East," *JNES* 2 (1943) 295-301.

*B[enjamin] Maisler, "The Scribe of King David and the Problem of the High Officials in the Ancient Kingdom of Israel," *BIES* 13 (1946-47) #3/4, IV-V.

*William F. Edgerton, "The Strikes in Ramses III's Twenty-Ninth Year," *JNES* 10 (1951) 137-145.

*Walter J. Fischel, "The Jewish Merchants, Called Radanites," *JQR, N.S.,* 42 (1951-52) 321-325.

*T. Fish, "The Smith at Lagash," *MCS* 1 (1951) 46-48.

Mark Wischnitzer, "Notes to a History of the Jewish Guilds," *HUCA* 33 (1950-51) 245-263.

*Rodolfo Mondolfo, "The Greek Attitude to Manual Labor," *P&P* #6 (1954) 1-5, *(Trans. by D. S. Duncan)*

*H. J. Katzenstein, "The House of Eliakim, a Family of Royal Stewards," *EI* 5 (1958) 89*-90*.

*Henry G. Fischer, "The Butcher *Pḥ-r-nfr,*" *Or, N.S.,* 29 (1960) 168-190.

Barbara Parker, "The Assyrian Civil Service," *Sumer* 16 (1960) 32-38.

*I. Mendelsohn, "The Corvee Labor in Ancient Canaan and Israel," *BASOR* #167 (1962) 31-35.

*D. G. Evans, "The Incidence of Labour-service in the Old Babylonian Period," *JAOS* 83 (1963) 20-26.

*Geoffrey Evans, "The Incidence of Labour-Service at Mari," *RAAO* 57 (1963) 65-78. [I. Work upon the canals and irrigation system; II. Agricultural corvées; III. Conclusions; IV. Periods of Labour-service]

Jack M. Sasson, "Instances of Mobility Among Mari Artisans," *BASOR* #190 (1968) 46-54.

*Eug Bogoslowskij, "Weaver's Managers in Egypt of the Sixteenth and Fifteenth Centuries B.C.," *VDI* (1968) #1, 96.

*R. Ye. Lyast, "Manumissions of Slave Craftsmen in the First Century B.C.," *VDI* (1968) #2, 120.

*Daniel Sperber, "Some Observations of Fish and Fisheries in Roman Palestine," *ZDMG* 118 (1968) 265-269.

Anson F. Rainey, "The Scribe at Ugarit. His Position and Influence," *PIASH* 3 (1969) 126-147.

§93 *2.3.3.2 Weaving, Dyeing and Clothing Production*

*(Mrs.) E. A. Finn, "Mosaic and Embroidery in the Old Testament," *PEFQS* 22 (1890) 189-193.

Clarence H. Young, "Practical Hints on Ancient Greek Dressmaking," *AJA* 4 (1900) 167-168.

*Myron R. Sanford, "The Material of the Tunica and Toga," *AJA* 5 (1901) 15-16.

Felix von Oefele, "Old Babylonian Linen Weaving," *JAOS* 36 (1916) 415.

*A. H. Sayce, "Assyriological Notes," *SBAP* 39 (1917) 207-212. [Imperial Purple, p. 210]

G[race] M. Crowfoot, "Models of Egyptian Looms," *AEE* 6 (1921) 97-101.

Grace M. Crowfoot and H. Ling Roth, "Were the Ancient Egyptians Conversant with Tablet-Weaving (*Brettchenweberei, Tissage aux Cartons*)?" *AAA* 10 (1923) 7-20.

*Ernest Mackay, "The Representation of Shawls with a Rippled Stripe in the Theban Tombs," *JEA* 10 (1924) 41-43.

S[tephen] Langdon, "Assyriological Notes," *RAAO* 22 (1925) 31-38. [I. *ŠUTUR = šuturu,* cloth in the roll, "hank", p. 31; II. *UTTUKU,* weaver, fuller, (male and female), pp. 32-36]

*Paul Haupt, "Sum. *azalak,* fuller, and Heb. *ašlāḡ,* fuller's earth," *BAVSS* 10 (1927) Heft 2, 268-270.

*Kate McK. Elderkin, "Buttons and their Use on Greek Garments," *AJA* 32 (1928) 333-345.

Gisela M. A. Richter, "Silk in Greece," *AJA* 33 (1929) 27-33.

G[race] M. Crowfoot, "The Mat Weaver from the Tomb of Khety," *AEE* 18 (1933) 93-99.

Grace M. Crowfoot, "The Mat Looms of Huleh, Palestine," *PEFQS* 66 (1934) 195-198.

*M. M. C., "An Egyptian Mummy Cloth," *UMB* 6 (1935-37) #4, 119-120.

*R. Campbell Thompson, "úKurangu and úLal(l)angu as possibly 'Rice' and 'Indigo' in Cuneiform," *Iraq* 6 (1939) 180-183.

H. Kurdian, "Kirmiz," *JAOS* 61 (1941) 105-107. *[Insects & Dyeing]*

Grace M. Crowfoot, "The Vertical Loom in Palestine and Syria," *PEQ* 73 (1941) 141-151.

Grace M. Crowfoot, "Handicrafts in Palestine. Primitive Weaving," *PEQ* 75 (1943) 75-88.

Grace M. Crowfoot, "Handicrafts in Palestine. Jerusalem Hammock Cradles and Hebron Rugs," *PEQ* 76 (1944) 121-130.

Grace M. Crowfoot, "The Tent Beautiful. A Study of Pattern Weaving in Transjordan," *PEQ* 77 (1945) 34-76.

Margrethe Hald, "Ancient Textile Techniques in Egypt and Scandinavia. A Comparative Study," *AA* 17 (1946) 49-98.

A. J. B. Wace, "Weaving or Embroidery?" *AJA* 52 (1948) 51-55, 452. [Corrections, *AJA* 54 (1950) p. 203]

*G. R. Driver, "Technical Terms in the Pentateuch," *WO* 2 (1954-59) 254-263. [II. חֹשֵׁב 'embroiderer'; חֵשֶׁב 'band', pp. 255-259; III. כָּלִיל 'woven in one piece', p. 259; VI. שָׁבֵץ 'lined, quilted', pp. 262-263]

Martin Levey, "Dyeing Auxiliaries in Ancient Mesopotamia," *Cent* 4 (1955-56) 126-131.

Trude Dothan, "Spinning Bowls," *EI* 6 (1960) 27*-28*.

Chrysoula Kardara, "Dyeing and Weaving Works at Isthmia," *AJA* 65 (1961) 261-266.

Trude Dothan, "Spinning Bowls," *IEJ* 13 (1963) 97-112.

Lloyd B. Jensen, "Royal Purple of Tyre," *JNES* 22 (1963) 104-118.

Harold B. Burnham, "Çatal Hüyük—The Textiles and Twined Fabrics," *AS* 15 (1965) 169-174.

*M. L. Ryder, "Report on Textiles from Çatal Hüyük," *AS* 15 (1965) 175-176.

*Diane Lee Carroll, "The Heddle in Greek Art," *AJA* 70 (1966) 185.

Diane Lee Carroll, "Patterned Greek Textiles," *AJA* 71 (1967) 184.

*Harry A. Hoffner Jr., "Ugartic *pwt:* A Term from the Early Canaanite Dyeing Industry," *JAOS* 87 (1967) 300-303.

*Eug Bogoslowskij, "Weaver's Managers in Egypt of the Sixteenth and Fifteenth Centuries B.C.," *VDI* (1968) #1, 96.

§94 *2.3.2 Wearing Apparel and Style*

Anonymous, "Transparent Dress of the Ladies," *MMBR* 17 (1804) 555-556.

*(Miss) Fanny Corbaux, "The Rephaim, and Their Connexion with Egyptian History," *JSL, 2nd Ser.,* 1 (1851-52) 151-172, 363-394; 2 (1852) 55-91, 303-340; 3 (1852-53) 87-116, 279-307. [Chap. 18 - Costumes of the Rephaim, pp. 291-307]

Samuel Sharpe, "On an Egyptian Shawl for the Head as worn on the Statues of the Kings," *SBAT* 4 (1875) 248-250.

*B. Pick, "The Rites, Ceremonies and Customs of the Jews," *HR* 17 (1889) 199-206. [II. The Fringes, pp. 200-201]

Claude R. Conder, "Notes by Major Conder R.E. IV. The so-called 'Hittite' Hat," *PEFQS* 21 (1889) 89.

*A. H. Sayce, "Miscellaneous Notes," *ZA* 4 (1889) 382-393. [30. The Accadian *sebi* "clothing", pp. 390-392]

F. W. Nicolson, "Greek Modes of Hair-cut, as set forth by Pollux (II 29 seqq.)," *PAPA* 22 (1890) x-xii.

*Stanley A. Cook, "The articles of dress in Dan. III.," *JP* 26 (1898-99) 306-313. [כרבלא ; פטש ; סרבל]

*Myron R. Sanford, "The Material of the Tunica and Toga," *AJA* 5 (1901) 15-16.

*E. W. G. Masterman, "Dress and Personal Adornment in Modern Palestine," *BW* 18 (1901) 167-175, 249-258.

*James A. Quarles, "Sociology of Joseph's Day," *CFL, N.S.,* 5 (1902) 97-108. [Dress, pp. 103-106]

Paul Carus, "The Evolution of Ornament," *OC* 17 (1903) 291-296.

Eb. Nestle, "'They Enlarge the Borders of Their Garments'," *ET* 20 (1908-09) 188.

Irmagarde Richards, "The Evidence of the Monuments for the Dress of Roman Women," *PAPA* 41 (1909) ci-cii.

*Robert Mond, "An Egyptian Funerary Cap," *AAA* 3 (1910) 137.

C. F. Ross, "Reconstruction of the Later Toga," *AJA* 14 (1910) 77-78.

Grace Palmerlee, "The Coiffure of Roman Women as Shown on Portrait Busts and Statues," *RP* 9 (1910) 167-176.

Thorold D. Lee, "The Linen Girdle of Rameses III," *AAA* 5 (1912-13) 84-96.

C. F. Lehmann-Haupt, "Note on the Linen Girdle of Rameses III," *AAA* 7 (1914-16) 50.

*Jacob Nacht, "The Symbolism of the Shoe with Special Reference to the Jewish Sources," *JQR, N.S.,* 6 (1915-16) 1-22.

Charles C. Torrey, "The Art of the Hairdresser in Ancient Babylonia," *AJA* 21 (1917) 85-86.

Felix von Oefelé, "A Babylonian belt buckle," *JAOS* 38 (1918) 308-309.

*H. J. D. Astley, "Ladies' Fashions in Jerusalem. Circ. 735 B.C.—Isa. III. 16-24," *ICMM* 16 (1919-20) 127-134.

Albert W. Barker, "Domestic Costumes of the Athenian Woman in the Fifth and Fourth Centuries, B.C.," *AJA* 26 (1922) 410-425.

Mary MacAlister, "Ancient Costume and Modern Fashion," *A&A* 15 (1923) 167-175.

Albert W. Barker, "The Costume of the Servant on the Grave-Relief of Hegeso," *AJA* 28 (1924) 290-292.

M. A. Murray, "Costume of Early Kings," *AEE* 11 (1926) 33-40.

*H. F. B. Compston, "Ladies' Finery in Isaiah iii," *CQR* 103 (1926-27) 316-330.

*Kate McK. Elderkin, "Buttons and their Use on Greek Garments," *AJA* 32 (1928) 333-345.

Leichester B. Holland, "Mycenaean Plumes," *AJA* 33 (1929) 173-205.

R. Engelbach, "A pecularity of Dress in the Old and Middle Kingdoms," *ASAE* 29 (1929) 31-32.

R. Engelbach, "The ancient Egyptian 'dress-bow'," *ASAE* 29 (1929) 40-46.

*A. Kenneth Graham, "Scientific Notes on the Finds from Ur," *MJ* 20 (1929) 246-257. [III. The Cosmetics of Queen Shubad, pp. 253-255]

*E. Douglas Van Buren, "Some Archaic Statuettes, and a Study of Early Sumerian Dress," *AAA* 17 (1930) 39-56.

A. Lucas, "Ancient Egyptian Wigs," *ASAE* 30 (1930) 190-196.

T. Eric Peet, "The so-called Ramesses Girdle," *JEA* 19 (1933) 143-149.

Carline M. Galt, "Veiled Ladies," *AJA* 35 (1931) 373-393.

*Wm. Stevenson Smith, "The Old Kingdom Linen List," *ZÄS* 71 (1935) 134-149.

*Simone Corbiau, "Sumerian Dress Lengths as Chronological Data," *Iraq* 3 (1936) 97-100.

Lillian B. Lawler, "Transparency of Garments in the Greek Dance," *AJA* 43 (1939) 309.

*J. W. Jack, "Recent Biblical Archaeology," *ET* 51 (1939-40) 420-423. [Shoes as Legal Symbols, pp. 422-423]

Mary Wallace, "Sutor Supra Crepidam," *AJA* 44 (1940) 213-221.

*J. W. Jack, "Recent Biblical Archaeology," *ET* 52 (1940-41) 229-233. [Dress and Apparel. 1. Loin-cloth and Plaid, 2. Tunic or Sleeved Garment, 3. Outer Garments, pp. 229-231]

G. M. Crowfoot and N. de G. Davies, "The Tunic of Tut'ankhamūn," *JEA* 27 (1941) 113-130.

*Martin P. Nilsson, "A Krater in the Cleveland Museum of Art with Men in Women's Attire," *AA* 13 (1942) 223-226.

Mary Wallace, "Sutor Resutus," *AJA* 46 (1942) 336-367. *[Footwear]*

E. A. Eisa, "A Study on the ancient Egyptian wigs," *ASAE* 48 (1948) 9-18.

Jan Macdonald, "Palestinian Dress," *PEQ* 83 (1951) 55-68.

(Mrs.) Charlotte R. Long, "Mycenaean Dress," *AJA* 58 (1954) 147-148.

Emile Marmorstein, "The Veil in Judaism and Islam," *JJS* 5 (1954) 1-11.

*E. Douglas Van Buren, "A Plaque of the Third Early Dynastic Period," *RAAO* 48 (1954) 142-145. *[Clothing]*

G. Ernest Wright, "How Israelites Dressed," *McQ* 8 (1954-55) #3, 3-6.

*J. Gwyn Griffiths, "The costume and insignia of the king in the *sed*-festival," *JEA* 41 (1955) 127-128.

Elizabeth Riefstahl, "Two Hairdressers of the Eleventh Dynasty," *JNES* 15 (1956) 10-17.

Ebba*[sic]* E. Kerrn, "The Development of the Ornamental 'Boatman's Fillet' in Old and Middle Kingdom in Egypt," *AO* 24 (1959) 161-188.

*Margarete Bieber, "Roman Men in Greek Himation (Roman Palliati). A Contribution to the History of Copying," *PAPS* 103 (1959) 374-417.

*Chrysoula Kardara, "ΕΠΜΑΤΑ ΤΡΙΓΛΗΝΑ ΜΟΡΟΕΝΤΑ," *AJA* 65 (1961) 62-64.

E[bbe] E. Kerrn, "Addendum to 'Boatman's Fillet'," *AO* 26 (1961-62) 93-95.

M. Levin and S. Horowitz, "The Textile Remains from the Caves of Naḥal Ḥever," *'Atiqot* 3 (1961) 163-164.

Stephen Bertman, "Tasseled Garments in the Ancient East Mediterranean," *BA* 24 (1961) 119-128.

Nelson Glueck, "Nabataean Torques," *BA* 25 (1962) 57-64.

*Margarete Bieber, "The Copies of the Herculaneum Women," *PAPS* 106 (1962) 111-134.

Lawrence Richardson and Emeline Hill Richardson, "Ad cohibendum bracchium toga," *AJA* 68 (1964) 199-200.

B. Goldman, "Origin of the Persian Robe," *IA* 4 (1964) 133-152.

Georgina Thompson, "Iranian Dress in the Achaemenian Period," *Iran* 3 (1965) 121-126.

John Boardman, "An Anatolian Greek Belt Handle," *AS* 16 (1966) 193-194.

P. R. S. Moorey, "Some Ancient Metal Belts: Their Antecedents and Relatives," *Iran* 5 (1967) 83-98.

Josef Klíma, "Kaunakes, Polos and some other Aspects of Mesopotamian Fashion," *NOP* 6 (1967) 164-168.

P. R. S. Moorey, "'Some Ancient Metal Belts'—a Retraction and a Cautionary Note," *Iran* 7 (1969) 155.

*Calvert Watkins, "A Latin-Hittite etymology," *Lang* 45 (1969) 235-242. [Lat. *uespillo* 'undertaker for the poorest classes' cognate with Hitt. *wašpaš* 'clothes']

§95 *2.3.2.1 Cosmetics and Jewelry*

†J. D. Fosbrooke, "Antiquity and Use of Gold Chains," *MMBR* 25 (1808) 515-516.

*J. William Dawson, "Notes on Useful and Ornamental Stones of Ancient Egypt," *JTVI* 26 (1892-93) 265-282. (Discussion, pp. 282-288) [1. Granitic, Dioritic, and Gneissic Rocks, 2. Basalt with Olivine, 3. The Nubian Sandstone, 4. Limestone, &c., 5. Miocene Quartzite of Jebel Ahmar, &c., 6. Various Stones and Gems, 7. Flint Flakes, Knives, Saws, &c.]

*Walter L. Nash, "An Ancient Egyptian Toilet-box belonging to W. L. Nash, F.S.A., with an Analysis of its contents by W. Gowland, F.C.S., F.S.A.," *SBAP* 20 (1898) 267-269.

†*J. Herbert Walker, "Analysis of Egyptian Cosmetic," *SBAP* 21 (1899) 79.

Anonymous, "The Oldest Discovered Specimens of Egyptian Jewelry," *AAOJ* 24 (1902) 188.

James H. Breasted, "Jewelry from the Tombs of Egypt," *BW* 22 (1903) 64-66.

Anonymous, "Jewels of Ta-Usert," *RP* 7 (1908) 126-127.

*H. F. De Cou, "Jewelry and Bronze Fragments in the Loeb Collection," *AJA* 15 (1911) 131-148.

G. A. Wainwright, "Pre-Dynastic Iron Beads in Egypt," *Man* 11 (1911) #100.

William N. Bates, "Note on a Roman Ring," *AJA* 16 (1912) 102.

Anonymous, "Pre-Dynastic Iron Beads in Egypt," *RP* 11 (1912) 52.

Reginald Engelbach, "The Jewellery of Riqqeh," *AEE* 1 (1914) 3-4.

H. R. Hall, "Egyptian Beads in Britain," *JEA* 1 (1914) 19.

William Copley Winslow, "Current Notes and News. An Amethyst Necklace of the Twelfth Dynasty," *A&A* 1 (1914-15) 260.

G. C. Pier, "Personal Ornaments of the Ancient Egyptians," *AJA* 20 (1916) 81-82.

H. E. Winlock, "Notes on the Jewels from Lahun," *AEE* 5 (1920) 74-87.

*Aylward M. Blackman, "On the Name of an Unguent used for Ceremonial Purposes," *JEA* 6 (1920) 58-60.

John Day, "A Gem from Tiryns," *AJA* 30 (1926) 442-443.

A. Lucas, "The necklace of Queen Aahhotep in the Cairo Museum of Antiquities," *ASAE* 27 (1927) 69-71.

Battiscombe Gunn, "A Pectoral Amulet," *ASAE* 29 (1929) 130-132.

Gustavus A. Eisen, "Lotus- and Melon-Beads," *AJA* 34 (1930) 20-43.

Gustavus A. Eisen, "Antique Fig-Beads," *AJA* 34 (1930) 190-196.

A. Lucas, "Cosmetics, Perfumes and Incense in Ancient Egypt," *JEA* 16 (1930) 41-53.

Grace H. Macurdy, "A Note on the Jewellery of Demetrius the Besieger," *AJA* 36 (1932) 27-28.

H. E. Winlock, "Elements from the Dahshūr jewelry," *ASAE* 33 (1933) 135-139.

E[dith] H. D[ohan], "A Pair of Earrings from Cyprus," *UMB* 5 (1934-35) #2, 41-44.

*D. B. Harden, "Pottery and Beads from near Nehavand, N.W. Persia, in the Ashmolean Museum," *AEE* 20 (1935) 73-81.

George M. A. Hanfmann, "Daidalos in Etruria," *AJA* 39 (1935) 189-194.

Otto Brendel, "The Great Augustus Cameo at Vienna," *AJA* 43 (1939) 307-308.

*J. W. Jack, "Recent Biblical Archaeology," *ET* 52 (1940-41) 112-115. [Jewellery, pp. 113-114]

*Gisela M. A. Richter, "Four Notable Acquisitions of the Metropolitan Museum of Art," *AJA* 44 (1940) 428-442. [3. A Set of Etruscan Jewelry, pp. 434-439]

Robert L. Scranton, "A Wreath in the Vassar Classical Museum," *AJA* 48 (1944) 135-142. *[Jewelry]*

Nils Ludvig Rasmusson, "Were Medals of Merit Used and Worn in Antiquity?" *AA* 16 (1945) 211-222.

*Doro Levi, "Gleanings from Crete," *AJA* 49 (1945) 270-329. [4. Jewellrey from the Idaean Cave, pp. 313-329]

George E. Mylonas, "A Signet-Ring in the City Art Museum of St. Louis," *AJA* 49 (1945) 557-569.

*Sedat Alp, "GIŠ *kalmuş* 'Lituus' and HUB.BI 'Earring' in the Hittite Texts," *TTKB* 12 (1948) 320-324.

Howard Comfort, "A Hoard of Greek Jewelry," *AJA* 54 (1950) 121-126.

*David M. Robinson, "Unpublished Greek Gold Jewelry and Gems," *AJA* 56 (1952) 176; 57 (1953) 5-19.

Hazel Palmer, "Vanity Box: *Third Century B.C.*," *Arch* 7 (1954) 179.

Carl H. Kraeling, "Hellenistic Gold Jewelry in Chicago," *Arch* 8 (1955) 252-259.

*Martin Levey, "Babylonian Chemistry: A Study of Arabic and Second Millenium B.C. Perfumery," *Osiris* 12 (1956) 376-389.

J. Gy. Szilágyi, "Some Problems of Greek Gold Diadems," *AAASH* 5 (1957) 45-93.

Helene J. Kantor, "Oriental Insitute Museum Notes, No. 8: Achaemenid Jewelry in the Oriental Institute," *JNES* 16 (1957) 1-23.

*Viggo Nielsen, "Famed for Its Many Pearls," *Kuml* (1958) 157-160.

William Culican, "Essay on a Phoenician Ear-Ring," *PEQ* 90 (1958) 90-103.

Olgo Tufnell, "Anklets in Western Asia," *ULBIA* 1 (1958) 37-54.

K. R. Maxwell-Hyslop, "The Ur Jewellery. *A re-assessment in the light of some recent discoveries*," *Iraq* 22 (1960) 105-115.

*Chrysoula Kardara, "ΕΠΜΑΤΑ ΤΡΙΓΛΗΝΑ ΜΟΡΟΕΝΤΑ," *AJA* 65 (1961) 62-64.

Christopher Hawkes, "Gold Ear-rings of the Bronze Age, East and West," *Folk* 72 (1961) 438-474.

Clark Hopkins, "The Aegina Treasure," *AJA* 66 (1962) 182-184.

Edward L. B. Terrace, "Ancient Egyptian Jewelry in the Horace L. Meyer Collection," *AJA* 67 (1963) 269-274.

W. Culican, "Spiral-end Beads in Western Asia," *Iraq* 26 (1964) 36-43.

Dorothy Kent Hill, "To Perfume The Etruscans and Latins," *Arch* 18 (1965) 187-190.

*J. V. Canby, "Early Bronze 'Trinket' Moulds," *Iraq* 27 (1965) 42-61.

*T. C. Skeat, "A fragment on the Ptolemaic perfume monopoly (P. Lond. Inv. 1849)," *JEA* 52 (1966) 179-180.

*George F. Bass, "A New Tie between Troy IIg and the Royal Cemetery at Ur," *AJA* 71 (1967) 183. *[Jewelry]*

S. M. Paul, "Jerusalem—A City of Gold," *IEJ* 17 (1967) 259-263. *[Jewelry]*

Jeanny Vorys Canby, "New Egyptian Jewelry at the Walters Art Gallery," *JARCE* 6 (1967) 111-112.

Susan Downey, "The Jewelry of Hercules at Hatra," *AJA* 72 (1968) 211-217.

Herbert Hoffmann, "'Greek Gold' Reconsidered," *AJA* 73 (1969) 447-451.

H. A. Hoffner Jr., "The 'City of Gold' and the 'City of Silver'," *IEJ* 19 (1969) 178-180.

P. R. S. Moorey, "Two Middle Bronze Age Brooches from Tell ed-Duweir," *L* 1 (1969) 97-99.

§96 *2.3.2.2 Gems and Minerals*

†Anonymous, "Precious Stones," *ERCJ* 124 (1866) 228-260. *(Review)*

†Anonymous, "Antique Gems," *ERCJ* 124 (1866) 511-552. *(Review)*

*Anonymous, "Antique Gems and Ancient Art," *DUM* 84 (1874) 513-524.

Anonymous, "Precious Stones," *BQRL* 67 (1878) 90-115. *(Review)* [Biblical Refs., pp. 91-92]

*Terrien de Lacouperie, "On Yakut Precious Stones from Oman to North China, 400 B.C.," *BOR* 6 (1892-93) 271-274.

H. B. Tristram, "Requests and Replies," *ET* 4 (1892-93) 295. [Bdellium]

Martha Adelaide Curl, "Ancient Gems," *AAOJ* 22 (1900) 284-291.

Anonymous, "Antique Gems," *QRL* 194 (1901) 416-434. *(Review)*

[Hermann] Zeller, "Precious Stones.—Translated from Zeller's Biblisches Wörterbuch," *ER* 15 (1864) 544-548. [1. Sardius; 2. Topaz; 3. Emerald; 4. Ruby; 5. Sapphire; 6. Diamond; 7. Ligure; 8. Agate; 9. Amethyst; 10. Turquoise; 11. Onyx/Beryl; 12. Japser]

W. J. Perry, "The Significance of the Search for Amber in Antiquity," *JMUEOS* #8 (1918-19) 71-80.

*Paul Haupt, "Philological and Archaeological Studies," *AJP* 45 (1924) 238-259. [4. The Median Lapis-lazuli Mountain, pp. 245-247]

*Kate McK. Elderkin, "Aphrodite Worship on a Minoan Gem," *AJA* 29 (1925) 53-58.

*George A. Barton, "On Binding-Reeds, Bitumen, and other Commodities in Ancient Babylonia," *JAOS* 46 (1926) 297-302.

G. A. Wainwright, "Obsidian," *AEE* 12 (1927) 77-93.

Paul Haupt, "Naphtha and Asphalt," *BAVSS* 10 (1927) Heft 2, 141-143.

A. Lucas, "The occurrence of natron in Ancient Egypt," *JEA* 18 (1932) 62-66.

*Clive H. Carruthers, "More Hittite Words," *Lang* 9 (1933) 151-161. [3. *kunkunuzzi* 'diorite', pp. 154-155]

*R. Campbell Thompson, "On Some Assyrian Minerals," *JRAS* (1933) 885-895.

*R. Campbell Thompson, "On the Assyrian words for 'whetstone' and 'corundum'," *JRAS* (1934) 343-346.

Campbell Bonner, "A Group of Gems," *AJA* 39 (1935) 112.

*C. R. Wason, "The Drill Style on Ancient Gems," *AAA* 23 (1936) 51-56.

Anonymous, "Multum in Parvo. An Exhibition of Newly Acquired Engraved Ancient Gems," *AJA* 46 (1942) 488-489.

A. Lucas, "Obsidian," *ASAE* 41 (1942) 271-275; 47 (1947) 113-123.

*(Mrs.) Linda S. Braidwood, "Preliminary Notes on the Jarmo Flint and Obsidian Industry," *Sumer* 7 (1951) 105-106.

Gisela M. A. Richter, "Unpublished Gems in Various Collections," *AJA* 61 (1957) 263-268.

*J. A. Thompson, "The Economic Significance of Transjordan in Old Testament Times," *ABR* 6 (1958) 143-168. [Mineral Resources in Transjordan, pp. 156-161]

Martin Levey, "Alum in Ancient Mesopotamian Technology," *Isis* 49 (1958) 166-169.

Martin Levey, "Gypsum, Salt and Soda in Ancient Mesopotamian Chemical Technology," *Isis* 49 (1958) 336-341.

*Philip C. Hammond, "The Nabataean Bitumen Industry at the Dead Sea," *AJA* 63 (1958) 188.

*Philip C. Hammond, "The Nabataean Bitumen Industry at the Dead Sea," *BA* 22 (1959) 40-48.

*Rutherford J. Gettens, "Minerals in Art and Archaeology," *SIR* (1961) 551-569.

*F. Charles Fensham, "Salt as a Curse in the Old Testament and the Ancient Near East," *BA* 25 (1962) 48-50.

John S. Harris, "An Introduction to the Study of Personal Ornaments of Precious, Semi-Precious and Imitation Stones used throughout Biblical History," *ALUOS* 4 (1962-63) 49-83.

Abd el-Mohsen el-Khachab, "A Collection of Gems from Egypt in Private Collections," *JEA* 49 (1963) 147-156.

J. E. Betts, "The Vapheio Gems: A Note of Clarification," *AJA* 70 (1966) 368-369.

Victore E. G. Kenna, "The Vapheio Gems—A Further Comment (*AJA* 70:4, October 1966, 368)," *AJA* 71 (1967) 409-410.

*Georgina Herrmann, "Lapis-Lazuli: The Early Phases of its Trade," *Iraq* 30 (1968) 21-57.

*Gary A. Wright and Adon A. Gordus, "Distribution and Utilization of Obsidian from Lake Van Sources betweeen 7500 and 3500 B.C.," *AJA* 73 (1969) 75-77.

*Gary A. Wright, "Obsidian Analyses and Prehistoric Trade: 7500 to 3500 B.C.," *UMMAAP* #37 (1969) i-v, 1-92.

§97 *2.3.3.3 Pottery Manufacturing*

*John Garstang, "A Pre-dynastic Pot-Kiln, recently discovered at Mahâsna, in Egypt," *Man* 2 (1902) #29.

Anonymous, "Ancient Pottery Furnaces," *RP* 6 (1907) 183-184.

*(Miss) Gisela M. A. Richter, "What an Archaeologist can Learn at a Modern Pottery School," *AJA* 22 (1918) 65.

*Stephen B. Luce, "An Early Potter's Wheel," *MJ* 11 (1920) 245-250.

*Randall MacIver, "On the Manufacture of Etruscan and other Ancient Black Wares," *Man* 21 (1921) #51.

Frederick D. Crane, "Materials and Methods of Early Potters," *AJA* 40 (1936) 116-117.

*R. Laird Harris, "A Mention of Pottery Glazing in Proverbs," *JAOS* 60 (1940) 268-269.

Marie Farnsworth and S. E. Q. Ashley, "The Technology of Black Attic Glaze," *AJA* 45 (1941) 92.

M. Stekelis, "A New Neolithic Industry: The Yarmukian of Palestine," *IEJ* 1 (1950-51) 1-19.

*Ruth Amiran, "The Millstone and the Potter's Wheel," *EI* 4 (1956) V.

Marie Farnsworth, "Types of Greek Glaze Failure," *Arch* 12 (1959) 242-250.

John Boardman, "Greek Potters at Al Mina?" *AS* 9 (1959) 169.

Martin Levey, "Clay and its Technology in Ancient Mesopotamia," *Cent* 6 (1959) 149-156.

Marie Farnsworth, "Draw Pieces as Aids to Correct Firing," *AJA* 64 (1960) 72-75.

*Ann Konrad Knudsen, "The Relation between the Pottery and Metal Vessel Industries of Gordion in the Eighth Century B.C.," *AJA* 65 (1961) 191.

Marie Farnsworth and Ivor Simmons, "Coloring Agents for Greek Glazes," *AJA* 67 (1963) 389-396.

Frederick R. Matson, "The Shoreline Excavation of a Kiln in Greece," *AJA* 72 (1968) 168.

Vronwy Hankey, "Pottery-Making at Beit Shebab, Lebanon," *PEQ* 100 (1968) 27-32.

Joseph V. Noble, "The Technique of Egyptian Faïence," *AJA* 72 (1968) 169.

Philip C. Hammond, "Ceramic Technology in the Mediterranian Littoral of Southwest Asia: Selected Iron II Period Sites," *AJA* 73 (1969) 236.

G. Kenneth Sams, "The Pottery Industry of Gordion at the Time of the Kimmerian Invasion," *AJA* 73 (1969) 244-245.

Peter Warren, "An Early Bronze Age Potter's Workshop in Crete," *Antiq* 43 (1969) 224-227.

A. S. K. Barky, "On the Mending of Pottery and Stone Vessels," *MDIÄA* 24 (1969) 43-50.

*L. A. Yelnitsky, "The Ancient Greek Wine Trade and Ceramics Production," *VDI* (1969) #3, 105.

§98 *2.3.3.4 Stonecutting, Quarry & Mining Industries*

( ) Newbold, "On the Process prevailing among the Hindus, and formerly among the Egyptians, of quarrying and polishing Granite; its uses &c; with a few Remarks on the tendency of the Rock in India to separate by Concentric exfoliation," *JRAS* (1843) 113-128.

*B. Harris Cowper, "The Mines and Metals of Antiquity: with Special Reference to the Bible," *JSL, 3rd Ser.,* 14 (1861-62) 257-268.

*W. O., "Copper Mines in the Sinaitic Peninsula," *JSL, 4th Ser.,* 1 (1862) 192.

*Anonymous, "The Land of Midian and its Mines," *PEFQS* 10 (1878) 141-145.

*J. William Dawson, "Notes on Useful and Ornamental Stones of Ancient Egypt," *JTVI* 26 (1892-93) 265-282. (Discussion, pp. 282-288) [1. Granitic, Dioritic, and Gneissic Rocks, 2. Basalt with Olivine, 3. The Nubian Sandstone, 4. Limestone, &c., 5. Miocene Quartzite of Jebel Ahmar, &c., 6. Various Stones and Gems, 7. Flint Flakes, Knives, Saws, &c.]

*C[onrad] Schick, "Letters from Baurath C. Schick," *PEFQS* 24 (1892) 9-25. [Chisel Marks in the Cotton Grotto in Jerusalem, pp. 24-25]

*Cyrus Adler, "The Cotton Grotto, and Ancient Quarry in Jerusalem," *JQR* 8 (1895-96) 384-391.

Archibald C. Dickie, "Stone Dressing of Jerusalem, Past and Present," *PEQFS* 29 (1897) 61-67.

C. R. Conder, "Remarks on Masonry," *PEFQS* 29 (1897) 145-147.

*H. W. Seaton-Karr, "How the Tomb Galleries at Thebes were cut and the limestone quarried at the Prehistoric flint-mines of the E. Desert," *ASAE* 6 (1905) 176-184.

*W. P. Jervis, "The Minerals and Metals Mentioned in the Old Testament. *Their paramount influence on the Social and Religious History of the Nations of Antiquity,*" *JTVI* 37 (1905) 259-280, 282. [(Discussion, pp. 280-281) (Remarks by G. Mackinlay, pp. 281-282)]

*Anonymous, "Gold Mines of Egypt," *MQR, 3rd Ser.,* 33 (1907) 612.

A. F. R. Platt, "The Ancient Egyptian Methods of Working Hard Stones," *SBAP* 31 (1909) 172-184.

Anonymous, "Ancient Egyptian Methods of Quarrying Stone," *RP* 9 (1910) 73.

Somers Clarke, "Cutting Granite," *AEE* 3 (1916) 110-113. {Note by W. M. F[linders] P[etrie], p. 113}

Anonymous, "Current Notes and News. King Solomon's Mines," *A&A* 9 (1920) 201-202.

*A. H. Sayce, "Geographical Notes," *JRAS* (1921) 47-55. [The Lead-Mines of Early Asia Minor, PP. 54-55]

Oscar S. Heizer and Steven T. Byington, "Copper Mines in the Territory of Judah," *PEFQS* 58 (1926) 56-58.

A. H. Sayce, "The Lead-mines of Early Asia Minor," *JRAS* (1921) 55-56.

*Elise Baumgärtel, "The Flint Quarries of Wady Sheykh," *AEE* 15 (1930) 103-108.

George M. Calhoun, "Ancient Athenian Mining," *JEBH* 3 (1930-31) 333-361.

*A. Barrois, "The Serâbît Expedition of 1930: II. The Mines of Sinai," *HTR* 25 (1932) 101-121.

*R. Engelbach, "The quarries of the Western Nubian Desert. A preliminary report," *ASAE* 33 (1933) 65-74.

Jaroslav Černý, "Semites in Egyptian Mining Expeditions to Sinai," *ArOr* 7 (1935) 384-389.

*Nelson Glueck, "The Copper Mines of King Solomon," *AJA* 40 (1936) 125. *[Arabah]*

O. G. S. C[rawford], "Tin-deposits in the Near East," *Antiq* 12 (1938) 79-81.

*R. Englbach, "The Quarries of the western Nubian desert and the ancient road to Tushka," *ASAE* 38 (1938) 369-390.

*Gisela M. A. Richter, "The Drove," *AJA* 47 (1943) 188-193.

*Anonymous, "Ancient Mining and Metallurgy," *Antiq* 24 (1950) 145.

Rosalind Moss, "Iron-mines near Aswān," *JEA* 36 (1950) 112-113.

*G. W. Murray, "A New Empire (?) copper mine in the Wadi 'Araba," *ASAE* 51 (1951) 217-218.

*A. E. Raubitschek, "The Mechanical Engraving of Circular Letters," *AJA* 55 (1951) 343-344.

*(Mrs.) Linda S. Braidwood, "Preliminary Notes on the Jarmo Flint and Obsidian Industry," *Sumer* 7 (1951) 105-106.

*K. Morgan, "*The Wadi Arabah:* Solomon's Mines," *AT* 5 (1960-61) #1, 9-12.

*K. Morgan, "*The Wadi Arabah:* Solomon's Industrial Port," *AT* 5 (1960-61) #2, 2-6.

*Anonymous, "Solomon's Mines," *AT* 5 (1960-61) #3, 14-15. *[Wadi Arabah]*

G. Ernest Wright, "More on King Solomon's Mines," *BA* 24 (1961) 59-62.

Perry A. Bialor, "The Chipped Stone Industry of Çatal Hüyük," *AS* 12 (1962) 67-110.

Hans Goedicke, "Some Remarks on Stone Quarrying in the Egyptian Middle Kingdom (2060-1786 B.C.)," *JARCE* 3 (1964) 43-50.

*Anson F. Rainey, "King Solomon's Mines," *JASA* 16 (1964) 18-19.

*C. Nylander, "Old Persian and Greek Stonecutting and the Chronology of Achaemenian Monuments. Achaemenian Problems I," *AJA* 69 (1965) 49-55.

Ian A. Todd and Giorgio Pasquare, "The Chipped Stone Industry of Avla Dağ," *AS* 15 (1965) 95-112.

V. Hankey, "A marble quarry at Karystos," *BMB* 18 (1965) 53-59.

*Carl Nylander, "The Toothed Chisel in Pasaradae: Further Notes on Old Persian Stonecutting," *AJA* 70 (1966) 373-376. [Achaemenian Problems II]

C. Nylander, "A Note on the Stonecutting and Masonry of Tel Arad," *IEJ* 17 (1967) 56-59.

L. Copeland and J. Waechter, "The Stone Industries of Abri Bergy, Lebanon," *ULBIA* 7 (1967) 15-36.

L. M. Gluskina, "The *Dikai Metallikai* in Attica in the Fourth Century B.C.," *VDI* (1967) #1, 59.

G[ary] A. Wright and A[don] A. Gordis, "Source Areas for Obsidian Recovered at Munhata, Beisamoun, Hazorea and El-Khiam," *IEJ* 19 (1969) 79-88.

M. W. Prausnitz, "The Sequence of Early to Middle Palaeolithic Flint Industries along the Galilean Littoral," *IEJ* 19 (1969) 129-136.

‡E. D. Stockton, "A Bibliography of the Flint Industries of Transjordan," *L* 1 (1969) 100-103.

Gary A. Wright and Adon A. Gordis, "Distribution and Utilization of Obsidian from Lake Van Sources between 7500 and 3500 B.C.," *AJA* 73 (1969) 75-77.

§99 *2.3.3.5 Metallurgy*

G. M. Bell, "On the Abundance of the Precious Metals in Ancient Times," *JSL, 1st Ser.*, 2 (1848) 267-280.

*B. Harris Cowper, "The Mines and Metals of Antiquity: with Special Reference to the Bible," *JSL, 3rd Ser.*, 14 (1861-62) 257-268.

*W. O., "Copper Mines in the Siniatic Peninsula," *JSL, 4th Ser.*, 1 (1862) 192.

*P. le Page Renouf, "On the metal [hieroglyphs]," *ZÄS* 11 (1873) 119-123. [Addenda, *ZÄS* 12 (1874) 105.

*Anonymous, "The Land of Midian and its Mines," *PEFQS* 10 (1878) 141-145.

*Anonymous, "Goldfields: Ancient and Modern," *WR* 120 (1883) 378-408. *(Review)*

Selah Merrill, "On the use of Gold and Silver among the Assyrians," *JAOS* 11 (1895) x-xi.

J. Magens Mello, "The Dawn of Metallurgy," *JTVI* 23 (1889-90) 277-294. [(Discussion, pp. 294-303) (Remarks by A. H. Sayce, p. 303; C. R. Conder, pp. 303-304)]

*J. H. Gladstone, "On Copper and Bronze of Ancient Egypt and Assyria," *SBAP* 12 (1889-90) 227-234.

A. Wiedemann, "Cobalt in Ancient Egypt," *SBAP* 13 (1890-91) 113-114.

*J. H. Gladstone, "On Metallic Copper, Tin, and Antimony from Ancient Egypt," *SBAP* 14 (1891-92) 223-227. (Remarks by Robert Austen, pp. 227-228)

*J. H. Gladstone, "Ancient Metals from Tell-el-Hesy," *SBAP* 16 (1893-94) 95-99.

J. H. Gladstone, "The Metals Used by the Great Nations of Antiquity," *PEFQS* 30 (1898) 252-254.

M. Berthelt, "Discovery of Platinum Among the Ancient Egyptian Metals," *AAOJ* 25 (1903) 114-116.

M. Berthelt, "Egyptian Gold," *AAOJ* 25 (1903) 178-179. *(Trans. by Charles A. Brassler)*

H. R. Hall, "Note on the Early Use of Iron in Egypt," *Man* 3 (1903) #86.

*W. P. Jervis, "The Minerals and Metals Mentioned in the Old Testament. *Their paramount influence on the Social and Religious History of the Nations of Antiquity,"* *JTVI* 37 (1905) 259-280, 282. [(Discussion, pp. 280-281) (Remarks by G. Mackinlay, pp. 281-282)]

H. R. Hall, "The Early Occurrence of Iron in Egypt," *Man* 5 (1905) #40.

Anonymous, "The Use of Metals by the Egyptians," *AAOJ* 28 (1906) 14-16.

Anonymous, "The Egyptian Metals," *MQR, 3rd Ser.,* 32 (1906) 383-384.

*Anonymous, "Gold Mines of Egypt," *MQR, 3rd Ser.,* 33 (1907) 612.

[William] Ridgeway, "The Beginnings of Iron," *RP* 6 (1907) 286-287.

*Claude R. Conder, "Notes on New Discoveries," *PEFQS* 41 (1909) 266-275. [Iron (Deut. 8:9; Num. 31:22; 1 Sam. 17:7), p. 271]

*William Frederic Badè, "The Iron-Taboo of the Hebrews," *PAPA* 43 (1911) lx.

*Anonymous, "The Philistines and Steel," *RP* 10 (1911) 295.

A. H. Sayce, "The Iron-Workers of the Sudan," *SBAP* 33 (1911) 96-97.

W. Belck, "The discoverers of the art of iron manufacture," *SIR* (1911) 507-521.

W. M. Flinders Petrie, "The Metals in Egypt," *AEE* 2 (1915) 12-23.

*Wilfred H. Schoff, "The Eastern Iron Trade of the Roman Empire," *JAOS* 35 (1915) 224-239.

G. Elliot Smith, "The Invention of Copper-making," *Man* 16 (1916) #18.

James Burt Willson, "The Use of Iron in Ancient Times," *PTR* 15 (1917) 250-276.

James Burt Willson, "Lead and Tin in Ancient Times," *PTR* 15 (1917) 443-450.

John Sebelien, "Early Copper and its Alloys," *AEE* 9 (1924) 6-15.

Anonymous, "Notes and Comments. Iron in Antiquity," *A&A* 23 (1917) 88.

A. Lucas, "Copper in Ancient Egypt," *JEA* 13 (1927) 162-170.

*Warren R. Dawson, "The Substance called *Didi* by the Ancient Egyptians," *JRAS* (1927) 497-503. *[Nubian Hæmatite(?)]*

H. Frankfort, "Sumerians, Semites, and the Origin of Copper-working," *AJ* 8 (1928) 217-235.

A. H. Sayce, "The Antiquity of Iron-Working," *Antiq* 2 (1928) 224-227.

Harold Peake, "The Copper Mountain of Magan," *Antiq* 2 (1928) 452-457.

A. Lucas, "Notes on the Early History of Tin and Bronze," *JEA* 14 (1928) 97-108.

A. Lucas, "Silver in Ancient Times," *JEA* 14 (1928) 313-319.

*O. Davies, "ΟΡΕΙΧΑΛΚΟΣ," *Man* 29 (1929) #21. *[Ancient Metallugy]*

J. Penrose Harland, "The Use of Iron in the Bronze Age," *AJA* 34 (1930) 59-60.

G. A. Wainwright, "Iron in Egypt," *JEA* 18 (1932) 3-15.

G. A. Wainwright, "The Occurrence of Tin and Copper near Byblos," *JEA* 20 (1934) 29-32.

Harry Craig Richardson, "Iron, Prehistoric and Ancient," *AJA* 38 (1934) 189-190, 555-583.

Thomas T. Read, "Metallurgical Fallacies in Archaeological Literature," *AJA* 38 (1934) 382-389.

*[W. M.] Flinders Petrie, "Copper or Bronze?" *AEE* 20 (1935) Supplement, 148.

G. A. Wainwright, "The Coming of Iron," *Antiq* 10 (1936) 5-24.

O. G. S. C[rawford], "The Discovery of Bronze," *Antiq* 10 (1936) 87-88.

Christopher Hawkes, "Early Iron in Egypt," *Antiq* 10 (1936) 355-357.

*Charles C. Torrey, "The Foundry of the Second Temple," *JBL* 55 (1936) 247-260.

Am. Hertz, "Iron Prehistoric and Ancient. An Answer to Mr. Richardson," *AJA* 41 (1937) 441-446.

Harry Craig Richardson, "Iron: Prehistoric and Ancient. A Reply to Madame Hertz" *AJA* 38 (1937) 447-451.

Herbert Maryon, "Prehistoric Soldering and Welding," *Antiq* 11 (1937) 208-209.

E. Wyndham Hulme, "Early Iron-Smelting in Egypt," *Antiq* 11 (1937) 222-223.

Homer A. Thompson, "The Metal Works of Athens and the Hephaisteion," *AJA* 42 (1938) 123.

G. Ernest Wright, "Iron in Israel," *BA* 1 (1938) 5-8.

T. A. Rickard, "The Primitive Smelting of Iron," *AJA* 43 (1939) 85-101.

G. Ernest Wright, "Iron: The Date of Its Introduction into Common Use in Palestine," *AJA* 43 (1939) 458-463.

H. H. Coghlan, "Some Experiments on the Origin of Early Copper," *Man* 39 (1939) #92.

*Gisela M. A. Richter, "A Greek Silver Phiale in the Metropolitan Museum And the Light It Throws On Greek Embossed Metalwork *(Toreutice)* of the Fifth Century B.C. and on the 'Calene' Phialai Mesomphaloi of the Hellenistic Period," *AJA* 45 (1941) 363-389.

H. H. Coghlan, "Prehistoric Iron prior to the Dispersion of the Hittite Empire," *Man* 41 (1941) #59, #63.

Herbert Maryon, "Welding and Soldcring," *Man* 41 (1941) #85.

V. Gordon Childe, "Prehistoric Iron," *Man* 41 (1941) #99.

*Dows Dunham and William J. Young, "An Occurrence of Iron in the Fourth Dynasty," *JEA* 28 (1942) 57-58.

G. A. Wainwright, "Early Records of Iron in Abyssina," *Man* 42 (1942) #43.

G. A. Wainwright, "Egyptian Bronze-making," *Antiq* 17 (1943) 96-98; 18 (1944) 100-102.

*Dows Dunham, "Notes on Copper-Bronze in the Middle Kingdom," *JEA* 29 (1943) 60-62.

G. A. Wainwright, "Early Tin in the Aegean," *Antiq* 18 (1944) 57-64.

*George G. Cameron, "The Babylonian Scientist and His Hebrew Colleague," *BA* 7 (1944) 21-29, 32-40. [Ancient Metallurgy, pp. 34-36]

G. A. Wainwright, "Rekhmirê's Metal-Workers," *Man* 44 (1944) #75.

A. Lucas, "The Origin of Early Copper," *JEA* 31 (1945) 96-97.

*Dorothy Kent Hill, "The Technique of Greek Metal Vases and Its Bearing on Vase Forms in Metal and Pottery," *AJA* 51 (1947) 248-256.

*Albrecht Goetze, "Contributions to Hittite Lexicography," *JCS* 1 (1947) 307-320. [(1) *kuwanna(n)* - "copper, azurite, (azurite) bead", pp. 307-310]

Herbert Maryon, "Metal Working in the Ancient World," *AJA* 53 (1949) 93-125.

*Alan Robinson, "God, the Refiner of Silver," *CBQ* 11 (1949) 188-190.

*Anonymous, "Ancient Mining and Metallurgy," *Antiq* 24 (1950) 145.

*James L. Kelso, "Ancient Copper Refining," *BASOR* #122 (1951) 26-27.

*T. Fish, "The Smith at Lagash," *MCS* 1 (1951) 46-48.

W. Rees Williams, "An Ancient Urn and Smelting Hearth in Kurdistan," *Sumer* 7 (1951) 46-48.

*R. J. Forbes, "Metals and Early Science," *Cent* 3 (1953-54) 24-31.

*G. R. Driver, "Babylonian and Hebrew Notes," *WO* 2 (1954-59) 19-26. [III. Three Hebrew Words (בדיל, מצהב, כסף), (i) בְּדִיל 'tin; antimony' and 'dross, slag'; (ii) נחשת מצהב 'orichalc'; (iii) כֶּסֶף 'silver'; pp. 21-26]

*G. R. Driver, "Technical Terms in the Pentateuch," *WO* 2 (1954-59) 254-263. [I. גַּבְלוּת 'welding', pp. 254-255]

R. North, "Metallurgy in the Ancient Near East," *Or, N.S.,* 24 (1955) 78-88.

*C. F. Cheng, and C. M. Schwitter, "Nickel in Ancient Bronzes," *AJA* 61 (1957) 351-365.

D. B. Stronach, "The Development and Diffusion of Metal Types in Early Bronze Age Anatolia," *AS* 7 (1957) 89-125.

Gisela M. A. Richter, "Ancient Plaster Casts of Greek Metalware," *AJA* 62 (1958) 369-377.

*Schyler V. R. Cammann, "The 'Bactrian Nickel Theory'," *AJA* 62 (1958) 409-414.

Jørgen Læssøe, "Akkadian Annakum: 'Tin' or 'Lead'?" *AO* 24 (1959) 83-94. [Sh 868]

E. Young, "Note on a hitherto unknown technique in Egyptian bronze-working," *JEA* 45 (1959) 104-106.

J. Vercoutter, "The Gold of Kush: Two Gold-washing Stations at Faras East," *Kush* 7 (1959) 120-153.

*Ann Konrad Knudsen, "Bronze Vessels from Gordion, and Evidence for Phrygian Metal-Working Techniques," *AJA* 64 (1960) 187.

Herbert Maryon, "Early Near Eastern Steel Swords," *AJA* 65 (1961) 173-184. [with technical reports by Mr. R. M. Organ, Dr. O. W. Ellis, Dr. R. M. Birch, Dr. R. Sneyers, Dr. E. E. Herzfeld, and Dr. F. K. Naumann]

*Ann Konrad Knudsen, "The Relation between the Pottery and Metal Vessel Industries of Gordion in the Eighth Century B.C.," *AJA* 65 (1961) 191.

*C. M. Schwitter, "Bactrian Nickel and Chinese Bamboo," *AJA* 66 (1962) 87-89. [Appendix by C. F. Cheng and C. M. Schwitter, pp. 89-92]

Schuyler Cammann, "On the Renewed Attempt to Revive the 'Bactrian Nickel Theory'," *AJA* 66 (1962) 92-94.

Beno Rothenberg, "Ancient Copper Industries in the Western Arabah," *PEQ* 94 (1962) 5-71.

A. Guillaume, "Metallurgy in the Old Testament," *PEQ* 94 (1962) 129-132.

*R. Knox, "Detection of Iron Carbide Structure in the Oxide Remains of Ancient Steel," *Archm* 6 (1963) 43-45.

*W. W. Hallo, "Lexical Notes on the neo-Sumerian Metal Industry," *BO* 20 (1963) 136-142.

*(Miss) Sylvia Benton, "No Tin from Kirsha in Phokis," *Antiq* 38 (1964) 138.

*Stuart Piggot, "Iron, Cimmerians and Aeschylus," *Antiq* 38 (1964) 300-303.

*J. Birmingham, N. F. Kennon, and A. S. Malin, "A 'Luristan' Dagger: An Examination of Ancient Metallurgical Techniques," *Iraq* 26 (1964) 44-49.

K. R. Maxwell-Hyslop and H. W. M. Hodges, "A Note on the Significance of the Technique of 'Casting On' as Applied to a Group of Daggers from north-West Persia," *Iraq* 26 (1964) 50-53.

*Robert H. Brill and J. Marion Wampler, "Isotope Studies of Ancient Lead," *AJA* 69 (1965) 165-166.

*J. Condamin and M. Picon, "Notes on Diffusion in Ancient Alloys," *Archm* 8 (1965) 110-114.

*J. V. Canby, "Early Bronze 'Trinket' Moulds," *Iraq* 27 (1965) 42-61.

*Beno Rothenberg and Alexandru Lupu, "Excavations in the Early Iron Age Copper Industry at Timna (Wadi Arabah, Israel), May 1964," *ZDPV* 82 (1966) 125-135.

*Colin Renfrew, "Cycladic Metallurgy and the Aegean Early Bronze Age," *AJA* 71 (1967) 1-20.

*Robert H. Brill and J. M. Wampler, "Isotope Studies of Ancient Lead," *AJA* 71 (1967) 63-77.

*Yu. B. Tsirkin, "The Tin Route and the Northern Trade of Massalia," *VDI* (1968) #3, 104.

*G. A. Melikishvili, "Names of Metals in Ancient Oriental and Caucasian Languages," *VDI* (1968) #4, 127.

P. R. S. Moorey, "Prehistoric Copper and Bronze Metallurgy in Western Iran (with special reference to Lūristān)," *Iran* 7 (1969) 131-153.

F. C. Fensham, "Iron in the Ugaritic Texts," *OA* 8 (1969) 209-213.

C. V. Golenko, "Anonymous Pontic Copper," *VDI* (1969) #1, 154.

§100 *2.3.4 Commerce, Economics & Business Transactions*

*F. M. Hubbard, "Commerce and Manufacturing of Ancient Babylon, intended to illustrate some parts of the Prophetic Scriptures," *BRCR* 7 (1836) 364-390.

F. M. Hubbard, "An Inquiry into the Commerce of Ancient Egypt," *BRCR* 10 (1837) 33-66.

Albert Barnes, "The Ancient Commerce of Western Asia," *BRCR, N.S.,* 4 (1840) 310-328; 5 (1841) 48-74.

*François Lenormant, "Money in Ancient Greece and Rome. A Chapter in the History of Political Economy," *ContR* 34 (1878-79) 504-523.

*Howard Osgood, "Prehistoric Commerce and Israel," *BQR* 7 (1885) 163-184.

*†Theo. G. Pinches, "Assyriological Notes," *SBAP* 8 (1885-86) 240-245. [Âgarrūtu, "workmen", p 241]

Theo. Mees, "Labor in the Light of the Bible," *ColTM* 6 (1886) 372-384.

Theo. G. Pinches, "Babylonian Banking-Houses," *ONTS* 9 (1889) 27-28.

W. St. C[had] Boscawen, "The Oldest Bank in the World," *BOR* 7 (1893-94) 241-246.

*W. St. Chad Boscawen, "The Merchants of Ur," *ET* 6 (1894-95) 120-122.

Anonymous, "The Origins of Political Economy," *SRL* 33 (1899) 353-371.

W. H. Bennett, "Wages in Ancient Israel," *ET* 13 (1901-02) 381-382.

*Joseph Clark Hoppin, "The Greek Colonial Movement as a Commercial Factor," *AJA* 7 (1903) 80-81.

J. T. Gracey, "Money, Bankers, and Hid Treasure in the Bible," *HR* 47 (1904) 277-279.

*Hermann Ranke, "Business House of Murashu Sons of Nippur," *RP* 3 (1904) 364-374.

*Maurice Thorner, "The Biblical Conception of Poverty and Riches," *HR* 49 (1905) 360-362.

*Anonymous, "The Excavations of Two Large Banking Houses," *MQR, 3rd Ser.,* 32 (1906) 184.

*William J. Hinke, "Legal and Commercial Transactions Chiefly from Nippur," *RP* 8 (1909) 11-19. *(Review)*

Albert T. Clay, "Babylonian Bookkeeping," *AJA* 14 (1910) 74.

*Anonymous, "Babylonian Legal and Business Documents," *RP* 9 (1910) 84-88. *(Review)*

Hugh Pope, "The Wealth of the Hebrews," *ITQ* 6 (1911) 414-426.

Allan Chester Johnson, "Studies in the Financial Administration of Athens," *AJP* 36 (1915) 424-452.

*William Notz, "Monopolies in the Ancient Orient," *BS* 74 (1917) 254-283.

A. C. Baird, "Early Babylonian Bills and Inventories," *GUOST* 4 (1913-22) 21-22.

*M. Rostovtzeff, "The Foundations of Social and Economic Life in Egypt in Hellenistic Times," *JEA* 6 (1920) 161-178.

W. M. Flinders Petrie, "The Rise of Price in Roman Egypt," *AEE* 7 (1922) 103-107.

*Mayer Sulzberger, "The Status of Labor in Ancient Israel," *JQR, N.S.,* 13 (1922-23) 397-459.

*Louis C. West, "Commerical Syria under the Roman Empire," *TAPA* 55 (1924) 159-189.

*Philip Vollmer, "Some Economic Principles of the Mosaic Law," *TZDES* 52 (1924) 264-272.

*T. Fish, "Sumerian Wage List of the Ur Dynasty," *BJRL* 9 (1925) 241-247.

*John E. McFadyen, "Poverty in the Old Testament," *ET* 37 (1925-26) 184-189.

J. G. Milne, "Double Entries in Ptolemaic Tax-Receipts," *JEA* 11 (1925) 269-283.

Ira M. Price, "The Laws of Deposit in Early Babylonia and the Old Testament," *JAOS* 47 (1927) 250-255.

A. H. Pruessner, "The Earliest Traces of Negotiable Instruments," *AJSL* 44 (1927-28) 88-107.

George M. Calhoun, "Risk in Sea Loans in Ancient Athens," *JEBH* 2 (1929-30) 561-584.

William Linn Westermann, "Warehousing and Trapezite Banking in Antiquity," *JEBH* 3 (1930-31) 30-54.

Henry Fr. Lutz, "Price Fluctuations in Ancient Babylonia," *JEBH* 4 (1931-32) 335-355.

Henry Fr. Lutz, "Babylonian Partnership," *JEBH* 4 (1931-32) 552-570.

*Eli Ginzberg, "Studies in the Economics of the Bible," *JQR, N.S.,* 22 (1931-32) 343-408. [I. Laws Pertaining to Slavery; II. The Sabbatical Year; III. The Jubilee Year; Appendix]

Tenney Frank, "The Public Finances of Rome 200-157 B.C.," *AJP* 53 (1932) 1-20.

G. A. Duncan, "Athenian Public Finance in the Fifth Century B.C.," *Herm* #47 (1932) 62-98.

*Elizabeth Grier, "The Accounts of Wages Paid in Kind in the Zenon Papyri," *TAPA* 63 (1932) 230-244.

Anonymous, "Notes and Comments. The Five-Day Week Four-Thousand Years Ago," *A&A* 34 (1933) 55.

*T. H. Robinson, "Some Economic and Social Factors in the History of Israel. II. In Domestic Relations," *ET* 45 (1933-34) 294-300.

Jaroslav Černý, "Fluctuations in Grain Prices During the Twentieth Egyptian Dynasty," *ArOr* 6 (1934) 173-178.

Michael I. Rostovtzeff, "The Hellenistic World and its Economic Development," *AmHR* 41 (1935-36) 231-252.

*W. H. McClellan, "Rich Men in Ancient Israel. I. The Patriarchal Period," *TRQU* 10 (1935-36) 437-452.

*W. H. McClellan, "Rich Men in Ancient Israel. II. The Patriarchal Period," *TRQU* 10 (1935-36) 602-620.

Waldo H. Dubberstein, "Comparative Prices in Later Babylonia (625-400 B.C.)," *AJSL* 56 (1939) 20-43.

A. Segrè, "The Ptolemaic Copper Inflation, *ca.* 230-140 B.C.," *AJP* 63 (1942) 174-192.

C. H. V. Sutherland, "Corn and Coin: A Note on Greek Commerical Monopolies," *AJP* 64 (1943) 129-147.

Charles C. Torrey, "The Evolution of a Financier in the Ancient Near East," *JNES* 2 (1943) 295-301.

*Fritz Mezger, "To hold (up) the head of the debtor," *JAOS* 64 (1944) 31-32.

*Samuel Atlas, "Rights of Private Property and Private Profit," *YCCAR* 54 (1944) 212-241. {Discussion by: [Jacob] Singer, pp. 241-242; [Herman I.] Pollack, p. 242; [Ferdinand M.] Isserman, pp. 242-243; Isaiah Sonne, pp. 243-246; Julius Gordon, pp. 246-247; [Moses] Landau, p. 247; [Abraham] Shinedling, pp. 247-248; Eric Werner, pp. 248-249; Solomon B. Freehof, p. 249; [Bernard] J. Bamberger, pp. 249-251; Reply by Samuel Atlas, pp. 251-256]}

*I. Mendelsohn, "Slavery in the Ancient Near East," *BA* 9 (1946) 74-88. [III. The Economic Role of Slavery, pp. 86-88]

A. Leo Oppenheim, "A Fiscal Practice of the Ancient Near East," *JNES* 6 (1947) 116-120.

Norman W. Porteous, "Aspects of Ancient Commerce," *GUOST* 13 (1947-49) 11-15.

*Henry R. Immerwahr, "An Athenian Wineshop," *TAPA* 79 (1948) 184-190.

Tony Reekmans, "Economic and Social Repercussions of the Ptolemaic Copper Inflation," *CdÉ* 24 (1949) 324-342.

*George W. Edwards, "The Maladjustment of Palestinian Economy Under Herod," *JAAR* 17 (1949) 116-119.

*Leicester B. Holland and Louise Adams Holland, "The Tiber in Primitive Commerce," *AJA* 54 (1950) 261-262.

W. F. Leemans, "The rate of interest in Old-Babylonian Times," *RIDA, 1st Ser.*, 5 (1950) 7-34.

*Walter J. Fischel, "The Jewish Merchants, Called Radanites," *JQR, N.S.*, 42 (1951-52) 321-325.

*J. G. Milne, "Roman coinage in Egypt in relation to the native economy," *Aeg* 32 (1952) 143-151.

*A. H. M. Jones, "The Economic Basis of the Athenian Democracy," *P&P* #1 (1952) 13-31.

S. Stein, "The Laws on Interest in the Old Testament," *JTS, N.S.*, 4 (1953) 161-170.

F. M. Heichelheim, "Recent Discoveries in Ancient Economic History," *HJAH* 2 (1953-54) 129-135.

*E[dward] Neufeld, "The Rate of Interest and the Text of Nehemiah 5.11," *JQR, NS.*, 64 (1953-54) 194-204.

Jaroslav Černý, "Prices and Wages in Egypt in the Ramesside Period," *JWH* 1 (1953-54) 903-921.

*Rodolfo Mondolfo, "The Greek Attitude to Manual Labor," *P&P* #6 (1954) 1-5. *(Trans. by D. S. Duncan)*

Lubor Matouš, "Some Remarks to the Economical Sources from Larsa (In margine*[sic]* of two publications by *W. F. Leemans*)," *ArOr* 23 (1955) 465-474.

*Siegfreid Stein, "The Development of Jewish Law on Interest from the Biblical Period to the Expulsion of the Jews from England," *HJud* 17 (1955) 3-40.

*E. Neufeld, "The Prohibitions against Loans at Interest in Ancient Hebrew Laws," *HUCA* 26 (1955) 355-412.

*Ferris J. Stephens, "Notes on some Economic Texts of the Time of Urukagina," *RAAO* 49 (1955) 129-136. [3. The Seizure of Property for Debt, pp. 132-134]

*Tom B. Jones, "Bookkeeping in Ancient Sumer," *Arch* 9 (1956) 16-21.

*E[phraim] A. Speiser, "Nuzi Marginalia," *Or, N.S.,* 25 (1956) 1-23. {*Entire article, especially:* [1. The Hurrian Equivalent of *sikiltu(m) [to accumulate savings],* pp. 1-4]}

*A. Ehrman, "Law and Equity in the Talmudic Concept of Sale," *JJS* 8 (1957) 177-186.

L. Jacobs, "The Economic Conditions of the Jews in Babylon in Talmudic Times Compared with Palestine," *JSS* 2 (1957) 349-359.

William McInnes, "Merchants and Markets in Babylon in the Second Millenium B.C.," *MH* 13 (1957-58) #2, 33-47.

*J. A. Thompson, "The Economic Significance of Transjordan in Old Testament Times," *ABR* 6 (1958) 143-168. [Pre-Israelite Transjordan; The Iron Age Kingdoms of Transjordan; Agriculture and Pastoral Pursuits in Transjordan in the Iron Age; Mineral Resources in Transjordan; Transjordan and the Caravan Routes; Supplementary Evidence from Assyria, Babylonia and Persia; Conclusion]

*G. R. Watson, "The Pay of the Roman Army. The Republic," *HJAH* 7 (1958) 113-120.

Julius Lewy, "Some Aspects of Commerical Life in Assyria and Asia Minor in the Nineteenth Pre-Christian Century," *JAOS* 78 (1958) 89-101.

*Gus W. Van Beek, "Frankincense and Myrrh in Ancient South Arabia," *JAOS* 78 (1958) 141-152. [Economic Effects of the Incense Trade, pp. 148-149]

Edward Neufeld, "Socio-economic background of Yōbēl and Š^{e}miṭṭā," *RDSO* 33 (1958) 53-124.

*I. M. Finley, "Was Greek Civilisation based on Slave Labor?" *HJAH* 8 (1959) 145-164.

John B. Curtis and William W. Hallo, "Money and Merchants in Ur III," *HUCA* 30 (1959) 103-139.

*Y. Yadin, "Recipients or Owners: A Note on the Samaria Ostraca," *IEJ* 9 (1959) 184-187.

*J. A. C. Thomas, "*Custodia* and *Horrea*," *RIDA, 3rd Ser.*, 6 (1959) 371-383. *[Laws of Liability of Warehousing]*

*James E. Pritchard, "Industry and Trade in Biblical Gibeon," *BA* 23 (1960) 23-29.

*Rivkah Harris, "Old Babylonian Temple Loans," *JCS* 14 (1960) 126-136.

*I. Mendelsohn, "The Corvee Labor in Ancient Canaan and Israel," *BASOR* #167 (1962) 31-35.

*Maria Jaczynowaska, "The Economic Differentiation of the Roman Nobility at the End of the Republic," *HJAH* 11 (1962) 486-499.

Klaus Baer, "The Low Cost of Land in Ancient Egypt," *JARCE* 1 (1962) 25-45.

*Albrecht Goetze, "Two Ur-Dynasty Tablets Dealing with Labor," *JCS* 16 (1962) 13-16.

*Anson F. Rainey, "Merchants at Ugarit and the Patriarchal Narratives," *CNI* 14 (1963) #2, 17-26.

A[nson] F. Rainey, "Business Agents at Ugarit," *IEJ* 13 (1963) 313-321.

*D. G[eoffrey] Evans, "The Incidence of Labour-service in the Old Babylonian Period," *JAOS* 83 (1963) 20-26.

*[D.] Geoffrey Evans, "The Incidence of Labour-Service at Mari," *RAAO* 57 (1963) 65-78. [I. Work upon the canals and irrigation system; II. Agricultural corvées; III. Conclusions; IV. Periods of Labour-service; V. Royal Policies upon labor service and land use, pp. 76-78]

*Bernard J. Meislin and Morris L. Cohen, "Backgrounds of the Biblical Law against Usury," *CSSH* 6 (1963-64) 250-267.

*Angelo P. O'Hagan, "Poverty in the Bible," *ABR* 12 (1964) 1-9.

*Pierre Biard, "Biblical Teaching on Poverty," *CC* 14 (1964) 433-440. *(Trans. by M. de Montfort)*

*Richard A. Parker, "A Demotic Property Settlement from Deir el Ballas," *JARCE* 3 (1964) 89-103.

*Derek Kinder, "Wealth," *TB* #15 (1964) 2-9.

*Paul E. Davies, "'The Poor You Have With You Always'. *(The Biblical View of Poverty)*," *McQ* 18 (1964-65) #2, 37-48.

Daniel Sperber, "Costs of Living in Roman Palestine," *JESHO* 8 (1965) 248-271.

*I. J. Gelb, "The Ancient Mesopotamian Ration System," *JNES* 24 (1965) 230-243.

*J. A. C. Thomas, "Return to 'Horrea'," *RIDA, 3rd Ser.*, 13 (1965) 353-368.

*G. M. Tucker, "Covenant forms and Contract Forms," *VT* 15 (1965) 487-503.

Mogens Weitemeyer, "Hiring of Workers. Dockets from the Old Babylonian Period," *AO* 29 (1965-66) 19-222.

Jack M. Sasson, "A sketch of north Syrian economic relations in the Middle Bronze Age," *JESHO* 9 (1966) 161-181.

Daniel Sperber, "Costs of Living in Roman Palestine II," *JESHO* 9 (1966) 182-211.

*Pierre Biard, "Biblical Teaching on Poverty," *TD* 14 (1966) 153-154. *(Synopsis)*

*B. De Vries, "Partial Admission," *Tarbiz* 36 (1966-67) #3, III-IV. *[Oaths concerning credit and debt]*

*James Kelly, "The Biblical Meaning of Poverty and Riches," *BibT* #33 (1967) 2282-2290.

*John H. Betts, "New Light on Minoan Bureaucracy. *A Re-examination of some Cretan Sealings*," *KZFE* 6 (1967) 15-40.

*Horst Klengel, "On the Economic Basis of Nomadism in Ancient Mesopotamia," *VDI* (1967) #4, 69-70.

*W. F. Leemans, "Old Babylonian letters and economic history. A review article with a digression on Foreign Trade," *JESHO* 11 (1968) 171-226. *(Review)*

Daniel Sperber, "Costs of Living in Roman Palestine III," *JESHO* 11 (1968) 233-274.

*I. M. Diakonoff, "Problems of Economics. The Structure of Near Eastern Society to the Middle of the Second Millenium B.C. 3. The Structure of the Communal Sector of the Economy in Western Asia," *VDI* (1968) #3, 26-27.

*I. M. Diakonoff, "Problems of Economics. The Structure of Near Eastern Society to the Middle of the Second Millenium B.C.," *VDI* (1968) #4, 38-40. [4. The Structure of the State Sector of the Economy in Western Asia; 5. General Conclusions. The Structure of Society and the Mode of Production]

Bezalel Porten and Jonas C. Greenfield, "The Guarantor at Elephantine-Syene," *JAOS* 89 (1969) 153-157.

*Henry T. Wright, "The Administration of Rural Production in an Early Mesopotamian Town," *UMMAAP* #38 (1969) i-xiii, 1-162.

§101 *2.3.7 Defense and Warfare [See Individual names of persons or places for Specific Campaigns; See also: Fortifications →]*

( ) Andreossi, "Observations on the Writings of Historians of all Ages and Countries chiefly with reference to their Knowledge of the Art of War," *MMBR* 22 (1806) 235-238, 325-327.

Ασπιδιωτης, "The Shields of the Mighty," *CongML* 20 (1837) 86-92, 172-176.

*Anonymous, "The Use of Elephants in War," *DUM* 21 (1843) 117-120. *(Review)*

*Anonymous, "Notes on Bishop Colenso's New Book," *JSL, 4th Ser.*, 2 (1862-63) 385-401. *(Review)* [II. Were the Israelites Armed? pp. 395-398]

*John Campbell, "The Hornets of Scripture, as connected with Jewish and Egyptian history," *PQPR* 4 (1875) 677-692. *[Insects in Warfare]*

*Herman Hager, "Army surgeons in ancient Greek warfare," *JP* 8 (1879) 14-17.

*Thomas W. Ludlow, "The Athenian Naval Arsenal of Philon," *AJP* 3 (1882) 317-328.

D. G. Hogarth, "The army of Alexander," *JP* 17 (1888) 1-26.

Terrien de Lacouperie, "The Tarshish Tats'in Navy," *BOR* 8 (1895-1900) 83-94.

*T. K. Cheyne, "Solomon's Armoury, Canticles, iv. 4," *ET* 9 (1897-98) 423-424.

George H. Chase, "Shield Devices among the Greeks," *AJA* 5 (1901) 26.

*James A. Quarles, "Sociology of Joseph's Day," *CFL, N.S.,* 5 (1902) 340-352. [Military, pp. 346-348]

*T. K. Frost, "The Navy of Tharshish and the Failure of Jehoshaphat," *ET* 16 (1904-05) 177-180.

*Arthur E. P. Weigall, "A Report on Some Objects recently found in Sebakh and other Diggings," *ASAE* 8 (1907) 40-50. [Prehistoric Celt from Gebelên, pp. 42-43; Archaic Celt from Saḳḳâra, p. 43]

*J. L. Myers, "A Tomb of the Early Iron Age, from Kition in Cyprus, containing Bronze Examples of the 'Sigynna' or Cypriot Javelin," *AAA* 3 (1910) 107-117.

*[Paul Carus], "Battle Scenes in Ancient Art," *OC* 26 (1912) 443-446.

H. M. Tirard, "The Soldiers of Ancient Egypt," *JEA* 2 (1915) 229-233.

*Somers Clarke, "Ancient Egyptian Frontier Fortresses," *JEA* 3 (1915) 155-179.

*Eduard König, "Israel's Attitude Respecting Alien-Right and Usages of War in Antiquity," *HR* 72 (1916) 184-189.

*Wallace N. Stearns, "Judas Maccabaeus as a Military Strategist," *IJA* #47 (1916) 53-54.

*S[tephen] Langdon, "Lexicographical and epigraphical notes," *RAAO* 13 (1916) 1-4. [The sign (*šita*), "Weapon, Mace", pp. 3-4]

*Joseph Offord, "Archaeological Notes on Jewish Antiquities. XXXVI. *The Israelite Wars against Damascus, and Recent Discoveries,*" *PEFQS* 49 (1917) 179-181.

H. R. James, "The Usages of War in Ancient Greece," *ERCJ* 227 (1918) 68-84.

H. F. Lutz, "The helmet of Eannatum," *JAOS* 38 (1918) 68-69.

*Paul Haupt, "Heb. talpî'ôṯ, Siege-towers," *JBL* 38 (1919) 186-187.

Stephen B. Luce, "Ancient Helmets from Italy," *MJ* 11 (1920) 68-76.

*Joseph Offord, "Archaeological Notes on Jewish Antiquities. LXI. *The Sukkiim*," *PEFQS* 52 (1920) 42.

*A. H. Burne, "Some Notes on the Battle of Kadesh. Being a Military Commentary on Professor J. H. Breasted's Book, *The Battle of Kadesh* (University of Chicago Press, 1903)," *JEA* 7 (1921) 191-195.

*W. J. Phythian-Adams, "Hittite and Trojan Allies 1290-1190 B.C.," *BSAJB* #1 (1922) 3-7.

*M. H. Segal, "David's War Against the Philistines," *PEFQS* 54 (1922) 74-78.

*S[tephen] Langdon, "Assyriological Notes," *RAAO* 22 (1925) 31-38. [III. *ILLURI: ILLULU*, javelin, boomerang, bow(?); pp. 36-37]

[W. M.] Flinders Petrie, "Supplies and Defence[sic]*," *AEE* 11 (1926) 15-23.

*William Hovgaard, "The Arsenal in Piraeus and the Ancient Building Rules," *Isis* 8 (1926) 12-20.

*Paul Haupt, "Ass. *mitpânu*, longbow," *BAVSS* 10 (1927) Heft 2, 144-145.

*Allan Chester Johnson, "Ancient Forests and Navies," *TAPA* 58 (1927) 199-209.

*S. Tolkowsky, "The Destruction of the Jewish Navy at Jaffa in the Year 68 A.D.," *PEFQS* 60 (1928) 153-163.

William Loftus Hare, "Greek Armorial Bearings," *A&A* 27 (1929) 59-63.

William Loftus Hare, "Greek Armorial Bearings: Part II," *A&A* 27 (1929) 136-140.

William Loftus Hare, "Greek Armorial Bearings: Part III," *A&A* 27 (1929) 169-174.

*William Nickerson Bates, "Two Inscribed Slingers' Bullets from Galatista," *AJA* 34 (1930) 44-46.

Clive H. Carruthers, "Some Hittite Etymologies," *Lang* 6 (1930) 159-163. [5. *šenah(h)aš* 'battle-line, army in the field(?)' pp. 162-163]

*W[illiam] F[oxwell] Albright, "Mitannian maryannu, 'chariot-warrior', and the Canaanite and Egyptian Equivalents," *AfO* 6 (1930-31) 217-221.

José Abelda Y Albert, "The Greek Helmet of Huelva," *A&A* 32 (1931) 166-168.

*N. P. Clarke, "Ancient Defences of Tell el Ajjūl," *AEE* 17 (1932) 10-12.

*Alexander David Fraser, "The Panoply of the Ethiopian Warrior," *PAPA* 63 (1932) lix.

*Theodor Gaster, "A Hittite Word in Hebrew," *JRAS* (1933) 909. [כּוֹבַע 'helmet' / קוֹבַע = Hittite kupaḫi]

Bengt Thordeman, "A Persian Splint Armour," *AA* 5 (1934) 294-296.

*A[lexander] D[avid] Fraser, "The Panoply of the Ethiopian Warrior," *AJA* 39 (1935) 35-45.

C. J. Gadd, "An Assyrian Camp-Scene," *Antiq* 9 (1935) 209-210.

C. A. Robinson, "Alexander's Army," *AJA* 40 (1936) 124.

*Dwight F. Putman, "War and Religion: An Unholy Alliance," *LCQ* 9 (1936) 197-205. [1. War and Religion in the Tribe of Dan, pp. 197-200]

*Harris Gary Hudson, "The Shield Signal at Marathon," *AmHR* 42 (1936-37) 443-459.

Lynn Harper Wood, "Archaeology and the Bible—The Evolution of Systems of Defense in Palestine," *JAAR* 5 (1937) 127-135.

Edward Robertson, "Assyrian Warfare," *JMUEOS* #21 (1937) 25-36.

Alfred Westholm, "Cypro-Archaic Splint Armour," *AA* 9 (1938) 163-173.

Lionel Cohen, "Evidence for the Ram in the Minoan Period," *AJA* 42 (1938) 486-494.

*Robert L. Scranton, "The Fortifications of Athens at the Opening of the Peloponnesian War," *AJA* 42 (1938) 525-536.

Guy Brunton, "Syrian connections of a composite bow," *ASAE* 38 (1938) 251-252.

*Nelson Glueck, "Ezion-Geber: Solomon's Naval Base on the Red Sea," *BA* 1 (1938) 13-16.

Ovid R. Sellers, "Sling Stones of Biblical Times," *BA* 2 (1939) 41-44.

*J. W. Jack, "Recent Biblical Archaeology," *ET* 51 (1939-40) 420-423. [Deadly Power of Ancient Arrows, The Arsenal of Official Archives, p. 421]

J. L. Myres, "The Structure and Origin of the Minoan Body-shield," *Man* 39 (1939) #37.

A. E. H. Love, "The Shape and Physical Qualities of the Minoan Shield," *Man* 39 (1939) #38.

*Grahame Clark, "Horses and Battle-axes," *Antiq* 15 (1941) 50-70.

*V. Gordon Childe, "Horses, Chariots, and Battle-axes," *Antiq* 15 (1941) 196-199.

R. O. Faulkner, "Egyptian Military Standards," *JEA* 27 (1941) 12-18.

*J. W. Jack, "Recent Biblical Archaeology," *ET* 53 (1941-42) 113-117. [Israelite Warfare, pp. 115-116]

*John Garstang, "Hittite Military Roads in Asia Minor: A Study in Imperial Strategy with a Map," *AJA* 47 (1943) 35-62.

Chester G. Starr Jr., "Coastal Defense in the Roman World," *AJP* 64 (1943) 56-70.

S. V[ernon] McCasland, "The Military Draft in the Bible," *JBL* 62 (1943) iii.

S. Vernon McCasland, "'Soldiers on Service:' The Draft Among the Hebrews," *JBL* 62 (1943) 59-71.

Torgny Säve-Söderbergh, "The Navy of the Eighteenth Egyptian Dynasty," *UUÅ* (1946) #6, i-iv, 1-94.

James Hornell, "Naval Activity in the Days of Solomon and Rameses III," *Antiq* 21 (1947) 66-73.

Merrill F. Unger, "Archeology and the Israelite-Aramaean Wars," *BS* 106 (1949) 178-186, 303-311.

Y. Yadin, "The Reorganization of the Army of Judah under Josiah," *BIES* 15 (1949-50) #3/4, III-IV.

Hugh Hencken, "Shields of the Herzsprung Type," *AJA* 54 (1950) 259.

*Hugh Hencken, "Herzsprung Shields and Greek Trade," *AJA* 54 (1950) 295-309.

*Robert L. Scranton, "Greek Arts in Greek Defense," *Arch* 3 (1950) 4-11.

E. A. Speiser, "On Some Articles of Armor and Their Names," *JAOS* 70 (1950) 47-49.

S. Yeivin, "Canaanite and Hittite Strategy in the Second Half of the Second Millennium B.C.," *JNES* 9 (1950) 101-107.

A[braham] Malamat, "The Last Wars of the Kingdom of Judah," *JNES* 9 (1950) 218-227.

*Thomas T. Hoopes, "A Crested Helmet from Italy," *AJA* 56 (1952) 174.

*M. Avi-Yonah, "The 'War of the Sons of Light and the Sons of Darkness' and the Maccabean Warfare," *IEJ* 2 (1952) 1-5.

D. H. Gordon, "Fire and Sword: the Technique of Destruction," *Antiq* 27 (1953) 149-152.

O. Tufnell, "The Shihan Warrior," *Iraq* 15 (1953) 161-166.

R. O. Faulkner, "Egyptian Military Organization," *JEA* 39 (1953) 32-47.

*A[braham] Malamat, "The War of Gideon and Midian. A Military Approach," *PEQ* 85 (1953) 61-65.

*Yigael Yadin, "Hyksos Fortifications and the Battering-ram," *BASOR* #137 (1955) 23-32.

*A[braham] Malamat, "Scales of Rationing in Pap. Anastasi I and the Bible," *BIES* 19 (1955) #3/4, ii.

*Yigael Yadin, "The Earliest Record of Egypt's Military Penetration into Asia? Some Aspects of the Narmer Palette, and the 'Desert Kites' and Mesopotamian Seal Cylinders," *IEJ* 5 (1955) 1-16.

*Yigael Yadin, "Goliath's Javelin and the מנור ארגים," *PEQ* 87 (1955) 58-69.

Y. Y. Rabinovitz, "Enrolled in the King's Army," *EI* 4 (1956) VII.

*William McKane, "The *Gibbôr Ḥayil* in the Israelite Community," *GUOST* 17 (1957-58) 28-37.

*A[braham] Malamat, "A New Record of Nebuchadrezzar's Palestinian Campaigns," *IEJ* 6 (1956) 246-256.

*William McKane, "The *Gibbôr Ḥayil* in the Israelite Community," *GUOST* 17 (1957-58) 28-37.

S. B. Gurewicz, "The Deuteronomic Provisions for Exemption from Military Service," *ABR* 6 (1958) 111-121.

Wallace E. McLeod, "An Unpublished Egyptian Composite Bow in the Brooklyn Museum," *AJA* 62 (1958) 397-401.

*G. R. Watson, "The Pay of the Roman Army. The Republic," *HJAH* 7 (1958) 113-120.

*F. Willesen, "The Philistine Corps of the Scimitar from Gath," *JSS* 3 (1958) 327-335.

*T. Wheildon Brown, "The Discovery of a Line of Ancient Fortifications on a Ridge to the East of the Rania Plain, Sulaimaniyah Liwa," *Sumer* 14 (1958) 122-124.

*Anonymous, "When Kings, Hunted Lions, and Men. No. 2. Palace Pictures of nearly 3000 years ago Support the Scriptures," *AT* 3 (1958-59) #3, 9-12.

*G. Ernest Wright, "Philistine Coffins and Mercenaries," *BA* 22 (1959) 54-66.

G. A. Reisner, "The Egyptian Forts from Halfa to Semna," *Kush* 8 (1959) 11-24. (Edited by Dows Dunham)

*R. MacMullen, "Inscriptions on Armor and the Supply of Arms in the Roman Empire," *AJA* 64 (1960) 23-40.

*Geoffrey Evans, "An Old Babylonian Soldier: Notes on the Archive of Ubarrum," *JCS* 14 (1960) 34-42.

*Albrecht Goetze, "The Beginning of the Hittite Instructions for the Commander of the Border Guards," *JCS* 14 (1960) 69-73.

A. van Selms, "The armed Forces of Israel under Saul and David," *OTW* 3 (1960) 55-66.

N. K. Sandars, "The first Aegean Swords and their Ancestry," *AJA* 65 (1961) 17-29. [Errata, p. 219]

*Herbert Maryon, "Early Near Eastern Steel Swords," *AJA* 65 (1961) 173-184. [with technical reports by Mr. R. M. Organ, Dr. O. W. Ellis, Dr. R. M. Birch, Dr. R. Sneyers, Dr. E. E. Herzfeld, and Dr. F. K. Naumann]

Henry George Fischer, "The Nubian Mercenaries of Gebelein during the First Intermediate Period," *Kush* 9 (1961) 44-80.

*George M. A. Hanfmann, "A Near Eastern Horseman," *Syria* 38 (1961) 243-256.

*Awni K. Dajani, "Some of the Industries of the Middle Bronze Period," *ADAJ* 6&7 (1962) 55-75. [Weapons, pp. 55-66]

Wallace E. McLeod, "Egyptian Composite Bows in New York," *AJA* 66 (1962) 13-19.

*Zane C. Hodges, "Conflicts in the Biblical Account of the Ammonite-Syrian War," *BS* 119 (1962) 238-243.

James B. Pritchard, "Civil Defense at Gibeon," *Exped* 5 (1962-63) #1, 10-17.

*Alan R. Schulman, "The *Nʿrn* at the Battle of Kadesh," *JARCE* 1 (1962) 47-53.

N. K. Sandars, "Later Aegean Bronze Swords," *AJA* 67 (1963) 117-153.

*J. K. Anderson, "The Statue of Chabrias," *AJA* 67 (1963) 411-413. *[Military Strategy]*

Albrecht Goetze, "Warfare in Asia Minor," *Iraq* 25 (1963) 124-130.

H. W. F. Saggs, "Assyrian Warfare in the Sargonid Period," *Iraq* 25 (1963) 145-154.

*V. Korošec, "The Warfare of the Hittites—from the Legal Point of View," *Iraq* 25 (1963) 159-166.

E. A. E. Reymond, "The Origin of the Spear. I," *JEA* 49 (1963) 140-146.

Mordechai Gichon, "The Defences of the Salomonic Kingdom," *PEQ* 95 (1963) 113-126.

*B[enjamin] Mazar, "The Military Élite of David," *VT* 13 (1963) 310-320.

A. F. Johns, "The military strategy of the sabbath attacks on the Jews," *VT* 13 (1963) 482-486.

George Radan, "Italic Helmets," *Exped* 6 (1963-64) #1, 28-33.

*Kate C. Lefferts, "Technical Notes on Another Luristan Sword," *AJA* 68 (1964) 59-62.

Bernard Goldman, "Late Scythian Parade Helmets," *AJA* 68 (1964) 194.

Stephen Foltiny, "Flange-hilted Cutting Swords of Bronze in Central Europe, Northeast Italy and Greece," *AJA* 68 (1964) 247-257.

*K. L. McKay, "Animals in War and ἰσονμία," *AJP* 85 (1964) 124-135.

Alan R. Schulman, "Some Remarks on the Military Background of the Amarna Period," *JARCE* 3 (1964) 51-69.

E. A. E. Reymond, "The Origin of the Spear. II," *JEA* 50 (1964) 133-138.

A. Gelston, "The Wars of Israel," *SJT* 17 (1964) 325-331.

James H. Turnure, "Etruscan Ritual Armor: Two Examples in Bronze," *AJA* 69 (1965) 39-48.

*Dorothy Kent Hill, "A Helmet Tomb-Group of the Trebenischte Type," *AJA* 69 (1965) 169. *["Illyrian" type Helmet]*

J. H. Young, "An Inscribed Helmet in Baltimore," *AJA* 69 (1965) 179.

Anonymous, "Recent Acquisitions by the Institute. A Hammer and Sling Stone from the Jerusalem Excavations of 1962-63.— Modern investigations throw light on a Bible Story," *BH* 2 (1965) #1, 3-8.

A. W. Lawrence, "Ancient Egyptian Fortifications," *JEA* 51 (1965) 69-94.

A[nson] F. Rainey, "The Military Personnel of Ugarit," *JNES* 24 (1965) 17-27.

*J. A. Brinkman, "Elamite Military Aid to Merodach-Baladan," *JNES* 24 (1965) 161-166.

Tariq Madhloum, "Assyrian Siege-engines," *Sumer* 21 (1965) 9-15.

*F. E. Winter, "Notes on Military Architecture in the Termessos Region," *AJA* 70 (1966) 127-137.

*Elizabeth MacNeil Boggess, "Ancient Horsemanship and Marathon," *AJA* 70 (1966) 183.

*G. Radan, "Attic Kylix with Four Warships," *Sefunim* 1 (1966) 35-39.

*Arie Ben-Eli, "Reconstruction of a Warship from a Wall Painting in a Catacomb in Jerusalem," *Sefunim* 1 (1966) 40-42.

J. Roy, The Mercenaries of Cyrus," *HJAH* 16 (1967) 287-323.

R. D. Milns, "*Miszelle.* Philip II and the Hypaspists," *HJAH* 16 (1967) 509-512.

Geoffrey Powell, "The Roman Legions and their Officers," *HT* 17 (1967) 785-764.

*Å. W. Sjöberg, "Contributions to the Sumerian Lexicon," *JCS* 21 (1967) 275-278. [1. á-sìg-ge(á-sìg) Akk. *assukku*, "sling stone, p. 275]

*J. Liver, "The Wars of Mesha, King of Moab," *PEQ* 99 (1967) 14-31.

*Lionel Casson, "The Emergency Rig of Ancient Warships," *TAPA* 98 (1967) 43-48.

G. Radan, "Helmet Found Near Ascalon," *Sefunim* 2 (1967-68) 46-49.

A. M. Khazanov, "Cataphractarii in the History of the Art of War," *VDI* (1968) #1, 191.

L. P. Marinovich, "Mercenaries During the Peloponnesian Wars," *VDI* (1968) #4, 90.

*N. N., "Additional Note to עָצוּר וְעָזוּב," *Lĕš* 33 (1968-69) #1, n.p.n.

David Blackman, "The Athenian Navy and Allied Naval Contributions in the Pentecontaetia," *GRBS* 10 (1969) 179-216.

Arnaldo Momigliano, "Cavalry and Patriciate. An Answer to Professor Alfödi," *HJAH* 18 (1969) 385-388.

M. L. Heltzer, "The Army of Ugarit and Its Organisation," *VDI* (1969) #3, 38.

§102 *2.3.6 Foreign Policy, Diplomatic Relations, International Influences and Interaction (Synchronism)*

*F. M. Hubbard, Commerce and Manufacturing of Ancient Babylon, intended to illustrate some parts of the Prophetic Scripture," *BRCR* 7 (1836) 364-390.

Anonymous, "Connection between Egyptian and Jewish History," *QCS, 3rd Ser.*, 8 (1836) 337-353.

*G. B., "The Dial of Ahaz and the Embassy from Merodach Baladan," *JSL, 3rd Ser.*, 2 (1855-56) 163-179.

*T. S. K[ing], "India in Greece," *UQGR* 9 (1857) 221-241. *(Review)*

A. H. Sayce, "The early relations of Egypt and Babylonia," *ZÄS* 8 (1870) 150-151.

†Anonymous, "Chinese Literature. Its connection with Babylonia," *QRL* 154 (1883) 124-150. *(Review)*

*Howard Osgood, "Prehistoric Commerce and Israel," *BQR* 7 (1885) 163-184.

Theo. G. Pinches, "The Babylonians and Assyrians as Maritime Nations.—I. Information supplied by the Bilingual inscriptions," *BOR* 1 (1886-87) 41-42.

T[errien] de Lacouperie, "Babylonia and China," *BOR* 1 (1886-87) 113-115.

Robert Young, "The Influence of Egypt on the Hebrews," *ERG, 9th Ser.*, 1 (1886-87) 338-342.

*D. G. Lyon, "Israelitish Politics as Affected by Assyrian, Babylonian and Early Achaemenian Kings," *ONTS* 6 (1886-87) 293-302.

*Frederic Gardiner, "Various Topics III. The Jew and the Greek," *JBL* 8 (1888) 150-151.

Terrien de Lacouperie, "From Ancient Chaldea and Elam to Early China: a Historical Loan of Culture," *BOR* 5 (1891) 32-44, 63-70, 79-86.

James Marshall, "Some Points of Resemblance between Ancient Nations of the East and West," *SBAP* 14 (1891-92) 4-16.

A. Lazarus, "Phoenician Influence on Palestine," *EN* 4 (1892) 475-476.

Morris Jastrow Jr., "Egypt and Palestine, 1400 B.C.," *JBL* 11 (1892) 95-124.

*Anonymous, "The Hebrews and the Sea," *ONTS* 14 (1892) 307.

Robert W. Rogers, "Assyria's First Contact with Israel," *MR* 77 (1895) 207-222.

Joseph Horner, "The Contact of Israel with Assyria," *MR* 77 (1895) 470-471.

*W. M. Flinders Petrie, "Egypt and Israel," *ContR* 69 (1896) 617-627.

*Hugh Pope, "Phoenicia and Israel," *IER, 4th Ser.*, 2 (1897) 488-499; 3 (1898) 38-59.

F. B. Welch, "The Influence of the Aegean Civilisation on South Palestine," *PEFQS* 32 (1900) 342-350.

Camden M. Cobern, "Early Intercourse Between the Hebrews and Other Ancient Peoples," *HR* 42 (1901) 105-112.

*William R. Harper, "Was Israel Really a Separate Nation?" *BW* 19 (1902) 163-167. *(Editorial)*

Camden M. Cobern, "Intercourse Between the Hebrews and Other Ancient Peoples—900-600 B.C. and Earlier," *HR* 44 (1902) 121-127.

*John E. McFadyen, "Hellenism and Hebraism," *AJT* 8 (1904) 30-47.

A. H. Sayce, "Babylonian Culture in Canaan," *AAOJ* 27 (1905) 317-320.

Robert Dick Wilson, "The Linguistic Evidence for Relations between Babylon and Israel," *CFL, 3rd Ser.,* 2 (1905) 324-340.

P. J. Boyer, "Assyria and Israel," *ICMM* 2 (1905-06) 208-213, 315-323.

*Andrew Craig Robinson, "The Bearing of Recent Oriental Discoveries on Old Testament History," *JTVI* 38 (1906) 154-176. {(Discussion, pp. 176-181.) [The Connection of Israel with Babylonia in the Early Times. *Abraham,* pp. 156-158; The Assyrians in Contact with Israel, pp. 175-176]}

*Anonymous, "Egyptian Images and Vases," *MQR, 3rd Ser.,* 32 (1906) 386.

F. J. Foakes-Jackson, "Foreign Influence upon Israel's Development," *ICMM* 3 (1906-07) 55-69.

F. J. Foakes-Jackson, "Israel and Babylon," *ICMM* 3 (1906-07) 126-140.

F. J. Foakes-Jackson, "Israel and Persia," *ICMM* 3 (1906-07) 257-272.

F. J. Foakes-Jackson, "Israel and Greece," *ICMM* 3 (1906-07) 388-404.

Percy E. Newberry, "The Petty-Kingdom of the Harpoon and Egypt's Earliest Mediterranean Port," *AAA* 1 (1908) 17-22.

J. C. Kinnaman, "The Relation of Egyptian to Classical Culture," *AAOJ* 30 (1908) 323-327.

George E. White, "Assyrian Influence in Asia Minor," *RP* 7 (1908) 250-251.

Edouard Montet, "Israel and Babylonian Civilization," *OC* 23 (1909) 619-631.

Anonymous, "Early Intercourse Between Greece and Italy," *RP* 8 (1909) 62-63.

S[tephen] Langdon, "The Relations of Canaan and Babylonia in the Hammurabi Epic," *OSHTP* (1909-10) 23-26.

*H. R. Hall, "The Discoveries in Crete and their Relation to the History of Egypt and Palestine," *SBAP* 31 (1909) 135-148, 221-238, 280-285 , 311-318.

*J. Rendel Harris, "Crete, the Jordan, and the Rhône," *ET* 21 (1909-10) 303-306. *[The Creatans, their linguistic influence]*

S[amuel*[sic]*] Langdon, "Relation between Canaan and Babylonia in the Hammurabi Epoch," *Exp, 7th Ser.*, 10 (1910) 128-147.

*A. H. Godbey, "The Influence of Alexander's Conquest upon Jewish Life," *BW* 38 (1911) 171-184.

*Alan S. Hawkesworth, "Sardinia's Connection with Babylon," *OC* 25 (1911) 447.

*H. R. Hall, "The Land of Alashiya and the Relation of Egypt and Cyprus Under the Empire. (1500-1100 B.C.)," *JMUEOS* #2 (1912-13) 33-45.

Clarence P. Bill, "Early Greek Influence on Asia Minor," *PAPA* 45 (1913) xvi.

A. J. Evans, "The Minoan and Mycenaean element in Hellenic Life," *SIR* (1913) 617-637.

W. M. Flinders Petrie, "Egypt in Africa," *AEE* 1 (1914) 115-127, 159-170.

Ed[uard] König, "Canaan and the Babylonian Civilization," *LCR* 33 (1914) 37-45.

T. Eric Peet, "The Early Relations of Egypt and Asia," *JMUEOS* #4 (1914-15) 27-48.

Stanley A. Cook, "An Egyptian List of Palestinian Ambassadors," *PEFQS* 47 (1915) 43-44.

Charles M. Watson, "Egypt and Palestine," *PEFQS* 47 (1915) 132-143.

*William Mitchell Ramsay, "The Intermixture of Races in Asia Minor: Some of its Causes and Effects," *PBA* 7 (1915-16) 359-422. [II. Immigrant Races in Ancient Times, pp. 362-374; III. Survival of Ancient Races and Ancient Customs or Law, pp. 374-381]

*Eduard König, "Israel's Attitude Respecting Alien-Right and Usages of War in Antiquity," *HR* 72 (1916) 184-189.

*G. Elliott Smith, "The Influence of Ancient Egyptian Civilization in the East and in America," *BJRL* 3 (1916-17) 48-77.

W. M. Flinders Petrie, "Egypt and Mesopotamia," *AEE* 4 (1917) 26-36.

*L. D. Barnett, "Commerical and Political Connexions of Ancient India with the West," *BSOAS* 1 (1917-20) #1, 101-105.

*Fletcher H. Swift, "Hebrew Education in School and Society. During the Period of Reaction to Foreign Influence," *OC* 32 (1918) 228-253.

*(Miss) Ida C. Thallon, "Some Balkan and Danubian Connections of Troy," *AJA* 23 (1919) 67-68.

A. T. Olmstead, "Kashshites, Assyrians, and the Balance of Power," *AJSL* 36 (1919-20) 120-153.

David Neumark, "The Beauty of Japhet in the Tents of Shem," *JJLP* 1 (1919) 5-17.

Maurice*[sic]* Jastrow Jr., "Mesopotamia and Greece," *PAPA* 50 (1919) xii-xiii.

*W[illiam] F[oxwell] Albright, "Menes and Narâm-Sin," *JEA* 6 (1920) 89-98. *[Synchronism of Chronology]*

*H. A. Ormerod, "Ancient Piracy in the Eastern Mediterranean," *AAA* 8 (1921) 105-124.

*H. R. Hall, "Egypt and the External World in the Time of Akhenaten," *JEA* 7 (1921) 39-53.

*W[illiam] F[oxwell] Albright, "Magan, Meluḫa, and the Synchronism between Menes and Narâm-Šin," *JEA* 7 (1921) 80-86.

G. W. Gilmore, "Early Babylonia Connected with Early Egypt," *HR* 83 (1922) 478.

*Raymond P. Dougherty, "Nabonidus in Arabia," *JAOS* 42 (1922) 305-316.

*H. R. Hall, "The Discoveries at Tell el 'Obeid in Southern Babylonia and Some Egyptian Comparisons," *JEA* 8 (1922) 241-257.

P. Boylan, "Egypt and Israel in the Days of Tutankhamon," *DR* 173 (1923) 94-111.

*G. A. Wainwright, "The Red Crown in Early Prehistoric Times," *JEA* 9 (1923) 26-33.

*Nora Griffith, "Akhenaten and the Hittites," *JEA* 9 (1923) 78-79.

Theophilus G. Pinches, "Assyro-Babylonians and Hebrews—Likenesses and Contrasts," *JTVI* 55 (1923) 182-199, 203-206. (Discussion, pp. 199-203)

S. Casson, "Mycenæan Elements in the North Ægean," *Man* 23 (1923) #107.

Ernest Mackay, "Sumerian Connexions with Ancient India," *JRAS* (1925) 697-701.

*G. W. B. Huntingford, "On the Connection Between Egyptian and the Masai-Nandi Group of East Africa," *AEE* 11 (1926) 10-11.

*Harold M. Weiner, "The Relation of Egypt and Israel and Judah in the Age of Isaiah," *AEE* 11 (1926) 51-53, 70-72.

[W. M.] Flinders Petrie, "Egypt and Mesopotamia," *AEE* 11 (1926) 102-103.

H. Frankfort, "Egypt and Syria in the First Intermediate Period," *JEA* 12 (1926) 80-99.

F. W. W. DesBarres, "Greek Influences in Palestine," *CJRT* 4 (1927) 420-429.

*J. Penrose Harland, "Aegean Influence in Sicily in the Bronze Age," *AJA* 33 (1929) 106-107.

Stephen Gaselee, "Greek Culture in Egypt," *ERCJ* 250 (1929) 318-328.

*George A. Barton, "The Origins of Civilization in Africa and Mesopotamia, their Relative Antiquity and Interplay," *PAPS* 68 (1929) 303-312.

*Alan Rowe, "A Comparison of Egyptian and Babylonian Civilizations and their Influence on Palestine," *PAPS* 68 (1929) 313-319.

*Edith M. Guest, "The Influence of Egypt on the Art of Greece," *AEE* 15 (1930) 45-54.

[W. M.] Flinders Petrie, "The Linking of Egypt and Palestine," *Antiq* 4 (1930) 279-284.

J. D. S. Pendlebury, "Egypt and the Aegean in the Late Bronze Age," *JEA* 16 (1930) 75-92.

Dorrance Stinchfield White, "Changes in Roman Diplomatic Practice," *PAPA* 61 (1930) xxiii-xxiv.

W. W. Cannon, "Israel and Moab," *Theo* 20 (1930) 184-196, 249-261.

Ernest Mackay, "Further Links between Ancient Sind, Sumer and elsewhere," *Antiq* 5 (1931) 459-473.

*Harold L. Craeger, "Cultural and Religious Influence of Babylonia and Assyria on Western Asia," *LCQ* 4 (1931) 345-367.

J. Penrose Harland, "Helladic vs. Minoan," *AJA* 36 (1932) 37.

*E. A. Speiser, "On Some Important Synchronisms in Prehistoric Mesopotamia," *AJA* 36 (1932) 465-471.

Ernest Mackay, "An Important Link between Ancient India and Elam," *Antiq* 6 (1932) 356-357.

*Sidney Smith, "An Egyptian in Babylonia," *JEA* 18 (1932) 28-32.

T. J. C. Baly, "The relations of the Eleventh Dynasty and the Heracleopolitans," *JEA* 18 (1932) 173-176.

*N. D. Mironov, "Aryan Vestiges in the Near East of the Second Millenary B.C.," *AO* 11 (1932-33) 140-217. [I. The Kassites, pp. 142-149; II. The Hyksos, pp. 150-170; III. Palestine and Syria (Amarna Letters), pp. 171-185; IV. The Mitanni, 186-205; V. The Hittites, pp. 205-215]

S. F. Hunter, "Assyrian Contacts with Judah and Israel," *NZJT* 2 (1932-33) 166-175.

Theodore Burton Brown, "Anatolian Relations with the Aegean before 2400 B.C.," *AAA* 20 (1933) 43-64.

*V. I. Avdief, "Egypt and Caucasus," *AEE* 18 (1933) 29-36.

*T. H. Robinson, "Some Economic and Social Factors in the History of Israel. I. In External Relations," *ET* 45 (1933-34) 264-269.

J. R. Towers, "The Syrian Problem in the El-Amarna Period," *AEE* 19 (1934) 49-55.

[W. M.] Flinders Petrie, "Links of Palestine and Egypt," *AEE* 20 (1935), *Supplement*, pp. 143-145.

Arthur Evans, "Crete and Egypt," *Antiq* 9 (1935) 216-217.

Alex Heidel, "Political Contacts of the Hebrews with Assyria and Babylon," *CTM* 7 (1936) 418-436, 481-497.

C. G. Seligman, "The Roman Orient and the Far East," *Antiq* 11 (1937) 5-30.

Claude Harrison, "Greek Culture and Rome," *IER, 5th Ser.*, 50 (1937) 156-161.

Robert H. Pfeiffer, "Hebrews and Greeks before Alexander," *JBL* 56 (1937) 91-101.

*W[illiam] F[oxwell] Albright, "The Egyptian Correspondence of Abimilki, Prince of Tyre," *JEA* 23 (1937) 190-203.

Joseph I. Schade, "Foreign Influences on Ancient Israel," *AER* 100 (1939) 510-522.

V. Gordon Childe, "India and the West Before Darius," *Antiq* 13 (1939) 5-15.

*Alan Rowe, "Addendum No. 1 on Egypto-Canaanite Contacts (*A Catalogue of Egyptian Scarabs, &c., in the Palestine Archaeological Museum*, 1936)," *QDAP* 8 (1939) 72-76.

*J. W. Jack, "Recent Biblical Archaeology," *ET* 51 (1939-40) 420-423. [Ras Shamra (Ugarit). Europe and Palestine connected *c.* 1900 B.C., p. 421]

Thorkild Jacobsen, "The Assumed Conflict between Sumerians and Semites in Early Mesopotamian History," *JAOS* 59 (1939) 485-495.

*Homer H. Dubs, "An Ancient Military Contact between Romans and Chinese," *AJP* 62 (1941) 322-330.

M. A. Murray, "Connexions between Egypt and Russia," *Antiq* 15 (1941) 384-386.

Kurt von Fritz, "The Mission of L. Caesar and L. Roscius in January 49 B.C.," *TAPA* 72 (1941) 125-156.

*Carl W. Blegen, "The Foreign Relations of Troy in the Bronze Age," *AJA* 46 (1942) 121.

Helene J. Kantor, "The Early Relations of Egypt with Asia," *JNES* 1 (1942) 174-213. [I. Egypt and Palestine, The Pre-Gerzean Period, the Gerzean and Semainean Periods; II. Later Predynastic Relationships with Mesopotamia; III. Egypt and Palestine, The First Dynasty; IV. Egypt and Syria; V. Summary]

Helene J. Kantor, "The Aegean and the Orient in the Second Millenium B.C.," *AJA* 51 (1947) 1-103.

*Raphael Patai, "Hebrew Installation Rites. A Contribution to the Study of Ancient Near Eastern-African Culture Contact," *HUCA* 20 (1947) 143-225.

Rhys Carpenter, "The Greek Penetration of the Black Sea," *AJA* 52 (1948) 1-10.

*Saul S. Weinberg, "Neolithic Figurines and Aegean Interrelations," *AJA* 54 (1950) 256-257.

W[illiam] F[oxwell] Albright, "Cilicia and Babylonia under the Chaldaean Kings," *BASOR* #120 (1950) 22-25.

Leslie H. Neatby, "Romano-Egyptian Relations During the Third Century B.C.," *TAPA* 81 (1950) 89-98.

*Saul S. Weinberg, "Neolithic Figurines and Aegean Interrelations," *AJA* 55 (1951) 121-133.

Clark Hopkins, "Hittite Influences and Etruscan Culture," *AJA* 56 (1952) 174.

Ruth B. K. Amiran, "Connections between Anatolia and Palestine in the Early Bronze Age," *IEJ* 2 (1952) 89-103.

*John A. Wilson, "Oriental History: Past and Present," *JAOS* 72 (1952) 49-55.

Helene J. Kantor, "Further Evidence for Early Mesopotamian Relations with Egypt," *JNES* 11 (1952) 239-250.

*W[illiam] F[oxwell] Albright, "The New Assyro-Tyrian Synchronism and the Chronology of Tyre," *AIPHOS* 13 (1953) 1-9.

*Roland E. Murphy, "Israel and Moab in the Ninth Century B.C.," *CBQ* 15 (1953) 409-417.

*J. L. Myers, "Persia, Greece and Israel," *PEQ* 85 (1953) 8-22.

*M. Dothan, "High, Loop-Handled Cups and the Early Relations between Mesopotamia, Palestine and Egypt," *PEQ* 85 (1953) 132-137.

R. E. Smith, "The Opposition to Agesialaus' Foreign Policy, 394-371 B.C.," *HJAH* 2 (1953-54) 274-288.

*Ephraim A. Speiser, "The Hurrian Participation in the Civilizations of Mesopotamia, Syria and Palestine," *JWH* 1 (1953-54) 311-327.

*John W. Wilson, "Egyptian Technology, Science, and Lore," *JWH* 2 (1954-55) 209-213. [Influences Through Israel, p. 212]

*Hildegard Lewy, "The Synchronism Assyria—Ešnunna—Babylon," *WO* 2 (1954-59) 438-453.

*Immanuel Ben-Dor, "Some Mediterranean Relations in the 8th Century B.C.—The Excavation of a Phoenician Cemetery in Palestine," *AJA* 59 (1955) 170.

*Yigael Yadin, "The Earliest Record of Egypt's Military Penetration into Asia? Some Aspects of the Narmer Palette, the 'Desert Kites' and Mesopotamian Seal Cylinders," *IEJ* 5 (1955) 1-16.

*Berta Segall, "Problems of Copy and Adaptation in the Second Quarter of the First Millenium, B.C. Some Syrian and 'Syro-Hittite' Elements in the Art of Arabia and of the West," *AJA* 60 (1956) 165-170.

Raymond V. Schoder, "The Roman Impress on North Africa," *AJA* 60 (1956) 183.

George E. Mylonas, "Mycenaean Greek and Minoan-Mycenaean Relations," *Arch* 9 (1956) 273-279.

V. Gordon Childe, "Anatolia and Thrace. Some Bronze Age Relations," *AS* 6 (1956) 45-48.

W[illiam] F[oxwell] Albright, "Further Light on Synchronisms Between Egypt and Asia in the Period 935-685 B.C.," *BASOR* #141 (1956) 23-27.

J. M. Munn-Rankin, "Diplomacy in Western Asia in the Early Second Millennium B.C.," *Iraq* 18 (1956) 68-110.

*S. Schuller, "Some Problems Connected with the Supposed Common Ancestry of Jews and Spartans and Their Relations During the Last Three Centuries B.C.," *JJS* 1 (1956) 257-268.

C[yrus] H. Gordon, "Colonies and enclaves," *SOOG* 1 (1956) 409-419.

*Louis Le Breton, "The Early Periods at Susa, Mesopotamian Relations," *Iraq* 19 (1957) 79-124.

Robert H. Pfeiffer, "Assyria and Israel," *RDSO* 32 (1957) 145-154.

Ann Perkins and Saul S. Weinberg, "Connections of the Greek Neolithic and the Near East," *AJA* 62 (1958) 225.

A[braham] Malamat, "The Kingdom of David & Solomon in Its Contact with Egypt and Aram Naharaim," *BA* 21 (1958) 96-102. (Correction, *BA* 22 (1959) p. 51)

J. Kaplan, "Connections between Palestine and Egypt in the Chalcolithic Period," *BIES* 22 (1958) #3/4, n.p.n.

Cyrus H. Gordon, "Indo-European and Hebrew Epic," *EI* 5 (1958) 10*-15*.

E. Badian, "The Unification of the Mediterranean: Cold War in the Ancient World," *HT* 8 (1958) 83-87.

E. Badian, "The Unification of the Mediterranean: Cold War in the Ancient World. Part II," *HT* 8 (1958) 170-176.

*Peter J. Parr, "Palestine and Anatolia: A Further Note," *ULBIA* 1 (1958) 21-23.

J. Kaplan, "The Connections of the Palestinian Chalcolithic Culture with Prehistoric Egypt," *IEJ* 9 (1959) 134-136.

S. Yeivin, "Did the Kingdoms of Israel have a Maritime Policy?" *JQR, N.S.,* 50 (1959-60) 193-228.

*John L. Caskey, "Lerna, the Cyclades, and Crete," *AJA* 64 (1960) 183.

S. Yeivin, "Early Contacts Between Canaan and Egypt," *IEJ* 10 (1960) 193-203.

*George F. Hourani, "Ancient South Arabian Voyages to India—A Rejoinder to G. W. Van Beek," *JAOS* 80 (1960) 135-136.

*G. A. Wainwright, "Meneptaḥ's Aid to the Hittites," *JEA* 46 (1960) 24-28.

*A. H. van Zyl, "Israel and the Indigenous Population of Canaan according to the Books of Samuel," *OTW* 3 (1960) 67-80.

H. G. Güterbock, "Mursili's accounts of Suppiluliuma's dealings with Egypt," *RHA* 18 (1960) 57-63.

*Stephen Foltiny, "Athens and the East Halstatt Region: Cultural Interrelations at the Dawn of the Iron Age," *AJA* 65 (1961) 283-297.

W. A. Ward, "Egypt and the East Mediterranean in the Early Second Millenium B.C.," *Or, N.S.,* 30 (1961) 22-45, 120-155.

*C. M. Schwitter, "Bactrian Nickel and Chinese Bamboo," *AJA* 66 (1962) 87-89. [Appendix by C. F. Cheng and C. M. Schwitter, pp. 89-92]

*Benjamin Mazar, "The Aramean Empire and its Relations with Israel," *BA* 25 (1962) 98-120.

William A. Ward, "Egypt and the East Mediterranian from Predynastic times to the end of the Old Kingdom," *JESHO* 6 (1963) 1-57.

*A[braham] Malamat, "Aspects of the Foreign Policies of David and Solomon," *JNES* 22 (1963) 1-17. [A. David and the Kingdom of Hadadezer; B. Israel and Hamath; C. David's and Solomon's Foreign Marriages; D. The Historical Implications of Solomon's Marriage with the Daughter of Pharaoh]

Cyrus H. Gordon, "The Mediterranean Factor in the Old Testament," *VTS* 9 (1963) 19-31.

J. Gwyn Griffiths, "Siberian Links with Egypt?" *Antiq* 38 (1964) 222-226.

*F. Charles Fensham, "The Treaty Between Israel and the Gibeonites," *BA* 27 (1964) 96-100.

*Anonymous, "Villas and Victuals," *BH* 1 (1964) #1, 3-7. *[Roman Culture in Palestine]*

C. Bradford Welles, Elias Kapetanopoulos, John F. Oates, & J. Frank Gilliam, "The Romanization of the Greek East," *BSAP* 2 (1964-65) 42-77. [Introduction; The Evidence of Athens; The Evidence of Egypt; The role of the Army; Conclusion]

Miriam Tadmor, "Contacts Between the 'Amuq and Syria-Palestine (Review-article)," *IEJ* 14 (1964) 253-269. *(Review)*

Hans Goedicke, "Diplomatical Studies in the Old Kingdom," *JARCE* 3 (1964) 31-41.

William A. Ward, "Relations between Egypt and Mesopotamia from Prehistoric times to the end of the Middle Kingdom," *JESHO* 7 (1964) 1-45, 121-135.

*L. M. Muntingh, "Political and international relations of Israel's neighbouring peoples according to the oracles of Amos," *OTW* 7&8 (1964-65) 134-142.

*A. E. Raubitschek, "The Peace Policy of Perikles," *AJA* 69 (1965) 174.

*Ruth Amiran, "A Preliminary Note on the Synchronisms Between the Early Bronze Strata of Arad and the First Dynasty," *BASOR* #179 (1965) 30-33.

*James H. Oliver, "Athens and Roman Problems around Moesia," *GRBS* 6 (1965) 51-55.

*(Mrs.) E. C. L. Caspers, "Further Evidence for Cultural Relations Between India, Baluchistan, and Iran and Mesopotamia in Early Dynastic Times," *JNES* 24 (1965) 53-56.

*Joseph Klíma, "The Periphery of Mesopotamian Culture," *NOP* 4 (1965) 17-19.

J. B. Ward-Perkins, "The Roman West and the Parthian East," *PBA* 51 (1965) 175-199.

Derek J. Mosley, "The Size of Embassies in Ancient Greek Diplomacy," *TAPA* 96 (1965) 255-266.

*Raphael Hallevy, "The Canaanite Period: A Culture Clash," *Tarbiz* 35 (1965-66) #2, I-II.

M. Seshadri, "Roman Contacts with South India," *Arch* 19 (1966) 244-247.

Hans Petersen, "New Evidence for the Relations Between Romans and Parthians," *Bery* 16 (1966) 61-69.

*T. C. Skeat, "A fragment on the Ptolemaic perfume monopoly," *JEA* 52 (1966) 179-180.

I. A. F. Bruce, "Athenian Embassies in the Early Fourth Century B.C.," *HJAH* 15 (1966) 272-281.

*D. J. Wiseman, "Some Egyptians in Babylonia," *Iraq* 28 (1966) 154-158.

*Jana Siegelová, "The Hittites and Egypt," *NOP* 5 (1966) 76-79.

*I. H. Eybers, "Relations between Jews and Samaritans in the Persian Period," *OTW* 9 (1966) 72-89.

*O. Tufnell and W. A. Ward, "Relations between Byblos, Egypt and Mesopotamia at the end of the third Millennium B.C. A Study of the Montet Jar," *Syria* 43 (1966) 165-241.

*Geo Widengren, "Iran and Israel in Parthian Times with Special Regard to the Ethiopic Book of Enoch," *Tem* 2 (1966) 139-177.

Cyrus H. Gordon, "Hellenes and Hebrews," *GOTR* 12 (1966-67) 134-140.

*Keith Branigan, "Further Light on Prehistoric Relations between Crete and Byblos," *AJA* 71 (1967) 117-121.

*Frank J. Frost, "A Friend of Ptolemy at Halicarnassus," *AJA* 71 (1967) 187.

*Briggs Buchanan, "A Dated Seal Impression Connecting Babylonia and India," *Arch* 20 (1967) 104-107.

Joseph M. Sola-Sole, "Semitic Elements in Ancient Hispania," *CBQ* 29 (1967) 487-494.

S. Yeivin, "Additional Note on Early Relations between Canaan and Egypt," *EI* 8 (1967) 74*.

Robert W. Benton, "The Philistines and the Early Kingdom of Israel," *GJ* 8 (1967) #1, 21-31.

*B[enjamin] Mazar, "The Philistines and the Rise of Israel and Tyre," *PIASH* 1 (1967) #7, 1-22.

*Sp. Marinatos, "Αἰώρα," *AASCS* 2 (1968) 1-14.

Ingomar Weiler, "Greek and Non-Greek World in the Archaic Period," *GRBS* 9 (1968) 21-29.

*George F. Dales, "Of Dice and Men," *JAOS* 88 (1968) 14-23.

Sh. Yeivin, "Additional Notes on the Early Relations Between Canaan and Egypt," *JNES* 27 (1968) 37-50.

*W. A. Sumner, "Israel's encounters with Edom, Moab, Ammon, Sihon, and Og According to the Deuteronomist," *VT* 18 (1968) 216-228.

William Stevenson Smith, "Influence of the Middle Kingdom of Egypt in Western Asia, Especially in Byblos," *AJA* 73 (1969) 277-281.

*Ruth Amiran, "A Second Note on Synchronisms Between the Early Bronze Arad and the First Dynasty," *BASOR* #195 (1969) 50-53.

*J[acob] Weingreen, "The pattern theory in Old Testament studies," *Herm* #108 (1969) 5-13.

Michael Grant, "The Greek Genius for Adaptation," *HT* 19 (1969) 93-100. *[Synchronism]*

*Wolf Wirgin, "Judah Maccabee's Embassy to Rome and the Jewish-Roman Treaty," *PEQ* 101 (1969) 15-20.

(Miss) M. S. Drower, "Early Connections Between Sumer and Egypt," *ULBIA* 8&9 (1968-69) 243-247.

A. I. Kharsekin, 'Etruscan-Carthaginian Relations in the Light of New Epigraphical Data," *VDI* (1969) #1, 107-108.

Hans Goedicke, "An Egyptian Claim to Asia," *JARCE* 8 (1969-70) 11-27.

§103 *2.3.8 Trade*

William Rideway, "The Greek Trade-Routes to Britain," *Folk* 1 (1890) 82-107.

C[laude] R. Conder, "Ancient Trade," *SRL* 19 (1892) 74-98.

*Terrien de Lacouperie, "On Yakut Precious Stones from Oman to North China, 400 B.C.," *BOR* 6 (1892-93) 271-274.

J. Kennedy, "The Early Commerce of Babylon with India," *JRAS* (1898) 241-288.

T. W. Rhys Davids, "Early Commerce between India and Babylon," *JRAS* (1899) 432.

*J. D. Murphy, "Ancient Commerce with East Africa and the 'Ophir' of King Solomon," *ACQR* 28 (1903) 157-173.

J. D. Murphy, "Ancient Commerce of the Phoenicians in the Mediterranean," *ACQR* 30 (1905) 331-345, 495-508.

*E. J. Pilcher, "The Himyaritic Script derived from the Greek," *SBAP* 29 (1907) 123-132.

Basil Weld, "'The Bridge of Asia'," *ICMM* 4 (1907-08) 202-212.

*Wilfred H. Schoff, "The Eastern Iron Trade of the Roman Empire," *JAOS* 35 (1915) 224-239.

*William Notz, "Monopolies in the Ancient Orient," *BS* 74 (1917) 254-283.

*L. D. Barnett, "Commerical and Political Connexions of Ancient India with the West," *BSOAS* 1 (1917-20) #1, 101-105.

Wilfred H. Schoff, "Biblical Foreign Trade Chapters," *HR* 78 (1919) 47.

*Walter Eugene Clark, "The Sandalwood and Peacocks of Ophir," *AJSL* 36 (1919-20) 103-119.

*Herbert H. Gowen, "Hebrew Trade and Trade Terms in O.T. Times," *JSOR* 6 (1922) 1-16.

George McLean Harper Jr., "A Study in the Commercial Relations between Egypt and Syria in the Third Century before Christ," *AJP* 49 (1928) 1-35.

Albert Gwynn, "Greek Sailors and the Indian Ocean," *TFQU* 4 (1929-30) 104-135.

M. Rostovtzeff, "Foreign Commerce in Ptolemaic Egypt," *JEBH* 4 (1931-32) 728-769.

*T. Fish, "The *DAM-QAR* (Trader?) in Ancient Mesopotamia," *BJRL* 22 (1938) 160-174.

J. G. Milne, "Trade between Greece and Egypt before Alexander the Great," *JEA* 25 (1939) 177-183.

*A. J. B. Wace and C. W. Blegen, "Pottery as Evidence for Trade and Colonisation in the Aegean Bronze Age," *Klio* 32 (1939-40) 131-147.

*J. W. Jack, "Recent Biblical Archaeology," *ET* 52 (1940-41) 454-458. [Shipping at Ugarit (Ras Shamra), pp. 456-457]

James Hornell, "Sea-trade in Early Times," *Antiq* 15 (1941) 233-256. [additional note, p. 386]

*J. W. Jack, "Recent Biblical Archaeology," *ET* 53 (1941-42) 210-211. [Ships of Tarshish, pp. 210-211]

*Sidney Smith, "The Greek Trade at Al Mina: A Footnote to Oriental History," *AJ* 22 (1942) 87-112.

Norman de G. Davies and R. O. Faulkner, "A Syrian Trading Venture to Egypt," *JEA* 33 (1947) 40-46.

*Martin P. Nilsson, "Oriental Import in Minoan and Mycenaean Greece," *ArOr* 17 (1949) Part 2, 210-212.

*Hugh Hencken, "Herzsprung Shields and Greek Trade," *AJA* 54 (1950) 295-309.

George F. Hourani, "Did Roman Commercial Competition Ruin South Arabia?" *JNES* 11 (1952) 291-294.

A. L. Oppenheim, "The Seafaring Merchants of Ur," *JAOS* 74 (1954) 6-17.

Lionel Casson, "The Grain Trade of the Hellenistic World," *TAPA* 85 (1954) 168-187.

*Charles Seltman, "The Wine Trade in Ancient Greece,"*HT* 5 (1955) 860-866.

*Richard D. Barnett, "Phoenicia and the Ivory Trade," *Arch* 9 (1956) 87-97.

Clark Hopkins, "Early Phoenican Trade in the Mediterranean," *AJA* 61 (1957) 183.

*J. A. Thompson, "The Economic Significance of Transjordan in Old Testament Times," *ABR* 6 (1958) 143-168. [Transjordan and the Caravan Routes, pp. 161-165; Supplementary Evidence from Assyria, Babylonia and Persia, pp. 165-167]

R. D. Barnett, "Early Shipping in the Near East," *Antiq* 32 (1958) 220-230.

*William L. Reed, "Caravan Cities of the Near East," *CollBQ* 35 (1958) #3, 1-16.

*Gus W. Van Beek, "Frankincense and Myrrh in Ancient South Arabia," *JAOS* 78 (1958) 141-152. [Ancient Trade Routes, pp. 144-148; Economic Effects of the Incense Trade, pp. 148-149; Political Effects of the Incense Trade, pp. 149-151]

*S. Yeivin, "Topographic and Ethnic notes," *'Atiqot* 2 (1959) 155-164. [A. Trade Routes in Israel in the First Half of the 2nd Millenium, pp. 155-159]

*Immanuel Ben Dor, "Phoenicians in Spain and Excavations at Riotinto, 1966," *AJA* 71 (1967) 183.

*Sara A. Immerwahr, "Mycenaean Trade and Colonization," *Arch* 13 (1960) 4-13.

*George F. Hourani, "Ancient South Arabian Voyages to India—Rejoinder to G. W. Van Beek," *JAOS* 80 (1960) 135-136.

Gus W. Van Beek, "Pre-Islamic South Arabian Shipping in the Indian Ocean—A Surrejoinder," *JAOS* 80 (1960) 136-139.

W. F. Leemans, "The trade relations of Babylonia and the question of relation with Egypt in the Old Babylonian Period," *JESHO* 3 (1960) 21-37.

*D. Cracknell, "*Abraham and Ur:* Mesopotamian Commerce and Religion," *AT* 5 (1960-61) #1, 6-8.

*W[illiam] F[oxwell] Albright, "Abram the Hebrew: A New Archaeological Interpretation," *BASOR* #163 (1961) 36-54. [I. The Negeb and Sinai in the Middle Bronze I; II. The Caravan Trade of the Early Second Millennium; III. Abraham and the Caravan Trade]

*Emmanuel Anati, "Prehistoric Trade and the Puzzle of Jericho," *BASOR* #167 (1962) 25-31.

*John B. Ward-Perkins and Peter Throckmorton, "New Light on the Roman Marble Trade: The San Pietro Wreck," *Arch* 18 (1965) 201-209.

*M. E. L. Mallowan, "The Merchants of Ancient Trade in Western Asia. Reflections on the location of Magan and Meluḫḫa," *Iran* 3 (1965) 1-7.

*A. L. Oppenheim, "Essay on Overland Trade in the First Millenium B.C.," *JCS* 21 (1967) 236-254.

*James Mellaart, "Anatolian Trade with Europe and Anatolian Geography and Culture Provinces in the late Bronze Age," *AS* 18 (1968) 187-202.

E. M. Blaiklock, "A Cargo of Ivory, Apes and Peacocks," *BH* 4 (1968) 43-44.

*Anonymous, "Trade Routes, Fortresses and the Queen of Sheba. Interesting and Enlightening Background Material from Archaeological Research," *BH* 4 (1968) 45-49.

*Georgina Herrmann, "Lapis-Lazuli: The Early Phases of its Trade," *Iraq* 30 (1968) 21-57.

*W. F. Leemans, "Old Babylonian letters and economic history. A review article with a digression on Foreign Trade," *JESHO* 11 (1968) 171-226.

*Yu. B. Tsirkin, "The Tin Route and the Northern Trade of Massalia," *VDI* (1968) #3, 104.

*Nimet Özgüç, "Assyrian Trade Colonies in Anatolia," *Arch* 22 (1969) 250-255.

*S. Yeivin, "Ostracon A1/382 from Hazor and its Implications," *EI* 9 (1969) 136. *[English Summary]*

*Reuven Yaron, "Foreign Merchants at Ugarit," *ILR* 4 (1969) 70-79.

*Gary A. Wright and Adon A. Gordus, "Distribution and Utilization of Obsidian from Lake Van Sources betweeen 7500 and 3500 B.C.," *AJA* 73 (1969) 75-77.

*Gary A. Wright, "Obsidian Analyses and Prehistoric Trade: 7500 to 3500 B.C.," *UMMAAP* #37 (1969) i-v, 1-92.

*L. A. Yelnitsky, "The Ancient Greek Wine Trade and Ceramics Production," *VDI* (1969) #3, 105.

§104 *2.3.12 Communications and Transportation, & Travel (includes Bridges)*

*M. L. Whately, "Chariots, Runners, & Torches," *ERG, 3rd Ser.,* 2 (1863-64) 289.

*Selah Merrill, "Modern Researches in Palestine," *PEFQS* 11 (1879) 138-154. [Bridges over the Jordan, p. 138]

*J. Leslie Porter, "The Old City of Adraha (Dera) and the Roman Road from Gerasa to Bostra," *PEFQS* 13 (1881) 77-79.

*Frank C. Roberts, "The Bridges of Ancient Rome," *AAOJ* 6 (1884) 145-155.

Wm. P. Alcott, "Letters and Posts of the Ancients," *ONTS* 4 (1884-85) 374-375.

A. H. Sayce, "The season and extent of the travels of Herodotos *[sic]* in Egypt," *JP* 14 (1885) 257-286.

B. Perrin, "Equestrianism in the Doloneia," *PAPA* 17 (1885) ix-x.

D. D. Heath, "Herodotus in Egypt," *JP* 15 (1886) 215-240.

Henry H. Harper, "'The Way of the Philistines'," *PEFQS* 22 (1890) 46.

*Selah Merrill, "Notes by Dr. Selah Merrill. Natural Bridge, Hot Spring, and Roman Road at Pella," *PEFQS* 23 (1891) 76.

*J. Elfreth Watkins, "The Transportation and Lifting of Heavy Bodies by the Ancients," *SIR* (1898) 615-619.

Andrew J. Gregg, "The Ancient Road from Near the Present Bab ez Zahare," *PEFQS* 31 (1899) 65.

Joseph Offord, "The Antiquity of the Four-wheeled Chariot," *SBAP* 24 (1902) 130-131.

J[oseph] Offord, "An Egyptian four-wheeled Chariot," *SBAP* 24 (1902) 308.

G. Bertrand, "The Chariot of Thotmes IV," *RP* 2 (1903) 344-346.

Anonymous, "An Etruscan Chariot," *RP* 2 (1903) 367-372.

*Anonymous, "An Etruscan Chariot Unearthed," *MQR, 3rd Ser.,* 30 (1904) 393-394.

George Adam Smith, "The Roman Road Between Kerak and Medeba," *PEFQS* 36 (1904) 367-377; 37 (1905) 39-48.

Anonymous, "Notes and Comments. The Highways of Bible Times," *ICMM* 1 (1905) 194-196.

Anonymous, "The Purpose of Travel in Old Testament Days," *ICMM* 1 (1905) 196-197.

Charles Knapp, "Travel in Ancient Times as seen in Plautus and Terence," *PAPA* 37 (1905) xlvii.

George Adam Smith, "Notes on 'The Roman Road Between Kerak and Medeba'," *PEFQS* 37 (1905) 148-149.

*A. H. Sayce, "Babylonian Tourist, of the Abrahamic Age, and His Map of the World," *AAOJ* 28 (1906) 334-338.

*A. H. Sayce, "A Babylonian Tourist of the Abrahamic Age and his Map of the World," *ET* 18 (1906-07) 68-73.

Charles H. Weller, "The Evidence for Strabo's Travels in Greece," *AJA* 10 (1906) 84.

*W. A. Harper, "Roman Bridges of the Tiber," *AAOJ* 30 (1908) 193-209.

*R. A. S. Macalister, "Notes and Queries. (3.) *A Bronze Object from Nablus,*" *PEFQS* 40 (1908) 340-341. *[Chariot]*

C. F. Ross, "Roman Milestones," *RP* 9 (1910) 8-15.

Anonymous, "Mail Delivery in Ancient Egypt," *RP* 9 (1910) 192.

Chas. Hallock, "Antediluvian Airships—The Fall of Icarus Not a Myth," *AAOJ* 35 (1913) 87-89.

A. S. F. Gow, "Hesiod's Wagon," *JP* 33 (1913-14) 145-153.

J. Grafton Milne, "Greek and Roman Tourists in Egypt," *JEA* 3 (1915) 76-80.

*Eugen von Merclin, "New Representations of Chariots on Attic Geometic Vases," *AJA* 20 (1916) 397-406.

James Henry Breasted, "The Earliest Boats on the Nile," *JEA* 4 (1916) 174-176.

Katharine Allen, "The Appian Way from Rome to Formia," *A&A* 6 (1917) 193-201.

*F. W. Read, "Boats or fortified villages," *BIFAO* 13 (1917) 145-151.

W. Boyd Dawkins, "The Maltese Cart Ruts," *Man* 18 (1918) #52.

E. G. Fenton, "The Maltese Cart Ruts," *Man* 18 (1918) #40, #69.

H. N. M. Hardy, "The Maltese Cart Ruts," *Man* 18 (1918) #93.

*Joseph Offord, "Archaeological Notes on Jewish Antiquities. LIII. *How Cedars were Transported,*" *PEFQS* 50 (1918) 181-183.

G. W. Murray, "The Roman Roads and Stations in the Eastern Desert of Egypt," *JEA* 11 (1925) 138-150.

Alan H. Gardiner, "The Ancient Military Road between Egypt and Palestine," *JEA* 6 (1920) 99-116.

E. G. Fenton, "Maltese Cart Ruts," *Man* 20 (1920) #54.

Marion E. Blake, "Roman Pavements of the Republican and Augustan Eras," *AJA* 30 (1926) 83-84.

*W. M. Ramsay, "Specimens of Anatolian Words," *OOR* 1 (1926) #2, 1-7. [V. The Wagon (Benna), pp. 2-4]

B. Vernon Bird, "Broadcasting in Old Testament Times," *ET* 38 (1926-27) 69-70.

T. Zammit, "Prehistoric Cart-tracts in Malta," *Antiq* 2 (1928) 18-25.

*M. Rostovtzeff, "Greek Sightseers in Egypt," *JEA* 14 (1928) 13-15.

*H. R. Hall, "The Oldest Representation of Horsemanship (?). An Egyptian Axe in the British Museum," *AAA* 18 (1931) 3-5.

*T. Eric Peet, "An Ancient Egyptian Ship's Log," *BIFAO* 30 (1931) 481-490.

*James B. Johnston, "The Chariot and the Pentateuch," *EQ* 3 (1931) 168-171.

E. M. P. Evans, "Maltese Cart-Ruts," *Antiq* 8 (1934) 339-342.

J. Hornell, "Malta: the So-called Cart-Ruts," *Man* 34 (1934) #105.

*R. Engelbach, "The Quarries of the western Nubian desert and the ancient road to Tushka," *ASAE* 38 (1938) 369-390.

F. W. Ogilvie, "The Tourist in Antiquity," *QRL* 270 (1938) 264-274.

*Paul C. Smither, "A Postal Register of the Ramesside Age," *JEA* 25 (1939) 103.

*J. W. Jack, "Recent Biblical Archaeology," *ET* 51 (1939-40) 420-423. [Houses, Streets, Gates, pp. 420-421]

*C. S. Jarvis, "To Petra from the West: a forgotten Roman highway," *Antiq* 14 (1940) 138-147.

*M. Hecker, "The Roman Road and the Swamps in the Emeq Zebulun," *BIES* 8 (1940-41) #3, I.

*V. Gordon Childe, "Horses, Chariots and Battle-axes," *Antiq* 15 (1941) 196-199.

*Alan H. Gardiner, "Ramesside Texts relating to the Taxation and Transportation of Corn," *JEA* 27 (1941) 19-73.

Norman J. DeWitt, "Rome and the 'Road of Hercules'," *TAPA* 72 (1941) 59-69.

*John Garstang, "Hittite Military Roads in Asia Minor: A Study in Imperial Strategy with a Map," *AJA* 47 (1943) 35-62.

*Zemach Green, "Restriction of Travel on New Moon Holidays in Biblical Judaism," *JBL* 63 (1944) v.

L[eon] L[egrain], "Horseback Riding in Mesopotamia in the Third Millenium B.C.," *UMB* 11 (1945-46) #4, 27-31.

*Cedric A. Yeo, "Land and Sea Transportation in Imperial Italy," *TAPA* 77 (1946) 221-244.

*William C. Hayes, "Ḥoremkha'uef of Nekhen and his Trip to It-towe," *JEA* 33 (1947) 3-11.

Hans Julius Wolff, "Registration of Conveyances in Ptolemaic Egypt," *Aeg* 28 (1948) 17-96.

*Osman R. Rostem, "Bridges in ancient Egypt with a report on a newly excavated bridge from the Old Kingdom, Giza," *ASAE* 48 (1948) 159-162.

R. G. Goodchild, "The Coast Road of Phoenicia and its Roman Milestones," *Bery* 9 (1948-49) 91-127.

*Louise Adams Holland, "Forerunners and Rivals of the Primitive Roman Bridge," *TAPA* 80 (1949) 281-319.

Armas Salonen, "Notes on Wagons and Chariots in Ancient Mesopotamia," *SO* 14 (1950) #2, 1-8.

*Anonymous, "Summary of Archaeological Research in Turkey, 1949-1950," *AS* 1 (1951) 9-20. [Explorations of Ancient Roads passing Karatepe, by Alkim U. Bahadir, pp. 19-20, (Note by W. M. Calder, p. 20)]

*T[ony] Reekmans and E. Van 'tDack, "A Bodleian Archive on Corn Transport," *CdÉ* 27 (1952) 149-195.

J. Lewy, "Studies in the Historic Geography of the Ancient East II. Old Assyrian Caravan Roads in the Valleys of the Hābūr and the Euphrates and in Northern Syria," *Or, N.S.,* 21 (1952) 265-292, 393-425.

*Albrecht Goetze, "An Old Babylonian Itinerary," *JCS* 7 (1953) 51-72.

H. S. Gracie, "The Ancient Cart-tracks of Malta," *Antiq* 28 (1954) 91-98.

J. H. Young, "Some Attic Roads," *AJA* 59 (1955) 175.

Selim Hassan, "The causeway of *Wnis* at Sakkara," *ZÄS* 80 (1955) 136-139.

Rhys Carpenter, "A Trans-Saharan Caravan Route in Herodotus," *AJA* 60 (1956) 231-242.

J. H. Young, "Greek Roads in South Attica," *Antiq* 30 (1956) 94-97.

Nelson Glueck, "Ancient Highways in the Wilderness of Zin," *PAPS* 100 (1956) 150-155.

Z. Kallai-Kleinmann, "Remants of the Roman Road near the Mevo-Beitar highway," *BIES* 21 (1957) #3/4 III.

A[lbrecht] Goetze, "The roads of Northern Cappadocia in Hittite times," *RHA* 15 (1957) 91-103.

M. H. Ballance, "Roman Roads in Lycaonia," *AS* 8 (1958) 223-234.

M. Harel, "The Roman Road at Maaleh-Aqrabbim," *BIES* 22 (1958) #3/4, n.p.n.

*Y. Aharoni, "Tamar and the Roads to Elath," *EI* 5 (1958) 91*.

Y[ehuda] Karmon, "The Historical Development of Routes in the Mountains of Safed," *BIES* 24 (1959-60) #4, II-III.

Kenneth D. Matthews Jr., "The Embattled Driver in Ancient Rome," *Exped* 2 (1959-60) #3, 22-27.

T. Jacobsen, "The Waters of Ur," *Iraq* 22 (1960) 174-185. *[Canal Transportation]*

*J. A. C. Thomas, "Carriage by Sea," *RIDA, 3rd Ser.*, 7 (1960) 489-505.

Y[ehuda] Karmon, "The Historical Development of Routes in the Mountains of Safed," *SGEI* #2 (1960) II-III.

J. M. Birmingham, "The Overland Route Across Anatolia in the Eighth and Seventh Centuries B.C.," *AS* 11 (1961) 185-195.

*Yehuda Karmon, "Geographical Influences on the Historical Routes in the Sharon Plain," *PEQ* 93 (1961) 43-60.

*Alexander Badway, "The transportation of the colossus of Djeḥutiḥetep," *MIO* 8 (1961-63) 325-332.

William A. McDonald, "Minoan and Mycenaean Highways," *AJA* 66 (1962) 198-199.

S. Frederick Starr, "Mapping Ancient Roads in Anatolia," *Arch* 16 (1963) 162-169.

Alan R. Schulman, "The Egyptian Chariotry: a Reexamination," *JARCE* 2 (1963) 75-98.

Lionel Casson, "Ancient Shipbuilding: New Light on an Old Source," *TAPA* 94 (1963) 28-33.

Awni Kh. Dajani, "Transportation in the Middle Bronze Periods," *ADAJ* 8&9 (1964) 56-67.

*William W. Hallo, "The Road to Emar," *JCS* 18 (1964) 57-88. [YBC 4499]

Åke Åkerström, "A Horseman from Asia Minor," *MB* #4 (1964) 49-53.

*A. Saarisalo, "Sites and Roads in Asher and Western Judah," *SO* 28 (1964) #1, 1-30.

*J. A. Bundgård, "Caesar's Bridges of the Rhine," *AA* 36 (1965) 87-103.

J. K. Anderson, "Homeric, British and Cyrenaic Chariots," *AJA* 69 (1965) 349-352.

*Anonymous, "The King's Highway. A study of ancient sites in the Transjordan by means of a surface survey helps determine the history of an ancient highway and resolves some doubts raised about two Bible narratives," *BH* 2 (1965) #1, 19-24.

Z. Kallai, "Remains of the Roman Road Along the Mevo-Beitar Highway," *IEJ* 15 (1965) 195-203.

Siegfried Mittmann, "The Roman Road from Gerasa to Adraa," *ADAJ* 11 (1966) 65-87. *(Trans. by F. Theis)*

A. Negev, "The Date of the Petra-Gaza Road," *PEQ* 98 (1966) 89-98.

M. Harel, "Israelite and Roman Roads in the Judean Desert," *IEJ* 17 (1967) 18-25.

Gladys Pike, "Pre-Roman land transport in the western Mediterranean region," *Man, N.S.,* 2 (1967) 593-605.

*H. W. Catling, "A Mycenaean Puzzle from Lefkandi in Euboea," *AJA* 72 (1968) 41-49. *[Cart in Transportation]*

§105 *2.3.15.1 Canals, Navigation & Ships*

†Anonymous, "Reports on the Navigation of the Euphrates," *QRL* 49 (1833) 212-228. *(Review)*

*Thomas W. Ludlow, "The Harbors of Ancient Athens," *AJP* 4 (1883) 192-203.

*William Hayes Ward, "The Ship-yard at Ancient Issus," *JBL* 5 (1885) 84.

W. St. Chad Boscawen, "Babylonian Canals," *BOR* 2 (1887-88) 226-233. [Explanatory Note, p. 263]

*Anonymous, "The Hebrews and the Sea," *ONTS* 14 (1892) 307.

*Mitchel Carroll, "Observations on the Harbors and Walls of Ancient Athens," *AJA* 8 (1904) 88-91. [I. Harbors, pp. 89-90]

*John C. Rolfe, "Some References to Seasickness in Greek and Latin Writers," *AJP* 25 (1904) 192-200.

*Christopher Johnston, "Assyrian Lexicographical Notes," *AJSL* 27 (1910-11) 187-189. [*b*) kalaku 'raft', pp. 187-188]

*G. Elliot Smith, "Ships as Evidence of the Migrations of Early Culture," *JMUEOS* #5 (1915-16) 63-102.

James Henry Breasted, "The Earliest Boats on the Nile," *JEA* 4 (1916) 174-176.

[Alan H. Gardiner], "The Earliest Boats on the Nile. A Supplementary Note by the Editor," *JEA* 4 (1916) 255.

*Paul Haupt, "Askari, *'soldier',* and Lascar, *'sailor',*" *JAOS* 36 (1916) 417-418.

*F. W. Read, "Boats or fortified villages," *BIFAO* 13 (1917) 145-151.

Wilfred H. Schoff, "Navigation to the Far East under the Roman Empire," *JAOS* 37 (1917) 240-249.

*Duncan Mackenzie, "The Port of Gaza and Excavations in Philistia," *PEFQS* 50 (1918) 72-87.

H. H. Brindley, "A Graffito of a Ship at Beit Jibrin," *PEFQS* 51 (1919) 76-78.

Somers Clarke, "Nile Boats and Other Matters," *AEE* 5 (1920) 2-9, 40-51.

*H. A. Ormerod, "Ancient Piracy in the Eastern Mediterranean," *AAA* 8 (1921) 105-124.

William F. Edgerton, "Ancient Egyptian Ships and Shipping," *AJSL* 39 (1922-23) 109-135.

E[rnest] S. Thomas, "The Branch on Prehistoric Ships," *AEE* 8 (1923) 97.

Ira Maurice Price, "Transportation by Water in Early Babylonia," *AJSL* 40 (1923-24) 111-116.

Warren R. Dawson, "Note on the Egyptian Papyrus Boat," *JEA* 10 (1924) 46.

J. Hornell, "Herodotus and Assyrian River Transport," *Man* 24 (1924) #123.

*William F. Edgerton, "An Ancient Egyptian Steering Gear," *AJA* 30 (1926) 82-83.

William F. Edgerton, "Ancient Egyptian Steering Gear," *AJSL* 43 1926-27) 255-265.

*S. Tolkowsky, "The Destruction of the Jewish Navy at Jaffa in the Year 68 A.D.," *PEFQS* 60 (1928) 153-163.

William F. Edgerton, "Dimensions of Ancient Egyptian Ships," *AJSL* 46 (1929-30) 145-149.

C. D. Jarrett-Bell, "Rowing in the XVIIIth Dynasty," *AEE* 15 (1930) 11-19.

William F. Edgerton, "Egyptian Seagoing (?) Ships of One Hundred Cubits," *AJSL* 47 (1930-31) #1, Part 1, 50-51.

*T. Eric Peet, "An Ancient Egyptian Ship's Log," *BIFAO* 30 (1931) 481-490.

G. D. Hornblower, "Reed-Floats in Modern Egypt," *JEA* 17 (1931) 53-54.

*G. R. Driver, "A Problem of River-traffic," *ZA* 40 (1931) 228-233.

*S. R. K. Glanville, "Records of a Royal Dockyard of the Time of Thutmosis III.: Papyrus British Museum 10056," *ZÄS* 66 (1931) 105-121; 68 (1932) 7-41.

George H. Allen, "Some Problems of Inland Navigation in the Roman Empire," *AJA* 36 (1932) 41.

[W. M.] Flinders Petrie, "Egyptian Shipping," *AEE* 18 (1933) 1-14, 65-75.

C. D. Jarrett-Bell, "Ancient Egyptian Ship Design; Based on a Critical Analysis of the XIIth Dynasty Barge," *AEE* 18 (1933) 101-111.

C. D. Jarrett-Bell, "The Obelisk Barge of Hatshepsut. A Conjectural Design Based on Rules Evolved from an Analysis of the Lines of the XIIth Dynasty Funeral Barge," *AEE* 19 (1934) 107-115.

Lionel Cohen, "Aegean and Mediterranean Ships of the Early Minoan Period: A Discussion of the Stem and Stern," *AJA* 40 (1936) 127.

James Hornell, "Origins of Plank-built Boats," *Antiq* 13 (1939) 35-44. [Ancient Egyptian Boats, pp. 40-43]

Edward Robertson, "Early Navigation: Its Extent and Importance," *BJRL* 24 (1940) 285-306.

R. O. Faulkner, "Egyptian Seagoing Ships," *JEA* 26 (1940) 3-9.

Leopold Halliday Savile, "Ancient Harbours," *Antiq* 15 (1941) 209-232.

R. O. Faulkner, "Egyptian Seagoing Ships: a Correction," *JEA* 27 (1941) 158.

*Nelson Glueck, "The Excavations of Solomon's Seaport: Ezion-Geber," *SIR* (1941) 453-478.

*J. W. Jack, "Recent Biblical Archaeology," *ET* 53 (1941-42) 208-212. [Ships of Tarshish, pp. 210-211]

Raphael Patai, "Jewish Seafaring in Ancient Times," *JQR, N.S.,* 32 (1941-42) 1-26.

Percy E. Newberry, "Notes on Seagoing Ships," *JEA* 28 (1942) 64-66.

James Hornell, "The Sailing Ship of Ancient Egypt," *Antiq* 17 (1943) 27-41.

James Hornell, "On the Carrying Capacity of Ramesside Grain-ships," *JEA* 29 (1943) 76-78.

Lionel Casson, "Note on a Nile Boat," *AJP* 63 (1944) 333-334.

*James Hornell, "The Role of Birds in Early Navigation," *Antiq* 20 (1946) 142-149.

*Cedric A. Yeo, "Land and Sea Transportation in Imperial Italy," *TAPA* 77 (1946) 221-244.

Lionel Casson, "Speed Under Sail of Ancient Ships," *TAPA* 82 (1951) 136-148.

*Sidney Smith, "The Ship Tyre," *PEQ* 85 (1953) 97-110.

Lionel Casson, "The Sails of the Ancient Mariner," *Arch* 7 (1954) 214-219.

*Chester G. Starr, "The Myth of the Minoan Thalassocracy," *HJAH* 3 (1954-55) 282-291.

Albrecht Goetze, "Archaeological Survey of Ancient Canals," *Sumer* 11 (1955) 127-128.

Benjamin W. Labaree, "How the Greeks Sailed into the Black Sea," *AJA* 61 (1957) 29-33.

B. Ludman, "The Problem of Ancient Oriental Shipping on the North Sea," *JNES* 16 (1957) 105-117.

Richard LeBaron Bowen Jr., Egypt's Earliest Sailing Ships," *Antiq* 34 (1960) 117-131.

T. Jacobsen, "The Waters of Ur," *Iraq* 22 (1960) 174-185. *[Canal Transportation]*

*J. A. C. Thomas, "Carriage by Sea," *RIDA, 3rd Ser.,* 7 (1960) 489-505.

*M[oshe] Dothan, "The Ancient Harbour of Ashdod," *CNI* 11 (1960) #1, 16-19.

George F. Dales Jr., "A Search for Ancient Seaports," *Exped* 4 (1961-62) #2, 2-10, 44.

*Robert J. Buck, "The Minoan Thalassocracy re-examined," *HJAH* 11 (1962) 129-137.

Lionel Casson, "The Earliest Two-Masted Ship," *Arch* 16 (1963) 108-111.

Lionel Casson, "Ancient Shipbuilding: New Light on an Old Source," *TAPA* 94 (19630 28-33.

*Anonymous, "Ezion-Geber Reconsidered. An excavator takes a new look at his findings at Solomon's seaport on the gulf of Aqabah," *BH* 2 (1965) #4, 17-19, 24.

*Arie Kindler, "Maritime Emblems on Ancient Jewish Coins," *Sefunim* 1 (1966) 15-20.

*Lionel Casson, "Galley Slaves," *TAPA* 97 (1966) 35-44.

*F. A. Fensham, "Shipwreck in Ugarit and Ancient Near East Law Codes," *OA* 6 (1967) 221-224.

*Lionel Casson, "The Emergency Rig of Ancient Warships," *TAPA* 98 (1967) 43-48.

*Irwin L. Merker, "The Harbor of Iulis," *AJA* 72 (1968) 383-384.

Clarence A. Wendel, "Land Tilting or Silting? Which Ruined the Ancient Aegean Harbors?" *Arch* 22 (1969) 322-324.

A. F. Tilley, "Odysseus and the Sirens: the Problem of the Trireme," *HT* 19 (1969) 792-794. [How the Greeks propelled a boat]

§106 *2.3.12.2 Colonization*

*Anonymous, "The Provinces of the Roman Empire," *SRL* 12 (1888) 293-330. *(Review)*

Thomas Robert Shannon Broughton, "Some Non-colonial Coloni of Augustus," *TAPA* 66 (1935) 18-24.

G. A. Short, "The Siting of Greek Colonies on the Black Sea Coasts of Bulgaria and Romania," *AAA* 24 (1937) 141-155.

*A. J. B. Wace and C. W. Belgen, "Pottery as Evidence for Trade and Colonisation in the Aegean Bronze Age," *Klio* 32 (1939-40) 131-147.

*Sh. Applebaum, "The Jewish Revolt in Cyrene in 115-117, and the Subsequent Recolonisation," *JJS* 2 (1950-51) 177-186. [I. Cyrene, Additional Evidence of Damage during the Revolt; II. The Other Towns of the Pentapolis and the Countryside]

*W. G. Forrest, "Colonisation and Rise of Delphi," *HJAH* 6 (1957) 160-175.

*R. Ross Holloway, "Tyndaris: Last Colony of the Sicilian Greeks," *Arch* 13 (1960) 246-250.

*Giorgio Buchner, "Pithekoussai: Oldest Greek Colony in the West," *Exped* (1965-66) #4, 5-12.

*Nimet Özgüç, "Assyrian Trade Colonies in Anatolia," *Arch* 22 (1969) 250-255.

*Briggs Buchanan, "The End of the Assyrian Colonies in Anatolia: The Evidence of the Seals," *JAOS* 89 (1969) 758-762.

A. Ye. Parshikov, "The Status of Athenian Colonies in the Fifth Century B.C.," *VDI* (1969) #2, 19.

§107 *2.3.17 Water Supply & Irrigation*

(   ) G., "Observations on the Fountains, Wells, and Cisterns of the ancient Hebrews, with a view to illustrate the scriptures," *QCS* 1 (1819) 237-241.

John Irwine Whitty, "Water Supply of Jerusalem—Ancient and Modern," *JSL, 4th Ser.*, 5 (1864) 133-157.

R. F. Hutchinson, "Note on the Pool of Bethesda," *PEFQS* 2 (1870) 331.

*Selah Merrill, "Modern Researches in Palestine," *PEFQS* 11 (1879) 138-154. [Water Supply and Irrigation, pp. 138-140]

W. F. Birch, "Note on the Two Pools," *PEFQS* 11 (1879) 179-180. *[Solomon's Pool & The Pool of Siloam]*

Charles Wright Barclay, "Jacob's Well," *PEFQS* 13 (1881) 212-214.

C[laude] R. Conder, "The Siloam Tunnel," *PEFQS* 14 (1882) 122-131.

*S. Beswick, "Siloam Tunnel," *PEFQS* 14 (1882) 178-183. {(Note by C. R. Conder, p. 183) [I. One Thousand Cubits; II. The Tablet-Maker's Cubit; III. Test Cases]}

W. F. Birch, "Siloam and the Pools," *PEFQS* 15 (1883) 105-107.

C[laude] R. Conder, "Notes. *Siloam*," *PEFQS* 15 (1883) 139.

C[onrad] Schick, "The Aqueducts at Siloam," *PEFQS* 18 (1886) 88-91. (Note by C. W. Wilson, p. 92)

C[onrad] Schick, "Second Aqueduct to the Pool of Siloam," *PEFQS* 18 (1886) 197-200.

Hugo Winckler, "Nebuchadnezzar's Artificial Reservior," *AJSL* 4 (1887-88) 174-175.

C[onrad] Schick, "Pool of Bethesda. I," *PEFQS* 20 (1888) 115-122.

C[onrad] Schick, "Pool of Bethesda. II," *PEFQS* 20 (1888) 122-124.

C. W. Wilson, "Pool of Bethesda. III," *PEFQS* 20 (1888) 124-131.

William Simpson, "The Conduit near the Pool of Bethesda," *PEFQS* 20 (1888) 259-260.

C[onrad] Schick, "Pool of Bethesda. IV," *PEFQS* 20 (1888) 131-134.

W. F. Birch, "The Valleys and Waters of Jerusalem," *PEFQS* 21 (1889) 38-44.

C[onrad] Shick, "Two Cisterns Near Jeremiah's Grotto," *PEFQS* 22 (1890) 11-12.

C[onrad] Shick, "Further Report on the Pool of Bethesda," *PEFQS* 22 (1890) 18-20.

Wiliam Simpson, "Irrigation and Water-Supply in Palestine," *PEFQS* 22 (1890) 55-57.

Gray Hill, "Irrigation and Water Supply in Syria," *PEFQS* 22 (1890) 72-73.

(Mrs.) E. A. Finn, "Irrigation and Water Supply in Palestine," *PEFQS* 22 (1890) 199.

*W. F. Birch, "The Pool that was Made," *PEFQS* 22 (1890) 204-208.

*C[onrad] Schick, "Herr Schick's Reports II. Ancient Bath and Cistern near Bethany," *PEFQS* 23 (1891) 9-11.

*C[onrad] Schick, "Herr Schick's Reports IV. The 'Second' Siloam Aqueduct," *PEFQS* 23 (1891) 13-18.

*C[onrad] Schick, "Herr Schick's Reports. V. The Height of the Siloam Aqueduct," *PEFQS* 23 (1891) 18-19.

William Simpson, "Irrigation and Water Supply in Palestine," *PEFQS* 23 (1891) 160-161.

*C[onrad] Schick, "Herr Schick's Reports. 4. *Watercourse providing the ancient City with Water from North-west,* " *PEFQS* 23 (1891) 278-280.

*C[onrad] Schick, "Letters from Baurath C. Schick," *PEFQS* 24 (1892) 9-25. [Old Pool in Upper Kedron Valley or 'Wady el Joz', pp. 9-13]

*C[onrad] Schick, "Letters from Herr Schick. II. A Pool Cleared Out," *PEFQS* 24 (1892) 289.

G. Schumacher, "Discoveries During the Construction of the Acre-Damascus Railway," *PEFQS* 25 (1893) 331.

*Theo. G. Pinches, "Water Rate in Ancient Babylonia," *SBAP* 17 (1895) 278-279.

*Edward Davies, "Certificate of Analysis," *PEFQS* 28 (1896) 47. *[Water from the Spring of Callirrhoe]*

Henry [J.] Bailey, "The Quality of the Water in Jacob's Well," *PEFQS* 29 (1897) 67-68.

H. Clay Trumbull, "The Water of Jacob's Well. I.," *PEFQS* 29 (1897) 149.

Ernest W. Gurney Masterman, "The Water of Jacob's Well. II," *PEFQS* 29 (1897) 149-151.

Henry J. Bailey, "The Water of Jacob's Well," *PEFQS* 29 (1897) 196-198.

*C[onrad] Schick, "Reports by Dr. Conrad Schick I. *The Columbarium or Cistern east of Zion Gate,* " *PEFQS* 30 (1898) 79-81.

*C[onrad] Schick, "Reports by Dr. Conrad Schick. II. *Another interesting Cistern,*" *PEFQS* 30 (1898) 81-82.

*W. F. Birch, "David's Tomb and the Siloam Tunnel," *PEFQS* 30 (1898) 161-167. (Note by C. Clermont-Ganneau, pp. 250-251)

Conrad Schick, "Birket es Sultan, Jerusalem," *PEFQS* 30 (1898) 224-229.

Gray Hill, "Discovery of a Sulphur Spring and Bath on the Bank of the Jabbok," *PEFQS* 31 (1899) 45.

Gray Hill, "A Remarkable Cistern and Newly Discovered Spring at Aisawiyeh," *PEFQS* 31 (1899) 45-47.

Andrew J. Gregg, "'The Upper Watercouse of Gihon'," *PEFQS* 31 (1899) 64.

*Andrew J. Gregg, "Note on Gibeon, Nob, Bezek and the High-Level Aqueduct to Jerusalem," *PEFQS* 31 (1899) 128-129. [3. The high-level aqueduct, p. 129]

*Conrad Schick, "Reports by Dr. Conrad Schick. Notes on the Discovery of a Large Cistern North-West of Jerusalem; of a Perpendicular Shaft in Bishop Blyth's Ground; of some Carved Stones in the Muristan," *PEFQS* 32 (1900) 144-145.

J. E. Hanauer, "Rock-Hewn Vats Near Bir Eyub," *PEFQS* 32 (1900) 361-364. (Note by Selah Merrill, pp. 364-365)

*Howard Crosby Butler, "The Roman Aqueducts as Monuments of Architecture," *AJA* 5 (1901) 175-200.

Père Léon Cré, "Discovery at the Pool of Bethesda," *PEFQS* 33 (1901) 163-165.

E. W. G. Masterman, "The Water Supply of Jerusalem, Ancient and Modern," *BW* 19 (1902) 87-112.

C. W. Wilson, "The Water Supply of Jerusalem," *JTVI* 34 (1902) 11-23. (Discussion, pp. 23-25)

Conrad Schick, "The Virgin's Fount," *PEFQS* 34 (1902) 29-35. (Note, p. 196)

E. W. G. Masterman, "The Recently-Discovered Aqueduct from the Virgin's Fountain," *PEFQS* 34 (1902) 35-38.

R. A. Stewart Macalister, "Reports by R. A. Stewart Macaslister, M.A., F.S.A. VIII. 'Ain el-Khanduk," *PEFQS* 34 (1902) 245-247.

M. H. Morgan, "Remarks on the Water Supply of Ancient Rome," *TAPA* 33 (1902) 30-37.

E. W. G. Masterman, "The Water Supply of Damascus," *BW* 21 (1903) 98-107.

Ernest W. G Masterman, "The Water Supply of Jerusalem," *JTVI* 35 (1903) 157-158. [(Remarks by Edward Hull, pp. 158-161; Reply by C. W. Wilson, pp. 161-162) (Discussion, pp. 163-166)]

Selah Merrill, "Notes from Jerusalem. 3. *A Bit of the Ancient Upper Gihon Aqueduct,*" *PEFQS* 35 (1903) 157-158.

*E. W. G. Masterman, "Notes on Some Ruins and a Rock-cut Aqueduct in the Wady Kumran," *PEFQS* 35 (1903) 264-267.

R. A. Stewart Macalister, "'Ain el Kus'ah," *PEFQS* 35 (1903) 268-270.

Anonymous, "Asia," *RP* 2 (1903) 317-318. *[Irrigation works in the Tigro-Euprates Valley]*

Selah Merrill, "An Ancient Sewer at Jerusalem," *PEFQS* 36 (1904) 392-393. (Note by C. W. Wilson, pp. 393-394)

*Charles Wilson, "Centurial Inscriptions on the Syphon of the High-level Aqueduct at Jerusalem," *PEFQS* 37 (1905) 75-77.

*Anonymous, "Ancient Irrigation Works in Central Asia," *RP* 4 (1905) 32.

Anonymous, "Ancient Babylonian Drainage," *RP* 4 (1905) 288.

*Theodore F. Wright, "The Siloam and Simplon Tunnels," *BW* 27 (1906) 468-472.

Anonymous, "Ancient Babylonian Drainage," *MQR, 3rd Ser.,* 32 (1906) 178-180.

*Lewis Bayles Paton, "Jerusalem in Bible Times: III. The Springs and Pools of Ancient Jeruslaem," *BW* 29 (1907) 168-182.

Hugues Vincent, "The Gezer Tunnel," *PEFQS* 40 (1908) 218-229.

R. A. S. Macalister, "Notes and Queries. (5.) *The depth of Jacob's Well,*" *PEFQS* 41 (1909) 74.

J. Sully, "The Upper Anio," *QRL* 211 (1909) 441-463. *(Review)*

G. Schumacher, "The Great Water Passage of Khirbet Bel'Ameh," *PEFQS* 42 (1910) 107-112.

Asad Mansur, "Jacob's Well," *PEFQS* 42 (1910) 131-137.

Asad Mansur, "'The Virgin's Fountain,' Nazareth," *PEFQS* 45 (1913) 149-153.

Frank Bigelow Tarbell, "The Pont du Gard," *A&A* 2 (1915) 45-47. *[Aqueduct]*

E. W. G. Masterman, "The Pool of Bethesda," *PEFQS* 53 (1921) 91-100.

*Evelyn Howell, "River Control in Mesopotamia," *QRL* 237 (1922) 68-84. *[Irrigation]*

*Albert Hiorth, "Concerning Irrigation in Ancient and Modern Times, the Cultivation and Electrification of Palestine with the Mediterranean as the Source of Power," *JTVI* 55 (1923) 133-144, 154-157. (Discussion, pp. 145-154)

*A. E. R. Boak, "Notes on Canal and Dike Work in Roman Egypt," *Aeg* 7 (1926) 215-219.

*William Foxwell Albright and R. P. Dougherty, "From Jerusalem to Baghdad down the Euphrates. I. From Jerusalem to Aleppo," *BASOR* #21 (1926) 1-10. [The Irrigation Culture of Northern Phoenicia, pp. 4-6]

*W. M. Ramsay, "Specimens of Anatolian Words," *OOR* 1 (1926) #2, 1-7. [VII. Paga and Kranna: Fountain, Water-Source, pp. 5-6]

I. O. Nothstein, "The Watercouse of Mt. Zion," *AugQ* 7 (1928) 273-274. *[Virgin's Fountain]*

Eli Edward Burriss, "The Use and Worship of Water Among the Romans," *A&A* 30 (1930) 221-228, 233.

S. Yeivin, "The Ptolemaic System of Water Supply in the Fayyûm," *ASAE* 30 (1930) 27-30.

Paul E. Kretzmann, "The Spring and Pool of Bethesda," *CTM* 3 (1932) 861-862.

D. C. Baramki, "An Ancient Cistern in the Grounds of Government House, Jerusalem," *QDAP* 4 (1935) 165-167.

D. C. Baramki, "Two Roman Cisterns at Beit Nattīf," *QDAP* 5 (1936) 3-10.

E. A. Werber, "The Technical Questions of the 'Huleh Problem'," *PEQ* 69 (1937) 258-259.

M. Hecker, "The Ancient Water Supply of Jerusalem," *BIES* 6 (1938-38) #1, II-III.

L. Picard, "Ground-Water in Palestine," *BIES* 7 (1939-40) #2, I-II; 8 (1940-41) #1, I.

*D. Ashbel, "Rain and water conditions in the Negev," *BIES* 8 (1940-41) #2, I.

*J. W. Jack, "Recent Biblical Archaeology," *ET* 53 (1941-42) 276-280. [Springs, Wells, pp. 276-279]

*J. W. Jack, "Recent Biblical Archaeology," *ET* 53 (1941-42) 367-370. [1. Pools, 2. Cisterns, pp. 367-368]

Grahame Clark, "Water in Antiquity," *Antiq* 18 (1944) 1-15.

A. S. Kirkbride and Lankester Harding, "The Seven Wells of Beni Murra," *QDAP* 11 (1945) 37-43.

Fuad Safar, "Sennacherib's Project for Supplying Erbil with Water," *Sumer* 3 (1947) 23-25.

Jørgen Laessøe, "The Irrigation System at Ulḫu, 8th Century B.C.," *JCS* 5 (1951) 21-32.

Jørgen Laessøe, "Reflexions on Modern and Ancient Oriental Water Works," *JCS* 7 (1953) 5-26.

James B. Prichard, "The Water System at Gibeon," *BA* 19 (1956) 66-75. [Cistern of the Roman Period; The Great Rock-cut Pool; The Tunnel]

*Robert M. Adams, "Survey of Ancient Water Courses and Settlements in Central Iraq," *Sumer* 14 (1958) 101-103.

*Millar Burrows, "The Conduit of the Upper Pool," *ZAW* 70 (1958) 221-227.

*Hans Helbaek, "Ecological Effects of Irrigation in Ancient Mesopotamia," *Iraq* 22 (1960) 186-196.

*Geoffrey Evans, "The Incidence of Labour-Service at Mari," *RAAO* 57 (1963) 65-78. [I. Work upon the canals and irrigation system; II. Agricultural corvées; III. Conclusions; IV. Periods of Labour-service]

A. Negev, "The High Level Aqueduct at Caesarea," *IEJ* 14 (1964) 237-249.

*Robert D. Biggs, "A Letter from Kassite Nippur," *JCS* 19 (1965) 95-102. *[Irrigation Problems]*

Russell Dell, "Man-made Water Systems in Palestine," *CCBQ* 9 (1966) #4, 3-31.

*Margarete Bieber, "The Aqua Marcia in Coins and in Ruins," *Arch* 20 (1967) 194-196.

*M. B. Rowton, "Watercourses and Water Rights in the Official Correspondence from Larasa and Isin," *JCS* 21 (1967) 267-274.

S. Graham, "Rock Pools (Gulut) and their Importance as Sources of Water in the Central Sudan in Past and Present Times," *Kush* 15 (1967-68) 299-307.

Paul Ward English, "The Origin and Spread of Qanats in the Old World," *PAPS* 112 (1968) 170-181.

William G. Dever, "The Water Systems at Hazor and Gezer," *BA* 32 (1969) 71-78. [The Hazor Water System; The Gezer Water System: Its Discovery; When Was It Built? How Was the System Designed and How Did it Function?]

Christian E. Hauer, "Water in the Mountain?" *PEQ* 101 (1969) 44-45.

§108 *2.3.18 Studies in Hebrew Religious Customs (not necessarily mentioned in the O.T.)*

Lyman Coleman, "The Festivals of the Christian Church Compared with those of other Ancient Forms of Religion," *BS* 4 (1847) 650-671. [Relation of the Festivals of the Christian church to those of the Jews, pp. 658-662]

Charles A. Brigham, "On the Jewish Ban," *JAOS* 8 (1866) xxix-xxx.

*M. Friedlander, "Jewish Lulab and Portal Coins," *JQR* 1 (1888-89) 282-284.

*B. Pick, "The Rites, Ceremonies and Customs of the Jews," *HR* 17 (1889) 199-206. [I. The Phylacteries; II. The Fringes; III. The Mezuzah, or sign on the Door-Post; IV. Circumcision; V. Redemption of the First-Born; VI. Marriage; VII. Daily Prayers and Confession of Faith; VIII. The Jewish Sabbath; IX. New Year's Day; X. The Day of Atonement; XI. Other Festivals; XII. In Death and After Death]

*I. M. Casanowicz, "Non-Jewish religious ceremonies in the Talmud," *JAOS* 16 (1894-96) lxxvi-lxxxii.

F. C. Spurr, "'Throwing a Stone at an Idol'," *ET* 8 (1896-97) 524.

J. A. Selbie, "The Laying on of Hands," *ET* 12 (1900-01) 454-455.

W. O. E. Oesterley, "A Great Heap of Stones," *ET* 15 (1903-04) 47-48.

J. H. A. Hart, "Corban," *JQR* 19 (1906-07) 615-650. [I. Introduction; II. Jewish Sacramental Meals; III. The Law of God and the Precepts of Men; IV. Corban]

B. W. Bacon, "The Festival of Lives Given for the Nation in Jewish and Christian Faith," *HJ* 15 (1916-17) 256-278.

Julian Morgenstern, "The Origin of Maṣṣoth and the Maṣṣoth-Festival," *AJT* 21 (1917) 275-293.

Julian Morgenstern, "Two Ancient Israelite Agricultural Festivals," *JQR, N.S.,* 8 (1917-18) 31-54.

Burton S. Easton, "Jewish and Early Christian Ordination," *ATR* 5 (1922-23) 308-319.

Burton S. Easton, "Jewish and Early Christian Ordination II," *ATR* 6 (1923-24) 285-295.

*Louis Finkelstein, "The Development of the Amidah," *JQR, N.S.,* 16 (1925-26) 1-43, 127-170.

*Robert H. Pfeiffer, "Three Assyriological Footnotes to the Old Testament," *JBL* 47 (1928) 184-187. [*3. The earliest reference to kiblah,* pp. 186-187]

Sol. B. Finesinger, "The Shofar," *HUCA* 8&9 (1931-32) 193-228.

*P. E. Kretzmann, "The Substitution of the Levites for the First-Born," *CTM* 4 (1933) 536.

Jacob Z. Lauterbach, "*Tashlik,* a Study in Jewish Ceremonies," *HUCA* 11 (1936) 207-340.

Samuel Krauss, "The Jewish Rite of Covering the Head," *HUCA* 19 (1945-46) 121-168.

Lou H. Silberman, "The Sefirah Season, A Study in Folklore," *HUCA* 22 (1949) 221-237.

Solomon Zeitlin, "The Second Day of the Holidays in the Diaspora," *JQR, N.S.,* 44 (1953-54) 183-193.

*Yithak Schalev, "The Holyday as an Experience of Time," *Jud* 5 (1956) 160-166.

*Alexander Scheiber, "The Mezuzah of the Egyptological Collection of the Hungarian Museum of Fine Arts," *JQR, N.S.,* 48 (1957-58) 6-12.

*Burton M. Leiser, The 'Mezuzah' Column in Hungary's Egyptological Collection," *JQR, N.S.,* 50 (1959-60) 365-370.

Shmuel Saphrai, "The Duty of Pilgrimage to Jerusalem and its Performance During the Period of the Second Temple," *Zion* 25 (1960) #2, I.

*K. A. Dickson, "A Note on the Laying on of Hands as a Sacrificial Rite," *GBT* 2 (1961-66) #7, 26-28.

*Joseph Heineman, "Birkath Ha-Zimmum and Havurah-Meals," *JJS* 13 (1962) 23-29.

B. J. van der Merwe, "The Laying on of Hands in the O.T.," *OTW* 5 (1962) 34-43.

Everett Ferguson, "Jewish and Christian Ordination," *HTR* 56 (1963) 13-19. [Laying on of Hands; Solemn Seating]

Hugo Mantel, "Ordination and Appointment in the Period of the Temple," *HTR* 57 (1964) 325-346.

*Gerald J. Blidstein, "Man and Nature in the Sabbatical Year," *Trad* 8 (1965-66) #4, 48-55.

Zeev Weisman, "The Biblical Nazarite, its Types and Roots," *Tarbiz* 36 (1966-67) #3, I.

Monford Harris, "Jewish Devotional Life," *C&C* 19 (1967) 23-34.

Julian Morgenstern, "*Lag Ba 'Omer*—Its Origin and Import," *HUCA* 38 (1967) 81-90.

Saul Levin, "The Traditional Chironomy of the Hebrew Scriptures," *JBL* 87 (1968) 59-70. *[Hand Movements]*

Solomon Zeitlin, "Korban: a Gift," *JQR, N.S.,* 59 (1968-69) 133-136.

§109 *2.3.18.1 Baptism*

Irah Chase, "Dr. Bushnell's Arguments for Infant Baptism. II. Jewish Proselyte Baptism, and the Conversation with Nicodemus," *CRB* 28 (1863) 510-520. *[Other articles #1, 3-7 not applicable]*

W. Barrows, "Jewish Baptism in the Times of Our Lord, as Related to Household Baptism," *CongR* 7 (1867) 502-521.

C. H. Toy, "Jewish Proselyte-Baptism," *BQ* 6 (1872) 301-332.

Jas. F. Latimer, "Baptism under the Two Dispensations," *PQ* 4 (1890) 169-187.

C. F. Rogers, "How Did the Jews Baptize?" *JTS* 12 (1910-11) 437-445; 13 (1911-12) 411-414.

I. Abrahams, "'How Did the Jews Baptize?'" *JTS* 12 (1910-11) 609-612.

R. A. Aytown, "The Mystery of Baptism by Moses bar Kepha compared with the Odes of Solomon," *Exp, 8th Ser.*, 2 (1911) 338-358.

*George A. Barton, "The Origin of the Thought-Pattern which survives in Baptism," *JAOS* 56 (1936) 155-165.

S. Zeitlin, "A Note on Baptism for Proselytes," *JBL* 52 (1933) 78-79.

L. Finkelstein, "The Institution of Baptism for Proselytes," *JBL* 52 (1933) 203-211.

H. H. Rowley, "Jewish Proselyte Baptism and the Baptism of John," *HUCA* 15 (1940) 313-334.

T. F. Torrance, "Proselyte Baptism," *NTS* 1 (1954-55) 150-154.

N. A. Dahl, "The Origin of Baptism," *NTTO* 56 (1955) 36-52.

T. M. Taylor, "The Beginnings of Jewish Proselyte Baptism," *NTS* 2 (1955-56) 193-198.

Pat E. Harrell, "Jewish Proselyte Baptism," *RestQ* 1 (1957) 159-165.

G. Vermes, "Baptism and Jewish Exegesis: New Light from Ancient Sources," *NTS* 4 (1957-58) 309-319.

§110 *2.13.8.2 Circumcision [see also: Exodus chap. 4 (in loc.)]*

*J. Offord Jr., "The 'Peoples of the Sea' of Merenptah," *SBAP* 10 (1887-88) 231. *[Circumcison]*

*Max Müller, "Supplementary Notes to 'Notes on the Peoples of the Sea' etc.," *SBAP* 10 (1887-88) 287-289.

*B. Pick, "The Rites, Ceremonies and Customs of the Jews," *HR* 17 (1889) 199-206. [IV. Circumcision, p. 201]

Aaron Hahn, "The Milath Gerim Question," *YCCAR* 2 (1891-92) 66-69. (Response by Isaac Schwab, pp. 69-84)

Henry Berkowitz, "Malath Guerim. An Open Letter to the Rabbis of the United States of America," *YCCAR* 2 (1891-92) 84-85. [Responses by: Isaac M. Wise, pp. 85-86; B. Felsenthal, pp. 86-95; M. Mielziner, pp. 95-96 (with appendix, pp. 96-98); S. Sonneschein, pp. 98-100; G. Gottheil, p. 100; A. Moses, pp. 100-101; Emmanuel Schreiber, pp. 101-113; Max Landsberg, pp. 113-114; S. Hecht, pp. 114-115; Published Opinions of: K. Kohler, pp. 115-117; M. Samfield, pp. 117-122; Henry Iliowizi, pp. 124-125; E. G. Hirsch, pp. 126-127]

Wm. [M.] F. Petrie, "Requests and Replies," *ET* 6 (1894-95) 81. *[Circumcision]*

*M. G. Kyle, "The Religion of Israel and Its Relation to the Religions of Contiguous Peoples," *CFL, N.S.,* 7 (1903) 17-23. [II. Circumcision]

Arthur E. Whatham, "The Origin of Circumcision," *AJRPE* 1 (1904-05) 301-315.

*Jacob Son of Aaron, "Circumcision Among the Samaritans," *BS* 65 (1908) 697-710.

G. Elliot Smith, "The Rite of Circumcision," *JMUEOS* #2 (1912-13) 75.

*G. Róheim, "The Passage of the Red Sea," *Man* 23 (1923) #96. *[Circumcision]*

Raymond F. Stoll, "The Circumcision," *AER* 110 (1944) 31-42.

*S. Talmon, "The 'Bloody Husband'," *EI* 3 (1954) IV.

*Ernest Kennaway, "Some Biological Aspects of Jewish Ritual," *Man* 57 (1957) #83. [Circumcision, pp. 65-68]

*Sidney B. Hoening, "Circumcision: The Covenant of Abraham," *JQR, N.S.,* 53 (1962-63) 322-334.

Jack M. Sasson, "Circumcision in the Ancient Near East," *JBL* 85 (1966) 473-476.

§111 *2.3.18.3 Fasting*

F. W. Farrar, "'Fasting' in the Holy Scripture," *Exp, 4th Ser.,* 1 (1890) 339-351.

John E. Godbey, "Is Fasting as a Religious Exercise Enjoined by the Bible?" *MQR, 3rd Ser.,* 19 (1895-96) 217-222.

Julius J. Price, "Fasting," *OC* 37 (1923) 751-761.

*A. Marmorstein, "The Amidah of the Public Fast Days," *JQR, N.S.,* 15 (1924-25) 409-418.

Israel Davidson, "Note to 'the Amidah of the Public Fast Days'," *JQR, N.S.,* 15 (1924-25) 507.

*S. Lowy, "The Motivation of Fasting in Talmudic Literature," *JJS* 9 (1958) 19-38.

Gerald E. Zuriff, "The History of Fasting in Judaism," *YR* 4 (1965) 62-79.

§112 *2.3.18.4 Phylacteries*

*B. Pick, "The Rites, Ceremonies and Customs of the Jews," *HR* 17 (1889) 199-206. [I. The Phylacteries, p. 200]

Anonymous, "Phylacteries," *ONTS* 15 (1892) 77.

John Bowman, "Phylacteries," *GUOST* 15 (1953-54) 54-55.

A. M. Habermann, "The Phylacteries in Ancient Times," *EI* 3 (1954) XI.

J[ohn] Bowman, "Phylacteries," *StEv* 1 (1959) 523-538.

Leopold Zunz, "Tephillin—A Contemplation," *Jud* 12 (1963) 351-354.

§113 *2.3.19 Burial Customs & Mourning [For burial places see: Tombs and Sepulchres →]*

Anonymous, "The Custom of Burial with the Head Towards the East," *DUM* 78 (1871) 705-709.

Hyde Clarke, "Niches for Skulls," *PEFQS* 7 (1875) 218.

*G. Maspero, "The Egyptian Documents relating to the Statues of the Dead," *SBAP* 1 (1878-79) 44.

Herman Hager, "How were the bodies of criminals at Athens disposed of after death?" *JP* 8 (1879) 1-13.

*G. Maspero, "Egyptian Documents relating to Statues of the Dead," *SBAT* 7 (1880-82) 6-36.

*Samuel Birch, "Observations on Canopic Vases from Tel-Basta, exhibited by F. G. Hilton-Price," *SBAP* 5 (1882-83) 98-100.

C[laude] R. Conder, "The Canaanites," *PEFQS* 19 (1887) 149. *[Burial Custom]*

*W. M. Flinders Petrie, "Egyptian Funereal Cones," *BOR* 2 (1887-88) 64-65.

*B. Pick, "The Rites, Ceremonies and Customs of the Jews," *HR* 17 (1889) 199-206. [XII. In Death and After Death, pp. 205-206]

M. Schlesinger, "Cremation from a Jewish Standpoint," *YCCAR* 2 (1891-92) 33-40.

Anonymous, "Funeral Customs Among the Ancient Jews," *EN* 4 (1892) 465-469.

E. Towry Whyte, "Notes on Pectorals," *SBAP* 15 (1892-93) 409-416.

*A. P. Bender, "Beliefs, Rites, and Customs Connected with Death, Burial and Mourning (as Illustrated by the Bible and Later Jewish Literature) I," *JQR* 6 (1893-94) 317-322.

*A. P. Bender, "Beliefs, Rites, and Customs Connected with Death, Burial and Mourning (as Illustrated by the Bible and Later Jewish Literature) II," *JQR* 6 (1893-94) 322-347.

*A. P. Bender, "Beliefs, Rites, and Customs Connected with Death, Burial and Mourning (as Illustrated by the Bible and Later Jewish Literature) III," *JQR* 6 (1893-94) 664-671.

L. C. Casartelli, "The Art of Burial," *DR* 114 (1894) 1-21.

*A. P. Bender, "Beliefs, Rites, and Customs Connected with Death, Burial and Mourning (as Illustrated by the Bible and Later Jewish Literature) IV," *JQR* 7 (1894-95) 101-118.

*A. P. Bender, "Beliefs, Rites, and Customs Connected with Death, Burial and Mourning (as Illustrated by the Bible and Later Jewish Literature) V," *JQR* 7 (1894-95) 259-269.

E. Towry Whyte, "Some Remarks on the Sepulchral Figures usually called Ushabti," *SBAP* 18 (1896) 138-146.

E. Towry Whyte, "Sepulchral Figures usually called Ushabti," *SBAP* 18 (1896) 161.

*Morris Jastrow Jr., "Dust, Earth and Ashes as Symbols of Mourning among the Ancient Hebrews," *JAOS* 20 (1899) 133-150.

*A[ngus] C[rawford], "Notes—Archæological, Etc.," *PER* 13 (1899-1900) 48-50. *[Dried Flowers in Mummy Wrappings]*

*James A. Quarles, "Sociology of Joseph's Day," *CFL, N.S.,* 5 (1902) 97-108. [Death, pp. 106-108]

*Morris Jastrow Jr., "Baring the Arm and Shoulder as a Sign of Mourning," *ZAW* 22 (1902) 117-120.

Tracy Peck, "The Personal Address in Roman Epitaphs," *AJA* 7 (1903) 88-89.

*E. W. G. Masterman, "Jewish Customs of Birth, Marriage, and Death," *BW* 22 (1903) 248-257.

C[laude] R. Conder, "Burial and Burning," *PEFQS* 35 (1903) 179-180.

*Anonymous, "Little Figures from Egyptian Tombs," *RP* 4 (1905) 128.

Anonymous, "Coffins for Mice," *RP* 6 (1907) 270.

J. Y. W. Macalsiter, "Notes and Queries. 2. *Dismemberment of the Dead at Gezer,*" *PEFQS* 41 (1909) 153-154.

*Claude R. Conder, "Notes on New Discoveries," *PEFQS* 41 (1909) 266-275. [Burning the Dead, p. 273]

Anonymous, "Beheading Corpses in Egypt," *RP* 8 (1909) 58.

*W. H. Wood, "Jar-Burial Customs and the Question of Infant Sacrifice in Palestine," *BW* 36 (1910) 166-175, 227-234.

*W. F. Badè, "Hebrew Funerary Rites as Survivals of Ancestor Worship," *PAPA* 42 (1910) lxxvii.

Alan H. Gardiner, "The colour of mourning," *ZÄS* 47 (1910) 162-163.

B. D. Eerdmans, "The Sepulchral Monument 'Maṣṣebah'," *JBL* 30 (1911) 109-113.

Anonymous, "Prehistoric Burials in Egypt," *RP* 10 (1911) 54.

Anonymous, "Burials in Jars on Island of Crete," *RP* 10 (1911) 116.

Anonymous, "Origin of Cremation Among the Greeks," *RP* 10 (1911) 238.

*E. Mahler, "Notes on the Funeral Statuettes of the Ancient Egyptians, commonly called Ushabti Figures," *SBAP* 34 (1912) 146-151, 179.

*Paul Pierret, The Ushabti Figures," *SBAP* 34 (1912) 247.

[(Ushebti)]

Alan H. Gardiner, "An Unusual Sketch of a Theban Funeral," *SBAP* 35 (1913) 229.

C. Leonard Woolley, "Hittite Burial Customs," *AAA* 6 (1913-14) 87-98.

G. Elliot Smith, "Ancient Egypt and the Persistence of Ancient Burial Customs in Nigeria," *JMUEOS* #3 (1913-14) 95.

*T. Eric Peet, "A Remarkable Burial Custom of the Old Kingdom," *JEA* 2 (1915) 8-9. *[Clay Balls containing Hair]*

Arthur E. P. B. Weigall, "An Ancient Funeral Ceremony," *JEA* 2 (1915) 10-11. [Note by F. Ll. Griffith, p. 11-12]

Aylward M. Blackman, "Libations to the Dead in Modern Nubia and Ancient Egypt," *JEA* 3 (1915) 31-34.

W. M. F[linders] Petrie, "Funereal Figures in Egypt," *AEE* 3 (1916) 151-162.

Aylward M. Blackman, "Some Notes on the Ancient Egyptian Practice of washing the Dead," *JEA* 5 (1918) 117-124.

*Moses Buttenwieser, "Blood Revenge and Burial Rites in Ancient Israel," *JAOS* 39 (1919) 303-321.

*Julius J. Price, "Rabbinic Conceptions about Death," *OC* 34 (1920) 440-448.

Northcote W. Thomas, "The Burial Rites of West Africa in Relation to Egypt," *AEE* 6 (1921) 7-13.

Ernest Thomas, "The Magic Skin. A Contribution to the Study of the 'Tekenu'," *AEE* 8 (1923) 3-8, 46-56. *[Egyptian Funeral Rite]*

Winfred S. Blackman, "An Ancient Egyptian Custom illustrated by a Modern Survival," *Man* 25 (1925) #38 *[Clay Balls containing Hair]*

H. Godden Cole, "Disposal of the Dead and the Origins of Piety," *OC* 39 (1925) 131-144.

F. Ll. Griffith, "Tomb-endowment in Ancient Egypt," *ZÄS* 60 (1925) 83-84.

*D. B. Harden, "Punic Cinerary Urns from the Precinct of Tanit at Carthage," *AJA* 31 (1927) 95.

*D. B. Harden, "Punic Urns from the Precinct of Tanit at Carthage," *AJA* 31 (1927) 297-310.

*H. E. Winlock, "Notes of the Reburial of Tuthmosis I," *JEA* 15 (1929) 56-68.

*Frank E. Brown, "Violation of Sepulture in Palestine," *AJP* 52 (1931) 1-29.

Alan W. Shorter, "The Study of Egyptian Funerary Amulets," *CdÉ* 6 (1931) 312-314.

Arthur Darby Nock, "Cremation and Burial in the Roman Empire," *HTR* 25 (1932) 321-359.

A. Marmorstein, "Some rites of mourning in Judaism," *SMSDR* 10 (1934) 80-94.

Hermann Ranke, "The Origin of the Egyptian Tomb Statue," *HTR* 28 (1935) 45-53.

P. Bar-Adon, "On the Custom of Secondary Burials," *BIES* 5 (1937-38) #3, IV. (Note by S. Yeivin, p. IV]

Maurice A. Canney, "More Notes on Boats and Ships in Temples and Tombs," *JMUEOS* #21 (1937) 45-49.

T. H. Gaster, "Rights and Beliefs of Samaritans Relating to Death and Mourning. From the Papers of the Late Dr. Moses Gaster," *JPOS* 19 (1939-40) 180-212.

G. Allon, "The Origin of an Ancient Jewish Burial Custom," *BIES* 8 (1940-41) #3, II.

Alfred O'Rahilly, "Jewish Burial," *IER, 5th Ser.*, 58 (1941) 122-135.

B[enjamin] Maisler, "Cremation of the Dead," *KSJA* 1 (1942) XI.

John A. Wilson, "Funeral Services of the Egyptian Old Kingdom," *JNES* 3 (1944) 201-218.

G. Ernest Wright, "Additional Remarks on Ancient Burial Customs," *BA* 8 (1945) 17-18.

*Nina M. Davies, "An Unusual Depiction of Ramesside Funerary Rites," *JEA* 32 (1946) 69-70.

George E. Mylonas, "Homeric And Mycenaean Burial Customs," *AJA* 52 (1948) 56-81.

Rodney S. Young, "Burials within the Walls of Athens," *AJA* 52 (1948) 377-378.

Jarslov Černý, "Organization of Ushabti-figures," *JEA* 34 (1948) 121.

*Elise Baumgartel, "Tomb and fertility," *JKF* 1 (1950-51) 56-65.

Alan [H.] Gardiner, "The benefit conferred by reburial," *JEA* 37 (1951) 112.

*G. R. Driver, "A Hebrew Burial Custom," *ZAW* 66 (1954) 314-315.

*M. A. Murray, "Burial Customs and Beliefs in the Hereafter in Predynastic Egypt," *JEA* 42 (1956) 86-96.

I. W. Cornwall, "The Pre-Pottery Neolithic Burials, Jericho," *PEQ* 88 (1956) 110-124.

L. V. Grinsell, "The Breaking of Objects as a Funerary Rite," *Folk* 72 (1961) 475-491.

Joseph A. Callaway, "Burials in Ancient Palestine: From the Stone Age to Abraham," *BA* 26 (1963) 74-91.

Vassos Karageorghis, "Horse Burials on the Island of Cyprus," *Arch* 18 (1965) 282-290.

Sp. E. Iakovidis, "A Mycenaean Mourning Custom," *AJA* 70 (1966) 43-50.

E. A. E. Reymond, "The God's *'IḪT*-Relics," *JEA* 53 (1967) 103-106.

John Bennett, "The Symbolism of a Mummy Case," *JEA* 53 (1967) 165-166.

*Barry J. Kemp, "Merimda and the Theory of House Burial in Prehistoric Egypt," *CdÉ* 43 (1968) 22-33.

*Jac. J. Janssen and P. W. Pestman, "Burial and inheritance in the community of the necropolis workmen at Thebes," *JESHO* 11 (1968) 137-170.

David Gilead, "Burial Customs and the Dolmen Problem," *PEQ* 100 (1968) 16-26.

J. Murtagh, "Mourning Customs in the Old Testament," *BibT* #44 (1969) 3047-3061.

G. R. H. Wright, "Strabo on Funerary Customs at Petra," *PEQ* 101 (1969) 113-116.

*T. L. Fenton, "Ugaritica—Biblica," *UF* 1 (1969) 65-70. *[Sackcloth & Ashes]*

*Alan D. Crown, "Theology, Eschatology and Law in Samaritan Funeral Rites and Liturgy," *GUOST* 23 (1969-70) 86-101.

§114 *2.3.19.1* *Mummies, Mummification* *[See also: Anthropology; Studies regarding specific remains →]*

*G. Seyffarth, "Three Lectures on Egyptian Antiquities, &c., delivered at th Stuyvesant Institute, New York, May 1856," *ER* 8 (1856-57) 34-104. [VII. The Apis-Mummies, pp. 72-76]

*J. E. Howard, "Egypt and the Bible," *JTVI* 10 (1876-77) 340-377. {(Appendicies, pp. 377-379) (Discussion, pp. 379-385) ["Appendicies. (A.) Mummy from Gournou, examined by A. B. Granville, M.D., F.R.S. &c. Read *April* 14, 1825, before the Royal Society," pp. 377-378]}

S. Birch, "On a Mummy opened at Stafford House on the 15th July, 1875," *SBAT* 5 (1876-77) 122-126.

[Stephen D. Peet], "The Egyptian Mummies," *AAOJ* 4 (1881-82) 65-68. *(Editorial)*

*E. A. Wallis Budge, "The Mummy and Coffin of Nes-Ames, Prophet of Ames and Chonsu," *SBAP* 8 (1885-86) 106-108.

[G.] Maspero, "Unrolling the Mummy of Rameses the Great," *ONTS* 6 (1886-87) 26-27. [From a translation (in the Sunday School Times of Aug. 14, 1886]

Anonymous, "Mummification," *MR* 76 (1894) 811-814.

*A[ngus] C[rawford], "Notes—Archæological, Critical and Expository: Mummy of Merenptah," *PER* 12 (1898-99) 460.

E. Towry Whyte, "Egyptian Bronze Mummy-case for a fish," *SBAP* 21 (1899) 82.

G. Elliot Smith, "Ouverture des momies provenant de la seconde trouvaille de Deir el-Bahari: II. Report on the four Mummies," *ASAE* 4 (1903) 156-160.

Anonymous, "Methods of Embalming," *RP* 7 (1908) 62-63.

Anonymous, "Trepanning Among Egyptian Mummies," *RP* 8 (1909) 263.

Anonymous, "Mummy of the Red Sea Pharaoh," *RP* 9 (1910) 343. *[Menephtah]*

*G. Elliot Smith, "'Heart and Reins' in Mummification," *JMUEOS* #1 (1911) 41-44 [Supplementary note, pp 45-48]

G. Elliot Smith, "The Earliest Evidence of Attempts at Mummification in Egypt," *JMUEOS* #2 (1912-13) 77-78.

*Jivanji Jamshedji Modi, "The Preservation, Among the Ancient Egyptians and Iranians, of Parts of the Body for Resurrection," *JMUEOS* #3 (1913-14) 73-76.

G. Elliot Smith, "Mummification and British Folklore," *JMUEOS* #3 (1913-14) 97.

A. Lucas, "The Use of Natron by the Ancient Egyptians in Mummification," *JEA* 1 (1914) 119-123.

G. Elliot Smith, "Egyptian Mummies," *JEA* 1 (1914) 189-196.

A. Lucas, "The use of Bitumen by the Ancient Egyptians in Mummification," *JEA* 1 (1914) 241-245.

Warren R. Dawson, "Making a Mummy," *JEA* 13 (1927) 40-49.

Warren R. Dawson, "References to Mummification by Greek and Latin authors," *Aeg* 9 (1928) 106-112.

M. L. Tildesley, "A Mummy-Head of Unusual Type," *JEA* 15 (1929) 158-159.

Warren R. Dawson, "A Note on the Egyptian Mummies in the Castle Museum, Norwich," *JEA* 15 (1929) 186-190.

Anonymous, "The Mummy Case of Neb-Neteru," *UMB* 1 (1930) #3, 26-27.

Anonymous, "Notes and Comments. Faked Mummies and the X-ray," *A&A* 31 (1931) 284-285.

A. Lucas, "'Cedar'-Tree Products employed in Mummification," *JEA* 17 (1931) 13-21.

A. Lucas, "The use of natron in mummification," *JEA* 18 (1932) 125-140.

Percy E. Spielmann, "To what extent did the ancient Egyptians employ bitumen for embalming?" *JEA* 18 (1932) 177-180.

Anonymous, "Notes and Comments. Her Teeth in Her Stomach," *A&A* 34 (1933) 105.

*Warren R. Dawson, "Pettigrew's Demonstrations upon Mummies. A Chapter in the History of Egyptology," *JEA* 20 (1934) 170-182.

Casper John Kraemer Jr. and Floyd Albert Spencer, "New Light on the Ταριχαντής in Augustan Egypt," *PAPA* 65 (1934) xlv.

B[attiscombe] G[unn], "The New Mummy Room," *UMB* 5 (1934-35) #4, 13-18.

M[ary] L[ouise] M[orton], "How Mummies Were Made," *UMB* 5 (1934-35) #4, 18-22.

*M. M. C., "An Egyptian Mummy Cloth," *UMB* 6 (1935-37) #4, 119-120.

*R. Engelbach, "Mummification. I.-Introduction: Herodotus with notes on his text," *ASAE* 41 (1942) 235-239.

D[ouglas] E. Derry, "Mummification. II.-Methods practised at different periods," *ASAE* 41 (1942) 271-275.

Ahmad Zaki and Zaky Iskander, "Materials and method used for mummifying the body of Amentefnekht, Saqqara 1941," *ASAE* 42 (1943) 223-250.

M. A. Stuckey, "The Art of Mummification in Ancient Egypt and Its Interesting Revelations," *TUSR* 5 (1956-58) 93-103.

John Dimick, "The Embalming House of the Apis Bulls," *Arch* 11 (1958) 183-189.

A. T. Sandison, "The Use of Natron in Mummification in Ancient Egypt," *JNES* 22 (1963) 259-267.

Klaus Parlasca, "A Painted Egyptian Mummy Shroud of the Roman Period," *Arch* 16 (1963) 264-268.

A. T. Sandison, "The Use of Natron in Mummification in Ancient Egypt," *JNES* 22 (1963) 259-267.

Zaky Iskander and Abd el Moeiz Shaheen, "Temporary stuffing materials used in the process of Mummification in Ancient Egypt," *ASAE* 58 (1964) 197-208.

P. H. K. Gray, "Embalmers' 'Restorations'," *JEA* 52 (1966) 138-140.

F. Filce Leek, "The Problem of Brain Removal during Embalming by the Ancient Egyptians," *JEA* 55 (1969) 112-116.

§115 *2.3.20 Modern Beliefs & Customs Illustrating the Ancient Near East & Old Testament*

†Anonymous, "Antes on Egypt," *BCQTR* 16 (1800) 667-678. *(Review) [Modern Customs]*

†*Anonymous, "Burder on Oriental Customs," *BCQTR* 23 (1804) 166-169. *(Review)*

†Anonymous, "Oriental Illustrations," *BCQTR, 4th Ser.*, 17 (1835) 445-477 *(Review)*

†*Anonymous, "Lane's *Manners and Customs of the Modern Egyptians*," *QRL* 59 (1837) 165-208. *(Review)*

*(   ) Y., "Traditions of the East—From Herder," *CTPR, N.S.*, 2 (1840) 208-210.

Henry A. Homes, "The Sect of Yezidies of Mesopotamia," *BRCR, N.S.* 7 (1842) 329-351. (Remarks of Father Lucas, pp. 350-351)

†Anonymous, "The Maronites and Druses," *DR* 18 (1845) 43-47. *(Review)*

†Anonymous, "Modern Syria," *BQRL* 19 (1854) 81-112. *(Review)*

†Anonymous, "Dr. Thomson's and Professor Osborn's Works on Palestine," *PQR* 7 (1858-59) 613-637. *(Review)*

*G. Octavius Wray, "A Singular Custom," *PEFQS* 1 (1869) 89. *["... my children are in bed with me" (cf. Luke 11:7)]*

*W. Robertson Smith, "Animal worship and animal tribes among the Arabs and the Old Testament," *JP* 19 (1880) 75-100.

*C[laude] R. Conder, "Captain Conder's Reports," *PEFQS* 14 (1882) 69-112. [XI. On Some Arab Folk-lore Tales, pp.90-99]

Jas. Neil, "Camp-Fires in the Holy Land," *ONTS* 3 (1883-84) 20-21.

G. Schumacher, "Arabic Proverbs," *PEFQS* 19 (1887) 192-195.

C[laude] R. Conder, "Samaritan Customs," *PEFQS* 19 (1887) 233-236.

James Richard Jewett, "Some Arabic proverbs; collected by Mr. James Richard Jewett," *JAOS* 13 (1889) cxxix-cxxii.

C[laude] R. Conder, "Reports on Answers to the 'Questions'," *PEFQS* 21 (1889) 120-133. *[Modern Customs]*

James Neil, "The Clapping of Hands," *TML* 1 (1889) 131-141.

George E. Post, "Essays on the Sects and Nationalities of Syria and Palestine. *Land Tenure, Agriculture, Physical, Mental and Moral Characteristics,*" *PEFQS* 23 (1891) 99-147. (Notes by C. R. Conder, pp. 252-254)

T. W. Davies, "The Modern Jew and His Synagogue," *ONTS* 13 (1891) 134-142, 200-208.

J. E. Hanauer, "Proverbs and Sayings among the Spanish Jews," *PEFQS* 23 (1891) 151-156.

Frederick Jones Bliss, "Essays on the Sects and Nationalities of Syria and Palestine," *PEFQS* 24 (1892) 71-83, 129-153, 207-218, 308-322. [The Maronites]

James Richard Jewett, "Arabic Proverbs and Proverbial Phrases, Collected, Translated and Annotated," *JAOS* 15 (1893) 28-120.

Philip J. Baldensperger, "Peasant Folklore of Palestine," *PEFQS* 25 (1893) 203-219. (Notes by C. R. Conder, pp. 323-324)

Philip J. Baldensperger, "Religion of the Fellahin of Palestine," *PEFQS* 25 (1893) 307-320. [Note by C. R. Conder, *PEFQS* 26 (1894) p. 82]

Philip J. Baldensperger, "Orders of Holy Men in Palestine. *(Answers to Questons.),*" *PEFQS* 26 (1894) 22-38.

Philip J. Baldensperger, "Birth, Marriage, and Death among the Fellahin of Palestine. *(Answers to Questons.),*" *PEFQS* 26 (1894) 127-144. (Notes by C. R. Conder, pp. 207-209)

*Samuel Bergheim, "Land Tenure in Palestine," *PEFQS* 26 (1894) 191-199.

G. Deutsch, "'The Scroll of the Law'," *YCCAR* 6 (1895-96) 68-77. (Remarks by M. Mielziner, pp. 77-78) *[The Writing of a Scroll of the Law]*

*Elkan N. Alder, "The Persian Jews: Their Books and Their Ritual," *JQR* 10 (1897-98) 584-625.

Bernard Pick, "Historical Sketch of the Jews Since their Return from Babylon," *OC* 11 (1897) 265-279, 337-364.

*P[hilip] J. Baldensperger, "Morals of the Fellahin," *PEFQS* 29 (1897) 123-134. (Notes by C. R. Conder, pp. 211-212)

*Philip J. Baldensperger, "Woman in the East," *PEFQS* 31 (1899) 132-160.

R. A. Stewart Macalister, "The Vocal Music of the Fellahin," *PEFQS* 32 (1900) 104-109.

*Philip J. Baldensperger, "Woman in the East. Part II," *PEFQS* 32 (1900) 171-190.

W. E. Jennings-Bramley, "Sport Among the Bedâwin," *PEFQS* 32 (1900) 369-376.

*Philip J. Baldensperger, "Woman in the East," *PEFQS* 33 (1901) 66-90, 167-184, 252-273.

A. Kingsley Glover, "Modern Jewish Customs as Possible Helps in Bible Study," *BW* 18 (1901) 7-12.

*R. A. S. Macalister, "Reports and Notes by R. A. S. Macalister, Esq. II. The Birak esh-Shinanir," *PEFQS* 33 (1901) 391-393.

Samuel Ives Curtiss, "The Physical Relation of Man to God Among the Modern Semites," *AJT* 6 (1902) 304-313.

Samuel Ives Curtiss, "Conceptions of God Among Modern Semites," *BW* 19 (1902) 122-131.

Samuel Ives Curtiss, "The Local Divinities of the Modern Semites," *BW* 19 (1902) 168-177, 288-298.

Henry Minor Huxley, "Syrian Songs, Proverbs, and Stories collected, translated, and annotated," *JAOS* 23 (1902) 175-188.

E. W. G. Masterman, "The Jews in Modern Palestine," *BW* 21 (1903) 17-26.

*W. Deans, "Tree-Worship and Similar Practices in China," *ET* 15 (1903-04) 384.

J. Parisot, "A Collection of Oriental Jewish Songs," *JAOS* 24 (1903) 227-264. *[Modern]*

Philip J. Baldensperger, "The Immovable East," *PEFQS* 35 (1903) 65-77, 162-170, 336-344; 36 (1904) 49-57, 128-137, 258-264, 360-367; 37 (1905) 33-38, 116-126, 199-205; 38 (1906) 13-23, 97-102, 190-197; 39 (1907) 10-21, 269-274; 40 (1908) 290-298; 41 (1909) 247-252; 42 (1910) 259-268; 44 (1912) 8-13, 57-62; 45 (1913) 124-132; 47 (1915) 10-22.

E. W. G. Masterman, "Feasts and Fast of the Jews in Modern Palestine," *BW* 23 (1904) 24-36, 110-121.

(   ) Hammond, "The Samaritan Passover of the Year *1861*," *JTVI* 36 (1904) 213-218. (Discussion, pp. 219-223)

R. A. Stewart Macalister and E. W. G. Masterman, "Occasional Papers on the Modern Inhabitants of Palestine," *PEFQS* 36 (1904) 150-160; 37 (1905) 48-61. *[Personal Names]*

J. E. Hanauer, "Palestine Animal Folk-lore," *PEFQS* 36 (1904) 265-274; 37 (1905) 152-155.

*Ghosn-el *[sic]* Howie, "Gezer Foundation Deposits and Modern Beliefs," *RP* 3 (1904) 212-216.

W. E. Jennings-Bramley, "The Bedouin of the Sinaitic Peninsula," *PEFQS* 37 (1905) 126-137, 211-219; 39 (1907) 22-33, 131-137, 279-284; 40 (1908) 30-36, 112-116; 41 (1909) 253-258; 42 (1910) 140-149; 43 (1911) 34-42, 172-181; 44 (1912) 13-20, 62-68; 45 (1913) 34-38, 79-84; 46 (1914) 9-18.

R. A. Stewart Macalister and E. W. G. Masterman, "Occasional Papers on the Modern Inhabitants of Palestine. A History of the Doings of the Fellahin During the First Half of the Nineteenth Century, from Native Sources," *PEFQS* 37 (1905) 343-356; 38 (1906) 33-50, 110-114, 221-225, 286-291.

(Miss) Gladys Dickson, "Notes on Palestinian Folk-lore," *PEFQS* 38 (1906) 67-69, 130-132; 39 (1907) 148-151; 40 (1908) 245-248.

R. Campbell Thompson, "The Folk-lore of Mossoul. I," *SBAP* 28 (1906) 76-86, 97-109.

(Mrs.) Hans H. Spoer (A Goodrich-Freer), "The Powers of Evil in Jerusalem," *Folk* 18 (1907) 54-76.

( ) Yusif, "Some Specimens of Fellah Wit and Humour," *PEFQS* 39 (1907) 274-279. *(Trans. by R. A. Stewart Macalister)*

R. Campbell Thompson, "The Folk-lore of Mossoul—*(continued),*" *SBAP* 29 (1907) 165-174, 282-288, 323-331.

(Mrs.) El Ghosu Howie, "Survival of Old Semitic Customs," *AAOJ* 30 (1908) 31-32. *[Thread charms as a "fleece"]*

*Jas. P. Conry, "Some Old Biblical Customs in Modern Palestine," *AER* 39 (1908) 169-175.

*Jacob Son of Aaron, "Circumcision Among the Samaritans," *BS* 65 (1908) 694-710.

( ) Yusif, "Further Tales of the Fellahin," *PEFQS* 40 (1908) 36-39. *(Trans. by R. A. Stewart Macalister)*

R. A. S. Macalister, "Notes and Queries. 4. *Fellah Supersitions,*" *PEFQS* 40 (1908) 165-167.

R. Campbell Thompson, "The Folk-lore of Mossoul (III)," *SBAP* 30 (1908) 30-33.

R. A. Stewart Macalister, "Some Miscellaneous Tales of the Fellahin," *PEFQS* 41 (1909) 219-227.

*Israel Friedlaender, "Bonfires on Purim," *JQR, N.S.*, 1 (1910-11) 257-258.

*Lewis Bayles Paton, "Survivals of Primitive Religion in Syria," *AJA* 15 (1911) 63-64.

Lewis Bayles Paton, "Modern Palestine and the Bible. *I. The Land*," *HR* 61 (1911) 8-12.

Lewis Bayles Paton, "Modern Palestine and the Bible. *II. The Races of Palestine*," *HR* 61 (1911) 108-112.

Lewis Bayles Paton, "Modern Palestine and the Bible. *III. Occupations of the Inhabitants*," *HR* 61 (1911) 190-195.

Lewis Bayles Paton, "Modern Palestine and the Bible. *IV. Food and Drink*," *HR* 61 (1911) 275-280.

Lewis Bayles Paton, "Modern Palestine and the Bible. *V. Clothing and Ornaments*," *HR* 61 (1911) 354-359.

Lewis Bayles Paton, "Modern Palestine and the Bible. *VI. Houses, Villages, and Towns*," *HR* 61 (1911) 439-443.

Lewis Bayles Paton, "Modern Palestine and the Bible. *VII. Family and Tribal Organization*," *HR* 62 (1911) 27-30.

Lewis Bayles Paton, "Modern Palestine and the Bible. *VIII. Social Life and Customs*," *HR* 62 (1911) 108-113.

*Lewis Bayles Paton, "Modern Palestine and the Bible. *IX. Survivals of Primitive Religion*," *HR* 62 (1911) 194-199.

*Lewis Bayles Paton, "Modern Palestine and the Bible. *X. The Religion of the Jews*," *HR* 62 (1911) 268-273.

J. P. Conry, "Biblical Memories in Palestine: Old Testament," *IER, 4th Ser.*, 29 (1911) 507-522.

W. W. Baker, "Ancient Ways in Modern Greece," *AJA* 16 (1912) 106-107.

*A. Mitchell Innes, "Love and the Law: A Study of Oriental Justice," *HJ* 11 (1912-13) 273-296. [I. The Two Systems; II. Until Seventy Times Seven; III. The Dogma of Divine Reciprocity; IV. Old and New]

*C. Ryder Smith, "Some Indian Parallels to Hebrew Cult," *JTS* 14 (1912-13) 424-432.

Edgar J. Banks, "The Awakening of Babylonia," *HR* 66 (1913) 93-96.

R. A. Stewart Macalister, "A Day in a Fellah Village," *PEFQS* 47 (1915) 29-34.

Philip J. Baldensperger, "The Immovable East. *Clothes and Fashions*," *PEFQS* 47 (1915) 66-72, 165-170; 48 (1916) 19-26.

E. W. G. Masterman and R. A. Stewart Macalister, "Occasional Papers on the Modern Inhabitants of Palestine," *PEFQS* 47 (1915) 170-179; 48 (1916) 11-19, 44-71, 126-137, 173-178; 49 (1917) 72-80, 119-125, 177-179.

William H. Worrell, "Ink, Oil and Mirror Gazing Ceremonies in Modern Egypt," *JAOS* 36 (1916) 37-53.

*Philip J. Baldensperger, "The Immovable East. *Toilet*, *PEFQS* 48 (1916) 71-77.

*Philip J. Baldensperger, "The Immovable East. *The General Characteristics of the Different Towns*," *PEFQS* 48 (1916) 165-172; 49 (1917) 12-17, 159-165; 50 (1918) 20-25.

George M. Mackie, "Proverbs of Oriental Wisdom," *ET* 28 (1916-17) 346-349.

A. Mishcon, "Proverbs of Oriental Wisdom," *ET* 28 (1916-17) 479-480.

Philip J. Baldensperger, "The Immovable East. IV. Hebron," *PEFQS* 50 (1918) 119-122.

E. Herman, "Pagan Survivals in Palestine," *HR* 77 (1919) 366.

E. W. G. Masterman, "A Jewish Feast. The Annual Feast of Rabbi Simeon ben Yokhai at Meron," *PEFQS* 51 (1919) 112-117.

Philip J. Baldensperger, "The Immovable East. Natural History Notes," *PEFQS* 51 (1919) 118-122.

Philip J. Baldensperger, "The Immovable East. Natural History Notes— *(continued). Serpents,*" *PEFQS* 51 (1919) 159-167.

Philip J. Baldensperger, "The Immovable East. Religion, Feasts, Processions," *PEFQS* 52 (1920) 161-166.

*E. N. Haddad, "Blood Revenge Among the Arabs," *JPOS* 1 (1920-21) 103-111.

*T. Canaan, "Haunted Springs and Water Demons in Palestine," *JPOS* 1 (1920-21) 153-170.

'Omar Effendi el-Barghuthi, "Judicial Courts Among the Bedouin of Palestine," *JPOS* 2 (1922) 34-65.

Philip G. Baldensperger, "The Immovable East. *Ceremonies and Beliefs,*" *PEFQS* 54 (1922) 23-32.

Philip G. Baldensperger, "The Immovable East. *Arab Life,*" *PEFQS* 54 (1922) 63-67, 161-172; 57 (1925) 80-90.

E. N. Haddad, "Methods of Education and Correction Among the Fellahin," *JPOS* 3 (1923) 41-44.

St[ephan] H. Stephan, "Palestinian Animal Stories and Fables," *JPOS* 3 (1923) 167-190.

R. Campbell Thompson, "Some Notes on Modern Babylonia," *JRAS* (1923) 233-242.

H. Hirschfeld, "Note on Some Arab Proverbs," *JRAS* (1923) 419-420.

Philip G. Baldensperger, "The Immovable East. *Arab Life,*" *PEFQS* 55 (1923) 173-184. [Tent Life, pp. 179-184]

'Omar Ṣâliḥ el-Barghuthi, "Rules of Hospitality (*Qānûn yḍ-Ḍiyâfeh),*" *JPOS* 4 (1924) 175-203.

G. W. B. Huntingford, "Egypt in Africa," *AEE* 10 (1925) 98-99.

Winifred S. Blackman, "Sacred Trees in Modern Egypt," *JEA* 11 (1925) 56-57.

Stephan H. Stephan, "Lunacy in Palestinian Folklore," *JPOS* 5 (1925) 1-16.

Stephan H. Stephan, "Animals in Palestinian Folklore," *JPOS* 5 (1925) 92-155; 8 (1928) 65-112; 9 (1929) 88-99.

Philip J. Baldensperger, "The Immovable East. *Raids*," *PEFQS* 58 (1926) 93-97.

T. Canaan, "The Child in Palestinian Arab Supersition," *JPOS* 7 (1927) 159-186.

*E. Power, "The shepherd's two rods in modern Palestine and in some passages of the Old Testament *(Ps. 23, 4; Zach. 11, 7 ss.; 1 Sam. 17, 43)*," *B* 9 (1928) 434-442.

T. Canaan, "Plant-lore in Palestinian Superstition," *JPOS* 8 (1928) 129-168.

Stephan H. Stephan, "Studies in Palestinian Customs and Folklore," *JPOS* 8 (1928) 214-222.

'Omar es-Saleh el-Barghuthy, "Traces of the Feudal System in Palestine," *JPOS* 9 (1929) 70-79.

*Philip J. Baldensperger, "The Immovable East. *Horses*," *PEFQS* 61 (1929) 183-189.

Julius J. Price, "Bible Quotations and Chinese Customs," *ET* 40 (1928-29) 165-168.

T. Canaan,"Water and 'the Water of Life' in Palestinian Superstition," *JPOS* 9 (1929) 57-69.

(Mrs.) A. M. Spoer, "Jewish Folklore from Palestine," *Folk* 42 (1932) 67-69.

T. Canaan, "Light and Darkness in Palestine Folklore," *JPOS* 11 (1931) 15-36.

T. Canaan, "Unwritten Laws affecting the Arab Woman of Palestine," *JPOS* 11 (1931) 172-203.

St[ephan] H. Stephan, "Palestinian Nursery Rhymes and Songs," *JPOS* 12 (1932) 62-85.

T. Canaan, "The Palestinian Arab House: Its Architecture and Folklore," *JPOS* 12 (1932) 223-247; 13 (1933) 1-83.

Winifred S. Blackman, "Some Further Notes on a Harvesting Scene," *JEA* 19 (1933) 31-32.

*A. S. Tritton, "Spirits and Demons in Arabia," *JRAS* (1933) 715-727.

*H. Frankfort, "A Tammuz Ritual in Kurdistan (?)," *Iraq* 1 (1934) 137-145.

T. Canaan, "Modern Palestinian Beliefs and Practices Relating to God," *JPOS* 14 (1934) 59-92.

T. Canaan, "The Curse in Palestinian Folklore," *JPOS* 15 (1935) 235-279.

*Edward Robertson, "The Days of the Week and of the Month in Arab Folk-Lore," *JMUEOS* #20 (1936) 19-24.

T. Canaan, "The Ṣaqr Bedouin of Bisān," *JPOS* 16 (1936) 21-32.

E. S. Drower, "Woman and Taboo in Iraq," *Iraq* 5 (1938) 105-117.

T. Torrance, "The Survival of Old Testament Religious Customs Among the Chiang People of West China," *JTVI* 71 (1939) 100-110, 114-116. [(Discussion, pp. 111-113) (Communication by H. S. Curr, pp. 113-114)]

Walter Cline, "Proverbs and Lullabies from Southern Arabia," *AJSL* 57 (1940) 291-301.

*S. P. T. Prideaux, "The Wisaga," *ET* 55 (1943-44) 278.

*Harold Garner, "Exodus, Prophet and West Africa," *ET* 58 (1946-47) 278-279.

Dayton S. Mak, "Some Syrian Arabic Proverbs," *JAOS* 69 (1949) 223-228.

*Henry Field, "Camel Brands and Graffiti from Iraq, Syria, Jordan, Iran, and Arabia," *JAOSS* #15 (1952) i-vi, 1-41.

Franz Landsberger, "The Origin of European Torah Decorations," *HUCA* 24 (1952-53) 133-150.

*Charles Lee Feinberg, "The Old Testament in Jewish Thought and Life," *BS* 111 (1954) 27-38, 125-136.

J. B. Segal, "Neo-Aramaic Proverbs of the Jews of Zakho," *JNES* 14 (1955) 251-270.

Aryeh Newman, "Yom Ha'atzma'ut—A New Festival in the Making," *Jud* 6 (1957) 219-223.

*J. N. Schofield, "Modern Issues in Biblical Studies. The Religion of the Near East and the Old Testament," *ET* 71 (1959-60) 195-198.

Franz Landsberger, "The Origin of the Decorated Mezuzah," *HUCA* 31 (1960) 149-166.

T. Canaan, "Superstition and Folklore about Bread," *BASOR* #167 (1962) 36-47.

Walter P. Zenner, "Saints and Piecemeal Supernaturalism Among the Jerusalem Sephardim," *AQW* 38 (1965) 201-217.

Paula G. Rubel, "Herd composition and social structure: on building models of nomadic pastoral societies," *Man, N.S.,* 4 (1969) 268-273.

Lucian Turkowski, "Peasant Agriculture in the Judaean Hills," *PEQ* 101 (1969) 21-33.

Lucian Turkowski, "Peasant Agriculture in the Judaean Hills *(concluded),*" *PEQ* 101 (1969) 101-112.

§116 *2.3.21 The Calendar and Studies in Reckoning of Time [See also: Qumran Calendar →]*

Anonymous, "The Great Year," *CongML* 14 (1831) 340-341.

*†Anonymous, "Ancient Chronology," *BCQTR, 4th Ser.*, 12 (1832) 120-141. *(Review) [Calendar]*

Henry Browne, "The Egyptian month Adrian," *JCSP* 2 (1855) 44-46.

*I. *[sic]* W. Bosanquet, "The Dial of Ahaz and Scripture Chronology," *JSL, 3rd Ser.*, 1 (1855) 407-413.

Jospeh P. Thompson, "The Egyptian Year," *BS* 14 (1857) 644-654.

*Gust. Geyffarth, "To the Author of the 'Queries in regard to Dr. Seyffarth's Lectures on Egyptian Antiquities,' in the Ev. Review, January 1857, p. 415," *ER* 9 (1857-58) 58-75. *[Calendar]*

A. H. Wratislaw, "Hebrew Division of the Day," *JSL, 3rd Ser.*, 14 (1861-62) 470-471.

*C. W. Goodwin, "The Calendar question I," *ZÄS* 5 (1867) 45-49, 57-60.

C. W. Goodwin, "The Calendar question," *ZÄS* 5 (1867) 78-82. *[Parts II-V]*

*Daniel Hy. Haigh, "Note on the calendar in Mr. Smith's papyrus," *ZÄS* 9 (1871) 72-73. *[Pap. Ebers]*

C. W. Goodwin, "On the symbolic Eye, Uta," *ZÄS* 10 (1872) 124. *[Egyptian Calendar]*

C. W. Goodwin, "Notes on the calendar in Mr. Smith's papyrus," *ZÄS* 11 (1873) 107-109. *[Pap. Ebers]*

*P. le Page Renouf, "Calendar of Astronomical Observations found in Royal Tombs of the XXth dynasty," *SBAT* 3 (1874) 400-421.

*Cedron, "The Ritual Temple. The Calendar," *CongL* 4 (1875) 161-167.

†Theo. G. Pinches, "Observations upon Calendars of the Ancient Babylonians, now in the British Museum," *SBAP* 4 (1881-82) 32-33.

B. S. Clarke, "The Reckoning of Days in Use among the Ancient Hebrews," *CM* 15 (1882) 43-55.

Francis Brown, "Babylonian Calendars," *PR* 3 (1882) 399.

*A. H. Sayce, "Miscellaneous Notes," *ZA* 2 (1887) 331-340. [17. Agricultural Calendar, pp. 333-335]

A. H. Sayce, "A Babylonian Saints' Calendar," *ONTS* 7 (1887-88) 134-135.

*M. Friedmann, "The New Year and Its Liturgy," *JQR* 1 (1888-89) 62-75.

Thomas Laurie, "Assyrian Months," *BS* 46 (1889) 564-565.

*C[laude] R. Conder, "The Hebrew Months," *PEFQS* 21 (1889) 21-24.

*Terrien de Lacouperie, "Hyspaosines, Kharacenian king, on a Babylonian Tablet dated 127 a.c. and the Arsacian era, 248 a.c.," *BOR* 4 (1889-90) 136-144.

*Benjamin Wisner Bacon, "Chronology of the account of the Flood in P.—A Contribution to the History of the Jewish Calendar," *AJSL* 8 (1891-92) 79-88.

*Benjamin Wisner Bacon, "II. The Calendar of Enoch and Jubilees," *AJSL* 8 (1891-92) 124-131.

Emmeline Plunket, "The Accadian Calendar," *SBAP* 14 (1891-92) 112-119.

F. L. Griffith, "The Ancient Egyptian Year," *SBAP* 14 (1891-92) 260-263. (Note by P. le Page Renouf, pp. 264-265)

*W. Muss-Arnolt, "The Names of the Assyro-Babylonian Months and Their Regents," *JBL* 11 (1892) 72-94, 160-176.

W. Marsham Adams, "Note on the Babylonian Kalendar*[sic]*," *BOR* 7 (1893-94) 66-67.

W. A. B., "The Egyptian Cycles—4677," *DownsR* 13 (1894) 172-180.

Rufus B. Richardson, "A Sacrificial Calendar from the Attic Epakria," *AJA, O.S.,* 10 (1895) 209-226.

T. Nicklin, "The Attic civil and sacred years," *JP* 24 (1895-96) 54-82.

*E[mmeline] M. Plunkett, "The Median Calendar and the Constellation Taurus," *SBAP* 19 (1897) 229-249. [Note by J[oseph] Offord, pp. 243-245]

*J. F. Hewitt, "The History of the Week as a Guide to Historic Chronology," *WR* 148 (1897) 8-22, 126-149, 237-250.

S. Poznanski, "Ben Meir and the Origin of the Jewish Calendar," *JQR* 10 (1897-98) 152-161.

*Charles Warren, "Dates on Which Paschal Full Moons Occur," *PEFQS* 32 (1900) 157-164.

J. A. Selbie, "The Seven Days' Week and the Names of its Days," *ET* 12 (1900-01) 70.

E. L. Butcher, "The Egyptian Month Abib," *ET* 12 (1900-01) 191.

John M. Mecklin, "The Calendar of the Hebrews," *CFL, N.S.,* 4 (1901) 329-336.

*Joseph Offord, "Araza and Aziza, and other Archæological Notes," *SBAP* 23 (1901) 244-247. [Median Calendar, pp. 245-246]

(Miss) E. M. Plunket, "The Chinese Calendar, with some remarks with reference to that of the Chaldeans," *SBAP* 23 (1901) 367-377.

George Melville Bolling, "Beginning of the Greek Day," *AJP* 23 (1902) 428-435.

Louis H. Gray, "The Origin of the Names of the Avesta Months," *AJSL* 20 (1903-04) 194-201.

M. A. Power, "Bishop Lightfoot and Professor Ramsay on Early Calendars," *ET* 15 (1903-04) 515-518.

J. K. Fotheringham, "The formation of the Julian Calendar, with reference to the astronomical year," *JP* 29 (1903-04) 87-99.

*E[dward] Mahler, "The *Ḥodeš Ḥ'abib* חדש האביב in which the Exodus took place: and its identification with the Epiphi of the Egyptian 'Nature-year'," *SBAP* 27 (1905) 255-259.

Anonymous, "Editorial Notes. The Jewish Calendar," *ICMM* 2 (1905-06) 237-241.

C. H. W. Johns, "The Amorite Calendar," *Exp, 7th Ser.,* 1 (1906) 123-132, 337-345.

Alan H. Gardiner, "Mesore as the first month of the Egyptian year," *ZÄS* 43 (1906) 136-144.

*G. Legge, "Is the a heliacal rising," *RTR* 31 (1908) 106-112.

*F. A. Jones, "The Ancient Year and the Sothic Cycle," *SBAP* 30 (1908) 95-106.

C. H. W. Johns, "On the Length of the Month in Babylonia," *SBAP* 30 (1908) 221-230.

*Mark Lidzbarski, G. B. Gray, and E. J. Pilcher, "An Old Hebrew Calendar-Inscription from Gezer," *PEFQS* 41 (1909) 26-34.

*Samuel Diaches, "Notes on the Gezer Calendar and Some Babylonian Parallels," *PEFQS* 41 (1909) 113-118.

W. S. Auchincloss, "The Year of Our Era," *RP* 8 (1909) 242-244.

*Morris Jastrow Jr., "Months and Days in Babylonian-Assyrian Astrology," *AJSL* 26 (1909-10) 151-155.

Emmeline Plunket, "The Accadian Calendar," *SBAP* 32 (1910) 11-17, 55-63.

*Martin Sprengling, "Chronological Notes from the Aramaic Papyri. The Jewish Calendar. Dates of the Achaemenians (Cyrus-Darius II)," *AJSL* 27 (1910-11) 233-266.

P. S. P. Handcock, "Fresh Light on the Jewish Calendar," *ET* 22 (1910-11) 500-502.

George A. Barton, "The Babylonain Calendar in the Reigns of Lugalanda and Urkagina," *JAOS* 31 (1910-11) 251-271.

H. C. Tomam, "Identification of the Ancient Persian Month Garmapada in the Light of the Recently Found Aramaic Papyrus Fragments," *AJP* 32 (1911) 444-445.

*G. Margoliouth, "The Calendar, The Sabbath, and the Marriage Law in the Geniza-Zadokite Document," *ET* 23 (1911-12) 362-365. [I. The Calendar]

*S[tephen] Langdon, "Astronomy and the Early Sumerian Calendar," *SBAP* 34 (1912) 248-256.

Theophilus G. Pinches, "The Babylonian Month-Names of the Fifth Series," *SBAP* 34 (1912) 292-295.

*M. Gaster, "The Feast of Jeroboam and the Samaritan Calendar," *ET* 24 (1912-13) 198-201.

George A. Barton, "Recent Researches in the Sumerian Calendar," *JAOS* 33 (1913) 1-9.

George A. Barton, "Kugler's Criterion for Determining the Order of the Months in the Earliest Babylonian Calendar," *JAOS* 33 (1913) 297-305.

Paul Haupt, "The Cuneiform Name of the Second Adar," *JBL* 32 (1913) 139-145.

*Paul Haupt, "The Names of the Months on SP. ii, 263," *JBL* 32 (1913) 273-274.

Theophilus G. Pinches, "Notes upon the Early Sumerian Month-Names," *SBAP* 35 (1913) 123-128.

Francis A. Cunningham, "The Sothic Cycle used by the Egyptians," *JAOS* 34 (1914) 369-373.

Paul Haupt, "The Grain Growing Month," *JBL* 33 (1914) 298.

F. W. Read, "Egyptian Calendars of Lucky and Unlucky Days," *SBAP* 38 (1916) 19-26, 60-69.

*S[tephen] Langdon, "Critical Notes. III. The Sign in the Name of the Fourth Month at Umma," *AJSL* 33 (1916-17) 48-49.

*C. C. Edgar, "On the dating of early Ptolemaic papyri," *ASAE* 17 (1917) 209-223. [§2. The Macedonian Calendar, pp. 219-222]

*Paul Haupt, "Heb. *Ämš*, Yesterday - Assyr. *Ina Mûši*," *JBL* 36 (1917) 147-148.

Joseph Offord, "Archaeological Notes on Jewish Antiquities. XXXII. *Palestinian and Phoenician Month Names*," *PEFQS* 49 (1917) 101-103.

E. Walter Maunder, "The Mosaic Calendar," *JTVI* 51 (1919) 136-160. [(Discussion, pp. 160-166.) (Communications by D. R. Fotheringham, p. 165; J. K. Fotheringham, pp. 167-170; A. H. Finn, pp. 170-172; G. Mackinlay, p. 172)]

*S[tephen] Langdon, "Assyrian Lexicographical Notes," *JRAS* (1920) 325-331. [1. Bararitu, *evening, first watch*, pp. 325-326]

St. H. Stephan, "The Division of the Year in Palestine," *JPOS* 22 (1922) 159-170.

*A. J. Wensinck, "The Semitic New Year and the Origin of Eschatology," *AO* 1 (1922-23) 158-199.

*F. W. Read, "Regnal Years and Calendar Years in Egypt," *AEE* 8 (1923) 111-115.

*Andrew C. Baird, "Babylonian Number Systems and the Origin of the Calendar," *GUOST* 5 (1923-28) 9-14.

Julian Morgenstern, "The Three Calendars of Ancient Israel," *HUCA* 1 (1924) 13-78. [I. The Problem; II. The time of the Transition from Calendar I to Calendar II; III. The Time of Transition from Calendar II to Calendar III; IV. The Date of Ṣukkoṯ-New Year's Festival; V. Ṣukkoṯ – New Year's Festival at the Time of Ezra and Nehemiah; VI. The Date of the Dedication of Solomon's Temple; VII. The Date of the Dedication of the Tabernacle in the Wilderness; VIII. The Date of the Passover Festival; IX. The Solar Character of Calendar I; X. The Luni-Solar Character of Calendar II; XI. The Relation of Calendar III to Calendar II; XII. Summary]

*A. Anselm Parker, "The Old Testament and the Jubilee Year," *AER* 73 (1925) 481-490. [I. Facts from the Old Testament, pp. 482-483]

Paul Haupt, "The Origin of the name Veadar," *JAOS* 45 (1925) 320-322. *[Babylonian Calendar]*

Julian Morgenstern, "Additional Notes on 'The Three Calendars of Ancient Israel'," *HUCA* 3 (1926) 77-107.

Warren R. Dawson, "Some Observations on the Egyptian Calendars of Lucky and Unlucky Days," *JEA* 12 (1926) 260-264.

*Andrew C. Baird, "Babylonian Number Systems and the Origin of the Calendar," *GUOST* 5 (1923-28) 9-14.

*K. Budde, "The Sabbath and the Week," *JTS* 30 (1928-29) 1-15.

W. Bell Dawson, "The Hebrew Calendar, and Time Periods," *JTVI* 61 (1929) 40-50, 58-59. [(Discussion, pp; 50-57) (Communication by Norman S. Denham, pp. 57-58)]

Cornelius C. Berning, "The Egyptian Calendar," *SS* 5 (1931) 46-53.

Kenneth Scott, "Greek and Roman Honorific Months," *YCS* 2 (1931) 199-278.

A[lexander] Pogo, "Calendars on coffin Lids from Asyut (Second half of the third millenium)," *Isis* 17 (1932) 6-24.

Allen B. West, "Correspondences Between the Delian and Athenian Calendars in the Years 443 and 442 B.C.," *AJA* 38 (1934) 1-9.

*Ferris J. Stephens, "Concerning Sumerian *mu-an-na*, 'Year'," *AJSL* 51 (1934-35) 48-49.

Julian Morgenstern, "Supplementary Studies in the Calendars of Ancient Israel," *HUCA* 10 (1935) 1-148.

Jotham Johnson, "Observations of the Equinox at Petra," *JAOS* 55 (1935) 464-465.

Cyrus H. Gordon, "The Names of the Months of the Nuzi Calendar," *RDSO* 15 (1935) 253-257.

*Edward Robertson, "The Days of the Week and of the Month in Arab Folk-Lore," *JMUEOS* #20 (1936) 19-24.

Alexander Pogo, "Three unpublished calendars from Asyut," *Osiris* 1 (1936) 500-509.

*S[tephen] Langdon, "Philological Notes," *RAAO* 33 (1936) 191-196. [VI. The length of daylight in each month, pp. 194-195]

*T. C. Skeat, "The Reigns of the Ptolemies. With Tables for Converting Egyptian Dates to the Julian System," *Miz* 6 (1937) 7-40. [Introduction; Instructions for Use of the Tables; Table of Regnal Years; On the Insertion of a Sixth Epegomenal Day; Table A; Table B; Notes to the Table of Reigns]

S. H. Taqizadeh, "An Ancient Persian Practice Preserved by a non-Iranian People," *BSOAS* 9 (1937-39) 603-619. [The Mandæan Calendar]

*Malcom F. McGregor, "The Last Campaign of Kleon and the Athenian Calendar in 422/1 B.C.," *AJP* 59 (1938) 145-168.

Arno Poebel, "The Names and the Order of the Old Persian and Elamite Months During the Achaemenian Period," *AJSL* 55 (1938) 130-141.

Cyrus H. Gordon and Ernest R. Lacheman, "The Nuzu Menology," *ArOr* 10 (1938) 51-64.

*J[ulian] Morgenstern, "The Calendar of Deuteronomy," *JBL* 57 (1938) viii.

*Carl W. Blegen, "Prosymna: Remains of Post-Mycenaean Date," *AJA* 43 (1939) 410-444. [Sun Dial, pp. 443-444]

Milton Giffler, "The Calendar of Cos," *AJA* 43 (1939) 445-446.

Julius Lewy, "The Assyrian Calendar," *ArOr* 11 (1939-40) 35-46.

H. E. Winlock, "The Origin of the Ancient Egyptian Calendar," *PAPS* 83 (1940) 447-464.

H. M. Hoenigswald, "On Etruscan and Latin Month-Names," *AJP* 62 (1941) 199-206.

*Sterling Dow, "Corinthiaca. I. The Month Phoinikaios," *AJA* 46 (1942) 69-72. *[Calendar]*

Grace Amadon, "Ancient Jewish Calendation," *JBL* 61 (1942) 227-280. [I. The Problem; II. Nature of the Ancient Jewish Calendar; III. Active Principles Governing the Moons of Ancient Jewish Time; IV. Why 30 A.D. Was Not the Crucifixion Date; V. Calendar Demonstration of the Crucifixion Date; VI. Other Scripture Synchronisms; VII. Conclusions]

T. Fish, "A New Detail Relating to the Drehem Calendar," *JMUEOS* #23 (1942) 21-23.

O. Neugebauer, "The Origin of the Egyptian Calendar," *JNES* 1 (1942) 396-403.

Hildegard Lewy and Julius Lewy, "The Origin of the Week and the Oldest West Asiatic Calendar," *HUCA* 17 (1942-43) 1-152c.

Walter F. Snyder, "When Was the Alexandrian Calendar Established?" *AJP* 64 (1943) 385-398.

J[aroslav] Černý, "The origin of the name of the month Tybi," *ASAE* 43 (1943) 173-181.

*W[illiam] F[oxwell] Albright, "The Gezer Calendar," *BASOR* #92 (1943) 16-26.

*George G. Cameron, "The Babylonian Scientist and His Hebrew Colleague," *BA* 7 (1944) 21-29, 32-40. [The Babylonian Calendar, pp. 26-27]

*Louis Finkelstein, "A Talmudic Note on the Word for Cutting Flax in the Gezer Calendar," *BASOR* #94 (1944) 28-29.

Julius Lewy, "Neo-Babylonian Names of the Days of the Week?" *BASOR* #95 (1944) 34-36.

R. A. Parker, "Ancient Jewish Calendation: A Criticism," *JBL* 63 (1944) 173-176.

Grace Amadon, "The Crucifixion Calendar," *JBL* 53 (1944) 177-190.

A. L. Oppenheim, "The Neo-Babylonian Week Again," *BASOR* #97 (1945) 27-29.

*Lynn H. Wood, "The Kahun Papyrus and the Date of the Twelfth Dynasty (with a Chart)," *BASOR* #99 (1945) 5-9.

*Alan H. Gardiner, "Regnal Years and Civil Calendar in Pharaonic Egypt," *JEA* 31 (1945) 11-28.

P. J. Heawood, "The Beginning of the Jewish Day," *JQR, N.S.,* 36 (1945-46) 393-401.

Solomon Zeitlin, "The Beginning of the Jewish Day During the Second Commonwealth," *JQR, N.S.,* 36 (1945-46) 403-414.

Kendrick Pritchett, "Months in Dorian Calendars," *AJA* 50 (1946) 358-360.

H. Torczyner, "A New Interpretation of the Gezer Calendar," *BIES* 13 (1946-47) #1/2, I-II.

*Julian Morgenstern, "The Chanukkah Festival and the Calendar of Ancient Israel," *HUCA* 20 (1947) 1-136.

P. J. Heawood, "The Beginning of the Jewish Day," *ET* 59 (1947-48) 250-251.

P. J. Heawood, "Correspondence. The Beginning of the Jewish Day During the Second Commonwealth," *JQR, N.S.,* 38 (1947-48) 215-216.

S[olomon] Zeitlin, Correspondence. The Beginning of the Jewish Day During the Second Commonwealth," *JQR, N.S.*, 38 (1947-48) 216-219.

Solomon Gandz, "Studies in the Hebrew Calendar," *PAAJR* 17 (1947-48) 9-17.

R. W. Sloley, "The origin of the 365-day Egyptian calendar," *ASAE* 48 (1948) 261-265.

Abd El-Mohsen Bakir, "The Cairo calendar of lucky and unlucky days *(Journal d'Entrée,* No. 86637)," *ASAE* 48 (1948) 425-431.

*Julian Morgenstern, "The Chanukkah Festival and the Calendar of Ancient Israel," *HUCA* 21 (1948) 365-496.

T. C. Skeat, "The Macedonian Calendar during the Reign of Ptolemy Euergetes I," *JEA* 34 (1948) 75-79.

Solomon Gandz, "Studies in the Hebrew Calendar I," *JQR, N.S.* 39 (1948-49) 259-280.

L. H. Wood, "Fifth-century Jewish Calendation as Shown by the Assuan Papyri," *JBL* 68 (1949) xvii.

Agnes Kirsopp Michels, 'The 'Calendar of Numa' and the Pre-Julian Calendar," *TAPA* 80 (1949) 320-346.

Solomon Gandz, "Studies in the Hebrew Calendar II," *JQR, N.S.* 40 (1949-50) 157-172, 251-277.

*Jaroslav Černý, "Philological and etymological notes," *ASAE* 51 (1951) 441-446. [III, 6. Age of the Egyptian month names, pp. 441-442]

*Jaroslav Černý, "Philological and etymological notes," *ASAE* 51 (1951) 441-446. [III, 8. The words for the first and the last day of the month, pp. 444-446]

*Albrecht Goetze, "On the Hittite Words of 'Year' and the Seasons and for 'Night' and 'Day'," *Lang* 27 (1951) 467-476.

T. Fish, "Drehem Calendar: Šulgi 34-46," *MCS* 1 (1951) 45.

S. H. Taqizadeh, "The Old Iranian Calendars Again," *BSOAS* 14 (1952) 603-611. [Correction by W. B. Henning, *BSOAS* 15 (1952) p. 39]

R[ichard] A. Parker, "Sothic Dates and the Calendar 'Adjustment'," *RÉg* 9 (1952) 101-108.

Solomon Gandz, "The Calendar of *Seder Olam*," *JQR, N.S.*, 43 (1952-53) 177-192, 249-270.

E. B. Smick, "Hebrew Menologies," *JBL* 72 (1953) viii-ix.

Richard A. Parker, "The Names of the Sixteenth Day of the Lunar Month," *JNES* 12 (1953) 50. *[Egyptian]*

S. H. Horn and L. H. Wood, "The Fifth-Century Jewish Calendar at Elephantine," *JNES* 13 (1954) 1-20.

T. G. H. James, "The date of the month *rkḥ wr*," *JEA* 41 (1955) 123.

Richard A. Parker, "Some Considerations on the Nature of the Fifth-Century Jewish Calendar at Elephantine," *JNES* 14 (1955) 271-274.

Alan [H.] Gardiner, "The Problem of the Month-Names," *RÉg* 10 (1955) 9-31.

B. L. van der Waerden, "Tables for the Egyptian and Alexandrian Calendar," *Isis* 47 (1956) 387-390.

Richard A. Parker, "The Lunar Dates of Tutmose III and Ramesses II," *JNES* 16 (1957) 39-43.

Richard A. Parker, "The Problem of the Month-Names: A Reply," *RÉg* 11 (1957) 85-107.

J. B. Segal, "Intercalation and the Hebrew Calendar," *VT* 7 (1957) 250-307.

*E. R. Leach, "A possible method of intercalation for the calendar of the Book of Jubilees," *VT* 7 (1957) 392-397.

Van L. Johnson, "Those Superstitions about the Nundinae," *AJA* 62 (1958) 223-224. *[Roman Calendar]*

*Joseph M. Baumgarten, "The Beginning of the Day in the Calendar of Jubilees," *JBL* 77 (1958) 355-360.

*George R. Hughes," The Sixth Day of the Lunar Month and the Demotic Word for 'Cult Guild'," *MDIÄA* 16 (1958) 147-160.

S. Talmon, "Divergences in the Calendar-Reckoning in Ephraim and Judah," *VT* 8 (1958) 48-75.

A. M. Bakir, "The groups with and in the light of the Cairo Calendar," *ASAE* 56 (1959) 203-206.

*P. Hulin, "A Hemerological Text from Nimrud," *Iraq* 21 (1959) 42-53. [ND. 5545]

Solomon Zeitlin, "The Beginning of the Day in the Calendar of Jubilees," *JBL* 78 (1959) 153-156. [Reply by Joseph M. Baumgarten, p. 157]

*John Bowman, "Is the Samaritan Calendar the Old Zadokite One?" *PEQ* 91 (1959) 23-37.

*Wolf Wirgin, "The Calendar Tablet from Gezer," *EI* 6 (1960) 9*-12*.

J. Drescher, "A new Coptic month," *JEA* 46 (1960) 111-112.

Einar, Gjerstad, "Notes on the Early Roman Calendar," *AA* 32 (1961) 193-214.

*Wolf Leslau, "The Names of the Week in Ethiopic," *JSS* 6 (1961) 62-70.

*J. B. Segal, "The Hebrew Festivals and the Calendar," *JSS* 6 (1961) 74-94.

F. S. North, "Four-month seasons of the Hebrew Bible," *VT* 11 (1961) 446-448.

*J. B. Segal, "'YRḤ' in the Gezar 'Calendar'," *JSS* 7 (1962) 212-221.

Maurice L. Zigmond, "The Jewish Calendar—A Dilemma," *CCARJ* 10 (1962-63) #2, 32-37.

*Joseph M. Baumgarten, "The Calendar of the Book of Jubilees and the Bible," *Tarbiz* 32 (1962-63) #4, I-II.

*Earle Hilgert, "The Jubilees Calendar and the Origin of Sunday Observance," *AUSS* 1 (1963) 44-51.

S. Talmon, "The Gezer Calendar and the Seasonal Cycle of Ancient Canaan," *JAOS* 83 (1963) 177-187.

Benjamin D. Meritt, "Athenian Calendar Problems," *TAPA* 95 (1964) 200-260.

Benjamin D. Meritt, "The Metonic Cycle in Athens," *AJA* 69 (1965) 171.

*Alan E. Samuel, "Year 27 = 30 and 88 B.C.," *CdÉ* 40 (1965) 376-400.

*J. M. Baumgarten, "The Counting of the Sabbath in Ancient Sources," *VT* 16 (1966) 277-286.

H. R. Stroes, "Does the Day Begin with Evening or Morning?" *VT* 16 (1966) 460-475.

*Solmon Zeitlin, "The Judaean Calendar during the Second Commonwealth and the Scrolls," *JQR, N.S.,* 57 (1966-67) 28-45.

*Robert F. Healey, "A Gennetic Sacrifice List in the Athenian State Calendar," *AJA* 71 (1967) 189.

Javier Teixidor, "The Calendar Used in the Texts of Hatra," *AJA* 71 (1967) 195.

Elias J. Bickerman, "The 'Zoroastrian' Calendar," *ArOr* 35 (1967) 197-207.

*Siegfried H. Horn, "The Babylonian Chronicle and the Ancient Calendar of the Kingdom of Judah," *AUSS* 5 (1967) 12-27.

Van L. Johnson, "The Primitive Basis of Our Calendar," *Arch* 21 (1968) 14-21.

§117 *2.3.21.1 The Zodiac & Horoscopes*

Samuel Henley, "Observations on the Zodiac at Dendera (anciently Tentyra)," *MMBR* 14 (1802) 295-300.

†Capel Lofft, "On Constellations commemorative of the Hebrew Cipher of the Heavens," *MMBR* 33 (1812) 315-317.

*†Anonymous, "Ancient Chronology," *BCQTR, 4th Ser.,* 12 (1832) 120-141. *(Review) [Zodiac]*

*G. Seyffarth, "Three Lectures on Egyptian Antiquities, &c., delivered at the Stuyvesant Institute, New York, May 1856," *ER* 8 (1856-57) 34-104. [IX. The Zodiac of Dendera, pp. 78-79]

*J. C. C. Clarke, "Jacob's Zodiac, " *ONTS* 2 (1882-83) 155-158.

*O. D. Miller, "Zodiacal Chronology," *AAOJ* 12 (1890) 313-328.

*Robert Brown Jr., "Remarks on the Euphratean Astronomical Names of the Signs of the Zodiac," *SBAP* 13 (1890-91) 246-271.

*(Miss) E. M. Plunket, "The Constellation Aries," *SBAP* 15 (1892-93) 237-242. *[Akkadian Calendar]*

*(Miss) E. M. Plunket, " (*Gu*), the Eleventh Constellation of the Zodiac," *SBAP* 18 (1896) 65-70.

*†(Miss) E. M. Plunket, "The Median Calendar and the Constellation Taurus," *SBAP* 19 (1897) 229-243. (Note by J. Offord, pp. 243-245; Additional Note by Miss E. Plunket, pp. 246-249)

*A. B. Grimaldi, "The Zodiacal Arrangement of the Stars: in its Historical and Biblical Connections," *JTVI* 38 (1906) 235-237. [(Discussion, pp. 237-239)(Communication by George Mackinlay, pp. 239-241)]

Paul Carus, "Zodiacs of Different Nations," *OC* 20 (1906) 458-483.

*Geo. St. Clair, "Israel in Camp: A Study," *JTS* 8 (1906-07) 185-217. *[The Twelve Tribes and the Zodiac]*

*C. J. Ball, C. H. W. Johns, Theophilus G. Pinches, and A. H. Sayce, "Communications on the 'Zodiac-Tablet' from Gezer," *PEFQS* 40 (1908) 26-30.

*George St. Clair, "Notes and Queries. 5. *The Zodiac-Tablet,*" *PEFQS* 40 (1908) 78-79.

*C[laude] R. Conder, "Notes and Queries. 1. *The Gezer Zodiacal Signs,*" *PEFQS* 40 (1908) 162-163.

*William J. Hinke, "The Significance of the Symbols on Babylonian Boundary Stones," *AJA* 20 (1916) 76-77. *[Zodiac]*

Nelson Glueck, "The Zodiac of Khirbet et-Tannûr," *BASOR* #126 (1952) 5-10.

A. Sachs, "Babylonian Horoscopes," *JCS* 6 (1952) 49-75.

B. L. van der Waerden, "History of the Zodiac," *AfO* 16 (1952-53) 216-230. [Introduction; Chapter I. The Babylonian Zodiac; Chapter II. The Greek Zodiac; Chapter III, The Egyptian Zodiac]

*I. Sonne, "The Zodiac Panel in the Bet-Alpha Synagogue," *JBL* 72 (1953) vi.

*O. Neugebauer, "Melothesia and Dodecatemoria," *SBO* 3 (1959) 270-275.

O. Neugebauer and Richard A. Parker, "Two Demotic Horoscopes," *JEA* 54 (1968) 231-235.

§118 *2.3.21.2 Date Formulae, Year Dates, Regnal Years, etc.*

*John D. Davis, "The Fourteenth Year of King Hezekiah," *PRR* 1 (1880) 100-105.

†*J. Oppert, "Eclipse, Ninety-one Years after the Death of Ahab, King of Israel," *SBAP* 8 (1885-86) 58-59.

*John A. Paine, "The Eclipse of the 7th year of Cambyses," *JAOS* 14 (1890) xc-xciii.

E. L. Curtis, "The Old Testament Reckoning of Regnal Years," *JBL* 14 (1895) 125-130.

*F. W. Read, "A Supposed Eclipse of the Moon under XXIInd Egyptian Dynasty," *SBAP* 21 (1899) 309-310.

C. H. W. Johns, "The Year Names of Samsu-iluna," *SBAP* 25 (1903) 325-326.

*C. H. W. Johns, "The First Year of Samsu-iluna," *SBAP* 30 (1908) 70-71.

*Stephen Langdon, "Miscellanea Assyriaca," *Baby* 7 (1913-23) 39-50. [I. Date Formulae of Larsa]

*F. W. Read, "Regnal Years and Calendar Years in Egypt," *AEE* 8 (1923) 111-115.

T. Eric Peet, "A Possible Year Date of King Ramesses VII," *JEA* 11 (1925) 72-75.

Jaroslav Černý, "A Note on the 'Repeating of Births'," *JEA* 15 (1929) 194-198. *[Year Dates]*

*J. A. Montgomery, "The Year-Eponymate in the Hebrew Monarchy," *JBL* 49 (1930) 311-319.

S[tephen] Langdon, "Double Dating in the Reigns of Rim-Sin and Hammurabi," *RAAO* 27 (1930) 79-82.

S[tephen] Langdon, "A Year Date of Ibi-Sin in an Historical Inscription," *RAAO* 31 (1934) 114.

*S[tephen] Langdon, "The Sumerian Word for 'Year' and Origin of the Custom of Dating by Events," *RAAO* 32 (1935) 131-149.

Ferris J. Stephens, "New Date Formulae of the Isin Dynasty," *RAAO* 33 (1936) 11-26.

*T. C. Skeat, "The Reigns of the Ptolemies. With Tables for Converting Egyptian Dates to the Julian System," *Miz* 6 (1937) 7-40. [Introduction; Instructions for Use of the Tables; Table of Regnal Years; On the Insertion of a Sixth Epegomenal Day; Table A; Table B; Notes to the Table of Reigns]

*W[illam] F[oxwell] Albright, "A Third Revision of the Early Chronology of Western Asia," *BASOR* #88 (1942) 28-36. [A Fixed Date in Early Hebrew History? pp. 33-36]

Francis R[ue] Steele, "Notes on Ur III Date Formulae," *JAOS* 63 (1943) 155-158.

Grace Amadon, "The Jewish Regnal Year under Babylonian and Persian Rule," *JBL* 64 (1945) v.

*Alan H. Gardiner, "Regnal Years and Civil Calendar in Pharaonic Egypt," *JEA* 31 (1945) 11-28.

Alan H. Gardiner, "The Accession Day of Sesostris I," *JEA* 32 (1946) 100.

Vaughn E. Crawford, "An Ishbī-Irra Date Formula," *JCS* 2 (1948) 13-19.

*Taha Baqir, "A Date-List of Isbi-Irra From An Unpublished Text in the Iraq Museum," *Sumer* 4 (1948) 103-114. [IM 11794]

*Alan [H.] Gardiner, "The Reading of the Word for Regnal Year," *JNES* 8 (1949) 165-171.

Taha Baqir, "Date-Formulae and Date-Lists," *Sumer* 5 (1949) 34-86.

Taha Baqir, "Supplement to the Date-Formulae from Harmal," *Sumer* 5 (1949) 136-143.

Francis Rue Steele, "The Date Formulae of Shu-ilishu of Isin," *BASOR* #122 (1951) 45-49.

Albrecht Goetze, "The Year Names of Abī-Ěsuḫ," *JCS* 5 (1951) 98-103.

*Barbara E. Morgan, "Dated Texts and Date-Formulae of some First Dynasty Kings," *MCS* 2 (1952)16-22.

Barbara E. Morgan, "Dated Texts and Date-Formulae of the Reign of Ammizaduga," *MCS* 2 (1952) 31-37.

Barbara E. Morgan, "Dated Texts and Date-Formulae of the Reign of Ammiditana," *MCS* 2 (1952) 44-53.

Barbara E. Morgan, "Dated Texts and Date-Formulae of Sinmuballit," *MCS* 3 (1953) 33-36.

Barbara E. Morgan, "Dated Texts and Date-Formulae of the Reign of Samsuiluna," *MCS* 3 (1953) 56-69.

Barbara E. Morgan, "Dated Texts of the Reign of Abiešuh," *MCS* 3 (1953) 72-76.

Barbara E. Morgan, "Dated Texts and Date-Formulae of the Reign of Samsuditana," *MCS* 3 (1953) 76-79.

Barbara E. Morgan, "The Year-Formulae of the First Dynasty of Babylon," *MCS* 4 (1954) 24-61.

*Barbara E. Morgan, "Index of Words and Phrases in the Year-Formulae of the First Babylonian Dynasty," *MCS* 4 (1954) 62-77.

Cyril Aldred, "Year Twelve at El-'Amārna," *JEA* 43 (1957) 114-117.

*William C. Hayes, "Varia from the Time of Hatshepsut," *MDIÄA* 15 (1957) 78-90. [1. Dated Inscriptions of "Reignal Year 7", pp. 78-80]

J. J. Finkelstein, "The Year Dates of Samsuditana," *JCS* 13 (1959) 39-49.

*Albrecht Goetze, "The Chronology of Šulgi Angain," *Iraq* 22 (1960) 151-156.

*H. W. Fairman, "The supposed Year 21 of Akhenaten," *JEA* 46 (1960) 108-109.

*Richard T. Hallock, "The 'One Year' of Darius I," *JNES* 19 (1960) 36-39.

Erica Reiner, "The Year Dates of Sumu-jamūtbāl," *JCS* 15 (1961) 121-124.

Jaroslav Černý, "Three Regnal Dates of the Eighteenth Dynasty," *JEA* 50 (1964) 37-39. [1. The supposed year 39 of Amenophis III; 2. The supposed year 7 of Smenkhkerē'; 3. The highest regnal date of Tut'ankhamūn]

*Alger F. Johns, "Did David Use Assyrian-Type Annals?" *AUSS* 3 (1965) 97-109.

Albrecht Goetze, "Date Formula of Iddin-Dagān of Isin," *JCS* 19 (1965) 56.

*H. K. Jacquet-Gordon, "The Illusory Year 36 of Osorkon I," *JEA* 53 (1967) 63-68.

*Ricardo A. Caminos, "An Ancient Egyptian Donation Stela in the Archaeological Museum of Florence (Inv. No. 7207)," *Cent* 14 (1969) 42-46. *[Regnal Year]*

§119 *2.3.21.4 Sabbatical and Jubilee Years*

*A. Anselm Parker, "The Old Testament and the Jubilee Year," *AER* 73 (1925) 481-490. [I. Facts from the Old Testament, pp. 482-483]

*Eli Ginsberg, "Studies in the Economics of the Bible," *JQR, N.S.,* 22 (1931-32) 343-408. [II. The Sabbatical Year, pp. 351-364; III. The Jubilee Year, pp. 364-391]

John B. Alexander, "A Babylonian Year of Jubilee," *JBL* 57 (1938) 75-80.

Solomon Zeitlin, "A Note on the Sabbatical Cycles," *JQR, N.S.,* 35 (1944-45) 238-239.

*Robert North, "The Biblical Jubilee and Social Reform," *Scrip* 4 (1949-51) 323-335.

*Gerald J. Blidstein, "Man and Nature in the Sabbatical Year," *Trad* 8 (1965-66) #4, 48-55.

Sidney B. Hoenig, "Sabbatical Years and the Year of Jubilee," *JQR, N.S.,* 59 (1968-69) 222-236.

§120 *2.3.21.5 Concepts of Time & Timekeeping Devices*

*(   ) R., "'Time' in the Old Testament," *ONTS* 3 (1883-84) 205-207.

C. M. Mead, "Is Time a Reality? An Examination of Professor Bowne's Doctrine of Time," *BS* 43 (1886) 601-631.

*John Q. Bittinger, "Septenary Time and the Origin of the Sabbath," *BS* 46 (1889) 321-342.

*C[laude] R. Conder, "The Hebrew Months," *PEFQS* 21 (1889) 21-24.

C[onrad] Schick, "Reports from Herr Baurath von Schick. 4. *Reckoning of time among the Armenians*," *PEFQS* 27 (1895) 110.

*W. W. Crump, "A Day's Journey, " *Exp, 6th Ser.,* 2 (1900) 211-215.

*Leslie J. Walker, "Time, Eternity and God," *HJ* 18 (1919-20) 36-48.

*E. J. Pilcher, "Portable Sundial from Gezer," *PEFQS* 55 (1923) 85-89.

R. W. Sloley, "Ancient Clepsydrae," *AEE* 9 (1924) 43-50. {Note by [W. M.] F[linders] P[etrie], p. 50} *[Water Clocks]*

*M[oses] Marcus, "Space and Time in Relation to the Existence of God According to the Talmud," *JIQ* 4 (1927-28) #1, 7-9.

Alfred T. Schofield, "Time and Eternity," *JTVI* 59 (1927) 281-291, 300-301. [(Discussion, pp. 291-297) (Communications by Miss C. Tindall, p. 297; W. Bell Dawson, pp. 297-298; John Tuckwell, pp. 298-300)]

*A. T. Richardson, "Time-Measures of the Pentateuch," *ET* 39 (1927-28) 515-519.

*A. T. Richardson, "'Time-Measures of the Pentateuch'," *ET* 41 (1929-30) 45-46.

*Solomon Gandz, "The Origin of the Term Gnomon or the Gnomon in Hebrew Literature," *PAAJR* 2 (1930-31) 23-28. *[Sundial]*

R. W. Sloley, "Primitive Methods of Measuring Time, with Special Reference to Egypt," *JEA* 17 (1931) 166-178.

A[lexander] Pogo, "Egyptian water clocks," *Isis* 25 (1936) 403-425.

*Henry S. Robinson, "The Tower of the Winds and the Roman Market-place," *AJA* 46 (1942) 123-124; 47 (1943) 291-305.

*Paul S. Minear, "The Conception of History in the Prophets and Jesus," *JAAR* 11 (1943) 156-161. [II. The Time-Consciousness of the Prophets and Jesus, pp. 158-160]

*O. Neugebauer, "Studies in Ancient Astronomy. VIII. The Water Clock in Babylonian Astronomy," *Isis* 37 (1947) 37-43.

Abraham J. Heschel, "Architecture of Time," *Jud* 1 (1952) 44-51.

Trude Weiss-Rosmarin, "Time and Space," *Jud* 1 (1952) 277-278.

Solomon Gandz, "The division of the hour in Hebrew literature," *Osiris* 10 (1952) 10-34.

Eric C. Rust, "Time and Eternity in Biblical Thought," *TT* 10 (1953-54) 327-356.

John F. Gates, "Time and Timeless God," *JASA* 8 (1956) #3, 15-17. (Comments by William W. Paul, p. 17)

*Yithak Schalev, "The Holyday as an Experience of Time," *Jud* 5 (1956) 160-166.

*J. D. Thomas, "Time and History," *RestQ* 1 (1957) 17-20.

*S. Lauer, "Philo's Concept of Time," *JJS* 9 (1958) 39-46.

*Robert G. Bratcher, "Weights, Money, Measures and Time," *BTr* 10 (1959) 165-174.

Edmund Perry, "The Biblical Viewpoint," *JAAR* 27 (1959) 127-132. *[Time]*

Charles H. Clark, "Time in Biblical Faith," *SEAJT* 1 (1959-60) #2, 37-44.

James Muilenberg, "The Biblical View of Time," *HTR* 54 (1961) 225-252.

*Truesdell S. Brown, "The Greek Sense of Time in History as suggested by their Accounts of Egypt," *HJAH* 11 (1962) 257-270.

*Arthur L. Merrill, "The Old Testament and the Future," *MHSB* 7 (1962) #1, 3-14. [Time, pp. 3-6]

*Eva Radanovsky, "Time: The Priceless Gift of God as Seen by Amos," *HQ* 4 (1963-64) 65-68.

S. G. F. Brandon, "Time as God and Devil," *BJRL* 47 (1964-65) 12-31.

E. M. Bruins, "The Egyptian Shadow Clock," *Janus* 52 (1965) 127-137.

*J. Licht, "Time and Eschatology in Apocalyptic Literature and in Qumran," *JJS* 16 (1965) 177-182.

*Joseph V. Noble and Derek J. de Solla Price, "The Water Clock in the Tower of the Winds," *AJA* 70 (1966) 193.

Alan E. Willingale, "Time in the Bible," *F&T* 96 (1967) #1, 25-53.

Joseph V. Noble and Derek J. de Prince, "The Water Clock in the Tower of the Winds," *AJA* 72 (1968) 345-355.

Jürgen Moltman, "Eternity," *Listen* 3 (1968) #2, 89-95.

Jerome Walsh, "Biblical Time and the Conjugal Metaphor," *LS* 2 (1968-69) 376-383.

*Derek J. De Solla Price, "Portable Sundials in Antiquity, including an Account of a New Example from Aphrodisias," *Cent* 14 (1969) 242-266.

Sidney Smith, "Babylonian Time Reckoning," *Iraq* 31 (1969) 74-81.

§121 *2.3.22 Systems of Measurement, Numeral Systems and Weights & Measures (Metrology)*

E. Norris, "On the Assyrian and Babylonian Weights," *JRAS* (1854) 215-226.

*G. Seyffarth, "Three Lectures on Egyptian Antiquities, &c., delivered at the Stuyvesant Institute, New York, May 1856," *ER* 8 (1856-57) 34-104. [XXII. The Egyptian & Hebrew Measures of Capacity, pp. 102-103]

Charles Warren, "List of Weights and Other Stones Found in the Shafts at Ophel, Robinson's Arch, and Elsewhere," *PEFQS* 2 (1870) 330.

George Smith, "On Assyrian weights and measures," *ZÄS* 10 (1872) 109-112.

*C. W. Goodwin, "On the [hieroglyph] šet, an Egyptian weight," ZÄS 11 (1873) 16-17.

Francis Roubiliac Conder, "Ancient Metrology," *SBAT* 4 (1875) 118-128.

C. R. Conder, "The Metrology of the Bible," *ONTS* 2 (1882-83) 117-118.

*James Gow, "The Greek Numerical Alphabet," *JP* 12 (1883) 278-284.

*†J. Oppert, "Weights and Measures written in Cuneiform," *SBAP* 8 (1885-86) 122-128.

*E. A. Wallis Budge, "On a Babylonian weight with a trilingual inscription," *SBAP* 10 (1887-88) 464-466.

*†A. H. Sayce, "Babylonian Weight," *SBAP* 11 (1888-89) 15. (Note by W. H. Rylands)

Albert L. Long, "A Small Collection of Babylonian Weights," *AJA, O.S.*, 5 (1889) 44-46.

William Hayes Ward, "On an inscribed Babylonian Weight," *JAOS* 13 (1889) lvi-lvii.

Thomas Chaplin, "An Ancient Hebrew Weight from Samaria," *PEFQS* 22 (1890) 267-268.

*F. L. Griffith, "The Metrology of the Medical Papyrus Ebers," *SBAP* 13 (1890-91) 392-406, 526-538.

C[laude] R. Conder, "Notes by Major Conder. II. The Hebrew Weights," *PEFQS* 23 (1891) 69-70.

F. L. Griffith, "Notes on Egyptian Weights and Measures," *SBAP* 14 (1891-92) 403-450. [I. Measures of Length; II. Measures of Area; III. Measures of Capacity; IV. Weights; Postscript]

C[onrad] Schick, "Letters from Herr Schick. III. An Ancient Stone Weight," *PEFQS* 24 (1892) 289-290.

F. L. Griffith, "Notes on Egyptian Weights and Measures," *SBAP* 15 (1892-93) 301-316. (Postscript by W. Spiegelberg, p. 315 *[German Text]*) [I. Measures of Length; II. Measures of Area; III. Measures of Capacity; IV. Weights; Addenda]

*F. Vigouroux, "Recent Discoveries in Palestine," *AER* 8 (1893) 241-250. *[Hebrew Weight, ie., Talent]*

A. H. Sayce, "On an Inscribed Bead from Palestine," *PEFQS* 25 (1893) 32-33. *[Weight]*

[C. Clermont-]Ganneau, "Note on Professor Theodore F. Wright's Inscribed Weight or Bead," *PEFQS* 25 (1893) 257.

C. Clermont-Ganneau, "Note on an Ancient Weight Found at Gaza," *PEFQS* 25 (1893) 305-306.

A. H. Sayce, S. R. Driver, Ed. König, Thomas Chaplin, W. Robertson Smith, "The Haematite Weight, with an Inscription in Ancient Semitic Characters, purchased at Samaria by Thomas Chaplin, Esq., M.D.," *PEFQS* 26 (1894) 220-231.

A. H. Sayce and Thomas Tyler, "The Ancient Haematite Weight from Samaria," *PEFQS* 26 (1894) 284-286. (Note by Thomas Chaplin, pp. 286-287)

*G. Schumacher, "Reports from Galilee," *PEFQS* 27 (1895) 110-114. [Weights, p. 112]

Ebenezer Davis, "Notes on the Haematite Weight from Samaria," *PEFQS* 27 (1895) 187-190.

Claude R. Conder, "The Haematite Weight," *PEFQS* 27 (1895) 191.

P. le Page Renouf, "Note on Length and Breadth in Egyptian," *SBAP* 17 (1895) 191.

George Reisner, "Notes on the Babylonian system of measures of area," *ZA* 11 (1896-97) 417-424.

George Reisner, "Old Babylonian Systems of Weights and Measures," *JAOS* 18 (1897) 366-374.

C. M. Watson, "Jewish Measures of Capacity," *PEFQS* 30 (1898) 103-110. (Note by C. Clermont-Ganneau, pp. 158-159)

*C. Clermont-Ganneau, "Note on the Inscribed Jar Handle and Weight Found at Tell Zakariya," *PEFQS* 31 (1899) 204-209. [2. The Weight of Tell Zakarîya, pp. 207-209]

Charles Warren, "The Ancient Standards of Measure in the East," *PEFQS* 31 (1899) 218-268, 357-371. (Note by C. R. Conder, pp. 353-354)

*A[ngus] Crawford, "Palestinian Antiquities," *PER* 12 (1898-99) 392-398. [Ancient Hebrew Weight from Samaria, pp. 393-394; Cast of a Bead or Inscribed Weight, p. 398]

C. H. W. Johns, "Babylonian Weights and Measures," *SBAP* 21 (1899) 308.

A. H. Sayce, "Notes on the December Number of the *Proceedings*," *SBAP* 22 (1900) 86. *[Ref. C. H. W. Johns - previous article]*

*Charles Warren, "Egyptian Weights and Measures Since the Eighteenth Dynasty and of the Rhind Mathematical Papyrus," *PEFQS* 32 (1900) 149-150.

C. M. Watson, "The Measurement of Eggs," *PEFQS* 33 (1901) 203-204.

A. E. Weigall, "Some Egyptian Weights in the Collection of Prof. Petrie," *SBAP* 23 (1901) 378-395.

Charles Warren, "Notes on 'Du Bimetallisme Chez les Hebreux'," *PEFQS* 34 (1902) 94.

C[laude] R. Conder, "Hebrew Weights and Measures," *PEFQS* 34 (1902) 175-195.

*W. [M.] Flinders Petrie, "Description of the Scarabs and Weights," *PEFQS* 34 (1902) 365. *[Weights and Scarabs found at Gezer]*

*Charles C. Torrey, "Semitic Epigraphical Notes," *JAOS* 24 (1903) 205-226. [II. An Inscribed Hebrew Weight, pp. 206-208; III. A Phoenician(?) Bronze Weight, pp. 208-209]

George A. Barton, "Two New Hebrew Weights," *JAOS* 24 (1903) 384-387. [1. A Unique Hebrew Weight; 2. A New נצף Weight]

W. Shaw-Caldecott, "The Linear Measures of Babylonia about B.C. 2500," *JRAS* (1903) 257-283.

A. H. Sayce, "Inscribed Weights," *PEFQS* 36 (1904) 357-358. (Note on Professor Sayce's Communication by R. A. S. Macalister, pp 358-360)

A. H. Sayce, "Notes and Queries. 2. *Cypriote Weights*," *PEFQS* 37 (1905) 88.

*George A. Barton, "Three Objects in the Collection of Mr. Herbert Clark, of Jerusalem," *JAOS* 27 (1906) 400-401. [A Hebrew weight; A Hittite(?) seal(?); A stone duck weight(?)]

Charles Warren, "Weights Found in Jerusalem. Consideration of the Ancient System of Weights, Showing the Derivation of the Stone Weights Found in the Excavations at Jerusalem in 1867-1870, at Ophel, Robinson's Arch, &c. (*P.E.F.Q.S.,* 1870, p. 336)," *PEFQS* 38 (1906) 182-190, 259-268. [(1) *Untitled;* (2) The Ancient Cubit and the Inch; (3) The Evolution of the Grain Troy; (4) The Four Ancient Systems of Weights and Measures; (5) The Gudean Shekel; (6) The Egyptian Kat; (7) The Addition to the Old Pounds of 1/15 Their Weight; (8) The Jerusalem Weights]

Anonymous, "Notes and Queries. 3. *Ancient Measures,*" *PEFQS* 39 (1907) 163.

*Stanley A. Cook, "Notes and Queries. (4) *Inscribed Objects from Gezer,*" *PEFQS* 39 (1907) 319-320. *[Weight]*

*L. W. King, "Nabû-shum-libur, king of Babylon," *SBAP* 29 (1907) 221. *[Weight]*

S[tanley] A. Cook, "Notes and Queries. (3.), *The inscribed Objects from Gezer,*" *PEFQS* 40 (1908) 76-77. *[Weights]*

*Christopher Johnston, "Assyrian Lexicographical Notes," *AJSL* 27 (1910-11) 187-189. [*d*) tikpu 'row, course of stone, or brick,' pp. 188-189] *[= 'a measure of length']*

*L. W. King, "On methods of expressing the tens of *ḳa* under the 'royal *gur*' system," *ZA* 25 (1911) 353-355.

A[rchibald] R. S. Kennedy, "A Recent Find of Jewish Measures," *ET* 24 (1912-13) 393-395.

A[rchibald] R. S. Kennedy, "Inscribed Hebrew Weights from Palestine," *ET* 24 (1912-13) 488-491, 538-542. [I. The Phoenician Standard; II. The Gezer Market Weight; III. The Inscribed בקע (Beḳa') Series of Weights; IV. The King's Weight; V. The X Series of Weights; VI. The נצף (Neẓeph?) Weights; VII. The Inscribed חמש (Ḥomesh) Weight; VIII. The פים (?) Weights; IX. Inscribed Weights of the Attic Standard; Summary of Results]

E. J. Pilcher, "Weights of Ancient Palestine," *PEFQS* 44 (1912) 136-144, 178-195. [1. Introduction; 2. The Phoenician Standard; 3. The Assyrian Standard; 4. The Persic Standard; 5. The Egyptian Standard; 6. The Philippic Silver Standard; 7. Conclusion]

E. J. Pilcher, "Weight Standards of Palestine," *SBAP* 34 (1912) 114-118.

E. J. Pilcher, "Notes and Queries. *A New Hebrew Weight,*" *PEFQS* 46 (1914) 99.

W. Riedel, "The Measure *Gar*," *SBAP* 36 (1914) 120-131.

Archibald R. S. Kennedy, "Hebrew Weights and Measures," *JTVI* 47 (1915) 277-297, 300. (Discussion, pp. 298-300)

M. H. Segal, "A New Hebrew Weight," *PEFQS* 47 (1915) 40-41.

C. M. Watson, "Babylonian Measures of Length," *SBAP* 37 (1915) 60-65.

Charles Watson, "Measures of Distance in Palestine," *PEFQS* 47 (1915) 179-186.

*S[tephen] Langdon, "Lexicographical and Epigraphical Notes," *RAAO* 13 (1916) 1-4. [[illegible]] *[a designation of measure]*

*E. J. Pilcher, "Hebrew Weights in the Book of Samuel," *PEFQS* 48 (1916) 77-85.

Joseph Offord, "Archaeological Notes on Jewish Antiquities. XXII. *The Weight* Karsha," *PEFQS* 48 (1916) 192-193.

W. Airy, "Miscellaneous Ancient Weights in the Palestine Exploration Fund Museum," *PEFQS* 48 (1916) 149-150.

*W. T. Pilter, "The Manna of the Israelites," *SBAP* 39 (1917) 155-167, 187-206. [The Capacity of the Omer, pp. 196-201]

C. H. W. Johns, "The Babylonian Measures of Capacity," *SBAP* 40 (1918) 136-140.

*George Macdonald, "The Silver Coinage of Crete: a Metrological Note," *PBA* 9 (1919-20) 289-318.

Samuel Raffaeli, "Two Ancient Hebrew Weights," *JPOS* 1 (1920-21) 22-24.

*S[tephen] Langdon, "Assyrian Lexicographical Notes," *JRAS* (1921) 573-582. [V. A *Mana* Stone Weight of the Period of Entemena, pp. 575-577]

E. J. Pilcher, "Bronze Weight from Petra," *PEFQS* 54 (1922) 71-73.

Charles Warren, "Notes on Ancient Weights and Measures," *PEFQS* 54 (1922) 119-131.

G. P. G. Sobhy, "An Eighteenth Dynasty Measure of Capacity," *JEA* 10 (1924) 283-284.

Herbert Thompson, "Length-Measures in Ptolemaic Egypt," *JEA* 11 (1925) 151-153.

Anonymous, "A Hebrew Weight," *PEFQS* 57 (1925) 107.

*R. Engelbach, "A Repaired Steelyard," *AEE* 14 (1929) 46.

N. C. Debevoise, "A Parthian Standard," *RAAO* 27 (1930) 137-139.

[W. M.] Flinders Petrie, "The Pendulum in Egypt," *AEE* 17 (1932) 110-111.

A. S. Hemmy, "A Statistical Treatment of Ancient Weights," *AEE* 20 (1935) 83-93.

[W. M.] Flinders Petrie, "The Study of Weights," *AEE* 20 (1935) Supplement, pp. 146-147.

A. S. Hemmy, "An Analysis of the Petrie Collection of Egyptian Weights," *JEA* 23 (1937) 39-56.

Thompson R. Campbell, "The Assyrian Kisal as the Origin of the Carat-Weight," *Iraq* 5 (1938) 23-30.

A. S. Hemmy, "The Weight-Standards of Ancient Greece and Persia," *Iraq* 5 (1938) 65-81.

*G. A. Wainwright, "Thoughts on Three Recent Articles," *JEA* 24 (1938) 59-64. [II. *Reference to:* An Analysis of the Petrie Collection of Egyptian Weights, pp. 62-63]

[W. M.] Flinders Petrie, "The Present Position of the Metrology of Egyptian Weights," *JEA* 24 (1938) 180-181.

*O. H. Myers, "Note on the Treatment of a Bronze Weight," *JEA* 25 (1939) 102-103.

A. Lucas and Alan Rowe, "Ancient Egyptian measures of capacity," *ASAE* 40 (1940-41) 69-92.

A. Lucas and Alan Rowe, "Addition to *Ancient Egyptian measures of capacity* (in *Annales du Service*, XL, pp. 82, 83," *ASAE* 41 (1942) 348.

David Diringer, "The Early Hebrew Weights found at Lachish," *PEQ* 74 (1942) 82-103.

A. Lucas, "Ancient egyptian measures of capacity," *ASAE* 42 (1943) 165-166.

*A. J. Sachs, "Some Metrological Problems in Old Babylonian Texts," *BASOR* #96 (1944) 29-39. [Miscellaneous Prefatory Remarks; I. The Old Babylonian Measures of Capacity; II. The Size of a GI-SA; III. Bricks]

*Hildegard Lewy, "Assyro-Babylonian and Israelite Measures of Capacity and Rates of Seeding," *JAOS* 64 (1944) 65-73.

Angelo Segre, "Babylonian, Assyrian and Persian Measures," *JAOS* 64 (1944) 73-81.

Hildegard Lewy, "A Propos of Babylonian Metrology," *BASOR* #98 (1945) 25-26. (Rejoinder by A. J. Sachs, pp. 26-27)

Angelo Segrè, "A Documentary Analysis of Ancient Palestinian Units of Measure," *JBL* 64 (1945) 357-375.

*E. L. Sukenik, "The Meaning of the 'Le-Melekh' Inscriptions," *KSJA* 2 (1945) VI.

*Virginia Grace, "Fractional Stamped Containers," *AJA* 52 (1948) 381. *[Units of Measure]*

A. Reifenberg, "The Legend 'Shekel' on Hebrew Weights," *BIES* 15 (1949-50), #3/4, I.

T. Fish, "Silver Equivalents of Copper," *MCS* 1 (1951) 49.

*H[ildegard] Lewy, "Studies in Assyro-Babylonian Mathematics and Metrology. B. On Some Metrological Pecularities of Old Akkadian Texts from Nuzi," *Or, N.S.,* 20 (1951) 1-12.

*N. Avigad, "Another *bat le-melekh* Inscription," *IEJ* 3 (1953) 121-122.

A. E. Berriman, "Some Marked Weights in the Petrie Collection," *JEA* 41 (1955) 48-50.

A. E. Berriman, "A New Approach to the Study of Ancient Metrology," *RAAO* 49 (1955) 193-201.

*Edmond, Sollberger, "Selected Texts from the American Collections," *JCS* 10 (1956) 11-31. [6. *gú* and *sa* as Measures, p. 20 (Emory University No. 45)]

Klaus Baer, "A Note on Egyptian Units of Area in the Old Kingdom," *JNES* 15 (1956) 113-117.

Richard T. Hallock, "The Nuzi Measure of Capacity," *JNES* 16 (1957) 204-206.

A. E. Berriman, "A Sumerian Weight-Standard in Chinese Metrology during the Former Han Dynasty (206 B.C.-A.D. 23)," *RAAO* 52 (1958) 203-207.

R. B. Y. Scott, "Weights and Measures of the Bible," *BA* 22 (1959) 22-40. [I. Linear Measures; II. Measures of Area; III. Measures of Capacity; IV. Weights]

R. B. Y. Scott, "The Shekel Sign on Stone Weights," *BASOR* #153 (1959) 32-35.

*Nelson Glueck, "A Seal Weight from Nebi Rubin," *BASOR* #153 (1959) 35-38.

*Robert G. Bratcher, "Weights, Money, Measures and Time," *BTr* 10 (1959) 165-174.

*J. Lewy, "The Old Assyrian Measure *Šubtum*," *SBO* 3 (1959) 216-226.

*J. Walter Graham, "The Minoan Unit of Length and Minoan Palace Planning," *AJA* 64 (1960) 335-341.

*William R. Lane, "Newly Recognized Occurrences of the Weight-name *PYM*," *BASOR* #164 (1961) 21-23.

*Yigael Yadin, "Ancient Judean Weights and the Date of the Samaria Ostraca," *SH* 8 (1961) 9-25.

*Erwin Reiflier, "The Evidence for the Near Eastern Origin of the Doric and the Parthenon Foot Standard," *AJA* 67 (1963) 216.

*Mabel Lang, "The Palace of Nestor Excavations of 1963. Part II Pylos Pots and the Mycenaean Units of Capacity," *AJA* 68 (1964) 99-105.

*Erwin Reifler, "The Metrological Reasons for the Difference in Aristotle's and Androtion's Statements about Solon's Change of Weight of the Mina," *AJA* 68 (1964) 202.

*R. B. Y. Scott, "Shekel-Fraction Markings on Hebrew Weights," *BASOR* #173 (1964) 53-64.

Hildegard Lewy, "The Assload, the Sack, and Other Measures of Capacity," *RDSO* 39 (1964) 181-197.

Hildegard Lewy, "The Assload and Other Old Measures of Capacity," *AAI* 2 (1965) 291-304.

Erwin Reifler, "Additional Evidence for a Prehistoric Link between the Measuring Sytems of Sumeria and the Indus Valley," *AJA* 69 (1965) 174.

A[nson] F. Rainey, "Royal Weights and Measures," *BASOR* #179 (1965) 34-36.

R. B. Y. Scott, "The Scale-Weights from Ophel, 1963-64," *PEQ* 97 (1965) 128-139.

J. Walter Graham, "Further Notes on the Minoan Foot," *AJA* 70 (1966) 190.

O. H. Myers, "Shorter Units of Length," *Antiq* 40 (1966) 230-232.

*Aharoni Yohanan, "The Use of Hieratic Numerals in Hebrew Ostraca and the Shekel Weights," *BASOR* #184 (1966) 13-19.

Vera I. Kerkhof, "An Inscribed Stone Weight from Shechem," *BASOR* #184 (1966) 20-21.

*R[euven] Yaron, "*ksp zwz*," *Lěš* 31 (1966-67) #4, n.p.n. *[Silver standard to* zuz*]*

Sh. Yeiven, "Weights and Measures of Various Standards in the Biblical Period," *Lěš* 31 (1966-67) #4, n.p.n.

Oscar Broneer, "The Foot on the Stadium," *AJA* 71 (1967) 184.

*Ivan Tracy Kaufman, "New Evidence for Hieratic Numerals on Hebrew Weights," *BASOR* #188 (1967) 39-41.

Eythan Shany, "A New Unpublished 'Beq'a' Weight in the Collection of the Pontifical Biblical Institute, Jerusalem, Israel," *PEQ* 99 (1967) 54-55.

*Isaac D. Gilsy, "Measurements as Rabbinical Ordinances," *Tarbiẕ* 37 (1967-68) #3, I-II.

N. Avigad, "A Sculptured Hebrew Stone Weight," *IEJ* 18 (1968) 181-187.

*R[euven] Yaron, "Minutiae Aramaicae," *JSS* 13 (1968) 202-211. [I. "Silver *zuz* to the Ten"]

Ayre Ben-David, "The Talmud Was Right! The Weight of the Biblical Sheqel," *PEQ* 100 (1968) 145-147.

Richard Parkhurst, "A Preliminary History of Ethiopian Measures, Weights, and Values (Part I)," *JES* 7 (1969) #1, 31-54.

Richard Parkhurst, "A Preliminary History of Ethiopian Measures, Weights, and Values (Part II)," *JES* 7 (1969) #2, 99-164.

Daniel Sperber, "A Note on Some Shi'urim and Graeco-Roman Measurements," *JJS* 20 (1969) 81-86.

S. Yeivin, "Weights and Measures of Varying Standards in the Bible," *PEQ* 101 (1969) 63-68.

Ayre Ben-David, "The 'Tartimar'," *PEQ* 101 (1969) 117-121.

§122 *2.3.22.1 Mathematics & Numbering Systems*

*†Anonymous, "Egyptian Method of Notation," *WR* 13 (1830) 227-239.

Anonymous, "Arithmetic,—Ancient and Modern," *LQHR* 11 (1858-59) 415-443. [Hebrew Number System, p. 428]

*C. W. Goodwin, "Notes on Egyptian Numerals," *ZÄS* 5 (1867) 94-95, 98-101; 6 (1868) 106-108.

*S. Birch, "Geometic Papyrus," *ZÄS* 6 (1868) 108-110.

*A. H. Sayce, "The Accadian Numerals," *ZDMG* 27 (1873) 696-702.

*George Bertin, "Notes on the Assyrian Numerals," *SBAP* 2 (1879-80) 37-38.

*George Bertin, "The Assyrian Numerals," *SBAT* 7 (1880-82) 370-389.

*A. H. Sayce, "Notes on the Assyrian Numerals," *SBAP* 4 (1881-82) 105-107.

*Theo. G. Pinches, "The Akkadian Numerals," *SBAP* 4 (1881-82) 111-116.

*†John P. Peters, "The Akkadian Numerals," *SBAP* 5 (1882-83) 120-121.

*A. H. Sayce, "Miscellaneous Notes," *ZK* 2 (1885) 399-405. [2. *Tisâ* "nine", p. 399]

*Robert Brown Jr., "Ugro-Altaic Numerals: One—Five," *SBAP* 10 (1887-88) 207-214.

S. H. Butcher, "The geometrical problem of the *Meno* (p. 86E-87A)," *JP* 17 (1888) 219-225. *[Greek Mathematics]*

*Robert Brown Jr., "The Etruscan Numerals," *ARL* 3 (1889) 376-410.

Hermann Schubert, "The Squaring of the Circle. An Historical Sketch of the Problem from the Earliest Times to the Present Day," *SIR* (1890) 97-120. [III. Historical Attempts: The Egyptian Quadrature; The Biblical and Babylonian quadratures; Among the Greeks; Among the Romans; pp. 104-110]

Hermann Schubert, "The Squaring of the Circle. An Historical Sketch of the Problem from Earliest Times to the Present Day," *Monist* 1 (1890-91) 197-228.

*F. L. Griffith, "The Rhind Mathematical Papyrus," *SBAP* 14 (1891-92) 26-31.

*F. L. Griffith, "The Rhind Mathematical Papyrus," *SBAP* 16 (1893-94) 164-173, 201-208, 230-248.

*David Künstlinger, "The Numeral 'Two' in the Semitic Language," *JQR* 10 (1897-98) 462-469.

*Edgar Johnson Goodspeed, "The Ayer Papyrus: A Mathematical Fragment," *AJP* 19 (1898) 25-39. *[Greek]*

*†August Eisenlohr, "Letter to Mr. Rylands referring to the Mathematical Papyrus," *SBAP* 21 (1899) 49-50.

*Charles Warren, "Egyptian Weights and Measures Since the Eighteenth Dynasty and the Rhind Mathematical Papyrus," *PEFQS* 32 (1900) 149-150.

Robert Brown Jr., "A Greek Circle of late times showing Euphratean Influence," *SBAP* 23 (1901) 255-257.

*J. F. C. Fuller, "Elohim and the Numeral π," *Monist* 17 (1907) 110-111.

Anonymous, "Hilprecht's Recent Researches. A Discussion," *AAOJ* 30 (1908) 78-80. *[The number 12,900,000]*

George Barton, "On the Babylonian Origins of Plato's Nuptial Number," *JAOS* 29 (1909) 210-219.

Alan S. Hawkesworth, "The Æonic Number in Babylon," *OC* 25 (1911) 511.

*L. W. King, "On methods of expressing the tens of *ḳa* under the 'royal *gur*' system," *ZA* 25 (1911) 353-355.

John Cameron, "The Origin of the Arabic Numerals," *GUOST* 4 (1913-22) 9-12. *(Review)*

Eugene Tavenner, "Three as a Magic Number in Latin Literature," *TAPA* 47 (1916) 117-143.

*B. Touraeff, The Volume of the Truncated Pyramid in Egyptian Mathematics," *AEE* 4 (1917) 100-102.

R. W. Sloley, "Ancient Egyptian Mathematics," *AEE* 7 (1922) 111-117.

T. Eric Peet, "Arithmetic in the Middle Kingdom," *JEA* 9 (1923) 91-95.

*Andrew C. Baird, "Babylonian Number Systems and the Origin of the Calendar," *GUOST* 5 (1923-28) 9-14.

Robert Morris, "Note on the Origin of the Arabic Numerals," *GUOST* 5 (1923-28) 43-44.

*Paul Haupt, "Philological Studies. 7. The Cuneiform Prototype of *Cipher* and *Zero*," *AJP* 45 (1924) 57-59.

*Anonymous, "Notes and Comments. Two Babylonian Multiplication Tablets in Ontario," *A&A* 26 (1928) 145-146.

*Battiscombe Gunn and T. Eric Peet, "Four Geometrical Problems from the Moscow Mathematical Papryus," *JEA* 15 (1929) 167-185.

*Kurt Vogel, "The Truncated Pyramid in Egyptian Mathematics," *JEA* 16 (1930) 242-249.

Thomas Eric Peet, "Mathematics in Ancient Egypt," *BJRL* 15 (1931) 409-441.

*W. R. Thomas, "Moscow Mathematical Papyrus, No. 14," *JEA* 17 (1931) 50-52.

*T. Eric Peet, "A Problem in Egyptian Geometry," *JEA* 17 (1931) 100-106.

*Solomon Gandz, "Hebrew Numerals," *PAAJR* 4 (1932-33) 53-112.

Quido Vetter, "Problem 14 of the Moscow Mathematical Papyrus," *JEA* 19 (1933) 16-18.

*Cyrus H. Gordon, "Numerals in the Nuzi Tablets," *RAAO* 31 (1934) 53-60.

Lancelot Hogben, "Mathematics in Antiquity," *Antiq* 9 (1935) 190-194.

*Louis C. Karpinski, "New Light on Babylonian Mathematics," *AJSL* 52 (1935-36) 73-80.

George Sarton, "Minoan mathematics," *Isis* 24 (1935-36) 375-381.

Raymond Clare Archibald, "Babylonian Mathematics," *Isis* 26 (1936) 63-81.

*Solomon Gandz, "Mene Mene Tekal Upharsin, a chapter in Babylonian mathematics," *Isis* 26 (1936) 82-94.

Solomon Gandz, "The Babylonian Tables of Reciprocals," *Isis* 25 (1936) 428-432.

*G. V. Bobrinskoy, "A Line of Brāhmī (?) Script in a Babylonian Contract Tablet," *JAOS* 56 (1936) 86-88. *[Arabic Numerals(?)]*

*Charles C. Torrey, "Note on the Line of Brāhmī (?) Script on a Babylonian Tablet," *JAOS* 56 (1936) 490-491. *[Arabic Numerals(?)]*

*T. C. Skeat, "A Greek Mathematical Tablet," *Miz* 3 (1936) 18-25.

L. C. Karpinski, "Is there progress in mathematical discovery and did the Greeks have analytic geometry?" *Isis* 27 (1937) 46-52.

*Jaroslav Černý, "The Gender of Tens and Hundreds in Late Egyptian," *JEA* 23 (1937) 57-59.

Solomon Gandz, "The origin and development of quadratic equations in Babylonian, Greek, and early Arabic algebra," *Osiris* 3 (1938) 405-557.

*Solomon Gandz, "Studies in Hebrew Mathematics and Astronomy," *PAAJR* 9 (1938-39) 5-50.

George Sarton, "Remarks on the study of Babylonian mathematics," *Isis* 31 (1939) 398-404.

Solomon Gandz, "Studies in Babylonian mathematics II: Conflicting interpretations of Babylonian mathematics," *Isis* 31 (1939) 405-425.

F. Thureau-Dangin, "Sketch of a history of the sexagesimal system," *Osiris* 7 (1939) 95-141.

Solomon Gandz, "Studies in Babylonian mathematics III: Isoperimetric Problems and the Origin of the Quadratic Equations," *Isis* 32 (1940) 103-115.

*O. Neugebauer, "On the Special Use of the Sign 'Zero' in Cuneiform Astronomical Texts," *JAOS* 61 (1941) 213-215. [[illegible]]

R. S. Williamson, "Geometric Series and the Rhind Papyrus," *JEA* 28 (1942) 67.

*George G. Cameron, "The Babylonian Scientist and His Hebrew Colleague," *BA* 7 (1944) 21-29, 32-40. [Mathematics, pp. 38-40]

*A. J. Sachs, "Some Metrological Problems in Old Babylonian Texts," *BASOR* #96 (1944) 29-39. [Miscellaneous Prefatory Remarks; I. The Old Babylonian Measures of Capacity; II. The Size of a GI-SA; III. Bricks]

R. S. Williamson, "Squaring the Circle: Suggested Basis of the Ancient Egyptian Rule," *JEA* 31 (1945) 112.

*Thorkild Jacobsen, "Mathematical Cuneiform Texts," *BASOR* #102 (1946) 17-19. *(Review)*

*Albrecht Goetze, "Number Idioms in Old Babylonian," *JNES* 5 (1946) 185-202.

*A. [J.] Sachs, "Notes on Fractional Expressions in Old Babylonian Mathematical Texts," *JNES* 5 (1946) 203-214.

*Hildegard Lewy, "Marginal Notes on a Recent Volume of Babylonian Mathematical Texts," *JAOS* 67 (1947) 305-320.

*A. J. Sachs, "Babylonian Mathematical Texts. I. Reciprocals of Regular Sexagesimal Numbers," *JCS* 1 (1947) 219-240.

Solomon Gandz, "Studies in Babylonian Mathematics I. Indeterminate analysis in Babylonian mathematics," *Osiris* 8 (1948) 12-40.

*G. R. Driver, "Gender in Hebrew Numbers," *JJS* 1 (1948-49) 90-104.

*Julius Lewy, "Apropos of the Akkadian Numerals *iš-ti-a-na* and *iš-ti-na*," *ArOr* 17 (1949) Part 2, 110-123.

Hildegard Lewy, "Origin and Development of the Sexagesimal System of Numeration," *JAOS* 69 (1949) 1-11.

*H. Lewy, "Studies in Assyro-Babylonian Mathematics and Metrology. A. A New Text of Babylonian Mathematical Texts," *Or, N.S.*, 18 (1949) 40-67, 137-170.

*O. Neugebauer, "Comments on Publications by Mrs. Hildegard Lewy on Mathematical Cuneiform Texts," *Or, N.S.*, 18 (1949) 423-426.

*Emmett L. Bennett Jr., "Fractional Quantities in Minoan Bookeeping," *AJA* 54 (1950) 204-222.

Robert Shafer, "Lycian Numerals," *ArOr* 18 (1950) Part 4, 251-261.

*Taha Baqir, "An Important Mathematical Problem Text from Tell Hamal (On the Euclidean Theorum)," *Sumer* 6 (1950) 39-54. [IM 55357]

A. C. Kennedy, "Digamma, Koppa, and San," *GUOST* 14 (1950-52) 61-62.

*H. Lewy, "Studies in Assyro-Babylonian Mathematics and Metrology. B. On Some Metrological Pecularities of Old Akkadian Texts from Nuzi," *Or, N.S.*, 20 (1951) 1-12.

*Friedrich Drenckhahn, "A Geometrical Contribution to the Study of the Mathematical Problem from Tell Harmal (IM. 55357) in the Iraq Museum, Bagdad," *Sumer* 7 (1951) 22-27.

*Taha Baqir, "Some More Mathematical Texts from Harmal," *Sumer* 7 (1951) 28-45.

*Albrecht Goetze, "A Mathematical Compendium from Tell Harmal," *Sumer* 7 (1951) 126-155.

*E. M. Bruins, "Comments on the Mathematical Tablets of Tell Harmal," *Sumer* 7 (1951) 179-185.

*Sterling Dow, "Greek Numerals," *AJA* 56 (1952) 21-23.

A. [J.] Sachs, "Babylonian Mathematical Texts II-III," *JCS* 6 (1952) 151-156. [II. Approximations of Reciprocals of Irregular Numbers in an Old-Babylonian Text; III. The Problem of Finding the Cube Root of a Number]

*E. M. Bruins, "Three Geometrical Problems," *Sumer* 9 (1953) 255-259.

*E. M. Bruins, "Some Mathematical Texts," *Sumer* 10 (1954) 55-61.

Alan H. Kelso de Montigny, "Delving into the mysteries of pre- and proto-Indo-European: A.—Origin of the world's numerals: 1) *On the numeral one,*" *IALR* 2 (1955-56) 145-157.

E. M. Bruins, "On the system of Babylonian geometry," *Sumer* 11 (1955) 44-49.

E. M. Bruins, "Pythagorean Triads in Babylonian Mathematics. The Errors on Plimpton 322," *Sumer* 11 (1955) 117-121.

E. M. Bruins, "The Technique of Areas in Babylonian Mathematics," *Janus* 46 (1957) 4-11.

*W. French Anderson, "Arithmetical Procedure in Minoan Linear A and Minoan-Greek Linear B," *AJA* 62 (1958) 363-368.

Charles F. Nims, "The Bread and Beer Problems of the Moscow Mathematical Papyrus," *JEA* 44 (1958) 56-65.

G. Sarfatti, "Arithmetical Fractions in Biblical and Mishnaic Hebrew," *Tarbiẕ* 28 (1958-59) #1, I-II.

E. M. Bruins, "Regular Polygons in Babylonian and Greek Mathematics," *Janus* 48 (1959) 5-23.

*W. K. Simpson, "The nature of the brick-work calculations in *Kah. Pap* XXIII, 24-40," *JEA* 46 (1960) 106-107.

*A. Draffkorn Kilmer, "Two New Lists of Key Numbers for Mathematical Operations," *Or, N.S.,* 29 (1960) 273-308.

*H. W. F. Saggs, "A Babylonian geometrical Text," *RAAO* 54 (1960) 131-146.

*John Wilkins, "Etruscan Numerals," *TPS* (1962) 51-79.

*R. B. Y. Scott, "Shekel-Fraction Markings on Hebrew Weights," *BASOR* #173 (1964) 53-64.

*Derek J. de Solla Price, "The Babylonian 'Pythagorean Triangle' Tablet," *Cent* 10 (1964-65) 1-13. [Plimpton 322]

Asger Aaboe, "Some Seleucid Mathematical Tables (Extended Reciprocals and Squares of Regular Numbers)," *JCS* 19 (1965) 79-86.

R. J. Gillings, "The Addition of Egyptian Unit Fractions," *JEA* 51 (1965) 95-106.

*Aharoni Yohanan, "The Use of Hieratic Numerals in Hebrew Ostraca and the Shekel Weights," *BASOR* #184 (1966) 13-19.

*Otto Neugebauer, "The Greek Mathematical Ostracon Crum 480," *CdÉ* 41 (1966) 160.

E. M. Bruins, "Format Problems in Babylonian Mathematics," *Janus* 53 (1966) 194-211.

*Ivan Tracy Kaufman, "New Evidence for Hieratic Numerals on Hebrew Weights," *BASOR* #188 (1967) 39-41.

Asger Aaboe, "Two Atypical Multiplication Tablets from Uruk," *JCS* 22 (1968-69) 88-91.

J. Walter Graham, "X=10," *AJA* 73 (1969) 236.

Richard A. Parker, "Some Demotic Mathematical Papyri," *Cent* 14 (1969) 136-141.

§123 *2.3.22.2 The Cubit*

J. F. Thrupp, "On the Hebrew Cubit," *JCSP* 1 (1854) 379-385.

S. Beswick, "The Sacred Cubit—Test Cases," *PEFQS* 11 (1879) 181-184.

Claude R. Conder, "Length of the Cubit," *PEFQS* 12 (1880) 98-100.

Chas. Whittlesey, "The Cubit of the Ancients," *AAOJ* 4 (1881-82) 262-269.

*S. Beswick, "Siloam Tunnel," *PEFQS* 14 (1882) 178-183. (Note by C. R. Conder, p. 183) [II. The Tablet-Maker's Cubit, pp. 180-181]

H. G. Wood, "The Boston Cubit," *AJA, O.S.,* 3 (1887) 269-270.

W. M. Flinders Petrie, "The Tomb-Cutter's Cubits at Jerusalem," *PEFQS* 24 (1892) 28-35.

C. M. Watson, "The Length of the Jewish Cubit," *PEFQS* 29 (1897) 201-203.

Charles Warren, "Derivatives of the Ancient Cubit of 20.6109 Inches," *PEFQS* 32 (1900) 145-149.

W. S. Caldecott, "The Biblical Cubit—A New Suggestion," *PEFQS* 34 (1902) 79-82.

W. M. Flinders Petrie, "An Old World Cubit in America," *AEE* 7 (1922) 98-99.

*S. R. K. Glanville, "Records of a Royal Dockyard of the Time of Thutmosis III: Papyrus British Museum 10056," *ZÄS* 66 (1931) 105-121; 68 (1932) 7-41. [III. Comparative table of measurements (in cubits) of timber, etc., p. 41; *Texts,* pp. 1*-8* *following p. 140;* Index of words discussed in the notes and of proper names, pp. 33-37]

George Sarton, "On a curious subdivision of the Egyptian cubit," *Isis* 25 (1936) 399-402.

R. B. Y. Scott, "The Hebrew Cubit," *JBL* 77 (1958) 205-214.

Abraham I. Lebowitz, "A Note on R. B. Y. Scott's 'The Hebrew Cubit'," *JBL* 78 (1959) 75-76. (Reply by R. B. Y Scott, p. 77)

R. B. Y. Scott, "Postscript on the Cubit," *JBL* 79 (1960) 368.

*Hubert Paulsen, "The Cubit—Remen Applied to the Geometry of the Cheops Pyramid," *AA* 40 (1969) 185-200.

§124 *2.3.22.3 Surveying*

Henry Lyons, "Two Notes on Land-Measurement in Egypt," *JEA* 12 (1926) 242-244.

Suzanne Berger, "A Note on some Scenes of Land-Measurement," *JEA* 20 (1934) 54-56.

Henryk Kupiszewski, "Surveyorship in the Law of Greco-Roman Egypt," *JJP* 6 (1952) 257-268.

A. W. Hanson, "A Field Plan," *MCS* 2 (1952) 1-3.

*A. W. Hanson, "Field Plans," *MCS* 2 (1952) 21-26.

F. Stephens, "A Surveyor's Map of a Field," *JCS* 7 (1953) 1-4.

*William W. Hallo, "The Road to Emar," *JCS* 18 (1964) 57-88. [YBC 4499]

§125 *2.3.23* *Ancient Monetary Systems*

[Augustin] Calmet, "On the Antiquity of Coined Money," *BibR* 2 (1826) 129-150.

R. L. Ellis, "Value of Roman Money," *JCSP* 1 (1854) 92-93.

*François Lenormant, "Money in Ancient Greece and Rome. A Chapter in the History of Political Economy," *ContR* 34 (1878-79) 504-523.

W. W. Goodwin, "The Value of the Attic Talent in modern Money," *PAPA* 17 (1885) xxii-xxiii.

C. H. W. Johns, "Did the Assyrians Coin Money?" *Exp, 5th Ser.,* 10 (1899) 389-400.

*Alan H. Gardiner, "Note on the 'ring' and its relation to the *dbn*," *ZÄS* 43 (1906) 45-47. *[Monetary Exchange]*

*Alfred Smythe, "Ancient Coinage from a Non-Commercial Standpoint," *WR* 174 (1910) 556-567.

J. G[rafton] Milne, "The Currency of Egypt under the Romans to the time of Diocletian," *AAA* 7 (1914-16) 51-66.

J. Laurence Laughlin, "Evolution of Money," *A&A* 26 (1927) 3-11, 35.

J. G[rafton] Milne, "The Currency Reform of Ptolemy II," *AEE* 13 (1928) 37-39.

S[tephen] Langdon, "The Silver Standard in Sumer and Accad," *JSOR* 12 (1928) 107-108.

J. Grafton Milne, "Greek Monetary Standards," *AAA* 17 (1930) 77-80.

Alfred R. Bellinger, "Corinthian Factional Currency," *YCS* 2 (1931) 185-198.

*T. Fish, "Aspects of Sumerian Civilization During the Third Dynasty of Ur, 4: Silver," *BJRL* 20 (1936) 121-133.

*T. Fish, "Aspects of Sumerian Civilisation During the Third Dynasty of Ur, 5: Silver," *BJRL* 20 (1936) 286-296.

J. G[rafton] Milne, "The Currency of Egypt under the Ptolemies," *JEA* 24 (1938) 200-207.

J. G[rafton] Milne, "Syriac Substitute Currencies," *Iraq* 6 (1939) 93-100.

A[lexander] S. Kirkbride, "Currencies in Transjordan," *PEQ* 71 (1939) 152-161.

Paul A. Clement, "Chronological Notes of the Issues of Several Greek Mints," *AJP* 62 (1941) 157-168.

Louis C. West, "The Roman Gold Standard and the Ancient Sources," *AJP* 62 (1941) 289-301.

W. F. Lofthouse, "Money in the Bible," *LQHR* 180 (1955) 6-13. [O.T. refs., pp. 10-13]

*Raphael Loewe, "The Earliest Biblical Allusion to Coined Money?" *PEQ* 87 (1955) 141-150.

L. H. Neatby and F. M. Heichelheim, "The Early Roman Currency in the Light of Recent Research," *AAASH* 8 (1960) 51-85.

Richard H. Pierce, "Notes on Obols and Agios in Demotic Papyri," *JEA* 51 (1965) 155-159. *[Gold to Silver Ratios]*

Daniel Sperber, "Palestinian Currency System During the Second Commonwealth," *JQR, N.S.,* 56 (1965-66) 273-301.

Ayre Ben-David, "The Standard of the Sheqel," *PEQ* 98 (1966) 168-169.

Jeremy U. Newman, "Ancient Money-Changers," *Shekel* 2 (1969) #1, 11, 31.

Edwin Mendelssohn, "Development of the Monetary System in Pre-Exilic Palestine," *Shekel* 2 (1969) #2, 17-19, 22-23; #3, 17, 22, 24.

§126 *2.3.23.1 Numismatics*

Anonymous, "An Essay on Medals; or an Introduction to the Knowledge of Ancient and Modern Coins and Medals, especially those of Greece, Rome, and Britain," *QRL* 1 (1809) 112-131. *(Review)*

*( ) K., "Jewish Coins and Hebrew Palæography," *TRL* 5 (1868) 244-259. *(Review)*

Ad. Ernan, "A Find of Coins in Jerusalem," *PEFQS* 12 (1880) 181-182.

*H. D. Rawnsley, "Note," *PEFQS* 13 (1881) 124-125. [Roman Coin]

*M. A. Stein, "Zoroastrian Deities on Indo-Scythian Coins," *BOR* 1 (1886-87) 155-166.

*C. de Harlez, "The Deities of the Indo-Scythic Coins," *BOR* 1 (1886-87) 206-207.

Ernest Babelon, "Review of Greek and Roman Numismatics," *AJA, O.S.,* 3 (1887) 75-86. *(Review)*

*Alex. Cunningham, "Deities on Indo-Scythian Coins," *BOR* 2 (1887-88) 40-44.

*E. W. West, "Notes on Indo-Scythian Coin-Legends," *BOR* 2 (1887-88) 236-239.

*M. Friedlander, "Jewish Lulab and Portal Coins," *JQR* 1 (1888-89) 282-284.

G. J. Chester, "Note on a Coin Engraved on p. 77 *Quarterly Statement,* 1889," *PEFQS* 21 (1889) 153.

J. E. Hanauer, "Letters from Rev. J. E. Hanauer. I. A Curious Coin," *PEFQS* 24 (1892) 198-199. (Note by C. R. Conder, p. 334)

Theodore E. Dowling, "A Short Descripton of Some Bible Coins Found in Palestine," *PEFQS* 28 (1896) 152-160.

Alfred Porcelli, "Bible Coins," *PEFQS* 28 (1896) 341-342. (Notes by C. R. Conder, and C. Clermont-Ganneau, p. 84)

Charles C. Torrey, "(2) A Hoard of Ancient Phoenician Silver Coins," *AJA* 6 (1902) 33-34.

George N. Olcott, "Numismatic Notes. 1. A Hoard of Roman Coins from Tarquinii," *AJA* 6 (1902) 404-409.

Anonymous, "Silver Coin of 800 B.C.," *RP* 3 (1904) 316.

C. Densmore Curtis, "Coins from Asia Minor," *AJA* 11 (1907) 194-195.

Anonymous, "Ancient Coined Money," *MQR, 3rd Ser.,* 33 (1907) 409.

Theodore E. Dowling, "Coinage of Ptolemais and Sycaminum," *PEFQS* 39 (1907) 158-159.

Percy Gardner, "The Gold Coinage of Asia Before Alexander the Great," *PBA* 3 (1907-08) 107-138.

J. Grafton Milne, "The Copper Coinage of the Ptolemies," *AAA* 1 (1908) 30-39.

Anonymous, "The History of Coins and Coins in History," *AAOJ* 30 (1908) 278-280.

A. W. Hands, "The Coinage of Simon Maccabaeus," *IJA* #13 (1908) 14-15.

Jeremiah Zimmerman, "Religious Character of Ancient Coins," *RP* 7 (1908) 15-22.

*E. J. Pilcher, "A Coin of Gaza, and the Vision of Ezekiel," *SBAP* 30 (1908) 45-52.

Charles R. Morey, "The Coinage of Bostra," *AJA* 14 (1909) 92.

E. J. Pilcher, "Notes and Queries. 4. *An Ancient Counterfeit Coin,*" *PEFQS* 41 (1909) 154-155.

Anonymous, "Hebrew Coin Found in Natal, South Africa," *RP* 8 (1909) 262.

J. Grafton Milne, "Report on Coins from Asia Minor," *AAA* 3 (1910) 86-98.

E. J. Pilcher, "Notes and Queries. 2," *PEFQS* 42 (1910) 79-80. *[Coin]*

Frederic Stanley Dunn, "A Study of Roman Coins of the Empire," *RP* 9 (1910) 31-52.

*Alfred Smythe, "Ancient Coinage from a Non-Commercial Standpoint," *WR* 174 (1910) 556-567.

Edgar Rogers, "The Shekels of Simon Maccabaeus," *IJA* #27 (1911) 68-70.

Percy Gardner, "The Earliest Coins of Greece Proper," *PBA* 5 (1911-12) 163-201.

Theodore E. Dowling, "Notes on Gaza Coins," *PEFQS* 44 (1912) 98-100.

Anonymous, "Greek Coin from the Isle of Wight," *RP* 12 (1913) 131.

Elizabeth H. Palmer, "Roman Coins as Illustrative Material," *A&A* 5 (1917) 213-220.

J. G[rafton] Milne, "Leaden Tokens from Memphis," *AEE* 2 (1915) 107-121. {Note by W. M. F[linders] P[etrie], p. 120}

Samuel Raffaeli, "Notes and Queries. 3. *Maccabaean Shekels*," *PEFQS* 47 (1915) 51-52.

E. J. Pilcher, "The Shekel of the Sanctuary," *PEFQS* 47 (1915) 186-195.

*Moses Gaster, "Jewish Coins and Messianic Traditions," *Exp, 8th Ser.*, 12 (1916) 241-259.

J. G[rafton] Milne, "Some Alexandrian Coins," *JEA* 4 (1916) 177-186.

George Edwin Howes, "The Story of Three Greek Coins," *A&A* 6 (1917) 181-190.

*Edgar Rogers, "Jewish Coins and Messianic Traditions. A Reply to Dr. Gaster," *Exp, 8th Ser.*, 13 (1917) 29-43.

*Anonymous, "The Symbolism of Ancient Jewish Coins," *HR* 73 (1917) 25.

E. T. Newell, "The Coinage of Ancient Palestine," *A&A* 7 (1918) 207-211.

Arthur C. Headlam, "Ancient Coinage," *CQR* 86 (1918) 354-361. *(Review)*

*George Macdonald, "The Silver Coinage of Crete: a Metrological Note," *PBA* 9 (1919-20) 289-318.

Samuel Raffaeli, "Classification of Jewish Coins," *JPOS* 1 (1920-21) 202-208.

E. J. Pilcher, "Philistine Coin from Lachish," *PEFQS* 53 (1921) 131-141.

Alan Johnston, "Archaeological Notes and Comments. The Potted Gold of Croesus," *A&A* 14 (1922) 107-108.

J. G[rafton] Milne, "The Coins from Oxyrhynchus," *JEA* 8 (1922) 158-163.

*Samuel Raffaeli, "The Epigraphy of Jewish Coinage," *PEFQS* 54 (1922) 154-156.

*Samuel Raffaeli, "A Supposed Hittite Deity," *PEFQS* 54 (1922) 179. *[Coins]*

*Samuel Raffaeli, "Jewish Coinage and the Date of the Bar-Kokhbah Revolt," *JPOS* 3 (1923) 193-196.

Edith Hall Dohan, "Coins from Magna Græcia and Sicily," *MJ* 14 (1923) 162-169.

*E. J. Pilcher, "The Supposed 'Hittite Deity'," *PEFQS* 55 (1923) 50. *[Coins]*

*Eugene S. McCartney, "The Symbolism of Pegasus on Aera Signata," *AJA* 28 (1924) 66.

Leon Legrain, "Coins from Nippur," *MJ* 15 (1924) 70-76.

J. Grafton Milne, "The Alexandria Coinage of Augustus," *JEA* 13 (1927) 135-140.

A. Reifenberg, "On the Chronology of Maccabaean Coins," *PEFQS* 59 (1927) 47-50.

C. Lambert, "A Hoard of Jewish Bronze Coins from Ophel," *PEFQS* 59 (1927) 184-187.

A. Marmorstein, "The Coins of Alexander Jannaeus," *PEFQS* 60 (1928) 48-50.

J. G[rafton] Milne, "Ptolemaic Coinage in Egypt," *JEA* 15 (1929) 150-153.

Charles T. Seltman, "A Philosophy and Coinage: Coinage and a Philosophy," *AJA* 34 (1930) 50.

George V. Edwards, "A Warranted Interpretation of a Denarius of Julius Caesar of 50 B.C.," *PAPA* 62 (1931) xliii.

H. Mattingly and E. S. G. Robinson, "The Date of the Roman Denarius and other Landmarks in Early Roman Coinage," *PBA* 18 (1932) 211-267.

*M. Narkiss, "A Dioscuri Cult in Sebustiya," *PEFQS* 64 (1932) 210-212. *[Coins]*

C. Lambert, "A Hoard of Phoenician Coins," *QDAP* 1 (1932) 10-20.

C. Lambert, "Note on the Obverse Type of the Tetradrachms of the Second Revolt of the Jews," *QDAP* 1 (1932) 69.

C. Lambert, "Coins of the Palestine Museum (*Local Varieties, unpublished or little known*). I.," *QDAP* 1 (1932) 70-73.

C. Lambert, "Coins of the Palestine Museum (*Local Varieties, continued from Vol. I, No. 2, pp. 70-3.*) II.," *QDAP* 1 (1932) 130-138.

*David M. Robinson, "A Typical Block of Houses at Olynthos with an Account also of Three Hoards of Coins," *AJA* 37 (1933) 111-113.

Charles Alexander Robinson Jr., "Notes on the Coinage of Eucratides," *AJA* 37 (1933) 116.

J. Grafton Milne, "The Beni Ḥasan Coin-hoard," *JEA* 19 (1933) 119-121.

G. F. Hill, "Ptolemaios, son of Lysimachos," *Klio* 26 (1933) 229-230. *[Coins]*

Eunice Burr Couch, "An Historical Background for the Study of the Coinage of Argos," *PAPA* 64 (1933) lv.

C. Lambert, "Egypto-Arabian, Phoenician, and Other Coins of the Fourth Century B.C. found in Palestine," *QDAP* 2 (1933) 1-10.

Allan C. Johnson, "Notes on Egyptian Coinage," *AJA* 38 (1934) 49-54.

J. G[rafton] Milne, "'Phocaean Gold' in Egypt," *JEA* 20 (1934) 193-194.

*E. L. Sukenik, "Paralipomena Palestinensia," *JPOS* 14 (1934) 178-184. [I. The Oldest Coins of Judaea, pp. 178-182, 184]

J. G[rafton] Milne, "Report on Coins found at Tebtunis in 1900," *JEA* 21 (1935) 210-216.

E. L. Sukenik, "More About the Oldest Coins of Judaea," *JPOS* 15 (1935) 341-343.

A. Reifenberg, "Rare and Unpublished Jewish Coins," *PEFQS* 67 (1935) 79-84.

*Helen Rosenau, "Some Aspects of the Pictorial Influence of the Jewish Temple," *PEFQS* 68 (1936) 157-162. *[Coins]*

T. R. S. Broughton, "A Significant Break in the Cistophoric Coinage of Asia," *AJA* 41 (1937) 248-249.

Agnes Baldwin Brett, "A New Cleopatra Tetradrachm of Ascalon," *AJA* 41 (1937) 452-463.

J. G[rafton] Milne, "The Origin of Certain Copies of Athenian Tetradrachms," *Iraq* 4 (1937) 54-58.

A[lexander] S. Kirkbride, "Notes on a New Type of Æ Coin from Petra," *PEFQS* 69 (1937) 256-257.

A. Reifenberg, "A Memorial Coin of Herod Agrippa I," *BIES* 5 (1937-38) #4, II.

Harold Mattingly, "The 'Romano-Campanian' Coinage: An Old Problem from a New Angle," *JWCI* 1 (1937-38) 197-203.

Paul Clement, "The Silver Coinage of the Chalcidic Mint at Alynthus," *AJA* 42 (1938) 124.

J. G[rafton] Milne, "The Coinage of Aradus and the Hellenisitic Period," *Iraq* 5 (1938) 12-22.

*G. A. Wainwright, "Thoughts on Three Recent Articles," *JEA* 24 (1938) 59-64. [II. *Reference to:* An Analysis of the Petrie Collection of Egyptian Weights, pp. 62-63]

J. G[rafton] Milne, "The Silver of Aryandes," *JEA* 24 (1938) 245-246. *[Coinage]*

G[eorge] Hill, "The Shekels of the First Revolt of the Jews," *QDAP* 6 (1938) 78-83.

George Hill, "Additional Note on 'The Shekels of the First Revolt of the Jews' *QDAP* VI, PP. 78-83) The Autonomous Shekels of Tyre," *QDAP* 7 (1938) 63.

W. Schwabacher, "Some Coins of Metapontum in the Royal Collection at Copenhagen," *AA* 10 (1939) 120-131.

Donald F. Brown, "New Identifications of Roman Temple Coin-Types," *AJA* 43 (1939) 308-309.

J. Baramki, "Coins in the Palestine Archaeological Musuem (*Local Varieties, unpublished or little known*), III.," *QDAP* 8 (1939) 77-80.

*Josephine Harris, "Numismatic Reflections on the History of Corinth," *AJA* 44 (1940) 112.

A. R. Bellinger and E. T. Newell, "A Seleucid Mint at Dura-Europos," *Syria* 21 (1940) 77-81.

W. Schwabacher, "Corinthian Contributions from Copenhagen," *AA* 12 (1941) 53-65.

Bruno Kisch, "Shekel Medals and False Shekels," *HJud* 2 (1941) 67-101.

J. G[rafton] Milne, "The Ṭūkh El-Ḳarāmūs Gold Hoard," *JEA* 27 (1941) 135-137.

A. Reifenberg, "A Jewish Coin of the Fifth Century B.C.," *BIES* 9 (1941-42) #2/3, II.

N. Breitenstein, "Studies in the Coinages of the Macedonian Kings," *AA* 13 (1942) 242-258.

Paulo Boneschi, "Three Coins of Judaea and Phoenicia," *JAOS* 62 (1942) 262-266.

Stella Ben-Dor, "Two New Seleucid Coins," *KSJA* 1 (1942) VII.

E. L. Kukenik, "On Some Coins of Agrippa I," *KSJA* 1 (1942) VIII.

W. Schwabacher, "Illyro-Paeonian Silver Coins in the Royal Collection," *AA* 14 (1943) 83-91.

*Sydney P. Noe, "Symbols for Cities," *Arch* 1 (1948) 188-189. *[Symbols on Coins]*

Millar Burrows, "Significant Recent Finds of Coins in Palestine," *BA* 6 (1943) 37-39.

J. G[rafton] Milne, "Pictorial Coin-types at the Roman Mint of Alexandria," *JEA* 29 (1943) 63-66.

*Paul Romanoff, "Jewish Symbols on Ancient Coins," *JQR, N.S.,* 33 (1942-43) 435-444; 34 (1943-44) 161-177, 299-312, 425-440.

Angelo Segrè, "Maneh-Obolos," *JQR, N.S.,* 34 (1943-44) 481-482.

A. Reifenberg, "A Hebrew Shekel of the Fifth Century B.C.," *PEFQS* 75 (1943) 100-104.

*Lily Ross Taylor, "Symbols of the Augurate on Coins of the Caecilii Metelli," *AJA* 48 (1944) 352-356.

F. M. Heichelheim, "From Aisa Minor to India," *AJP* 63 (1944) 91. *[Coinage]*

B. Kirschner, "Numismatic Section: The 'Umbrella' coins of Agrippa I," *BIES* 11 (1944-45) #3/4, IV.

A. Reifenberg, "Numismatic Section: Note on a Coin of King Agrippa," *BIES* 11 (1944-45) #3/4, IV.

Meriwether Stuart, "The Denarius of M'. Aemilius Lepidus and the Aqua Marcia," *AJA* 49 (1945) 226-251.

J. G[rafton] Milne, "Alexandrian Coins Acquired by the Ashmolean Museum, Oxford," *JEA* 31 (1945) 85-91.

J. Baramki, "Coin Hoards from Palestine," *QDAP* 11 (1945) 30-36, 86-90.

A. Reifenberg, "A Hoard of Tyrian and Jewish Shekels," *QDAP* 11 (1945) 83-85.

B. Kirschner, "A Mint of Bar-Kokhba?" *BIES* 12 (1946) XI.

Stella Ben-Dor, "Some New Seleucid Coins," *PEQ* 78 (1946) 43-48.

E. I. Sukenik, "A Hoard of Coins of John Hyrcanus," *JQR, N.S.,* 37 (1946-47) 281-284.

C. H. V. Sutherland, "The Personality of the Mints under the Julio-Claudian Emperors," *AJP* 68 (1947) 47-63.

Alexander S. Kirkbride, "Some Rare Coins from Transjordan," *BASOR* #106 (1947) 4-9.

A[rie] Kindler, "Jewish Lead Coins," *BIES* 14 (1947-48) #1/2, IV.

E. L. Sukenik, "Some Unpublished Coins of Aelia Capitolina," *JQR, N.S.,* 38 (1947-48) 157-160.

Stella Ben-Dor, "Some New Seleucid Coins II," *PEQ* 80 (1948) 59-63.

Aline Abaecherli Boyce, "Coins of Roman Alexandria," *Arch* 2 (1949) 181-183.

*Leo Mildenberg, "The Eleazer Coins of the Bar Kochba Rebellion," *HJud* 11 (1949) 77-108.

*H. Hamburger, "Caesarea Coin-Finds and the History of the City," *BIES* 15 (1949-50) #3/4, II.

A. Reifenberg, "Ancient Jewish Coins," *JPOS* 19 (1939-40) 59-81, 286-313.

Harold Mattingly, "Zephyritis," *AJA* 54 (1950) 126-128. *[Coins]*

Dorothy Markham, "Coins from Terenouthis, Egypt," *AJA* 54 (1950) 257-258.

David M. Robinson, "A New Peloponnesian Hoard of Alexander and Ptolemaic Silver Coins," *AJA* 54 (1950) 259-260.

Margaret Thompson, "The 'Owls' of Athens," *Arch* 3 (1950) 151-154. *[Coins]*

*Helen Wade Smith, "Sculptural Style on Ptolemaic Portrait Coins," *Bery* 10 (1950-53) 21-36.

B. Kanael, "The Beginning of Maccabean Coinage," *IEJ* 1 (1950-51) 170-175.

A. Reifenberg, "Unpublished and Unusual Jewish Coins," *IEJ* 1 (1950-51) 176-178.

J. G[rafton] Milne, "Pictorial Coin-types at the Roman Mint of Alexandria: a Supplement," *JEA* 36 (1950) 83-85.

Alfred R. Bellinger, "Greek Coins from the Yale Numismatic Collection," *YCS* 11 (1950) 305-316.

Alfred R. Bellinger, "Greek Coins from the Yale Numismatic Collection, II," *YCS* 12 (1951) 251-264.

Alfred R. Bellinger, "Greek Coins from the Yale Numismatic Collection, III, A Hoard of Bronze Coins of Cyzicus," *YCS* 13 (1952) 159-169.

*E. Bammel, "Syrian Coinage and Pilate," *JJS* 2 (1950-51) 108-110.

Alfred R. Bellinger, "An Alexander Hoard from Byblos," *Bery* 10 (1950-53) 37-49.

David M. Robinson, "An Unpublished Hoard of Silver Coins from Carystus," *AJA* 55 (1951) 151-152.

Aline Abaecherli Boyce, "Parva Ne Pereant," *Arch* 4 (1951) 172-174. *[Coins]*

Leslie H. Neatby, "The 'Bigatus'," *AJA* 55 (1951) 241-244. *[Coins]*

B. Kanael, "The Greek Letters on the Coin of the Jehochanan the High-Priest," *BIES* 16 (1951) #3/4, VI.

B. Kirschner, "Two Observations on Ancient Jewish Coins," *BIES* 16 (1951) #3/4, VII. [1. An expression of 'Terra Marique' on a Coin of Alexandria Jannaeus; 2. The Year of the First Procurators' Coin]

J. G[rafton] Milne, "Pictorial Coin-types at the Roman Mint of Alexandria: A Second Supplement," *JEA* 37 (1951) 100-102.

Baruch Kanael, "The Coins of King Herod of the Third Year," *JQR, N.S.,* 42 (1951-52) 261-264.

*J. G[rafton] Milne, "Roman coinage in Egypt in relation to the native economy," *Aeg* 32 (1952) 143-151.

Aline Abaecherli Boyce, "The Coins of Pompey's Pirate City," *AJA* 56 (1952) 171-172.

A[rie] Kindler, "Restruck Mints of the First Revolt," *BIES* 17 (1952-53) #1/2, IV.

M. Narkiss, "The Sepphorenes and Vespasian," *BIES* 17 (1952-53) #3/4, III-V. *[Coins]*

A[rie] Kindler, "Rare and Unpublished Hasmonaen Coins," *IEJ* 2 (1952) 188-189.

B. Kanael, "The Greek Letters and Monograms on the Coins of Jehohanan the High Priest," *IEJ* 2 (1952) 190-194.

*Cecil Roth, "The Priestly Laver as a Symbol on Ancient Jewish Coins," *PEQ* 84 (1952) 91-93.

*David Magie, "Egyptian Deities in Asia Minor in Inscriptions and on Coins," *AJA* 57 (1953) 163-187.

B. Kanael, "The Historical Background of the Coins 'Year Four. . . .of the Redemption of Zion,'" *BASOR* #129 (1953) 18-20.

A[rie] Kindler, "Some Unpublished Coins of King Herod," *IEJ* 3 (1953) 239-241.

G. K. Jenkins and R. A. G. Carson, "Greek and Roman Numismatics 1940-1950," *HJAH* 2 (1953-54) 214-234.

Michael Grant, "Antony and Cleopatra," *Arch* 7 (1954) 47. *[Coins with a bust of both]*

*Antonine DeGulielmo, "The Religious Life of the Jews in the Light of Their Coins," *CBQ* 16 (1954) 171-188.

L. Kadman, "The Hebrew Coin Script," *IEJ* 4 (1954) 150-169.

A[rie] Kindler, "The Jaffa Hoard of Alexander Jannaeus," *IEJ* 4 (1954) 170-185.

J. Meyshan (Mestschanski), "The Coinage of Agrippa the First," *IEJ* 4 (1954) 186-200.

H. Hamburger, "A Hoard of Syrian Tetradrachms and the Tyrian Bronze Coins from Gush Ḥalav," *IEJ* 4 (1954) 201-226.

Alfred R. Bellinger, "The Drachmae of Alexander the Great," *AJA* 59 (1955) 170.

Eunic Work, "A City's Coinage: The Mint of Camarina," *Arch* 8 (1955) 102-107.

W. P. Wallace, "The Coinage of the Euboian League," *Arch* 8 (1955) 264-267.

H. Hamburger, "Minute Coins from Caesarea," *'Atiqot* 1 (1955) 115-138.

James W. Curtis, "Pictorial Coin Types at the Roman Mint of Alexandria: A Third Supplement," *JEA* 41 (1955) 119-120.

*Raphael Loewe, "The Earliest Biblical Allusion to Coined Money?" *PEQ* 87 (1955) 141-150.

Margaret Thompson and Alfred R. Bellinger, "Greek Coins in the Yale Collection IV: A Hoard of Alexander Drachms," *YCS* 14 (1955) 3-45.

*H. St. J. Hart, "The face of Baal: the interest of ancient coins types and legends for biblical studies," *OSHTP* (1955-56) 35-36.

A[rie] Kindler, "More Dates on the Coins of the Procurators," *IEJ* 6 (1956) 54-57.

H. Hamburger, "An Unknown Syrian Tetradrachm of Caracalla," *IEJ* 6 (1956) 188-190.

J. Walker, "A Palmyrene tessera," *SOOG* 2 (1956) 601-602. *[Coin]*

A. Spijkerman, "A Supplemental Study of the Coinage of Aelia Capitolina (Jerusalem)," *SBFLA* 7 (1956-57) 145-164.

*Arie Kindler, "Coins as Documents for Israel's Ancient History," *A&S* 2 (1957) #2/3, 225-236.

Cornelius [C.] Vermeule [III], "Minting Greek and Roman Coins," *Arch* 10 (1957) 100-107.

James W. Curtis, "Coinage of Pharaonic Egypt," *JEA* 43 (1957) 71-76.

L. Kadman, "A Coin Find at Masada," *IEJ* 7 (1957) 61-65.

J. F. Healy, "The Cyrene Half-Shekel," *JSS* 2 (1957) 377-379.

Harold Mattingly, "Roman Numismatics: Miscellaneous Notes," *PBA* 43 (1957) 179-210.

Kenan Erim, "Morgantina," *AJA* 62 (1958) 79-90. *[Coins]*

*Schuyler V. R. Cammann, "The Bactrian Nickel Theory," *AJA* 62 (1958) 409-414. *[Coins]*

Rena Evelpides, "Stelae and Coins," *Arch* 11 (1958) 55-56.

*J. Meyshan, "The Canopy Symbol on the Coins of Agrippa I," *BIES* 22 (1958) #3/4, n.p.n.

Cornelius C. Vermeule III, "Greek Numismatic Art 400 B.C.—A.D. 300," *GRBS* 1 (1958) 97-117.

R. M. Cook, "Speculations on the Origins of Coinage," *HJAH* 7 (1958) 257-262.

G. K. Jenkins, "Hellenistic Coins from Nimrud," *Iraq* 20 (1958) 158-168.

A. Spijkerman, "A Hoard of Syrian Tetradrachms and Eastern Antoniniani from Capharnaum," *SBFLA* 9 (1958-59) 283-329.

Otto Mørkholm, "A South Anatolian Coin Hoard," *AA* 30 (1959) 184-200.

B. Oestreicher, "A New Interpretation of Dates on Coins of the Procurators," *IEJ* 9 (1959) 193-195.

*Josef Meyshan (Mestschanski), "The Symbols on the Coinage of Herod the Great and Their Meanings," *PEQ* 91 (1959) 109-121.

*John Walker, "The Liḥyānite Inscription on South Arabian coins," *RDSO* 34 (1959) 77-81.

J. Meyshan, "A New Coin Type of Herod Archelaus," *BIES* 24 (1959-60) #1, VI.

H. Strauss, "A New Interpretation of the Amphora on Ancient Jewish Coins," *BIES* 24 (1959-60) #1, VI.

*W. Wirgin, "Numismatics and the Dead Sea Scrolls," *RdQ* 2 (1959-60) 69-74..

*Andrew Alföldi, "Diana Nemorensis," *AJA* 64 (1960) 137-144. *[Coins]*

R. Ross Holoway, "The Crown of Naxos and the Coming of the Persians," *AJA* 64 (1960) 186. *[Coins]*

*Cecil Roth, "Star and Anchor: Coin Symbolism and the End of Days," *EI* 6 (1960) 13*-15*.

L. Kadman, "The Hebrew Coin Script. *A Study in the Epigraphy and Palaeography of Ancient Jewish Coins,*" *EI* 6 (1960) 30*-31*.

*L. Y. Rahmani, "The Maon Synagogue (The Small Finds and Coins)," *EI* 6 (1960) 29*.

*Josef Meyshan (Mestschanski), "Chronology of the Coins of the Herodian Dynasty," *EI* 6 (1960) 31*-34*.

B. Kirshcner, "New Views in Jewish Numismatics," *EI* 6 (1960) 34*-35*.

Edith Porada, "Greek Coin Impressions from Ur," *Iraq* 22 (1960) 228-234.

Otto Mørkholm, "Greek Coins from Failaka," *Kuml* (1960) 205-207.

Harold Mattingly, "Roman Numismatics: Further Miscellaneous Notes," *PBA* 46 (1960) 249-266.

Nehemia Tzori, "On Two Rare Coins from Scythopolis (Beth-Shan)," *PEQ* 92 (1960) 70.

*L. Y. Rahmani, "The Ancient Synagogue of Ma'on (Nirim). B. The Small Finds and Coins," *RFEASB* 3 (1960) 14-18.

Donald Kagan, "Pheidon's Aeginetan Coinage," *TAPA* 91 (1960) 121-136.

Margaret Thompson, "A Monetary Liturgy in Hellenisitic Athens," *AJA* 65 (1961) 192. *[Coins]*

V. Clain-Stefanelli, "Comparative Die Studies: A Method of Numismatic Investigation and its Historical Significance," *AJA* 65 (1961) 187-188.

J. Meshorer, "An Attic Archaic Coin from Jerusalem," *'Atiqot* 3 (1961) 185.

L. Y. Rahmani, "The Coins from Naḥal Ṣeelim and Naḥal Hardor," *IEJ* 11 (1961) 63-64.

J. Meyshan, "A New Coin Type of Agrippa II and Its Meaning," *IEJ* 11 (1961) 181-183.

Harold J. Mattingly, "The Athenian Coinage Decree," *HJAH* 10 (1961) 148-188.

*Abd el-Mohsen el-Khachab, *"Ο 'ΚΑΡΑΚΑΛΛΟΣ' ΚΟΣΜΟΚΡΑΤΩΡ," JEA* 47 (1961) 119-133. *[Coins]*

*R. R. Williams, "An Early Coin from Qumran," *NTS* 8 (1961-62) 334-335.

*T. V. Buttrey Jr., "The Morgantina Excavations and the Date of the Roman Denarius," *AJA* 66 (1962) 195.

*Bluma L. Trell, "The Naophoroi of Greek Imperial Coins," *AJA* 66 (1962) 200.

O. R. Sellers, "Coins of the 1960 Excavation at Shechem," *BA* 25 (1962) 87-96.

C. Roth, "The Historical Implications of the Jewish Coinage of the First Revolt," *IEJ* 12 (1962) 33-46.

L. Y. Rahmani, "The Expedition to the Judean Desert, 1961. The Coins from the Cave of Horror," *IEJ* 12 (1962) 200.

A. Spijkerman, "Some Rare Jewish Coins," *SBFLA* 13 (1962-63) 298-318.

Miriam S. Balmuth, "Epigraphical Imitations of Early Coinage in the Near East," *AJA* 67 (1963) 208.

Baruch Kanael, "Ancient Jewish Coins and Their Historical Importance," *BA* 26 (1963) 38-62. *(Corr., p. 140)*

J. Meshorer, "An Unpublished Coin of Aelia Capitolina," *IEJ* 13 (1963) 59-60.

Harold Mattingly, "Various Numismatic Notes," *PBA* 49 (1963) 313-343.

Daniel Sperber, "A Note on a Coin of Antigonus Mattathias," *JQR, N.S.,* 54 (1963-64) 250-257.

A. Spijkerman, "Observations on the coinage of Ælia Capitolina," *SBFLA* 14 (1963-64) 245-260.

V. Clain-Stefanelli, "New Quarter-Shekel of the First Jewish War against the Romans," *AJA* 68 (1964) 193.

R. Ross Holloway, "Parian Marble and Parian Drachms," *AJA* 68 (1964) 195-196.

*Erwin Reifler, "The Metrological Reasons for the Difference in Aristotle's and Androtion's Statements about Solon's Change of the Weight of the Mina," *AJA* 68 (1964) 202.

L. Y. Rahmani, "A Hoard of Alexander Coins," *EI* 7 (1964) 168*.

*Josef Meysha, "Jewish Coins in Ancient Historiography," *PEQ* 96 (1964) 46-52.

K. de B. Codrington, "The Origin of Coinage," *ULBIA* 4 (1964) 1-24.

Otto Mørkholm, "A Greek Coin Hoard from Susiana," *AA* 36 (1965) 127-156.

J. H. Jongkees, "Primitive Images Maiorum of Coins of the Roman Republic," *AA* 36 (1965) 232-239.

*T. C. Yao and F. H. Stross, "The Use of Analysis by X-ray Fluorescence in the Study of Coins," *AJA* 69 (1965) 154-156.

Alfred R. Bellinger, "Electrum Coins from Gordion," *AJA* 69 (1965) 164-165.

Wesley E. Thompson, "The Date of the Athenian Gold Coinage," *AJP* 86 (1965) 159-174.

Michael Cheilik, "Numismatic and Pictorial Landscapes," *GRBS* 6 (1965) 215-225.

G. K. Jenkins, "Coin Hoards from Pasargadae," *Iran* 3 (1965) 41-52.

*D[aniel] Sperber, "A Note on Hasmonean Coin-Legends. Heber and Rosh-Heber," *PEQ* 97 (1965) 85-93.

Miriam S. Balmuth, "From Wappenmünzen to Owls," *AJA* 70 (1966) 183.

V. Clain-Stefanelli, "An Application of Physics in Ancient Numismatics: Detection of certain counterfeit Aegina staters through X-ray diffraction analysis," *AJA* 70 (1966) 185.

Y[aakjov] Meshorer, "A New Type of YHD Coin," *IEJ* 16 (1966) 217-219.

D. M. Metcalf, "Ptolemaic and Roman Coins found in Nubia," *Kush* 14 (1966) 334-335.

*Arie Kindler, "Maritime Emblems on Ancient Jewish Coins," *Sefunim* 1 (1966) 15-20.

K. de B. Codrington, "The Basis of Coinage," *ULBIA* 6 (1966) 15-28.

Theodore V. Buttrey, "Halved Coins of the Late First Century B.C.," *AJA* 71 (1967) 184.

*Susan Handler, "The Architecture of Alexandria in Egypt as seen on the Bronze Alexandrian Coinage of the Roman Imperial Period," *AJA* 71 (1967) 188.

Bluma L. Trell, "A Numismatic Solution of Two Problems in Euripides," *AJA* 71 (1967) 195.

*Margaret Bieber, "The Aqua Marcia in Coins and in Ruins," *Arch* 20 (1967) 194-196.

A[rie] Kindler, "The Mint of Tyre—The Major Source of Silver Coins in Ancient Palestine," *EI* 8 (1967) 79*.

J. Meyshan, "What is a Prutah?" *EI* 8 (1967) 79* *[Coins]*

Peter A. Clayton, "The Coins from Tell Rifa'at," *Iraq* 29 (1967) 143-154.

*Daniel Sperber, "Numismatic Hapax-Legomena," *Muséon* 80 (1967) 265-268.

Daniel Sperber, "Catalogue of Coins in the Jewish Museum (London)," *PEQ* 99 (1967) 106-113.

K. V. Golenko, "Little Known Coins of Late Hellenistic Chersonesus," *VDI* (1967) #2, 174.

James A. Dengate, "A Mint for the Coinage of the Ionian Revolt," *AJA* 72 (1968) 164.

Richard S. Stewart, "Findings from a Check-list of Tesserae Nvmuvlariae," *AJA* 72 (1968) 173.

A. Muehsam, "Letter to the Editor," *AJA* 72 (1968) 201-202. *[Coins]*

Michael Crawford, "Coins from a Cemetery at Malignano," *AJA* 72 (1968) 281-282.

J. Naveh, "Dated Coin of Alexander Janneus," *IEJ* 18 (1968) 20-25. (Appendix: A Selected List of Coins, by H. Hirsch, p. 26)

A[rie] Kindler, "Addendum to the Dated Coins of Alexander Janneus," *IEJ* 18 (1968) 188-191.

W. Wirgin, "A Note on the 'Reed' of Tiberias," *IEJ* 18 (1968) 248-249. *[Coins]*

Yaakov Meshorer, "The Seafaring Commemorative Coin: The Jewel of Israel's Crowns," *Shekel* 1 (1968) #1, 16-17.

Matthew J. Vand Der Voort, "Shalom to A.I.N.A. from Amsterdam," *Shekel* 1 (1968) #1, 28, 45. *[Article on Shekel]*

Mel Wacks, "Judacan *[sic]* Jottings: The Jewish Shekel," *Shekel* 1 (1968) #1, 32-33, 40.

‡Mel Wacks, "Judaean Jottings: A Short Bibliography of Ancient Jewish Numismatics," *Shekel* 1 (1968) #2, 15-16, 39-40.

Yaakov Meshorer, "The Mint of King Herod The Great?" *Shekel* 1 (1968) #2, 29-31.

Stanley Lechner, "The Story of Minting," *Shekel* 1 (1968) #3, 18-20, 25.

Mel Wacks, "Judaean Jottings: A Starter Set of Ancient Judaean Coins," *Shekel* 1 (1968) #4, 21-23.

P. J. Bicknell, "An Early Incuse Stater of Kroton Overstruck on a Pegasus," *AASCS* 3 (1969) 1-4.

Andrew Alföldi, "The Diadem of Caesar," *AJA* 73 (1969) 231.

*Gerald D. Hart, "The Diagnosis of Disease from Ancient Coins," *AJA* 73 (1969) 236.

Robert L. Hohlfelder, "The Coins of Kenchreai," *AJA* 73 (1969) 237.

*Bluma L. Trell, "Architectura Numismatica Orientalis," *AJA* 73 (1969) 246.

*G. F. Carter, "Preparation of Ancient Coins for Accurate X-Ray Fluorescene Analysis," *Archm* 7 (1964) 106-113.

*P. Meyers, "Non-Destructive Activation Analysis of Ancient Coins Using Charged Particles and Fast Neutrons," *Archm* 11 (1969) 67-83.

Mel Wacks, "Judaean Jottings: Who Issued the First Jewish Coins?" *Shekel* 2 (1969) #1, 16-17, 28-31.

*Aaron Hendin, "Jewish History as Portrayed in Coins," *Shekel* 2 (1969) #1, 25; #2, 24-25; #3, 15, 22; #4, 8-9, 25.

Arie Kindler, "Numismatics in Israel—Ancient and Modern. An Address to the A.I.N.A. Convention Tel-Aviv, Israel," *Shekel* 2 (1969) #2, 11-13, 22.

Anonymous, "The First Jewish Coin? Important Find of the 'YEHUD' Coin May Shed Light on Long Standing Dilemma," *Shekel* 2 (1969) #2, 12.

Mel Wacks, "Judaean Jottings: Who Issued the First Jewish Coins? Part II," *Shekel* 2 (1969) #4, 10-12, 23.

§127 *2.3.20 Administration, Government, Jurisprudence, Politics, & Law in Israel - General Studies*

*W. B. O. P., "The Character and Institutions of Moses, considered with particular Reference to their Bearing on the Science of Government and Civil Liberty," *CE* 21 (1836) 1-21.

*Anonymous, "The Primitive Jews and Their Moral Code," *FBQ* 2 (1854) 67-84.

*Hermann Hupfeld, "The Political Principles of the Old Testament Prophets," *AThR, N.S.,* 2 (1864) 223-233.

*[S. N. Tufts], "The Hebrew Lawgiver," *FBQ* 15 (1867) 430-445; 16 (1868) 143-161.

Francis Roubiliac Conder, "Ewald's History of the Hagiocracy in Israel," *TRL* 12 (1875) 70-92. *(Review)*

†S[igmund] Louis, "The Poor Laws of the Hebrews," *SBAP* 5 (1882-83) 95-97.

S[igmund] Louis, "The Poor-Laws of the Hebrews," *ONTS* 3 (1883-84) 119-120.

James E. Sime, "Law and Legislation Among the Hebrews," *ONTS* 3 (1883-84) 258-259.

Sigmund Louis, "The Poor Laws of the Ancient Hebrews," *SBAT* 8 (1883-84) 30-41.

*A. H. Sayce, "The Politics of Isaiah and Jeremiah," *ET* 1 (1889-90) 65.

G. S., "Political Parties in Israel," *ONTS* 15 (1892) 72-73.

*W. St. Chad Boscawen, "The Laws of the Family," *ET* 6 (1894-95) 371-372.

*Thomas Nixon Carver, "Moses as a Political Economist," *MR* 74 (1892) 598-605.

Charles Foster Kent, "Characteristics of Israelitish Political Life," *BW* 7 (1896) 520-529.

*J. F. McCurdy, "Light on Scriptural Texts from Recent Discoveries. Assyrian Politics and Israel's First Captivity.—2 Kings xv. 29," *HR* 32 (1896) 119-121.

B. M. Palmer, "The Ancient Hebrew Polity," *PQ* 12 (1898) 153-169.

Julius Silversmith, "The Administration of Laws and Justice in Early Jewish and Christian Eras. From Talmudic and Post-Biblical Records," *BW* 13 (1899) 170-175.

*David Werner Amram, "Zekenim or council of elders," *JBL* 19 (1900) 34-52.

C. F. Kent, "The Humanitarian Element in the Old Testament Legislation," *BW* 18 (1901) 270-283, 338-351.

*Joseph Offord, "The Myths and Laws of Babylonia, and the Bible," *AAOJ* 25 (1903) 258-261.

Anonymous, "The Hebrew Secular Law in the Light of Comparative Jurisprudence," *OC* 18 (1904) 630-633.

Wentworth Webster, "Precedent Cases and 'Fazanias' in Bible History," *ET* 15 (1904-05) 424-426.

Gabriel Oussani, "The Administration of Law and Justice in Ancient Israel," *NYR* 1 (1905-06) 739-761.

*Milton G. Evans, "Biblical Teaching on the Righteous Acquisition of Property," *BW* 27 (1906) 275-285.

*Willard Brown Thorp and J. W. A. Stewart, "Biblical Teaching on the Righteous Acquisition of Property: Comment and Criticism," *BW* 27 (1906) 359-361.

G. A. Smith, "The Jewish Constitution from Nehemiah to the Maccabees," *Exp, 7th Ser.,* 2 (1906) 193-209.

G. A. Smith, "The Jewish Constitution from the Maccabees to the End," *Exp., 7th Ser.,* 2 (1906) 348-364.

Harold M. Wiener, "Israel's Laws and Legal Precedents'—A Review," *CFL, 3rd Ser.,* 8 (1908) 268-273. *(Review)*

*Harold M. Wiener, "The Legislations of Israel and Babylonia," *JTVI* 41 (1909) 139-163. (Discussion, pp. 163-166)

Mayer Sulzberger, "The Polity of the Ancient Hebrews," *JQR, N.S.* 3 (1912-13) 1-81.

Bernard Revel, "Notes on 'The Polity of the Ancient Hebrews,' by Judge Sulzberger," *JQR, N.S.* 3 (1912-13) 315-316.

*P. T. Forsyth, "Land Laws of the Bible," *ContR* 104 (1913) 496-504.

*Nahum Slousch, "Representative Government Among the Hebrews and Phoenicians," *JQR, N.S.* 4 (1913-14) 303-310.

Mayer Sulzberger, "The Ancient Hebrew Law of Homicide," *JQR, N.S.,* 5 (1914-15) 127-161, 289-344, 559-614.

*Harold M. Wiener, "Professor Weismann on Talion and Public Punishment in the Mosaic Law," *BS* 73 (1916) 485-496. *(Review)*

*H. S. Linfield, "The Relation of Jewish to Babylonian Law," *AJSL* 36 (1919-20) 40-66.

Herbert H. Gowen, "Were the Hebrews Democratic?" *ATR* 3 (1920-21) 137-140.

Harold M. Wiener, "The Law of Change in the Bible," *BS* 78 (1921) 73-102.

*Leroy Waterman, "Pre-Israelite Laws in the Book of the Covenant," *AJSL* 38 (1921-22) 36-54.

Samuel A. B. Mercer, "New Evidence on the Origin of Israel's Laws," *ATR* 4 (1921-22) 314-324.

Israel Herbert Levinthal, "The Jewish Law of Agency," *JQR, N.S.,* 13 (1922-23) 117-191.

*W. F. Lofthouse, "Tablet B. M. 21,901 and Politics in Jerusalem," *ET* 35 (1923-24) 454-456.

Thiselton Mark, "The Progressiveness of the Law. An Old Testament Study. (*From a Popular Study of the Bible in Preparation*)," *ICMM* 20 (1923-24) 229-236.

*Bernard Revel, "Some Anti-Traditional Laws of Josephus," *JQR, N.S.,* 14 (1923-24) 293-301.

V. Aptowitzer, "Observations on the Criminal Law of the Jews," *JQR, N.S.,* 15 (1924-25) 55-118.

*Julian Morgenstern, "Trial by Ordeal Among the Semites and in Ancient Israel," *HUCA, Jubilee Volume* (1925) 113-144.

*William F. Albright, "The Administrative Divisions of Israel and Judah," *JPOS* 5 (1925) 17-54.

*Samuel Teitelbaum, "The Political and Social Ideas of the Prophets," *JIQ* 2 (1925-26) #2, 15-17.

Harry J. Brevis, "Asmaktha and Babylonian Influence," *JIQ* 5 (1928-29) #2, 24-27.

Solomon Zeitlin, "Asmaka or Intention, A Study in Tannaitic Jurisprudence," *JQR, N.S.,* 19 (1928-29) 263-273.

*Sheldon H. Blank, "The LXX Renderings of Old Testament Terms for Law," *HUCA* 7 (1930) 259-283.

L. Blau, "Asmakta or Intention," *JQR, N.S.,* 21 (1930-31) 321-326.

*Frank E. Brown, "Violation of Sepulture in Palestine," *AJP* 52 (1931) 1-29.

*Eli Ginzberg, "Studies in the Economics of the Bible," *JQR, N.S.,* 22 (1931-32) 343-408. [I. Laws Pertaining to Slavery; II. The Sabbatical Year; III. The Jubilee Year; Appendix]

*Harold L. Creager, "A Comparison of the Hebrew and Greek Ideals of Democracy," *LCQ* 5 (1932) 312-325.

Hyman Klein, 'The Hadrianic Persecution and the Rabbinic Law of Sale," *JQR, N.S.,* 23 (1932-33) 211-231.

Murray V. McInerney, "Natural Law," *RJ* 1 (1935-38) 316-319.

H. J. Randall, "Law and Archaeology," *Antiq* 10 (1936) 154-161. *(Review)*

*Louis Finkelstein, "The Beginnings of the Prophetic Doctrine of Peace," *JBL* 55 (1936) xviii-xix.

Leon Nemoy, "A Tenth Century Disquisition of Suicide According to the Old Testament (From the *Kitāb Al-Anwār* of Ya'qūb Al-Qirqisānī)," *JBL* 57 (1938) 411-420.

*Martin Buber, "Samuel and the Evolution of Authority in Israel," *Zion* 4 (1938-39) #1, I-II.

*Solomon Gandz, "The dawn of literature. Prolegomena to a history of unwritten literature," *Osiris* 7 (1939) 261-522. [Chapter XVII.— *The Hebrews. The Unwritten Law*, pp. 438-474]

*Th. Laetsch, "The Prophets and Political and Social Problems," *CTM* 11 (1940) 241-258, 337-351.

*J. W. Jack, "Recent Biblical Archaeology," *ET* 51 (1939-40) 420-423. [Shoes as Legal Symbols, pp. 422-423]

Solomon Gandz, "The Hall of Reckonings in Jerusalem," *JQR, N.S.,* 31 (1940-41) 383-404.

*James A. Montgomery, "Law and Religion in the Ancient World as Illustrated in the Bible," *ATR* 23 (1941) 293-306.

I. Rapaport, "The Origins of Hebrew Law," *PEQ* 73 (1941) 158-167.

E. L. Allen, "The Biblical Roots of International Law," *LQHR* 168 (1943) 328-332.

Solomon Zeitlin, "A Note on the Doctrine of Asmakhta," *JQR, N.S.,* 34 (1943-44) 494-495.

Jacob J. Rabinowitz, "A Note on the Doctrine of Asmakhta," *JQR, N.S.,* 34 (1943-44) 491-494.

David Daube, "Some Forms of Old Testament Legislation," *OSHTP* (1944-45) 36-45.

Simon Greenberg, "Democracy in Post-Biblical Judaism," *CJ* 1 (1945) #2, 1-8.

Solomon Goldman, "The Legal Fiction in Jewish Law," *SSO* 2 (1945) 54-72.

*Solomon Zeitlin, "The Political Synedrion and the Religious Sanhedrin," *JQR, N.S.,* 36 (1945-46) 109-140.

*Harry Wolfson, "Synedrion in Greek Jewish Literature and Philo," *JQR, N.S.,* 36 (1945-46) 303-306.

*Solomon Zeitlin, "Synedrion in the Judeo-Hellenistic Literature and Sanhedrin in Tannaitic Literature," *JQR, N.S.,* 36 (1945-46) 307-315.

C. Umhau Wolf, "Traces of Democracy in Israel," *JBL* 65 (1946) vi.

Anton-Hermann Chroust, "The Function of Law and Justice in the Ancient World and the Middle Ages," *JHI* 7 (1946) 298-320.

*Sidney B. Hoenig, "Synderion in the Attic Orators, the Ptolmaic Papyri and Its Adoption by Josephus, the Gospels and Josephus," *JQR, N.S,* 37 (1946-47) 179-187.

C. H. Dodd, "Natural Law in the Bible," *Theo* 49 (1946) 130-133, 160-167. [O.T. refs., pp. 162-167]

*B[enjamin] Maisler, "The Scribe of King David and the Problem of High Officials in the Ancient Kingdom of Israel," *BIES* 13 (1946-47) #3/4, IV-V.

*Solomon Zeitlin, "Synedrion in Greek Literature, the Gospels and the Institution of the Sanhedrin," *JQR, N.S.,* 37 (1946-47) 189-198.

*Boaz Cohen, "Some Remarks on the Law of Persons in Jewish and Roman Jurisprudence," *PAAJR* 16 (1946-47) 1-37.

R. Gordis, "Democratic Origins in Israel," *JBL* 66 (1947) vi.

C. Umhau Wolf, "Traces of Primitive Democracy in Ancient Israel," *JNES* 6 (1947) 98-108.

*Julien L. Tondriau, "Comparisons and Identifications of Rulers with Deities in the Hellenistic Period," *RR* 13 (1948-49) 24-47.

*David Daube, "Concerning Methods of Bible-Criticism. Late Law in Early Narratives," *ArOr* 17 (1949) part 1, 88-99.

*Paul Ramsey, "Elements of a Biblical Political Theory," *JR* 29 (1949) 258-283. [I. Covenant, pp. 258-272; II. Justice, pp. 272-283]

*Boaz Cohen, "Contrectatio in Jewish and Roman Law," *RIDA, 1st Ser.,* 2 (1949) 133-156.

David Daube, "Error and Accident in the Bible," *RIDA, 1st Ser.,* 2 (1949) 189-213.

*A. Van Selms, "The Goring Ox in Babylonian and Biblical Law," *ArOr* 18 (1950) Part 4, 321-330.

*G. Ernest Wright, "The Israelite Law for the Common Life," *McQ* 4 (1950-51) #4, 7-10.

*Leo Adler, "The Natural Boundaries of the Aministrative Divisions of Israel under Solomon," *BIES* 16 (1951) #1/2, II.

Boaz Cohen, "Peculium in Jewish and Roman Law," *PAAJR* 20 (1951) 135-233.

*E[dward] Neufeld, "The status of the male minor in Talmud," *RIDA, 1st Ser.,* 6 (1951) 121-140.

*G. Mendenhall, "Israelite Law in the Period of the Judges," *JBL* 71 (1952) vi.

H. S. Gerhan*[sic],* "Natural Law and the Old Testament," *JBL* 71 (1952) viii. *[Author's Last Name should be* "Gehman"*]*

Cyrus H. Gordon, "Marginal Notes on the Ancient Middle East," *JKF* 2 (1952-53) 50-61. [V. Hebraica: d. The Wrestling Belt, pp. 55-56] *[Trial by Ordeal]*

*G. E. Mendenhall, "Ancient Oriental and Biblical Law," *BA* 17 (1954) 26-46. [Legal and Religious Obligation, Religious Obligation is Sanctioned by the Deity Himself; Covenant as the Foundation of Religious Obligation, Types of "Law"; Israelite Law, The Laws of the Covenant Code, The Law of the Monarchy, The Reform of the Law; Epilogue]

*Joseph H. Heinemann, "The Status of the Labourer in Jewish Law and Society in the Tannaitic Period," *HUCA* 25 (1954) 263-325.

*J. A. Wilson, E. A. Spieser, H. G. Güterbock, I. Mendelsohn, D. H. H. Ingalls and D. Bodde, "Authority and Law in the Ancient Orient," *JAOSS* #17 (1954) 1-55. [Authority and Ancient Lawin Canaan-Israel, by I. Mendelsohn, pp. 25-33]

*Cohen Boaz, "Ususfructus in Jewish and Roman Law," *RIDA, 3rd Ser.,* 1 (1954) 173-193.

*E. Shochat, "Political Motives in the Stories of the Patriarchs," *Tarbiẕ* 24 (1954-55) #3, I-II.

*Siegfried Stein, "The Development of Jewish Law on Interest from the Biblical Period to the Expulsion of the Jews from England," *HJud* 17 (1955) 3-40.

*Mordecai Roshwald, "Ancient Hebrews and Government," *Jud* 4 (1955) 167-174.

*A. L. Oppenheim, "A Note on *ṣôn barzel*," *IEJ* 5 (1955) 89-92. *[Legal Idiom concerning Husbandry]*

*Cohen Boaz, "Self-Help in Jewish and Roman Law," *RIDA, 3rd Ser.,* 2 (1955) 107-133.

*E. Douglas Van Buren, "The Sceptre, its Origin and Significance," *RAAO* 50 (1956) 101-103.

*Elias J. Bickerman, "Two Legal Interpretations of the Septuagint," *RIDA, 3rd Ser.,* 3 (1956) 81-104. [I. DOS (Gen. 34, 12; Ex. 22, 16); II. Actio de Pastu (Exod. 22, 4)]

*Jaes G. Leovy Jr. and Greer M. Taylor, "Law and Social Development in Israel," *ATR* 39 (1957) 9-24.

Jonah Ostrow, "Tannaitic and Roman Procedure in Homicide," *JQR, N.S.,* 48 (1957-58) 352-370.

*E. E. Hallewy, "The Entry of a Field of Sale," *Tarbiẕ* 27 (1957-58) #1, IV-V. *[Law in the Talmud and Tosefta]*

*Gus W. Van Beek, "Frankincense and Myrrh in Ancient South Arabia," *JAOS* 78 (1958) 141-152. [Political Effects of the Incense Trade, pp. 149-151]

*Elias J. Bickerman, "The Altars of the Gentiles: A Note on the Jewish 'ius sacrum'," *RIDA, 3rd Ser.,* 5 (1958) 137-164.

*Boaz Cohen, "Arbitration in Jewish and Roman Law," *RIDA, 3rd Ser.,* 5 (1958) 165-223.

*Boaz Cohen, "Concerning Jewish and Roman Law. 'Specificato' in Jewish and Roman Law," *RIDA, 3rd Ser.,* 5 (1958) 225-290.

Edward Neufeld, "Self-help in Ancient Hebrew Law," *RIDA, 3rd Ser.,* 5 (1958) 291-298.

*Moshe Greenberg, "The Biblical Concept of Asylum," *JBL* 78 (1959) 125-152.

*F. C. Fensham, "The Judges and Ancient Israelite Jurisprudence," *OTW* 2 (1959) 15-22.

*R. Yaron, "Jewish Law and Other Legal Systems of Antiquity," *JSS* 4 (1959) 308-331.

*Zeev W. Falk, "Hebrew Legal Terms," *JSS* 5 (1960) 350-354.

Arthur L. Merrill, "Law in Ancient Israel," *MHSB* 6 (1960) #1, 5-17.

*F. C. Fensham, "A Few Aspects of legal practices in Samuel in Comparison with legal material from the Ancient Near East," *OTW* 3 (1960) 18-27.

*Zeev W. Falk, "Two Symbols of Justice," *VT* 10 (1960) 72-74.

*Zeev W. Falk, "Testate Succession in Jewish Law," *JJS* 12 (1961) 67-77.

*Edward Neufeld, "*Ius redemptionis* in Ancient Hebrew Law," *RIDA, 3rd Ser.,* 8 (1961) 29-40.

*Stanley Gevirtz, "West-Semitic curses and the Problem of the origins of Hebrew Law," *VT* 11 (1961) 137-158.

D. Daube, "Direct and indirect causations in Biblical Law," *VT* 11 (1961) 246-270.

Jonah Ostrow, "Tannaitic and Roman Procedure in Homicide," *JQR, N.S.,* 52 (1961-62) 160-167, 245-263.

*Milton H. Polin, "Genesis as a Source of Law," *Trad* 4 (1961-62) 36-43.

*E. Mary Smallwood, "High Priests and Politics in Roman Palestine," *JTS, N.S.,* 13 (1962) 14-34.

*L. Johnston, "The Prophets and Politics," *Scrip* 14 (1962) 43-47.

*Abraham Malamat, "Kingship and Council in Israel and Sumer: A Parallel," *JNES* 22 (1963) 247-253.

Cecil Roth, "The Constitution of the Jewish Republic of 66-70," *JSS* 9 (1964) 295-319.

*D. McKenzie, "Juridicial Procedure at the Town Gate," *VT* 14 (1964) 100-104.

*E. E. Ubrach, "The Laws Regarding Slavery as a Source for Social History of the Period of the Second Temple, the Mishnah and Talmud," *PIJSL* 1 (1964) 1-94.

*Fredrick L. Moriarty, "Hezekiah, Isaiah and Imperial Politicis," *BibT* #19 (1965) 1270-1276.

*Simon Cohen, "The Political Background of the Words of Amos," *HUCA* 36 (1965) 153-160.

*Stephen M. Passamaneck, "The Talmudic Conception of Defamation," *RIDA, 3rd Ser.,* 12 (1965) 21-54.

John F. Hemmer, "The Natural Law and the Old Testament," *SS* 17 (1965) #2, 3-40.

*Menaḥem Stern, "The Politics of Herod and Jewish Society towards the End of the Second Commonweatlh," *Tarbiẓ* 35 (1965-66) #3, III.

*J. R. Porter, "The Legal Aspects of the Concept of 'Corporate Personality' in the Old Testament," *VT* 15 (1965) 361-380.

*Menaḥem Stern, "The Politics of Herod and the Jewish Society towards the End of the Second Commonwealth," *Tarbiẓ* 35 (1965-66) #3, III.

*H. Reviv, "The Government of Shechem in the El-Amarna Period and in the Days of Abimelech," *IEJ* 16 (1966) 252-257.

*Reuven Yaron, "The Goring Ox in Near Eastern Laws," *ILR* 1 (1966) 396-406.

*D. Geoffrey Evans, "Rehoabam's Advisers at Shechem, and Political Institutions in Israel and Sumer," *JNES* 25 (1966) 273-279. [I. The Elders of Israel and Judah under King David; II. The Crisis of Succession; III. The Councils at Shechem; IV. The Assemblies at Uruk]

*Bruce Vawter, "Church and State in Ancient Israel," *Focus* 3 (1966-67) #2, 5-17.

*Joshua Brand, "The Title אשר על הבית," *Tarbiẓ* 36 (1966-67) #3, I-III.

*Samuel Amirtham, "Prophecy and Politics in Jeremiah," *BTF* 1 (1967) #2, 1-22.

*G. Ernest Wright, "The Provinces of Solomon (I Kings 4:7-19)," *EI* 8 (1967) 58*-68*.

*Z[eev] W. Falk, "Hebrew Legal Terms II," *JSS* 12 (1967) 241-244.

*George Buccellati, "Cities and nations of ancient Syria, an essay on political institutions with special reference to the Israelite kingdoms," *SSR* 26 (1967) 1-264.

*Eugene B. Borowitz, "Judaism and the Secular State," *JR* 48 (1968) 22-34.

*Thomas Tompson and Dorothy Thompson, "Some Legal Problems in the Book of Ruth," *VT* 18 (1968) 79-99.

Millard C. Lind, "The Concept of Political Power in Ancient Israel," *ASTI* 7 (1968-69) 4-24.

Hayim Tadmor, "'The People' and the Kingship in Ancient Israel: The Rise of Political Institutions in the Biblical Period," *JWH* 11 (1968-69) 46-68.

W. Ze'ev Falk *[sic]*, "Conditions in Biblical Law," *Tarbiz* 38 (1968-69) #4, I.

‡Anonymous, "Current Bibliography of Hebrew Law No. 8," *DI* 1 (1969) xxxi-xxxix.

*Z[eev] W. Falk, "Hebrew Legal Terms III," *JSS* 14 (1969) 39-44.

*Leo Landman, "Law and Conscience: The Jewish View," *Jud* 18 (1969) 17-29.

Samuel Morell, "The Halachic Status of Non-Halachic Jews," *Jud* 18 (1969) 448-457. *[Offender of the Law]*

*F. C. Fensham, "Aspects of Family Law in the Covenant Code in Light of Ancient Near Eastern Parallels," *DI* 1 (1969-70) v-xix.

*Solomon Zeitlin, "Studies in Talmudic Jurisprudence: Possession, Pignus and Hypothec," *JQR, N.S.*, 60 (1969-70) 89-111.

*Sh. M. Paul, "Type of Formulation in Biblical and Mesopotamian Law," *Lĕš* 34 (1969-70) #4, n.p.n.

§128 *2.3.20.1 The Theocracy in Israel*

E. C. Wines, "The Hebrew Theocracy," *BRCR, 3rd Ser.*, 6 (1850) 575-599.

M. P., "The Divine Government.—Its General Principles," *JSL, 5th Ser.*, 2 (1867-68) 385-427.

Leonard Bacon, "The Hebrew Theocracy," *DTQ* 1 (1875) 161-171.

*Franklin Carter, "The Study of the Hebrew Theocracy in the College," *ONTS* 7 (1887-88) 11-15.

§129 *2.3.20.2 "The Law" in Israel - Specifically [See also: The Decalogue →]*

*†Anonymous, "The Law of Moses viewed in connexion with the History and Character of the Jews, with a Defense of the Book of Joshua against Professor Leo of Berlin; being the Hulsean Lecture for 1833," *BCQTR, 4th Ser.,* 17 (1835) 310-332. *(Review)*

*W. B. O. P., "The Character and Institutions of Moses, considered with particular Reference to their Bearing on the Science of Government and Civil Liberty," *CE* 21 (1836) 1-21.

T. W., "Spirit of the Mosaic Laws. By J. E. Cellerier, the younger," *CE* 26 (1839) 319-343. *(Review)*

Henry M. Field, "Humane Features of the Hebrew Law," *BS* 10 (1853) 340-366.

Enoch Pond, "Commentaries on the Laws of the Ancient Hebrews, by E. C. Wines," *TLJ* 6 (1853-54) 223-236. *(Review)*

[Joseph Levin] Saalschutz, "The Representative System in the Constitution of Moses," *BS* 15 (1858) 825-844. *(Trans. by S. Tuska)*

James Harper, "Secondary Uses of the Ceremonial Law," *UPQR* 1 (1860) 278-300.

J. B. Sewall, "Humaneness of the Mosaic Code," *BS* 19 (1862) 368-384.

*G. S. Drew, "On the Social and Sanitary Laws of Moses," *ContR* 2 (1866) 514-534.

*Russell Martineau, "The Legislation of the Pentateuch," *TRL* 9 (1872) 474-487. *(Review)*

*T[homas] B. Thayer, "The Land-Laws of Moses," *UQGR, N.S.,* 9 (1872) 220-228.

*Frederic Gardiner, "The Relation of Ezekiel to the Levitical Law," *JBL* 1 (1881) 172-205.

*Anonymous, "On the Development of Dogmatic Teaching Regarding the Old Law in the Lifetime of the Apostles," *IER, 3rd Ser.,* 2 (1881) 455-467.

*F[rederic] Gardiner, "The Relation of Ezekiel to the Levitical Law," *BFER* 32 (1883) 150-177.

*Frederic Gardiner, "The Relation of Ezekiel to the Levitical Law," *DTQ, N.S.,* 2 (1883) 17-47.

S. Schechter, "The Law and Recent Criticism," *JQR* 3 (1890-91) 754-766.

*W. D. Meyer, "The Relation of the New Testament to the Mosaic System," *ONTS* 13 (1891) 143-146.

( ) G., "The Ideal in Hebrew Legislation," *ONTS* 14 (1892) 244.

L. H. Hastings, "'The Mistakes of Moses'," *CT* 10 (1892-93) 32-47.

Dwight Goddard, "The Decard Structure of the Earliest Mosaic Law," *HSR* 3 (1892-93) 225-251.

John Poucher, "The Humane Spirit in Hebrew Legislation," *MR* 77 (1895) 39-56.

D. Farbstein, "On the Study of Jewish Law," *JQR* 10 (1897-98) 177-181.

*I. Abrahams, "Professor Schürer on Life under the Jewish Law," *JQR* 11 (1898-99) 626-642.

*I. Abrahams, "Professor Schürer on Life under the Jewish Law," *OSHTP* (1898-99) 33-37.

Epapharoditus Peck, "The Development of the Hebrew Law," *BW* 16 (1900) 351-361.

Robert Hastings Nichols, "Provisions for Mercy in Israelitish Law," *CFL, N.S.,* 6 (1902) 286-297.

Herman Cohen, "Some Notes on Resemblances of Hebrew and English Law," *JQR* 20 (1907-08) 784-797.

Harold M. Wiener, "'Israel's Laws and Legal Precedents'," *BS* 65 (1908) 97-131. *(Review)*

*W. F. Lofthouse, "The Social Teaching of the Law," *Exp, 7th Ser.,* 5 (1908) 449-469.

*Anonymous, "Editorial Notes," *ICMM* 5 (1908-09) 1-12. [The Growth of Laws; Babylon—the Earliest Home of Law; Hammurabi's Code; The Bridge Between Hammurabi's and Israel's Law; Hebrew "Torah"; The Divine Authority of Israel's Laws; Israelitish Laws were the subject of Growth; The Authors of the Israelitish Laws; The Different Decalogues Written on Sinai; The Same Argument Retold More Simply; The Value of this View of the Growth of Law; The Relation of the Law-giver to Prophet; The Study of the Prophets; Ezekiel; Jeremiah]

*Charles Edward Smith, "Ethics of the Mosaic Law," *BS* 66 (1909) 267-277.

Alexander R. Gordon, The Spirit of Freedom in the Law," *BW* 33 (1909) 260-271.

Charles Edward Smith, "Were the Mosaic 'Statutes' Right?" *CFL, 3rd Ser.,* 11 (1909) 167-171.

William G. Moorehead, "The Mosaic Laws Direct from God," *CFL, 3rd Ser.,* 11 (1909) 175-178.

W. W. Moore, "Moses' Provision to Perpetuate His Great System," *CFL, 3rd Ser.,* 11 (1909) 179-182.

Anonymous, "The Law of Moses," *MQR, 3rd Ser.,* 35 (1909) 259-268.

*A. [E.] Cowley, "Ezra's Recension of the Law," *JTS* 11 (1909-10) 542-545.

V. Apotwitzer, "The Influence of Jewish Law on the Development of Jurisprudence in the Christian Orient," *JQR, N.S.,* 1 (1910-11) 217-229.

A. H. McNeil, "Law, Sin, and Sacrifice in the Old Testament," *ICMM* 9 (1912-13) 376-383.

*Harold M. Wiener, "The Mosaic Authenticity of the Pentateuchal Legislation," *LQHR* 123 (1915) 264-277. (Reply by W. F. Lofthouse, pp. 277-278)

Robert H. Kennett, "The Law," *ICMM* 12 (1915-16) 32-40.

*Israel Lebendiger, "The Minor in Jewish Law. I-III," *JQR, N.S.,* 6 (1915-16) 459-493.

*Harold M. Wiener, "Professor Weismann on Talion and Public Punishment in the Mosaic Law," *BS* 73 (1916) 485-496. *(Review)*

*Israel Lebendiger, "The Minor in Jewish Law," *JQR, N.S.,* 7 (1916-17) 89-111, 145-174. *(Parts IV-VI)*

*Robert Dick Wilson, "Scientific Biblical Criticism," *PTR* 17 (1919) 190-240, 401-456. [B. Laws in the Pentateuch, pp. 198-218]

Gay Morrison, "The Law," *MQR, 3rd Ser.,* 50 (1924) 500-512.

*Philip Vollmer, "Some Economic Principles of the Mosaic Law," *TZDES* 52 (1924) 264-272.

Louis Larson, "The Origin and Scope of the Mosaic Laws," *TTM* 11 (1927-28) 81-100, 181-203, 272-294.

*A. Mackenzie, "The Law of God. With Special Reference to the Third Commandment," *AusTR* 2 (1931) 33-59.

*Boaz Cohen, "The Classification of the Law in the Mishneh Torah," *JQR, N.S.,* 25 (1934-35) 519-540.

*O. T. Allis, "Modern Dispensationalism and the Law of God," *EQ* 8 (1936) 272-289.

J. O[liver] B[ushwell], "Were the Old Testament Saints Under the Law?" *CFL, 3rd Ser.,* 43 (1937) 5-8.

*Ernest Findlay Scott, "The Conception of God's Law in the Prophets and in Jesus," *JAAR* 11 (1943) 152-155.

James McKee Adams, "Archaeology and the Laws of Moses," *R&E* 42 (1945) 165-182.

J. van der Ploeg, "Studies in Hebrew Law," *CBQ* 12 (1950) 248-259.

J. van der Ploeg, "Studies in Hebrew Law: II. The Style of the Laws," *CBQ* 12 (1950) 416-427.

J. van der Ploeg, "Studies in Hebrew Law III. Systematic Analysis of the Contents of the Collection of Laws in the Pentateuch," *CBQ* 13 (1951) 28-43.

J. van der Ploeg, "Studies in Hebrew Law IV. The Religious Character of the Legislation," *CBQ* 13 (1951) 164-171.

J. van der Ploeg, "Studies in Hebrew Law V. Varia. Conclusions," *CBQ* 13 (1951) 296-307.

Johannes Hempel, "On the Problems of Law in the Old and New Testaments," *ATR* 34 (1952) 227-231.

*R. McL. Wilson, "Nomos: The Biblical Significance of the Law," *SJT* 5 (1952) 29-35.

Alva J. McClain, "What Is 'The Law'?" *BS* 110 (1953) 333-341.

B. D. Napier, "Community Under Law. On Hebrew Law and Its Theological Presuppositions," *Interp* 7 (1953) 404-417.

B. Gemser, "The importance of the motive clause in Old Testament law," *VTS* 1 (1953) 50-66.

Roy L. Aldrich, "Has the Mosaic Law Been Abolished?" *BS* 116 (1959) 322-335.

P. J. Verdam, "Mosaic law in practice and study throughout the ages," *FUQ* 6 (1959) 31-84.

*D. Daube, "Concessions to Sinfulness in Jewish Law," *JJS* 10 (1959) 1-14.

*R[euven] Yaron, "Jewish Law and Other Legal Systems of Antiquity," *JSS* 4 (1959) 308-331.

*Zvi E. Kurzweil, "Three Views on Revelation and Law," *Jud* 9 (1960) 291-298.

F. Muliyil, "Torah—Nomos—Law," *BTr* 13 (1962) 117-120.

*Edward Heppenstall, "The Law and the Covenant at Sinai," *AUSS* 2 (1964) 18-26.

*Eliezer Berkovits, "Faith and Law," *Jud* 13 (1964) 422-430.

*Lawrence E. Toombs, "Love and Justice in Deuteronomy. *A Third Approach to the Law,*" *Interp* 19 (1965) 399-411.

*Edward E. Erpelding, "An Investigation of the Israelite Concept of Law Expressed in the Covenant Code," *SS* 17 (1965) #2, 41-67.

*Paul J. Camp, "The Attitudes of the Pharisees Toward the Law at the Time of Christ," *SS* 17 (1965) #2, 68-88. [Introduction; The Law; History of the Pharisees; The Social Milieu of the Pharisees; Theoretical Attitudes Toward the Law; A Dichotomy in the Face of the Law; Unmooring the Law; Practical Attitudes; The Pharisees and Politics; St. Paul, the Ideal Pharisee]

*Walther Eichrodt, "Covenant and Law. *Thoughts on Recent Discussion,*" *Interp* 20 (1966) 302-321.

Charles C. Ryrie, "The End of the Law," *BS* 124 (1967) 239-247.

*Henry Wansbrough, "Event and Interpretation. II. Desert Encounter," *CIR* 52 (1967) 929-937. [The Law, pp. 936-937]

*Henry Piorkowski, "Law and Love in the Old Testament," *Scotist* 23 (1967) 33-46.

*Horace D. Hummel, "Law and Grace in Judaism and Lutheranism," *LQ, N.S.,* 21 (1969) 416-429.

*Alan D. Crown, "Theology, Eschatology and Law in Samaritan Funeral Rites and Liturgy," *GUOST* 23 (1969-70) 86-101.

§130 *2.3.20.3 Comparison of the Mosaic Law with other Law Codes and in particular with the Laws of Hammurabi*

*C. H. W. Johns, "The Code of Hammurabi, Fresh Material for Comparison with the Mosaic Code," *JTS* 4 (1902-03) 172-183.

*Hugh Pope, "The Code of Hammurabi and the Code of Moses," *AER* 28 (1903) 502-515.

*James Henry Stevenson, "The Hammurabi Code and Hebrew Legislation," *MQR, 3rd Ser.,* 30 (1904) 513-525.

*C. M. Cobern, "Moses and Hammurabi and Their Laws," *MR* 86 (1904) 697-703.

*John R. Sampey, "The Code of Hammurabi and the Laws of Moses," *R&E* 1 (1904) 97-107, 233-243.

*Hewlett Johnson, "The Code of Hammurabi and the Laws of Israel," *ICMM* 1 (1905) 133-145.

*Max Kellner, "The Hammurabi Code and the Code of the Covenant," *RP* 4 (1905) 99-118. [I. The Discovery of the Hammurabi Stele; II. The Origin of the Code; III. An Analysis of the Code; IV. The Code of the Covenant; V. The Covenant Code and the Code of Hammurabi, Treatment of Slaves, Accidental Homicide, Attack on Parents, Man-Stealing, Bodily Injuries, Criminal Negligence, House-Breaking, Trespass and Loss, Seduction, Pledge, Judicial Integrity; VI. Conclusion]

*Gabriel Oussani, "The Code of Hammurabi and the Mosaic Legislation," *NYR* 1 (1905-06) 488-510.

*Gabriel Oussani, "The Code of Hammurabi and the Mosaic Legislation. (II)," *NYR* 1 (1905-06) 616-639.

*J. E. Godbey, "Hammurabi and Moses," *MQR, 3rd Ser.,* 32 (1906) 461-475.

D. H. Müller, "The Mosaic Law and the Code of Hammurabi," *Monist* 16 (1906) 313.

Lewis N. Dembitz, "Babylon in Jewish Law," *JQR* 19 (1906-07) 109-126.

*J. Robertson Buchanan, "The Code of Hammurabi and Israelitish Legislation: A Comparison of the Civil Codes in Babylonia and Israel," *GUOST* 3 (1907-12) 25-27.

*Anonymous, "Editorial Notes," *ICMM* 5 (1908-09) 1-12. [The Growth of Laws; Babylon—the Earliest Home of Law; Hammurabi's Code; The Bridge Between Hammurabi's and Israel's Law; Hebrew "Torah"; The Divine Authority of Israel's Laws; Israelitish Laws were the subject of Growth; The Authors of the Israelitish Laws; The Different Decalogues Written on Sinai; The Same Argument Retold More Simply; The Value of this View of the Growth of Law; The Relation of the Law-giver to Prophet; The Study of the Prophets; Ezekiel; Jeremiah]

*Eduard König, "Relations of Babylonian and Old Testament Culture. *IV. The Legislation of the Old Testament and Its Relation to that of Babylon*," *HR* 57 (1909) 443-447.

Perry Wayland Sinks, "The Laws of Plato Compared with the Laws of Moses," *BS* 91 (1934) 65-77, 204-210.

*Cohen Boaz, "The Relationship of Jewish to Roman Law," *JQR, N.S.*, 34 (1943-44) 267-280, 409-424.

*A. E. Guilding, "Notes on the Hebrew Law Codes," *JTS* 49 (1948) 43-52.

P. Peters, "Luther on the Form and Scope of the Mosaic Law," *WLQ* 45 (1948) 98-113.

*Robert A. Bartels, "Law and Sin in Fourth Esdras and Saint Paul," *LQ, N.S.*, 1 (1949) 319-330.

*M. David, "The Codex of Hammurabi and its Relation to the Provisions of Law in Exodus," *OTS* 7 (1950) 149-178.

*R[euven] Yaron, "Jewish Law and Other Legal Systems of Antiquity," *JSS* 4 (1959) 308-331.

*Jacob J. Rabinowitz, "Manumission of Slaves in Roman Law and Oriental Law," *JNES* 19 (1960) 42-44.

*Jacob J. Rabinowitz, "Neo-Babylonaian Legal Documents and Jewish Law," *JJP* 13 (1961) 131-175.

§131 *2.3.21 Laws of Retaliation, Retribution & Revenge [Blood Feuds]*

Austin Abbott, "The Use of Retaliation in the Mosaic Law," *CT* 7 (1889-90) 321-333.

Albert A. Isaacs, "Retribution," *EN* 3 (1891) 481-483.

*Fritz Hommel, "Assyriological Notes," *SBAP* 19 (1897) 78-90.

[§27. *Tuktû,* "blood, vengance" = ቱክቶ (*tektô*) "blood (of the woman)", pp. 87-88.

Walter M. Patton, "Blood-Revenge in Arabia and Israel," *AJT* 5 (1901) 703-731.

Alexander H. Harley, "Blood-Feud Among the Semites," *GUOST* 3 (1907-12) 23-25.

David Werner Amran, "Retaliation and Compensation," *JQR, N.S.,* 2 (1911-12) 191-211.

Robert Burnett, "The Law of Retaliation in the East," *GUOST* 4 (1913-22) 82-84.

Politicus, "Biblical Legislation Concerning Reprisal and Punishment," *HR* 75 (1918) 364-366.

*Moses Buttenwieser, "Blood Revenge and Burial Rites in Ancient Israel," *JAOS* 39 (1919) 303-321.

*E. N. Haddad, "Blood Revenge Among the Arabs," *JPOS* 1 (1920-21) 103-111.

S. U. Turnipseed, "Blood Revenge and Trial by Jury," *MQR, 3rd Ser.,* 50 (1924) 103-110.

Otto A. Piper, "Vengeance and the Moral Order," *TT* 5 (1948-49) 221-234. [II. The Old Testament, pp. 225-229]

Herbert G. May, "Individual Responsibility and Retribution," *HUCA* 32 (1961) 107-120.

Henry McKeathing, "Vengence is Mine. A Study of the Pursuit of Vengeance in the Old Testament," *ET* 74 (1962-63) 239-245.

V. N. Yarkho, "Blood Vengeance and Divine Retribution in the 'Oresteia' of Aeschylus," *VDI* (1968) #4, 68-69. *[Greek]*

Pinchas Doron, "A New Look at an old Lex," *JANES* 1 (1968-69) #2, 21-27. *[Law of Retaliation]*

§132 *2.3.25 Taxation - General Studies*

*A. H. Sayce, "Jewish Tax-gatherers in Thebes," *JQR* 2 (1889-90) 400-405.

Allen B. West, "Aristidean Tribute in the Assessment of 421 B.C.," *AJA* 29 (1925) 135-151.

*Allen B. West, "Methone and the Assessment of 430," *AJA* 29 (1925) 440-444.

*W. L. Westermann, "Orchard and Vineyard Taxes in the Zenon Papyri," *JEA* 12 (1926) 38-51.

Mostafa Khan Fateh, "Taxation in Persia: A Synopsis from the Early Times to the Conquest of the Mogols," *BSOAS* 4 (1926-28) 723-743.

George McLean Harper Jr., "Tax-Contractors and their Relation to Tax-Collection in Ptolemaic Egypt," *PAPA* 64 (1933) lix.

G[eorge] M[cLean] Harper Jr., "Tax Contractors and their Relation to Tax Collection in Ptolemaic Egypt," *Aeg* 14 (1934) 49-64.

*G[eorge] M[cLean] Harper Jr., "The Relation of Ἀρχώνης, Μέτοχοι, and Ἔγγυοι to each other, to the Government and to the Tax Contract in Ptolemaic Egypt," *Aeg* 14 (1934) 269-285.

*Sherman Leroy Wallace, "Census and Poll-Tax in Ptolemaic Egypt," *AJP* 59 (1938) 418-442.

*Alan H. Gardiner, "Ramesside Texts relating to the Taxation and Transport of Corn," *JEA* 27 (1941) 19-73.

*Victor Tcherikover, "*Syntaxis* and *Laographia,*" *JJP* 4 (1950) 179-207. *[Poll Tax]*

A. Mittwoch, "Tribute and Land-tax in Seleucid Judea," *B* 36 (1955) 352-361.

J. A. S. Evans, "The Poll-tax in Egypt," *Aeg* 37 (1957) 259-265.

*J. Liver, "The Half-Shekel in the Scrolls of the Judean Desert Sect," *Tarbiẕ* 31 (1961-62) #1, III-IV.

*Moshe Beer, "Were the Babylonian Amoraim Exempt from Taxes and Customs?" *Tarbiẕ* 33 (1963-64) #3, III-IV.

*I. Shifman, "Royal Service Obligations in Palestine in the First Half of the First Millenium B.C., according to Biblical Tradition," *VDI* (1967) #1, 48.

§133 *2.3.22 The Institution of Kingship*

F. W. Buckler, "The Oriental Despot," *ATR* 10 (1927-28) 238-249.

Erwin R. Goodenough, "The Political Philosophy of Hellenistic Kingship," *YCS* 1 (1928) 55-102.

*Percy E. Newberry, "The Shepherd's Crook and the so-called 'Flail' or 'Scourge' of Osiris," *JEA* 15 (1929) 84-94. *[Symbol of Royalty]*

Militza Matthiew, "A Note on the Coronation Rites in Ancient Egypt," *JEA* 16 (1930) 31-32.

Maurice A. Canney, "The Magic of Kings," *JMUEOS* #17 (1932) 41-45.

H. G. Baynes, "On the Psychological Origins of Divine Kingship," *Folk* 47 (1936) 74-104.

*W. J. Ferrar, "The Jewish Kingship and the Sacred Combat," *Theo* 32 (1936) 37-43.

Anonymous, "Kingship in Sumeria," *BJRL* 21 (1937) 17.

Theodore H. Gaster, "Divine Kingship in the Ancient Near East: A Review Article," *RR* 9 (1944-45) 267-281. *(Review)*

*Raphael Patai, "Hebrew Installation Rites. A Contribution to the Study of Ancient Near Eastern-African Culture Contact," *HUCA* 20 (1947) 143-225.

*M. E. L. Mallowan, "Kingship and the Gods: a review," *Antiq* 23 (1949) 93-99. *(Review)*

*Geo Widengren, "The King and the Tree of Life in Ancient Near Eastern Religion (King and Saviour IV)," *UUÅ* (1951) #4, 1-79.

T. Fish, "Some Aspects of Kingship in the Sumerian City and Kingdom of Ur," *BJRL* 34 (1951-52) 37-43.

E. Douglas Van Buren, "Homage to a Deified King," *ZA* 50 (1952) 92-120.

F. E. Adcock, "Greek and Macedonian Kingship," *PBA* 39 (1953) 163-180.

*Matitiahu Tsevat, "Marriage and Monarchical Legitimacy in Ugarit and Israel," *JSS* 3 (1958) 237-243.

*J. G. Macqueen, "Hattian Mythology and Hittite Monarchy," *AS* 9 (1959) 171-188.

*Julian Morgenstern, "The King-God Among the Western Semites and the Meaning of Epiphanes," *VT* 10 (1960) 138-197.

Richard N. Frye, "The charisma of kingship in ancient Iran," *IA* 4 (1964) 36-54.

*Barnabas Lindars, "Gideon and Kingship," *JTS, N.S.,* 16 (1965) 315-326.

C. G. Thomas, "The Roots of Homeric Kingship," *HJAJ* 15 (1966) 387-407.

*D. Geoffrey Evans, "Rehoabam's Advisers at Shechem, and Political Institutions in Israel and Sumer," *JNES* 25 (1966) 273-279. [I. The Elders of Israel and Judah under King David; II. The Crisis of Succession; III. The Councils at Shechem; IV. The Assemblies at Uruk]

*Matitiahu Tsevat, "The Biblical Narrative of the Foundation of Kingship in Israel," *Tarbiz* 36 (1966-67) #2, I.

Mohiy E. A. E. Ibrahim, "Miscellaneous Passages about King and Kingship according to the Inscriptons of the Temple of Edfu," *ASAE* 60 (1968) 297-300.

§134 *2.3.22.1 The Monarchy in Israel*

†Anonymous, "History of the Hebrew Monarchy," *BQRL* 8 (1848) 26-61. *(Review)*

Anonymous, "Hebrew History," *CTPR, 3rd Ser.*, 4 (1848) 1-33. *(Review) [The Monarchy]*

†Anonymous, "The Old Testament: *Newman* and *Greg*," *NBR* 16 (1851-52) 119-148. *(Review) [History of the Hebrew Monarchy]*

J. H. A., "Newman's Hebrew Monarchy," *UQGR* 13 (1856) 5-33. *(Review)*

Anonymous, "The Hebrew Monarchy—Its Origins and Objects," *BFER* 10 (1861) 318-338. *(Review)*

George H. Schodde, "The Origin of the Royal Government in Israel," *LQ* 11 (1881) 178-183.

C. H. Toy, "The King in Jewish Post-exilian Writings," *JBL* 18 (1899) 156-168.

*Walter R. Betteridge, "The Attitude of Amos and Hosea Toward the Monarchy," *BW* 20 (1902) 361-369, 457-464.

*B. K. Ratty, "Samuel and the Monarchy," *ICMM* 8 (1911-12) 428-435.

Edward Day, "Was the Hebrew Monarchy Limited?" *AJSL* 40 (1923-24) 98-110.

James Oscar Boyd, "Monarchy in Israel: The Ideal and the Actual," *PTR* 26 (1928) 41-64.

C[hristopher] R. North, "The Old Testament Estimate of the Monarchy," *AJSL* 48(1931-32) 1-19.

* C[hristopher] R. North, "The Religious Aspect of Hebrew Kingship," *ZAW* 50(1932) 8-38.

*W. J. Ferrar, "The Jewish Kingship and the Sacred Combat," *Theo* 32 (1936) 37-43.

*S. Yevin, "The Beginnings of the Davidids," *Zion* 9 (1943-44) #3, I.

*Raphael Patai, "Hebrew Installation Rites. A Contribution to the Study of Ancient Near Eastern-African Culture Contact," *HUCA* 20 (1947) 143-225.

*A. R. Johnson, "Living Issues in Biblical Scholarship. Divine Kingship in the Old Testament," *ET* 62 (1950-51) 36-42.

Stanley Chesnut, "A Review of the Bible Concept of Kingship," *TUSR* 2 (1951-52) 2-16.

S. H. Hooke, "Biblical Studies. 2. Sacred Kingship in Israel," *CQR* 157 (1956) 386-392. *(Review)*

*W. Stewart McCullough, "Israel's Kings, Sacral and Otherwise," *ET* 68 (1956-57) 144-148.

*Aubrey R. Johnson, "Old Testament Exegesis Imaginative and Unimaginative. A Reply to Professor McCullough's article, 'Israel's Kings, Sacral and Otherwise'," *ET* 68 (1956-57) 178-179.

*Geo Widengren, "King and Covenant," *JSS* 2 (1957) 1-32.

E. I. J. Rosenthal, "Some Aspects of the Hebrew Monarchy," *JJS* 9 (1958) 1-18.

*Matitiahu Tsevat, "Marriage and Monarchical Legitimacy in Ugarit and Israel," *JSS* 3 (1958) 237-243.

*Wallace I. Wolverton, "The King's 'Justice' in Pre-exilic Israel," *ATR* 41 (1959) 276-286. [The *Shafaṭ* Function of Rule; The Early Period; The King's *Mishpaṭ;* The Eighth Century Prophets and *Mishpaṭ; Mishpaṭ* and Messiah; Conclusions]

*Cyril S. Rodd, "Kingship and Cult," *LQHR* 184 (1959) 21-26.

*A. G. Hebert, "The Idea of Kingship in the Old Testament," *RTR* 18 (1959) 34-45.

Joseph Bourke, "The Ideal King of Judah," *Scrip* 11 (1959) 97-110.

*Eugene H. Maly, "The Jotham Fable—Anti-Monarchical?" *CBQ* 22 (1960) 299-305.

*C. S. Mann, "Sacral Kingship—An Ashanti Footnote," *JSS* 5 (1960) 378-387.

*Julian Morgenstern, "The King-God Among the Western Semites and the Meaning of Epiphanes," *VT* 10 (1960) 138-197. [II. The King-God in Israel, pp. 176-197]

*Nicol Milne, "Prophet, Priest and King and Their Effect on Religion in Israel," *Abr-N* 2 (1960-61) 55-67.

Raphael Hallevy, "Charismatic Kingship in Israel," *Tarbiẕ* 30 (1960-61) #3, V-VII.

*Gerald Cooke, "The Israelite King as Son of God," *ZAW* 73 (1961) 202-225.

R. N. Whybray, "Some Historical Limitations of Hebrew Kingship," *CQR* 163 (1962) 136-150.

*Raphael Hallevy, "The Place of the Monarchy in the Israelite Religion," *Tarbiẕ* 32 (1962-63) #3, I-II.

*Abraham Malamat, "Kingship and Council in Israel and Sumer: A Parallel," *JNES* 22 (1963) 247-253.

T. C. G. Thornton, "Charismatic Kingship in Israel and Judah," *JTS, N.S.,* 14 (1963) 1-11.

A. E. Cundall, "Antecedents of the Monarchy in Ancient Israel," *VE* 3 (1964) 42-50.

*Abraham Malamat, "Organs of Statecraft in the Israelite Monarchy," *BA* 28 (1965) 34-65.

*Martin Noth, "God, King, People in the Old Testament: A Methodological Debate with a Contemporary School of Thought," *JTC* 1 (1965) 20-48. *(Trans. by Alice F. Carse)*

*D. Geoffrey Evans, "Rehoabam's Advisers at Shechem, and Political Institutions in Israel and Sumer," *JNES* 25 (1966) 273-279. [I. The Elders of Israel and Judah under King David; II. The Crisis of Succession; III. The Councils at Shechem; IV. The Assemblies at Uruk]

*L. M. Muntingh, "Some aspects of West-Semitic kingship in the period of the Hebrew patriarchs," *OTW* 9 (1966) 106-115.

*I. Shifman, "Royal Service Obligations in Palestine in the First Half of the First Millenium B.C., according to Biblical Tradition," *VDI* (1967) #1, 48.

J. H. Eaton, "The King as God's Witness," *ASTI* 7 (1968-69) 25-40.

E. E. Hallewy, "The Authority of Kingship," *Tarbiz* 38 (1968-69) #3, II-III.

*G. W. Ahlström, "Solomon, the Chosen One," *HRel* 8 (1968-69) 93-110.

Neil D. Isaacs, "Royal Robes and Regicide: A Preliminary Study of Literary Vestiges of Rule Rituals," *Folk* 80 (1969) 199-215.

*N. B. Jankowska, "Communal self-government and the king of the state of Arrapḫa," *JESHO* 12 (1969) 233-282.

*G. G. Giorgadze, "The Order of Succession to the Throne in the Old Hittite Kingdom (On the interpretation of §28 in the 'Decree of Telipinu')," *VDI* (1969) #4, 83.

*Arthur E. Cundall, "Sacral Kingship—The Old Testament Background," *VE* 6 (1969) 31-41.

§135 *2.3.23 Government, Politics & Law (outside Israel)*

*Anonymous, "Essays on the Institutions, Government, and Manners of the States of Ancient Greece," *QRL* 22 (1819-20) 163-203. *(Review)*

*Anonymous, "Outlines of History," *QRL* 45 (1831) 350-471. *[Subtitled:* "Subversion of Ancient Governments"*]*

G[eorge] H. E[merson], "Progress, as exhibited in the Government of Ancient Greece," *UQGR* 9 (1857) 113-129.

G[eorge] H. E[merson], "Progress, as exhibited in the Government of Ancient Rome," *UQGR* 9 (1857) 329-355.

Anonymous, "Ancient Political Economy," *WR* 68 (1857) 1-32.

†Anonymous, "Maine's *Ancient Law*," *QRL* 110 (1861) 114-138. *(Review)*

*August Eisenlohr, "On the Political of Egypt before the Reign of Ramses III; *probably in connection with the establishment of the Jewish Religion.* From the Great Harris Papyrus," *SBAT* 1 (1872) 355-384.

*†Anonymous, "Aristotle and the Athenian Constitution," *ERCJ* 173 (1891) 470-494. *(Review)*

Abby Leach, "The Athenian Democracy in the Light of Greek Literature," *AJP* 21 (1900) 361-177.

*James A. Quarles, "Sociology of Joseph's Day," *CFL, N.S.*, 5 (1902) 340-352. [Political, pp. 340-346]

W. S. Ferguson, "Athenian politics in the early third century," *Klio* 5 (1905-06) 155-179.

*Harold M. Wiener, "The Legislations of Israel and Babylonia," *JTVI* 41 (1909) 139-163. (Discussion, pp. 163-166)

*William Scott Ferguson, "Legalized Absolution en Route from Greece to Rome," *AmHR* 18 (1912-13) 29-47.

*Nahum Slousch, "Representative Government Among the Hebrews and Phoenicians," *JQR, N.S.,* 4 (1913-14) 303-310.

*James A. Montgomery, "Brief Communications," *JBL* 33 (1914) 78-80. [3. TARWAḤ, Sachau's Elephantine Papyrus 7, p. 80] *[Foreign Law]*

A. T. Olmstead, "The Political Development of Early Babylonia," *AJSL* 33 (1916-17) 283-321.

Arthur E. R. Boak, "The Extraordinary Commands from 80 to 48 B.C.: A Study in the Origin of the Principate," *AmHR* 24 (1918-19) 1-25.

*H. S. Linfield, "The Relation of Jewish to Babylonian Law," *AJSL* 36 (1919-20) 40-66.

Wilfred H. Schoff, "Regencies in Babylon," *JAOS* 42 (1922) 371-372.

Joseph William Hewitt, "The Development of Political Gratitude," *TAPA* 55 (1924) 35-51.

[W. M.] Flinders Petrie, "Justice and Revenue," *AEE* 10 (1925) 45-54. *[Staff of officers managing the Country of Egypt]*

Frank Burr Marsh, "Roman Parties in the Reign of Tiberius," *AmHR* 31 (1925-26) 233-250.

*Henry Roy William Smith, "A Political Cartoon of the Sixth Century B.C.," *PAPA* 57 (1926) xxii-xxiii.

George McLean Harper Jr., "Village Administration in the Roman Province of Syria," *YCS* 1 (1928) 105-168.

W. W. Tarn, "Seleucid-Parthian Studies," *PBA* 16 (1930) 105-135.

H. I. Bell, "The Problem of the Alexandrian Senate," *Aeg* 12 (1932) 173-184.

*Harold L. Creager, "A Comparison of the Hebrew and Greek Ideals of Democracy," *LCQ* 5 (1932) 312-325.

*Clive H. Carruthers, "More Hittite Words," *Lang* 9 (1933) 151-161. [1. *kutrus* 'witness', pp. 151-152]

Kurt Latte, "The Origin of the Roman Quaestorship," *TAPA* 67 (1936) 24-33.

M. P. Charlesworth, "The Virtues of a Roman Emperor: Propaganda and the Creation of Belief," *PBA* 23 (1937) 105-133.

R. L. Gilbert, "The Origin and History of the Peregrine Praetorship, 242-166 B.C.," *RJ* 2 (1939-41) 50-58.

*Kurt von Fritz, "Pompey's Policy before and after the Outbreak of the Civil War of 49 B.C.," *TAPA* 73 (1942) 145-180.

Herbert Liebesny, "The Administration of Justice in Nuzi," *JAOS* 63 (1943) 128-144.

*T. Fish, "The Place of the Small State in the Political and Cultural History of Ancient Mesopotamia," *BJRL* 18 (1944) 83-98.

*Saul Lieberman, "Roman Legal Institutions in Early Rabbnics and in the Acta Martyrum," *JQR, N.S.,* 35 (1944-45) 1-57.

Hans Julius Wolff, "The Origin of Judicial Litigation Among the Greeks," *Tr* 4 (1946) 31-87.

William F. Edgerton, "The Government and the Governed in the Egyptian Empire," *JNES* 6 (1947) 152-160.

C. Bradford Welles, "The Ptolemaic Administration of Egypt," *JJP* 3 (1949) 21-47.

Kurt von Fritz, "The Reorganisation of the Roman Government in 366 B.C. and the so-called Licinio-Sextian Laws," *HJAH* 1 (1950) 3-44.

Victor Ehrenberg, "Origins of Democracy," *HJAH* 1 (1950) 515-548.

*A. H. M. Jones, "The Economic Basis of the Athenian Democracy," *P&P* #1 (1952) 13-31.

William C. Hayes, "Notes on the Government of Egypt in the Late Middle Kingdom," *JNES* 12 (1953) 31-39.

*J. A. Wilson, E. A. Spieser, H. G. Güterbock, I. Mendelsohn, D. H. H. Ingalls and D. Bodde, "Authority and Law in the Ancient Orient," *JAOSS* #17 (1954) 1-55. [Authority and Ancient Law in Egypt, by J. A. Wilson, pp. 1-7; Authority and Law in Mesopotamia, by E. A. Spieser, pp. 8-15; Authority and Law in the Hittite Kingdom, by H. G. Güterbock, pp. 16-24; Authority and Law in Canaan-Israel, by I. Mendelsohn, pp. 25-33]

Hugh Last, "The *Praefectus Aegypti* and his Powers," *JEA* 40 (1954) 68-73.

A. H. M. Jones, "Imperial and Senatorial Jurisdiction in the Early Principate," *HJAH* 3 (1954-55) 464-488.

*John W. Wilson, "Egyptian Technology, Science, and Lore," *JWH* 2 (1954-55) 209-213. [Government and Society, pp. 210-212]

John H. Collins, "Caesar and the Corruption of Power," *HJAH* 4 (1955) 445-465.

G. E. M. de St. Croix, "The Constitution of the Five Thousand," *HJAH* 5 (1956) 1-23. *[Greek Government]*

E. T. Salmon, "The Evolution of Augustus' Principate," *HJAH* 5 (1956) 456-478. *[Roman Government]*

*Hans Julius Wolff, "Roman Law as Part of Ancient Civilization: Reflections on Leopold Wenger's Last Work," *Tr* 11 (1956) 381-394. *(Review)*

Thorkild Jacobsen, "Early Political Development in Mesopotamia," *ZA* 52 (1957) 91-140.

Ronald Syme, "Imperator Caesar. A Study in Nomenclature," *HJAH* 7 (1958) 172-188.

Geoffrey Evans, "Ancient Mesopotamian Assemblies," *JAOS* 78 (1958) 1-11

Geoffrey Evans, "Ancient Mesopotamian Assemblies—an addendum," *JAOS* 78 (1958) 114-115.

*Gus W. Van Beek, "Frankincense and Myrrh in Ancient South Arabia," *JAOS* 78 (1958) 141-152. [Political Effects of the Incense Trade, pp. 149-151]

*Andrew Alföldi, "Hasta—Summa Imperii. The Spear as Embodiment of Sovereignty in Rome," *AJA* 63 (1959) 1-27.

M[ohammad] Abdul-Ḳader Mohammad, "The Administration of Syro-Palestine during the New Kingdom," *ASAE* 56 (1959) 105-137. *[Egyptian Government]*

Ann Boddington, "The Original Nature of the Consulare Tibunate," *HJAH* 8 (1959) 356-364.

*P. A. Brunt, "Charges of Provincial Maladministration under the Early Principate," *HJAH* 10 (1961) 189-227.

*Abd el-Mohsen el-Khachab, "*Ο 'ΚΑΡΑΚΑΛΛΟΣ' ΚΟΣΜΟΚΡΑΤΩΡ*," *JEA* 47 (1961) 119-133. *[Politics]*

*A. F. Rainey, "Administration in Ugarit and the Samaria Ostraca," *IEJ* 12 (1962) 62-63.

*‡John A. Brinkman, "A Preliminary Catalogue of Written Sources for a Political History of Babylonia: 1160-722 B.C.," *JCS* 16 (1962) 83-109.

*S. Safrai, "The Status of Provincia Judea after the Destruction of the Second Temple," *Zion* 27 (1962) #3/4, VII.

*D. R. Dudley, "Stocism and Roman Politics: Introduction and Prospects," *HT* 13 (1963) 767-773.

Jacob Neusner, "Parthian Political Ideology," *IA* 3 (1963) 40-59.

J. A. Brinkman, "Provincial Administration in Babylonia under the second dynasty of Isin," *JESHO* 6 (1963) 233-242.

*Abraham Malamat, "Kingship and Council in Israel and Sumer: A Parallel," *JNES* 22 (1963) 247-253.

*E. A. Speiser, "Cuneiform Law and the History of Civilization," *PAPS* 107 (1963) 536-541.

J. David Thomas, "The Theban Administrative District in the Roman Period," *JEA* 50 (1964) 139-143.

H. Lewy, "Notes on the Political Organization of Asia Minor at the Time of the Old Assyrian Texts," *Or, N.S.,* 33 (1964) 181-198.

Erich S. Gruen, "Politics and the Courts in 104 B.C.," *TAPA* 95 (1964) 99-110.

*D. McKenzie, "Juridical Procedure at the Town Gate," *VT* 14 (1964) 100-104.

A. E. Raubitschek, "The Peace Policy of Perikles," *AJA* 69 (1965) 174.

*Donald White, "Demeter's Sicilian Cult as a Political Instrument," *GRBS* 5 (1965) 261-279.

Jerzy Linderski, "Constitutional Aspects of the Consular Elections in 59 B.C.," *HJAH* 14 (1965) 423-442.

M. Abdul-Qader Muhammed, "The Hittite Provincial Administration of conquered Territories," *ASAE* 59 (1966) 109-142.

*Erich S. Gruen, "Political Persecutions in the 90's B.C.," *HJAH* 15 (1966) 32-64.

*D. Geoffrey Evans, "Rehoabam's Advisers at Shechem, and Political Institutions in Israel and Sumer," *JNES* 25 (1966) 273-279. [I. The Elders of Israel and Judah under King David; II. The Crisis of Succession; III. The Councils at Shechem; IV. The Assemblies at Uruk]

Nels Bailkey, "Early Mesopotamian Constitutional Development," *AmHR* 72 (1966-67) 1211-1236.

Richard A. Henshaw, "The Office of *Šaknu* in Neo-Assyrian Times. I," *JAOS* 87 (1967) 517-525.

*T. J. Luce, "Political Propaganda on Roman Republican Coins: circa 92-82 B.C.," *AJA* 72 (1968) 25-39.

*R. W. Davies, "Police Work in Roman Times," *HT* 18 (1968) 700-707.

Richard A. Henshaw, "The Office of *Šaknu* in Neo-Assyrian Times. II," *JAOS* 88 (1968) 461-483.

Rivkah Harris, "Some Aspects of the Centralization of the Realm under Hammurapi and his Successors," *JAOS* 88 (1968) 727-732.

A. I. Dovatur, "Two *Aporiai* in the 'Politics' of Aristotle," *VDI* (1968) #3, 63.

K. M. Kolobova, "Problems Connected with the Rise of the Athenian State," *VDI* (1968) #4, 55.

*Naphtali Lewis, "The Limited Role of the Epistrategos in Liturgic Appointments," *CdÉ* 44 (1969) 339-344.

John Briscoe, "Early Policy and Senatorial Politics 168-146 B.C.," *HJAH* 18 (1969) 49-70. [I. The Dipolmacy of the Senate (a) Egypt (b) Syria (c) Pergamum and Bithynia (d) Cappadocia (e) Rhodes and the Aegean (f) The Greek Mainland; II. Supporters and Opponents of Senatorial Policy; III. Political Alignments]

*N. B. Jankowska, "Communal self-government and the king of the state of Arrapḫa," *JESHO* 12 (1969) 233-282.

H. Reviv, "On urban representative institutions and self-government in Syria-Palestine in the second half of the second millenium B.C.," *JESHO* 12 (1969) 283-297.

*Michael C. Astour, "The Partition of the Confederacy of Mukiš-Nuḫašše-Nii by Šuppiluliuma. A Study in Political Geography of the Amarna Age," *Or., N.S.,* 38 (1969) 381-414.

§136 *2.3.24 Laws of Foreign Countries - Specifically*

†Anonymous, "Legal Oratory of Greece," *QRL* 29 (1823) 313-338. *(Review)*

†Anonymous, "Greek Courts of Justice," *QRL* 33 (1825-26) 332-356. *(Review)*

Anonymous, "The Quarterly Review: 'Greek Courts of Justice.' No. 66," *WR* 7 (1827) 227-268.

†Anonymous, "Roman Law," *WR* 8 (1827) 384-423. *(Review)*

†Anonymous, "Corn-Laws of Athens and Rome," *ERCJ* 83 (1846) 351-374. [Additional note, *ERCJ* 85 (1847) p. 259] *(Review)*

Anonymous, "Roman Civil Law," *DUM* 37 (1851) 126-130. *(Review)*

*( ) G., "The Prince of Persia; The Law of the Medes and Persians; and the Chronology of the Jewish Writer Demetrius," *JSL, 3rd Ser.*, 12 (1860-61) 446-456; 13 (1961) 153-175.

*George M. Towle, "International and Ancient Law," *CongR* 5 (1865) 142-161.

†Eugene Revillout, "A Lawsuit tried before the *Laocrites* during the reign of Ptolemy Soter," *SBAP* 1 (1878-79) 33-34.

Perceval M. Laurence, "Judges and Litigants," *JP* 8 (1879) 125-132.

*August C. Merriam, "Law Code of the Kretan Gortyna," *AJA, O.S.*, 1 (1885) 324-350; 2 (1886) 24-45, 424. *[Greek Law Codes on Adoption & Property Rights]*

A[ugust] C. Merriam, "The Law Code of the Creatan Gortyna," *PAPA* 17 (1885) xxxiv-xxxv.

W. W. Goodwin, "The Relation of the Πρόεδροι to the Πρυτάνεις in the Attic Senate," *PAPA* 17 (1885) xxxv-xxxvi.

A[ugust] C. Merriam, "The Law Code of the Kretan Gortyna," *AJA, O.S.*, 2 (1886) 424.

Frank B. Tarbell, "The Relation of ΨΗΦΙΣΜΑΤΑ to NOMOI at Athens in the Fifth and Fourth Centuries, B.C.," *AJP* 10 (1889) 79-83.

*(Miss) M. A. Murray, "The Descent of Property in the Early Periods of Egyptian History," *SBAP* 17 (1895) 240-245.

*Joseph Offord, "The Myths and Laws of Babylonia, and the Bible," *AAOJ* 25 (1903) 258-261.

*Theophilus G. Pinches, "The Laws of the Babylonians, as Recorded in the Code of Hammurabi," *JTVI* 35 (1903) 237-247. (Discussion, pp. 247-255)

A. H. Sayce, "The Legal Code of Babylonia," *AJT* 8 (1904) 256-266.

*James Henry Stevenson, "The Hammurabi Code and Hebrew Legislation," *MQR, 3rd Ser.,* 30 (1904) 513-525.

*C. M. Cobern, "Moses and Hammurabi and Their Laws," *MR* 86 (1904) 697-703.

*John R. Sampey, "The Code of Hammurabi and the Laws of Moses," *R&E* 1 (1904) 97-107, 233-243.

*Max Kellner, "The Hammurabi Code and the Code of the Covenant," *RP* 4 (1905) 99-118. [I. The Discovery of the Hammurabi Stele; II. The Origin of the Code; III. An Analysis of the Code; IV. The Code of the Covenant; V. The Covenant Code and the Code of Hammurabi, The Treatment of Slaves, Accidental Homicide, Attack on Parents, Man-Stealing, Bodily Injuries, Criminal Negligence, House-Breaking, Trespass and Loss, Seduction, Pledge, Judicial Integrity; VI. Conclusion]

*J. E. Godbey, "Hammurabi and Moses," *MQR, 3rd Ser.,* 32 (1906) 461-475.

Anonymous, "Laws of Ancient Babylonia," *MR* 88 (1906) 315-318.

*J. Robertson, Buchanan, "The Code of Hammurabi and Israelitish Legislation: A Comparison of the Civil Codes in Babylonia and Israel," *GUOST* 3 (1907-12) 25-27.

*Eduard König, "Relations of Babylonian and Old Testament Culture. *IV. The Legislation of the Old Testament and Its Relations to that of Babylon,*" *HR* 57 (1909) 443-447.

*W. T Pilter, "A Legal Episode in Ancient Babylonian Family Life," *SBAP* 32 (1910) 81-92, 129-142.

William Scott Ferguson, "The Laws of Demetrius of Phalerum and their Guardians," *Klio* 11 (1911) 265-276.

V. Aptowitzer, "The Controversy Over the Syro-Roman Code," *JQR, N.S.,* 2 (1911-12) 55-74.

W. D. Strappini, "Babylonian Legislation 4500 Years Ago," *AER* 47 (1912) 161-172.

Marcus N. Tod, "International Abritration in the Greek World," *JTVI* 44 (1912) 275-292. (Discussion, pp. 292-296)

[Paul Carus], "Hammurabi and the Salic Law," *OC* 26 (1912) 577-583.

Alan H. Gardiner, "A Political Crime in Ancient Eygpt," *JMUEOS* #2 (1912-13) 57-64.

P. Koschaker, "The Scope and Methods of a History of Assyrio-Babylonian Law," *SBAP* 35 (1913) 230-243.

*Anonymous, "Ancient Semitic Law," *MR* 97 (1915) 968-972. *[Code of Hammurabi]*

*A. H. Sayce, "Assyriological Notes," *SBAP* 39 (1917) 207-212. [The Hittite Code of Laws, p. 211]

*M. Cary, "The land legislation of Caesar's first consulship," *JP* 35 (1919-20) 174-190.

*S[tephen] Langdon, "The Sumerian Law Code Compared with the Code of Hammurabi," *JRAS* (1920) 489-515.

*V. Schiel, "The Oldest Written Code," *MJ* 11 (1920) 130-132.

*George A. Barton, "An Important Social Law of the Ancient Babylonians—A Text Hitherto Misunderstood," *AJSL* 37 (1920-21) 62-71. *[Prostitution, and the rights of Prostitutes]*

*John A. Maynard, "The Assyrian Law Code," *JSOR* 6 (1922) 17-20.

G. R. Driver and John [C.] Miles, "Koschaker's theory of the 'Old Assyrian Laws'," *Baby* 9 (1926) 41-64.

Alfred P. Dorjahn, "Legal Precedent in Athenian Courts," *PAPA* 58 (1927) xxviii-xxix.

Raymond P. Dougherty, "The Babylonian Principle of Suretyship as Administered by Temple Law," *AJSL* 46 (1929-30) 73-103.

*S[tephen] Langdon, "Note on the Legal Commentary *Ana itti-šu*," *AJSL* 48 (1931-32) 51-53.

I. Lourie, "A Note on Egyptian Law-Courts," *JEA* 17 (1931) 62-64.

*Ira M. Price, "The Relation of Certain Gods to the Equity and Justice in Early Babylonia," *JAOS* 52 (1932) 174-178.

Clyde Pharr, "The Interdiction of Magic in Roman Law," *TAPA* 63 (1932) 269-295.

*George A. Barton, "An Obscure passage in the Hittite Laws," *JAOS* 53 (1933) 358-359.

*Nathaniel Julius Reich, "The Codification of the Egyptian Laws by Darius and the Origin of the 'Demotic Chronicle'," *Miz* 1 (1933) 178-185.

*G[eorge] M[cLean] Harper Jr., "The Relation of Ἀρχώνης, Μέτοχοι, and Ἔγγυοι to each other, to the Government and to the Tax Contract in Ptolemaic Egypt," *Aeg* 14 (1934) 269-285.

*J. Capart, A. H. Gardiner, and B. van de Walle, "New Light on the Ramesside Tomb-Robberies," *JEA* 22 (1936) 169-193.

*Jaroslav Černý, "Restitution of, and Penalty attaching to, Stolen Property in Ramesside Times," *JEA* 23 (1937) 186-189.

A. Billheimer, "Amendments in Athenian Decrees," *AJA* 42 (1938) 456-485.

*G. A. Wainwright, "Thoughts on Three Recent Articles," *JEA* 24 (1938) 59-64. [I. *Reference to:* "New Light on the Ramesside Tomb Robberies", pp. 59-62]

James H. Oliver, "On the Ephesian Debtor Law of 85 B.C.," *AJP* 60 (1939) 468-469.

*Russel M. Geer, "Notes on the Land Law of Tiberius Gracchus," *TAPA* 70 (1939) 30-36.

*G. R. Driver and John C. Miles, "Ordeal by Oath at Nuzi," *Iraq* 7 (1940) 132-138.

Herbert Liebesny, "Evidence in Nuzi Legal Procedure," *JAOS* 61 (1941) 130-142.

E. L. Allen, "The Biblical Roots of International Law," *LQHR* 168 (1943) 328-332.

*Boaz Cohen, "The Relationship of Jewish to Roman Law," *JQR, N.S.,* 34 (1943-44) 267-280, 409-424.

*Boaz Cohen, "Some Remarks on the Law of Persons in Jewish and Roman Jurisprudence," *PAAJR* 16 (1946-47) 1-37.

*Hans Julius Wolff, "Marriage Law and Family Organization in Ancient Athens: A Study in the Interrelation of Public and Private Law in the Greek City," *Tr* 2 (1944) 43-96.

*Gisela M. A. Richter, "Peisistratos' Law Regarding Tombs," *AJA* 49 (1945) 152.

‡A. Arthur Schiller, "Bibliography of Anglo-American Studies in Roman, Greek, and Greco-Egyptian Law and Related Sciences (1939-1945)," *SAENJ* 3 (1945) 75-94.

‡Adolf Berger and A. Arthur Schiller, "Bibliography of Anglo-American Studies in Roman, Greek, and Greco-Egyptian Law and Related Sciences, II (1945-1947)," *SAENJ* 5 (1947) 62-82.

*Rafael Taubenschlag, "Customary Law and Custom in the Papyri," *JJP* 1 (1946) 41-54.

Hans Julius Wolff, "Consensual contracts in the papyri?" *JJP* 1 (1946) 54-79.

Hans Julius Wolff, "The Origin of Judicial Litigation Among the Greeks," *Tr* 4 (1946) 31-87.

Henry S. Robinson, "Notes on the Code of Solon," *AJA* 52 (1948) 373-374.

Franklin F. Russell, "Note on a Recent Greek Work in Greek Legal History," *SAENJ* 6 (1948) 77-88.

*Leopold Wenger, "Observations concerning the Papyrus Baraize and the Right of Redemption in Hellenistic Law," *JJP* 3 (1949) 9-20.

Albrecht Goetze, "Mesopotamian Laws and the Historian," *JAOS* 69 (1949) 115-120.

*Boaz Cohen, "Contrectatio in Jewish and Roman Law," *RIDA, 1st Ser.,* 2 (1949) 133-156.

A. Arthur Schiller, "The jurists and praefects of Rome," *RIDA, 1st Ser.,* 3 (1949) 319-359.

H. F. Jolowicz, "The judex and the arbitral principle," *RIDA, 1st Ser.,* 2 (1949) 477-492.

E. Neufeld, "Notes on Hittite Laws," *ArOr* 18 (1950) Part 4, 116-130.

*Rafael Taubenschlag, "The Inviolability of Domicle in Greco-Roman Egypt," *ArOr* 18 (1950) Part 4, 293-297.

*A. Van Selms, "The Goring Ox in Babylonian and Biblical Law," *ArOr* 18 (1950) Part 4, 321-330.

Rafael Taubenschlag, "Τευημ̣ατογραφία in Greco-Roman Egypt," *JJP* 4 (1950) 77-82.

*Josef Klima, "The *patria potestas* in the Light of the Newly Discovered pre-Hammurabian Sources of Law," *JJP* 4 (1950) 275-288.

John C. Miles, "The Court in Phreatto," *RIDA, 1st Ser.,* 5 (1950) 219-224.

R[afael] Taubenschlag, "The Law of Associations in Greco-Roman Egypt," *RIDA, 1st Ser.,* 5 (1950) 509-514.

*†M. D. W. Jeffreys, "A remark concerning the Laws of Eshnunna," *Sumer* 6 (1950) 194-195.

L. R. Palmer, "The Indo-European Origins of Greek Justice," *TPS* (1950) 149-168.

P. Artiz, "Two Pre-Hammurabi Codes Newly Discovered," *BIES* 16 (1951) #1/2, II.

H. H. Figulla, "Lawsuit concerning a Sacrilegious*[sic]* Theft at Erech," *Iraq* 13 (1951) 95-101.

Rafael Taubenschlag, "The Provisional Legal Protection in the Papryi," *JJP* 5 (1951) 143-154.

David Daube, "Concerning the Classification of Interdicts," *RIDA 1st Ser.,* 6 (1951) 23-78.

A. F. L. Beeston, "A Sabaean Penal Law," *Muséon* 64 (1951) 305-315.

Józef Modrzejewski, "Private Arbitration in the Law of Greco-Roman Egypt," *JJP* 5 (1952) 239-256.

Rafael Taubenschlag, "Introduction to the Law of the Papyri," *RIDA, 2nd Ser.,* 1 (1952) 279-376. [Chapter I. Egyptian, Greek and Roman Law and their Interrelation; Chapter II. Private Law; Chapter III. Penal Law; Chapter IV. Procedure and Execution; Chapter V. Political Law; Chapter VI. Administrative Law; Chapter VII. Administrative Procedure and Administrative Execution]

F. Pringsheim, "The Decisive Moment for Aedilician Liability," *RIDA, 2nd Ser.,* 1 (1952) 545-556.

*Manfred R. Lehmann, "Abraham's Purchase of Machpelah and Hittite Law," *BASOR* #129 (1953) 15-18.

Adolf Berger, "Encyclopedic Dictionary of Roman Law," *TAPS, N.S.,* 43 (1953) 333-808.

Józef Modrzejewski, "Additional Provisions in Private Legal Acts in Greco-Roman Egypt," *JJP* 7&8 (1953-54) 211-229.

S[amuel] N[oah] Kramer, "Ur-Nammu Law Code," *Or, N.S.,* 23 (1954) 40-48. (Appendix: notes by Adam Falkenstein, pp. 49-51)

*Boaz Cohen, "Ususfructus in Jewish and Roman Law," *RIDA, 3rd Ser.,* 1 (1954) 173-193.

E. Stuart Staveley, "The Conduct of Elections during an *Interregnum,*" *HJAH* 3 (1954-55) 193-211. [Addendum: The Supposed 'Violations of the Licinio-Sextian Plebiscite, pp. 208-211]

*Boaz Cohen, "Self-Help in Jewish and Roman Law," *RIDA, 3rd Ser.,* 2 (1955) 107-133.

John [C.] Miles, "Some Remarks on the Origins of Testacy, with Some References to the Old Babylonian Laws," *RIDA, 3rd Ser.,* 1 (1954) 119-124.

*M. I. Finley, "Marriage, Sale and Gift in the Homeric World," *RIDA, 3rd Ser.,* 2 (1955) 166-194.

Cezary Kunderewicz, "The Problem of *Anefang* in Certain Ancient and Medieval Laws," *JJP* 9&10 (1955-56) 401-430. [II. The Greek Law, pp. 410-413; III. The Law of Egypt, pp. 413-417; IV. The Code of Hammurabi, pp. 417-426; V. The Roman Law, pp. 426-429]

Julius Lewy, "On Some Institutions of the Old Assyrian Empire," *HUCA* 27 (1956) 1-79.

*Hans Julius Wolff, "Roman Law as Part of Ancient Civilization: Reflections on Leopold Wenger's Last Work," *Tr* 11 (1956) 381-394. *(Review)*

G. G. Garner, "Writing and the Bible: Dodging The Law," *AT* 1 (1956-57) #4, 3-4.

Gertrude Smith, "More Recent Theories on the Origin and Interrelation of the First Classifications of Greek Laws," *JWH* 3 (1956-57) 173-195.

*Jacob J. Rabinowitz, "A Legal Formula in Egyptian, Egyptian-Aramaic, and Murabba'at Documents," *BASOR* #145 (1957) 33-34. *[On the sale of Property]*

Donald H. Gard, "Power for Life. *The Rise of Organized Law in Mesopotamia,*" *Interp* 11 (1957) 41-47.

A. S. Diamond, "An Eye for an Eye," *Iraq* 19 (1957) 151-155.

F. Pringsheim, "Some causes of codification," *RIDA, 3rd Ser.,* 4 (1957) 301-311.

Reuven Yaron, "Some Remarks on 'Donatio Mortis Causa'," *RIDA, 3rd Ser.,* 3 (1957) 493-512.

A. L. Boegehold, "Athenian Law Courts and Tokens," *AJA* 62 (1958) 222.

*Boaz Cohen, "Arbitration in Jewish and Roman Law," *RIDA, 3rd Ser.,* 5 (1958) 165-223.

*Boaz Cohen, "Concerning Jewish and Roman Law 'Specificato' in Jewish and Roman Law," *RIDA, 3rd Ser.,* 5 (1958) 225-290.

*Reuven Yaron, "Notes on Aramaic Papryi," *RIDA, 3rd Ser.,* 5 (1958) 299-310. [(A) The Interpretation of P. Brooklyn 1; (B) The *Kyrieia*-Clause in P. Brooklyn 12; (C) The Two Beginnings of P. Brooklyn 12]

J.A . Iliffe, "'Thirty days hath Lex Aquilla'," *RIDA, 3rd Ser.,* 5 (1958) 493-506.

*R[euven] Yaron, "Jewish Law and Other Legal Systems of Antiquity," *JSS* 4 (1959) 308-331.

*J. A. C. Thomas, "*Custodia* and *Horrea,*" *RIDA, 3rd Ser.,* 6 (1959) 371-383. *[Laws on Liability]*

T. Jacobsen, "An Ancient Mesopotamian Trial for Homicide," *SBO* 3 (1959) 130-150.

Kathleen M. T. Atkinson, "Constitutional and Legal Aspects of the Trials of Marcus Primus and Varro Murena," *HJAH* 9 (1960) 440-473.

M. I. Finley, "The Servile Statuses of Ancient Greece," *RIDA, 3rd Ser.*, 7 (1960) 165-189.

Hans Julius Wolff, "Plurality of Laws in Ptolemaic Egypt," *RIDA, 3rd Ser.*, 7 (1960) 191-223.

Kathleen M. T. Atkinson, "'Restitutio in integrum', and 'iussum Augusti Caesaris' in an inscription at Leyden," *RIDA, 3rd Ser.*, 7 (1960) 227-272.

*J. A. C. Thomas, "Carriage by Sea," *RIDA, 3rd Ser.*, 7 (1960) 489-505. *[Liability]*

*J. J. Finkelstein, "Ammiṣaduqa's Edict and the Babylonian 'Law Codes'," *JCS* 15 (1961) 91-104.

*Jacob J. Rabinowitz, "Neo-Babylonian Legal Documents and Jewish Law," *JJP* 13 (1961) 131-175.

Alan Watson, "The Form and Nature of 'acceptilatio' in Classical Roman Law," *RIDA, 3rd Ser.*, 8 (1961) 391-416.

Hans G. Güterbock, "Further Notes on Hittite Laws," *JCS* 16 (1962) 17-23.

*F. Charles Fensham, "Widow, Orphan and the Poor in Ancient Near Eastern Legal and Wisdom Literature," *JNES* 21 (1962) 129-139.

Reuven Yaron, "Forms in the Laws of Eshnunna," *RIDA, 3rd Ser.*, 9 (1962) 137-153.

Kathleen M. T. Atkinson, "The *Constitutio* of Vedius Pollio at Ephesus and its analogies," *RIDA, 3rd Ser.*, 9 (1962) 261-289.

*W. M. Gordon, "Interruption of *Usucapio*," *RIDA, 3rd Ser.*, 9 (1962) 325-333.

Peter Stein, "Generations, Life-spans and Usufructs," *RIDA, 3rd Ser.*, 9 (1962) 335-355.

Alan Watson, "Consensual *Societas* between Romans and the Introduction of *formulae*," *RIDA, 3rd Ser.*, 9 (1962) 431-436.

*David Asheri, "Laws of Inheritance, Distribution of Land and Political Constitutions in Ancient Greece," *HJAH* 12 (1963) 1-21.

*V. Korošec, "The Warfare of the Hittites—from a Legal Point of View," *Iraq* 25 (1963) 159-166.

*E. A. Speiser, "Cuneiform Law and the History of Civilization," *PAPS* 107 (1963) 536-541.

Reuven Yaron, "On Section II 57 (=172) of the Hittite Laws," *RIDA, 3rd Ser.*, 10 (1963) 137-146.

*Roland F. Willetts, "Observations on Leg. Gort. II. 16-20," *KZFE* 3 (1964) 170-176.

Lujo Margetić, "The Judge-Affixer in the Judicial Procedure of Athens," *RIDA, 3rd Ser.*, 12 (1965) 149-155.

William E. Brynteson, "Roman Law and New Law: The Development of a Legal Idea," *RIDA, 3rd Ser.*, 12 (1965) 203-223.

*J. A. C. Thomas, "Return to 'Horrea'," *RIDA, 3rd Ser.*, 13 (1965) 353-368.

*Edward E. Erpelding, "An Investigation of the Israelite Concept of Law Expressed in the Covenant Code," *SS* 17 (1965) #2, 41-67. [Ancient Near Eastern Law, pp. 57-64]

Ronald S. Stroud, "Drakon's Law on Homicide," *AJA* 70 (1966) 195.

*Reuven Yaron, "The Goring Ox in Near Eastern Laws," *ILR* 1 (1966) 396-406.

*J. J. Finkelstein, "Sex Offenses in Sumerian Laws," *JAOS* 86 (1966) 355-372.

*Albrecht Goetze, "On §§163, 164/5 and 176 of the Hittite Code," *JCS* 20 (1966) 128-132.

Richard Holton Pierce, "Affixer and Allotment Machine at Athens," *RIDA, 3rd Ser.*, 14 (1966) 155-156.

B. M. Levick, "Imperial Control of the Elections under the Early Principate: Commendatio, Suffragatio and 'Nominatio'," *HJAH* 16 (1967) 207-230.

*M. B. Rowton, "Watercourses and Water Rights in the Offical Correspondence from Larasa and Isin," *JCS* 21 (1967) 267-274.

*L. M. Muntingh, "The Social and Legal Status of a Free Ugaritic Female," *JNES* 26 (1967) 102-112.

*F. A. Fensham, "Shipwreck in Ugarit and Ancient Near East Law Codes," *OA* 6 (1967) 221-224.

Lily Ross Taylor, "The Dating of Major Legislation and Elections in Caesars' First Consulship," *HJAH* 17 (1968) 173-193. [I. The First Agrarian Law; II. The Lex Vatinia de impero Caesaris; III. The Election of Magistrates for the year 58]

J. J. Finkelstein, "The Laws of Ur-Nammu," *JCS* 22 (1968-69) 66-82. [U. 7739; U. 7740]

*David Sperling, "The Akkadian Legal Term *dīnu u dabābu*," *JANES* 1 (1968-69) #1, 35-40.

Solomon Grayzel, "The Jews and Roman Law," *JQR, N.S.,* 59 (1968-69) 93-117.

Peter Garnsey, "Legal Privilege in the Roman Empire," *P&P* #41 (1968) 3-24.

J. A. C. Thomas, "*Furtum* of Documents," *RIDA, 3rd Ser.,* 15 (1968) 429-444.

*M. A. Dandamayev, "The Testimony of Slaves in Babylonian Courts," *VDI* (1968) #1, 12.

*Reuven Yaron, "Foreign Merchants at Ugarit," *ILR* 4 (1969) 70-79.

*Albrecht Goetze, "Hittite *šek- / šak-* '(legally) recognize', in Treaties," *JCS* 22 (1968-69) 7-8.

*Harry A. Hoffner Jr., "Some Contributions of Hittitology to Old Testament Study," *TB* #20 (1969) 27-55. [B. Hittite Law and the Old Testament, pp. 37-44]

*V. P. Popov, "The Status of Slaves in the Hittite Kingdom (based on §§ 93-99 of the Hittite laws)," *VDI* (1969) #3, 81.

*Sh. M. Paul, "Types of Formulation in Biblical and Mesopotamian Law," *Lěš* 34 (1969-70) #4, n.p.n.

§137 *2.3.25 Civil Liberty, Citizenship, Patriotism, Censorship & Propaganda*

*W. B. O. P., "The Character and Institutions of Moses, considered with particular Reference to their Bearing on the Science of Government and Civil Liberty," *CE* 21 (1836) 1-21.

†Anonymous, "Restrictions on the Diffusion of Opinion among the Ancients," *WR* 24 (1836) 135-155.

John Poucher, "The Israelite View of Patriotism," *BW* 4 (1894) 32-37.

*Eduard König, "Israel's Attitude Respecting Alien-Right and Usages of War in Antiquity," *HR* 72 (1916) 184-189.

M. Radin, "Freedom of Speech in Ancient Athens," *AJP* 48 (1927) 215-220.

*Moses Buttenwieser, "The Prophets and Nationalism," *YCCAR* 37 (1927) 271-291.

J. Murphy, "The development of Individuality in the Ancient Civilizations," *AIPHOS* 4 (1936) 867-883.

Clarence A. Forbes, "Books for Burning," *TAPA* 67 (1936) 114-125. *[Practice of Burning Books]*

*W. S. Ferguson, "*Polis* and *Idia* in Periclean Athens. The Relation between Public Service and Private Activities," *AmHR* 45 (1939-40) 269-278.

*Robert Henry Pfeiffer, "The Patriotism of Israel's Prophets," *HDSB* 7 (1941-42) 45-54.

*H. A. Wolfson, "Philo on Jewish Citizenship in Alexandria," *JBL* 63 (1944) 165-168.

Bernard J. Bramberg, "Individual Rights and the Demands of the State: The Position of Classical Judaism," *YCCAR* 54 (1944) 197-211.

Frederick H. Cramer, "Bookburning and Censorship in Ancient Rome: A Chapter from the History of Freedom of Speech," *JHI* 6 (1945) 157-196.

*O. W. Reinmuth, "The Ephebate and the Citizenship in Attica and Egypt," *TAPA* 78 (1947) 433-434.

*A[ntony] E. Raubitschek, "The Origin of Ostracism," *AJA* 54 (1950) 258-259.

Antony E. Raubitschek, "The Origin of Ostracisim," *AJA* 55 (1951) 221-229.

C. A. Robinson Jr., "Cleisthenes and Ostracism," *AJA* 56 (1952) 23-26.

Anton-Hermann Chroust, "Treason and Patriotism in Ancient Greece," *JHI* 15 (1954) 280-288.

Irving A. Agus, "The Rights and Immunities of the Minority," *JQR, N.S.*, 45 (1954-55) 120-129.

*W. den Boer, "Political Propaganda in Greek Chronology," *HJAH* 5 (1956) 162-177.

M. A. H. el-Abbadi, "The Alexandrian Citizenship," *JEA* 48 (1962) 106-123.

*William W. Hallo, "Royal Hymns and Mesopotamian Unity," *JCS* 17 (1963) 112-118.

C. Bradford Welles, "Greek Liberty," *JJP* 15 (1965) 29-47.

*J. R. Porter, "The Legal Aspects of the Concept of 'Corporate Personality' in the Old Testament," *VT* 15 (1965) 361-380.

*A. van Selms, "Church and state according to the Old Testament prophets," *Min* 7 (1966-67) 155-159.

E. Ferenczy, "The Censorship of Appius Claudius Caecus," *AAASH* 15 (1967) 27-61.

*T. J. Luce, "Political Propaganda on Roman Republican Coins: circa 92-82 B.C.," *AJA* 72 (1968) 25-39.

*R. W. Davies, "Police Work in Roman Times," *HT* 18 (1968) 700-707.

§138 *2.3.26 Studies concerning Covenants, Contracts, Curses, Oaths, Treaties & Vows [See also: Covenants (Theological Studies); and Israel as the "Chosen People" →]*

†Anonymous, "Origin, Nature and History of Oaths," *BCQTR, 4th Ser.*, 16 (1834) 43-55. *(Review)*

†Anonymous, "Tyler *on Oaths*," *ERCJ* 59 (1834) 446-474. *(Review)*

J. Romeyn Berry, "The Vows of Scripture," *AThR* 5 (1867) 419-437.

Adolph Rahn, "The Relation of the Mosaic to the Christian Economy," *RChR* 18 (1871) 607-628.

Paul J. Turquand, "The Oaths of the Old Testament Scriptures," *CongL* 12 (1883) 292-297.

*J. Max Hark, "Blood-Covenanting and Atonement," *AR* 5 (1886) 375-389.

*H. Clay Trumbull and Edmund M. Vittum, "Correspondence," *AR* 5 (1886) 559-563. *[Blood-Covenanting and Atonement]*

*E. Revillout and V. Revillout, "*Sworn Obligations* in Egyptian and Babylonian Law," *BOR* 1 (1886-87) 101-104.

E. Revillout and V. Revillout, "Sworn Obligations in Babylonian Law," *BOR* 2 (1887-88) 22-24.

*H. H. Hawes, "The Covenants of Genesis XV. and XVII.," *USR* 4 (1892-93) 112-114.

J. N. Fradenburgh, "The Covenant of Salt," *MR* 80 (1898) 937-954.

James Silvester, "The Two Covenants," *HR* 38 (1899) 543-545.

*F. J. Coffin, "Third commandment," *JBL* 19 (1900) 166-188. [VI. The Oath, pp. 183-187]

Luther Link, "The Abrahamic Covenant," *PQ* 14 (1900) 520-531.

*E. G. King, "The Covenant of Creation in the Psalms," *ICMM* 8 (1911-12) 410-421.

*Samuel A. B. Mercer, "The Oath in Cuneiform Inscriptions: The Oath in Babylonian Inscriptions of the Time of the Ḫammurabi Dynasty," *AJSL* 29 (1912-13) 65-94. *[Part II]*

*Samuel A. B. Mercer, "The Oath in Cuneiform Inscriptions," *JAOS* 33 (1913) 33-50. *[Part I]*

*Samuel A. B. Mercer, "The Oath in Cuneiform Inscriptions: III. The Oath in the Inscriptions Since the Time of the Ḫammurabi Dynasty," *AJSL* 30 (1913-14) 196-211.

*Duncan Cameron, "The Covenants in the Psalter," *GUOST* 4 (1913-22) 27-29, 84.

*James A Montgomery, "Babylonian *niš* 'oath' in West-Semitic," *JAOS* 37 (1917) 329-330.

E. J. Pilcher, "The Covenant Ceremony among the Hebrews," *SBAP* 40 (1918) 8-14.

(   ) McClure, "A Note on the Covenant Ceremony among the Hebrews," *SBAP* 40 (1918) 41.

M. Cary, "The early Roman treaties with Tarentum and Rhodes," *JP* 35 (1919-20) 165-173.

*S[tephen] Langdon and Alan H. Gardiner, "The Treaty of Alliance between Ḫattušili, King of the Hittites, and the Pharaoh Ramesses II of Egypt," *JEA* 6 (1920) 179-205.

*S. Prentice, "Elijah and the Tyrian Alliance," *JBL* 42 (1923) 33-38.

Ira M. Price, "The Oath in Court Procedure in Early Babylonia and the Old Testament," *JAOS* 49 (1929) 22-29.

*Clive H. Carruthers, "More Hittite Words," *Lang* 9 (1933) 151-161. [1. *kutrus* 'witness', pp. 151-152]

*S[tephen] Langdon, "Note on the Aramaic Treaty of Bar-ga'ya and Mati'el," *JRAS* (1933) 23-24.

*Allen B. West, "Prosopographical Notes on the Treaty between Athens and Haliai," *AJP* 56 (1935) 72-76.

Samuel Rosenbalatt, "The Relations Between Jewish and Muslin Laws Concerning Oaths and Vows," *PAAJR* 7 (1935-36) 229-243.

Jacob Z. Lauterbach, "The Belief in the Power of the Word," *HUCA* 14 (1939) 287-302.

*G. R. Driver and John C. Miles, "Ordeal by Oath at Nuzi," *Iraq* 7 (1940) 132-138.

*P. E. Kretzmann, "The Chronology of the Two Covenants (Gal. 3:17 cp. with Ex. 12:40)," *CTM* 12 (1941) 606-610.

Herbert Liebsny, "The Oath of the King in the Legal Procedcure of Nuzi," *JAOS* 61 (1941) 62-63.

*P. E. Kretzmann, "The Chronology of the Two Covenants," *CTM* 15 (1944) 767-771.

John A. Wilson, "The Oath in Ancient Egypt," *JNES* 7 (1948) 129-156.

G. T. Griffith, "The Union of Corinth and Argos (392-386 B.C.)," *HJAH* 1 (1950) 236-256.

Sheldon H. Blank, "The Curse, the Blasphemy, the Spell, the Oath," *HUCA* 23 (1950-51) Part 1, 73-95.

A. R. Johnson, "The Covenant with the House of David," *OSHTP* (1951-52) 20-21.

*George E. Mendenhall, "Puppy and Lettuce in Northwest-Semitic Covenant Making," *BASOR* #133 (1954) 26-30.

Paul G. Bretscher, "The Covenant of Blood," *CTM* 25 (1954) 1-27, 109-125, 199-209.

P. Van Imschoot, "Covenant in the Old Testament," *TD* 2 (1954) 86-89.

*F. M. Heichelheim, "New Evidence on the Ebro Treaty," *HJAH* 3 (1954-55) 211-219.

*Paul E. Brown, "The Basis for Hope. *The Principle of the Covenant as a Biblical Basis of a Philosophy of History*," *Interp* 9 (1955) 35-40.

*E[phraim] A. Speiser, "Nuzi Marginalia," *Or, N.S.*, 25 (1956) 1-23. [5. The terminology of the oath by the gods, pp. 15-23]

*J[acob] J. Rabinowitz, "The Aramaic Papyri, the Demotic Papyri from Gebelên and Talmudic Sources," *B* 38 (1957) 269-274. *[False Oaths]*

*Moshe̱ Greenberg, "The Hebrew Oath Particle *ḤAY/ḤĒ*," *JBL* 76 (1957) 34-39.

*Geo Widengren, "King and Covenant," *JSS* 2 (1957) 1-32.

Saul Lieberman, "On Adjurations among the Jews," *Tarbiẕ* 27 (1957-58) #2/3, VIII.

*Matitiahu Tsevat, "The Neo-Assyrian and Neo-Babylonian Vassal Oaths and the Prophet Ezekiel," *JBL* 78 (1959) 199-204.

M. B. Rowton, "The Background of the Treaty between Ramesses II and Ḫattušiluš III," *JCS* 13 (1959) 1-11.

J. A. Thompson, "Covenant Patterns in the Ancient Near East and their Significance for Biblical Studies," *RTR* 18 (1959) 65-75.

*J. A. Thompson, "Non-Biblical Covenants in the Ancient Near East and their Relevance for Understanding the Covenant Motif in the Old Testament," *ABR* 8 (1960) 39-45.

*F. Charles Fensham, "The Treaty between Solomon and Hiram and the Alalakh Tablets," *JBL* 79 (1960) 59-60.

*G. A. Wainwright, "Meneptaḥ's Aid to the Hittites," *JEA* 46 (1960) 24-28.

J. W. Roberts, "Exegetical Helps. Some Notes on Swearing," *RestQ* 4 (1960) 30-34. [Oaths in the Old Testament, pp. 30-32]

*F. C[harles] Fensham, "The Possibility of the Presence of Casuistic Legal Material at the Making of the Covenant at Sinai," *PEQ* 93 (1961) 143-146.

*Stanley Gevirtz, "West-Semitic Curses and the Problem of the Origins of Hebrew Law," *VT* 11 (1961) 137-158.

*I. M. Grintz, "The Treaty with the Gibeonites," *Zion* 26 (1961) #2, I.

*F. Charles Fensham, "Salt as a Curse in the Old Testament and the Ancient Near East," *BA* 25 (1962) 48-50.

Edward Neufeld, "Inalienability of Mobile and Immobile Pledges in the Laws of the Bible," *RIDA, 3rd Ser.*, 9 (1962) 33-44.

F. Charles Fensham, "Malediction and Benediction in Ancient Near Eastern Vassal-Treaties and the Old Testament," *ZAW* 74 (1962) 1-9.

*Sidney B. Hoening, "Circumcision: The Covenant of Abraham," *JQR, N.S.*, 53 (1962-63) 322-334.

*F. Charles Fensham, "The Wild Ass in the Aramean Treaty between Bar-ga'ayah and Mati'el," *JNES* 22 (1963) 185-186.

*J. A. Thompson, "The Significance of the Ancient Near Eastern Treaty Pattern," *TB* #13 (1963) 1-6.

*F. Charles Fensham, "Clauses of Protection in Hittite Vassal-Treaties and the Old Testament," *VT* 13 (1963) 133-143.

*F. Charles Fensham, "Common Trends in the Curses of Near Eastern Treaties and *Kudurr*—Inscriptions Compared with the Maledictions of Amos and Isaiah," *ZAW* 75 (1963) 155-175.

Virgil H. Todd, "The Covenant: Its Significance for Biblical Study," *CS* 10 (1963-64) #2, 1-4, 9-10.

*A. D. Crown, "Aposiopesis and the O.T. and the Hebrew Conditional Oath," *Abr-N* 4 (1964) 96-111.

*Edward Heppenstall, "The Law and the Covenant at Sinai," *AUSS* 2 (1964) 18-26.

*F. Charles Fensham, "Did a Treaty Between the Israelites and the Kenites Exist?" *BASOR* #175 (1964) 51-54.

Delbert R. Hillers, "A Note on Some Treaty Terminology in the Old Testament," *BASOR* #176 (1964) 46-47.

*Dennis J. McCarthy, "Three Covenants in Genesis," *CBQ* 26 (1964) 179-189.

B. de Vries, "The Testimony of Witness and the Instantaneous Delivery of the Confessed Amount (הילך)," *Tarbiz* 34 (1964-65) #4, V-VI.

Meredith G. Kline, "Oath and Ordeal Signs," *WTJ* 27 (1964-65) 115-139.

*M. Weinfeld, "Traces of Assyrian Treaty Formulae in Deuteronomy," *B* 46 (1965) 417-427.

*Dennis J. McCarthy, "Notes on the Love of God in Deuteronomy and the Father-Son Relationship between Yahweh and Israel," *CBQ* 27 (1965) 144-147. *[Covenant]*

Dennis J. McCarthy, "Covenant in the Old Testament: The Present State of Inquiry," *CBQ* 27 (1965) 217-240.

*R. Frankena, "The Vassal-Treaties of Esarhaddon and the Dating of Deuteronomy," *OTS* 14 (1965) 122-154.

*G. M. Tucker, "Covenant forms and Contract Forms," *VT* 15 (1965) 487-503.

*Jonas C. Greenfield, "Studies in Western Semitic Inscriptions I. Stylistic Aspects of Sefire Treaty Inscriptions," *AO* 29 (1965-66) 1-18.

Meredith G. Kline, "Oath and Ordeal Signs—II," *WTJ* 28 (1965-66) 1-37.

A. E. Raubitschek, "The Peace Policy of Pericles," *AJA* 70 (1966) 37-41.

*Herbert B. Huffmon, "The Treaty Background of Hebrew *Yāda'*," *BASOR* #181 (1966) 31-37.

*Herbert B. Huffmon and Simon B. Parker, "A Further Note on the Treaty Background of Hebrew *Yāda'*," *BASOR* #184 (1966) 36-37.

Gene M. Tucker, "Witness and 'Dates' in Israelite Contracts," *CBQ* 28 (1966) 42-45.

*Joseph Blenkinsopp, "Are there Traces of the Gibeonite Covenant in Deuteronomy?" *CBQ* 28 (1966) 207-219.

*Walther Eichrodt, "Covenant and Law. *Thoughts on Recent Discussion*," *Interp* 20 (1966) 302-321.

*Philip B. Harner, "Exodus, Sinai, and the Hittite Prologues," *JBL* 85 (1966) 233-236.

Ray F. Chester, "Covenant Types," *RestQ* 9 (1966) 285-289.

*B. De Vries, "Partial Admission," *Tarbiz* 36 (1966-67) #3, III-IV. *[Oaths concerning Credit and debt]*

E. E. Hallewi*[sic]*, "The Oath (A Chapter in the History of the Halakha)," *Tarbiz* 37 (1967-68) #1, III-IV.

*Albrecht Goetze, "Hittite *šek-/šak-* '(legally) recognize' in the Treaties," *JCS* 22 (1968-69) 7-8.

*A. F. Campbell, "An Historical Prologue in a Seventh Century Treaty," *B* 50 (1969) 534-535.

*S. Talmon, "*Amen* as an Introductory Oath Formula," *Text* 7 (1969) 124-129.

F. C[harles] Fensham, "The treaty between the Israelites and Tyrians," *VTS* 17 (1969) 71-87.

Manfred R. Lehmann, "Biblical Oaths," *ZAW* 81 (1969) 74-92.

*F. C[harles] Fensham, "Aspects of Family Law in the Covenant Code in Light of Ancient Near Eastern Parallels," *DI* 1 (1969-70) v-xix.

*David [Noel] Freedman, "A New Approach to the Nuzi Sistership Contract," *JANES* 2 (1969-70) 77-85.

*C. D. Jathanna, "The Covenant and Covenant Making in Pentateuch," *BTF* 3 (1969-71) #1, 27-54. [Scholar's outlook from Richard Kraetzschmar to Gerhard von Rad; Etymology of *Berith;* Secular usage of *Berith* in JE Acts of covenant-making between men; The covenant in Western-Semitic Texts; Religious usage of *Berith* in JE: God's Covenant with Abraham; The Covenant between God and His People, I. The Sinai Covenant, II. The Covenant-making in Deuteronomy, III. The covenant in Priestly Writings]